Eighteenth-century Economics

Peter Groenewegen is one of the world's foremost scholars of eighteenth-century economics – the era that saw the effective 'mainstreaming' of the discipline in the work of Smith, Turgot and Quesnay. This collection of essays amounts to the definitive guide to eighteenth-century economics and is a must for any economist's bookshelves.

Eighteenth-century Economics represents four decades of Peter Groenewegen's research of that period. Presented in chronological order, the essays read not only as an authoritative summary of the period, but also as a guide to the evolution of Groenewegen's writings down the years. There can be no doubt that this book is truly indispensable to any serious economist and will prove a valuable resource for students of the history of economic thought.

Peter Groenewegen is Professor of Economics at the University of Sydney.

Routledge Studies in the History of Economics

1 **Economics as Literature**
Willie Henderson

2 **Socialism and Marginalism in Economics 1870–1930**
Edited by Ian Steedman

3 **Hayek's Political Economy**
The Socio-economics of Order
Steve Fleetwood

4 **On the Origins of Classical Economics**
Distribution and Value from William Petty to Adam Smith
Tony Aspromourgos

5 **The Economics of Joan Robinson**
Edited by Maria Cristina Marcuzzo, Luigi Pasinetti and Alesandro Roncaglia

6 **The Evolutionist Economics of Léon Walras**
Albert Jolink

7 **Keynes and the 'Classics'**
A Study in Language, Epistemology and Mistaken Identities
Michel Verdon

8 **The History of Game Theory, Vol. 1**
From the Beginnings to 1945
Robert W. Dimand and Mary Ann Dimand

9 **The Economics of W. S. Jevons**
Sandra Peart

10 **Gandhi's Economic Thought**
Ajit K. Dasgupta

11 **Equilibrium and Economic Theory**
Edited by Giovanni Caravale

12 **Austrian Economics in Debate**
Edited by Willem Keizer, Bert Tieben and Rudy van Zijp

13 **Ancient Economic Thought**
Edited by B. B. Price

14 **The Political Economy of Social Credit and Guild Socialism**
Frances Hutchinson and Brian Burkitt

15 **Economic Careers**
Economics and Economists in Britain 1930–1970
Keith Tribe

16 **Understanding 'Classical' Economics**
Studies in the Long-period Theory
Heinz Kurz and Neri Salvadori

17 **History of Environmental Economic Thought**
E. Kula

18 **Economic Thought in Communist and Post-communist Europe**
Edited by Hans-Jürgen Wagener

19 **Studies in the History of French Political Economy**
From Bodin to Walras
Edited by Gilbert Faccarello

20 **The Economics of John Rae**
Edited by O. F. Hamouda, C. Lee and D. Mair

21 **Keynes and the Neoclassical Synthesis**
Einsteinian versus Newtonian Macroeconomics
Teodoro Dario Togati

22 **Historical Perspectives on Macroeconomics**
Sixty Years after the 'General Theory'
Edited by Philippe Fontaine and Albert Jolink

23 **The Founding of Institutional Economics**
The Leisure Class and Sovereignty
Edited by Warren J. Samuels

24 **Evolution of Austrian Economics**
From Menger to Lachmann
Sandye Gloria

25 **Marx's Concept of Money**
The God of Commodities
Anitra Nelson

26 **The Economics of James Steuart**
Edited by Ramón Tortajada

27 **The Development of Economics in Europe since 1945**
Edited by A. W. Bob Coats

28 **The Canon in the History of Economics**
Critical Essays
Edited by Michalis Psalidopoulos

29 **Money and Growth**
Selected Papers of Allyn Abbott Young
Edited by Perry G. Mehrling and Roger J. Sandilands

30 **The Social Economics of Jean-Baptiste Say**
Markets and Virtue
Evelyn L. Forget

31 **The Foundations of Laissez-faire**
The Economics of Pierre de Boisguilbert
Gilbert Faccarello

32 **John Ruskin's Political Economy**
Willie Henderson

33 **Contributions to the History of Economic Thought**
Essays in Honour of R. D. C. Black
Edited by Antoin E. Murphy and Renee Prendergast

34 **Towards an Unknown Marx**
A Commentary on the Manuscripts of 1861–63
Enrique Dussel

35 **Economics and Interdisciplinary Exchange**
Edited by Guido Erreygers

36 **Economics as the Art of Thought**
Essays in Memory of G. L. S. Shackle
Edited by Stephen F. Frowen and Peter Earl

37 **The Decline of Ricardian Economics**
Politics and Economics in Post-Ricardian Theory
Susan Pashkoff

38 **Piero Sraffa**
His Life, Thought and Cultural Heritage
Alessandro Roncaglia

39 **Equilibrium and Disequilibrium in Economic Theory**
The Marshall-Walras Divide
Edited by Michel de Vroey

40 **The German Historical School**
The Historical and Ethical Approach to Economics
Edited by Yuichi Shionoya

41 **Reflections on the Classical Canon in Economics**
Essays in Honor of Samuel Hollander
Edited by Sandra Peart and Evelyn Forget

42 **Piero Sraffa's Political Economy**
A Centenary Estimate
Edited by Terenzio Cozzi and Roberto Marchionatti

43 **The Contribution of Joseph A. Schumpeter to Economics**
Richard Arena and Cecile Dangel

44 **On the Development of Long-run Neo-classical Theory**
Tom Kompas

45 **F. A. Hayek as a Political Economist**
Economic Analysis and Values
Edited by Jack Birner, Pierre Garrouste and Thierry Aimar

46 **Pareto, Economics and Society**
The Mechanical Analogy
Michael McLure

47 **The Cambridge Controversies in Capital Theory**
A Study in the Logic of Theory Development
Jack Birner

48 **Economics Broadly Considered**
Essays in Honor of Warren J. Samuels
Edited by Steven G. Medema, Jeff Biddle and John B. Davis

49 **Physicians and Political Economy**
Six Studies of the Work of Doctor-economists
Edited by Peter Groenewegen

50 **The Spread of Political Economy and the Professionalisation of Economists**
Economic Societies in Europe, America and Japan in the Nineteenth Century
Massimo Augello and Marco Guidi

51 **Historians of Economics and Economic Thought**
The Construction of Disciplinary Memory
Steven G. Medema and Warren J. Samuels

52 **Competing Economic Theories**
Essays in memory of Giovanni Caravale
Sergio Nisticò and Domenico Tosato

53 **Economic Thought and Policy in Less Developed Europe**
The Nineteenth Century
Edited by Michalis Psalidopoulos and Maria-Eugenia Almedia Mata

54 **Family Fictions and Family Facts**
Harriet Martineau, Adolphe Quetelet and the Population Question in England 1798–1859
Brian Cooper

55 **Eighteeth-century Economics**
Turgot, Beccaria and Smith and their Contemporaries
Peter Groenewegen

Eighteenth-century Economics

Turgot, Beccaria and Smith and their contemporaries

Peter Groenewegen

ROUTLEDGE
Taylor & Francis Group

London and New York

First published 2002
by Routledge
11 New Fetter Lane, London EC4P 4EE

Simultaneously published in the USA and Canada
by Routledge
29 West 35th Street, New York, NY 10001

Routledge is an imprint of the Taylor & Francis Group

Typeset in Goudy by Taylor & Francis Books Ltd
Printed and bound in Great Britain by MPG Books Ltd, Bodmin

British Library Cataloguing in Publication Data
A catalogue record for this book is available from the British Library

Library of Congress Cataloging in Publication Data
A catalog record has been requested for this title

ISBN 0–415–27940–2

Contents

PART III

Illustrations

Figures

Tables

Preface

There comes a time in life when past work can be reviewed with an eye to making it accessible in a new form. My long academic career in the history of economics makes me think that this might well be the case with my essays in this field, contributed over four decades to academic journals, books and conference proceedings. The contents of the material here reprinted is discussed in detail in the subsequent Prelude, together with my reasons for choosing them for inclusion. My Acknowledgments convey my thanks to former publishers and those who assisted with this publication. However, I might here take the opportunity to offer a general thanks to my teachers in the history of economics, formal and informal. Their specific contributions are generally indicated in an appropriate footnote. However, their willingness to comment on material in draft, occasionally from someone whom they had never met, is praiseworthy. It indicates one type of unpaid work many academics are willing to do in the advancement of their discipline. This is one of the many joys of academic life that needs regular celebration.

Long may this tradition continue.

Peter Groenewegen
The University of Sydney

Acknowledgements

For permission to reprint material (articles or chapters in books) from publications over which they hold the copyright, I gratefully acknowledge permission to reprint the items specifically mentioned from the following publishers: for permission to reprint Chapters 3, 7, 17, 20, 21, 22, Blackwells Ltd; for permission to reprint Chapters 16 and 19, Duke University Press; for permission to reprint Chapter 18, Kenzei Kenkyu, Hitotsubashi University, Japan; for permission to reprint Chapter 10, Libraire Droz S.A. (Geneva); for permission to reprint Chapter 6, Presses universitaires de France; for permission to reprint Chapter 23, Milelle edizione, Lecce; for permission to reprint Chapters 8 and 9, Routledge (Taylor & Francis); for permission to reprint Chapter 15, Storia del pensiero economico, and for permission to reprint Chapter 5 in English, Verlag Wirtschaft und Finanzen (Verlagsgruppe Handelsblatt Gmbh, Dusseldorf). In addition, I wish to thank Rebecca Leung and Jannine Cradick for preparing the material for the publishers; to Tony Aspromourgos for commenting on the original proposal and consenting to reproduce the part of Chapter 8 which he had written; and finally to the staff of Routledge, particularly Robert Langham and Terry Clague, for their cooperation and assistance in bringing this project to a successful conclusion.

Peter Groenewegen
University of Sydney
November 2001

Prelude

The essays on eighteenth-century economics collected in this volume represent four decades of my research on this subject. These began with my postgraduate studies in the 1960s and have continued as part of my activities as a university teacher at the University of Sydney specialising in the history of economics. In 1961 and 1962, I wrote a Master of Economics thesis at the University of Sydney on the Economics of A.R.J. Turgot; in 1963–5 I completed a Ph.D. thesis at the London School of Economics on the history of the theory of value, production and distribution from 1650 to 1776. Many of the articles reprinted in this volume – particularly Chapters 4, 7, 8, 16, 17, 18 and 20 – derive from this graduate research although, not surprisingly, in each case they embody a great deal of additional work and reflect the impact of advice from eminent scholars in the history of economics.

In 1976, I spent a period of study leave from Sydney at the University of Florence in Piero Barucci's history of economics department. There I worked on eighteenth-century Italian economics, particularly that of Beccaria, Verri, Genovesi and Galiani, as reprinted in the Custodi edition of Italian economic classics. Some fruits of this research are visible in Chapters 1 and 15. In 1982, I began a series of reprints of classics in economics, largely, but not totally, drawn from the eighteenth century. Chapters 13 and 14 present extracts from introductions to two of these reprints, while Chapter 10 recounts some of my early experiences in this venture. When in 1989 I formed a Centre for the Study of the History of Economic Thought at the University of Sydney, with the encouragement and support from its then Vice Chancellor, the late Professor J. M. Ward, the reprints were published under its auspices. The series was completed in 2000 with a reprint of a work by Boisguilbert, his 1704 *A Treatise on the Nature of Wealth, Money and Taxation*. The Centre also organised a number of one-day (or longer) workshops and conferences, of which Chapter 11 marks an early instance. The proceedings of many of the later meetings tended to be published in book form, including a study on women and economics (1994), economics and ethics (1996) and one on physicians and political economy (2001). The most recent in fact also covers much early economics by investigating the links between medicine and economics by way of six case studies of physician-economists, only one of whom lived in the nineteenth century.

The chapters not mentioned so far in nearly all cases derive from conference presentations or from public addresses, published subsequently either in the official proceedings of these conferences, or in refereed journals, or both. Chapter 2 is an exception, since it has never before been published. It deals with the emergence of economics as a science, one of the more formal problems in the history of economics, examining the various time periods selected in other historical studies, partly in terms of the preferred definition of economics (or political economy) which they implied. This paper had been presented in 1972 at a British History of Economic Thought Conference organised at Birmingham by T. W. Hutcheson and subsequently (1973) in much revised form at the Third Conference of Economists in Adelaide (Australia). A decade and a half later I used some of its contents in Chapter 3, a review article on the origins of modern economics (appropriately concentrating on a book by Hutcheson which had appeared in 1988). However, there is no real overlap between these two essays as reprinted here. The lapse of a quarter century from its first writing to its re-editing meant that I felt free to change much of its contents, greatly condensing the argument and improving the style, while at the same time conserving what was valuable among the ideas on that topic by their presentation in a more coherent, concise and simplified form. The degree of success I have achieved in this task can be left to the judgement of my readers. Chapters 6, 9, and 23 are also papers from conferences, presented in Paris, Grenoble and Lecce respectively; Chapters 12 and 22 were both originally presented as public lectures. The first was sponsored by Macquarie University (Sydney, Australia) as its first Henry George Memorial Lecture (subsequent Henry George Memorial Lecturers have included eminent historians of economics such as Mark Blaug). The second, more significantly, was presented on the occasion of the bicentenary of the publication of the *Wealth of Nations*, at a meeting sponsored by the Economic Society of Australia (New South Wales Branch). It deals with Smith's almost unique starting point for his economic treatise, the division of labour, placing it in its historical setting on the basis of what was then contemporary division of labour research. Finally, Chapters 5 and 21, which do not neatly fall into these categories, originated respectively as part of the introduction for a German facsimile reprint of a scarce tract, and as a review article for the *Economic Record*.

Omissions from this volume

Two other issues at least ought to be raised in this prelude. First, in making this selection, what items from my published work on eighteenth-century economics have been omitted? Two broad sets of omissions immediately suggest themselves, though some potential inclusions were excluded for reasons of duplication or lack of requisite quality. First, I have not included any of my entries for major books of reference dealing with aspects of eighteenth-century economics, of which my substantial number of articles for the *New Palgrave Dictionary* are by far the most important. Their relative brevity in many instances provides a good rationale for such non-inclusion, while in the case of relevant longer pieces, there is considerable duplication with some of the essays here included (for example, my articles on 'Division of Labour' and on 'Turgot' for the *New Palgrave* overlap considerably with essays included in this volume, especially in the case of the second). The other major omissions are from my book reviews, as distinct from review articles. I have been an ardent book reviewer since the early 1960s, most frequently of books devoted to the history of economic thought. Again, their relative brevity precluded them from being included in this collection, even if many of them embody themes drawn from eighteenth-century economics.

A number of specific omissions may also be mentioned. These include my first scholarly publication on the history of economics in a non-Australian journal, namely a brief note on the authorship of *The Natural and Political Observations upon the Bills of Mortality*. This appeared in the *Journal of the History of Ideas* in 1967, but was written, and first submitted, during 1964. It is very short. A paper on the 'International Foundations of Political Economy. An Alternative Perspective', included in a volume on *Pre-Classical Economic Thought* (edited by S. Todd Lowry) in 1987 has been omitted because its contents somewhat duplicate those of Chapter 6 on 'The French connection'. Duplication likewise explains the following omissions: my introduction to Turgot's 'Reflections' for the facsimile reprint of this text in the 'Klassiker der National Ökonomie' series (1990); the chapter on Quesnay in the *Physicians and Political Economy* book (2001); my article 'Boisguilbert: Theory of Money, Circular Flow, Effective Demand, Distribution of Wealth', which appeared in *History of Economics Review* (2001); a review article, 'Professor Vaggi and the Physiocrats', for *Research in the History of Economic Thought and Methodology* (1992); and two papers on Verri's *Meditazione* for conferences on Italian economics whose proceedings were published in 1994 and 1999.

A chronological table of contents in terms of writing the essays

It has been suggested to me that it would also be of interest to readers of this volume to have a listing of the essays included in this volume in the order in which they were written. A table of contents constructed in this way is provided below, following this Prelude. The following comments on this listing elaborate on aspects of the development of my research interests in eighteenth-century economics, and also provide further relevant background to the writing of each piece included.

A review article opens the chronological list. I was offered Mizuta's catalogue of Adam Smith's Library to review for the *Economic Record* and requested whether I could submit it at article length. I had become interested in the contents of Smith's library through my work on Turgot, in which I had researched possible influences of his work on Smith. The final section of the review deals specifically with this topic, and therefore acts as a good lead-in to the third of the essays in chronological order, 'Turgot and Adam Smith' (Chapter 22). That essay reviewed the Turgot/Smith controversy by examining in turn the evidence on their meetings in Paris, the issue of their alleged correspondence, and Smith's actual access to Turgot's major writings. It also examined some points of similarity in their economics, both in terms of specific theoretical contributions and the structure of their treatises. It concluded that similarities in their work derived largely from their shared heritage in economic literature, a type of explanation for this type of issue encountered in several other essays in this volume. I might add that this essay had a long gestation period, and greatly benefited from comments by Jacob Viner, Ronald Meek (the external examiner of my Ph.D.) and Andrew Skinner.

The second essay published in 1969 (Chapter 4) drew heavily on a chapter of my Ph.D. thesis, and was commissioned by an editor of the journal in which it appeared. It examines attitudes to labour in the writings of the classical economists, with specific reference to the association between wages and prices as a sort of classical view on cost-push explanations of inflation, and the denial of such a link by Ricardo and Wicksell. It also looked at the impact of wages on productivity as a potential offsetting factor in this relationship, by examining in turn 'the economy of high, and low wages' arguments, and the effects of wage costs on introducing more capital-intensive methods of production. Its publication sparked off the fifth essay chronologically (Chapter 7) since the editor of the *Journal of Industrial Relations* (who had read and enjoyed my article on attitudes to labour) asked me to submit a paper on a similar theme for his journal. The employment and machinery topic fitted the bill, the first part of which also drew heavily on the contents of my Ph.D. thesis.

During the late 1960s I also drew further for journal articles on the contents of my Master's thesis on Turgot. Originally, I had intended to follow the model of Meek's *Economics of Physiocracy* (1962) of combining a set of translations (in my case of Turgot's work) with a set of my own essays on that subject. In the event, the translations were published without the essays (Groenewegen, 1977) but a number of Turgot essays were completed and published: on the theory of value, exchange and price for *History of Political Economy* (1970) and one on his theory of capital and interest for the *Economic Journal* (1971). From the same period comes my essay on the emergence of economics as a science, which exploited my knowledge of pre-Smithian economics and an interest in the methodology of the history of economics. It may be recalled that the late 1960s and early 1970s showed considerable interest in such methodology issues but my paper missed the bus, as it were, and was never published, despite several attempts to secure publication in its original and rather lengthy form.

During these years, I began work on a secondary research interest, which was also useful for my teaching: public finance in general, and taxation reform in particular. For much of the second half of the 1970s, I was busily engaged in writing a public finance text for Australian students, and my public finance research in fact distracted me from much publishing in the history of economics until the end of the 1980s. With one exception, what was published in this field between 1977 and 1989 reflected invitations to contribute a paper by editors of journals, often to commemorate centenaries of economic works. Thus my 1977 'Adam Smith and the Division of Labour' (Chapter 22) was a lecture given to the Economic Society of Australia (New South Wales Branch) to celebrate the bicentenary of the publication of the *Wealth of Nations*; the 1983 article in *History of Political Economy* (Chapter 19) commemorated the bicentenary of Turgot's death. The 1982 Turgot article (Chapter 18) was an invited contribution to a Japanese journal to commemorate the same event. The essay 'Turgot, Beccaria and Smith' (1983) was my contribution to a volume on *Italian Economics Past and Present* edited with Joseph Halevi for the University of Sydney Foundation of Italian Studies with which I was involved, while the lecture on the Physiocrats and the single tax (1984) resulted from an invitation from Macquarie University to give the first Henry George Memorial Lecture.

The piece on Quesnay's first economic publication, the article 'Fermier', marks a further step in my academic career as historian of economics: the publishing of a series of reprints of classics in the history of economics. I had started this in 1982, and the Quesnay translation to which this item (Chapter 13) was an introduction was the second in a series, it will be recalled, eventually completed in 2000. It explains the background to Quesnay's activities as an economist for the decade 1756–66, and reflected my long standing interests in Physiocracy. It was also a desire to repair the omission of a translation of Quesnay's first article on economics from Meek's Quesnay translations published in his *Economics of Physiocracy* (1962), despite its importance for history of capital theory reasons. The 1987 reflections on Pietro Verri's political economy (Chapter 15) written at the request of Pierro Roggi, drew on the work I had done on Verri for the fourth reprint (published in 1986), a translation of Verri's *Meditazione sulla economia politica*. The 1989 piece on the origins of modern economics (Chapter 3) was a review article inspired by Hutcheson's *Before Adam Smith*. For some of its chapters, this had drawn extensively on my entries for *The New Palgrave Dictionary*, which I was also then preparing for publication in 1987.

The last eight essays were all published during the 1990s. The essay on laissez-faire (1991) and the paper on the 'French connection' (1994) were both designed to highlight the importance of French writers during the formative period of economics of the decades before Adam Smith, all too frequently played down by English speaking historians of economics (Chapters 11 and 6 respectively). The 1992 essay on editing the classics recounted difficulties experienced by an antipodean editor and was presented at a European conference devoted to examining the nature of such editorial tasks. The first of the 1998 essays (Chapter 14) produces the fruits of one of the more recent efforts in my reprint series, the translation of Du Pont's essay on the origins and progress of a new science. The other 1998 essay (Chapter 5) is also an introduction to a reprint of an economic classic: this time of Boisguilbert's *Le Détail de la France sous le règne de Louis XIV* by the Verlag Wirtschaft und Finanzen, and originally appeared in German. This leaves the three 1999 essays. The one on Steuart and Cantillon (Chapter 9) was prepared for a conference on Steuart organised by Ramòn Tortajada at the Chateau de Vizille in 1995 (it was the English version, originally published by Routledge; the French version appeared in *Economies et Sociétés* nos. 11 and 12). The second article, with Tony Aspromourgos (Chapter 8) was written for the essays in honour of Pierangelo Garegnani (edited by Gary Mongiovi and Fabio Petri) as a historical contribution to a key aspect of the classical surplus approach to economic theorising. The final essay (Chapter 23), which is also the last in this volume, was one of two lectures on the classical theory of economic growth given at the University of Lecce (southern Italy) at the invitation of Cosimo Perrotta. It looked at Smith's optimistic view of economic growth possibilities, supported by his faith in the virtually unlimited possibilities opened up by a modern, industrial division of labour and the rises in labour productivity which this generated. This burst of publication in the history of economics was greatly assisted by my position as an Australian Research Council Senior Research Fellow during the first half of the 1990s, which enabled concentration on history of economics research and eliminated much of my teaching and administrative responsibilities.

Design

Finally, I note that the design of this collection reflects a belief (perhaps immodest) of the enduring value of these contributions as studies on an important era in the history of economics. Much of its contents has not been widely available before. This applies particularly strongly to most of the first ten chapters, if not the first fifteen, and perhaps likewise to the final three. On the other hand, four of the five Turgot pieces are quite well known, having been published in widely disseminated journals (*Economic Journal, History of Political Economy, Scottish Journal of Political Economy*); those published in Australian, French, German, Italian and Japanese publications have had a far more limited exposure. Whether such wider circulation of these pieces is of as great a value as I presume it to be, can also be left to my readers to decide. In any case, I wish them an enjoyable journey through the vagaries of eighteenth-century and occasionally earlier economic thought, as reflected in the following pieces, thereby repeating an earlier voyage enjoyed by myself over the last four decades.

Peter Groenewegen,
Sydney, August 2001

References

Groenewegen, Peter (1967) 'Authorship of the *Natural and Political Observations upon the Bills of Mortality*', *Journal of the History of Ideas*, 28(4) Oct-Dec, pp. 601–2.

——(1977) *The Economics of A. R. J. Turgot*, The Hague: Martinus Nijhoff.

——(1987) 'International Foundations of Political Economy: An Alternative Perspective', in *Pre-Classical Economic Thought*, ed. S. Todd Lowry, Dordrecht: Kluwer, pp. 211–20.

——(1990) 'Über Turgot's Réflexions', in *Kommentar zur Faksimile Ausgabe von Anne Robert Jacques Turgot, Réflexions sur la formation et la distribution des richesses*, Düsseldorf: Verlag Wirtschaft und Finanzen, pp. 62–88.

——(1992) 'Professor Vaggi and the Physiocrats: New Explorations in the Classical Theory of Value and Distribution', *Research in the History of Economic Thought and Methodology*, no. 9, pp. 209–19.

——(1994) 'Pietro Verri's Mature Political Economy of the Meditazioni', in *Political economy and National Realities*, eds Manuella Alberetone and Alberto Masoero, Turin: Einaudi Foundation, pp. 107–25.

——(1999) 'The Significance of Pietro Verri's *Meditazioni* in the History of Economic Thought: The Wider European Influences', in *Pietro Verri e il suo tempo*, ed. Carlo Capra, Milan: Cisalpino, vol. 2, pp. 693–708.

——(2001) 'From Prominent Physician to Major Economist: Some Reflections on Quesnay's Switch to Economics in the 1750s', in *Physicians and Political Economy*, London: Routledge, pp. 93–115.

——(2001) 'Boisguilbert's Theory of Money, Circular Flow, Effective Demand and Distribution of Wealth', *History of Economics Review*, no. 33, pp. 33–43.

Groenewegen, Peter (ed.) (1994) *Feminism and Political Economy in Victorian England*, Aldershot: Edward Elgar.

——(1996) *Economics and Ethics*, London: Routledge.

——(2001) *Physicians and Political Economy*, London: Routledge.

Hutcheson, Terrence (1988) *Before Adam Smith*, Oxford: Blackwell.

Meek, R. L. (1962) *The Economics of Physiocracy*, London: Allen and Unwin.

Chronological table of contents

Part I

1 Turgot, Beccaria and Smith[1]

Introduction

It is well known and documented (Winch, 1970; Schumpeter, 1959) that the third quarter of the eighteenth century marks perhaps the most important period in the history of economic thought, since it is at the end of this period that economics emerged as a separate and new science (cf. Shackle, 1967, p. 2). During the 1760s and 1770s political economy gradually distinguished and emancipated itself from its roots in moral and political philosophy, and from the fragmented economic literature produced in the previous two centuries by merchants and administrators, which constituted its foundations (Schumpeter, 1954, esp. ch. 1). This period, with one major exception (Cantillon, 1959) saw the publication of the first general treatises on the subject, and the construction of systems of classical political economy which emphasised the reproduction of annual wealth, capital accumulation, value, distribution and growth. Such systems concentrated considerably less on the earlier preoccupations of economic writers, that is, matters of trade, money, credit and public finance, the practical issues which had inspired the earlier pamphleteers. In addition, this period saw the publication of the first economic journals, the establishment of the first chairs in political economy at European universities,[2] and the gradual beginning of what can be described as an economics profession.

The reasons for the timing of this phenomenon in the history of political economy are substantially found in the developments in general intellectual thought which took place in the eighteenth century. As Leslie Stephen (1902) has convincingly demonstrated, the mid-eighteenth century marks the beginning of secular social science freed from the theological encumbrances which had hampered its development in earlier centuries. The great landmark of this liberation is Montesquieu's *l'Esprit des Lois* published in 1748. This birth of a secular social science is confirmed in the blossoming of intellectual inquiry in fields such as history, sociology, politics, jurisprudence and political economy which flourished particularly in France and Scotland (the Enlightenment), but whose influence was spread over the whole civilised (European) world. The quality of this inquiry was enhanced by the growing acceptance of scientific method in the social sciences, pioneered at the end of the seventeenth century by the scientific and philosophic endeavours of Newton and Locke, whose influence was spread over the whole of Europe during the eighteenth century (for its influence on economics, see Letwin, 1963). As Pope put it so effectively in the eighteenth century:

> Nature and Nature's laws lay hid in night.
> God said: 'Let Newton be', and all was light.[3]

The fruits of the new physical theory of knowledge which owed its existence to Newton and Locke were reaped as far as the social sciences were concerned in the rich harvest produced by the Enlightenment in this area during the second half of the eighteenth century (see Cassirer, 1951, esp. ch. 2).

In the history of political economy, three figures of the Enlightenment stand out at the end of the third quarter of the century: Turgot, Beccaria and Smith.[4] Turgot, the philosopher, administrator and economist, at this time reached the greatest heights of his illustrious career in his position as Finance Minister (Contrôleur-général) of France from 1774 to 1776. Beccaria, philosopher, academic and administrator, was by then prominent as a social reformer and administrator following his period as professor of economics from 1768 to 1771 at the Palatine school in Milan. Adam Smith, the philosopher and academic, was putting the finishing touches to his *magnum opus* in political economy, which was published in 1776 as *An Inquiry into the Nature and Causes of the Wealth of Nations*. Of these three figures from the Enlightenment who all wrote extensively on political economy, only one, Adam Smith, has been given a prominent place in the history of economic thought. Turgot has generally been given a more minor, but nevertheless relatively important place, while Beccaria has been almost totally ignored in the histories of economics.

One major exception[5] to this last proposition is the work of Schumpeter (1959) who spoke of the great 'triumvirate' of Turgot, Beccaria and Smith (p. 245) and who provides interesting comparisons of these three economists on a number of occasions (pp. 179–80, 245, 248–9). The following quotations illustrate the basis on which these comparisons were made:

> For the moment, we concentrate upon Beccaria, the Italian, and A. Smith. The similarity between the two men and their performances is indeed striking. There is even some similarity in their social backgrounds and locations. There is similarity in their lives – and in those attitudes that are conditioned by one's pursuits – though Beccaria was much more a public servant than A. Smith. … Both were sovereign lords of a vast intellectual realm that extended far beyond what, even then, was possible for ordinary mortals to embrace. Beccaria presumably knew more mathematics than A. Smith, but A. Smith seems to have known more astronomy and physics. Neither was merely an economist … Turgot's brilliant achievements, his unchallenged place in the history of our science, and his evident title to membership in the triumvirate in which Beccaria and A. Smith are his colleagues are sufficient reasons why it is desirable to look for a moment at

> the man and his career ... If we now try to compare Turgot's scientific personality with those of Beccaria and A. Smith, significant similarities strike us first: all three were polyhistoric in learning and range of vision: all three stood outside the arena of business and political pursuits: all three displayed single-minded devotion to the duty in hand. Turgot was undoubtedly the most brilliant of the three, though his brilliance was somewhat tinged with superficiality, not in economics, but in his outlying intellectual domains. The main difference, from the standpoint of their scientific achievement, is that A. Smith expended very little of his energies on non-scientific work, Beccaria very much, and Turgot, from 1761 on, almost all he had. During the thirteen years at Limoges, Turgot can have had but scanty leisure; during his (nearly) two years of ministerial office, practically none: his creative work must have been done between the ages of 18 and 24. And this explains all there is to explain, not indeed about the comparative merits of the three works in question, but about the different degrees to which they were finished works at all.
>
> (Schumpeter, 1959, pp. 179–80, 245, 248)

The broad comparison of the work, life and personalities of these three major economists from Italy, France and Scotland at the end of that quarter century during which economics emerged as a science, which Schumpeter draws only in bold outlines in his remarks quoted above, provides a major part of the purpose for this paper. The main emphasis, not surprisingly, will be on their economics (and in particular the sources of that economics) and thereby this paper will improve the understanding of this crucial period in the development of the science. This task is achieved as follows. The second section of the paper provides a biographical sketch of the three economists, giving details of their respective careers with considerable concentration on their intellectual pursuits. The third provides a comparative outline of the economic systems they constructed in their major treatises on the subject.[6] The fourth section looks at the basic sources of this economics, particularly the common sources, and the final section elicits some of the conclusions which can be derived from this comparative study in the history of economic thought.

The purpose of this paper is, however, wider than a mere comparison of these three authors. Its more substantial aim is by such a comparison to illuminate the origins of classical political economy and to delineate its major characteristics, as contained in these three formulations of the classical system of political economy in the eighteenth century. By demonstrating first the unity of ideas in the economic systems of Turgot, Beccaria and Smith, the distinction between pre-Adamite (Blaug, 1962, ch. 1) and classical political economy starting with Smith, becomes less meaningful, and support is given to Marx's more perceptive contention (Marx, 1859, pp. 52–3) that classical political economy developed from the works of Petty and Boisguilbert in the mid-to-late seventeenth century and more or less concluded with the works of Ricardo and Sismondi in the 1820s. Although this paper does not demonstrate agreement with all of Marx's contentions in this context, it does support the broad thrust of his argument as far as the eighteenth century is concerned, as the final section of the paper makes clear.

Three philosophers of the eighteenth century

In order to provide a simple overview of the lives of Smith, Turgot and Beccaria which facilitates comparison, Table 1.1 gives a chronology of their lives which emphasises the dates of publication of their major works, the details of their education and appointments, and additional chronological information which places them in context. This table is not intended to be comprehensive, since its purpose is to provide reference material used in the discussion of this and the fourth section of the paper.

The first point to be noted is that Turgot, Beccaria and Smith were all complete products of the eighteenth century. All three were born and died within that century. Of the three, Smith had by far the longest life (sixty-seven years) and was also first born (1723). Beccaria, who survived Smith by nearly four years, lived for fifty-six years, while of the three Turgot had the shortest life: he died in 1781 at the age of fifty-three. As Schumpeter indicated in the passage quoted, these data are not unimportant. It may also be noted that despite their different birth years they nevertheless produced the work for which they became famous during their lifetime in the late 1750s and early 1760s. At the age of thirty-six, Smith made his name with the publication of the *Theory of Moral Sentiments*, the first edition of which was published in 1759; Beccaria, at only twenty-six, published his *Dei Delitti e delle Pene* in 1764; while Turgot at age twenty-nine had clearly established his substantial intellectual reputation with his *Encyclopédie* articles published in 1756 and 1757. From the chart, it can also be deduced that Turgot was the most precocious of the three: his first piece on economics which has been preserved[7] was written at the age of twenty-one (the letter to l'Abbé de Cicé on paper money); Beccaria's first work on economics appeared when he was twenty-four, while Smith's first published work, the review of Samuel Johnson's *Dictionary*, did not appear until 1755 when he was thirty-one.

Interesting comparisons can also be made on their educational experience. All three enjoyed extensive formal education at schools and at universities, but some differences may be noted. There are variations in the length of their formal education, and the same can be said about the extent to which they enjoyed the educational experience of foreign travel.

What details there are on Smith's education have been chronicled by Rae (1895) as supplemented by Scott (1937). These can be briefly summarised. Smith attended the Burgh school of Kirkcaldy for approximately seven years (1730–7), a school described by Rae (p. 5) as 'one of the best secondary schools of Scotland at that period'.[8] He commenced Latin probably in 1733, and was 'marked' during this period of his schooling, as Rae (p. 8) put it, for 'his studious disposition, his love of reading, and his power of memory'. At the age of fifteen

Table 1.1 Biographical chronology of Adam Smith, Turgot and Beccaria

	Adam Smith	*A. R. J. Turgot*	*C. Beccaria*	*Works on Economics published*	*Other related and relevant events*
1720					End of Law's System in France. South Sea Bubble.
1721				Charles King, *The British Merchant*.	Montesquieu, *Lettres Persanes* published.
1723	June 5:Birth at Kirkcaldy. Father: Adam Smith. Mother: Margaret Douglas				Bernard de Mandeville, *Fable of the Bees*, second enlarged edition, first edition: 1705.
1724				Uztariz, *Traité du Commerce*.	
1727		10 May:Birth at Paris. Father: Michel Etienne. Mother: Magdeleine François Martineau.			Death of Sir Isaac Newton.
1729				Joshua Gee, *Trade and Navigation of Great Britain Considered*.	Publication of Part II of *Fable of the Bees* by Bernard de Mandeville.
c. 1730	Commences education at Kirkcaldy Burgh School (till 1737).			Richard Cantillon, *Essay on the Nature of Commerce in General* written.	
1734				Jacob Vanderlint, *Money Answers all Things*. Melon, *Essai Politique sur le Commerce*.	Voltaire publishes *Lettres sur les Anglais*. Death of Richard Cantillon.

Table 1.1 continued

	Adam Smith	*A. R. J. Turgot*	*C. Beccaria*	*Works on Economics published*	*Other related and relevant events*
1735				G. Berkeley, *The Querist.*	
c. 1736		Early education at Collège du Plessis and Collège de Bourgogne till 1745.			
1738	Smith attends University of Glasgow till 1740.		15 March: Birth at Naples. Father: Giovanni Saverio. Mother: Maria Visconti de Saliceto.	Du Tot, *Reflèxions Politiques sur les Finances et le Commerce.*	
1739					David Hume publishes *Treatise of Human Nature.*
1740	Smith graduates M.A. at Glasgow University. Wins Snell Exhibition to Oxford. At Balliol College till 1746.			B. de Ulloa, *Traité du Commerce.*	
1743		Turgot enters Séminaire de Saint-Sulpice to study theology.			
1746	Smith leaves Oxford. Lives with mother at Kirkcaldy till 1748.		Starts education at Jesuit College in Parma till 1754.		

	Adam Smith	*A. R. J. Turgot*	*C. Beccaria*	*Works on Economics published*	*Other related and relevant events*
1748	Smith goes to Edinburgh to give lectures on Belles-Lettres. Edits poems of Hamilton.	Graduates Bachelor of Theology from Saint-Sulpice.		Josiah Tucker, *Essays on Commercial Subject.*	Montesquieu publishes *l'Esprit des Lois*. Birth of Jeremy Bentham.
1749		Turgot enters Sorbonne, writes first economic work.		Turgot, *Lettre sur la Papier Monnaie* written.	
1750	Smith gives lectures on jurisprudence which include economic material. Meets Hume c.1750–51.	Elected Prior at Sorbonne, gives lecture on progress of human mind, benefits of Christianity.		F. Galiani, *Della Moneta* J. Massie, *Natural Rate of Interest.*	
1751	January: elected Professor of Logic at Glasgow University.	Abandons ecclesiastical career.		M. Postlethwayt *Universal Dictionary of Trade and Commerce.*	First volume of *Encyclopédie*, edited by Diderot and D'Alembert, published.
1752	April: appointed to Chair of Moral Philosophy at Glasgow.	Appointed Substitute Attorney-General and Member, Parliament of Paris.		Hume's *Economic Essays* published.	Benjamin Franklin discovers lightning conductor.
1753		Appointed Master of Requests. First meets Gournay. Prepares outline for work on Commerce and Wealth.		Nicholas Magens, *The Universal Merchant.*	

Table 1.1 continued

	Adam Smith	*A. R. J. Turgot*	*C. Beccaria*	*Works on Economics published*	*Other related and relevant events*
1754		Accompanies Gournay on tours of inspection of French industry and trade till 1756.	Enters University of Pavia to study Law.	Forbonnais, *Eléments du Commerce*.	Genovesi appointed as first Professor of Political Economy at University of Naples.
1755	Smith publishes two articles in first Edinburgh Review: review of Samuel Johnson, *Dictionary* and letter to the Editors which includes review of the *Encyclopédie*.	Translates Josiah Tucker's *Questions Importants sur le Commerce*.		Josiah Tucker, *Elements of Commerce and Theory of Taxes*. Posthumous publication of Cantillon's *Essay* and Hutcheson's *System of Moral Philosophy*.	Death of Montesquieu. J. J. Rousseau publishes *Discours sur la Inégalité*. Voltaire publishes *Abrégé de l'Histoire Universelle*.
1756		Publishes 'Etymologie', 'Existence' and 'Expansibilité' in *Encyclopédie*.		Mirabeau, *L'ami des Hommes*, F. Quesnay, 'Fermiers' published in *Encyclopédie*.	
1757		Publishes 'Foire' and 'Fondation' in *Encyclopédie*.		Quesnay writes 'Hommes' and 'Impôt'. Joseph Harris, *An Essay Upon Money and Coins*.	Beginning of physiocracy with meeting of Quesnay and Mirabeau at Entresol.
1758	Quaestor of Glasgow University Library.		Graduates *cum laude* in Law – University of Pavia.	Quesnay completes first editions of *Tableau économique*.	Helvétius publishes *De l'Esprit*. Hume starts *History of England*.
1759	First Edition of *Theory of Moral Sentiments* published.	Writes *Eloge de Gournay*.			Voltaire publishes *Candide*.

	Adam Smith	*A. R. J. Turgot*	*C. Beccaria*	*Works on Economics published*	*Other related and relevant events*
1760	Dean of Faculty of Arts till 1763.	Visits Voltaire at Ferney.		Mirabeau, *Théorie de l'Impôt*.	
1761	Vice Rector, Glasgow University. Second Edition of *Theory of Moral Sentiments*, including *Considerations Concerning First Formulation of Languages*.	Appointed Intendant of Limoges: full time administrative position till 1774.	Marries Teresa Blasco. Two daughters from marriage.		Diderot publishes *Rameau's Nephew*, J. J. Rousseau publishes *La Nouvelle Héloise*.
1762	Made Burgess of Glasgow. Conferred Glasgow L.L.D.		Publishes first book: *Del Disordine e de' Remedi Delle Monete nello Stato di Milano*.		Rousseau publishes *The Social Contract* and *Emile*. Hume completes last volume of *History of England*.
1763	Smith resigns Chair. Leaves for Europe as Tutor of Duke of Buccleugh: Paris; Toulouse.	Turgot writes 'Plan for a Paper on Taxation in General' for Bertin. Meets Du Pont de Nemours.		Mirabeau, *Philosophie Rurale*.	
1764	Commences *Wealth of Nations* at Toulouse, visits Voltaire.		Publishes *Dei Delitti e delle Pene*; writes for *Il Caffè* till 1766.		Voltaire publishes *Philosophical Dictionary*.
1765			Publishes 'Tentativo Analitico su I Contrabbandi' in *II Caffè*.		First volume of *Ephémeridés du Citoyen* published.

Table 1.1 continued

	Adam Smith	*A. R. J. Turgot*	*C. Beccaria*	*Works on Economics published*	*Other related and relevant events*
1766	Visits Paris till October: meets Turgot in Paris (July). Returns to London (November).	Writes 'Réflexions sur la Formation et Distribution des Richesses' (completed November).	Travels abroad: visits Paris October–December.	Quesnay publishes *Analyse* form of *Tableau Economique*.	D'Holbach publishes *Le Christianisme Dévoilé*. Birth of T. R. Malthus.
1767	In London: assists Townsend with taxation policy.	Corresponds with Hume on taxation. Writes 'Observations' on Graslin and Saint-Péravy.	Negotiates with Catherine the Great to enter Russian public service.	Mercier de la Rivière, *L'Ordre Naturel et Essentiel des Sociétés Politiques*; Sir James Steuart, *Principles of Political Economy*; Du Pont de Nemours, *Physiocratie*. Forbonnais, *Principles et Observations Economiques*.	Adam Ferguson, *Essay on the History of Civil Society*. Birth of J. B. Say.
1768			Appointed Professor of Political Economy at Milan.	Du Pont, *De l'Origine et des Progrès d'une Science Nouvelle*. Genovesi, *Lezioni di Commercio*.	First volumes of *Encyclopedia Britannica*.
1769		Writes 'Valeurs et Monnaies' for Morellet's *Dictionnaire du Commerce*; 'Réflexions' (Parts I and II) published in November, December issues of *Ephémérides du Citoyen*.	Publishes *Piano d'Istruzione e Piano di Lezioni di Economia Pubblica*.		

	Adam Smith	A. R. J. Turgot	C. Beccaria	Works on Economics published	Other related and relevant events
1770		Third part of 'Réflexions' published. Turgot writes letters on grain trade to L'Abbé Terray, and 'Mémoire sur les Préss d'argent'.	Publishes *Ricerche Interne Sullo Stile*.		Cook discovers Australia's East Coast. D'Holbach publishes *Système de la Nature*.
1771			Writes *Elementi di Economia Pubblica* (not published till 1804). Enters public service.	P. Verri, *Meditazione sulla Economia Politica*.	
1772					Birth of David Ricardo.
1773	Smith goes to London to finish *Wealth of Nations*. Admitted as Fellow of Royal Society.	Writes 'Lettre sur la Marque des Fers'.			Goethe writes *Sorrows of Young Werther*. Birth of James Mill.
1774		Appointed Minister of Navy (June); Contrôleur-Général (Minister of Finance) in August.	Second marriage: to Donna Anna Bardo (one son from marriage).		Death of François Quesnay.
1776	March 9: publication of first edition of *Wealth of Nations*.	Six edicts and Dismissal. Retirement.		Condillac, *Le Commerce et le Gouvernement*.	Start of American War of Independence. Death of David Hume. Gibbon publishes first volumes of *Decline and Fall of Roman Empire*.
1777				Le Trosne, *De l'Ordre Social*.	

Table 1.1 continued

	Adam Smith	*A. R. J. Turgot*	*C. Beccaria*	*Works on Economics published*	*Other related and relevant events*
1778	Appointed Commissioner for Customs of Scotland and Commissioner for Salt Duties.	Elected President of Académie des Belles Lettres et des Inscriptions.	Appointed Officer of the Mint. Member of inquiry into monetary reform.		Death of Voltaire.
1781		18 March – Dies in Paris aged 53.		Isnard, *Traité des Richesses*.	Kant, *Critique of Pure Reason*
1783	Foundation Member, Royal Society of Scotland.				Death of D'Alembert.
1784	Smith's mother dies. Third edition of *Wealth of Nations*.				Death of Diderot.
1786			Appointed Head, Department of Agriculture, Industry and Commerce.		
1787	Consulted by Pitt on taxation. Made Lord Rector of Glasgow till 1789.			J. Bentham, *Defence of Usury*.	
1789	Fifth and last edition of *Wealth of Nations*.		Head of Department of Justice.		July 14: Storming of Bastille – beginning of French Revolution.
1790	17 July: dies in Edinburgh, aged 67 years.				Death of Benjamin Franklin. Edmund Burke, *Reflections on the Revolution in France*.
1794			Dies: 56 years old.	Jeremy Bentham writes *Manual of Political Economy*.	

he matriculated and entered the University of Glasgow, where he took his M.A. with distinction in 1740, having studied mathematics and natural philosophy,[9] as well as the classics, logic and moral philosophy. Here he was influenced by Dunlop in Latin and Greek, Simpson in mathematics, and especially by the 'never-to-be forgotten Hutcheson' in philosophy, an influence which must have been of considerable importance in developing his interest in economic questions (see Taylor, 1965). In 1740 he was awarded a Snell exhibition to Balliol College, Oxford for over six years, a period which according to Rae he never regretted. Rae adds that his sojourn in Oxford allowed him the leisure for private reading of the classics as well as of modern literature: these included the Italian poets whom he could 'quote easily' and the French classics 'on account of their style' (Rae, 1895, pp. 22–3); Scott, 1937, p. 40). In 1746, he gave up the Snell exhibition because he could not accept its condition of taking holy orders in the Anglican church, and with that decision his formal education of sixteen years concluded.

Details of Turgot's schooling are as follows. His early schooling was at the Colleges of Duplessis and Bourgogne, and at the latter he was introduced to the work of Newton and Locke, the fathers of experimental science. In 1743 he entered the Séminaire de Saint-Sulpice, from which he obtained the Bachelor of Theology in 1748 with distinction. His thesis was regarded as brilliant. This allowed him to enter the Sorbonne in June 1749, where he was elected Prior for 1750. During this period (1749–50) he composed the two orations[10] on the *Benefits of Christianity* and on the *Successive Advances of the Human Mind*, as well as a number of other philosophical works which have been preserved and which demonstrate his familiarity with Lockean philosophy and Newtonian physics.[11] As in the case of Smith, his contemporaries recollected his prodigious memory, his love of reading and his studious disposition. He was versed in seven foreign languages (Greek, Latin, Hebrew, Spanish, German, Italian and English, the last three of which he spoke fluently) as well as his native French. Early in 1751, he left the Sorbonne because he did not want the ecclesiastical career which as a third son was the choice made for him. The length of Turgot's formal education is difficult to assess, since no dates are available for his early schooling. As in the case of Smith, this may be estimated to have lasted for six to eight years, which together with his higher education at Saint-Sulpice (five years) and the Sorbonne (two years) gives a total of thirteen to fifteen years (see Dakin, 1965, pp. 7–13).

The details of Beccaria's education are even more fragmentary but they appear to have followed a similar pattern. His early schooling took place at the Farensiano Jesuit College in Parma, where he specialised in mathematics, Newtonian physics and languages, particularly French. This period, as Venturi (1965, pp. 458–9) put it, demonstrated his lucidity and his precocious intelligence. His preliminary schooling lasted from 1746 till 1754. He then entered the University of Pavia, where he graduated in law on 13 September 1758.[12] Although his preliminary education was therefore of similar duration to that of Turgot and Smith, his university education lasted for only four years as compared with seven for Turgot and nine for Smith (Romagnoli, 1958, I, p. XCIV; Venturi, 1965, pp. 458–9).

In the context of education it is also of interest to mention the travel experiences of the three authors, where, rather surprisingly it turns out that Smith was the more experienced traveller. As is well known, the greater part of Smith's life was spent in Scotland (Kirkcaldy, Glasgow and Edinburgh). In addition he lived for some time in Oxford and in London. His famous travels to France as tutor to the Duke of Buccleugh took place in the three years 1764–6, but were largely spent in Paris (February 1764 and December 1765 to October 1766) and Toulouse (February 1764 to September–October 1765), apart from a short visit to Geneva largely for the purpose of visiting Voltaire (October–December 1765). Turgot travelled widely within France, particularly in the years 1753 to 1756, when he accompanied Gournay on a tour of inspection of French industry which covered Bourgogne, Lyonnais, Dauphiné, Provence, Languedoc, le Maine, Anjou and Bretagne (see Say, 1887, p. 59) and also within the intendancy of Limoges on official duties from 1761 to 1774. The major part of his life was spent in Paris. He apparently experienced only one short trip abroad in 1760, when he visited the Swiss Alps and Geneva, the latter largely for a visit to Voltaire. Beccaria's travels were extensive if his tours in Italy and Vienna on official duties are included. His foreign travel otherwise was confined to a three-month visit to France (October–December 1766) which included time spent in Paris where he was feted by D'Alembert, Diderot, d'Holbach and Helvétius.[13]

The details of their respective subsequent careers can be more quickly provided. Certain important differences can be noted here which, as Schumpeter has pointed out, influenced the quality of their performance in economics.

Adam Smith followed his departure from Oxford in 1746 with two years in Kirkcaldy with his mother, a period about which virtually nothing is known. In 1748 he moved to Edinburgh to earn his living as a freelance lecturer. In the winter of 1748–9, and the two subsequent winters, he lectured on rhetoric and *belles-lettres*, but these lectures were supplemented, at least during 1750–1, with lectures on more philosophical topics. These have been variously described as dealing with jurisprudence, or the 'history of civil society' or the history of philosophy, and appear to have included economic material. In 1751 he was appointed Professor of Logic at the University of Glasgow, a chair he exchanged for that of Moral Philosophy in April 1752. In the later years of his academic career he busied himself with university administration (as Quaestor of the Library from 1758 to 1760, Dean of Arts from 1760 to 1763 and Vice Rector from 1761 to 1763). He resigned his chair early in 1764 on becoming tutor to the Duke of Buccleugh during the latter's travels in Europe; this position ended in November 1766 and provided him with an income of £300 per annum for life (an income, to put it in perspective, double his early Glasgow professorial earnings of approximately £150). This annuity allowed him a leisurely life in London and Kirkcaldy, essential for writing the *Wealth of Nations*. This book was commenced in the first half of 1764 (when Smith was bored during his prolonged stay at Toulouse) and finally sent to press in the second half of 1775, eleven years later. In 1778 he obtained the position of Commissioner of Customs for Scotland (£500 per annum) and of Salt Duties (£100 per annum), positions which though they were not strenuous, occupied much of his time and energy. During this period, as Rae put it, 'his mother, his friends, his books – these were Smith's great joys'. But his mother's death deprived him of the first in 1784, and ill health thereafter gradually deprived him of the other two. In short, Smith's life was devoted to intellectual pursuits in his thirteen years in the chair at Glasgow, his ten years of writing the *Wealth of Nations* and, to a lesser extent, his twelve years as a government official.

Turgot's career can be briefly described. After leaving the Sorbonne early in 1751, he obtained a number of legal positions in 1752 and 1753, stepping-stones to the position of intendant which he aimed for, but did not procure until 1761. In that year Bertin assigned him the district of Limoges, the province he administered until 1774. In May 1774 he was appointed first as Minister of the Navy, and then from the end of August 1774 to May 1776 as Finance Minister. This position left him no leisure whatsoever. The last five years of his life were spent in retirement in Paris, where he busied himself with scientific experiments, particularly in meteorology, with reading and with his friends. During his retirement his health rapidly deteriorated, particularly from the attacks of gout he had suffered since 1760, and which eventually caused his death in March 1781. Fifteen of Turgot's thirty years of life after leaving the university were spent in important administrative posts; of the remaining fifteen, five were spent in retirement and ten in the comparative leisure of his minor legal positions from 1751 to 1761.

Beccaria's career reveals considerable similarities to those of Smith and Turgot. For ten years after graduating from the university. Beccaria enjoyed the life of a 'literato' and philosopher, being (by his own account) converted to the new philosophy in 1761 through a reading of Montesquieu's *Lettres Persanes* (Beccaria to Morellet, 26 January 1766, in Romagnoli, 1958, II, p. 865). From 1764 to 1766 he contributed essays to the journal, *Il Caffè*, founded by himself and his friends Pietro and Alessandro Verri on the model of *The Spectator*. In addition, he published the work on crime and punishment that made him famous in European intellectual society. After his trip to France in 1766 and negotiations in 1767 with the Russian court to enter the service of Catherine the Great, he was offered the new chair of cameral science at Milan in 1768, a position he held till March 1771. From that time onwards, Beccaria was involved in administrative government positions relating to economic affairs, health and the administration of justice, until his death in 1794. Like Turgot, Beccaria followed his university education with a decade of comparative leisure filled with intellectual pursuits and then full-time government administration; like Smith he was a full-time academic, but for a much shorter period of time.

Their literary output must also be briefly compared. As Schumpeter points out, all three were polymaths whose intellectual interests ranged over the whole of learning from mathematics and the natural sciences to many aspects of what are now called the social sciences. These wide interests are reflected in their published writings, but it can be said at the outset that only Smith published lengthy books. By contrast, Turgot and Beccaria produced only relatively short works.

Smith's collected works, now published in six hefty volumes together with a volume of correspondence, include as major parts the work which made him famous during his lifetime: *The Theory of Moral Sentiments* (first published in 1759 with later editions in 1761, 1767, 1774, 1781 and the sixth definitive revised and enlarged edition of 1791) and his *Wealth of Nations*, which takes up two volumes in the collected works (first published 1776, with further editions in 1778, 1784, 1786, 1789 and a posthumous edition of 1791). Apart from these he published in 1748 an edition of William Hamilton's *Poems on Several Occasions* to which he contributed a short preface, two essays for the *Edinburgh Review* in 1755 (one a perceptive review of Samuel Johnson's *A Dictionary of the English Language*, the other a plea to the editors of that short-lived journal for reviews of non-Scottish books, written in the form of a comparative essay on the state of learning in Britain and Europe), an essay entitled 'Considerations Concerning the First Formation of Languages', published in 1761 with the second edition of *Theory of Moral Sentiments*, and finally his *Essays on Philosophical Subjects*, published posthumously in 1795, covering astronomy, physics, classical philosophy, poety, painting, sculpture, music and dancing as well as an analysis of the external senses. The final two volumes of his works consist of his lectures on rhetoric and *belles-lettres* (delivered in Edinburgh) and his lectures on jurisprudence delivered during the last two years of his professorship at Glasgow, the contents of which cannot be easily summarised.[14]

The most complete edition of Turgot's works (edited by Schelle in 1913–23) is made up of five large volumes which contain his writings as well as documents relating to his life and official activities. A perusal of its contents will reveal no large books, very few works published during his lifetime,[15] a number of unfinished manuscripts and, by far the greatest part, memoranda produced in his official capacity as Intendant of Limoges and Finance Minister. The wide range of his interests is revealed in his early works produced at Saint-Sulpice and the Sorbonne, and during the ten years before he became fully occupied in the public service.[16] It can be illustrated by the entries he wrote and was asked to write for the *Encyclopédie*: 'Etymologie', 'Existence' and 'Expansibilité'; were published in 1756, 'Foire' and 'Fondations' in 1757. In 1759 Diderot asked him to contribute 'Humiditée', 'Idée', 'Idéalisme', 'Intérêt de l'argent', 'Impôt', 'Immatérialisme', 'Inspecteur' and 'Intendant de province'. Du Pont suggests he was also asked to contribute those on 'Grammaire générale', 'Hôpital', 'Inspecteurs', 'Origine des langues', 'Mendacité', 'Probabilité'; and 'Sensations' (see Groenewegen, 1977, p. xv, n27, n28). In addition, his interests can be gauged from the extraordinary list of projected works which he produced in his youth: these range from a tragedy to a treatise on luxury, and include as well works on universal history, origin of languages, love and marriage, political geography, natural theology, morality, economics and the natural sciences.

What is remarkable about this list, as Meek (1973, p. 2) put it, is that he managed to contribute to most of these subjects or at least to maintain an active interest in them during his short lifetime of fifty-four years.

Beccaria's readily available work is contained in the two volumes edited by Romagnoli (1958), one of which is virtually wholly devoted to memoranda written when he was a public servant, and to his correspondence. The first volume contains the works produced during the ten years when he was living the life of a philosopher and academic during the 1760s. These commence with his pamphlet on the monetary problems of Milan (published in 1762), his treatise 'Of Crime and Punishment' (first published in 1764 but reprinted and translated frequently during his lifetime), his contributions to the periodical *Il Caffè* (published between 1764 and 1766) which deal with subjects as diverse as the Pharaohs, the sense of smell, smuggling,[17] style, periodicals as a form of publication, and the delights of the imagination, and conclude with his book *Investigations Concerning the Nature of Style* (published in 1770). The last three works in this volume, only one of which was published during his lifetime, relate to his professorship in Milan: they are his plan for the teaching of political economy (written in 1769), his inaugural lecture (delivered on 9 January 1769 and published contemporaneously), and his lectures not published till 1804, under the title *Elementi di Economia Pubblica*. The sixty-odd documents which form the contents of the second volume are devoted to matters of economic administration, monetary questions, public health and penal and law reform. They also include some juvenile verse ('The Bibliomaniac', 'The Earthquake of Lisbon' and 'The Harvest') and fragments from manuscripts which include thoughts on matter, on barbarism and on civilisation of nations and the primitive state of mankind, and on the customs and habits of nations. These last works illustrate the interest in change and progress which he shared with Turgot and Smith, and which are evaluated later in this chapter.

This exercise in comparative biography[18] supplements the broad comparative picture of this 'triumvirate' as presented by Schumpeter, and highlights the similarities as well as the differences in their respective lives. To the similarities noted by Schumpeter a few can be added. All three received a good education which included an early introduction and training in the new scientific methodology pioneered by Newton and Locke. All three were greatly interested in literature and language, including style, grammar, etymology and the origins of language. All three explored the idea of historical progress and the cause of the change which transformed humankind from a savage state to civilisation, and the effects of such changes on customs, manners, institutions and the arts, and they contributed to these subjects in varying degrees. In addition, all three had linguistic abilities of a high order, prodigious memories, studious dispositions and were widely read. Viewed in this perspective they were all sublime products of their age, gatherers of and contributors to the fruits of enlightenment. Finally, they all combined this knowledge in the construction of systems of political economy, completed in varying degrees, which are now considered part of their crowning intellectual achievements. The major difference in their lives (as noted by Schumpeter) – the comparison of their economic systems – is discussed in the next section.

Three systems of classical political economy

The economic systems of Turgot, Beccaria and Smith were all produced within the decade commencing in 1765, and although there are differences between the theoretical skeletons on which these systems were constructed, they share the common feature of being primarily concerned with the production and reproduction of wealth. Turgot's major economic work, 'Reflections on the Production and Distribution of Wealth', was hurriedly composed and completed in November 1766; it is a short work of 101 paragraphs or sections, and was not intended as a major work at all (for details of its writing see Groenewegen, 1977, pp. xvi–xxi). Beccaria's *Elementi* was written during 1771–2 as his lecture notes; this is a much larger work than that of Turgot but is clearly unfinished, since the best available version of the text (Romagnoli, 1958) does not include the fifth part on the subject of 'police' (that is, on public regulation, science, education, law and order) or the material on taxation in Part IV on finance which Beccaria announced in his introduction (Romagnoli, 1958, pp. 383–5). Smith's *Wealth of Nations*, commenced in 1764 and completed over eleven years (nine of which were virtually completely devoted to it) is by far the largest of the three and was of course a finished and highly polished product, which moreover had the benefit of one substantial revision in the four editions subsequent to the first which were published during Smith's lifetime. As Schumpeter has suggested, this type of background should be remembered in comparing the scientific merit of the three works.

To make such a comparison, the logical sequence on which their argument is constructed must be briefly set out. As already indicated, all three economists regarded the reproduction and the increase of wealth as the primary objective of their inquiries. Smith and Turgot acknowledged this explicitly in their respective titles. Beccaria stated this by defining 'economia pubblica' as the art of preserving and increasing the wealth of nations and of putting it to its best possible use (Beccaria, 1958, I, p. 383). The manner in which this common subject matter is developed in the three works is, however, different. To facilitate the analysis of these three different approaches, Table 1.2 provides a comparative table of contents of the three works, which allows a convenient overview of their theoretical framework but which, unfortunately, cannot really explain the rationale behind the manner in which the three developed their subject matter. This rationale must therefore be briefly discussed.

Smith's inquiry into the nature and causes of the wealth of nations, or to put it another way, his analysis of the principal object of political economy (see Smith, 1776, p. 428) is conducted by first elucidating the principles underlying economic development, then analysing its historical progress, then critically investigating the policy principles developed by alternative systems of political economy, before concluding with a discussion of the role and share of the state

Table 1.2: Comparative table of contents of Smith's *Wealth of Nations*, Turgot's 'Reflections' and Beccaria's *Elementi*

A. Smith: *Wealth of Nations*	Turgot: *Reflections*	Beccaria: *Elementi*
Introduction and plan of the work	Part I [of agricultural society]	Part I – Principles and general view
Book I – Of the causes of improvement of the productive powers of labour, and of the order according to which its produce is naturally distributed among the different ranks of the people.	Sections 1–4: Origins of commerce, inequality of property, diversity of soil, multiplicity of wants and division of labour Section 5: Pre-eminence of husbandman Section 6: Wages	Introduction and plan Chapter 1: General principles: capital, reproduction, division of labour, exchange, value, sectors in production of wealth
Chapters I–3: The division of labour Chapter 4: Origins and use of money Chapter 5: Measure of value Chapter 6–7: Value and price Chapter 8–11: Wages, profit and rent (theory of distribution)	Section 7–18: Origins and characteristics of classes in agricultural society: proprietors, artisans and husbandmen Sections 19–28: Historical analysis of how the proprietors extract the agricultural surplus; by wage labour (section 20), slaves (21–2), bondage to the soil (23), vassalage (24), sharecroppping (25), tenant farming (26)	Chapter 2: The nature of labour and consumption, value, wages and profits Chapter 3: Of population, its increase, decrease and measurement Part II – of agriculture [primary industry]
Book II – Of the nature of accumulation and employment of stock	Part II [of capitals, commerce, money and interest]	Chapter 1: Obstacles to the improvement of agriculture and their remedies
Chapter 1: Division of stock Chapter 2: Money, credit, banking and capital Chapter 3: Productive, unproductive labour and capital accumulation Chapter 4: Interest Chapter 5: Different employments of capital	Section 29: Introduction Section 30: Gold and silver in commerce Section 31: Commerce and value Section 32–3: Determination of value and prices Sections 34–39: Measure of value and money	Chapter 2: Of small-scale and large-scale cultivation of the soil Chapter 3: Plan for the improvement of agriculture Chapter 4: of the proportions between the different methods of cultivation Chapter 5: Of regulations in staple commodities

Table 1.2 continued

A. Smith: Wealth of Nations	Turgot: Reflections	Beccaria: Elemeti
Book III – Of the natural progress of opulence in the different nations	Sections 40–7: Origins and use of money	Chapter 6: Of the cultivation of other types of foodstuffs
	Sections 48: Use of money and division of Labour	Chapter7: Of pastoral activity
Chapter 1: Of the natural progress of opulence	Sections 49–50: Accumulation of capital	Chapter 8: Of mining, fishing and hunting
Chapter 2: Discouragement of agriculture in the ancient state of Europe	Sections 51–8: Necessity for, and sources of capital	
Chapter 3: Rise and progress of cities and towns	Sections 59–71: Of the employments of capital, that is industry (59–60), agriculture (62–4) commerce (66–7) and lending at interest (71); division of artisans and husbandmen into capitalists and wage labourers (65)	Part III – Of arts and manufacturing
Chapter 4: Interrelationship of town and country		
Book IV – Of systems of political economy		Introduction
Introduction		Chapter 1: Of the different parts of arts and manufactures and their varying aspects
Chapter 1: Principle of mercantile system	Part III [interest and wealth]	Chapter 2: The causes which weaken and ruin the arts and the means to strengthen them
Chapters 2–5: Of restraints on trade that is, imports, drawbacks, bounties	Sections 72–6: False and true principles on the interest of money	
Chapter 6: Of treatises of commerce	Sections 77–80: Two values of money: interest and exchange value	Chapter 3: Of the preferment and distribution of the various types of arts and manufactures
Chapter 7: Of colonies		
Chapter 8: Conclusions on mercantile system	Sections 81–2: Variations in the rate of interest	Chapter 4: Of the requirements by which the arts can be practised
Chapter 9: Agricultural system or critique of physiocracy	Sections 83–90: Variations in interest and interrelationship with employment of capital	
Book IV – Of the revenue of the sovereign or commonwealth	Sections 91–2: Methods of estimating national wealth	Part IV – Of commerce
Chapter 1: Government expenditure on defence, law and order and public works	Sections 93–9: Interest and disposable surplus, implications for class analysis	Introduction
		Chapter 1: Of value and price
Chapter 2: Sources of revenue, that is public domain and taxation	Sections 100–1: Capital, land, savings and money	Chapter 2: Of money
Chapter 3: Public debt		Chapter 3: Of circulation and competition
		Chapter 4: Of commerce
		Chapter 5: Of luxury
		Chapter 6: Of the interest of money
		Chapter 7: Of exchange rates
		Chapter 8: Of banking and credit
		Chapter 9: Of public credit

Table 1.2 continued

A. Smith: Wealth of Nations	Turgot: Reflections	Beccaria: Elemeti
Chapter 2: Sources of revenue, that is public domain and taxation Chapter 3: Public debt	Sections 100–1: Capital, land, savings and money	[Part V – Finance] [Part VI – of police] N.B. It should be noted that the contents of the *Elementi* as actually published vary substantially from the plan of lectures produced *circa* 1769 (Romagnoli, 1958, I, pp. 342–9) which largely follows the contents of Cantillon's *Essai* except for adding material on manufactures and the state. This plan is divided into the following five parts: I: Principles and general view (11 chapters) II: Agriculture (4 chapters) III: Commerce (8 chapters) IV: Of manufactures (6 chapters) V: Of finance [i.e. public finance] This last part was intended to deal with the principles of public finance, including need for statistical information, taxation, public administration and public goods, and different types of government

in economic development. Book I therefore deals with the productivity of labour and the distribution of wealth, the subject matter covered in the first three and final four chapters of the book. This links the major cause of the wealth of nations with the first objective of political economy: how the people secure a revenue or subsistence for themselves. The apparent digression on money and value in the four intervening chapters is part of a logical chain of reasoning which links labour productivity to the division of labour (ch. 1), the division of labour to exchange and the extent of the market (chs 2–3), the development of exchange to the origin and use of money (ch. 4), the theory of money to the problem of value measurement (ch. 5), the measure of value to the theory of value and the determination of market and natural price (chs 6–7) and finally the three component parts of price to wages, profit and rent, the means by which the three classes of society obtain their subsistence and which Smith defined as the problem of the distribution of wealth. Book II on capital theory is immediately linked to the division of labour in its introduction, tackling its subject matter of 'the nature, accumulation and employment of stock' in chapters 1, 3 and 5 and in addition examining the relationship between money and stock, banking and credit (ch. 2) and the determination of the rate of interest (ch. 4). Book III applies these basic principles in the construction of a historical survey of economic development in Europe from the fall of the Roman Empire, and thereby provides the bridge between principles and their application in economic policy. Book IV critically evaluates the principles for enriching the people (and the state) developed by contemporary systems of political economy, partly in the light of the principles already developed in the earlier books, before Smith analyses his own prescriptions for the involvement of the state in economic progress (Book V). This is an impressive and highly effective method of analysing how economic growth affects the revenue and welfare of the various classes of society and of the state, and constitutes a major contribution to the economic dynamics of the evolution of civil society.

Turgot's analytical framework is similarly concerned with the theory of economic development in civil society, but his analysis is confined to the final two stages of that development – agricultural and commercial (capitalist) society – and to its effects on the classes of society rather than on the state.[19] If the division of the 'Reflections' into parts, adopted by Du Pont for its publication in the *Ephémérides*, is followed (as is done in Table 1.3), then Part I can be described as dealing with the characteristics of agricultural society, while Parts II and III deal with the changes in these characteristics induced by its transformation into commercial or capitalist society. The key features of this analysis are the manner in which the development of trade and money, and especially the accumulation of capital, alter the composition of national wealth, the annual revenue, the class structure in society and the manner in which these classes obtain their subsistence. The order in which this material is developed indicates Turgot's essentially materialistic approach to the economic development of civil society, as the summary in the following paragraphs indicates.

Table 1.3 Sources and authorities known to Smith, Turgot and Beccaria

Authorities cited in Wealth of Nations	*Present in Turgot's library*	*Cited elsewhere by Turgot*	*Cited by Beccaria*
Cantillon, *Essai sur la Nature du Commerce en Général* (1755)	Item 2704	S III 500	R 1 340 (a)
Child, Josiah, A *New Discourse of Trade* (1694)		S 1 372–76	
Davenant, Charles, *Political and Commercial Works* (1711)			
Decker, Matthew, *Essay on the Causes of the Decline of Foreign Trade* (1740)	Items 2229–2231*		
Du Tot, *Réflexions Politiques sur les Finances et le Commerce* (1738)	Item 2740	G 11–2	R II 845
Fleetwood, William, *Chronicon Preciosum* (1707)	Item 2217		
Gee, Joshua, *Trade and Navigation of Great Britain Considered* (1729)	Item 2224*		
Hobbes, T., *Leviathan* (1651)	Item 2546		R I 18
Hume, David, *History of England* (1754 and 1778)	Items 2171–4, 2183*	G 107 S III 150	
Essays Moral Political and Literary (1752)	Item 603 4002–03	G 100	R I 29, 376, II, 864–869
Hutcheson, Frances, A *Short Introduction in Moral Philosophy* (1747)	Item 2569		
A System of Moral Philosophy (1755)			
King, Charles, *The British Merchant* (1721)	Item 2223*		
King, Gregory, *Natural and Political Observations* (1688)			R I 422
Law, John, *Money and Trade Considered* (1705)		G 2, 3, 4, 5, 7	R I 599
Locke, John, *Essay on Civil Government (1690)*			
Considerations on the Consequences of Covering Interest and Raising the Value of Money(1691)	In works (1767)	G 47	R I 13 187, 203, 536
Further Considerations Concerning Raising the Value of Money(1696)	Item 4677	G 4, 11	R I 8
Magens, Nicolas, *Universal Merchant* (1753)			

Table 1.3 Continued

Authorities cited in Wealth of Nations	*Present in Turgot's library*	*Cited elsewhere by Turgot*	*Cited by Beccaria*
Mandeville, Bernard, *Fable of the Bees* (1723)			
Melon, V.F., *Essai Politique sur le Commerce* (1734)	Item 4447	S III, 500	R I 375–376, II 845
Mercier, de la Rivière, *L'Ordre Naturel et Essentiel des Sociétés Politiques* (1767)	Items 556–557		
Mirabeau, V.R., *L'ami des Hommes* (1756)	Item 2644	G 123	
Théorie de l'impôt (1760)	Item 2677	G 106, 107, 108, 123	
Philosophie Rurale (1766)	Item 2650	G 106, 118, 123	
Montesquieu, *l'Esprit des Lois* (1748)	Items 556, 567	G 152, 159	RI 9, 10, 46, 63, 204, 375
Mun, Thomas, *England's Treasure by Forraign Trade* (1664)			
Quesnay, François, *Physiocratie* (Ed. Du Pont) (1767–1768)	Item 571	S II 676–677	(b)
Steuart, Sir James, *Principles of Political Oeconomy* (1767)	Item 2636		
Tucker, Josiah, Not listed as authority but well represented in Smith's Library, M 147–8	Items 225, 2218, 2713		
Turgot, *Reflections on the Production and Distribution of Wealth* (1766)	Item 2668		
Uztariz, *Theory and Practice of Commerce* (1751)	Item 2705*		R I 376
WORKS IN SMITH'S LIBRARY NOT LISTED AS AUTHORITIES			
Beccaria, *Opere* M 71			
Berkeley, George, *The Querist* (1735) M 71			
Condillac, Le Commerce et le Gouvernement (1776) M 83	Item 2709		RI 203, 222 II 866, 868 (c)
Ephémérides Du Citoyen (1761–1769) M 91	Item 2466		
Forbonnais, *Éléments du Commerce* (1754) M 94	Item 2703		R I 12, 14 and R II 845

Table 1.3 Continued

Authorities cited in Wealth of Nations	*Present in Turgot's library*	*Cited elsewhere by Turgot*	*Cited by Beccaria*
Principles et Observations Economiques (1767) M 94	Item 2640		R II 845
Recherche et Consid[r1]érations sur les Finances(1758) M94	Item 2061		R II 845
Harris, Joseph, *Essay Upon Money and Coins* (1757) M 101			
Herbert, C.J., *Essai sur le Police Générale des Grains* (1755) M 102	Item 2985		
Le Trosne, *Receuil de Plusieurs Morceaux Economiques* (1760) M 112	Item 2722		
Verri, P., *Meditazione Sulla Economia Politica* (1771) M 149			(d)

Notes:
Column on Smith: M = Mizuta (1967) plus page reference.
Column on Turgot: Item number in Tsuda (1974)* denotes the work was present in Turgot's library in translation; S = Schelle (1913–23) volume and page reference; G = Groenewegen (1977) page reference.
Column on Beccaria: R = Romagnoli (1958), volume and page reference; (a) Although Cantillon is not cited directly the influence of his work on Beccaria is so striking that he must have been studied by Beccaria, as Romagnoli points out in the pages cited; (b) Beccaria cites Quesnay's article 'Fermiers' from the *Encyclopédie* R I 451; (c) All general references to Condillac; (d) Although not cited by Beccaria, he must have read it.
* Denotes works in French translation only in Turgot's Library.

In an agricultural society, although there is already a need for division of labour and exchange (sections 1–4), the non-agricultural occupations are still relatively unimportant. Society is therefore divided into proprietors who own the land, the people concerned with agricultural production who produce the greater part of national wealth, and finally the artisans who produce the non-agricultural commodities required by the first two classes and who receive their subsistence in return (section 5, pp. 7–18). Two types of income share arise in such a society: the surplus product or rent for the landowners, who are the sole owners of the national wealth (section 19) and the wages, reduced to subsistence by competition, for those who have no property except for their ability to work (section 6). The extraction of the surplus from the working classes by the proprietors has changed according to the various modes of agricultural production which have been practised (sections 20–8), that is, slavery, bondage to the soil, vassalage, sharecropping and, finally, the leasing of land to farmers who supply their own capital for the cultivation of the land for which they pay a regular and pre-determined money rent. This last method, as Turgot put it, is only utilised by countries which are already developed and wealthy; the fourth method was used by less developed and less wealthy areas. Hence France was in a stage of agricultural transition, since both of these methods were used in various parts of the country (sections 26–7). The discussion of the principle of capitalist farming leads Turgot naturally into a discussion of capital and the nature of commercial (capitalist) society.

The second part of the 'Reflections' opens with the statement that there is a further way of earning a revenue, which depends neither on work nor on land ownership: this is living off the revenue from money or interest. This requires a discussion of money (section 30), value and exchange (sections 31–48) and a discussion of capital accumulation, the need for capital in all sections of industry and the origin of profit (sections 49–55, 59–60, 62–71). Since this form of property permits the receipt of an income without labour, it has to be distinguished from the other form, land (sections 56–8) and consequently the division of society into classes presented in the first part is modified. With the advent of capital, society is divided into landlords who draw a revenue from their property in moveable wealth, and finally those without property who draw a revenue from their labour (sections 61 and 65). The third part discusses the legitimacy and determination of interest (sections 72–90), the division of wealth into real and personal property – land and capital from which the principal of loans has to be eliminated to avoid double counting (sections 91–2) – and the question of whether the revenue of capital is as disposable as that of land (sections 93–9); it then concludes with further remarks on the savings/investment process and the role of money therein (sections 100–1). In his 'Reflections', Turgot demonstrates that the progress of wealth takes place through the accumulation of capital, which transforms production in all sectors of the economy and which in addition transforms the division of social classes from that appropriate in an agricultural society to that of landlords, capitalists and labourers. Many of the details of this picture of the history of civil society can be filled in from Turgot's other economic work, in particular in relation to his views of the state and its role in economic development.

Beccaria views the object of political economy in a manner very similar to that of Smith. It is defined as that part of the science of legislation and politics which is used to increase the opulence of the subjects and of the state (Beccaria, 1958, I, p. 34) and which concerns itself with the art of maintaining and increasing the wealth of the nation which can only be achieved by the labour of useful and productive men (*ibid.*, pp. 350–1). This science embraces four important subjects, namely agriculture, manufactures, commerce, and finance or the perception and use of the revenue of the people and of the sovereign (*ibid.*, p. 341).[20] The elements of the subject therefore divide themselves naturally into four parts according to these four branches of economic activity, but just as all science has universal principles, this discussion must be preceded by the general principles of political economy (*ibid.* p. 385). In addition, the ordering of this material is important: the foundation of all economic activity is agriculture, which provides the basic food, clothing and lodging for humankind and is therefore discussed first; most of these prime materials have to be altered and modified by 'industrious hands' to make them suitable for other uses, hence manufacture is the second part of political economy. The growth of production creates abundance and hence trade, value, circulation and money – the third part of political economy, which follows naturally from agriculture and manufacturing. This labour of man, whether in agriculture or manufacture or in their mutual exchange, can only take place in peace and tranquillity, that is, under protection of 'arms and the law' against external aggression and against the 'greed of their fellow citizens'. This requires taxation to meet the cost of such protection and gives rise to the fourth part of the subject: (public) finance. Finally, these activities of humankind must be guided by laws moral and physical and hence by science, education, good order, security and public peace – in short, all that is included under the heading of 'Police' – for the fifth and last part of political economy (*ibid.*, pp. 383–5).

Since Beccaria regards political economy as the science of the legislator and statesman, much advice is proffered in the discussion of the first two objects of political economy for the improvement of agriculture and manufactures in order to increase national wealth. Beccaria's discussion of agriculture, for example, is therefore largely an analysis of the causes of its decline and the policy remedies for this, an argument which is largely conducted on physiocratic lines.[21] The decline of agriculture is ascribed to the low price of produce, poverty and low living standards and hence insufficient incentives for rural workers, deficiencies in transportation and other impediments to the circulation of agricultural produce such as the prohibition of foreign trade, lack of capital in agriculture and a system of taxation which frequently more than exhausts the net product of agriculture (Beccaria, 1958, I, pp. 437–47). The remedies are free trade in corn, the basic agricultural commodity, taxation of the net rather than the gross product, and improvements in transport in order to improve the returns on farming and thereby to provide the means to transform agriculture from small- to large-scale farming (*ibid.*, pp. 452–7). Similarly, in Part III dealing with manufactures, there is an analysis of the causes of the decline in manufactures, which include artificial government regulations and restrictions, high taxes, as well as lack of investment in manufactures because of the attractiveness of high interest rates paid by the banks, which diverts capital to less productive uses. The remedies here are the encouragement of free competition by removing restrictive practices such as guilds, the regulation of industry, excessive taxes, restrictions on trade and a low rate of interest. In addition, a flourishing agriculture is seen as providing the best possible stimulus to manufactures (*ibid.*, pp. 528–38).

Beccaria's *Elementi* is not, however, exclusively concerned with practical policy prescriptions for the improvement of agriculture, manufactures and trade. His treatment of commerce in the last completed part of the work, which he himself described as the most interesting part of the subject after agriculture (*ibid.*, p. 551), contains theoretical discussions of value, money, credit, interest, the foreign exchanges, and circulation and competition, which provide a more detailed elucidation of the principles underlying the policy prescriptions of earlier parts, and which were only hastily sketched in the introductory chapters of the first part. The introduction to Part IV provides a further justification of the order of the contents: commerce is fostered by the extension of man's types of want; such wants are limited in societies of hunters, are expanded but still quite limited in pastoral society, and do not really come into their own until the development of agriculture stimulates manufactures and trade. Beccaria therefore also subscribed to the four stages theory which had been developed by Turgot and Smith,[22] and it is this historical consideration, as has already been indicated, which inspired the design of the book. In addition, the analysis of commerce provides the principles which tie together the various branches of political economy dealing with private activities in agriculture and manufactures, and with state activities in the areas of public finance and 'police'.

The differences in these approaches should not obscure the tremendous similarity underlying their organisational framework which has just been outlined. All three developed the principles of political economy within the historical framework provided by the four stages theory, in which the principles of commercial society, which all three saw emerging within their respective countries (albeit in different degrees), are carefully analysed. In this analysis, all three emphasise the role of the economic surplus (net product or net revenue) as the key factor in economic development, because this surplus provides the means by which industry in general can be improved, living standards raised for the people as a whole, commerce expanded, and revenue supplied for the necessary activities of the state in providing the essential services of defence and justice and the preservation of property required for such development. All three, moreover, emphasise the obstacles to such development by pointing to the legacy of policy mistakes in restrictions on trade and competition, taxation, transport and communications which had created obstacles to capital accumulation and hence the improvement of agriculture and manufactures. The vision of the three economists, to use Schumpeter's concept, is essentially the same: it basically provides for the same scope in the subject and clearly contains all the basic characteristics which define classical political economy.

The similarities between the three books are not confined to these broad principles: the treatment of particular aspects of political economy is also frequently very similar. This is particularly so in the case of the theory of value, which may serve as an illustration of the manner in which the three writers almost simultaneously reached similar conclusions, and may at the same time allow some reflections on differences in their work. Similar comparisons could be provided on their theory of money, exchange rates, and so on, but space does not permit such detailed analysis.

The basic feature of the theory of value and price which Smith, Beccaria and Turgot held in common is a dual influence in the determination of prices: the market and the cost of production. Smith's discussion of price determination in the *Wealth of Nations* is so well known that it requires no further elucidation, but it should be noted that its essential features were already included in the accounts of his *Lectures* at Glasgow which have been preserved. In the *Lectures*, Smith distinguished the market price from the natural price, analysed the market price in terms of demand (including therein the wealth of buyers) and the relative scarcity of the good in question, and then defined the natural price as the necessary cost of production, especially labour costs but including the profits of stock. The interrelationship between the two prices is also clearly expressed in the accounts of the *Lectures* (Meek *et al.*, pp. 353–61, 495–9). Similarly, Turgot (though not in his 'Reflections') distinguished a fundamental value and an exchange value, the first being determined by cost of production (raw materials, labour costs and interest on advances), the second by supply and demand. As in the case of Smith, the interrelationship between these prices is clearly explained (Groenewegen, 1977, p. 120, n16; and see Groenewegen, 1982, pp. 128–9). Likewise, Beccaria analyses value and price in terms of exchange in the market where competition between the buyers and sellers determines the price, but where that market price is ultimately regulated by the labour costs of the good, including that of raw materials and transportation (Beccaria, 1958, I, pp. 388–9, 555–62).

A difference between Smith on the one hand, and Turgot and Beccaria on the other in the context of value should also be noted. Both Turgot and Beccaria place far more emphasis in their analysis of value on the manner in which commodities are traded, and both provide models of isolated exchange under various assumptions to illustrate how the exchange ratio between two isolated individuals trading wine and wheat is determined. They explain the considerations which enter into such exchanges and the inferences to be drawn from the mean valuation of the commodities which are traded (Beccaria, 1958, pp. 556–8). Turgot in like manner in the 'Reflections' (sections 31–3) examines the price formation of an isolated exchange, and carries out this analysis much more extensively in his unfinished paper 'Value and Money' (in Groenewegen, 1977, pp. 144–8). This type of analysis, with its apparently greater emphasis on subjective considerations in the determination of value, has no real counterpart in the writings of Smith, which can be partly explained by differences in their education.[23]

Before concluding this section, a few other points of comparison relevant to the purpose of this paper must be noted. In the first place, there are differences between the work of Beccaria and that of Smith and Turgot which have so far not been noted. One of these is the extensive treatment of population in Beccaria, which has no counterpart in the work of either Smith or Turgot. On the other hand, although Beccaria is fully aware of the importance of capital in production, which he derived from Quesnay's work as has already been mentioned, his analysis of capital is nowhere systematically developed in the manner in which it is by Turgot and Smith. Furthermore, Beccaria presents no systematic treatment of the theory of distribution as an analysis of the manner in which national revenue is distributed among the classes of society. There are remarks which support a subsistence theory of wages (Beccaria, 1958, I, pp. 398–9, 522–3); there is material on the rate of interest and rent; but there is no general discussion of income shares. It is of course possible that such a discussion may have been presented if Beccaria had analysed problems of taxation in the context of his proposed outline.[24]

A difference between Smith's work and that of Turgot and Beccaria which should also briefly be noted is the difference in treatment of the division of labour in their analysis of economic progress. Smith's heavy emphasis on this factor, and his detailed analysis of both the social division of labour and the industrial division of labour, are not matched in the work of the other two, though both were clearly aware of its importance and discussed it right at the beginning of their work (see Beccaria, 1958, part I, ch. 1, section 9; Turgot, sections 3–4). There are also differences in their support of free trade and laissez-faire: Turgot was here perhaps the most dogmatic, Smith less so, and Beccaria least of all. Nevertheless, all three regarded the removal of many of the existing barriers to trade and other artificial restrictions on industry, such as those of the guilds, as important policy measures to enhance the improvement of agriculture and manufactures.

The key similarity between the three major systems of political economy which have just been examined is their classical content. In their respective analyses of the reproduction of wealth, Turgot, Beccaria and Smith emphasised the role of economic surplus, its distribution among social classes and its disposal within this reproductive process, thereby indicating that they had appreciated the major contribution of Quesnay (and prior to him, though to a lesser extent, that of Cantillon) which had emphasised the interdependence of production, circulation and distribution. In addition, their works embodied the classical dichotomy between market price and natural price as one of the foundations of the classical theory of reproduction. This tradition can be traced back to the work of Petty. Furthermore, all three placed their analyses firmly within the schema of historical progress, and thereby demonstrated their faith in the application (to the social sciences) of the new experimental method of Newton and Locke. The three thus made history their laboratory. These issues are further explored in the concluding sections.

The international foundations of classical political economy

In an earlier comparison of Turgot and Adam Smith (Groenewegen, 1969, p. 287; below p. 373) it was concluded that the striking similarities which had been observed in the economic works of these two men could be explained by the common intellectual heritage which they shared. That conclusion, which was highly relevant to the settlement of the old Turgot/Smith controversies, can now be expanded and enriched when in addition the economic work of Beccaria is compared with that of his two illustrious contemporaries. Such a comparison, as Schumpeter to some extent indicated, sheds light on the qualities which were required to produce the three great works in the literature of political economy which were written in that crucial period of the third quarter of the eighteenth century, when economics emerged as a science. The similarity in thrust of the three works under consideration, combined with an analysis of the intellectual influences of the three authors under consideration, can be shown to be an important factor in explaining the birth of classical political economy.

Such an inquiry moreover transcends the earlier inquiries into the 'nationality of political economy' (e.g. Jevons, 1881) by demonstrating the role of the international transmission of ideas in this period, and hence explaining aspects of the sociology of the new science of political economy in the 1760s and 1770s.

Material regarding influences on the three economists in question is now relatively abundant. For Smith, there is the careful editorial documentation of his sources in the recent edition of his *Lectures* (Meek *et al.*, 1978) and *Wealth of Nations* (Campbell *et al.*, 1976), the catalogue of his library (Mizuta, 1967) and the information contained in his collected correspondence (Mossner and Ross, 1977) and in his early works, particularly the second of his two articles for the *Edinburgh Review* (Lindgren, 1967, pp. 15–28). For Turgot, apart from the evidence contained in his works and in his extensive correspondence (Schelle, 1913–23) there is the annotated three-volume edition of the catalogue of his library (Tsuda, 1974). For Beccaria, although there is unfortunately no library catalogue available, there is considerable evidence of the influence on his work and particularly on his economics, which he himself provided in his inaugural lecture of 1769 and in his intellectual autobiographical letter to l'Abbé Morellet written in 1766 (Romagnoli, 1958, I, pp. 365–77 and II, pp. 862–70). Taken together with the biographical details already given, these data provide a great deal of information from which the major sources of their economics can be deduced.

Before proceeding to a detailed treatment of the sources of their economics, a more general observation on their intellectual background must be made. In the introduction to this chapter it was indicated that the roots of the Enlightenment lay in the scientific revolution achieved at the end of the seventeenth century in England through the work of Newton and Locke, which was carried over into Europe partly through the efforts of Voltaire (1733, especially letters 12–17). It was shown in the second section of this chapter that in their early education Smith, Turgot and Beccaria were all exposed to the thoughts of these important authors, and had absorbed this new experimental method which guided the scientific thought and practice of the age. This is demonstrated by their appeal to history and its use in their work on the social sciences. All three were therefore products of the Enlightenment in the full sense of the word, as a result of their early introduction to the scientific advances which brought about the age of reason in the eighteenth century. Moreover, they all carried the implications of this scientific revolution over into their work on the social sciences.[25]

Progress in the development of the social sciences during the second half of the eighteenth century was given an additional boost by the publication in 1748 of Montesquieu's masterpiece, *l'Esprit des Lois*, which liberated the social sciences from their former theological encumbrances and which induced enormous activity in history, sociology, political philosophy, jurisprudence and, of course, political economy. The impact of Montesquieu's work on Smith, Beccaria and Turgot is both great and demonstrable, but in some ways also quite different in each of the three cases, since the work appeared when there were substantial differences in the degree of maturity they had attained (Beccaria was only ten years old, Turgot was twenty-one, Smith twenty-five). This influence of Montesquieu on the three writers, which in a sense is already part of the influence on their economics, must be discussed in more detail because it is such an important part of their common heritage.

The influence of Montesquieu on Smith has been well documented by Smithian scholars and was also clearly recognised by his contemporaries. Scott (1937, p. 112) reports that Smith was writing his 'final course' of Edinburgh lectures when Montesquieu's work appeared in 1748, but provides no real appraisal of his influence on these lectures apart from – and this is in the context of the controversy over plagiarism between Ferguson and Smith[26] – quoting Alexander Carlyle's statement that Ferguson 'had derived many notions from a French author [i.e. Montesquieu] and that Smith had been there before him' (*ibid.*, p. 119). John Millar, who was Smith's student at Glasgow, puts the matter of Montesquieu's influence in better perspective: 'Upon this subject [i.e. the lectures on jurisprudence] he followed the *plan* that seems to be suggested by Montesquieu, endeavouring to trace the gradual progress of jurisprudence … from the rudest to the most refined ages' (cited in Meek *et al.*, 1978, p. 3). The index of authorities produced in the edition of the two versions of Smith's Glasgow *Lectures* (*ibid.*, pp. 32, 605, which lists well over twenty entries on Montesquieu) confirms Millar's view that Smith frequently used Montesquieu as an authority in constructing the *Lectures*. Similarly, the index of authorities in the *Wealth of Nations* (Campbell *et al.*, 1976, p. 1015) clearly indicates that Montesquieu was a source much used in that book. There can be no doubt about the fact that Smith's work on the social sciences derived considerable inspiration from Montesquieu's pioneering project.

Montesquieu's influence on Turgot can also be easily documented and is reflected in his first piece on economics, the 'Letter on Paper Money' written in early April 1749, that is, within less than six months of the publication of *l'Esprit des Lois* (in Groenewegen, 1977, p. xii, n12). Even earlier, in 1748, Turgot had prepared critical notes on Montesquieu's emphasis on the influence of climate which permeates his *l'Esprit des Lois*. These criticisms were developed in Turgot's fragment on 'Universal History' (see Meek, 1973, pp. 5–6, 89, which provides an English text of this work: in it Turgot was critical of Montesquieu's climate explanation of the differences in the development of nations). Turgot's profound admiration for Montesquieu's contribution to political economy is expressed in a letter to Caillard (Schelle 1913–23, III, pp. 499–501) where he is listed as one of the pioneers of the science,[27] and it is further demonstrated by the fact that Turgot continued to regard him as an authority in his later work. (Montesquieu is cited, for example, in Turgot's 1770 'Paper on Lending at Interest', in Groenewegen, 1977, pp. 52, 159). Turgot's excursions into the social sciences clearly owed much to Montesquieu.

Beccaria's indebtedness to Montesquieu as an influence on the development of his thought is in many ways even more striking than that of Turgot and Adam Smith. In the autobiographical letter to Morellet (26 January 1766) already referred to, Beccaria wrote that he owed his conversion to philosophy in 1761, when he was twenty-three, to a reading of Montesquieu's *Lettres Persanes* (Romagnoli, 1958, II, p. 865). In an earlier letter to Carli (dated 4 August 1762), written when he had just published his first work on economics – the study of the monetary problems of Milan – he praises the genius of Montesquieu on monetary questions (*ibid.*, II, p. 845). Indeed, Beccaria's first work quotes several times from Montesquieu's *l'Esprit des Lois* (*ibid.*, I, pp. 8, 10) while his later works in their introductions refer to the important contributions of the 'immortal' Montesquieu. (See introduction to *Dei Delitti e delle Pene* in *ibid.*, I, p. 46; opening chapter of *Ricerche Intorno alla Natura dello Stile* in *ibid.*, I, p. 204; and his tribute to early economists given in his inaugural lecture at Milan, in *ibid.*, I, p. 376).[28] There is, however, only one direct reference to Montesquieu in the *Elementi* (*ibid.*, I, p. 405) and this occurs on the subject of population.

These general influences – that is, those provided by the new scientific spirit initiated by Newton and Locke and by the historical approach of Montesquieu – have clearly left their mark on the whole of the work of Smith, Turgot and Beccaria. These influences provided a major inspiration and offered a method by which to tackle social science investigations in general. This common background, which they of course shared with all the (second generation)[29] social thinkers of the eighteenth century in varying degrees, also greatly influenced their approach to political economy, and is undoubtedly one of the reasons for the similarity in the thrust of their writings on the subject, discussed in the previous section.

Such broad influences, however, tell only part of the story. Just as their general approach to political economy was inspired by the vision of the age with its belief in the experimental method and its usefulness in explaining the history of civil society, so in the development of their views on certain crucial topics of political economy, they shared a common heritage in many of the classics of economic literature which were available at the time they were writing. By the end of the 1750s and the early 1760s, there existed a number of recognised authorities in the economic writings of Europe which formed the foundations on which the new science of political economy was created in the next decade. The existence of such recognised authorities and their importance for the economic writings of Smith, Turgot and Beccaria can be easily demonstrated.

Both Turgot and Beccaria provided explicit opinions on the important contributions to this literature: the former in a letter to Caillard already cited, the latter in his inaugural lecture. These general statements must be briefly examined before proceeding to a more detailed discussion of the economic heritage. In the context of Du Pont's criticism of Melon,[30] Turgot wrote: 'a person who entered the world after Montesquieu, Hume, Cantillon, Quesnay and M. de Gournay, is less struck by Melon's merit of being first [to write on economic matters in France] because he does not appreciate it' (Turgot to Caillard, 1 January 1771, in Schelle 1913–23, III, p. 500). Turgot in this comment identified Cantillon, Montesquieu, Hume, Quesnay and Gournay as the most important persons in advancing the state of economic knowledge in the 1750s and 1760s. Beccaria in his inaugural lecture paid tribute to Bacon, Vauban, Melon, the 'immortal' Montesquieu, Uztariz, Ulloa, Hume and Genovesi, a selection of names which was probably partly inspired by his desire to present the new science in which he had just been appointed a professor as an internationally recognised one (Romagnoli, 1958, I, pp. 375–6).

Smith left no similar remarks. However, a good indication of the existence of generally recognised economic authorities in the 1750s and 1760s is obtained if the list of those authorities cited in the *Wealth of Nations* is compared with those known to have been familiar to Turgot (either from the catalogue of his library or from other sources) and those cited by Beccaria in his works on economics or referred to by him in his correspondence. From such an analysis (the results of which are presented in Table 1.3) it can be seen that the authors explicitly selected as particularly important in the development of political economy by Turgot and Beccaria were also highly regarded by Adam Smith, while in addition it can be demonstrated that there was a striking similarity (as well as some differences) in the sources on which these three authors drew in the construction of their political economy.

Table 1.3 also demonstrates a number of common authors on economics who had been studied by Turgot, Smith and Beccaria. These include particularly Richard Cantillon, Montesquieu, David Hume and François Quesnay as well as Locke, but in addition Du Tot, Forbonnais, Hobbes, Law, Melon and Uztariz. The common sources for Turgot and Smith are even more striking – nearly every important work on economics cited by Adam Smith was also familiar to Turgot, while a full and detailed comparison of the contents of their libraries would reveal that the same conclusion would apply to many less important sources cited in the *Wealth of Nations*.

It need hardly be demonstrated that key features from the work of Locke, Cantillon, Montesquieu, Hume and Quesnay provided the major building blocks from which the new science of political economy was constructed in the succeeding decades by Turgot, Smith and Beccaria. Locke, apart from providing some important doctrines on value, money and trade, more importantly supplied a political framework based on liberty and private property. Cantillon provided an integrated picture of trade and commerce which revealed the interdependence of classes, population, production, circulation, trade, value and money, and thereby provided the first general treatise on economics. Montesquieu in his *l'Esprit des Lois* put forward the ideas for the basic historical framework into which the economic material could be inserted. Hume's essays elaborated and improved on the earlier theories of trade, money, interest and credit, and consequently, by solving many of the contemporary problems in trade and monetary theory, cleared the way for concentrating on production. Similarly, his history influenced all three. Finally, and perhaps most importantly, Quesnay demonstrated the importance of capital and accumulation in agricultural production, and completed Cantillon's system of interdependence in his scheme of the annual circulation, distribution and reproduction of wealth, and the role of surplus in this process.

The manner in which Smith, Turgot and Beccaria put these elements together was discussed in the previous section. Some of the differences can now be partly explained by the sources of their respective systems. Take first the major difference between Beccaria on the one hand, and Turgot and Smith on the other, i.e. the lack of an effective distribution theory in Beccaria's work. This omission from Beccaria's political economy can be explained by his much lesser acquaintance with the literature of physiocracy, which seems paradoxical in the light of the strong physiocratic flavour in the second part of the *Elementi*. From a knowledge of the sources he used, that paradox is easily explained. Much of the apparent physiocratic flavour in Beccaria's work was derived from Cantillon's *Essai*, which stressed the role of the landlords in influencing the direction of economic activity and the manner in which this could be analysed in terms of the circular flow (Cantillon, 1959, I, chs 12–15, II, ch. 3). This was further enhanced by Beccaria's knowledge of Quesnay's article 'Fermiers', with its emphasis on capital requirements in distinguishing between 'la grande et la petite culture' which clearly influenced some of the chapters in Part II of the *Elementi*. His discussion of the regulation of trade in staple commodities (Beccaria, 1958, part II, ch. 5) was probably influenced by Quesnay's second article in the *Encyclopédie*, 'Grains', which Beccaria also would have read, since he had access at least to the early volumes of that work. From the evidence in his writing, and particularly from that contained in his inaugural lecture, it can be concluded that this was probably as far as his acquaintance with physiocratic economics went,[31] and hence the absence of treatment of distribution theory is explained by his lack of knowledge of the *Tableau* in its published forms in the second edition of *l'Ami des Hommes*, in *Philosophie Rurale* and in Du Pont's *Physiocratie*. On the other hand, in the material on value, money, banking, credit and commerce, where he shared the basic sources with Turgot and Smith, there are only few substantial differences between the three economists.

This comparative analysis also sheds light on an issue which puzzled the late Ronald Meek (1973, pp. 30–3): why did Turgot analyse a society in which 'the capitalist system has consolidated itself in all fields of economic activity'? (*ibid.*, p. 31). Meek's final paragraph in this discussion (*ibid.*, p. 33) in which it is argued that Turgot's capitalism 'was still relatively backward as compared with Adam Smith's', is not convincing, particularly in the light of Meek's own discussion in the two preceding paragraphs (*ibid.*, pp. 32–3). Turgot's class division for capitalist society into 'Entrepreneurs, Manufacturers and Master-craftsmen, *all owners of large capitals* which they invest profitably as advances for setting men at work' and the class of 'simple artisans who have no other property than their arms, who advance only their daily labour, and receive no profit but their wages' ('Reflections', section 61) is just as 'modern' as that of Adam Smith, particularly when it is remembered that Turgot commenced Part II of his 'Reflections' with the statement that modern society produces another way of being rich, '*without labouring* and without possessing lands' ('Reflections', section 29) which significantly alters the distribution of wealth in agricultural society. These arguments from the 'Reflections' clearly destroy Meek's inferences concerning Turgot's 'capitalists' (Meek, 1973, p. 33), as was fully realised by Marx (1962, pp. 54–9). Turgot's 'modernity' in this matter is explained by his considerable knowledge of industry in France, which he derived from the tours of inspection of industry and commerce which he made together with Gournay in the mid-1750s, and from his acquaintance with the industrial problems of the iron industry in Limoges, which he discussed in a number of papers (e.g. his 'Paper on Lending at Interest' in Groenewegen, 1977, pp. 149–50). Given his superb historical sense as illustrated by the development of the four stages theory, these observations would have impressed him greatly as the distinguishing characteristics between the fourth stage of capitalist society and the third stage of agriculture which was beginning to fade away.[32]

A further conclusion which can be derived from this comparative analysis relates to the sociology of science in what has been described as its formative stage (Kuhn, 1970, esp. chs 1 and 2). The evidence about sources used by Turgot, Beccaria and Smith provides the material for two important inferences relating to the emergence of economic science. In the first place, it clearly shows that by the early 1760s the key elements of the new science of political economy had all been developed in the internationally recognised classics on the subject – especially the works of Locke, Cantillon, Hume and Quesnay. All that remained was to put them together into a coherent system, and this was done by Turgot, Beccaria and Smith. The success of Smith's version of this system is explained by the fact that it was the most polished, most elaborate and most coherent, a consequence (as Schumpeter argued) of the fact that he had the time to devote nearly a decade of uninterrupted work to its construction. Second, the 1760s were a highly propitious period for the development of such a system of political economy to emerge as a new science: there was the rapid international transmission of new ideas which was a feature of the Enlightenment (see Mornet, 1967, pp. 19–25; Hazard, 1954, pp. 100–12, 467–9) and which is reflected in the international flavour of the common sources in Turgot, Beccaria and Smith. There was also the increasing official awareness of the importance of the science of political economy in that period, reflected in the creation of chairs, in the publication of journals and in the use made of consultant 'economists' by government.[33] These institutional developments greatly aided the spread of the new science.

The shared heritage of Turgot, Beccaria and Smith with its international composition, as illustrated in Table 1.3, allows a simple conclusion to Jevons' question about the nationality of political economy raised earlier. The authorities on which classical political economy was constructed were as international as the three authors who raised it to its greatest heights during the eighteenth century. The nationalistic quarrels over this question fought in the journals at the end of the nineteenth century were therefore as redundant as they were fruitless, as Jevons (1881, p. 183) had already suggested in his concluding paragraph.

The nature and origins of classical political economy

The comparison of the works and lives of Turgot, Beccaria and Smith sheds light on the still controversial question of the definition of classical political economy. (For a short technical definition which distinguishes classical political economy from the new economics developed in the late nineteenth century, see Groenewegen, 1982, pp. 121–4) It is well known that three definitions based on different theoretical justifications can be found in the literature. The most common is that implicit in the discussion of the largely British classical political economy commencing with the work of Smith in 1776 and concluding with J. S. Mill's *Principles of Political Economy*, which thereby dates the decline and fall at either 1848 or 1871, depending on the edition selected. The latter date allows an association between this decline and the 'marginal revolution', and had other merits as well. The second definition is that of Keynes (1936, p. 1, n1) who made the critique of 'Say's Law' his dividing line and who recognised the 'underworld' precursors in his controversial notes on mercantilism and so on (1936, ch. 23). As indicated in the last paragraph of the first section, the third definition is that of Marx (1859) which in its broad outlines is here supported, at least insofar as its starting point is concerned.[34]

This historiographical conclusion can be made more explicit in some final concluding comments to this comparative study of three great classical economists of the eighteenth century. First, their conception of the scope of political economy as the reproduction, distribution and circulation of wealth, and the focus therein on the role of economic surplus, is a conception which gradually developed from the work of Petty and Boisguilbert in the seventeenth century. It ultimately reached its first climax in the late 1760s and 1770s. Economic milestones in this century of progress in political economy are the works of Locke, Cantillon, Montesquieu, Hume and Quesnay. These constructed the foundations of classical political economy, which were fully elaborated on in Smith's highly polished and systematic exposition of the new science. He, therefore, is the most prominent of the eighteenth-century economists, but the significance of these foundations was just as fully appreciated by Turgot and Beccaria in their much less finished work.

This conclusion suggests a further important inference from the foregoing investigation. A major break occurred in the development of classical political economy at the turn of the century. It can be argued that much of this break may be associated with the political and social traumas arising from the French Revolution and the Napoleonic wars.[35] A second peak in classical political economy can therefore be noted in the work of Ricardo, which although almost totally within the classical tradition of political economy, was transformed in its conclusion by an emphasis on diminishing returns in agriculture. This turned the optimism of the economists of the Enlightenment into the dismal science of Carlyle in the 1840s. Further elaboration of this additional conclusion cannot of course be given in this already lengthy chapter. If the questions they raise inspire further research on these issues, this will add to the lustre here bestowed on three eighteenth-century giants of political economy: Turgot, Beccaria and Smith.

Notes

1 Paper given at the first Australian Conference of Historians of Economic Thought held at Armidale in May 1981. This paper has been revised in the light of subsequent discussion. I particularly acknowledge the contribution and encouragement of Bob Coats, Walter Eltis, Roberto Finzi, Arnold Heertje, Gianni Vaggi and Franco Venturi.

2 Three chairs in political economy were established during the eighteenth century: two in Italy and one in Sweden. The first was founded in Naples in 1754 with Genovesi as the first appointee; the second was founded at Uppsala in the 1760s (held by P. N. Christiernin): the third at Milan in 1768 for Beccaria, who held it till 1771. Malthus obtained the first English chair in political economy in 1805 at the East India College at Hertford Castle (see McLeod, 1863, p. 253; Petersen, 1979, p. 31; Eagly, 1963, p. 626, n1).

3 It is interesting to note that Turgot had translated Pope's epitaph of Newton into French:

> L'obscure nuit couvrait l'univers ignoré
> Dieu dit: que Newton soit, et tout fût éclairé.
> (Schelle, 1913–23, II, p. 703)

4 It could be objected (and indeed has been) that Sir James Steuart should have been included among this trio of great economic treatise writers of the third quarter of the eighteenth century. A number of reasons, one of which was space, made me decide against this. More substantially, Steuart's exclusion from the trio here discussed can be justified on the grounds that he was far less important a figure in the general Enlightenment than Turgot, Beccaria or Smith.

5 There are articles on Beccaria in Palgrave's *Dictionary* (1899), the *Encyclopedia of the Social Sciences* (Seligman, 1938) and the *International Encyclopedia of the Social Sciences* (Sills, 1968), the latter largely discussing Beccaria in his role as penal reformer, and a lengthy article in McLeod's *Dictionary* (1863). McCulloch's *Literature of Political Economy* (1845) includes his work as printed in the Custodi collection, while his influence on the growth of philosophical radicalism is documented in Halevy (1955).

6 These treatises are respectively 'Réflexions sur la Formation et la Distribution des Richesses' (1766), *Elementi di Economia Pubblica* (circa 1770, first published 1804) and *An Inquiry into the Nature and Causes of the Wealth of Nations* (1776). The editions of these works to be used are the Groenewegen translation (1977), the text of the *Elementi* in the edition of Beccaria's work edited by Romagnoli (1958) and the bicentenary Glasgow edition (1976). The author has already provided some comparison between Turgot and Adam Smith (Groenewegen, 1969) and an analysis of the sources of Smith's economics based on the contents of Smith's library as catalogued by Mizuta (Groenewegen, 1968) (both works are included in this volume, as Chapters 20 and 21 respectively).

7 For a comparison such as this, the qualification is essential. Many of Turgot's manuscript writings were preserved for posterity in the family archives at Lantheuil and by his friend Du Pont de Nemours, both for the publications of his *Oeuvres de Turgot* (1808–11) and among his papers now housed at the Eleutherian Mills Historical Library in Greenville, Delaware, from where they were partly retrieved and published by Schelle (1913–23) in the most complete edition of Turgot's

Oeuvres. Smith systematically destroyed his unpublished papers shortly before his death, so that his juvenilia and other unfinished writings can no longer be discussed (Rae, 1895, p. 434). In the context of Beccaria's papers, it should be noted that many of his unpublished papers are not included in the edition of the *Works* edited by Romagnoli (1958). Franco Venturi has told me that a new (hopefully definitive) edition of Beccaria's *Works* is now in preparation. [This edition, under the direction of Luigi Firpo, was published by Mediobanca, Milan, in seven volumes which appeared from 1984 to 1990.]

8 This can only be described as a misnomer by Rae, since secondary schooling in the sense in which that term is understood today did not exist in the eighteenth century; I have therefore used the term 'preliminary education' to describe pre-university education, although this was far from elementary insofar as syllabus was concerned. It should also be noted that his attendance at the Burgh school cannot be precisely dated: neither Rae nor Scott provide details; Viner (1965, p. 139) gives *circa* 1730–7, Mossner and Ross (1977, p. xix) give *circa* 1732–7. See also Stewart (1853), pp. xii–xiii.

9 Smith's knowledge of 'natural philosophy' is illustrated in his *Essays on Philosophical Subjects*, posthumously published in 1795, particularly the *Principles which Lead and Direct Philosophical Enquiries Illustrated by the History of Astronomy*, and the *History of Ancient Physics*. These were referred to in a letter to Hume (16 April 1773, in Mossner and Ross, 1977, pp. 40, 168).

10 These were preserved, and as Meek (1973) has shown in the context of the second, formed the foundations of Turgot's materialist conception of history which he developed in his four stages theory.

11 In 1748 Turgot wrote a critique of Buffon on the basis of arguments derived from Newtonian physics, in 1750 and 1751 he composed a long critique of Maupertuis' *Réflexions Philosophiques sur l'Origine des Langues*, a refutation of Berkeley's philosophy, a paper on the 'Causes of the Progress and Decline of the Sciences and the Arts', a fragment of 'Universal History' and his comments on Madame de Graffigny's *Lettres Péruviennes*. All these early works are reprinted in Schelle (1913–23), I.

12 This fact is provided by Romagnoli (1958, I, p. XCIX, and II, p. 937); Venturi provides only the date of graduation. In conversation, Professor Venturi confirmed that Beccaria studied law at the University of Pavia, so that the article in the second edition of the *Encyclopedia of Social Sciences* (1968) is even more deficient than has already been noted (note 5 above) because it is there claimed that he wrote his famous *Dei Delitti e delle Pene* without any formal legal training.

13 It would be tempting, from the fact that all three were in Paris in 1766, to deduce therefore that they may have met. This is, however, very unlikely. Beccaria did not arrive in Paris till 18 October (letter to Teresa Beccaria Blasco, 19 October 1766, in Romagnoli [1958], II, p. 882). Smith left Paris at the end of October (his last letter from Paris to Lady Frances Scott is dated 19 October 1766, in Mossner and Ross [1977], p. 121, who also state that he arrived in Dover on 1 November 1766). Turgot's correspondence provides no evidence for his presence in Paris in October 1766, but no evidence against this either. The possibility of a meeting between Turgot, Beccaria and Smith arises from their mutual friendship with Morellet and their known presence at the house of Baron d'Holbach during this year.

14 An indication of the contents of these lectures is provided in Meek *et al.* (1978, pp. 24–7), which reveals them as dealing with justice and 'police': the first deals with the principles, origins and development of government, domestic law and private law, the second with cleanliness and security, cheapness and plenty. This last part presents the major economic content and deals with growth, the division of labour, value, money and trade.

15 Turgot's published works include his translation of Tucker published in 1755, the five *Encyclopédie* articles published in 1756 and 1757, translations from the poems of

Gessner published in 1761 and 1762, letters on poetry published in 1754 and 1768, a theological tract published anonymously in 1767 (that is, *Les 37 Vérités Opposées aux 37 Impiétés de Bélisaire*) and a number of contributions to the *Ephémérides du Citoyen*, namely 'Des Caractères de la Grande et de la Petite Culture', 1767, no. 6, pp. 77–97; 'Mémoire ... sur la Propriété des Carrières et des Mines', 1767, no. 7, pp. 33–118; 'Lettre Circulaire ... aux Officiers de Police des Lieux où il y a des Marchés de Grains', 1768, no. 7, pp. 107–28; 'Réflexions sur la Formation et la Distribution des Richesses', 1769, nos. 11 and 12; 1770, no. 1 (this was also separately issued in 1770 and translated into German in 1775), and 'Instructions Générales pour les Ateliers de Charité', 1772, no. 2, pp. 195–206. The last book that appeared during his lifetime was a translation in metrical verse of the fourth book of Virgil's *Aeneid*, published in 1774.

16 For a list see notes 11 and 15 above. To these must be added the *Eloge de Gournay* written in 1759 and partly published by Marmontel in the August issue of the *Mercure*, 1759.

17 That is, 'Tentativo Analitico su i Contrabbandi', which presented an algebraic solution to the problem of tariff construction caused by the encouragement of smuggling by too high a tariff. See Theocharis (1961, pp. 21–4) and Beccaria (1958, I, pp. 164–6).

18 An area in the personal life of the three which provides for similarity as well as difference is their marital status. Beccaria, unlike Smith and Turgot, was married and had children: in 1761 he married Teresa Blasco; in 1774 after the death of his first wife, he married Anna Bardo. Although Smith sought several ladies in marriage, none accepted him (see Scott, 1937, p. 65). Turgot was similarly slighted in his proposals of marriage: he was rejected by Mlle de Ligniville, who married Helvétius, and it appears he was rejected a second time when she had become a widow. He also had an amorous friendship with the Duchesse D'Enville (see Cazes, 1970, p. 7, n1). If any inferences can be drawn from this type of biographical detail, they are left to the reader.

19 In his early works written in 1750–1, Turgot had developed the four stages theory of human progress, in which the savage society of hunters was replaced by that of shepherds, which in turn was replaced by agricultural society and finally by commercial society. In this theory the progress towards civilisation was predicated on the different manners in which humankind obtained its subsistence. For a discussion of these early texts see Meek (1973, introduction; 1976, pp. 68–76). A succinct reference to the four stages theory which illustrates the historical nature of the 'Reflections' is given in section 54 (see Groenewegen, 1977, p. 66). Turgot's views on the state were given in other works.

20 Beccaria's definitional comments on political economy closely resemble those of Adam Smith in the introduction to Book IV of the *Wealth of Nations*, where political economy is defined as

> a branch of the science of a statesman or legislator [which] proposes two distinct objects; first, to provide a plentiful revenue or subsistence for the people, or more properly to enable them to provide such a revenue or subsistence for themselves; and secondly, to supply the state or commonwealth with a revenue sufficient for the publick services.
>
> (Smith, 1776, p. 428)

It should be noted that Smith may have been aware of Beccaria's definition, since he owned a three-volume edition of his works published in Naples in 1770–1. This included Beccaria's 1769 inaugural lecture which contains these views (see Mizuta, 1967, p. 4).

21 Beccaria's support of physiocratic views is particularly clearly illustrated in Part II, chapter 2, of the *Elementi*, entitled 'Della Piccola e Grande Coltura delle Terre', which produces some of the argument from Quesnay's article, 'Fermiers', and bases the distinction between these two types of cultivation on ploughing by horses rather than oxen. It should also be noted here that Beccaria referred approvingly to this article by Quesnay in the *Encyclopédie*, though Quesnay's name is not mentioned (Beccaria, 1958, p. 451). The fourth section of this chapter provides further discussion of Beccaria's association with physiocracy.

22 See Beccaria, 1958, pp. 551–2. By the early 1770s this stadial theory was already a commonplace in many works, including Goguet's *De l'Origine des Loix, des Arts, et des Sciences et de Leurs Progrès chez Anciens Peuples*, which Beccaria cited in the introduction to the *Elementi* (1958, I, pp. 386, 388). For a discussion of Goguet's use of the theory, see Meek (1976, pp. 94–7). I find it therefore surprising that Meek argued (*ibid*., p. 30) that no real trace of the theory can be found in Beccaria, and can only explain this statement by the fact that he had not read his works, a supposition confirmed by his bracketing of Beccaria with Petty and Bolingbroke in his discussion of the *pre-history* of the theory.

23 As Thurlings (1978, p. 12) points out, such analyses of isolated exchange were common in medieval scholastic literature, and since only Turgot and Beccaria (particularly Turgot in a seminary) would have had solid grounding in these writings, it is not surprising that they had absorbed this type of analysis. Smith's protestant upbringing and education would have kept him more isolated from such work. Cf. also Groenewegen, 1982, pp. 129–30 (below, pp. 323–4).

24 At this point some part of the discussion in the fourth section of this chapter can be anticipated. It should be indicated that despite Beccaria's familiarity with Quesnay's work, this was confined to the early economic writing of the *Encyclopédie* articles of 1756 and 1757, and excluded the more important work from the point of view of the theory of distribution in the *Tableau*. It should also be noted that the major analytical influence on Beccaria's economics was Cantillon, as is apparent in the outline of his lectures (Romagnoli, 1958, I, pp. 341–9) which follow the content order of Cantillon's *Essai* very closely.

25 Smith's tremendous awareness of the importance of Newton and Locke for the scientific development of the eighteenth century is clearly indicated in his 'Letter to the Authors of the Edinburgh Review' (Lindgren, 1967, esp. pp. 15–16). His support of their method is abundantly demonstrated in his brilliant 'History of Astronomy', while a tribute to his own mastery of that method (by Pownall in his letter to Smith on the publication of the *Wealth of Nations*) in his exposition of the 'laws of motion ... which are the source of, and give direction to, the labour of man in the individual' (Mossner and Ross, 1977, p. 337) provides final evidence of the importance of this for his work in the social sciences. Turgot's absorption of Newtonian physics is demonstrated in his critique of Buffon, while his appreciation of Locke's sensationalist philosophy is clearly visible in his critique of Maupertuis on the origin of languages and in his comments on Mme de Graffigny's *Lettres Péruviennes* (see references in note 11 above). Beccaria refers to the contribution of Newton and Locke in some of his early essays for *Il Caffè* (Romagnoli, 1958, I, pp. 158, 168, 187) but more importantly he pays tribute to their methodological contributions and innovations in a passage in the *Elementi* (*ibid*., I, p. 536).

26 See W. R. Scott (1937, pp. 118–19) which is derived from Dugald Stewart's *Memoir of the Life of Adam Smith*; Viner (1965, pp. 33–7) sums up all the evidence on this famous controversy. Similar charges of plagiarism from Smith in the context of his philosophical views on history and progress were made in connection with William Robertson's *History of Charles V*, Part I, especially section 1 on 'View of the Progress of Society in Europe, with reference to Interior Government, Laws and Manners'. See Mossner and Ross (1977, p. 192, n2).

27 This letter appears to have been a comment on Du Pont's critical notes included with Beccaria's inaugural lecture as published in the *Ephémérides* in 1769, in which Du Pont was particularly offended at Beccaria's praise of Melon, who had been the private secretary of John Law till 1720 and who had published an account of Law's system in 1738 under the title *Réflexions politiques sur le commerce*. Du Pont's attack on Melon, largely directed at the latter's support of indirect taxes and the regulation of the domestic grain trade, inspired a defence of Melon by his son, and it is this controversy which Turgot discussed with Caillard in the letter cited, and in which Montesquieu is mentioned as an important early economist. See also McLain (1977), pp. 90–9, where Du Pont's views on the subject are set out.

28 See note 27 above, where it is shown that Turgot's brief comments on the importance of Montesquieu in the development of economics were indirectly inspired by Beccaria's views in his inaugural lecture.

29 Turgot, Smith and Beccaria are second generation as compared with Montesquieu (1689–1755), Voltaire (1694–1778), Quesnay (1694–1774) and perhaps even Hume (1711–1776).

30 See note 27 above.

31 This would explain the fact that in his historical commentary on earlier contributors to political economy, he omitted the names of Quesnay, Mirabeau and other physiocrats, despite his obvious sympathies with their work, because the *Encyclopédie* articles were both published anonymously. See the references in note 27 above.

32 It should be remembered in this context that in many ways Smith and Turgot were pre-Industrial Revolution writers and that in the period when they were formulating their economic ideas, the differences between the economies in France and England were not nearly as marked as they were to become some decades later.

33 See note 2 above with regard to chairs; the other institutional features are documented in Table 1.1.

34 Marx controversially dated this decline to the 1830s on the basis of the rising importance of class struggle which he saw in this decade. There has been substantial debate over this proposition ever since, particularly between the late Ronald Meek and Maurice Dobb on the side of Marx, and Hutchison opposing. For reasons which cannot be elaborated here. I think that Marx's date for the decline of classical political economy is more or less correct, but not for the reasons he suggested.

35 There are three important associations between these major events in world history and the transformation of political economy between Smith and Ricardo. The first are the major advances in monetary theory which occurred in the bullion controversies in England and which were the direct consequence of the 1797 suspension of specie payments by the Bank of England for war purposes. The second is the explicit development of Say's Law and Mr Mill's 'principle', which occurred during the Napoleonic wars in debates over trade. The third and most important is Malthus' essay on population, with its emphasis on diminishing returns in food production, which had its direct origin in the political controversy over the French Revolution, and which simultaneously drew a sharp line between the optimism of the Enlightenment and early nineteenth-century thought.

References

Beccaria, Cesare (1771–2, 1958) *Elementi di Economia Pubblica*, in S. Romagnoli, *Cesare Beccaria: Opere*, 2 vols, Florence: Sansoni.

Blaug, Mark (1962) *Economic Theory in Retrospect*, 1st edn, Homewood IL: Irwin.

Campbell, R. H., Skinner, A. S. and Todd, W. B. (eds) (1976) Adam Smith, *An Inquiry into the Nature and Causes of the Wealth of Nations*, Oxford: Clarendon Press.

Cantillon, R. (1959) *Essay on the Nature of Commerce in General*, ed. H. Higgs for the Royal Economic Society, London: Frank Cass.

Cassirer, Ernst (1951) *The Philosophy of the Enlightenment*, Boston: Beacon Press.

Cazes, Bernard (ed.) (1970) *Turgot, Ecrits Economiques*, Paris: Calmann-Levy.

Dakin, Douglas (1965) *Turgot and the Ancien Régime in France*, New York: Octagon Books.

Eagly, R. V. (1963) 'Money, Employment and Prices: A Swedish View 1761', *Quarterly Journal of Economics*, vol. 77, November, 626–36.

Groenewegen, P. D. (1968) 'A New Catalogue of Adam Smith's Library', *Economic Record*, vol. 44, December, 498–506 (below, Chapter 21).

——(1969) 'Turgot and Adam Smith', *Scottish Journal of Political Economy*, vol. XVI, 271–87 (below, Chapter 20).

——(1977) *The Economics of A. R. J. Turgot*, The Hague: Martinus Nijhoff.

——(1982) 'Turgot: Forerunner of Neo-classical Economics?', *Kenzei Kenkyu*, 33(2) April, 119–33 (below, Chapter 18).

Halevy, Eli (1955) *The Growth of Philosophical Radicalism*, Boston MA: Beacon Press.

Hazard, Paul (1954) *European Thought in the Eighteenth Century*, Harmondsworth: Penguin Books.

Jevons, W. S. (1881) 'Richard Cantillon and the Nationality of Political Economy', *Contemporary Review*, January, reprinted in W. S. Jevons (1905) *The Principles of Economics and Other Papers*, London: Macmillan, and in Cantillon, R. (1959) *Essay on the Nature of Commerce in General*, ed. H. Higgs for the Royal Economic Society, London: Frank Cass, 333–60.

Keynes, J. M. (1936) *The General Theory of Employment, Interest and Money*, London: Macmillan.

Kuhn, T. S. (1970) *The Structure of Scientific Revolutions*, 2nd edn, enlarged, Chicago: University of Chicago Press.

Letwin, William (1963) *The Origins of Scientific Economics. English Economic Thought, 1660–1776*, London: Methuen.

Lindgren, J. Ralph (1967) *The Early Writings of Adam Smith*, New York: Augustus M. Kelley.

McCulloch, J. R. (1845) *The Literature of Political Economy*, London: LSE Reprint, 1936.

McLain, James J. (1977) *The Economic Writings of Du Pont De Nemours*, Newark DE: University of Delaware Press.

McLeod, H. D. (1863) *A Dictionary of Political Economy*, London: Longman Brown, Longmans and Roberts.

Marx, K. H. (1859, 1971) *A Contribution to the Critique of Political Economy*, new edn, London: Lawrence and Wishart.

——(1962) *Theories of Surplus Value*, Part I, Moscow: Foreign Languages Publishing House.

Meek, R. L. (ed.) (1973) *Turgot on Progress, Sociology and Economics*, Cambridge: Cambridge University Press.

——(1976) *Social Science and the Ignoble Savage*, Cambridge: Cambridge University Press.

Meek, R. L., Raphael, D. D. and Stein, P.G. (eds) (1978) *Adam Smith Lectures on Jurisprudence*, Oxford: Clarendon Press.

Mizuta, Hiroshi (1967) *Adam Smith's Library*, Cambridge: Cambridge University Press for Royal Economic Society.

Mornet, Daniel (1967) *Les Origines Intellectuelles de la Révolution Française 1715–1787*, Paris: Armand Colin.

Mossner, E. C. and Ross, I. S. (1977) *The Correspondence of Adam Smith*, Oxford: Clarendon Press.

Palgrave, R. H. Inglis (ed.) (1899) *Palgrave's Dictionary of Political Economy*, London: Macmillan.

Petersen, William (1979) *Malthus*, London: Heineman.

Rae, John (1895, 1965) *Life of Adam Smith*, in Viner, Jacob *Guide to John Rae's Life of Adam Smith*, including reprint of Rae, *Life of Adam Smith*, New York: Augustus M. Kelley.

Romagnoli, S. (1958) *Cesare Beccaria: Opere*, 2 vols, Florence: Sansoni.

Say, Léon (1887) *Turgot*, Paris: Hachette.

Schelle, G. (1913–23) *Oeuvres de Turgot et Documents le concernant*, Paris: Felix Arcan.

Schumpeter, J. A. (1954) *Economic Doctrine and Method*, London: Allen & Unwin.

——(1959) *History of Economic Analysis*, London: Allen & Unwin.

Scott, W. R. (1937, 1965) *Adam Smith as Student and Professor*, reprinted New York: Augustus M. Kelley.

Seligman, E. R. A. (ed.) (1938) *Encyclopedia of the Social Sciences*, 1st edn, New York: Macmillan.

Shackle, G. L. S. (1967) *The Years of High Theory*, Cambridge: Cambridge University Press.

Sills, David L. (1968) *International Encyclopedia of the Social Sciences*, 2nd edn, New York: Macmillan and Company and the Free Press.

Smith, Adam (1853) *The Theory of Moral Sentiments* to which is added *A Dissertation on the Origin of Languages*, London: Bohn Standard Library.

——(1776, 1976) *An Inquiry into the Nature and Causes of the Wealth of Nations*, eds Campbell, R. H., Skinner, A. S. and Todd, W. B., Oxford: Clarendon Press.

Stephen, Leslie (1902, 1962) *History of English Thought in the Eighteenth Century*, 3rd edn, New York: Harbinger Books.

Stewart, Dugald (1853) 'Biographical and Critical Memoir of Adam Smith', in Smith, Adam, *The Theory of Moral Sentiments* to which is added *A Dissertation on the Origin of Languages*, London: Bohn Standard Library.

Taylor, W. L. (1965) *Francis Hutcheson and David Hume as Predecessors of Adam Smith*, Durham NC: Duke University Press.

Theocharis, R. D. (1961) *Early Developments in Mathematical Economics*, London: Macmillan.

Thurlings, Th. L.M. (1978) *Turgot en zijn tijdgenoten*, Wageningen: H. Veenman en Zonen.

Tsuda, Takumi (1974) *Catalogue des Livres de la Bibliothèque de Turgot*, Tokyo: Institut d'Etudes Economiques, Hitotsubashi University.

Turgot, A. R. J. (1766, 1977) 'Réflexions sur la Formation et la Distribution des Richesses', in Groenewegen, P. D., *The Economics of A. R. J. Turgot*, The Hague: Martinus Nijhoff.

Venturi, F. (1965) 'Cesare Beccaria', in *Dizionario Biografico Degli Italiani*, vol. 7, Rome.

Viner, Jacob (1965) *Guide to John Rae's Life of Adam Smith*, including reprint of Rae, *Life of Adam Smith*, New York: Augustus M. Kelley.

Voltaire, François-Marie Arouet (1733) *Letters on England*, trans. Leonard Tancock, Harmondsworth: Penguin Classics, 1980.

Winch, Donald (1970) 'The Emergence of Economics as a Science 1750–1870', *Fontana Economic History of Europe*, vol. 3, section 9, London: Collins.

2 Thoughts on the emergence of economics as a science[1]

> The historical interpretation and explanation of theories put forward in the past is the first and foremost task which the historian of political economy has to fulfill. But besides this great problem, which might be called his material problem, he is confronted with several others more or less formal in character. Three of them are of outstanding importance. They are indicated by the following questions: When did political economy arise? What were the phases in its evolution? How can it be defined and divided from other fields of thought? … The first problem – the problem of origin – naturally and necessarily arises with regard to any science, but it is especially intricate in political economy.
>
> (Stark 1944: p. 59)

The above quotation is useful as a starting point for this chapter because it places its subject matter in some perspective. In reflecting on the emergence of economics as a science, this chapter discusses a formal question in the history of economics of considerable importance, and one which, unfortunately, has not received a great deal of attention in the past.[2] Most historians of economics – as issues of the journals clearly testify – have been more concerned with the 'historical interpretation and explanation of theories put forward in the past'.

It should be noted that in the discussion of the emergence of economics, Stark's other two formal problems cannot be ignored. In fact, this can be put more strongly: these two other problems must of necessity be treated in a discussion of the emergence of economics as a science. Much of the content of this chapter illustrates this proposition.

The argument may be briefly stated as follows. A study of the literature of the history of economics quickly reveals that the question of the emergence of economics as a science has been treated in different ways, and that these different ways not infrequently can be explained by differences in the scope, subject matter and objectives of economics accepted by the historian. Hence there is a strong relationship between the treatment of the emergence of economics as a science, and the definition of economics as a science, different definitions generally, but not always, leading to different periods of time, and to different individuals or groups to whom or to which the emergence can be assigned. At the same time, it appears also self-evident that the problem of the separation of economics from other fields of enquiry is closely related to the problem of the emergence of economics as a science (cf. Schumpeter 1952; 1959: pp. 9–10; Kuhn 1970: section II esp. pp. 18–20).

The study of the literature further reveals that, broadly speaking, two approaches to the question of the emergence of economics as a science are discernible. The first argues that the question cannot be given a meaningful answer and that it should therefore be ignored.[3] The other suggests the fact that a definite – though a different one for different historians – time period can be assigned to the emergence of economics. The most frequently mentioned time periods in this context include the final decades of the seventeenth century, the quarter century preceding the publication of the *Wealth of Nations*, and the final decades of the nineteenth century.

Examination of the histories favouring these three time periods, together with arguments presented for rejecting the issue of emergence, reveals the strong connection between exploring that emergence and the problem of identifying phases in the development of economics, that is, the problem of periodisation.

An examination of various approaches to the question of the emergence of economics as a science is undertaken in the first section of this chapter. In this examination, attitudes to the definitional question and to the problem of periodisation implicit in these approaches are particularly emphasised. The second section shows that for a variety of reasons the quarter century prior to the publication of Smith's *Wealth of Nations* can best be described as the period during which economics emerged as a science.

I

The argument that the problem of the emergence of economics as a science is a non-question, because it is a question incapable of yielding precise or meaningful answers, is implied in much of the literature on the history of economics by a failure to explicitly justify their starting point in any way. Sometimes the argument is made explicit. It is then claimed that a definite starting point cannot be assigned, and that since economics in one form or another has been present among the ancients, it is best to start the discussion with them. Examples drawn from two distinguished histories of economics will make this clear.

The first of these examples, rather appropriately, is drawn from one of the first histories of political economy, that by J. A. Blanqui (1838). In his introduction, he clearly illustrates the dilemma posed by the question of the emergence of economics when he explains that in writing his history, two courses were essentially open to him.

> I could follow the beaten track, develop the preliminary discourses of J. B. Say, M. de Sismondi, and Mr. McCulloch, on the course of political economy since Quesnay, adding a few words of politeness for the preceding

> centuries, or I could go further back, and connect political economy with general history, noting their reciprocal influence from the ancients to our day.
> (Blanqui 1838: p. xxxiv)

Past practice by Say, Sismondi and McCulloch is rejected on several grounds, of which the following is the major one. These authors, Blanqui (1838: p. xxv) argued,

> of the treatises of political economy, without exception, traced its origins no further back than the first attempts of Quesnay and Turgot; as if never before the works of these celebrated men, had any systematic writings called the attention of savants and statesmen to the phenomenon of the production of wealth.

The traditional starting point is rejected by Blanqui because there must have been 'systematic writing' on economics before the middle of the eighteenth century.

From his own historical investigations, Blanqui (1838: p. xxvi) concludes the following. First, 'there was a political economy among the ancients, as there is among the moderns, not a systematic or formulated political economy, but one arising from facts, and practised before being written'. Second, it is an error to believe that even if we take no account of 'the systems attempted by governments, political economy dates simply from the second half of the eighteenth century because more than two hundred years before, Italy had very remarkable treatises on a multiple of special subjects which depended on political economy' (pp. xxxi–xxxii). Several starting points other than the middle of the eighteenth century can therefore be suggested.

That Blanqui's argument depended very much on the meaning ascribed to political economy is clear from the above. When political economy is identified with economic institutions, as Blanqui tended to do, its history can start with the ancients, but then it can no longer be described as intellectual history. It then becomes economic history, as much of Blanqui's history in fact really is (cf. Ingram 1888: pp. 2–3).

This definitional proposition is combined with the argument that the emergence of economics must be traced back at least as far as the Greeks and Romans. Because these societies had economic systems and economic institutions, there must have been people discussing economic questions. (Blanqui 1838: ch. I, esp. pp. 2–3). However, when Blanqui defines political economy as writings on economic subjects, then the Italian treatises become his starting point.[4] If political economy is defined as 'systematic writing on the production of wealth', a definition not pursued by Blanqui in this context, a different answer (and one approximating the 'preliminary discourses' of Say, Sismondi and McCulloch) would have been more appropriate.

An argument resembling that of Blanqui was presented a century later by Schumpeter (1952). This is illustrated in the following quotation, which explicitly treats the emergence of economics as a non-question:

> our original definition ('tooled knowledge') indicates the reason why it is in general impossible to date – even by decades – the origins, let alone the 'foundation' of a science as distinguished from the origins of a particular method or the 'foundation' of a school. Just as sciences grow by slow accretion, gradually differentiating themselves under the influence of favorable and inhibiting environmental and personal conditions, from their common-sense background and sometimes also from other sciences. Research into the past, clarifying these conditions, can and does reduce the time range within which it is in each case about equally justifiable to aver or to deny the existence of a body of scientific knowledge. But no amount of research can eliminate altogether a zone of doubt that has always been broadened by the historian's personal equation. As regards economics, bias or ignorance alone can explain such statements as that A. Smith or F. Quesnay or Sir William Petty or anyone else 'founded' that science, or that the historian should begin his report with one of them.
>
> (Schumpeter 1952: p. 9)

At a later stage this argument is clarified by Schumpeter, and thereby for all practical purposes negated. At the beginning of (Schumpeter 1952: Part II) the actual starting point of the history, Schumpeter repeats his argument that the birth of a science cannot be precisely dated, nor, in the sense that he has defined it, can it ever be related to the work of a single individual or group. The start he himself makes with the Greeks (neglecting his brief comments on Babylonians and Egyptians), is justified on the ground that here are the beginnings of economic analysis. The process of economic tool accumulation started, although as a 'very minor element', in the systematic work of the Greek philosophers, and 'is the fountainhead of practically all further work' (Schumpeter 1952: p. 53).

In addition to this concept of 'beginnings', Schumpeter (1952: p. 51) introduced two other historical categories which relate to the emergence of economics. These are the 'process' of the rising into 'recognised existence' of economics, which took place between the middle of the seventeenth and the end of the eighteenth century; and second, the concept of the 'classical situation'. Although this second concept is not really defined,[5] the following quotation shows its relevance for this discussion:

> Such a classical situation emerged in the second half of the eighteenth century and no such classical situation had ever emerged before. Availing ourselves of this, we might be tempted to start somewhere between 1750 and 1800, perhaps with the peak performance of the epoch, A. Smith's *Wealth of Nations* (1776). But every classical situation summarises or consolidates the work – the really original work – that leads up to it, and cannot be understood by itself. Therefore, we shall try to cover in this part, as best as we can, the whole span of more than 2000 years that extends from the 'beginnings' to about twenty years after the publication of *Wealth of Nations*.
>
> (Schumpeter 1952: pp. 51–2)

Schumpeter's historical views on early economics can be summarised by means of the interrelationship between these three historical concepts. The first of these, that is, 'the beginnings' or the slow accretion of 'tooled knowledge' which started with the Greeks, together with the second concept, the slow process in which economics gained 'a recognised existence' through the writings of the pamphleteer merchants and administrators of the seventeenth and eighteenth centuries, provides the source of explanation for the third, that is, the first 'classical situation', which 'emerged in the second half of the eighteenth century'. Unlike his earlier *Economic Doctrine and Method* (Schumpeter 1912), this perspective disguises the qualitative change which took place in the later part of the eighteenth century.[6]

Which of these concepts of periodisation coincides with the actual emergence of economics as a science substantially depends on the definition of economics adopted by the historian. If 'recognised existence' of a discipline and 'classical situation' are more important in the history of science, then to start as he did with the Greek philosophers can be explained partly by the historian's urge to trace everything back to their ultimate starting point, in order to aid the understanding of the phenomenon in which he is really interested (cf. Letwin 1963: pp. vii–viii).

There is, however, another explanation for this emphasis on early beginnings in the history. This arises from Schumpeter's dogmatic positivist position, so apparent in the methodological introduction. To commence with the Greeks reinforces the positivist belief that scientific knowledge grows by the gradual accumulation of truth, while at the same time it depreciates the relativist approach which is implicit in the more dialectical approaches to intellectual history. As Blaug (1964) and Viner (1953) have pointed out in their comment on Schumpeter, this dogmatic positivism is not sustained in the actual history itself, since Schumpeter found it virtually impossible to separate the economic analysis from the economic thought.

Furthermore, it seems to me that those who start with the Greek or other ancient philosophers evade the question of the emergence of economics, perhaps as a consequence of this historical zeal. It rests also on definitional confusions: In the case of Blanqui on a confusion between economics and economic institutions, and between writings with economic content and systematic economic writings; in the case of Schumpeter, between 'economic analysis as a minor element … in systematic work', and economics as a science.

Schumpeter's second historical concept, which is based on the suggestion that 'economics rose … into recognised existence between the middle of the seventeenth and the end of the eighteenth century' (Schumpeter 1952: p. 51) serves as a useful starting point for a discussion of the views of two historians of economics who have looked for the emergence of economics in the second half of the seventeenth century. One of these authors is Marx (1859), the other is Letwin (1963), in a study specifically addressed to this problem.

In a well known passage at the beginning of some historical notes on the analysis of commodities, Marx (1859) gave a definition of classical political economy in terms of the period of its existence, thereby indicating by implication its starting point. According to Marx, classical political economy began with Sir William Petty in England and with Boisguilbert in France, and ended with Ricardo in Britain and with Sismondi in France. Furthermore, the work on political arithmetic by Petty, one of the founders of classical political economy, is explicitly described as 'the first form in which political economy is treated as a separate science'. (Marx 1859: pp. 52–4). This proposition, together with the reference to Boisguilbert, tends to suggest that Marx regarded the end of the seventeenth century as the period in which classical political economy emerged as a science. Marx's reasons for this opinion need to be looked at briefly.

Some definitional comments are helpful at this stage. Marx viewed classical political economy as the second of three stages in the development of economics. It followed the monetary or mercantile system of political economy, and was in turn followed by vulgar or bourgeois political economy. Political economy itself was defined as the 'theoretical analysis of modern bourgeois society', and in its historical development reflected the development of capitalist society in its various forms. Political economy was inseparable from capitalism in Marx's view.[7]

Petty and Boisguilbert, but especially Petty, can be regarded as the founders of political economy, because their analysis formed the starting point for a correct scientific method in political economy. They discovered a 'few abstract general relations such as labour, division of labour, money, and value' which 'concretised historical experience' and which thereby facilitated the theoretical analysis of society. From Marx's point of view, which at this stage emphasises *method* rather than content, scientific political economy began with Petty and Boisguilbert at the end of the seventeenth century.[8]

A similar conclusion is reached by Letwin (1963). This result is partly a consequence of Letwin's specific views on the process of scientific development in general, and partly follows from his definition of scientific economics. In the introduction to his work, Letwin (1963: pp. vii–ix) criticises studies 'that locate the beginnings of economics at the very beginnings of history', because they confuse 'economic thought' with 'economic theory' (or with 'scientific economic thought' or 'economics', terms which Letwin seems to treat as synonymous). Before economics could become a science, it had to become an explanatory system, that is, 'scientific theory'. This is shown by the following quotation which sharply contrasts with Schumpeter's view of scientific development:

> A scientific theory, being a system, cannot grow by mere idle accumulation, but must be produced by an act of invention. There can be no period when a science was partly in existence: someone either has or has not brought together into an ordinary whole enough principles and effects to qualify as a science, however, rudimentary and fallacious. In the case of economics, although its fundamental principles had all been dimly recognised for centuries, the connections between them and their logical implications were not set down till the end of the seventeenth century. Then, as is often

> the case with inventions, a number of men devised slightly different but basically similar theories within a few decades. Before 1660 economics did not exist; by 1776 it existed in profusion.
>
> (Letwin 1963: pp. viii–ix)

Letwin rejects the hypothesis that the general interest in 'science and trade' so widespread in England at the end of the seventeenth century provides the explanation for this conclusion, because the bulk of the economic writings of the time do not really display a 'scientific' or 'detached attitude'. He perceives his task therefore as demonstrating 'how practical and often mercenary objectives led certain men to build a new science' (1963: p. ix) The remainder of his study is devoted to an analysis of the origins of scientific economics as revealed in the application of scientific method to economic policy questions.

Letwin (1963) ascribes the successful application of scientific method to economic policy at the end of the seventeenth century to three causes. The first of these (described in his chapter 3) is the discovery of a 'taut deductive system that infers its conclusions from a set of simple principles' and thereby guarantees objectivity (*ibid.*: esp. p. 97) The other two causes are Petty's (and Collins') introduction of Bacon's 'inductive empiricism' into economics (Letwin 1963: chs 4, 5), and second, the scientific methodology of the philosophical tradition, as exemplified by Locke's economic work (ch. 6).

Letwin's treatment of the origins of scientific economics appears to confuse economics as a science (that is, as 'an explanatory system of economic phenomena') on the one hand, and economic science as the application of scientific method to economic policy questions on the other. These two things are not the same, though the application of scientific method is of course a precondition for creating a science of economics. The practical identification of these two approaches to economic science in much of Letwin's work explains his lack of a definite conclusion in the final chapter on eighteenth-century developments. A reading of that chapter leaves the distinct impression that the question of whether the origins of scientific economics are to be found in the seventeenth century, in the work of Locke, Petty, North and Barbon, or in the eighteenth century in that of Cantillon and Smith, is largely left unresolved (Letwin 1963: esp. pp. 207–8, 218–19, 227–8).

Other criticism of this final chapter can be advanced. First, there is his total neglect of economic literature other than British' economics in this chapter, despite the obvious fact that the economics of Smith, and earlier that of Cantillon, drew on French economics as well as the British tradition of the seventeenth century to which Letwin's analysis is confined.

Furthermore, apart from a casual observation in connection with North (Letwin 1963: p. 204), Letwin does not discuss the influence of his six case studies on later developments in economics. Now, as far as my knowledge of the eighteenth-century literature goes, it seems correct to ascribe a great deal of such influence to Locke – the bearer of the important philosophical tradition – a good deal less to Child and Petty, and virtually nothing to Barbon, Collins and North.[9] In that case their legacy is rather restricted, and it can be said that the origins of economics re-emerge in terms of Schumpeter's (1912) two strands of thought: moral and political philosophy on the one hand, and the pamphlet literature of merchants, statesmen and administrators on the other. This consideration destroys the importance of the one really novel element in Letwin's argument: the deductive tradition, as exemplified by North, which aimed to increase the objectivity of policy discussions.

Finally, there is the question of the scope of economics, which seems to be deliberately left vague in Letwin's account. Letwin (1963) argues correctly that 'trade' had wider connotations than this word has at present; that the topics discussed under that heading fall within the proper domain of economic discussion as commonly understood, but he does not show that some of the more important subjects with which economists were to concern themselves in the late eighteenth and the whole of the nineteenth century, were completely omitted in these seventeenth- and early eighteenth-century treatises on trade. One of the differences between the economics of Cantillon and that of Smith (to take the strongest case possible) is the former's comparative neglect of questions of production and distribution, and his much greater emphasis on matters relating to international trade and monetary theory. This substantive shift in emphasis between the 'science of trade' and the 'science of political economy' is blurred over, despite the fact that it is clearly evident when the literature from these periods is compared.[10] There is an important qualitative difference between the economics of the end of the seventeenth century and that of the end of the eighteenth century, which is of great relevance to the question of the emergence of scientific economics. The end of the seventeenth century must therefore be rejected as the period in which economics emerged as a science, unless this is rather narrowly defined as the application of 'scientific method' to economic problems.

This brings the discussion to the eighteenth century. Here it is arguable that if the question of the emergence of scientific economics were to be settled by the votes of authority, then the physiocrats would probably have to be called the founders of economics. A look at the writings of some of the economists who pre-empted that important place for physiocracy – the system or science of the 'economistes' – also illustrates the importance of the definition of economics in such inquiries.

That the physiocrats were the founders of a new science was, not surprisingly, the opinion of Du Pont de Nemours, the first 'historian' of economics who inquired into its origin and progress. This is abundantly illustrated in the following quotation:

> About thirteen years ago [i.e. about 1754], a man of the greatest genius (*Quesnay*), skilled in profound meditations, already known for some excellent books and for success in an art [medicine] in which the highest qualifications consist in the observation and in a regard for nature, conjectured that nature did not confine her *physical* laws to those at present studied

> in our colleges and academies, but that, when she gave ants, bees and beavers the ability of submitting themselves of their own accord and in their own interest, to a good, stable, and unvarying government, she did not refuse to mankind the power to obtain for itself the same advantage. Urged on by the importance of this discovery and by the prospect of the important consequences which could be derived therefrom, he applied the whole of his penetrating mind to the research into nature's physical laws applicable to society, and finally succeeded in ascertaining the unshakeable foundation of these laws, in grasping their harmony, in developing their interconnection, and in extracting and demonstrating their results. All this was very new doctrine … [In 1756] Quesnay provided the *Encyclopédie* with the articles 'Fermiers' and 'Grain', the first published work in which he began the exposition of the science he had discovered. Shortly afterwards, he invented the *Tableau économique*, that astonishing model which depicts the rise, distribution and reproduction of wealth, and which can be used to calculate the effects of every transaction related to wealth with such a degree of certainty, speed, and precision. This model, together with its explanation, and the *Maximes générales du gouvernement économique* were printed at Versailles in 1758.
>
> (Du Pont de Nemours 1768: pp. 338–9; cf. Schelle 1888: pp. 46, 402)

In some respects, Du Pont's opinion can give no real guidance to the problem of the emergence of economics as a science, since the new science, the formation of which he so eloquently described, was only loosely related to what is now generally understood by the science of economics. Physiocracy, as envisaged by the physiocrats themselves, had a much broader aim: it attempted to provide a science of society as a whole.

Nevertheless, and as indicated earlier, physiocracy is widely regarded as a crucial landmark in the beginnings of the science of economics, if not as the beginning of that discipline itself. This view is held by authorities as diverse as McCulloch, Marx, Marshall and Schumpeter. What makes their views of special interest to the argument in this chapter is that they assigned this important place to the physiocrats for quite different reasons. These, in turn, were dependent on their view of what economics was all about. This proposition is easily illustrated as follows:

> But what the English writers [that is, Child, Locke, North, Vanderlint, Hume, Harris] had left undone was now attempted by a French philosopher, equally distinguished for the subtlety and originality of his mind, and the integrity and simplicity of his character. This was the celebrated M. Quesnay, a physician, attached to the Court of Louis XV. It is to him that the merit belongs of having first attempted to investigate and analyse the sources of wealth, *with the intention of ascertaining the fundamental principles of political economy*, and who thus gave it a systematic form, and raised it to the rank of a science.[11]
>
> (McCulloch 1824: pp. 41–2)

> The analysis of *capital*, within the bourgeois horizon, is essentially the work of the Physiocrats. It is this service which makes them the true fathers of modern political economy. In the first place, they analysed the various *material components* of which capital exists and into which it resolves itself in the course of the labour process. … [Second,] the Physiocrats established the forms which capital assumes in circulation (fixed capital, circulating capital, even though as yet they give them other names). … [Finally,] the Physiocrats transferred the enquiry into the origin of surplus value from the sphere of circulation into the sphere of direct production, and thereby laid the foundation for the analysis of capitalistic production.[12]
>
> (Marx 1969: pp. 44–5)

> The first systematic attempt to form an economic science on a broad basis was made in France about the middle of the eighteenth century by a group of statesmen and philosophers under the leadership of Quesnay. … They were the first to proclaim the doctrine of free trade as a broad principle of action. Their work has but little direct value, but its indirect influence on the present position of economics has been very great. For firstly, the clearness and logical consistency of their arguments have caused them to exercise a great influence on later thought. And secondly, the chief motive of their study was not, as it had been with most of their predecessors, to increase the riches of merchants, and to fill the exchequors of kings; it was to diminish the suffering and degradation which was caused by extreme poverty. They thus gave to economics its modern aim of seeking after such knowledge as may help raise the quality of human life.
>
> (Marshall 1890: app. B, pp. 756–7)[13]

> We have seen that our science like all others originated in individual researches into striking facts which appeared as problems even to laymen. As long as men confined themselves to such research and so long as the central phenomenon of economics itself remained more or less in the darkness of instinctive and practical knowledge, scientific analysis could never fully set to work, it could not, as it were, make full use of its vital powers. … It was, however, the Physiocrats, or 'Economists', who made the great breach, through which lay all further progress in the field of analysis, by the discovery and intellectual formulation of the circular flow in economic life.
>
> (Schumpeter 1912: pp. 42–3)[14]

The physiocrats, on the basis of this wide range of opinion quoted, therefore deserve an important place in the story of the emergence of economics as a science.[15]

First of all, they helped change the nature of economic discussion by emphasising production and distribution economics rather than matters of money and trade. Second, they introduced the analysis of capital into economics. Third, they developed the first model of the circular flow from which they drew important theoretical and policy conclusions; while, in addition, they were also the first school of thought to vigorously campaign for free trade in nearly all aspects of economic life, a policy deduced from their systematic economic inquiry. Yet, as argued below, to explain the emergence of economics as a science simply in terms of their efforts, can be seen as a mistake.

This leaves the question whether the emergence of economics as a science can best be dated to the end of the nineteenth century. Although there are few historians who have specifically opted for this alternative,[16] reasons can be advanced to support such a contention. Given that part of this essay's purpose is to argue that the question of 'emergence' is very dependent on issues of definition and periodisation, the claims for the end of the nineteenth century need to be briefly canvassed.

The first of these reasons is definitional. In his *Essay on the Nature and Significance of Economic Science*, on the specific ground that definitions generally follow the creation of a new science, Robbins (1935) showed that economics was in need of a new definition which more precisely reflected its scope and method. He therefore proposed to substitute the definition, 'Economics is the science which studies human behaviour as a relationship between ends and scarce means which have alternative uses' (Robbins 1935: p. 16) for the classical definitions which related economics 'to the study of the causes of material welfare', or more simply, to the production, distribution, and consumption of wealth (1935: p. 4).[17]

The whole of Robbins' (1935) first chapter, especially the arguments specifically supporting the new definition, tends to suggest that this definition derives from the 'new' economics of the 'more recent theories of value', and has little to do with the economics of the classical school. The very way in which the definition is phrased evokes the language of marginalism, of 'maximising' satisfactions and of 'minimising' costs. This impression is reinforced by the list of the four necessary and sufficient conditions for making human action susceptible to economic analysis: that is, that the ends are multiple and can be ranked in order of priority, and that the means to achieve the ends are limited and have alternative uses. Examples to illustrate these conditions were the stock-in-trade of all early neo-classical economists; they cannot really be found in the works of Smith, Ricardo, Say, McCulloch or John Stuart Mill.[18]

A conclusion from Robbins (1935) is that those who accept his definition of economics, need to acknowledge the end of the nineteenth century as the formative period of the new science of economics.[19] As a corollary, the earlier economic literature then constitutes a rich, but unscientific prehistory, leading up to the period when economics finally emerged as a (positive) science following the analytical results of the *marginal* revolution. This is another illustration of the manner in which the logic of a definition carries specific implications for the history of that science.[20]

Robbins' definitional exercises also draw attention to features of economic science which link it with this period rather than with earlier ones. The new developments turned economics even more into a highly deductive science, while they also turned it into a mathematical science whose major problems could logically, and easily, be tackled by an application of the calculus. It is therefore not surprising that at the end of the nineteenth century, economists with a mathematical bent became predominant among the leading theorists.[21] Furthermore, by 'defending the neutrality of ends' in economic analysis, Robbins put forward the view that economics is a 'positive', 'value-free' science, in line with the change of name of the discipline which occurred towards the end of the century.[22]

Aspects of Schumpeter's definitions of science tend to reinforce the argument that the end of the nineteenth century is really the period in which economics emerged as a science. Science, for Schumpeter (1952) is

> any field of knowledge in which there are people, so-called research workers or scientists or scholars, who engage in the task of improving upon the existing stock of facts and methods, and who, in the process of doing so, acquire a command of both that differentiates them from the 'layman' and also eventually from the mere 'practitioner'.
>
> (Schumpeter 1952: 7)

Schumpeter's argument invokes professionalisation of a science, making the presence of a community of scholars and research workers almost a necessary condition for the existence of a science. If the characteristics of such professionalisation are described in terms of 'the formation of specialised journals, the foundation of specialised societies, and a claim for a special place in the curriculum' (Kuhn 1970: p. 19), this likewise points to the end of the nineteenth century as the period when economics emerged as a science.[23]

Kuhn (1970), from which these characteristics of the professionalisation of a science were drawn, continued by arguing that 'in the sciences (though not in the fields of medicine, technology and law). ... these characteristics have usually been associated with the group's first reception of a single paradigm' (*ibid.*: pp. 18–20). If this argument is accepted, such sociology-of-science type reasons for dating the emergence of economics as a science at the end of the nineteenth century merge with the definitional reason generated by Robbins' (1935) essay. The last is easy to depict as the 'paradigm' of neo-classical economics, if not much of modern, 'positive' economics.[24] Are these sufficient reasons to date the emergence of economics as a science to the end of the nineteenth century, after the pioneering work of Jevons, Menger and Walras, had made such developments possible?

Present-day economists who hanker after the comforts of a Robbinsian definition of economics will be tempted to agree with this proposition. However, when a different definition is adopted, the historical net has to be cast differently. In fact, when the traditional mid-nineteenth century definition is adopted (see appendix to this chapter), the emergence of economics as a science can be discovered in the eighteenth century, in that quarter-century which culminated in the publication of the *Wealth of Nations*. The following section examines other reasons which lend support to such a conclusion.

II

The critical excursion through the literature on the emergence of economics as a science has shown the relationship between this question and problems associated with definition and periodisation. The selection of a particular time period for the emergence of economics as a science generally reveals a particular view of 'economics', or of 'science', or of 'economics as a science', while it furthermore implies that a distinction can be drawn between the period before and after the selected time. This, it was shown, applied to those who selected the end of the seventeenth- or of the nineteenth century for this purpose, or who associated it with the work of the physiocrats during the second half of the eighteenth century. Even those who, for some reason or other, deny the possibility of finding a particular period for the emergence of economics, start their historical investigations with 'beginnings', no matter how primitive, on the basis of a more or less specific definition.

In what follows, four sets of arguments are presented to show that 'there was a remarkable concentration of scientific effort in the three decades after 1750 … and [that] the appearance of many works of great quality in such a relatively brief period indicates some kind of conjuncture in the history of economics' (Winch 1970: pp. 9–10). Taken together, these suggest that it is appropriate to take the third quarter of the eighteenth century as the period during which economics emerged as a science.

General characteristics of concentrated scientific effort

The first thing which strikes the historian of economics who studies the period of the century before the publication of the *Wealth of Nations* is the tremendous amount of high-quality material which was published in the last quarter-century of this period. Although it stretches the time period a little, this acceleration in the rate and quality of economic publication commenced in 1748 with the publication of Montesquieu's *L'Esprit des Lois*, a work which was followed by a wide range of other important publications in both England and France.[25]

In 1752, Hume published his *Political Discourses* which, with the exception of the essay 'Of the Jealousy of Trade', contained all his economic essays. In 1754, Forbonnais published his *Elémens du Commerce*. In 1755 there were two important posthumous publications: Frances Hutcheson's *A System of Moral Philosophy* and Richard Cantillon's *Essai sur la Nature du Commerce en Général* (though this had been written about thirty years earlier). 1755 also saw the publication of the ambitious (but never completed) *Elements of Commerce and Theory of Taxes* by Josiah Tucker. In 1756, Quesnay published his first economic work in the *Encyclopédie* of Diderot and D'Alembert, in 1757, Joseph Harris his *Essay*

Upon Money and Coins; in 1758 the most important physiocratic publication, Quesnay's *Tableau Economique*, made its first appearance, while the decade closed on a high note with the publication of Turgot's *Eloge de Gournay* in 1759.

The remainder of the quarter-century saw the expansion and consolidation of this work from the 1750s. In 1760 and 1763, Mirabeau produced his *Théorie de l'Impôt* and *Philosophie Rurale* respectively, in 1766 Turgot wrote, and three years later published, his 'Réflexions sur la Formation et la Distribution des Richesses', 1767 produced Mercier de la Rivière's *L'Ordre Naturel et Essentiel des Sociétés Politiques*, Sir James Steuart's *Inquiry into the Principles of Political Economy* and Forbonnais' *Principles et Observations Economiques*. The period closed with Condillac's *Le Commerce et le Gouvernement* in France, and with the final triumph of this epoch, Smith's *An Inquiry into the Nature and Causes of the Wealth of Nations*.

When this record is compared with the previous century's output, a number of conclusions can almost immediately be drawn. In the first place, the above list of publications contained the first general treatises on economics, no such general works having been published in earlier periods. Second, a comparison of the authors of these works and of this period with those of the previous century discloses their quite different background, the important implications of which are explained later. Third, the basic quality of this work is much higher than that of the previous century. All three considerations may be explored further.

General treatises in economics were unknown until 1755, when Cantillon's *Essai* and Tucker's *Elements* were published, although the first of them was written in the 1730s. The literature prior to this period was predominantly pamphlet literature devoted to one or more particular topics (though often with a varied number of digressions on more general points). A comparison with such 'general' works on trade as Sir Josiah Child's *A New Discourse of Trade*, published in 1694, and John Cary's *A Discourse of Trade*, published in 1717, shows how the scope of economic inquiry had expanded over this time. If these tracts are compared with works such as Steuart's *Principles* and Turgot's 'Réflexions', not to mention Smith's *Wealth of Nations*, the contrast is even more striking. It is as if a completely different world is entered. The quarter-century ending in 1776 produced the first general, systematised accounts of economic phenomena, which transcended the policy-oriented literature of earlier periods.

An analysis of the background of the authors writing on economics in the century before 1750 and those from the quarter-century thereafter, discloses some quite dramatic changes. A sample of fifty of the more important British economic writers of these periods[26] indicates that, whereas about one half of the authors whose major work was produced in the period prior to 1750 were merchants or connected with manufactures, only one fifth of those from the quarter-century before 1776 fall into this group. At the same time, the writers drawn from the professions (church, law, universities, medicine) doubled from about 30 per cent before 1750 to 60 per cent of those in the period before 1776. It is no wonder that special pleading in favour of specific commercial interests considerably declined, and that more general, scientific inquiry of economic phenomena was on the rise.

This changing authorial background, which has implications for the authors' educational backgrounds, also explains the general rise in the quality of the economic literature of the period. As Letwin (1963: pp. viii–ix) argued, only little high-quality economic literature existed in the seventeenth century, while it existed quite profusely in the decades before Adam Smith's *Wealth of Nations*. This increased quality reveals itself in a greater use and acceptance of scientific method in the writing of economics, and in the more extensive and better use of factual material. It is also apparent in the more systematic treatment of economic questions which, during the period, became increasingly based on a broad analytical framework such as the circular flow model of Quesnay's *Tableau Economique*. Finally, this higher quality is reflected in a more scholarly and detached approach to the treatment of economic questions.

These considerations about the nature of the economic literature before Smith suggest an important qualitative difference between the economics of before and after 1750, hence illustrating one type of reason why this period has generally been regarded as so tremendously significant in the history of economics.

The widening scope and changing emphasis in economics

A second, and no less important differentiating feature which distinguishes the economics of before 1750 from that after that date, concerns the subject matter of economics. This change can be concisely captured as a decline in emphasis on problems of trade and money, and growing emphasis on developing a theory of exchange, production and distribution.

This shift in emphasis is already apparent in the change of title by which the economic subject matter was being described. The treatises and discourses of trade and commerce – of which Cantillon's *Essai* is at once the exception, and the last and most distinguished example – were replaced during this quarter-century by principles of political economy, and by treatises or reflections on the nature and causes, and the production and distribution, of wealth. These changes in name do not signify a mere titular change for the same subject matter; they indicate a new approach to the scope of economics, an approach which, in varying degrees, was to be followed in most further works on theoretical economics over the next century and a half.

This changed emphasis is also illustrated in the treatment of problems of value, production and distribution in the literature before and after 1750. For example, in Sir William Petty's *Treatise of Taxes and Contributions*, a fairly sophisticated labour theory of value, and a rudimentary wages and rent theory are enunciated as a digression, or series of digressions, in a work basically devoted to more practical problems (Petty 1899: I, pp. 43–51). The problem of market price determination analysed in terms of supply and demand, or of utility and scarcity, were discussed in the work of Locke (1696: p. 45–6), Barbon

(1690: pp. 1–6), Law (1705: pp. 4–5) and Jocelyn (1718: pp. 1–12) as background material to monetary problems.

In connection with distribution theory, the same thing is found in the pre-1750 literature. The analysis of wages, what little there is of this, was conducted largely in the context of export prices, and of a perceived need for increasing national competitiveness aboard (see for example Furniss 1920). The first analyses of rent occur in pamphlet literature on trade prohibitions with respect to exporting English wool, or importing foreign corn or Irish cattle. Explanations of interest arose largely from debates about the legal abatement of interest rates, which were also rooted in the needs of trade as envisaged by merchants (see Tucker 1960: chs 1–2). The idea of distribution theory as such did not occur in the literature until after 1750 (see Cannan 1953; Meek 1954).

Emphasis on value, production, distribution, accumulation and growth distribution as problems in their own right, is very visible in the theoretical frameworks of Turgot and Smith at the end of the period. It is also interesting to note that in their discussion of these problems, they seek explanations in the conditions of production instead of trade. This applies particularly to Smith's treatment of value, and to his and Turgot's theories of wages, interest and profits. Furthermore, both examined increases in the wealth of nations in terms of domestic production, and never in terms of the gains from international trade through a favourable trade balance.

This change in focus can be explained by several reasons, some of which have already been mentioned. The changing nature of the economic writers is one; the more systematic approach to economic questions making reduced emphasis on trade, and greater emphasis on production problems, is another. It can also be argued, at least for Turgot and Smith, that the superb theoretical work of Cantillon and Hume on the quantity theory of money, banking and credit, and their enunciation of the automatic mechanism of specie distribution, provided satisfactory solutions to some old problems, so that little further work was required in these areas.

Thus many of the trade problems of the pre-1750 literature faded away. Notable examples are concern over the adequacy of the money supply and the balance of trade. Both were shown to be non-problems (at least in the long run) in Hume's essay 'Of the Balance of Trade'. Simultaneously, protection policies were strongly attacked by arguments which gradually gained general acceptance among economists. Arrival at a general doctrine of the benefits of free trade based on the moral principle that individuals know their own interests better than any government could, so that prohibitions in economic matters could be described as socially harmful infringements of individual liberty, was one such argument. The second derived from the benefits of the international division of labour, particularly forcefully advanced by Smith (1776).

Finally, and perhaps the crucial reason for this shift in emphasis, changes in the economic circumstances of Britain made discussion of money and trade matters of less urgency in the quarter-century following 1750. Reform of the coinage, and improvements in banking and credit creation, eliminated relevance of concerns over the scarcity of money as a circulating medium, and the quality of the coinage, until the 1797 inconvertibility crises drew the attention of economic writers once more to broad monetary issues. Similarly, the rising supremacy of Britain in international trade relative to Holland and France lowered concerns over the competitiveness of exports abroad. The issue of colonial trade, which rose to prominence as a result of the revolt of the American colonies at the end of the period, partly replaced them.

However, growing interest in production and distribution economics is difficult to relate directly to contemporary industrial developments in Britain. Only the better economists – on both sides of the Channel – were sufficiently aware of changes in the production environment to draw conclusions from this for their economic theory. The majority of economic writers of the time took no notice of this, and probably were not even aware of such changes.[27]

The analysis of capital and the development of a three factor model

A third, and probably the most important theoretical distinguishing feature separating the economic analysis of the two periods, is that prior to 1750 there was no threefold classification of the factors of production. Problems of value, and of production theory if discussed, were only discussed in terms of land and labour, the 'original' factors.[28] Similarly, in the theory of distribution, the rate of profit as such was rarely analysed, while the rate of interest was explained either in monetary terms, or in terms of supply and demand for commercial stock, or in terms of the rate of return to land.[29] Capital, as a factor of production, was not really discussed before 1750.[30]

This two factor model of the production of wealth greatly affected the period's economic theory and policy discussion. The tremendous emphasis in the literature of 1650–1750 on the need for a large population, on the wastefulness of large numbers of able-bodied but unemployed poor, on better land utilisation, and on raising labour productivity, all illustrate the fact that increases in the quality and quantity of the 'original factors' were seen as the driving force behind economic growth. Capital accumulation was ignored as a relevant factor.

Repairing this omission was the work of three economists. Capital advances were first recognised as an important factor of production by Quesnay who, in his many works on economics, discussed the role of this 'new' factor of production in detail. He failed to recognise, however, that stressing this new, productive agent, also entailed the introduction of a new class into economic society: the owners of capital, and that this new class was entitled to a share in the annual revenue in the form of a 'new' income category, the profits of stock. Quesnay's scheme of distribution was still in terms of net product or rent on the one hand, and on the other reproduced expenditures which included the payment of wages and of capital charges such as depreciation. Interest was still connected by him with the rate of return to land, while profits, he argued, had no long-run existence under competitive conditions (see Quesnay 1958: esp. pp. 427–58, 763–8, 793–812; Meek 1962: pp. 297–312; Marx 1969: ch. 1).

Quesnay's omissions were remedied by his two contemporaries, Turgot and Smith. Signalling their full appreciation of the implications of Quesnay's capital analysis, their economic work introduced capitalists as the suppliers of advances of wages, raw materials, and even fixed capital, and profits as the income of these capitalists. Henceforth, value, production and distribution theory were discussed with reference to *three* requisites of production and in terms of *three* basic income shares.[31]

The explanation for the discovery of capital as a useful concept in economic analysis is to be found partly in the economic circumstances of eighteenth-century Scotland and France, and partly in the biographical details of Quesnay, Turgot and Smith.[32] Quesnay, for instance, 'discovered' capital in his analytical comparison of 'la grande culture' in the north with 'la petite culture' in the rest of France (see Quesnay 1958: pp. 427–58). This comparison may not have been made if Quesnay had not had a personal interest in agriculture and farming (see Quesnay 1958: pp. 245–6).

Turgot further developed and extended Quesnay's analysis of 'la grande et la petite culture' in an article in *Ephémérides* (1767, VI, pp. 77–97), and in his 'Réflexions' (Turgot 1766: pp. 22–4, 45–8). Turgot's extensions of Quesnay's views by his application of capital analysis to the whole sphere of production (see Turgot 1766: Part II) probably owed something to his tours of commercial and industrial centres with Vincent de Gournay in the second half of the 1750s, and to his knowledge of the industry within his own generality of Limoges (see Turgot 1970: pp. 254–5). Smith, as Meek (1954) has shown, saw the emergence of the new class and the new income share in the rapid economic development of Glasgow in the 1750s (which, in contrast to the relative stagnation and underdevelopment of most of the rest of Scotland, would have emphasised their importance to him).

The fundamental importance of this distinguishing feature for the later developments in economics should not be underrated. For Marx (1969), as was shown previously, it marked the beginning of modern political economy; for Harrod (1951: pp. 464–5), it had the following significance:

> The history of economic science ... has largely been the history of the formation of appropriate concepts. Our thinking about economic matters was revolutionised, for instance, when it was pointed out that all the multifarious costs of production could be grouped under the three heads of land, labour and capital. This made immense progress possible, and the whole of classical economics was based on this classificatory improvement.

The development of some general, unifying principles

It has already been argued that the third quarter of the eighteenth century produced the first general treatises on economics, which provided systematic accounts of economic phenomena. During this period economics also became more clearly defined as a 'separate branch of study' with an inter-connected body of theories and principles, and this considerably aided the presentation of 'a new science in a single book', the manner in which Gibbon greeted the *Wealth of Nations* on publication.[33]

Three factors which aided this unification of subject matter, and whose origins can be largely ascribed to the economic writings of the third quarter of the eighteenth century, may be mentioned. The first of these is the discovery of the concept of the circular flow by Quesnay; the second is the analysis of the effects on resource allocation of changes in market prices and the development of the notion of competitive equilibrium; the third is the argument that all individuals, knowing their own interests best, should be left free to pursue them, and implementing this policy yields the greatest prosperity.[34]

The importance of the concept of the circular flow in unifying the subject matter of economics need hardly be stressed. Quesnay's *Tableau Economique* showed the interconnection between the production, the circulation and the distribution of wealth and the role of three economic classes of society in this process. Moreover, it demonstrated the notion of equilibrium in economic society by analysing the uninterrupted production of wealth. Above all, this economic model clearly demonstrated the essential unity of economic phenomena, the aspect taken over, and generalised, by Adam Smith.

Extensive appreciation of the notion of competitive equilibrium was also a feature of this period. The same applies to the implications of competition for price determination and resource allocation. For example, Turgot and Adam Smith analysed supply variations induced by a divergence of market price from cost of production, thereby illustrating the tendency to equilibrium in a competitive market.[35] Other effects of price variations on resource allocation were discussed, sometimes with a great deal of elegance. For example, Turgot discussed the effects on the degree of capitalisation in production of changes in the market rate of interest, and showed that such changes warranted new equilibrium positions (Turgot 1766: pp. 85–6). Smith analysed resource allocation distortions resulting from monopolies, thereby linking the concept of the competitive market and the improved resource allocation more clearly for policy discussion (Smith 1776: pp. 61–2, 423–30).

Finally, the decades after 1750 accorded greater recognition of the postulate that individuals, knowing their own interests best, should be left free to pursue them, and that in this pursuit, they will maximise their means of enjoyment by increasing the conveniences of life. From this, it was easy to argue that general economic freedom contributes to the greatest possible increase in national wealth. This maxim of economic policy was later described by McCulloch as the 'general theorem' of political economy.[36]

It need not be demonstrated that these three developments in economic analysis in the eighteenth century, which came to the forefront of economic discussion only after 1750, remain at the core of much of modern economics, and that they, to a very large extent, provide the basis for the unity of its subject matter. This is a final reason for distinguishing the economics of before 1750 from that which came afterwards, and for giving special significance to the third quarter of the eighteenth century in the development of economics.

Are these reasons sufficient to describe the third quarter of the eighteenth century as the period during which economics emerged as a science, or are they only characteristics which divide one period in the development of economics from another? The answer to this question is implied in the nature of these characteristics and distinguishing features, in association with the preferred definition of the nature and scope of economics. This proposition needs to be further investigated as essential to the argument of this chapter.

It has already been argued that certain specific views of the nature of economic science carry implications for the dating of the emergence of economics. Emphasis on scientific method in the study of economic phenomena (to the exclusion of the presence of a systematised body of economic knowledge) suggests the end of the seventeenth century as the period during which economics emerged as a science, as argued by Letwin and Marx. Emphasis on multiple ends and scarce means *à la* Robbins focuses attention on the 'marginal revolution' and places the emergence of economics at the end of the nineteenth century, contrasting thereby a 'positive' economics with an older (and by implication, obsolete) form of political economy. What definitional consequences arise if the third quarter of the eighteenth century is selected as the period of emergence?

Two definitional considerations arise in this case. First, dating the emergence of economics as a science in the third quarter of the eighteenth century, links economics strongly with the classical definition of its subject matter, that is, as the science of the production and distribution of wealth. Second, by relating the emergence of economics to the period of emerging capitalism, it links economics to a definitional feature emphasised by authorities as diverse as Marx and Knight (see appendix below). These considerations strengthen the already strong case for depicting the third quarter of the eighteenth century as the period when economics emerged as a science. As Stark (1944) hinted, dating the emergence of a science rests largely on the manner in which that science has been defined.

Appendix

Some definitions of economics and political economy

Since much of the argument of this paper turns on definitions of economics, a short digest of some leading definitions is useful. The following definitions are ranked in chronological order and offered without further comment.

Sir James Steuart (1767: I, pp. 15, 16) 'Oeconomy in general, is the art of providing for all the wants of a family, with prudence and frugality. … What economy is in a family, Political Oeconomy is in a state'.

Adam Smith (1776: p. 397) 'Political oeconomy … [is] … a branch of the science of a statesman or legislator [and] proposes two distinct objects: first, to provide a plentiful revenue or subsistence for the people … and, secondly, to supply the state or commonwealth with a revenue sufficient for the public services'.

F. Engels (1839: p. 218) 'Political economy is … the theoretical analysis of modern bourgeois society'.

John Stuart Mill (1844: p. 140) 'Political economy, then may be defined as follows; and the definition seems to be complete: – "The science which traces the laws of such of the phenomena of society as arise from the combined operations of mankind for the production of wealth, in so far as these phenomena are not modified by the pursuit of any other object"'.

Henry Sidgwick (1887: p. 12) 'Political Economy … is now almost universally understood to be a study or enquiry concerned with the Production, Distribution, and Exchange of Wealth'.

Alfred Marshall (1890: p. 1) 'Political Economy or Economics is a study of mankind in the ordinary business of life; it examines that part of individual and social action which is most closely connected with the attainment and with the use of the material requisities of well-being'.

Lionel Robbins (1935: p. 16) 'Economics is the science which studies human behaviour as a relationship between ends and scarce means which have alternative uses'.

F. H. Knight (1951: p. 6) 'Modern economics is an aspect of modern thought and of the individualistic or 'liberal' outlook on life, of which 'capitalism' or the competitive system, or free business enterprise, is the expression upon the economic side, as democracy is on the political'.

Paul Samuelson (1970: p. 4) 'Economics is the study of how men and society choose, with or without the use of money, to employ scarce productive resources, which could have alternative uses, to produce various commodities over time and distribute them for consumption, now and in the future, among various people and groups in society'.

Notes

1 This essay is a revised version of a paper presented at the fifth Conference of Historians of Economics at Birmingham in September 1972. Revision of this essay has benefited greatly by its discussion at this conference.

2 Two recent contributions on this subject are Letwin (1963) and Winch (1970).

3 In practice, this group starts their histories with a treatment of the economics of the ancients, since a start has to be made somewhere. This starting point has implications for their view on the emergence of economics, as shown below in more detail.

4 These Italian treatises referred to by Blanqui include 'A Discourse of the Doge Moncenigo' and a 'Budget of Florence', as well as the monetary writings of Davanzati, Serra and others (Blanqui 1838: pp. 192–3, 204–6, 260–1). In actual fact, written material of this type has a much longer history than indicated by Blanqui.

5 Schumpeter 1952: p. 51, n1 – written by E. B. Schumpeter. In her note, classical situations are defined as 'the achievement of substantial agreement after a long period of struggle and controversy'. This 'catastrophic' view of scientific change contrasts sharply with the gradual 'accretion' notion stressed more frequently by Schumpeter.

6 Schumpeter 1952: pp. 51–2. In the earlier history he had argued as follows:

> The science of economics, as it took shape towards the end of the eighteenth century, had grown from two roots which must be clearly differentiated from one another. ... One of these originated in the study of the philosophers in the widest sense of the term ... the other had been accumulated by people of various types whose primary motive had been their interest in practical question.
>
> (Schumpeter 1912: pp. 9–10)

In his review of Schumpeter (1952), Robbins praised the periodisation and classification of the earlier work which placed the discussion of ultimate sources in the first chapter, and the emergence of the classical situation in the second, thereby emphasising their qualitative difference (Robbins 1955: pp. 53–4).

7 Thus the 'monetary system' is related to the 'primitive accumulation' stage of nascent capitalism, while a 'comparative study of Petty's and Boisguilbert's writings would illuminate the social divergence' and the similarities between English and French society in their time. See Marx (1859: pp. 52–5 and notes). The definition of political economy quoted in the above paragraph is from Engels (1859: p. 218).

8 See extracts from *Grundrisse* in Marx (1859: esp. pp. 205–6) and Engels (1859: pp. 354–63). Petty and Boisguilbert were only the founders of *classical* political economy, not of *modern* political economy. The founders of the latter were the physiocrats. On this, see below, and Marx 1859: ch. 1.

9 Some casual empiricism based on a survey of the *Kress Catalogue through 1776* suggests that while Child and Petty were fairly frequently reprinted in the eighteenth century, and Locke's economics (in his *Collected Works*) was readily available, the works of Collins, Barbon and North were not widely available, and hence infrequently, if at all, quoted. In addition, Locke and Child were also available in French translation.

10 Cf. Cannan 1898: ch. 1. This difference links the economic literature of these periods to their environment, as is discussed more fully in Part II. The 'agricultural revolution' and the beginnings of the 'industrial revolution' emphasised certain aspects of capitalistic production, which produced progress and interest in the economics of production and distribution, and hence in the theory of value as contrasted with the theory of market price.

11 McCulloch's definition of political economy (McCulloch 1824) explains why he regarded the physiocrats as the founders of the science: the object of political economy, according to him,

> is to point out the means by which the industry of man may be rendered most productive of those necessaries, comforts, and enjoyments of life, which constitute *wealth*; to ascertain the proportions in which the wealth is divided among

> the different classes of the community, and the mode in which it may be most advantageously consumed.

This is what Quesnay had attempted to do in the *Tableau Economique*.

12 It should be noted that the physiocrats are described as the founders of modern and not of classical political economy, because they discovered the foundation of the analysis of capitalistic production, which must be the starting point, according to Marx, for political economy as the theoretical analysis of modern bourgeois society. Cf. Marx (1859: pp. 20–1).

13 In earlier editions, this passage appeared in Book I, chapter IV. The last two sentences in the quotation give undoubtedly what would be Marshall's more personal reasons for naming the physiocrats as the founders of modern economics, since it is well known that his interest in economics was sparked off by his concern with the problem of poverty. See for example Keynes 1924: pp. 136–8.

14 For this reason the physiocrats (and Adam Smith) get the second chapter in Schumpeter (1912) all to themselves, as noted previously. This emphasises the tremendous importance of their contribution, but cf. the remarks made in note 6 above. Another reason why Schumpeter regarded Quesnay with such admiration is the (indirect) link between the *Tableau* and Walrasian general equilibrium analysis. See Schumpeter 1952: p. 242.

15 Cf. Meek (1962: p. 9):

> The French Physiocrats are at once the most exciting, the most contemporary group of economists in the whole history of economic thought. The most exciting, because the birth of Physiocracy was in fact the birth of the science of economics in the broad general form in which it has come down to us today. The most contemporary, because the Physiocrats' major preoccupations, in both the theoretical and the practical fields, were strikingly similar to those of present day economists.

The only historian of economics hostile to this praise of the physiocrats whom I know of, is Robbins. See for example Robbins 1935: pp. 54–5.

16 Donald Winch (1970: pp. 63–4) comes close to this when he states:

> 1870 witnessed the demise of political economy and the birth of economics. ... attention shifted. ... towards the narrower and more precise inquiry into the determination of relative prices. Economics became a quasimathematical science in which the important problems were posed as scarcity or choice problems involving the maximisation or minimisation of strategic economic quantities under specified conditions.

Is this a description of a landmark in economics, a break, a concept of periodisation, or is this 'the birth of economics as a science'? Similar issues were raised at the Bellagio Conference in August 1971. See Goodwin 1972.

17 That is, the definition of McCulloch (quoted in note 11 above), and that of J. S. Mill and Marshall. See appendix to this chapter on definitions of political economy and economics, and cf. Smith (1962), which presents a series of essays by prominent British economists of the nineteenth- and early twentieth century on the scope and method of political economy.

18 The references cited by Robbins in support of his definition are Menger's *Grundsatze* and von Mises' *Die Gemeinwirtschaft* (Robbins 1935: p. 16 n1). Others have more specifically related this definition to Walras and to the school of Lausanne; see for example, Stark (1944: p. 61 n2) and Napoleoni (1972: ch. 2, esp. pp. 31–2). The examples referred to in the text, which illustrate the four conditions underlying

Robbins' definition, relate to the distribution of a given and divisible stock of a particular commodity (say bags of corn) among alternative uses ranked in order of priority. Such examples can be found in the work of Menger, Böhm-Bawerk, von Wieser, Wicksell, Walras and Wicksteed, as well as in Marshall and Jevons. To my knowledge, the classical literature contains no examples of this nature; the question was in fact alien to their way of thinking on economic problems. Yet, interestingly enough, many students are still being brought up to think of Robbins' definition as *the* economic problem.

19 Stigler's use of the 'The Formative Period' as subtitle to his book on *Production and Distribution Theories*, is revealing, since it covers neo-classical contributions only.

20 The implications of positive economics for the historian of economic thought need more detailed treatment.

21 If the economists selected by Stigler (1941) together with Irving Fisher and Vilfredo Pareto are taken as a representative sample of the leading early neo-classical theorists, then the mathematicians are in a majority of 8 to 4. See also Stigler 1972.

22 Marshall's (1890) is a favourite example. Walras' treatise mentions 'pure economics' in its title; Pantaleoni's *Manuale di Economica Pura* (1889) was translated as *Pure Economics* in 1898. But Wicksell, Wicksteed, and Edgeworth, as late as 1926 preferred the title political economy (cf. Wicksell 1934: introduction, esp. p. 4), while neither Wicksteed nor Edgeworth found it necessary to explain their preference for the older terminology in the title of their work.

23 For evidence of this see Stigler (1941: pp. 32–44; 1972: pp. 576–86), as well as Schumpeter (1952: pp. 753–7). Schumpeter's warning that too much emphasis on 'chairs, research funds, organisation', etc. because that would place British performance in economics during the nineteenth century at the bottom of the international scale, is of particular relevance here.

24 In this connection it is interesting to note that the article 'Economics' in the *International Encyclopeadia of the Social Sciences*, vol. 4, p. 472, published as recently as 1968, still uses the Robbinsian definition (though modified a few paragraphs later to take account of the Keynesian revolution, and the new developments in macroeconomics). When that part of the definition that is generally quoted can account for less than half of the subject matter of a scientific discipline, the definition should be scrapped, as Joan Robinson reminded the 1971 Annual Meeting of the American Economic Association in her Ely Memorial Lecture.

25 Much important work was done in Italy in this period, by the Milanese School of Verri and Beccaria, and by the Venetian Ortes. See Schumpeter 1952: pp. 177–81, where Beccaria's *Elementi* is more than favourably compared with Smith's *Wealth of Nations*. (For my more subsequent excursions into Italian economics, see Chapters 1 and 15.)

26 That is, Sir William Petty, Thomas Mun, Sir Thomas Culpeper the Younger, Roger Coke, Samuel Fortrey, Rice Vaughan, Andrew Yarranton, Thomas Papillion, Thomas Firmin, John Houghten, Sir Mathew Hale, Sir Josiah Child, Nicholas Barbon, John Locke, Sir Dudley North, John Cary, Sir Francis Brewster, Charles Davenant, John Asgill, John Pollexfen, John Bellers, William Paterson, Daniel Defoe, John Law, William Fleetwood, Bernard de Mandeville, J. Jocelyn, Charles King, Joshua Gee, Richard Cantillon, Jacob Venderlint, George Berkeley, Sir Mathew Decker, Joseph Massie, Sir John Barnard, Henry Fielding, Malachy Postlethwayt, David Hume, Roger North, Nicholas Magens, Robert Wallace, Josiah Tucker, Frances Hutcheson, Francis Fauquier, Joseph Harris, William Temple, Sir William Mildmay, Sir James Steuart, Arthur Young, and Adam Smith.

27 It is difficult to provide a few short references to substantiate these historical generalisations, but see Ashton (1964), Deane (1967) and Dean and Cole (1969). The supposition that the majority of writers were unaware of these changes can be explained by the fact that most of them lived in London, or other towns where these

changes were not apparent, or that, even when they travelled widely, they did not appear to notice these changes. A study of Arthur Young's travels of the period (Young 1769; 1770; 1771) clearly illustrates this: Young was only really interested in the agricultural developments, and showed little interest in manufacturing in the places he visited.

28 This is illustrated in the following quotations: 'Labour is the Father and Active Principle of Wealth, as Lands are the Mother' (Petty 1899: I, p. 68). 'Land and Labour are the Foundation of Riches' (Bellers 1699: p. 12). 'Whether the four Elements, and Man's Labour therein, be not the true Source of Wealth?' (Berkeley 1751: Part I, p. 3). 'The Land is the Source of Matter from whence all Wealth is produced. The Labour of Man is the Form which produces it' (Cantillon 1959: p. 3).

29 For monetary theories of interest, see Locke (1696) and Law (1705); for those explaining interest by supply and demand for commercial stock, see Barbon (1690) and North (1691); for fructification theory, Petty (1899: I, 48; II, 447–8) and Hutcheson (1755: II, pp. 71–3).

30 The article, 'Capital', given by Postlethwayt (1751: I, p. 448) is especially illuminating. It 'signifies', according to Postlethwayt, 'the sum of money which individuals bring to make up the common stock of a partnership, when it is first formed'. The meaning of capital as an agent of production is not discussed, and the entire article is confined to one paragraph.

31 See Groenewegen 1969: pp. 278–9; and 1971 (below: Chapters 17, 20). Cf. Meek 1954: p. 140:

> it was apparently not until the third quarter of the eighteenth century that profit on capital, as a new generic type of class income, became so clearly differentiated from other types of income that economists were able to grasp its full significance and delineate its basic characteristics.

In this early paper, Meek emphasised the British contributions to this subject; to the neglect of those of Quesnay and Turgot. Meek (1962; 1973) corrected this omission.

32 In view of the clash on the subject of the importance of biography to historians of economics, between William Jaffé and George Stigler at Bellagio, this point is of some interest. See Goodwin 1972: pp. 613–18; Jaffé 1965.

33 Gibbon to Adam Ferguson, March, 1776, in Rae 1965: p. 287.

34 It is interesting to note that these discoveries are in turn connected with 'the theory of equilibrium via the market mechanism' and with the 'postulate of the maximising individual in a relatively free market', which have been described as the one and only paradigm in economics. See Gordon (1965: pp. 123, 292).

35 See Turgot 1970: p. 218 n1, pp. 226–8; Smith 1776: pp. 55–60. These sort of results were also recognised by Quesnay (1958: p. 530) and by Steuart (1767: Book II, ch. IV).

36

> Thus, it is an admitted principle in the science of Morals, as well as of Political Economy, that by far the largest proportion of the human race have a much clearer view of what is conducive to their own interests, than it is possible for any other man, or select number of men to have, and consequently that it is sound policy to allow every individual to follow the bent of his inclination, and to engage in any branch of industry he thinks proper. This is the general theorem.
>
> (McCulloch 1824: pp. 10–11)

According to Cannan (1898: introduction, pp. l–liv), Smith's discovery of this principle owed much to Mandeville's notion of 'self-love' and Hutcheson's notion of 'natural liberty'. For other statements of this principle in the period between 1750 and 1776, see Turgot (1770: pp. 88–9); Mercier de la Rivière (1767: p. 447) and Smith (1776: p. 423 and Book I, ch. II).

References

Ashton, T. S. (1964) *An Economic History of England: The Eighteenth Century*, London: Methuen.

Barbon, N. (1690, 1934) *A Discourse of Trade*, London, reprinted and edited by J. H. Hollander, Baltimore: Johns Hopkins Press.

——(1696) *A Discourse Concerning Coining the New Money Lighter*, London.

Bellers, John (1699) *Essays about the Poor, Manufactures, Trade, Plantations and Immortality*, London.

Berkeley, George (1751) *The Querist*, Dublin.

Blanqui, J. A. (1838, 1880) *History of Political Economy in Europe*, translated from the fourth French edition by E. J. Leonard, New York: Putnam.

Blaug, M. (1964) *Economic Theory in Retrospect*, London: Heinemann.

Cannan, Edwin (1898, 1953) *History of the Theories of Production and Distribution from 1776 to 1848*, London: Staples Press.

Cantillon, Richard (1959) *Essai sur la Nature du Commerce en Général*, edited with an English translation by H. Higgs, London: Frank Cass.

Coats, W. A. (1969) 'Is there a "Structure of Scientific Revolutions" in Economics?', *Kyklos*, 22(2).

——(1972) 'Retrospect and Prospect', in Goodwin, C. D. W. (ed.) (1972) 'Papers on the Marginal Revolution in Economics', *History of Political Economy*, 4(2) fall, 603–24.

Deane, Phyllis (1967) *The First Industrial Revolution*, Cambridge: Cambridge University Press.

Deane, Phyllis, and Cole, W. A. (1969) *British Economic Growth 1688–1959*, Cambridge: Cambridge University Press.

Du Pont De Nemours, P. S. (1768, 1846) *De l'Origine et des Progrès d'une Science Nouvelle*, reprinted in Daire, E. (ed.) *Physiocrates*, Part I, Paris: Guillaumin.

Engels, F. (1859, 1971) 'Review of *Contribution to the Critique of Political Economy* by K. Marx', *Das Volk*, 6/8/1859, reprinted in Marx, K. H., *A Contribution to the Critique of Political Economy*, ed. M. H. Dobb, London: Lawrence and Wishart.

Furniss, E. S. (1920) *The Position of the Labourer in a System of Nationalism*, Boston MA and New York: Heffner.

Goodwin, C. D. W. (ed.) (1972) 'Papers on the Marginal Revolution in Economics', *History of Political Economy*, 4(2) fall.

Gordon, D. F. (1965) 'The Role of the History of Economic Thought in the Understanding of Modern Economic Theory', *American Economic Review*, 15, May, 119–27.

Groenewegen, P. D. (1969) 'Turgot and Adam Smith', *Scottish Journal of Political Economy*, 16, November, 271–87 (below, Chapter 20).

——(1971) 'A Re-Interpretation of Turgot's Theory of Capital and Interest', *Economic Journal*, 81, June, 327–40 (below, Chapter 17).

Harrod, R. F. (1951) *Life of John Maynard Keynes*, London: Macmillan.

Hutcheson, Francis (1755) *A System of Moral Philosophy in three Books*, Glasgow.

Ingram, J. K. (1888) *History of Political Economy*, Edinburgh: A&C Black.

Jaffé, William (1965) 'Biography and Economic Analysis', *Western Economic Journal*, 3(3) summer, 223–32.

Jocelyn, J. (1718) *An Essay Upon Money and Bullion*, London: B. Lintot.

Keynes, J. M. (1924, 1961) *Essays in Biography*, London: Mercury Books.

Knight, F. H. (1951, 1956) 'Economics', in *On the History and Method of Economics*, Chicago: University of Chicago Press, 3–33.

Kuhn, T. S. (1970) *The Structure of Scientific Revolutions*, 2nd edn, Chicago: University of Chicago Press.

Law, John (1705) *Money and Trade considered, with a Proposal for supplying the Nation with Money*, Edinburgh: Andrew Anderson.

Letwin, W. (1963) *The Origins of Scientific Economics*, London: Methuen.

Locke, John (1696) *Some Considerations of the Consequences of the Lowering of Interests and Raising the Value of Money*, 2nd edn, London.

McCulloch, J. R. (1824) *A Discourse on the Rise, Progress, Peculiar Objects and Importance of Political Economy*, London: Alex Murray.

Marshall, A. (1890, 1920) *Principles of Economics*, 8th edn, London: Macmillan.

Marx, K. H. (1859, 1971) *A Contribution to the Critique of Political Economy*, ed. M. H. Dobb, London: Lawrence and Wishart.

——(1969) *Theories of Surplus Value*, Part I, Moscow: Foreign Languages Publishing House.

Meek, R. L. (1954) 'Adam Smith and the Classical Concept of Profit', *Scottish Journal of Political Economy*, I, 138–53.

——(1962) *The Economics of Physiocracy*, London: Allen & Unwin.

——(1973) *Turgot on Progress, Sociology and Economics*, Cambridge: Cambridge University Press.

Mercier de la Rivière (1767) *l'Ordre Naturel et Essential des Sociétés Politiques*, folio edn, Paris.

Mill, John Stuart (1844, 1948) *Essays on some Unsettled Questions of Political Economy*, LSE Reprint, London: London School of Economics and Political Science.

Napoleoni, C. (1972) *Economic Thought in the Twentieth Century*, London: Martin Robertson.

North, Sir Dudley (1691, 1954) *Discourses Upon Trade*, reprinted in J. R. McCulloch (ed.) *Early English Tracts on Commerce*, Cambridge: Cambridge University Press.

Petty, Sir William (1899) *Economic Writings*, ed. C. H. Hull, Cambridge: Cambridge University Press.

Postlethwayt, Malachy (1751) *Universal Dictionary of Trade and Commerce*, London: W. Strahan *et al.*

Quesnay, François (1958) *François Quesnay et la Physiocratie*, Paris: Institut National d'Etudes Démographiques.

Rae, John (1965) *Life of Adam Smith*, re-issued with an introduction by Jacob Viner, New York: Augustus M. Kelley.

Robbins, L. (1935) *An Essay on the Nature and Significance of Economic Science*, 2nd edn, London: Macmillan.

——(1955, 1970) 'Schumpeter on the History of Economic Analysis', in *The Evolution of Modern Economics*, London: Macmillan.

Samuelson, Paul (1970) *Economics*, Australian edn, Sydney: McGraw Hill.

Schelle, G. (1888) *Du Pont de Nemours et l'Ecole Physiocratique*, Paris.

Schumpeter, J. A. (1912, 1954) *Economic Doctrine and Method*, London: Allen & Unwin.

——(1952, 1959) *History of Economic Analysis*, London: Allen & Unwin.

Sidgwick, Henry (1887) *Principles of Political Economy*, 2nd edn, London: Macmillan.
Smith, Adam (1766, 1937) *An Inquiry into the Nature and Causes of the Wealth of Nations*, ed. E. Cannan, Modern Library edition, New York: Random House.
Smyth, R. L. (ed.) (1962) *Essays in Economic Method*, London: Duckworth.
Stark, W. (1944) *The History of Economics in its Relation to Social Development*, London: George Unwin.
Steuart, Sir James (1767, 1966) *An Inquiry into the Principles of Political Oeconomy*, ed. A. Skinner, London and Edinburgh: Oliver and Boyd.
Stigler, G. J. (1941) *Production and Distribution Theories: The Formative Period*, New York: Macmillan.
——(1965) 'Statistical Studies in the History of Economic Thought', in *Essays in the History of Economics*, Chicago: University of Chicago Press.
——(1972) 'The Adoption of the Marginal Utility Theory', in Goodwin, C. D. W. (ed.) 'Papers on the Marginal Revolution in Economics', *History of Political Economy*, 4(2) fall, 571–86.
Tucker, G. L. S. (1960) *Progress and Profits in British Economic Thought, 1650–1850*, Cambridge: Cambridge University Press.
Turgot, A. R. J. (1766, 1965) 'Reflections on the Formation and Distribution of Riches', trans. W. J. Ashley, New York: Augustus M. Kelley.
——(1970) *Ecrits Economiques*, with an introduction by Bernard Cazes, Paris: Calman-Levy.
Viner, Jacob (1953, 1958) 'Schumpeter's History of Economic Analysis', in *The Long View and the Short*, Glencoe IL: University of Illinois Press.
Wicksell, K. (1934) *Lectures on Political Economy*, London: Routledge and Kegan Paul.
Winch, D. (1970) 'The Emergence of Economics as a Science 1750–1870', in *The Fontana History of Europe*, vol. 3, section 9, London: Collins.
Young, Arthur (1769) *A Six Week Tour through the Southern Countries of England and Wales*, 2nd edn, London.
——(1770) *A Six Months' Tour thro' the North of England*, London.
——(1771) *The Farmer's Tour through the East of England*, London.

3 New light on the origins of modern economics[1]

> The historical interpretation and explanation of theories put forward in the past is the first and foremost task which the historian of political economy has to fulfil. But besides this great problem, which might be called the material problem, there are several others that are more or less formal in character. Three of them are of outstanding importance. They are indicated by the following questions: When did political economy arise? What were the phases in its evolution? How can it be defined and divided from other fields of thought? The first problem – the problem of origin – naturally and necessarily arises with regard to any science, but it is especially intricate in political economy.
>
> (Stark, 1944, p. 59)

> The process of 'secularization' manifested itself most significantly through the emergence of differentiated intellectual disciplines, each with its own expertise and, in time, with its own special experts. It was in jurisprudence and political philosophy, rather than in metaphysics, moral philosophy, economics, or even natural science, that 'human reason' first gained a large measure of autonomy from theology and the effective exercise of ecclesiastical authority.
>
> (Viner, 1978, pp. 113, 115)

The origins of modern economics continue to attract attention from a variety of scholars. Such interest is not only inspired by the importance of this formal question for the historian of economic thought,[2] or for its relevance to understanding that broader secularization process with which Viner was concerned. The question of the emergence and origin of economics has the additional use of illuminating aspects of the development of economics after the well recognized breakthrough by Adam Smith and his contemporaries. The pre-Smithian period, for example, sheds light on the development of what is called the surplus approach to value and distribution (Garegnani, 1984), a view alternative to the perspective provided by some prominent writers (such as Hollander, 1986) who analyse post-Smithian development as a continuous completion and improvement of a supply-and-demand-inspired general equilibrium approach to value and distribution. In addition, study of the pre-Smithian era draws attention to historical problems and philosophical difficulties in interpreting the relevance of what is often described as the rise of economic liberalism (cf.

Walther, 1984; Haakonnsen, 1988). This gives both a polemical and a political flavour to a discussion of the origins of economics which would not normally be expected in the examination of this type of issue, and likewise links it to contemporary debate in economics.

The focus of this chapter is on both the formal historical questions raised by its subject matter, and the issues it illuminates for more contemporary discussions of developments in economics. The former are addressed in the first two sections, and a third concluding section addresses links between the origins of economics and more modern debate. This raises the relevance of pre-Smithian economics for understanding an identified dichotomy in the foundations to economic reasoning (see Baranzini and Scarrieri, 1986) and for grasping more fully associations between twentieth-century economic liberalism and the analyses of economic order based on unrestrained self-interest in a 'system of natural liberty', to use Smith's famous phrase. Discussion of these objectives is greatly assisted by a number of new books which have appeared on the subject since 1970. These include new studies of what Marx (1859 p. 52) described as the founders of Classical Political Economy: Sir William Petty and Boisguilbert (Roncaglia, 1977; Faccarello, 1986). In addition there have been important studies of the development of eighteenth-century economics, covering individuals and groups. These deal with Cantillon (Murphy, 1986); the physiocrats (Eltis, 1984, chs 1 and 2; Vaggi, 1987); the Scottish Enlightenment and the development of political economy (Campbell and Skinner, 1982; Hont and Ignatief, 1983); Turgot (Bordes and Morange, 1981); and the Italian classical school of economics (Parisi Aquaviva, 1984). The enormous output generated by the *Wealth of Nations* bicentenary likewise addressed many of the issues relevant to this inquiry. Last, but not least, two books are explicitly devoted to the subject matter of this chapter. Lutfalla (1981) provides a French perspective on the origins of economic thought, and Hutchison (1988) gives a detailed and international examination of the emergence of political economy before Adam Smith, taking as his starting point the publication of Petty's *Treatise of Taxes and Contributions* in 1662. A recent collection of surveys of economics before Adam Smith (Todd Lowry, 1987) can also be noted in this context, though it contributes only implicitly to the subject of this chapter by highlighting the importance of the pre-Smithian (1776) period for the development of economics. In short, this survey and review of recent contributions to an important problem in the history of economic thought intends also to demonstrate the potential relevance of such an inquiry for contemporary debate.

One further preliminary matter has to be covered by way of introduction. Both quotations at the head of this chapter imply the need for at least a preliminary indication of what constitute the distinctive analytical characteristics of political economy as a separate field of inquiry which distinguish it from work in moral philosophy, for example. Systematic discussion of the enrichment of the people through analysis of the production, distribution and circulation of wealth is here taken as this basic distinguishing characteristic; the qualifying objective 'systematic' refers to the requirement of discussion based on theoretical principles developed within the confines of a unified treatise. This definition allows the identification of a specific era as the period in which economics emerged as a separate area of discourse.

I

The emergence of a science generally required a new area of specialization or division of scientific labour. This links it directly with the process of the secularization of knowledge as discussed in Viner's account of religious thought and economic society (Viner, 1978). Two aspects of the origins of economics to which recent literature draws attention illustrate the relevance of the secularization process to the problem at hand. One is associated with the impact of Jansenist thought, particularly in the writings of Pierre Nicole and Jean Domat, on the economic thought of Boisguilbert and, possibly, Mandeville (see Viner, 1978, pp. 130–40; Faccarello, 1986, esp. chs 2, 3; Hutchison, 1988, pp. 100–3). The other is the secularization of social and political thought inherent in the Scottish Enlightenment and derived at least in part from the lead in this matter given by Montesquieu's *l'Esprit des Lois* (1748).

The importance of Jansenist thought, especially that of Nicole and Domat, for the process of 'the secularization of economic ethics' was to my knowledge first brought to the attention of historians of economic thought by Jacob Viner (1978, pp. 131, 134 n37). This Jansenist thought distinguished sharply between 'virtue' and 'vice', where 'virtue' referred to actions in doing good for the pure love of God, that is charity; 'vice' was everything else. In this context of classifying human action, both Nicole and Domat examined the role of enlightened self-interest (*amour-propre éclairé*) in considerable detail. Nicole expounds the potential for the flourishing condition of temporal society under the motivation of enlightened self-interest, through the medium of commerce acting as mutual exchange of services, thereby enabling the provision of all the needs of earthly life without the intervention of charity. Enlightened self-interest is thus the way to a well ordered, secular society. Although Domat presents this argument more systematically and rigorously in his writings, as Viner (1978, p. 139) explicitly argued, both authors represent 'a strong anticipation of Adam Smith's economic philosophy' if their stress on 'the presence of subjective sin in objectively virtuous behaviour' is eliminated from their writings. More generally, if emphasis on providential design is omitted, the Jansenist doctrine in these writings is strongly reminiscent of the literature of nineteenth-century economic liberalism.[3] Comparisons such as this are fraught with historical difficulties because they are so susceptible to the anachronistic practice of reading more modern meanings into specific terms. This is clearly pointed out by Walther (1984) and Haakonssen (1988) in discussing problems in interpreting seventeenth-and eighteenth-century precursors to the notion of economic liberalism not developed until the late nineteenth century or early twentieth centuries. A similar caveat applies to remarks made in the subsequent paragraph.

None of this would be of particular importance for the subject of this chapter, except for the fact that it can be shown that this Jansenist perspective on economic order exerted considerable influence on a number of important economists of the late seventeenth- and early eighteenth centuries. Faccarello (1986) has analysed the importance of these ideas for the writings of Boisguilbert, the person who according to Marx founded classical political economy in France, and who was hailed by later French eighteenth-century writers as a great pioneer of economic liberalism. Hutchison (1988, pp. 100–3, 107–26) makes Faccarello's research accessible to a non-French reading audience. In addition, he emphasizes more fully the likely influence of Nicole and Domat on Mandeville, whose study of vice and virtue in *The Fable of the Bees* is familiar to many students of economics. Viner's comment on the resemblance between Smith's economic philosophy and that of the two Jansenists may therefore help to explain the similarity between Smith's *Wealth of Nations* and Boisguilbert's work, which Hazel van Dyke Roberts (1935) noted at length. It is interesting to observe in this context that Smith had at least one work by Nicole in his library (Mizuta, 1967, pp. 3, 68).

More interesting links between Jansenism and English thought have been suggested. Viner (1978, p. 135) mentioned the influence of Nicole on the work of Hobbes, remarking that Nicole is superior to the English philosopher in expounding 'the objective attractions of a society flourishing temporally under the motivation of self-interest'. Locke, as Cranston (1985, pp. 175–6) notes, translated a number of Nicole's works into English and it is therefore not surprising that works by Nicole were well represented in his library (Harrison and Laslett, 1971, p. 195). No student of the economics of Locke, as far as I am aware, has noted this matter, which may be quite significant for understanding Locke's strong belief in the order imposed by free markets, and the origins of that belief.[4]

Although its full ramifications need more investigation, the Jansenist connection with economic liberalism is undoubtedly one of the ways in which a secularization process influenced economic thinking at a crucial stage in its development. The other, better known influence of secularization on economic thinking is its role in transforming the political and social thinking of the leaders of the Scottish Enlightenment, who were partly inspired in this area by the pioneering work of Montesquieu. This has been well documented for Hume and Smith (see especially Hont and Ignatieff, 1983, chs 5–7, 9; Campbell and Skinner, 1982, chs 7, 8, 11, 12; Skinner and Wilson, 1976, essays vi, ix), and in this context only two further comments need to be made.

First, attention needs to be drawn to a view presented by Rashid (1987, pp. 258–9) that the secularist domination of the Scottish Enlightenment may have been overstated by the emphasis given to Hume and Adam Smith, clearly the crucial figures for the development of economics. Rashid notes that the 'doctrine of unintended consequences' – the idea that beneficence and order are obtainable from action motivated by self-interest and without specifically virtuous intentions – is not only present as the invisible hand of the *Wealth of Nations*, but also features in other contexts in sermons by Ferguson and Blair. Rashid then recalls the statement by Jacob Viner 'that laissez faire was simply the application to economics of concepts long familiar to theologians and moral philosophers', implying that this subject requires further investigation and reinterpretation. It seems strange that Hutchison (1988), who stresses the Jansenist theological influence on the liberal element in the thought of Boisguilbert and Mandeville, fails to explore more fully the potential for such theological influence on its English counterpart from the work of Locke, Davenant and North up to and including Adam Smith and David Hume.[5] Needless to say, Smith's application of such ethical doctrines to economic matters, in particular, reveals the process of secularization at work in liberating political economy from other subjects of study.

Second, the importance of the liberating influence of secular history for the development of political economy cannot be easily overstated. The historical excellence of the Scottish Enlightenment needs no documentation; a specific aspect of it, the four stages theory of economic development put forward by Smith and many of his contemporaries, has been dealt with in considerable detail by Meek (1976; see also Finzi, 1981, and, for some specific Italian developments ignored by Meek, Venturi, 1983, pp. 347–9). It is interesting that Hutchison (1988) largely avoids this aspect of the emergence of economics, presumably because its methodological implications have been 'denounced by some philosophers and historians' as antithetical to liberty and individualism (see Hutchison, 1988, pp. 357–8). Furthermore, he neglects to mention the importance of the four stages theory for the interpretation of Turgot's work, despite his familiarity with Finzi (1981) and my entry on Turgot (Groenewegen, 1987). The reasons of this omission are presumably their damaging implications for Hutchison's view of the role of Turgot's subjective value and exchange theory on the development of eighteenth-century economics (see esp. Hutchison, 1988, pp. 376–8).[6]

An obvious conclusion can be drawn from this discussion. Religious thought has been exhaustively discussed in connection with the rise of capitalism from a wide variety of perspectives and, in the end, with relatively little fruit (cf. Viner, 1978, ch. 4). Perhaps in this context a plea can be made for further discussion and research on the relationship between moral theology, secularization and the rise of economic liberalism, which, on the available evidence, may be a more fruitful enterprise in the context of understanding some important aspects of the origins of modern economics. Such research, however, requires careful study of the changes in the way in which 'economic liberalism' was conceived during the seventeenth and eighteenth centuries. This is essential if it is to have a useful application in assessing the role played in these origins by contemporaneous critical examination of the government's responsibilities in the process of enrichment of the population.

II

Hutchison (1988) covers the whole of the 1662–1776 period in his study, but subdivides it into four periods: a period dominated by English thought from 1660 to 1770; a leaner period with a variety of international contributions from

1700 to 1746; and then a boom period of thirty years subdivided into two phases – the emergence of a subject from *circa* 1746 to 1756, followed by a period of two decades (1756–76) described as 'French Pre-eminence, Milanese Enlightenment and Scottish Ascendancy'. This boom period is similar to what Schumpeter (1954, pp. 51–2) called the first classical situation in economics 'somewhere between 1750 and 1800', and what Groenewegen (1973) precisely dated from 1748 (the publication of Montesquieu's *l'Esprit des Lois*) to 1776, and called the 'crucial third quarter' of the eighteenth century. The apparent similarity between Hutchison's approach and my own disguises some important differences, which I highlight after making some observations on aspects of his earlier periods.

Like Letwin (1963), and following Marx and Sir George Clark, Hutchison (1988, pp. vi, 3–4) rightly draws attention to the importance of the second half of the seventeenth century for understanding the origins of economics, although he acknowledges there were earlier important economic writings in England and elsewhere (Hutchison, 1988, ch. 2). Petty's place of honour in this period is merited by the quality of his thinking, his profound theoretical modelling of the beginnings of a surplus approach to economic theory (see Aspromourgos, 1986) and his considerable influence over the subsequent development of economics, both directly and indirectly via Cantillon's *Essai*. Although English (as distinct from Scottish, Irish and European) writings dominate this period, Hutchison also points to beginnings in continental Europe and writings on Colbertism, cameralism, moral philosophy and natural law. An example is Boisguilbert's first published economic work (1695) which was related to his correspondence with French finance ministers over the 1690s. Boisguilbert therefore straddles the first and second periods in Hutchison's chronological subdivisions, and cannot be exclusively assigned to the second period as Hutchison does. This classification of Boisguilbert may be ascribed to Hutchison's desire to separate his work from that of Petty (an association which Marx drew in his discussion of the founders of classical political economy), and to link it more explicitly (see Faccarello, 1986) with economic order, enlightened self-interest and the work of Mandeville (the Domat-Nicole connection).

In addition, the seventeenth century already reveals cross-fertilization across national boundaries. Locke is the most important example of English recognition by French and Italian thought. Widespread citation of English economics (as shown by Hecht, 1966, pp. 160–1 and n1, who refers to citations from Davenant, King, Petty, Locke, Temple, Child and Mun) was practised by Dubos (1703). Unfortunately this is not mentioned in Hutchison (1988).

As a separate field of inquiry, economics cannot be said to have fully emerged in this period, a proposition which does not detract from its importance for understanding the origins of economics and the form which it eventually took as a new science in the following century. A number of reasons can be advanced for this non-controversial proposition. First of all, although this period saw the application of a variety of scientific methods to discussions of specific matters of economic policy (see Letwin, 1963), there were few, if any, attempts at comprehensive explanations of the behaviour of an economy on the basis of general principles. The foundations on which such principles could be constructed were, however, laid in this period in various ways by Petty, Locke and possibly North. The total absence of a systematic treatise in this period is part of the justification for the statement with which this paragraph commenced. Second, although Petty (1963, p. 24) in particular stressed the novelty of what he was doing, he tended in this context to stress his innovations in method as his original contribution. Hutchison (1988, pp. 56–8, cf. pp. 185–9) describes the 1690s as a boom period in English economic discussion before its decline in the eighteenth century, from which it did not really recover until the nineteenth century. Unlike later booms in economics, the developments of this period focused on discussion of specific economic problems, and did not climax (except perhaps indirectly in Cantillon's *Essai*) in a 'single, epoch-making publication'.

Hutchison's subsequent period, 1700–46, is rather barren but much more cosmopolitan. Apart from Cantillon, who wrote his famous *Essai* in the early 1730s, the authors whom Hutchison selects for detailed treatment are Mandeville and Vanderlint (both Dutchmen living in London), Gervaise (a French Huguenot living in London), a Scottish exile in France (John Law), and then, as Rashid (1987, p. 256) also reminds us, the important Irish contributions of Berkeley, Swift, Francis Hutcheson and minor figures like Dobbs, Prior and Madden, who are not mentioned by Hutchison. Finally, Hutchison discusses developments in mathematical economics in this period by Ceva in Italy (1988, pp. 178–81) and announces his discovery of a neglected economist, Ernst Ludwig Carl. Carl's *Traité de la Richesse des Princes et de leurs Etats* (1722–3) is virtually elevated by Hutchison (1988, p. 156) to the status of Cantillon's important work, without convincing argument.[7] In addition, though Hutchison does not deal with their work in any detail, these decades include publications by Melon and Dutot on money, credit and finance, and the work of Boisguilbert and Vauban, with which he does deal but which, chronologically speaking, fit more appropriately into the previous period. Leaving aside the tricky problems raised by Cantillon's treatise, two questions about this period need further explanation. Why were these first decades of the eighteenth century such a barren period in economic writing in general, and why did English contributions of great quality virtually disappear? For the latter there is perhaps an all-too-simple explanation. Increasing prosperity in England, including the general elimination of unfavourable trade balances and monetary scarcity by the development of greater sophistication in banking and other financial institutions, eliminated the need to write on economic subjects. Exceptions are periods of controversy, such as the excise campaign of the early 1730s, the 1738 abatement of interest campaign, and the perennial problem of the poor. The commercial successes of the Dutch in the seventeenth century have likewise left little by way of an economic literature.[8]

Both the timing and subdivision of Hutchison's boom period from 1746 to 1776 have a number of dubious qualities. Its starting date has no explained significance, and is perhaps only justifiable in terms of the round three decades it demarcates before the publication of the *Wealth of Nations*. Moreover, it unnecessarily detracts from the importance of the publication of Montesquieu's *l'Esprit des Lois*, which , as noted earlier, gave such a tremendous international impetus to the secularization of social inquiry. However, Hutchison's subsequent discussion (1988, pp. 185–6) implies that his starting date may have been designed to allow inclusion of the 1747 English translation of Hutcheson's *A Short Introduction to Moral Philosophy*, thereby giving greater prominence to the subjective value considerations in the work of Hutcheson's teacher, Gershom Carmichael. If Hutcheson is to be included in this 'period of boom', this can only be justified from the posthumous 1755 publication of his lectures as a *System of Moral Philosophy*.[9]

Hutchison's (1988, p. 188) subdivision of the boom period into a phase of international mid-century efflorescence (1747–55) and French predominance (1756–70) is likewise peculiar. Hutchison suggests that these periods 'can, and should be, distinguished, though they merged into one another, and are not very sharply separable'. Reasons for the necessity of this distinction are not really given. It seems to me that 'international efflorescence' can describe the whole period even if, early on, the French gained a predominance in the field which they lost for a while to the Scots with the publication of the *Wealth of Nations* in 1776.

One reason for Hutchison's subdivision of the 1740s–1770s period may be the practical need to subdivide the wealth of material to which it gave rise into two parts in the book, thereby making these parts more similar in size to the previous two parts which cover half-centuries. Another, more important reason can be inferred. This subdivision enables Hutchison to separate the work of Quesnay and the physiocrats (chapter 16) from the 'period of French pre-eminence' (chapter 18) identified with the more 'liberal writings' of Turgot and Condillac. The latter can of course both be classified as non-physiocrats, and even as critics of important parts of physiocratic doctrine. However, in other ways their work was inspired by Quesnay's contributions. In addition, Hutchison's insertion of a chapter on the economics of the Milanese Enlightenment (chapter 17) drives a further wedge between Quesnay's work and that of his French contemporaries, Turgot and Condillac. This ordering implies that in Hutchison's view Quesnay's work should not really be included in the period of French pre-eminence. Such an impression is further strengthened by Hutchison's clear preference for the work of anti-physiocrat Verri relative to that of his contemporary Beccaria, who was influenced in part by aspects of Quesnay's economics (see Groenewegen, 1983a, pp. 43–4, 58, n20). Hutchison's purpose in this implicit downgrading of the physiocratic contribution is examined later.

In contrast, Hutchison's careful discussion of the significance of the internationalisation of economic discourse during this period can be fully endorsed. First, he points to the enormous amount of translation of economic literature into French, Italian and even German. Murphy (1986, ch. 15) has highlighted

Gournay's very important role in this when, during the early and mid-1750s, Gournay instigated the publication and translation of a number of important English works, of which the publication of Cantillon's *Essai* in 1755 is undoubtedly the most important. The Kress catalogue of Italian works on economics (Barucci and Carpenter, 1985) facilitates an appreciation of the amount of work translated into Italian from the French and the English, some of it under the auspices of noted economists like Genovesi. Even the English were translating, though on a more limited scale. Examples of French and Italian work of the period rendered into English include translations of a Mirabeau (1766) version of the *Tableau Economique* and Beccaria's (1769) inaugural lecture. The linguistic abilities of key figures in the development of economics during this period, such as Steuart, Turgot and Smith, enhanced the international transmission and absorption of ideas even further.

Hutchison's other examples of the internationalization of the subject can be mentioned more briefly. First they include the establishment of a number of specialist, but short-lived economic journals, particularly in France. Second, they refer to Paris as the international capital of economic discourse, in which Scots (Hume, Smith, Steuart), Americans (Franklin) and Italians (Galiani, Beccaria) could mingle with the leading French economic thinkers of the period, either in Quesnay's entresol at Versailles, or at Mirabeau's famous 'Thursdays' or, more generally, the salons of Mlle de l'Espinasse, Baron d'Holbach and Mme de Boufflers. Correspondence shows that letter contact between economists was also important; the Verri correspondence, for example, reveals plans for contact with Forbonnais, the Trudaines and Condillac during the 1760s, while Pietro Verri's list of persons to whom he wanted to send his *Meditazioni* includes a number of important contemporary economic thinkers (Verri, 1771). Last, but not least, is the creation of several chairs in political economy (or perhaps, more accurately, in cameral science) in Sweden, Germany and Italy, which indicates official recognition of public education in economics as an important aspect of the science of government (Hutchison, 1988, p. 190; Tribe, 1984; Groenewegen, 1983a, p. 55, n1; Verri, 1771, p. 107 and n64). This extraordinary international interaction, rarely repeated in the case of economics, is clearly one important sign that the subject was emerging as a separate area of inquiry during this period. As discussed more fully in the concluding section, these aspects of an apparent professionalization in economics were not sustained in subsequent decades, unlike similar developments in professionalization which took place at the end of the nineteenth century.

More important, however, is the formalization of the subject matter of political economy in a number of general treatises. Prior to the 1750s, only Cantillon's *Essai* deserves the title of systematic economic analysis embodied in a treatise.[10] From the 1750s, and particularly during the 1760s, the number of such systematic treatises started to multiply, and they were increasingly recognized as contributions to a new science. In 1754 Forbonnais published an *Elémens du Commerce*. In 1755 Josiah Tucker published the (unfinished)

Elements of Commerce and Theory of Taxes, and Justi his *Staatswirtschaft*. This year also marks the publications of Cantillon's *Essai* at the instigation of Gournay. Not until after a decade of strong activity in production of monographs and articles do treatises begin to be written again, if works by Mirabeau with Quesnay's collaboration, such as the second edition of *l'Ami des Hommes* and *Philosophie Rurale* (respectively 1760 and 1763) are ignored.

The decade 1766–76 started with Turgot's brief 'Reflections on the Production and Distribution of Wealth' (written in November 1766 but not published till 1769–70), and continued in 1767 with the publication of Forbonnais' *Principes et Observations Oeconomiques*, Mercier de la Rivière's *Ordre Naturel et Essentiel des Sociétés Politiques* (the key treatise of physiocracy) and Steuart's *Principles of Political Oeconomy*, while Du Pont published Quesnay's collected economic papers under the title *Physiocratie*. In 1768 Genovesi published *Delle Lezioni di Commercio o sia d'Economia Civile*; in 1769 Beccaria wrote his *Elementi di Economia Pubblica* (but only posthumously published by Custodi in 1802); and in 1771 Verri published *Meditazioni sulla Economia Politica*. The period ends in 1776 with the publication of Condillac's *Le Commerce et le Gouvernement* and Smith's *Wealth of Nations*. Sonnenfells published the three volumes of his *Grundsätze der Polizei, Handlungs- und Finanzwissenschaft* in Vienna in 1765, 1769 and 1776. Furthermore, by 1768 Du Pont de Nemours could publish an article on the origin of a new science from the perspective of French physiocratic dominance in the economic thought of the 1760s, with a history which he traced back to Boisguilbert and Vauban. In 1776 Gibbon and Ferguson could congratulate Adam Smith on creating a new science between the proverbial two covers of a single book. Work in this decade saw political economy mature increasingly as a study of the production, distribution and circulation of wealth.

Brief comments on this revised scope of the subject are in order. Production and circulation, as well as the elements of distribution, had been analysed with increasing clarity and precision from the time of Sir William Petty, who had laid firm foundations for such systematic investigations in his *Treatise of Taxes and Contributions* of 1662 (see Aspromourgos, 1986). Such analysis was carried further in the work of Cantillon, especially with respect to the theory of circulation and value. For the last, Cantillon explicitly enunciated a relationship between a fundamental price of production ('intrinsic value') and a more ephemeral (but visible) market price determined by supply and demand, a relationship which became the hallmark of the classical theory of price (Murphy, 1986, ch. 13). The economic theory of production was significantly strengthened by the work of Quesnay. It introduced capital and, benefiting from work of Boisguilbert and Cantillon in constructing the *Tableau Economique*, interlinked production and circulation with the distribution of the product. Quesnay defined distribution in terms of the division of total product into two parts. The first was considered essential for the reproduction of subsequent periods and was destined for wages, profits and capital replacement. The second, a disposable surplus or net product, accrued to landlords, church and state and was available for luxury consumption, for accumulation or for both. Turgot formalized the distribution theory further, extending it to commercial or capitalistic society. Finally, Smith provided his more radical modification of the physiocratic analytical innovations in the core of his *Wealth of Nations* of 1776.

In defining and clarifying the research agenda for the new science of political economy, the work of the physiocrats systematized the rich economic legacy of predecessors like Petty, Locke, Boisguilbert, Cantillon and Hume, to name the more important. Quesnay's great contribution is twofold. First, his analysis of capital allowed the transformation of production theory from an essentially land and labour orientation which had dominated the discussion until then. Second, his various written contributions systematized the analysis of production, distribution and circulation of surplus from both the perspective of a theory of value *and* a theory of growth. Eltis (1984, chs 1–3, 9) has strikingly demonstrated the enormous similarity between Quesnay's and Smith's formal theories of growth, while Vaggi (1987) has emphasized the crucial role of value theory in physiocratic analysis, thereby linking value, surplus, profits, accumulation and growth in this important reinterpretation of the physiocratic system. As Vaggi (1987, p. 190) concisely puts it in the concluding chapter of his book: 'Thus Quesnay bequeathed to classical economics the idea that a theory of wealth, founded on the notions of surplus and reproduction, cannot be isolated from a study of prices and markets'. That part of physiocracy was also fully absorbed and appreciated by Turgot and, more particularly, by Adam Smith, in their different ways.

Hutchison's (1988) discussion of Quesnay and the physiocrats does not adequately reflect such considerations. His treatment of the *Tableau* (despite his acquaintance with Eltis' 1984 work) is perfunctory and only notes its 'macroeconomic connotations' of 'circular flow of payments' and 'aggregate equilibrium and general interdependence' as vehicles for a disequilibrium analysis of growth and decline (Hutchison, 1988, pp. 178–9). Neither Quesnay's theory of value, nor his theory of profit (so clearly set out in Vaggi, 1987) are shown to be part of this analysis. In fact, Hutchison switches quickly from physiocratic economics, with which he is rather uncomfortable, to the physiocratic view of society, where Quesnay's despotism and his dogmatism are contrasted unfavourably with the more liberal and tolerant attitudes of contemporaries such as Galiani, Turgot and Smith.[11] In his final evaluation of Quesnay and the physiocrats, Hutchison (1988, pp. 295–7) sharply distinguishes their technical and conceptual contributions, which 'were of the greatest and most fundamental value' from their 'proto-totalitarianism', 'false individualism' and, more accurately on Hutchison's part, their lack of historical sense. Hence for him 'there are large items on both the credit and the debit sides of the intellectual account of Quesnay and his school'.

Hutchison's downgrading of the physiocrats[12] has some important implications for his handling of intellectual comparisons and intellectual sequences. It explains the systematic omission of production and distribution theory in his account of the final decades before the publication of Smith's *Wealth of Nations*. It is emphasized in the elevation of Galiani (chapter 15) because of his subjective value theory, his demonstration of the necessity of a monetary and pricing system to provide order in a more complex form of economic society and, perhaps most importantly, for his historically relativist critique of physiocracy.[13] Hutchison's downgrading of the physiocrats also explains his rejection of Schumpeter's instructive comparison between Turgot, Beccaria and Smith (cf. Groenewegen, 1983a) which highlights crucial features of the emergence of economics. More importantly, Hutchison plays down what Schumpeter called the important sequence of Petty-Cantillon-Quesnay, with its implications for the analysis of reproduction and the surplus approach. Instead Hutchison emphasizes the development of a notion of interdependence between economic harmony, equilibrating tendencies and freedom of trade. This, he argues (1988, pp. 10–12, ch. 7, p. 375), developed from Petty, was more clearly stated by North and Martyn, treated quite systematically by Nicole, Boisguilbert and Mandeville and then, through the work of others, came to its full flowering in the writings of Hume, Galiani, Quesnay, Turgot and Smith.

More interestingly, Hutchison draws attention to what he calls aborted lines in the development of economics during its emergence period. The first is the historical method of the Scottish school, represented particularly by Hume, Steuart and Smith; but Hutchison fails to mention its use by Turgot and Beccaria, and its partial origins in Montesquieu's work. Second, here is the utility and scarcity approach to value of the natural law school (Pufendorf, Carmichael, Hutcheson) and others (especially Galiani, Turgot and Condillac). Third, there are contributions on the theory of money, employment and effective demand developing from Petty, Boisguilbert, Law and Cantillon to Sir James Steuart and, to a more limited extent, Hume. This tradition was eventually swamped by versions of Say's Law and the classical dichotomy in Turgot and Adam Smith. Finally, Hutchison refers to an emphasis on uncertainty, ignorance and erroneous expectations which can be traced from Boisguilbert (as Faccarello [1986] does) to Cantillon (with less justification) and then to Condillac (Hutchison, 1988, p. 376). These final considerations have further controversial implications for Hutchison's comprehensive history, explored in the concluding section.

The evidence marshalled by Hutchison reinforces the now widely held belief that economics emerged as a separate science during the period of just over a quarter of a century ending with the publication of the *Wealth of Nations* in 1776, even though Hutchison's explanations of the precise nature of this course of events are not always convincing and sometimes plainly wrong. The book likewise highlights the complexity and cosmopolitan nature of the phenomenon, thereby rejecting once and for all the possibility that a study like economics originated in a single nation. The intellectual effort in this direction which took place in England during the second half of the seventeenth century was not sufficiently strong to maintain itself over the subsequent half-century. The conjunction of events from the end of the 1740s in a number of European nations eventually brought the new science of political economy into being in a process taking over a quarter of a century.

III

Guillebaud (1971, p. 96) reports Marshall's response to a then contemporary economic argument concerning the need to 'go behind Ricardo to Adam Smith': Marshall said that he would go further, because it was essential to go 'back before Adam Smith'. Unfortunately Guillebaud failed to ask Marshall to amplify his statement. What precisely Marshall meant is not easily inferred. However, the sentiment reflected in this anecdote about the importance of pre-Smithian economics and, by implication, the dangers of its neglect, provide one illustration of the relevance of this topic to subsequent generations of economists. Hutchison (1988) and the many other recent works on this subject which have been referred to in the previous two sections, testify to the fact that this matter continues to attract the attention of contemporary economists.

Hutchison's discussion of four fundamental lines of thinking 'initiated, or significantly developed between 1662 and 1776' (1988, pp. 375–81) but excluded from English classical orthodoxy, may perhaps partly explain Marshall's proposition on the importance of pre-Smithian thought. First, modern economists can still learn (as they could in Marshall's time) from the institutional-relativist critique which underpinned the historical method of the Scottish school (Hume, Steuart and Smith) or from its witty and effective employment by Galiani in debunking the physiocratic faith in deregulating the grain market. Second, there are contemporary dangers in repeating the mistake of nineteenth-century English mainstream economics in ignoring the business cycle as an important phenomenon, or abandoning macroeconomic solutions to unemployment and low levels of economic activity. Third, full recognition of the importance of uncertainty and the unknowable in analysing economic processes is an eighteenth-century heritage (from Boisguilbert, Cantillon and especially Condillac) which cannot be emphasized too often, particularly when it is frequently tempting to dismiss such problems by assumptions which recognize their importance but effectively assume their influence away. Examples can be found in the Rational Expectations literature. Last, but not on Hutchison's ranking (1988, pp. 379–810), is the utility and subjective value heritage for price and exchange theory which, in his view, had to await its application until the 1870s.[14] Such examples show that economics is a subject where fashions in research programmes are not unknown, and an examination of the questions which agitated predecessors can pay positive dividends. Before discussing other links between pre-Smithian economics and modern economic thought and analysis, some points for further historical research may be noted.

The first of these relates to the barren period in England which followed the rich crop of economic discussion in the Restoration period and in the decade starting with the 1688 revolution. Why did English economics decline after this period for virtually the whole of the eighteenth century, and why was there a resurgence in economic thinking in other parts of the British Isles such as Ireland? The Scottish hegemony of the late eighteenth- and even much of the early nineteenth century, is perhaps explicable in terms of that Scottish Enlightenment which for a while made Edinburgh the 'Athens of the North'.

A 'material' explanation for the declining interest of the English in economic issues was suggested in the previous section in terms of growing commercial prosperity reflected in increasingly favourable trade balances. Particularly from the 1720s onwards, this tended to remove traditional concerns over adverse trade balances and related monetary scarcity, thereby greatly reducing the pamphlet flow from merchants and other practical persons as compared with the previous half century. Exceptions to this literary trend (as given in note 7 below) relate to contemporary policy issues like the excise and interest abatement controversies of the 1730s. Whatever its worth as an explanation for the decline in English economic argument in the eighteenth century, this raises the question of what general, 'material' influences can be associated with the origins of economics at this time. Is there, for example, an association with what in this context can be loosely described as the 'Industrial Revolution'?[15] More narrowly, can these matters be related to development in agricultural productivity as Lutfalla (1981) attempts to do? In Lutfalla's argument, rising agricultural productivity had the potential, if it was not actually successful in doing so, for removing regular grain scarcities and localized famines from the policy agenda, thereby making the case for free trade in that staple more plausible, and hence assisting the deregulation of trade in this and other areas. Furthermore, rising agricultural productivity increased the potential surplus to raise either living standards or accumulation, or both, and in addition enabled attention to be focused on the production or supply side of economic growth.

To some extent the argument in the previous paragraph points to an association between relevance of economic discourse and the state of economic development reached by a nation. Such an association conforms to the major concerns of Sir James Steuart, and those of Italian economic reformers such as Verri[16] and Beccaria in Milan and Genovesi in the Kingdom of Naples. Specific aspects of the general economic literature of the period – for example, attitudes to labour – remind one of similar concerns in the economic development literature of the post World War II period. Commercial prosperity, on the other hand, as existed in seventeenth-century Holland and eighteenth-century England, was not a soil which nurtured this type of economic literature.

Before commenting on another aspect of the association between stages of economic development and the encouragement of economic inquiry in the eighteenth century, a matter which clearly needs further research,[17] a further aspect of the material background needs to be pursued, namely the institutional features associated with the origins of economics during the 1750s and 1760s mentioned in the previous section. International transmission of ideas through the establishment of journals and correspondence, the role of Paris as an intellectual centre and even the creation of chairs were mentioned in this context. These were features more frequently associated with the professionalization of economics from the late nineteenth century. Comments on two aspects of the eighteenth-century manifestations of the phenomenon are in order. First, it was relatively short-lived. It declined sharply in importance and perhaps disappeared from the 1780s onwards, if not before. Second, and this partly explains the short-lived nature of the phenomenon, the cosmopolitan dimension to economic inquiry in this period was a product of that general philosophical Enlightenment of which it forms a minor part. The Enlightenment itself put Paris at the forefront of philosophical discourse in general, and encouraged systematic investigation in many areas of human knowledge, including the field that emerged as political economy at the conclusion of the Enlightenment. The *magnum opus* of that wide-ranging intellectual movement, the *Encyclopédie* of Diderot and d'Alembert, epitomizes this association between economic and more general inquiry in the impetus it provided to the economic speculations of Quesnay, Turgot, Forbonnais, and less directly, thinkers in Scotland and Italy (Groenewegen, 1983a).

The association between the emergence of economic development and economics as a separate discourse also provides the means whereby pre-Smithian economics can be linked to contemporary economic debate. Such an association in part informs the identification of a surplus approach or, more generally, a production-and-reproduction oriented approach as an opposite and dual to an exchange-oriented supply-and-demand approach in economic reasoning (see Pasinetti, 1981; 1986; Quadrio-Curzio and Scazzieri, 1986). Historically, and also more clearly indicating its associations with Scraffa's rehabilitation of classical economics, such a surplus approach to the economics of value and distribution, originating from production and reproduction concerns, can be demonstrated to have existed in the economic writings of Quesnay, Smith, Ricardo and Marx, especially the last two (Garegnani, 1984). Further research has been able to show what Marx himself had partly realized: the foundations for such a surplus approach to political economy were visible in writings going back to Petty (Aspromourgos, 1985; 1986). Such a dichotomy in approaches to economic thinking, which commenced with the beginnings of the subject, persists until today. As systems of thought, there is an inherent conflict between these two approaches, deriving from their different perspectives on the relationship between production, distribution and exchange, and as a consequence, on the function of prices in an economic system. As pieces of apparatus by which to analyse specific economic problems, both appear capable of assisting solutions when appropriately applied. Such a vision of dual development in a field of inquiry is generally not congenial to its practitioners, but its presence throughout the development of economics from the beginnings leaves little room for doubting that it actually exists.

In his account of pre-Smithian economics, Hutchison fails to note this production and reproduction aspect of the surplus approach in economics, side-tracking it in the case of physiocrats to what he perceives to be its detrimental social consequences.[18] His preferred focus is on the development of economics in terms of increased systematization of 'economic harmony, tendencies to equilibrium and free trade' in all markets. From this perspective, progress in economic thinking requires an analysis of the competitive market as the provider of economic progress, and an emphasis on the overriding importance of freedom of choice and enlightened self-interest in economic activity. This explains Hutchison's regret, for example, at the manner in which Smithian value theory swamped the subjective approaches which he found in French and Italian eighteenth-century economic thought. For him, Turgot, Galiani and Condillac were forerunners of that French school which Jevons depicted as the repository of economic truth.[19]

It is a moot point whether such a perspective makes the emergence of economics in the eighteenth century explicable simply in terms of the search for a secular moral philosophy of economic and social order, a process perhaps traceable to secular modifications of Jansenist theology. More importantly, it raises questions about the real potential for associating 'economic liberalism' with the origins of economics, as is done in some popular versions of its history. These see the starting-point of economics as a self-regulating free enterprise market economy. Such historical crudities, to which even some distinguished Nobel laureates in economics have not always been immune, as Winch (1988, p. 94) demonstrates, are dispelled by more careful study of both Smith's and pre-Smithian economic thought. This effectively combats a tendency to anachronistic error inherent in tracing precursors to the late nineteenth- and early twentieth century idea of economic liberalism in thinkers of the seventeenth and eighteenth centuries, with their different worlds and problematics (see Walther, 1984; Haakonssen, 1988; and, with respect to Smith's politics, Winch, 1978). This should make wearers of Adam Smith ties (of whom there must be a few among readers of this book) more wary of displaying a (multiple) image of this Scottish philosopher-economist. After all, many aspects of Smith's views sit uneasily with their popular depiction which justifies the peculiar sartorial homage they render him as an icon of their beliefs (see Letwin, 1988; cf. Viner, 1927).

These remarks on modern controversy inspired by a review and survey of recent literature on pre-Smithian economics, with special reference to Hutchison's important new book, allow one final and perhaps also timely reminder. In a profession which rarely cites material published more than ten years previously, the importance for the modern student of economics of studying economic classics needs to be kept constantly in mind. Like those involved in subjects such as art or philosophy, economists cannot safely neglect their roots, and can only benefit from the study of earlier systems of thought (Quadrio-Curzio and Scazzieri, 1986, p. 377). An excursion into that pre-Smithian economics to which Hutchison (1988) provides a useful but imperfect guide, not only reminds practising economists of the traditional links in their subject with practical policy concerns, ethical and moral values, and the systematic explanation of economic phenomena. It likewise reminds one of that historical relativity in economic thinking which makes the now far too prevalent view of universal applicability of *the* economic theory an inherently nonsensical viewpoint. As Marshall hinted to his nephew, a visit to the work of Adam Smith and before is not irrelevant to the modern practitioner, provided it is done in a spirit of willingness to learn rather than to correct or misapply.

Notes

1 A survey of some new literature on this subject produced since the early 1970s and specifically inspired by a critical reading of Hutchison's (1988) *Before Adam Smith: The Emergence of Political Economy 1662–1776* (Oxford: Blackwell). This chapter has been adapted from a paper on the emergence of economics as a science presented to a seminar at the History of Ideas Unit, Australian National University, in June 1988. For assistance in this transformation I am indebted to participants at that seminar (especially Knud Haakonssen, Eugene Kamenka and Melvin Richter) and in addition to Tony Aspromourgos, Terence Hutchison, Michael White, Philip Williams and an anonymous referee.

2 During 1972 and 1973 the present author (see Groenewegen, 1973) prepared papers on this subject for presentation at two conferences, but both of these contained problems not easy to resolve. A closer examination of some of these difficulties inspired the earlier version of this paper.

3 I have heavily relied on Viner (1978) in preparing this summary of Nicole and Domat's views on enlightened self-interest, the significance of which only became apparent when my attention was drawn to them in the context of the origins of Boisguilbert's economics by Terence Hutchison at a 1987 colloquium on economic liberalism at Verona.

4 Both Nicole and Domat were well represented in Turgot's very extensive library (Tsuda, 1975, items 181, 182, 222, 223, 253, 310–12, 318, 319, 335, 343, 2459, 3498, 3520, 3521 for Nicole; 702–4 for Domat), a sign of the importance assigned to their works by a French intellectual of the Enlightenment. Melvin Richter has drawn my attention to the article on 'Economie Politique' in *Handbuch Politsch-sozialer Grundbegriffe in Frankreich 1680–1820*, Munich, vol. 8, 1988, p. 75, which provides additional references to French material on Nicole's influence on late seventeenth- and early eighteenth-century economics.

5 In this context Hutchison (1988) also ignores what Ashley (1900) – and subsequently Beer (1939) – called the Tory origins of free trade policy. This suggests a specifically secular (political) catalyst in the process of the evolution of economic liberalism, which had clearly an important part in the emergence of economics as a science. Laski's (1936) still very readable study of the rise of European liberalism mentions these theological factors, but not the Jansenist contributions referred to by Viner (1978). In discussion, Haakonssen drew my attention to the need to investigate the degree of influence Domat and Nicole may have exerted on the Scottish Enlightenment, but preliminary investigations unearthed little of use in this respect.

6 These implications arise from the savage society context in which Turgot placed his more sophisticated value and exchange theory, as I point out in some detail in Groenewegen (1982a, pp. 128–9). Similar considerations apply to the interpretation of that early and rude society in Smith's account of natural price. Two further points may be noted in this context. First, my 1982 interpretation of Turgot on value allows him to be more firmly placed within the mainstream of classical value and price theory, which distinguishes market prices from the more 'fundamental' natural prices (see second section of this chapter). Second, the similarity which Hutchison (1988, pp. 300–1) notes between Beccaria and Turgot on value theory is probably explicable by the fact that Morellet's *Prospectus for an Economic Dictionary* (1769), which he sent Beccaria, contains a long article on value and money which either derives from the paper on that subject by Turgot or else was written by Turgot himself (see Groenewegen, 1977, pp. xxvi–xxvii). Since Turgot explicitly cited Galiani in this context, this makes it more difficult to speak of an independent subjective value tradition of the eighteenth century, particularly since both Condillac and Le Trosne (the last not dealt with by Hutchison [1988]) would also have been familiar with some of Turgot's work on value.

7 Carl's treatise is not mentioned in Schumpeter (1954) and, having not studied his work myself, I cannot comment directly on the accuracy of Hutchison's judgement about its quality. In the light of Hutchison's account of Carl's views (1988, pp. 157–63), a comparison with Cantillon seems to be the 'puffing' of a neglected author who, moreover, never seems to have enjoyed a substantial reputation, unlike Cantillon's tremendous influence on the economics of the second half of the eighteenth century.

8 The more important English writers of this period, ignored by Hutchison, are Gee, whose work on trade was widely read; King's *The English Merchant*, a work frequently translated, and the prolific and often interesting output of Defoe. Sir William Pulteney, to whom I have ascribed the very interesting *Some Thoughts on the Interest of Money in General* (1738), also contributed to the excise controversy (see Groenewegen, 1983b, introduction). John Cary, a Bristol merchant whose work on trade had also been translated, straddled the earlier and later periods. Hutchison (1988, p. 189) explains the decline of English economics referred to in the text partly in terms of an English 'isolationism' which he sharply contrasts with Scottish cosmopolitanism during this period; and partly in terms of an absence of important stimuli on economic thinking from urgent policy questions, unlike the 1690s with their debates on recoinage, interest abatement and national banking (Hutchison, 1988, p. 187).

9 Hutcheson's *Short Introduction* appears to have had little influence on the development of economics, only Turgot being acquainted with it among non-English economists; at least he had it in his library (Tsuda, 1975, item 2569). Hutcheson's death in 1746 seems to place him much more neatly in the previous period.

10 It is doubtful whether Carl (1722–3) deserves this accolade, as observed above in note 7.

11 An example of the lengths to which Hutchison takes his criticism of Quesnay's political views in his derivation of the comment that only the absence of 'psychiatric clinics' in eighteenth-century Paris prevented their use by the physiocrats 'for dealing with such madmen', from Quesnay's remarks on the 'freedom of madmen' in disobeying natural laws (1988, pp. 281–2).

12 Hutchison's perception of their work contrasts with the extensive praise of the physiocrats and Quesnay by earlier historians of economics to whose views I drew attention in my earlier reflections (Groenewegen, 1973). These range from McCulloch to economic writers as diverse as Marx, Schumpeter and Marshall.

13 Hutchison's emphasis on Galiani may be more important than his attempt to focus attention on Carl (1722–3). Both Einaudi and Dmitriev (see Hutchison, 1988, p. 270) depicted Galiani as a most important eighteenth-century economist, while his 'Vician' antecedents seem also worthy of further study. However, my study of Galiani's value theory fails to discover the 'marginalist aspects' which are of importance in seeing him as an *important* precursor of the dominant economics which emerged at the end of the nineteenth century.

14 The importance of this subjective value heritage for the new economics is not easy to assess, particularly when emphasis is placed on the marginal in the revolution in economic thinking which occurred in the 1870s (see note 13, where this point is made with respect to Galiani, while Turgot's links with neo-classical economics were questioned earlier in this paper in note 6). Only Menger's work revealed substantial knowledge of these French and Italian thinkers when it was published in 1871, unlike the first editions of Jevons and Walras' new theories.

15 My doctoral research on value, production and distribution theory from 1650 to 1776 was in part addressed to answering this question, but reached only negative results. Kindleberger (1976) yields a similar result with respect to Adam Smith.

16 Verri's (1771, p. 112) explicit dichotomy between public economy and finance, where the first has the objective of raising annual reproduction to the highest

possible level, while the second deals with taxation and government finance in general, is not only relevant to this association between economics and economic development; it also highlights in some respects the breach his writing made between cameral science as conceived of in Germany and Austria, and more modern political economy as it was then developing elsewhere in Europe. As an official in Austrian-controlled Milan and a child of the French and Italian Enlightenment, Verri was particularly well placed to make such a distinction. For a comprehensive perspective on cameralism in this context, see Tribe (1984).

17 Another area on which more research seems required is the background to the origins of physiocracy, particularly with respect to the events which brought Quesnay to study economics and for which there are still no really satisfactory explanations (see Groenewegen, 1983b, pp. viii–xii).

18 The extravagant expressions to which the thought of such consequences tend to move Hutchison are illustrated in note 11 above with respect to Quesnay. An equally fantastic comparison is his description of Sraffa's economics as the economics of the Gulag (see Hutchison, 1978, p. 231).

19 A statement of which Hutchison kindly reminded me in correspondence about aspects related to an earlier version of this paper. The statement is in Jevon's second edition preface to the *Theory of Political Economy* (1879).

References

Ashley, W. J. (1900) 'The Tory Origin of Free Trade Policy', in W. J. Ashley, *Surveys Historic and Economic*, London: Longman, Green, 269–303.

Aspromourgos, Anthony (1985) 'Sir William Petty and the Origins of Classical Political Economy in England', Ph.D. thesis, University of Sydney.

——(1986) 'Political Economy and the Social Division of Labour', *Scottish Journal of Political Economy*, 33(1) February, 28–45.

Baranzini, Mauro and Scazzieri, Roberto (1986) *Foundations of Economics. Structure of Inquiry and Economy Theory*, Oxford: Blackwell.

Barucci, P. and Carpenter, K. (1985) *Italian Economic Literature in the Kress Library 1475–1850*, Rome: Banco di Roma and Boston MA: Kress Library, Harvard.

Beccaria, Cesare (1769) *A Discourse on Public Economy and Commerce*, London.

Beer, Max (1939) *An Inquiry into Physiocracy*, London: Allen & Unwin.

Bordes, Christina and Morange, Jean (1981) *Turgot, Economiste et Administrateur*, Paris: Presses Universitaires de France.

Campbell, R. H. and Skinner, A. S. (1982) *The Origins and Nature of the Scottish Enlightenment*, Edinburgh: John Donald.

Carl, Conseiller de Prince de Brandenburg (1722–3) *Traité de la Richesse, des Princes et de leurs Etats*, 3 vols, Paris.

Cranston, Maurice (1985) *John Locke, A Biography*, Oxford: Oxford University Press.

Dubos, J. B. (1703) *Les Intérests de l'Angleterre Malentendus dans la Guerre Présente*, Amsterdam (i.e. Paris).

Eltis, Walter (1984) *The Classical Theory of Economic Growth*, London: Macmillan.

Faccarello, Gilbert (1986) *Aux origines de l'Economie Politique Libérale: Pierre de Boisguillebert*, Paris: Editions Anthropos.

Finzi, Roberto (1981) 'Turgot, l'Histoire et l'Economie', in Bordes, Christina and Morange, Jean, *Turgot, Economiste et Administrateur*, Paris: Presses Universitaires de France, 3–18.

Garegnani, P. (1984) 'Value and Distribution in the Classical Economists and Marx', *Oxford Economic Papers*, 36(4) 291–325.

Groenewegen, P. D. (1973) 'Thoughts on the Emergence of Economics as a Science', paper presented at Third Conference of Economists, Adelaide, August (above, Chapter 2).

——(1977) *The Economics of A. R. J. Turgot*, The Hague: Martinus Nijhoff.

——(1982a) 'Turgot, Forerunner of Neo-classical Economics', *Kenzei Kenkyu*, 33(2) 119–33 (below, Chapter 18).

——(1982b) Introduction to [Sir William Pulteney] *Some thoughts on the Interest of Money in General*, Sydney: Department of Economics, University of Sydney, Reprint of Economics Classics, series 2, no. 1, v–xviii.

——(1983a) 'Turgot, Beccaria and Smith', in P. Groenewegen and J. Halevi (eds) *Italian Economics Past and Present*, Sydney: Frederick May Foundation of Italian Studies, 31–78 (above, Chapter 1).

——(1983b) Introduction to *Quesnay, 'Fermiers' (1756) and Turgot, 'Sur le grande et la petite culture' (1767)*, Sydney: Department of Economics, University of Sydney, Reprint of Economics Classics, series 2, no. 2, vii–xxv (below, Chapter 13).

——(1987) 'Turgot, A. R. J.', in *The New Palgrave*, London: Macmillan, IV, 707–12.

Guillebaud, C. W. (1971) 'Some Personal Reminiscences of Alfred Marshall', *History of Political Economy*, 3(1) 1–8, reprinted in J. C. Wood (ed.) *Alfred Marshall, Critical Assessments*, London: Croom Helm, vol. 1, 91–7.

Haakonssen, Knud (1988) *Traditions of Liberalism: Essays on John Locke, Adam Smith and John Stuart Mill*, Sydney: Centre for Independent Studies, xi–xxi.

Harrison, John and Laslett, Peter (1971) *The Library of John Locke*, London: Oxford University Press.

Hecht, Jacqueline (1966) *La vie de Pierre le Pesant, Seigneur de Boisguillebert*, in *Pierre de Boisguillebert ou la Naissance de l'Economie Politique*, Paris: Institute National d'Etudes Démographiques, 121–244.

Hollander, Samuel (1986) *Classical Economics*, Oxford: Blackwell.

Hont, Istvan and Ignatieff, Michael (1983) *Wealth and Virtue: The Shaping of Political Economy in the Scottish Enlightenment*, Cambridge: Cambridge University Press.

Hutchison, Terence (1978) *Revolutions and Progress in Economic Knowledge*, Cambridge: Cambridge University Press.

——(1988) *Before Adam Smith: The Emergence of Political Economy 1662–1776*, Oxford: Blackwell.

Jevons, W. S. (1879) *Theory of Political Economy*, 2nd edn, London: Macmillan.

Kindleberger, C. P. (1976) 'The Historical Background, Adam Smith and the Industrial Revolution', in Thomas Wilson and Andrew Skinner (eds) *The Market and the State*, Oxford: Clarendon Press, 1–15.

Laski, Harold H. (1936) *The Rise of European Liberalism*, London: Allen & Unwin.

Letwin, William (1963) *The Origins of Scientific Economics*, London: Methuen.

——(1988) 'Was Adam Smith a Liberal?', in Haakonssen, Knud, *Traditions of Liberalism: Essays on John Locke, Adam Smith and John Stuart Mill*, Sydney: Centre for Independent Studies, 65–80.

Lutfalla, Michel (1981) *Aux Origines de la Pensée Economique*, Paris: Economica.

Marx, K. H. (1859, 1971) *A Contribution to the Critique of Political Economy*, with an introduction by Maurice Dobb, London: Lawrence and Wishart.

Meek, Ronald L. (1976) *Social Science and the Ignoble Savage*, Cambridge: Cambridge University Press.

Mirabeau, Victor Riquetti (1766) *The Oeconomical Table by the Friend of Mankind* [i.e. Mirabeau] London: W. Owen.

Mizuta, Hiroshi (1967) *Adam Smith's Library*, Cambridge: Cambridge University Press.

Murphy, Antoin E. (1986) *Cantillon: Entrepreneur and Economist*, Oxford: Clarendon Press.

Parisi, Aquaviva, Daniela (1984) *Il Pensiero Economico Classico in Italia (1750–1860)*, Milan: Università Cattolica.

Pasinetti, Luigi L. (1981) *Structural Change and Economic Growth*, Cambridge: Cambridge University Press.

——(1986) 'Theory of Value: A Source of Alternative Paradigms in Economic Analysis', in Baranzini, Mauro and Scazzieri, Roberto, *Foundations of Economics. Structure of Inquiry and Economy Theory*, Oxford: Blackwell, 409–31.

Petty, Sir William (1963) *The Economic Writings*, ed. C. H. Hull, New York: Augustus M. Kelley.

Quadrio-Curzio, Alberto and Scazzieri, Roberto (1986) 'The Exchange-Production Duality and the Dynamics of Economic Knowledge', in Barazini, Mauro and Scazzieri, Roberto, *Foundations of Economics. Structure of Inquiry and Economy Theory*, Oxford: Blackwell, 377–407.

Rashid, Salim (1987) 'The Scottish Enlightenment: Evaluation and Origins', in Todd Lowry, S., *Pre-Classical Economic Thought*, Boston MA: Kluwer Academic, 256–63.

Roberts, Hazel van Dyke (1935) *Boisguillebert, Economist of the Reign of Louis XIV*, New York: Columbia University Press.

Roncaglia, Alessandro (1977, 1985) *Petty. The Origins of Political Economy*, Cardiff: University College Cardiff Press.

Schumpeter, J. A. (1954) *History of Economic Analysis*, London: Allen & Unwin.

Skinner, A. S. and Wilson, T. (1976) *Essays on Adam Smith*, Oxford: Clarendon Press.

Stark, W. (1944) *The History of Economics in its Relation to Economic Development*, London: Allen & Unwin.

Todd Lowry, S. (1987) *Pre-Classical Economic Thought*, Boston MA: Kluwer Academic.

Tribe, Keith (1984) 'Cameralism and the Science of Government', *Journal of Modern History*, 56(23) June, 263–84.

Tsuda, Takumi (1975) *Catalogue des Livres de la Bibliothéque de Turgot*, Tokyo: Institute d'Etudes Economiques, Université Hitotsubashi.

Vaggi, Gianni (1987) *The Economics of François Quesnay*, London: Macmillan.

Venturi, Franco (1983) 'Scottish Echoes in Eighteenth Century Italy', in Hont, Istvan and Ignatieff, Michael, *Wealth and Virtue: The Shaping of Political Economy in the Scottish Enlightenment*, Cambridge: Cambridge University Press, 345–62.

Verri, Pietro (1771, 1986) *Reflections on Political Economy*, trans. Barbara McGilvray with an introduction by Peter Groenewegen, Sydney: Department of Economics, University of Sydney, Reprints of Economic Classics, series 2, no. 4.

Viner, Jacob (1927) 'Adam Smith and Laissez-faire', *Journal of Political Economy*, 35, April, 198–232.

——(1978) 'Religious Thought and Economic Society', four chapters of an unfinished work, eds Jacques Melitz and Donald Winch, *History of Political Economy*, 10(1) spring, 1–192.

Walther, Rudolf (1984) 'Economic Liberalism', *Economy and Society*, 13(2) 178–207.

Winch, Donald (1978) *Adam Smith's Politics: An Essay in Historiographic Revision*, Cambridge: Cambridge University Press.

——(1988) 'Adam Smith and the Liberal Tradition', in Haakonssen, Knud, *Traditions of Liberalism: Essays on John Locke, Adam Smith and John Stuart Mill*, Sydney: Centre for Independent Studies, 83–104.

Part II

4 Labour and the classical economists

An interesting aspect of labour history is the attitude to labour adopted by the great classical economists, Smith, Ricardo, Hume, North and others. It is also instructive to compare their views with what modern economists have to say about wages and the role of labour in production.

In twentieth-century economic literature there has been a great deal of discussion on the relationship between wages and prices as an explanation of inflation, as well as discussions on the role of productivity in this 'cost-push' theory, as it has been called.[1] In most of these arguments, a definite relationship between wages and prices is posed, often with the assumption that either labour productivity is constant or that it is rising at a constant rate, and generally with the implicit assumption that there is complete independence between rising money wage rates and rising productivity.[2] In a closed economy, especially one with a high degree of monopoly in its market structure, it is then argued that rising money wages will increase prices, provided that the rate of increase in wages is greater than that of productivity.[3] At the same time, the policy objectives of 'price stability' and 'external viability' demand a zero or moderate rate of inflation in order to preserve living standards of those on fixed incomes and the competitiveness of domestic products in overseas markets.[4]

It is interesting to note that these particular arguments are not new. The relationship between wages and prices and its relevance for international trade policy was an important tenet of seventeenth- and eighteenth-century economic policy; while in the literature of this period there were also discussions on the relationship between wages and productivity. However, although most writers at this time condemned rising wages for their effects on commodity prices and on the competitiveness of those commodities abroad,[5] there were other writers[6] who argued that rising money wages could lead to increased industriousness or productivity of the labourers. In the second case, the price effects assumed by the first group of writers would not necessarily follow. The first section of this chapter will examine this aspect of the debate.

A controversy of the nineteenth century has also some relevance in this connection. In his *Wealth of Nations*, Adam Smith had discussed the relationship between wages and prices, and had come to the conclusion that rising wages would lead to rising prices.[7] This opinion was strongly attacked by David Ricardo in his *Principles of Political Economy and Taxation*, in the curious argument which is now known as the 'Ricardo effect': that is, that rising wages, although causing rising prices in labour-intensive commodities, would cause falling prices in capital-intensive commodities. Furthermore, rising money wages, according to Ricardo, would in themselves be an incentive to more capital-intensive production and the application of machinery.[8] This argument was expanded by the Swedish economist Knut Wicksell, who argued that under certain conditions rising wages would cause extensions of the period of production, increase capital intensity and hence increased productivity.[9] This particular aspect of the problem will be dealt with in the second section of this chapter.

The belief in a relationship between money wages and prices after corrections for changes in productivity, which is so often put forward by economists, is therefore not as simple as it appears at first sight. Far from believing that productivity and money wages were independent variables, the classics argued that there was a definite relationship between the two, and that, under certain conditions, rising money wages would have a beneficial effect on labour productivity. The significance of the conclusions which can be derived from this study of two classical controversies will form the basis for the third and final section of this chapter.

I

As stated above, the seventeenth- and eighteenth-century writers on trade were well aware that there was a relationship between production costs and prices, and that when production costs – especially labour costs – were high, prices would be high and English commodities would be undersold by foreign competitors in overseas markets.[10] Andrew Yarranton, one of these writers, argued, for example, that in order to compete with the Dutch, provision prices would have to be lowered as 'Cheap Drink and cheap Bread at all times will make [low wages] and cheap Commodities'.[11] Roger Coke maintained that 'where men labour more industriously and upon less terms upon any thing, this thing is cheaply managed'[12] and, that as this was the case in Holland, it explained why the Dutch could outsell the English. Thomas Manley, pointing to the higher wage rates prevailing in England as compared to other countries, deduced from this that 'over-valuing our wages … is the capital reason that all forraigners under-sell us'.[13] Cost reductions and, consequently, price reductions, would allow the increase of exports.

Since these writers were generally also concerned with the policy objective of a favourable balance of trade, they were eager to formulate policies which would increase the competitiveness of English commodities abroad, and as costs were regarded then, as now, as the major factor in the expansion of exports, policies to reduce costs were formulated by many of the economists of the period. The debates on the desirability of the policy of reducing the legal rate of interest may be regarded as part of this export drive,[14] as can many of the wage policies formulated during this era. It is of course only with the latter that this chapter is concerned.

For people acquainted with the wage-fixing tribunals and wage legislation of medieval and Tudor England, a wage policy based on the relationship between wage rates and provision prices was easily and quickly discovered. The *Statute of Apprentices, 5 Eliz. c. 4*, had made provision for wage fixing by the Justices of the Peace and in connection with this it had been urged that attention should be paid to the prices of provisions.[15] The statute *1 Jac. I c. 6*, which expanded on this piece of Elizabethan legislation, stated explicitly that wages should be set 'according to the plenty, scarcity, necessity and respect of the time'.[16] Wage fixing in London in 1586, for example, had to be carried out in a manner closely resembling the modern calculations of a rise in the cost of living, by referring to the 'prices of all kinds of victuals, full raiment and apparel, both linnen and woollen and also of house rent'.[17] Despite the rapid disappearance of the wage-fixing tribunals and the virtual elimination of their effectiveness in the second half of the seventeenth- and the whole of the eighteenth century,[18] the idea persisted that wages ought to be regulated with reference to the price of subsistence, and that any increase in the cost of living was unjustifiable from a policy point of view.[19]

The argument that foreign trade policy demanded the regulation of wages based on changes in the cost of living was attacked on several grounds. Many economic writers, especially merchants and manufacturers, argued that if wages were geared to the cost of living all incentives to work and effort would disappear and labourers would become lazy and less productive. This particular line of thinking has been called the 'economy of low wages' argument and should now be considered.

This argument depended on the implicit assumption that the supply curve of labour was backward-bending; in other words, on the view that after a certain wage rate had been reached, any further wage increases would not lead to increases in the quantity of time worked but to increased leisure, as at that particular wage rate the wants of the labourers in terms of goods would be completely satisfied, and the additional income earned from extra work would be less preferable than additions to leisure.

Most authors who held this view backed up their argument with empirical evidence about the consumption patterns of the 'labouring poor', which, they argued, were confined to the necessities of life as well as to such 'stupefying' commodities as spirits, coffee, tea and tobacco. If basic food prices were low, and money wages remained at their old level, these necessities could be purchased with a minimum effort by the labourer, the luxuries mentioned could be purchased with some additional effort, after which the remainder of the working week would be spent in leisure. Increased real income for the labourers above a certain level meant a decreased supply of labour and lower labour productivity.[20]

This argument was already widely held in the economic literature of the seventeenth century.[21] During the eighteenth century, possibly due to the increased competition in foreign trade caused by England's new commercial rival, France, this argument gained in popularity, since by expressing the desire for lower wages it would at the same time ensure an increase in the competitiveness of exports by reducing their price. Mandeville may be regarded as an early spokesman of the century on this matter, as is shown in the following quotation:

> Everybody knows that there is a vast number of Journey-Men, Weavers, Taylors, Clothworkers, and twenty other Handicrafts; who if by four days Labour in a Week they can maintain themselves, will hardly be perswaded to work the fifth, and that there are Thousands of Labouring Men of all sorts who will, tho' they can hardly subsist, put themselves to fifty inconveniences, disoblige their Masters, pinch their Bellies, and run in Debts to make Holidays.[22]

This type of statement was repeated again and again by the advocates of a low 'real' wages policy (i.e. wages measured in purchasing power). These advocates were generally connected with trade and manufacturing interests and therefore had a direct concern in the matter of low wage costs.[23] Others argued that high real wages caused drunkenness and vice among the 'lower orders' which in turn impaired their efficiency and caused a loss in working hours. High real wages, through this drunkenness effect, would cause a real loss in labour productivity.[24]

These types of argument are embodied in the work of William Temple, a clothier from Trowbridge, who, in several pamphlets, argued that high provision prices and low money wages were the best policy for a trading nation as it would increase the 'industry of the poor' and make them 'sober, frugal, and thrifty'. This is illustrated in the following quotation from his work:

> The best spur to industry is necessity. The mass of the labourers work only to relieve their present wants and are such votaries to indolence, ease and voluptuousness, that they sacrifice all in consideration to the pleasures of the present moment, regardless of sickness and old age. … If a labourer can produce by his wages or plenty, all the necessaries of life, and afterwards have a residuum, he would expend the same, either on gin, rum, brandy, or strong beer; luxurise on great heaps of fat beef or bacon, and eat perhaps till he spewed; and having gorged and gotten dead drunk, lie down like a pig, and snore till he was fresh. … The common conduct of the labouring populace in times of plenty proves, that the easier the means of acquiring necessities, the less work is generally done, and the dearer the necessaries are, the more they labour.[25]

There were, however, other writers who held a different view of the effect of high real wage rates on the 'industriousness of the poor' or labour productivity. Their attitude pointed towards a distinct 'economy of *high* wages' argument. This reasoning depended on the assumption of the normal upward sloping supply curve of labour, where increases in the wage rate would ensure increases in the quantity and in the intensity of time worked.

This policy was justified on the ground that economic welfare did not necessarily depend on a favourable balance of trade, and on a consequent increase in the wealth of merchants and manufacturers, but that it depended much more on adequate living standards for the majority of members of society, that is, the labourers. This was therefore an essentially new attitude to the aim of economic activity.

This more liberal attitude to the welfare of the labourers did not, however, mean the abandonment of a wages policy for trade. High money wages and low provision prices were not incompatible with such a policy, these authors argued, since the higher standard of living, by extending the range of wants of the working class, would provide them with new incentives to work harder, and thereby raise their labour productivity. The following quotations illustrate this more enlightened position with regard to wages:

> The main spur to Trade, or rather to Industry and Ingenuity, is the exorbitant appetites of Men, which they will take pains to gratifie, and so be disposed to work, when nothing else will incline them to it; for did Men content themselves with bare Necessities we should have a poor World.[26]

> Whether the creating of Wants be not the likeliest Way to produce Industry in a People? Whether comfortable Living does not produce Wants, and Wants Industry, and Industry Wealth? Whether the Way to make Men industrious be not to let them taste the Fruits of their Industry? And whether the labouring Ox should be muzzled?[27]

> Everything in the world is purchased by labour; and our passions are the only cause of labour. … It is a violent method, and in most cases impracticable, to oblige the labourer to work. … Furnish him with manufactures and commodities, and he will do it of himself.[28]

These three quotations clearly indicate that in the view of North, Berkeley and Hume, high wages, resulting in higher living standards for the people, would affect the 'industry' or labour productivity favourably. Low or subsistence wages, by taking away incentives, would be a poor policy for a nation.

Daniel Defoe, in very precise language, defended this attitude to the 'economy of *high* wages' by showing clearly that higher living standards resulted in higher labour productivity. Competitiveness in international trade did therefore not depend on low wages, but on high labour productivity which in turn was caused by high wages. This argument is expressed in the following quotation:

> It is true, that our People, generally speaking, live better, and earn more money than the French, or than the labouring Poor of any other Nation. But then it is true, that they do more work than the Poor of any Nation of

> the World do or can do. ... Why do our People fare better, &c.? It is because they do more Work. And why do they do more Work than other Nations? It is because they fare better.[29]

It is interesting to note that both arguments, that is, the 'economy of low wages' and that of 'high wages', depend on a link between changing money wages and labour productivity, and that both do not assume independence between these two variables. Changes in money wages, through incentive effects, affect labour productivity, so that on this ground alone it cannot be supposed, as contemporary economic theory appears to do, that these two things are not related. The classics demonstrated that the two were linked, although they disagreed among themselves on the precise nature of this interconnection.

II

The controversy on the same subject in the nineteenth century was on a considerably higher level of analysis. As stated previously, it arose from Adam Smith's exposition of the relationship between wages and prices which was severely criticised by David Ricardo. It was this criticism of Ricardo, and its development by Wicksell, that provided further classical arguments on the relationship between a rise in wages and a rise in productivity.

Adam Smith's position on the relationship between wages and prices was similar to that of the authors discussed in the previous section. Wages, together with profit and rent, were component parts of the natural price, from which it could be concluded that a rise in wages would cause a rise in prices.[30] In his chapter on wages, this analysis is reaffirmed in the last paragraph where it is argued: 'The increase in the wages of labour necessarily increases the price of many commodities, by increasing that part of it which resolves itself into wages, and so far tends to diminish their consumption both at home and abroad'.[31] Although he occasionally qualified this proposition,[32] on the whole it can be said that Smith, like his contemporaries of the eighteenth century, adhered to it in his writings.

Smith's proposition was severely criticised by Ricardo in the chapter dealing with the subject of value. His position is made clear in the following quotation, which at the same time indicates the novelty of Ricardo's thought on this subject:

> it may be proper to observe, that Adam Smith, and all the writers who have followed him, have, without one exception that I know of, maintained that a rise in the price of labour would be uniformly followed by a rise in the price of all commodities. I hope I have succeeded in showing, that there are no grounds for such an opinion, and that only those commodities would rise which had less fixed capital employed upon them than the medium in which the price was estimated, and that all those which had more, would

> positively fall in price when wages rose. On the contrary, if wages fell, those commodities only would fall, which had a less proportion of fixed capital employed on them, than the medium in which the price was estimated; all those which had more, would positively rise in price.[33]

Ricardo's proposition on the relationship between wages and prices was discussed in detail in the first chapter of his *Principles*. In his proof, Ricardo assumed two men investing a certain quantity of labour in the production of a machine, and one investing the same quantity of labour in corn production. At the end of the year the value of the output will be the same in each case. In the following year, the owners of the machines employ the same quantity of labour together with the machines in cloth production, while the third man uses it once more to produce corn. In this case the output of the cloth producers 'will be more than twice the value of the corn, for the profit on ... [their] ... capital for the first year has been added to their capitals, while that of the farmer has been expended and enjoyed'.[34]

If it is further assumed that one hundred labourers are annually employed by each of the men, that the wage rate is £50 per annum, and that the rate of profit is 10 per cent, then the value of the output at the end of the first year is £5,500. At the end of the second year, the value of the output of the corn producer remains at £5,500, but that of the cloth manufacturers will rise to £6,050, being £5,500 for wages and profit on the circulating capital and £550 for profit on the fixed capital. The 'corn is not of the same value as ... [the cloth] ... because it is produced, as far as regards fixed capital, under different circumstances'.[35]

The next step in Ricardo's analysis is to assume a rise in the price of labour which causes a fall in the rate of profit from 10 to 9 per cent. This means that the cloth manufacturers can now only add £495 as profit on their fixed capital to the common value of their output of £5,500, so that the value of the annual output of cloth falls from £6,050 to £5,995. The value of the annual output of corn would continue to be £5,500.[36] From this argument, Ricardo drew the following conclusion:

> The degree of alteration in the relative value of goods, on account of a rise or fall of labour, would depend on the proportion which the fixed capital bore to the whole capital employed. All commodities which are produced by very valuable machinery, or in very valuable buildings, or which require a great length of time before they can be brought to market, would fall in relative value, while all those which were chiefly produced by labour, or which would be speedily brought to market would rise in relative value.[37]

For the purpose of this chapter, Ricardo drew an even more important conclusion from his analysis. Rises in wages will provide a strong incentive to the application of machinery, and therefore stimulate rises in labour productivity. As he put it himself:

> We here see why it is that old countries are constantly impelled to employ machinery, and new countries to employ labour. With every difficulty of providing for the maintenance of men, labour necessarily rises, and with every rise in the price of labour, new temptations are offered to the use of machinery.[38]

It was this particular part of the argument that was praised and further developed by Wicksell. According to Wicksell,

> Ricardo had correctly understood the sequence of cause and effect; if money wages rise ... then the introduction of machines which before proved unproductive will now become more profitable ... According to the more modern terminology, this means that every increase of wages encourages a lengthening of the period of production, which occupies more time but is more productive, whereby the wage increase is partly compensated.[39]

This particular aspect of the problem was fully treated by Wicksell in his own discussion of capital and wages, where he showed that rises in wages, by encouraging increased capital intensity in production, thereby also raise labour productivity, which partly compensates for the rise in wages.

In his mathematical exposition of Böhm-Bawerk's theory of interest, Wicksell established the precise relationships between wages, interest, product and the period of production under stationary conditions, a given single productivity function, a given constant supply of factors and perfect competition.[40] From this analysis it can be concluded that:

> at each level of wages a period of production of a certain length proves to be the most advantageous to the entrepreneur-capitalists, since it promises the greatest possible interest ... if more labour is demanded than is available, wages must rise. At the new level of wages a new, and what is more, a *longer* period of production proves at once to be the most profitable, as is evident, and the superfluous capital is absorbed partly by the rise in wages, and partly by the lengthening of the period of production.[41]

This conclusion is basically similar to the analysis presented by Ricardo, as Wicksell himself pointed out.[42] A rise in wages has, as consequence, the adoption of more capitalistic or more roundabout methods of production which lead to increased productivity, 'the lengthening of the period of production is seen to be a *reaction* on the part of the capitalists against the increase in wages which has taken place and the low interest *which results therefrom*'.[43] This, then, is the second classical demonstration of the favourable reaction of labour productivity to a rise in wages: when wages rise there is a strong incentive to use more capital-intensive methods of production, which in turn raise labour productivity. Once more, according to the classics, these two phenomena cannot be treated as independent.

III

The two classical arguments which have been discussed above both relate rises in wages to changes in labour productivity through the incentive effects of rising money wages. The first argument, that of North, Defoe, Berkeley and Hume, contributed the fact that rising money wages could stimulate labourers to greater effort, and in this way increase labour productivity. The second argument, that of Ricardo and Wicksell, showed that rising money wages, in a competitive system, provided incentives for the capitalists to use labour-saving devices and more capital-intensive processes which would raise labour productivity. The two arguments are therefore quite different: one depends on incentives for labour, the other on incentives for greater use of capital.

It is difficult to say how important these two arguments are in actual practice: a case could be made both for and against them. It seems fairly plausible that incentive effects for labour of higher wages are likely, but this proposition would be very difficult to test. Furthermore, in support of their existence, it may be argued that they must be important since these material incentives are the supposed foundation of the free enterprise economy, and one of its alleged superior features over the socialist economy. If this is indeed true, then there are probably productivity effects of this type at work in our society.

The second argument seems to be even more plausible under modern conditions, although once again it would be extremely difficult to test its validity. In the first place, this is because the argument depends on a high degree of competition which is absent in the Australian economy except in certain sectors of the rural industry.[44] Second, because it is extremely difficult to get measures of productivity in the economy which are independent of money wage rates.[45] Nevertheless, this is a hypothesis which, in my opinion, needs to be tested by those interested in the effects of rising money wages.

The testing of the classical arguments relating wages and productivity was, however, not the aim of this chapter; its purpose was merely to present them for consideration, and this has now been done. As such, they may serve a useful purpose for economists by reminding them of the possibility of interdependence between wages and productivity as put forward by some of the classical economists. In any case, they serve to illustrate a particular aspect of labour history in that they reveal part of the attitude to labour of some of the classical economists.

Notes

1 For a survey of this literature see M. Bronfenbrenner and F. D. Holzman (1965) 'A Survey of Inflation Theory', *Surveys of Economic Theory*, New York, vol. I, pp. 46–107.

2 See, for example, K. Lancaster, 'Productivity Geared Wage Policies', *Economica*, n.s., vol. 25, August 1958, esp. pp. 199–201.

3 See *Report of the Committee of Economic Inquiry* (Melbourne, 1965) vol. I, pp. 122–3 and note.

4 *Ibid*., pp. 36–7; these objectives are of course not confined to Australia. See *Council on Prices, Productivity and Incomes, First Report* (London, 1958) p. 1; *The Report of the*

U.S. Commission on Money and Credit (Homewood, 1961), pp. 13–17, 43–5 and dissenting notes.

5 This subject has been treated by E. S. Furniss (1920) *The Position of the Labourer in a System of Nationalism*, New York, esp. pp. 180ff.

6 For example, Dudley North, Daniel Defoe and David Hume. See the second section of this paper.

7 Adam Smith esp. pp. 47–54, 86.

8 David Ricardo (1953) 'Principles of Political Economy and Taxation', in P. Scraffa (ed.) *Collected Works of David Ricardo*, vol. I, Cambridge, pp. 38–43, 214–17.

9 Knut Wicksell (1954) *Value, Capital and Rent*, trans. S. H. Frowein, London, pp. 37–8, 120–30.

10 See E. S. Furniss (1920) *The Position of the Labourer in a System of Nationalism*, New York, pp. 159, 180ff; T. E. Gregory, 'The Economics of Employment in England, 1660–1713', *Economica*, vol. I, Jan. 1921, pp. 50f; R. L. Meek (1958) *Studies in the Labour Theory of Value*, London, pp. 18–24.

11 Andrew Yarranton (1677) *England's Improvement by Sea and Land*, London, vol. I, p. 168.

12 Roger Coke p. 51.

13 Thomas Manley (1669) *Usury at Six per Cent. Examined*, London, p. 17.

14 See, for example, Sir Josiah Child (1668) *Brief Observations Concerning Trade and Interest of Money*, London, p. 15; this whole question is discussed by G. L. S. Tucker (1960) *Progress and Profits in British Economic Thought*, Cambridge, esp. chs I and II.

15 *5 Eliz. c. 4, Clause XI*, reprinted in A. E. Bland, P. A. Brown and R. H. Tawney (1914) *English Economic History*, London, p. 328.

16 Reprinted in *ibid.*, p. 342.

17 Cited by Heckscher (1955) *Mercantilism*, London, I, p. 229.

18 See Lipson (1961) *Economic History of England*, London, III, pp. 264–71.

19 For examples of these views see the following: Rice Vaughan (1675) *A Discourse of Coin and Coinage*, London, p. 108; Charles Davenant (1771) 'An Essay on the Probable Method of Making the People the Gainers of the Balance of Trade', in *Works*, Whitworth edition, London, II, p. 199; John Cary (1695) *An Essay on the State of England in Relation to Trade*, Bristol, pp. 144–5; Jacob Vanderlint (1734) *Money Answers All Things*, London, pp. 6–7, 15; Joseph Massie (1760) *Reasons Humbly Offered against the Laying any further Tax on Malt and Beer*, London, p. 10.

20 Cf. Dorothy Marshall (1926) *The English Poor in the Eighteenth Century*, London, pp. 32–3.

21 Roger Coke (1670) *A Discourse of Trade*, London, p. 15; Sir William Petty (1899) *Economic Writings*, Hull edition, Cambridge, pp. 87, 274; Sir Josiah Child (1690) *A Discourse of Trade*, London, pp. 15–16; John Houghton (1681)*A Collection of Letters*, London, 1681), II, p. 184; Thomas Manley (1669) *Usury at Six per Cent. Examined*, London, 1669), pp. 19–20.

22 Bernard de Mandeville (1714) *The Fable of the Bees*, London, pp. 173–4.

23 See e.g. Joshua Gee (1729) *The Trade and Navigation of Great Britain Considered*, London, p. 38; George Lowe (1768) *Considerations on the Effects of the Bounties granted on Corn, Malt and Flour*, London, p. 25; *The Weavers' Pretences Examined*, London, 1719, pp. 12–13; *Some Thoughts on the Interest of Money in General*, London, 1738, p. 73; and J. Cunningham (1765) *Considerations on Taxes as they are supposed to affect the Price of Labour*, London, which is completely devoted to this subject.

24 Josiah Tucker (1751) *An Impartial Enquiry in to the Benefits and Damages arising … from the … Use of Low-priced Spirituous Licquors*, London; Thomas Alcock (1752) *Observations on the Defects of the Poor Laws*, London, p. 50.

25 William Temple (1758) *A Vindication of Commerce and the Arts*, London, pp. 27, 31, 40.

26 Sir Dudley North (1690) *Discourse Upon Trade*, London, reprinted in J. R. MacCulloch (ed.) (1954) *Early English Tracts on Commerce*, p. 528.
27 George Berkeley (1752) *The Querist*, London, pp. 3, 12, 38.
28 David Hume (1955) 'Of Commerce', in *Economic Writings*, Rotwein edition, London, pp. 11–12.
29 Daniel Defoe (1714) *Mercator*, 20–22 April, no. 143, p. 2.
30 Adam Smith (1937) *An Inquiry into the Nature and Causes of the Wealth of Nations*, Modern Library edition, New York, Book I, ch. VI.
31 Adam Smith, *op. cit.*, p. 86. It is interesting to note that Adam Smith criticised the 'economy of low wages' argument because it was based on false premises (*ibid.*, pp. 82–5), and that he favoured high wages as a general policy. The reasons given for the latter were two: first of all, high wages were desirable from the point of view of general welfare, as 'No society can surely be flourishing and happy, of which the far greater part of the members are poor and miserable' (*ibid.*, p. 79). Second, high wages were desirable because of their effect on 'industry':

> The wages of labour are the encouragement of industry, which, like every other human quality, improves in proportion to the encouragement it receives. A plentiful subsistence increases the bodily strength of the labourer, and the comfortable hope of bettering his condition, and of ending his days perhaps in ease and plenty, animates him to exert that strength to the utmost. Where wages are high, accordingly, we shall always find the workmen more active, diligent, and expeditious, than where they are low.
>
> (*ibid.*, p. 81)

32 For example, in a discussion of taxes on wages of country it is argued that price is not raised in 'proportion to the tax' (*ibid.*, p. 817). In the chapter on wages it is argued that the cause of rising wages diminishes prices, since 'the increase of stock', which raises wages, increases the 'productive powers' of labour (*ibid.*, p. 86).
33 David Ricardo (1953) 'Principles of Political Economy and Taxation', in P. Scraffa (ed.) *Collected Works of David Ricardo*, vol. I, Cambridge, p. 46; cf. pp. 104–5, 302, 307, 315. The crux of his proof lies in his definition of 'the medium in which the price was estimated', and this definition provides the crucial assumption for his argument. In the first edition of the *Principles*, this argument was even more strongly stated. See *ibid.*, pp. 61–3.
34 Ricardo, *op cit.*, pp. 33–4.
35 *Ibid.*, p. 34. The calculation of the value of the output of the cloth manufacturers is based on the implicit assumption that the machines have an indefinite life, so that no allowance has to be made for their depreciation. The comparison is therefore made between one commodity produced without any fixed capital, and one produced with a great deal of fixed capital.
36 *Ibid.*, p. 35. This argument is incomplete since no details of the wage rise are given. Assume that wages rose from £50 to £55 per annum; the value of corn would then be £5,500 for the wage bill plus £495 for the profit thereon, making a total of £5,995. The value of the cloth output will be £5,500 for wages, £495 for the profit thereon, and £495 for the profit on the fixed capital. Both commodities have therefore risen in absolute value, but since the price rise of corn is greater than that of cloth, cloth has fallen in value relative to corn, the labour-intensive commodity.
37 David Ricardo (1953) 'Principles of Political Economy and Taxation', in P. Scraffa (ed.) *Collected Works of David Ricardo*, vol. I, Cambridge, p. 35.
38 Ricardo, *op. cit.*, p. 41n. In an argument similar to the one presented above, Ricardo shows that 'machines would not rise in price, in consequence of a rise in wages' (*ibid.*, p. 41).
39 Knut Wicksell (1954) *Value, Capital and Rent*, trans. S. H. Frowein, London, pp. 37–8.

40 Wicksell, *op. cit.*, pp. 120–6; cf. F. Lutz (1967) *The Theory of Interest*, Dordrecht, mathematical appendix, 1.
41 Wicksell, *op. cit.*, p. 127.
42 Knut Wicksell (1951) *Lecturers on Political Economy*, translated from the Swedish by E. Classen, London, I, pp. 167–8.
43 Knut Wicksell (1954) *Value, Capital and Rent*, trans. S. H. Frowein, London, pp. 127–8.
44 It is interesting to note that it is precisely in these sectors that productivity gains appear to have been highest, presumably because here entrepreneurs have been forced to adopt more capital-intensive methods in the face of rising money wages. See *Report of Committee of Economic Inquiry* (Melbourne, 1965) I, Table 5.2.
45 See *Report of the Committee of Economic Inquiry* (Melbourne, 1965) II, esp. pp. 549–50, I, 96. This difficulty is greatest in the 'other industry' category.

5 Boisguilbert and eighteenth-century economics

Introduction

Boisguilbert is now very much a neglected economist, particularly in the English speaking world. None of his economic work has so far been translated into English and many general histories of economics pass his work silently by. Only more specialist English histories seem to mention him as an important seventeenth-century economic writer (for example, Hébert, 1987, pp. 187–91; Hutchison, 1988, pp. 107–15). In the nineteenth century, Marx (1859, pp. 54–5) described Boisguilbert together with Sir William Petty as one of the founders of classical political economy, but his assessments of Boisguilbert as an economic writer are largely confined to this work and are not included, for example, in his *Theories of Surplus Value* (for a discussion, see Groenewegen, 1987, pp. 28–30). The definitive edition of Boisguilbert's economic contributions published by the Institut National d'Etudes Démographiques (Boisguilbert, 1966) is, in the spirit of Marx, appropriately subtitled 'La Naissance de l'Economie Politique', but this claim, generally speaking, would be regarded in many Anglo-Saxon circles as typical French nationalistic bombast. An American scholar (Hazel Van Dyke Roberts, 1935) pioneered English work on Boisguilbert during the twentieth century, for which she was honoured at an international symposium on Boisguilbert in 1975 (Hecht, 1989). Since Van Dyke Roberts' pioneering study, detailed work on Boisguilbert has appeared in Nagels (1970), Spengler (1984) and Faccarello (1986) to name the more important work not yet mentioned.

This introduction to the facsimile reproduction of Boisguilbert's first important economic text, *Le Détail de la France sous le Règne de Louis XIV*, focuses on the century when Boisguilbert's work was most influential. It does so in three main sections. The first examines Boisguilbert's influence on British thought, with special reference to Mandeville, Cantillon and Smith. The second looks briefly at Boisguilbert's impact on French thought, with special references to the physiocrats; while the third section looks at his influence on the Tuscan, Neapolitan and Milanese schools of political economy in Italy. A final section offers some brief conclusions from this discussion in the context of assessing Boisguilbert's place in the history of economic thought.

The previous paragraph should not be taken to imply that Boisguilbert's influence did not extend beyond these major countries in which political economy flourished during the eighteenth century. There seems to be good reason to believe that he may have exerted some influence on Polish economists during the eighteenth century (Lipinski, 1989, pp. 245–64), a not surprising situation given that French influence on that eighteenth-century central European kingdom was particularly great. He is also said to have influenced the German economic writer Ernst Ludwig Carl (Hecht, 1989, pp. 455–6; Hutchison, 1988, p. 151). However, the spread of Boisguilbert's work to even these parts of Europe further emphasises the validity of associating Boisguilbert's writings with the birth of classical political economy in Europe in the late seventeenth century.

Boisguilbert and British political economy

The impact Boisguilbert's economic writings made on British economics during the eighteenth century is not easy to assess. Much of this type of assessment depends on circumstantial evidence. Earlier literature has suggested the possibility of Boisguilbert's influence on Mandeville, on Cantillon (Hecht, 1966, p. 520; Groenewegen, 1994, pp. 18–19) and on Smith (Van Dyke Roberts, 1935, chs XVI, XVII). It is to these three authors that this section is largely devoted after commenting briefly on the association between De Souligné's (1697) pamphlet, *The Desolation of France Demonstrated* and Boisguilbert's *Détail*. Even the last is doubtful (Hecht, 1966, p. 571) since De Souligné (1697) differs in important respects from Boisguilbert's views on population, for example. It also fails to raise underconsumption issues, though it is possible that its chapter 4 on destruction of the French capital stock and chapter 6 on taxation may have owed something to Boisguilbert's work which, however, is not cited (cf. Hutchison, 1988, p. 392 n5).

By the end of the 1720s, Boisguilbert's writings on economics were, however, not scarce. They had been reprinted in various collected editions in 1707. This included one edition published under the misleading title *Testament Politique de Monsieur Vauban*, an edition reissued in 1708 and again in 1712. Other collected editions appeared in 1712 and 1716. As Van Dyke Roberts (1935, p. 100 n6) indicates, these numerous editions over a period of ten years indicate that Boisguilbert's writings must have been widely read at this time by a variety of people. However, the fact that the collected works were either published without the author's name, or, in three cases, sheltered under the name of Boisguilbert's more illustrious contemporary, marshall Vauban, makes identification of subsequent references to them even more difficult than it would be in any case, given the slender proclivities to acknowledging work by others in the literature of the time (Van Dyke Roberts, 1935, p. 323).

Whether Mandeville was influenced by aspects of Boisguilbert's work is difficult to say. Boisguilbert is twice cited in Kaye's (1924, pp. c, cii–ciii) introduction to Mandeville's *Fable of the Bees* in the context of free trade and on the influence of self interest on social harmony. As Kaye (1924, pp. vii–viii, ciii) explicitly warns, these cannot be taken as influence, particularly the last, since 'Boisguilbert is comparatively halfhearted [on this point] … nor does he work out the details of this harmony as Mandeville does'. Later, and under the general *caveat* that such citations do not constitute reasons for suspecting influence, Kaye (1924, pp. 110n, 152n) cites Boisguilbert on his definition of wealth which disassociates it from bullion, and on his use of a remark by Seneca on wealth also mentioned by Mandeville.

The potential link between Boisguilbert and Mandeville, and reasons for the way in which their thought has been related, lie probably in two shared influences on their thought, particularly on the point about the impact of self interest and self love on social harmony. These influences came from the Jansenist theologians and moral philosophers Nicole and Domat, and were not only exerted on Mandeville (see Viner 1953, pp. 180–1, 185; 1978, p. 136 n31) but also on Boisguilbert (Faccarello 1986; Hutchison, 1988, pp. 107, 111–13), who had come under Jansenist influence at an early stage during his education. Boisguilbert's argument on the providential role of competition in securing social harmony, a viewpoint which particularly links his work with Mandeville and with Smith (on which, see below) may have its roots in a common ancestry of seventeenth-century theological thought. However, the possibility that Mandeville may have studied Boisguilbert's works at some time during the period before 1714 when the first edition of his *Fable of the Bees* appeared as a commentary on his 1705 poem about the 'grumbling hive', cannot be eliminated, particularly since these were the years when Boisguilbert's works were in the public eye, as evidenced by their fairly frequent reprinting.

The possibility of influence by Boisguilbert on Cantillon's *Essai* is more easy to document. Spengler (1954, p. 285 n16) indicates that Cantillon had cited Boisguilbert's 'Etat de la France' rather than that by Boulainvilliers as Higgs had surmised in his edition of the *Essai* (for details see Groenewegen, 1994, pp. 17–18, n8). Given the fact that from 1714 to 1717 Cantillon was living in Paris in his position as banker, and that in 1708 he had taken out French nationality there, he was, as it were, on the spot for purchasing a copy of Boisguilbert's works which were so frequently reissued over these years. The last surmise would explain obvious similarities in their work, as in their definition of wealth, their views on the limitations of the quantity theory, and even their greater emphasis on the dual of market price and 'intrinsic' value based on cost of production. Cantillon could more easily have obtained the last from Boisguilbert's work than from that of Petty, its other potential source (cf. Van Dyke Roberts, 1935, pp. 245–6 n9). In addition, the emphasis on landlords and their social importance as trendsetters in consumption, particularly in the court circles of the capital (cf. Hutchison, 1988, p. 114) and most importantly, the concept of a circular flow between town and country, agriculture and manufactures, which plays such an interesting role in the second part of Cantillon's *Essai*, may easily have obtained their initial inspiration from Boisguilbert's writings which linked both monetary and commodity circulation to prosperous and to depressed conditions. In fact, Boisguilbert's work is almost certainly the inspiration for the great emphasis on circulation in French economic writing of the first half of the eighteenth century, including the very influential works of Melon and Du Tot (see Groenewegen, 1994, pp. 21–3). None of this speculation detracts in any way from Cantillon's originality; it merely enhances his great reputation for adapting in a critical and constructive way the best of the economic thought available to him, and thereby constructing a new system on the basis of the old.

A similar conclusion can be advanced with respect to the claims that have been made on the likelihood of Boisguilbert's influence on Adam Smith (Van Dyke Roberts, 1935; cf. Spengler 1984, p. 69). No copy of Boisguilbert's works has as yet been placed in Smith's library, but the circumstantial evidence is strong that Smith may have used Boisguilbert's writings among his hundreds of sources for the *Wealth of Nations*. The reader wishing to investigate this claim in detail should carefully study Van Dyke Roberts' book, not only in the two chapters largely devoted to this quest, but also on the many occasions in the text elsewhere where such comparisons are made (for example, Van Dyke Roberts, 1935, pp. 105 n13, 135 n31, 149, n3, on the canons of taxation; and especially p. 132 n23 on their joint use of the 'happiness of the climate' in a similar context). Particularly striking is a long opening paragraph of Smith's chapter on the physiocrats (Smith, 1976, Ivix3, pp. 663–4). It discusses the problems of Colbertism as a fundamental reason for the creation of an 'agricltural system' of economics in France, especially via the 'discouragement and depression' Colbertism had induced in French agriculture in 'more or less every part of the country'. It then mentions 'many different inquiries [which] were set on foot concerning the causes of it [the decline of agriculture]'. Van Dyke Roberts (1935, p. 172; cf. p. 321) treats this last remark almost as if it could only refer to Boisguilbert and Vauban (a person, incidentally, to whom Smith also makes no reference and whose work on economics was not in his library). Given its position in the book, it could of course equally well refer to the inquiries by Quesnay and his followers who, after all, were the main subject of this chapter.

Be that as it may. Although influence of Boisguilbert's work cannot be ruled out in England without very detailed study, it is interesting to note that the only British author for which direct evidence of influence exists by way of citation is an Irish economist who became a French citizen and who probably wrote his major treatise in the language of his adopted country. This comparative neglect fits in well with the general neglect Boisguilbert has suffered in Anglo-Saxon hands in later years (he is, for example, not mentioned among the literature of political economy in McCulloch [1845]), perhaps to be blamed as much on the anonymity of his work as on what, by the nineteenth century, must have been its comparative scarcity. However, those familiar with French eighteenth-century writings could have no such excuse, since Boisguilbert was recognised in his own country as a considerable prophet, even if such praise was largely confined to those who shared the essentials of his views.

Boisguilbert and French political economy

In his *Siècle de Louis XIV*, Voltaire mentions Boisguilbert briefly as the author of *Le Détail de la France*, acknowledging both its 1695 edition and 1707 version as part of the works. Voltaire claims Boisguilbert to be in error when stating that France had been in continual decay since 1660 and that, consequently, its national stock had been diminished over that period by no less than 1,500 million livres. Just as in England when at its most flourishing, hundreds of broadsheets are published to proclaim its ruin, Voltaire continued, Boisguilbert's account of the state of France during Louis XIV's reign must be held to be false if not entirely untrue (Voltaire, 1910, pp. 590–1). Much to Van Dyke Roberts' annoyance (1935, pp. 93–4), Voltaire failed to include Boisguilbert among the great writers of the time and ultimately spoke favourably of him only once in his voluminous writings (Hecht 1966, pp. 575–6). However, Voltaire's inclusion of *Le Détail de la France* at the start of the chapter on finance and regulations, a chapter which has been described as a eulogy of Colbert, can also be seen as a tribute to the importance of Boisguilbert as a courageous economic writer in the sense that his contribution just cannot be ignored in a history of the reign of Louis XIV. It was of course as courageous reformer that Boisguilbert was in fact recognised by many in eighteenth-century France, especially in those circles which also appreciated the profundity of his economic reasoning.

Spengler (1984, esp. pp. 72, 82–4, 85–7) has placed Boisguilbert's work within the context of some of the other reformers in France at the turn of the century, that is, Vauban, Fénelon, Boulainvilliers and l'Abbé de Saint-Pierre. Among other things, Spengler (1984, p. 79) concluded from this comparison that unlike the case of Boisguilbert, these French writers 'anticipated few if any analytical concepts'. It may, however, be noted here that Vauban (1707, p. 3) in his preface (apparently already in draft by 1698 according to Hecht, 1966, p. 574) suggested that his diagnoses on taxation 'perfectly corresponded with what had been written about them by the author of *Le Détail de la France*', a tribute which may have inspired the printing of Boisguilbert's works under the title of *Political Testament of Vauban* either by himself or, more likely, by some of his publishers. The many readers of Vauban's *Dîme Royale* would therefore have had their attention drawn to the existence of similar opinions and facts in the work of a contemporary author. However, Boisguilbert disagreed with Vauban's solution to the problems (see Van Dyke Roberts, 1935, p. 35, n9) just as Vauban (1707, pp. 3–4) had disagreed with aspects of Boisguilbert's treatment of the topic. Nevertheless Vauban's admiration for Boisguilbert's work was so great that he strongly expressed the desire to meet him personally, a matter apparently arranged on more than one occasion. It seems therefore just to speak of Boisguilbert's considerable influence on Vauban (see Van Dyke Roberts, pp. 53–4, n38, 109).

Given the previous remarks in the context of Boisguilbert's influence on Cantillon on the importance of circulation in Boisguilbert's system, it seems useful to comment on Boisguilbert's possible impact on Melon in this regard. Apart from some brief remarks, Spengler (1984, pp. 70–1, n5) left this subject alone, perhaps largely because on this matter Law's financial system and its effects were more important as influences on Melon than Boisguilbert's work. Melon did not cite Boisguilbert in his work. However, he did mention Vauban's *Dîme Royale* on several occasions (Melon, 1734, pp. 814, 821, 824, 932) and also, perhaps even more interestingly in the context of what was said on Mandeville, made reference to the Jansenist moral philosopher and theologian Nicole (Melon, 1734, p. 821). There are a number of passages which recall some of Boisguilbert's arguments. These deal with taxation, including an interesting remark on the impact of the *aides* on the prosperity of the wine industry (Melon, 1734, pp. 741, 827), on wealth (pp. 711, 801); on commerce as the exchange of superfluities (pp. 709–10); on aspects of the grain trade including the price pattern of grain in the context of abundant harvests and harvest failure (ch. II); on some historical material on France's national debt (pp. 773–4, n1) and, most interestingly, on a number of aspects in connection with circulation. Melon (1734, p. 802) drew attention to circulation and its necessary interconnection with consumption; mentioned lack of appropriate circulation as the cause of agricultural depression (p. 805) while, more generally, the association between spending and good circulation and prosperity is illustrated by way of examples, some of which relate to Rouen, Boisguilbert's home province (pp. 818–19). Melon's references to circulation just mentioned link the concept more to Boisguilbert's concerns than to those of Law, which guide the greater part of Melon's discussion on the subject. This, together with the accessibility of Boisguilbert's works in the early part of the century, make it difficult to believe that Melon did not study the work of this predecessor, particularly given the praise it was accorded by Vauban's *Dîme Royale*, which Melon did cite on various occasions.

Another pre-physiocratic author who should be mentioned is Claude-Jacques Herbert, whose *Essai sur la Police Générale des Grains* had appeared in 1753. This cited Boisguilbert's *Le Détail de la France* on the fact that its author, sixty years previously, had advanced the proposition that the more grain is sold abroad, the more secure are the national harvests (Herbert, 1755, p. 42, n1; cf. preface pp. v–vi). This reference is important because it shows that in some circles neither the name of Boisguilbert nor his writings were forgotten; and its seems likely that Herbert's work, which was widely known to the physiocrats, including Quesnay, and to the school of Gournay (cf. Turgot 1759, p. 29)[1] induced the laudatory recognition as an important precursor given to Boisguilbert by the physiocrats including Mirabeau and Du Pont.

Before dealing with these eulogies of Boisguilbert by physiocracy's most ardent apostles, some reference needs to be made to Quesnay's acknowledgments of Boisguilbert's work. The first of these occurs in the third edition of the *Tableau Economique* of 1759, in a note on its maxim XXIV of the general maxims for the good government of an agricultural kingdom, a note subsequently reproduced with the version of the maxims printed by Du Pont in his

Physiocratie, that is, the collected economic essays by Quesnay. This mentioned Boisguilbert's *Le Détail de la France* in the context of what by then had become maxim XXVI, the maxim which admonished rulers to be more attentive to the revenue of the soil than to increasing the population, since the first will ensure the second (Quesnay, 1767, p. 956). The note attached thereto mentioned that Boisguilbert had correctly recognised this proposition during the 1690s, and that he had equally correctly ascribed the halving of French agricultural incomes between 1660 and 1699 to the incorrect imposition of taxes, particularly the taille (Quesnay, 1767, p. 976). In a manuscript note to Mirabeau's *Théorie de l'Impôt* a year later (1760), Quesnay suggested to Mirabeau that he give clear recognition to Boisguilbert, together with Vauban and Fénelon, as meritorious precursors of physiocratic tax policy and who, for their contribution, deserved due recognition by the nation (cited by Hecht, 1966, p. 565). Quesnay therefore seems to have recognised Boisguilbert as an important precursor, especially on taxation. However, it seems doubtful that he was strongly influenced by Boisguilbert's works in the construction of his own system, unless it can be shown that he had studied them in the years before 1756 when he started publishing on economics.

It seems that Turgot never cited Boisguilbert in his writings; however, his library contained no less than three editions of the *Testament Politique de Vauban* as well as a 1707 edition of Boisguilbert's works (Tsuda, 1974, items 600, 1948, 1672, 1673). It will be recalled that all of these were anonymous, so that this lack of recognition may have been from ignorance rather than deliberate.

Turgot's silence on Boisguilbert is all the more surprising given the praise bestowed on Boisguilbert's *Le Détail de la France* by Du Pont de Nemours in 1769. However, this had not been done in Du Pont's initial essay on the writings which had contributed to the science of political economy in France, in which he had omitted Boisguilbert's name, but in his final article on the topic. Correction of the earlier omission was probably due to Mirabeau. Du Pont's eulogy is quoted in full from the English translation by Van Dyke Roberts (1935, p. 324) because it so neatly sums up the qualified veneration with which the physiocrats looked on Boisguilbert:

> We just now recall a book that it is indeed astonishing that we should have forgotten, as it is one of the first that we have read and as we possess two copies of it. This book is *Le Détail de la France*, by M. Pierre le Pesant, Seigneur de Bois-Guilbert, attorney general of the Court of Aides in Normandy. This work, of which the title it is true, is not very clear, and of which the reading is a little fatiguing because the style is incorrect and diffuse, is, nevertheless, singularly precious on account of the sagacity with which the author understood all that of which the world in his time was ignorant: The necessity to respect the advances of useful labor, *and the advantages of liberty of commerce*. If he had seen that land and waters were the sole sources from which the labor of man can obtain wealth, and that labor of conservation, of manufacture, of exchange, etc., that have been

> quite improperly confounded under the generic term of industrial labor, did nothing except to exert itself on wealth already produced without adding anything thereupon; if he had recognised the existence of the net product, and distinguished it from the costs of reproduction; if he had combined these truths with the others that he senses, the honor of originating the principles of economic science would be due him.
>
> (Du Pont de Nemours, *Notice Abrégé*, 1769, cited by Van Dyke Roberts, 1935, p. 324)

Aspects of the physiocratic praise of Boisguilbert suggest that Boisguilbert's work had to be rediscovered during the late 1750s and 1760s. Hecht (1966, p. 554) surmises that Quesnay first drew Mirabeau's attention to Boisguilbert's work, an opinion which is supported by the manuscript note Quesnay had written on Mirabeau's *Théorie de l'Impôt*, as mentioned previously. Mirabeau first mentioned Boisguilbert in some explanations to the *Tableau Economique* included in the second edition of *l'Ami des Hommes* in 1760, that is, it will be recalled, after Quesnay had done so in his note to maxim XXIV appended to the third edition of the *Tableau* in 1759. It will also be recalled that Mirabeau alerted Du Pont de Nemours to his omission of Boisguilbert in his original review of French economic thought, an omission subsequently handsomely repaired. In his *Eloge Funèbre de M. François Quesnay* (Mirabeau, 1775, esp. p. 10) further attention is drawn to Boisguilbert's work, as was done in his earlier *Extraits des Eloges des Hommes à Célebrer* (Mirabeau, 1774, p. 59). A manuscript, *Elogue Historique de Vauban*, dated 1772 and preserved in the French National Archives, declared Mirabeau's intention to honour Boisguilbert as the author of *Le Détail de la France*, an intention only fulfilled in an unpublished letter by Mirabeau to the Italian Longo in September 1775. Its handsome praise of Boisguilbert can be quoted in full:

> The *Détail de la France* of Boisguilbert is a very good and noble piece; it is the true and sole precursor of the Economists [that is, physiocrats]. It only lacks [the concept of] the net product, [a discovery] reserved for the doctor [that is, Quesnay] and such a construction [without the net product] effectively throws things into disorder. That set aside, you have to admire the stamp of genius and the mind of the author.
>
> (Mirabeau, 1775, cited in Hecht, 1966, p. 555)

Hecht (1966) lists a number of other eighteenth-century French books which cited or were influenced by Boisguilbert's writings. The more important among these were by (Dutchman) Isaac de Pinto (Hecht, 1966, p. 561) and by Du Tot (Hecht, 1966, pp. 530–1), because Forbonnais, the most famous French economic writer from among this group, only mentioned Boisguilbert's work to criticise it, though he conceded it had a degree of merit (Hecht, 1966, p. 533). In short, Boisguilbert's works received considerable attention and recognition in France during the eighteenth century, even if it was not always flattering. Not surprisingly, those associated with the physiocrats praised him most. It is likely, however, that this recognition would have been much greater had his works not been published anonymously or, perhaps even more confusing, seemingly under the prominent name of marshall Vauban.

Boisguilbert and Italian political economy

Hecht (1966, pp. 511, 559) mentions two Italian economists of the eighteenth century who were influenced to a considerable extent by Boisguilbert's writings. The first was a Florentine archbishop, Bandini, whose *Discorso Economico* was posthumously published in 1775, having been written in 1737. It drew extensively on the fiscal reform measures of both Boisguilbert and Vauban, often reproducing large parts of their works verbatim. However, unlike Boisguilbert, Bandini was not a committed free trader. He wished to preserve a system of import duties, and, perhaps more significantly, was not quite sufficiently liberated from a fear of dearth to follow Boisguilbert's policy of unrestricted exports of grain as the best way of securing adequate grain supplies for the nation. The second author, Pascoli (Hecht, 1966, p. 559), another Tuscan economic writer hailing from Florence and writing in the 1730s, published his *Testamento Pubblico* in 1733. This also drew heavily on Boisguilbert's writings; even its title owes something to the one under which some of Boisguilbert's works were later published, though again, he departed from Boisguilbert's policies in various ways. Free grain exports were to be restricted when grain shortages were feared, trade barriers were only to be removed domestically while, more generally, trading policies were to be regulated on mercantilist lines less liberal than those which were developing in England at this time. Despite these lapses from Boisguilbert's views on what might be regarded as crucial points, Cossa (1893, pp. 214–16) described the work of these authors as that of Boisguilbert's 'school', and argued that this had greater influence in Italy than was exerted by the followers of Melon. Some of this carried over into the writings of Italian economists associated with the Neapolitan and Milanese schools.

Two authors from the Neapolitan school who have been linked with Boisguilbert can be mentioned first. Genovesi[2] mentioned *Le Détail de la France* on three occasions in a free translation of John Cary's *Discourse*, which was published in Naples in 1758 under the title *Storia del Commercio Della Gran Brettagna*. The first refers the reader to 'un libro eccelente, *Détail de la France*' (Genovesi, 1757–8, I, p. 294); the second mentions Boisguilbert's *Détail* among a number of other worthwhile books on the regulation of the grain trade, and the third refers to him on the deleterious effects of the arbitrary taille (Genovesi, 1757–8, I, pp. 382, 455, n13). Genovesi subsequently introduced a translation of Herbert (1753) in which the praise of Boisguilbert by the French author (and mentioned in the previous section) was left fully in the Italian version. Cossa (1893, p. 214) takes this as further evidence of the influence of the Boisguilbert school in Italy, since he appears to have counted Herbert as a bearer of that tradition.

The second famous member of the Neapolitan school of economics of relevance here is Galiani. Foley (1973, p. 141) appears to hint at a connection between Boisguilbert's metaphor on the flow of money in the economy in terms of the flow of a river through reservoirs and lakes on its way to the sea (Boisguilbert, 1966, pp. 869–71) and Galiani's rather similar metaphor in *Della Moneta* (Galiani, 1751, p. 55). However, *Della Moneta* made no direct reference to Boisguilbert's writings, but did rather frequently mention the work of l'Abbé de Saint-Pierre and other French writers on money and banking. It can, of course, not be ruled out that Galiani consulted Boisguilbert's works, some of which are largely devoted to monetary topics. More interesting is the possible indirect reference to Boisguilbert in Galiani's subsequent dialogues on the grain trade. From its fifth dialogue onwards, Galiani augmented the three original discussants by a fourth, described as 'M. le Président de *** P du P de B' (Galiani, 1770, p. 62). It would be too much of a coincidence that this belated entrant to the debate on the grain trade described by Galiani is not intended to refer to Boisguilbert. After all, Boisguilbert's full name was Pierre le Pesant, Sieur de Boisguilbert, and at one time he was a président du magistrature in his district of Rouen. When some of the phrases Galiani puts into the mouth of M. le Président are examined, it is easy to show that they match many of the views of Boisguilbert.[3] In this context it may be noted that Friedrich Melchior Grimm, an associate of Galiani and enemy of the physiocrats, had corresponded with Diderot on Boisguilbert (Hecht, 1989, pp. 466–7) and may in fact have suggested to Galiani to incorporate Boisguilbert into the dialogue in this way.

Boisguilbert's work was also known to the Milanese school of economists. For Pietro Verri, this was in the context of the grain trade. In his *Riflessioni sulle Legge Vincolante Principalmente nel Commercio de' Grani*, written in 1769 but not published until 1797, Verri cited 'marshall Vauban, in his Political Testament, printed in 1708' on the usefulness of permitting grain exports freely and on the risks to the lives of the poor from grain prices which are too low (Verri, 1769, pp. 301–2). Subsequently, Verri (1769, p. 306) cited the author of *Détail de la France*, printed at Rouen in 1696, on the benefits to grain cultivation and viniculture from free exports of agricultural produce.

The confusion between Vauban and Boisguilbert arising from the strategy to publish Boisguilbert's works under the title of Vauban's political testament, so evident in Verri (1769), is also visible in Beccaria's writing. In Beccaria's *Prolusione del 1769*, the inaugural lecture he gave when taking up the new chair of public economy at Milan, Beccaria praised marshall Vauban. His precise words appear to indicate that he was thinking of more than the author of just *Dîme Royale* and was including the writings published subsequently as Vauban's *Political Testament*, to enable him to reach the judgment that Vauban was the founder of French economics, an opinion for which later he was severely taken to task by Du Pont de Nemours.[4] No specific references to Boisguilbert or his work can be found in Beccaria's writings, but it seems likely that in a way similar to that of his friend Verri, he knew the significance of Boisguilbert's contribution from the writings disguised as the work of the famous marshall Vauban.

It is very likely that greater knowledge of the Italian eighteenth-century economic literature than I have will disclose more references to or acknowledgments of Boisguilbert's work. Enough has been said in this section to indicate the extent of that recognition by some of the more famous names of the time. His influence on Tuscan economics in the 1730s was undoubtedly the greatest (see also Acquaviva, 1984, pp. 74n, 105–6 n150), but his importance, particularly as a founder and continuing authority on certain economic questions, was also recognised in Naples and Milan. If my hypothesis about Galiani's *Dialogues* on the grain trade is correct, then his importance in late eighteenth-century debate appears to have been even greater, though it should be mentioned here that the context was France rather than Italy. The Italian examples studied also most strikingly reveal the difficulty of assessing the recognition given to Boisguilbert during the century from the anonymity under which his works were published, and worse, from the confusion their publication caused when presented as the political testament of Vauban.

Conclusions

The above survey of the recognition accorded to Boisguilbert by writers on economics in England, France and Italy reveals a mixed picture. Influence from Boisguilbert's writings, in the fuller sense of the word, was probably only exerted during the first half of the eighteenth century. This is most clearly illustrated in the context of the Tuscan writers, but more importantly, by their potential impact on a writer like Melon, and, most significantly, Cantillon. It is particularly interesting that the only demonstrable influence on a writer of British (Irish) extraction was on one long resident in France. Subsequently, from the 1750s onwards, Boisguilbert was recognised as an important precursor in the emerging science of political economy, partly on agricultural policy and on the grain trade, partly on tax reform, a recognition accorded to him strongly by obvious sympathisers such as the leading physiocrats and earlier, Herbert, but also by their critics such as Forbonnais and, probably, Galiani. Although therefore confined to the earlier part of the century, the influence was not negligible, particularly since it involved such an influential and widely read economist during the second half of the eighteenth century as Cantillon was. Moreover, his influence on Mandeville, an equally widely read author, remains possible.

Spengler (1984) has depicted Boisguilbert partly as an important concept builder, and it is for this in particular that his influence has been important. In his diffuse writings he tossed out many ideas on a wide variety of issues, in a manner not unlike Sir William Petty, and often these were capable of development by later sympathetic and more systematic authors. Perhaps most important for the subsequent development of economic theory are his stress on the importance of circulation, on the impact on economic activity of disturbances in the relationship between market prices and prices based on costs of production (something from which Quesnay particularly may have learned much if he had studied Boisguilbert's works early enough) and on the possibility of deficient demand through maldistribution of income and interruptions to the circular flow such as hoarding. However, especially in France and Italy, and perhaps even in England, he was largely recalled as a major reformer of France's iniquitous, inefficient and ineffective tax system, a proposer of improved agricultural policy, particularly with reference to the impact on rural prosperity of free trade on agricultural produce, including corn. It was for matters like this that the physiocrats were to praise him, and that even Voltaire was ultimately willing to assign him some grudging praise amidst heaps of criticism. Only in the nineteenth century did he come to be seen as a major French liberal precursor of laissez-faire and a staunch anti-mercantilist.

The excessive praise bestowed on Boisguilbert by the physiocrats may in fact be one reason why Boisguilbert's economics fell so quickly into oblivion. It either came to be looked on as something equally in error on agricultural policy or as equally praiseworthy for its liberal and anti-Colbertist views. However, as Hecht (1966) abundantly shows, in France his works continued to be studied by historians and a wider perception of its importance sometimes appeared. In addition, as this survey equally abundantly demonstrates, anonymity and the appearance of his works as the political testament of Vauban also made him a mysterious figure only known or recognised by a few. Even his first work, here reprinted in its 1697 edition, has no name on the title page, hence facilitating the many references to the author of *Le Détail de la France*. That this was unjust, even if understandable, has also been clearly indicated.

The potential influence of the rich content of Boisguilbert's works made Marx's verdict quite correct when describing him, together with Sir William Petty, as one of the founders of classical political economy. Understanding the full significance of Marx's judgement, however, requires further work, particularly through closer study of Boisguilbert's impact on Cantillon and, potentially, that on Mandeville, Melon, Galiani or even on Adam Smith. Boisguilbert is therefore a major figure intimately involved in the birth of economics because, on the evidence, his impact during its formative period was never negligible. Voltaire was doubly wrong when saying that 'if one was guided by Boisguilbert's beautiful systems, the kingdom [also of ideas] would be as impoverished and mean-spirited as Boisguilbert himself was' (cited in Hecht, 1966, p. 576). The last word can be given to an anonymous owner of the 1707 edition of Bolisguilbert's *Le Detail de la France*, now in the collection of Arnold Heertje, who noted in this copy: 'par Boisguillbert, le Christoph Colomb du monde économique'.

Notes

1 One of whom, Cliquot de Blervache, in *Le Réformateur*, apparently also praised Boisguilbert's work in the 1750s (see Van Dyke Roberts, 1935, p. 167), but this authorship attribution is apparently false (Hecht, 1966, p. 510).

2 I owe these references to Genovesi's comments on Boisguilbert to Paul Augimeri.

3 For example, Galiani (1770, pp. 69–70) on the merits and bliss of agricultural life; p. 87 on trade as the exchange of superfluities; p. 90 on taxes and the problem of their imposition; pp. 92–3, 105, on the impact of free trade in grain on increasing cultivation, and hence its description as a means to that end; p. 97, on the importance of a corn surplus for the trade, wealth and happiness of France; and so on. The parallels are very striking.

4 In the *Ephémérides*, 1769. Recall, however, that Du Pont himself was criticised by Mirabeau for failing to recognise satisfactorily the great merits of Boisguilbert, an ironic outcome given Beccaria's likely confusion between Boisguilbert and Vauban.

References

Acquaviva, Daniela Parisi (1984) *Il Pensiero Economico Classico in Italia (1750–1860)*, Milan: Università Cattolica.

Beccaria, Cesare (1769) 'Prolusione del 1769', in *Opere*, Vol. 1, ed. Sergio Romagnoli, Florence: Sansoni, 365–77.

Boisguilbert, Pierre de (1966) *Pierre de Boisguilbert ou la Naissance de l'Economie politique*, Paris: Institut National d'Etudes Démographiques.

Cossa, Luigi (1893) *An Introduction to the Study of Political Economy*, London: Macmillan.

De Souligné (1697) *The Desolation of France Demonstrated*, London: John Salsbury.

Faccarello, Gilbert (1986) *Aux Origines de l'Economie Politique Libéral: Pierre de Boisguilbert*, Paris: Editions Anthropos.

Foley, V. (1973) 'An Origin of the *Tableau Economique*', *History of Political Economy*, 5(1) 121–50.

Galiani, Ferdinando (1751) *Della Moneta*, reissued Milan: Feltrinelli (1963).

——(1770) *Dialogues sur les Commerce des Blés*, in *Mélanges d'Economie Politique*, vol. 2, ed. G. de Molinari, Paris: Guillaumin (1848) 7–202.

Genovesi, Antonio (1757–58) *Storia del Commercio della Gran Brettagna, Scritta da John Cary*, in M. L. Perna (ed.) (1983) *Antonio Genovesi, Scritti Economici*, 2 vols, Naples: Istituto Italiano per gli studi Filosofici.

Groenewegen, P. D.(1987) 'Marx's Conception of Classical Political Economy: An Evaluation', *Political Economy: Studies in the Surplus Approach*, 3 (1) 19–35.

——(1994) 'La "French Connection": Influences Françaises sur l'Economie Britannique', *Dix-Huitième Siècle*, no. 26, 15–36 (below, Chapter 6).

Hébert, Robert F. (1987) 'In Search of Economic Order: French Predecessors of Adam Smith', in S. Todd Lowry (ed.) *Pre-Classical Economic Thought*, Boston MA: Kluwer Academic, 185–211.

Hecht, Jacqueline (1966) 'Bibliographique Commentée', in Boisguilbert, Pierre de, *Pierre de Boisguilbert ou la Naissance de l'Economie Politique*, Paris: Institut National d'Etudes Démographiques, 507–79.

Hecht, Jacqueline (ed.) (1989) *Boisguilbert Parmi Nous*, Paris: Institut National d'Etudes Démographiques.

Herbert, Claude-Jacques (1755) *Essai sur la Police Générale des Grains*, ed. Edgard Dépitre, Paris: Paul Geuthner (1910).

Hutchison, T. W. (1988) *Before Adam Smith*, Oxford: Blackwell.

Kaye, F. B. (ed.) (1924) *The Fable of the Bees*, Oxford: Clarendon Press.

Lipinski, Edward (1989) 'Boisguilbert et la Pensée Economique Polonaise', in Hecht, Jacqueline (ed.) *Boisguilbert Parmi Nous*, Paris: Institut National d'Etudes Démographiques, 245–64.

McCulloch, J. R. (1845) *The Literature of Political Economy*, London: Longman, Brown, Green and Longmans.

Marx, K. H. (1859) *A Contribution to the Critique of Political Economy*, trans. N. I. Stone, Chicago: Charles H. Kenn (1913).

Melon, Jean-François (1734) *Essai Politique sur le Commerce*, in E. Daire (ed.) (1843) *Economistes-Financiers du XVIIIe Siècle*, Paris: Guillaumin, 707–836.

Mirabeau, Victor Riqueti, Marquis de (1774) *Extraits des Hommes à Celebrer*, Stockholm: H. Fougt, reprinted facsimile in Hecht, Jacqueline (ed.) (1989) *Boisguilbert Parmi Nous*, Paris: Institut National d'Etudes Démographiques, 380–440.

——(1775) *Eloge Funèbre de M. François Quesnay*, in August Oncken (ed.) (n.d.) *Oeuvres Economiques et Philosophiques de François Quesnay*, reissued New York: Burt Franklin, 3–14.

Nagels, Jacques (1970) *Reproduction du Capital selon Karl Marx, Boisguilbert, Quesnay, Leontiev*, Brussels: Université Libre, Institut de Sociologie.

Quesnay, François (1767) 'Maximes Générales du Gouvernement Economique d'un Royaume Agricole', in *François Quesnay et la Physiocratie*, Paris: Institut National d'Etudes Démographiques (1958) 949–76.

Seligman, E. R. A. (1930) 'Boisguilbert, Pierre le Pesant, Sieur de (1646–1714)', in E. R. A. Seligman (ed.) *Encyclopaedia of the Social Sciences*, vol. 2, New York: Macmillan, 619–20.

Smith, Adam (1976) *An Inquiry into the Nature and Causes of the Wealth of Nations*, eds R. H. Campbell and A. S. Skinner, Oxford: Clarendon Press.

Spengler, J. (1954) 'Richard Cantillon: First of the Moderns', *Journal of Political Economy*, 62, 281–95, 406–24.

Spengler, J. J. (1984) 'Boisguilbert's Economic Views *vis-à-vis* those of Contemporary *Réformateurs*', *History of Political Economy*, 16(1) spring, 69–88.

Tsuda, Takumi (1974) *Catalogue des Livres de la Bibliothèque de Turgot*, Tokyo: Institut d'Etudes Economiques, Hitotsubashi University.

Turgot, Anne Robert Jacques (1759) 'Eloge de Gournay', in P. D. Groenewegen (ed.) (1977) *The Economics of A. R. J. Turgot*, The Hague: Martinus Nijhoff, 20–42.

Van Dyke Roberts, Hazel (1935) *Boisguilbert: Economist of the Reign of Louis XIV*, New York: Columbia University Press.

Vauban, Sebastien le Prestre (1707) *Projet d'une Dîme Royale*, n.p.

Verri, Pietro (1769) 'Riflessioni sulle Legge Vincolante Principalmente nel Commercio de' Grani', in *Del Piacere e del Delore ed Altri Scritti*, Milan: Feltrinelli (1964) 265–408.

Viner, Jacob (1953) 'Introduction to Bernard Mandeville, A Letter to Dion', in Jacob Viner (1989) *Essays on the Intellectual History of Economics*, ed. Douglas A. Irwin, Princeton: Princeton University Press, 176–88.

——(1978) 'Religious Thought and Economic Society', eds Jacques Melitz and Donald Winch, *History of Political Economy*, 10(1) spring, 1–192.

Voltaire, François Arouet de (1910) *Siècle de Louis XIV*, Paris: Hachette.

6 The French connection

Some case studies of French influences on British economics in the eighteenth century

French contributions in the eighteenth century hold a unique place in the history of economics, in the sense that for substantial segments of that century they dominated thinking in the subject. Part of this dominance was associated with the Enlightenment, during which French thought reigned supreme over virtually every field of scientific endeavour. With special reference to economics, the leading position of French thought in the eighteenth century is explained by a number of factors. As shown by Hutchison,[1] part of the explanation lies in the relative decline in importance of English economics from the end of the seventeenth century, a position not recovered until almost a century after the Scottish ascendancy which began in the middle of the eighteenth century. More importantly, especially during the 1750s and 1760s, were the theoretical developments in French economics largely associated with physiocracy. These placed it in the forefront of economic theory over these two decades. The varying importance of French economics over the eighteenth century can be demonstrated statistically using data on the relative rate of publication and similar measures.[2] It can also be illustrated by using case studies of selected British writers, as a device for assessing the degree of French economic influence on such writers in greater depth. The last is the method adopted in this chapter to highlight the influence of French economics on the English-speaking writers in the eighteenth century.

The case studies have been selected to illustrate both the specific forms French influence took in the eighteenth century and the differing degrees of its importance. The first deals with Richard Cantillon, an economist of British birth but French nationality and writing on economics, probably in France and in French, in the late 1720s.[3] Cantillon's case is interesting since despite his undoubted French connections, the major influences on his economics are English, reflecting the dominance of English thinking at the time. However, the identifiable French influences on his work are intriguing. The second case study concerns David Hume, another writer with very good French connections, having spent his initial period as writer (1734–7) in France. Hume's economic essays, written approximately two decades after Cantillon's *Essai*, reflect the type of French economic influence existing at this time. His main period of residence in France, as secretary to the British Embassy in Paris (1763–6), during which he became personally acquainted with many of the leading contemporary French economists, was of course well after his economic writings had been completed,[4] and at best reveal a 'negative influence' in some of his correspondence. In his case, it is the French influences from the 1730s and 1740s and before, which are the focus of the discussion. The last case study involves Steuart and Smith, who started writing their respective treatises in the 1750s and 1760s, publishing them in the subsequent decade. Both spent significant periods in France prior to producing their major economic work. The controversial nature of the decidedly French influence on their work, exerted on both during the decades of prime importance of French economics in the development of the subject, make a particularly fitting finale to this chapter on French influence on British economics in the eighteenth century.

A methodological point should also be raised by way of introduction. This concerns what is meant by influence and the nature of the evidence deemed sufficient to suggest potential influence. Influence for this study entails the exerting of any effect on the writing of the person influenced, whether major or minor, on a point likely to have been absent without the influence in question. Influence is tested by either citation of the relevant work or, more circumstantially, by evidence that the author was in fact acquainted with the work from which influence on him is suspected. Such acquaintance may be the presence of the book in question in that person's library, or access to the relevant source in some other, clearly identifiable way. In short, influence by one author on another is ascribed by impact from an identifiable source with which the influenced author is demonstrably acquainted.

In what follows, the chapter is divided into four sections. The first three deal with the three case studies respectively, and a final section draws some general conclusions from the argument.

Cantillon and French economics

As has been frequently pointed out,[5] Cantillon's *Essai* drew systematically on a number of theoretical writings from the previous century, of which English seventeenth-century writers were by far the more important. From a theoretical perspective, as Aspromourgos[6] in particular has highlighted, much of Cantillon's analytical thrust derived from Petty, whose work was explicitly cited on no less than three occasions in Cantillon's *Essai*. Cantillon frequently critically analysed Petty's theoretical constructions, in order to either develop or reject them. Examples of the former are Cantillon's elaboration of Petty's analysis of velocity of circulation; of the latter, Cantillon's rejection of Petty's theory of the 'par'. Locke's economic writings are likewise used by Cantillon in a critical manner, while it was probably the statistical inquiries with special reference to demography and the social division of labour, in which Cantillon gained most from his access to work by Gregory King and Charles Davenant. In line with the relative paucity of English thinking on economics in the early decades of the eighteenth century, particularly when compared with the 'boom years' of the 1690s, the only English work from that century Cantillon cited is Sir Isaac Newton's 1717 report on the British Mint. John Law's work, not mentioned by Cantillon directly, for reasons explained by Antoin Murphy,[7] was clearly an important influence as well, particularly in a negative way with respect to Cantillon's account of banking and credit.

For an author who became French by choice and lived in France for a substantial part of his life, Cantillon also drew on the far smaller number of French authors then writing on the subject. Jean Boizard (died c. 1705) the monetary authority whose *Traité des Monnoies* went through several expanded editions (1692; 1711; 1714; 1723) at the turn of the seventeenth century, is cited on technical aspects of silver refining for monetary purposes. However, Boizard's work contains little of theoretical interest from which Cantillon could have gained. A more important reference is to Vauban's *Dîme Royale*, a work published in 1707, which obtained considerable fame for its proposals to reform national taxation. Cantillon criticised Vauban's tax proposals in passing, arguing proportional taxation of rent was fairer than Vauban's proposal for a royal tithe to be levied on all income. However, as Cantillon considered taxation to be outside his subject, his criticism of Vauban was not developed.

The final reference to a French author in Cantillon is both the most important and most intriguing. This is the reference to the author of an *Etat de la France*, who attributed the falls in the rents between 1660 and 1700 of vineyards near Mantes to 'defective consumption'. Again, Cantillon is critical of the author, suggesting the defective consumption can only be attributed to the scarcity of money in France, while the author as quoted by him suggests that the amount of silver money in this period had increased in France.[8]

Higgs attributed this *Etat de la France* to Boulainvilliers, thereby making him the author to whom Cantillon probably referred. Jacqueline Hecht, however, more correctly, argues that the type of argument to which Cantillon referred is more easily found in Boisguilbert's work, *Le Détail de la France*.[9] This is a 'State of France', to use the contemporary idiom, which covers the requisite period and, more importantly, frequently illustrates its argument by data drawn from vineyards in the election of Mantes. In addition, Boisguilbert was a noted early underconsumptionist. Hecht also points out that Cantillon may have learnt more from Boisguilbert's work than the remarks he chose to quote from the *Etat* suggest. In particular, Cantillon may have absorbed aspects of the notion of circulation which plays an important part in Boisguilbert's work, to develop them into a more sophisticated form.

There are many subjects on which Cantillon's knowledge of Boisguilbert's economics would have enriched his understanding of an economic system by supplementing what he had learned from British sources. The European, and more specifically French, slant of many of Cantillon's illustrations in all parts of the *Essai* heightens the plausibility of such influence. A few examples can be given. In Boisguilbert's work, the importance of the growth of the social division of labour is quantitatively illustrated by a comparison between primitive and modern society. This indicated that the two different types of professions present in primitive society are multiplied into 200 in its modern counterpart. Fundamental changes associated with this greatly expanded social division of labour are twofold. First, there is a tremendous increase in interdependence of economic agents. Second, it strengthens the tendency of a division of society into classes, in which one 'does nothing while enjoying all the pleasures', while the other class 'works from morn till night only to be deprived of the overplus above its essential consumption'. Private property in land for the few, obtained largely by violence, is Boisguilbert's explanation of this social division. The owning, landlord class, comprising nobility and church, is therefore the dominant sector in Boisguilbert's picture of contemporary France, a vision developed and elaborated on by Cantillon in the economic system he presented in Part I of the *Essai*. Growing interdependence between sections of the economy, with its geographic, inter-temporal and social implications for the relationship between national and individual interest, is mediated through the market. The last is expressed by relating prices set in that market by competition with necessary costs for producing commodities, a process in which Boisguilbert distinguished real flows from their monetary counterparts. This is formalised by his development of a simple notion of an economic circuit of output, income and consumption in which imbalances between the variables cause ruptures in these price relationships and between the monetary and real flows.[10]

All in all, the French influence on Cantillon is therefore significant, contrary to the view presented by Brewer.[11] This case study in addition supports Marx's profound conjecture that classical political economy has a dual origin, from France as well as from England, with Boisguilbert and Petty the respective founders of these two streams.[12] Cantillon's work is an early indication of the benefits to be derived from the merging of these two streams in the eighteenth century. However, despite the fact that French influence was not negligible in Cantillon's work as so often surmised, it is dwarfed by the much greater theoretical heritage he derived from the rich seventeenth-century English literature and from its efforts in political arithmetic. An alteration in the balance of influence between these two streams becomes somewhat more important with the work of Hume.

David Hume and French economics

David Hume's economic essays included with his 'political discourses' were largely written from the end of the 1740s to the early 1750s, being first published, with one exception, in the 1752 edition of his *Essays*. Intended as a critical commentary on major issues in economic policy and economic debate, with special reference to monetary theory, interest theory, market regulation, international trade, taxation and public credit, it is not surprising that they drew on experience from both sides of the channel, especially because their author had resided for some time in France during a formative period in his life. This makes French influence on his economics very likely. The last prospect is enhanced by the fact that during the 1730s and 1740s some important French contributions were published on the subjects in which Hume was particularly interested; partly to evaluate, and sometimes to defend, the famous financial system established by John Law during the Regency years of 1715–20. Most prominent among these authors were Melon and his adversary Du Tot, whose books were rapidly translated. Other, lesser lights in France likewise contributed to economic debate during these decades for which the evidence enables a judgement that France contributed more substantial work to the subject than the English-speaking world.[13] In addition, and of substantial importance to Hume's economics, the late 1740s when he wrote the economic essays coincided with the publication, in 1748, of Montesquieu's great and influential *l'Esprit des Lois*.

Hume mentions Melon's work on no less than three occasions in his *Essays*, while a fourth, indirect reference to Melon can also be identified. The first reference occurs in the essay 'Of Commerce', in which Melon's estimate of the social division of labour in France is queried. Melon suggested that if French society is subdivided into twenty parts, sixteen would be husbandmen, two artisans, and of the remaining two parts one belonged to law, church and nobility, the other to merchants, financiers and 'masters'. Hume rejected such a division on the ground that in 'France, England and indeed most parts of Europe, half of the inhabitants lived in cities; and even of those who lived in the country, a great number are artizans, perhaps above a third'.[14] In criticising these remarks, Hume missed the significance Melon attached to such calculations. They were required for maintaining the requisite balance between classes in society, an implicit emphasis on the implications of interdependence for social equilibrium, in the style of Boisguilbert. Melon is next mentioned in Hume's 'Of Money', in the company of Du Tot and Paris du Verney, two other important commentators on Law's 'system'. Again, the context is critical, since Hume disparages the three French writers for their failure to notice the benefits, in terms of stimulating levels of economic activity, of a mild inflation from 'a gradual and universal encrease of the denomination of money'.[15] Although Melon himself was critical of such reductions in the 'value of money' through debasing the currency, because they conferred benefits largely to debtors, he deplored the effects of deflation even more as a discouragement to production.[16] This blanket reference to Melon's work sits in any case rather uneasily with Hume's later reference to Melon and Du Tot, now in the company of John Law himself, on their frequent references to the benefits of 'circulation' without further explanation.[17] Once again, this seems a little misplaced. Melon's succinct exposition of Law's system alludes to the favourable and unfavourable consequences of good and bad 'circulation' respectively, on the basis of experience in particular countries.[18] A final, albeit indirect reference to Melon's work is made in Hume's essay 'Of Public Credit',[19] with its allusion that some writers treat this as unimportant when the debt is held internally, because then it involves but a transfer from the left to the right hand.[20]

The critical tone Hume adopted to Melon's work in the four cases just documented suggests a wider type of influence Melon's work may have exerted on the composition of Hume's essays. The overall thrust of Melon's work possibly provided the inspiration for the issues on which Hume concentrated when designing his project of economic essays as general criticism of contemporary economic debate. Melon's well known study can be described as the perfect foil to set off the contents of Hume's critical essays on economic issues.[21] No other single writer of the 1730s and 1740s meets such qualifications, even though Hume's essays are, in part at least, also directed at specific English authors, of whom Gee's well known *Trade and Navigation of Great Britain Considered*, is perhaps the best example.

Two of the references Hume made to Du Tot's *Réflexions Politiques sur les Finances et le Commerce*, were mentioned above. There is no doubt that, as in the case of Melon, Hume is correct in arguing that Du Tot presents little by way of explaining the benefits of a good circulation, except by his explicit association of this with improved consumption. He simply takes these benefits for granted, and does not even take the trouble to clarify what he means by 'circulation', for example, by distinguishing monetary circulation from that of commodities.[22] Similar to his treatment of Melon, Hume is wrong in suggesting that Du Tot failed to appreciate the benefits for trade and activity from a gradual increase in the quantity of money. In fact, Du Tot's defence of Law's 'system' provides clear support for the contrary view.[23] Finally, it is difficult to substantiate Hume's claim of factual indebtedness to Du Tot with respect to price effects from debasement of the coinage during the last year of the reign of Louis XIV. Hume seems, however, more correct in being generally sceptical of Du Tot's presentation of facts and, in his recognition of the value of Du Tot's general observation, 'that the augmenting of the money in France does not at first proportionably augment the prices'.[24] Taken with his use of Melon, Hume's comments on Du Tot suggest that his acknowledgement of the dual consequences of monetary increase, an aspect of his argument Keynes stressed in the *General Theory*, may well have been inspired by his detailed study of the consequences of Law's system, as reported by Melon and Du Tot, where these dual effects could be observed in its successive phases.[25]

Hume's reference to Law is too general, and his indebtedness to Montesquieu too well known, to warrant further comment.[26] However, his references to two French authorities from the first decade of the eighteenth century require some further notice. It is interesting that Hume had to 'learn from L'Abbé du Bos [the common English fear] that Scotland would soon drain them [the English] of their treasure' after the Union with Scotland had been effected in 1705. Hume denied such a supposition since the 'money' in a nation was invariably relative to its 'commodities, labour, and industry'.[27] The same applies to the fact that Hume illustrated the detrimental consequences of internal tariffs by citing Vauban's discussion of the import duties imposed by Brittany and Normandy on wine from southern provinces like Languedoc and Guienne.[28] It is also interesting to note that Hume fails to refer to Vauban's work in the essay 'Of Taxes'.

Hume's 'Of Taxes' was later seen as an attack on the taxation doctrines of the physiocrats and as such criticised by Turgot. The latter protested against

Hume's general advocacy of indirect taxes on commodities, which occupied the greater part of the essay. Much more specifically, Turgot criticised in depth Hume's presumption that workers could not pass on higher taxes on wage goods through higher wages, absorbing taxes instead by reduced consumption and increased work. The last touched the cornerstone of the physiocratic conclusion that all taxation was effectively paid by the landlord from the net product on land. Turgot's second letter to Hume on this subject in particular addressed Hume's denial of the proposition that 'wages increase in proportion to taxes' on the ground that this contravened the principle of supply and demand and was contrary to all experience. Turgot's argument drew on the dual nature of prices, that is, current prices, set in the market by supply and demand, and fundamental prices, the costs of the commodity to the producer, including his ordinary gain. Fundamental prices set the floor to market prices in the longer run, since any prolonged period where market prices did not cover costs implies a reduction in supply, as traders and producers leave the industry in response to the losses they were making. This eventually raised market price back to fundamental price. Wages, set by subsistence, were the fundamental price of labour, and set the floor to competitive wage determination by supply and demand. Hence in the short run, it was possible for the worker to respond to taxes on subsistence by consuming less and working more; in the longer run wages would respond to the increased price of essential wage goods and return to their 'natural' level of fundamental price. Hume's reply to Turgot, if indeed he wrote one, has not been found, nor did Hume take account of such criticism in the three editions of his essays which followed this correspondence. Hume's vehement hostility to the physiocrats would in any case have prevented any concessions to their position on his part.[29]

The case study of Hume's French connection is interesting in that it indicates that one of the major mid-century economic performances owed much to the French, and may in fact even have been inspired as to scope by the contents of one of the more famous economic publications of the previous two decades. Melon's work, to much of the argument of which Hume's essays appears to be implicitly directed, with the explicit critique documented therefore only the tip of the proverbial iceberg, is now no longer highly regarded, or even mentioned in the contemporary literature on the history of economics. It is interesting to note that Turgot appreciated the value of Melon's work for the development of economics during the eighteenth century, precisely because of the faults it contained. Turgot praised Melon's work as 'an intellectual feat … despite the errors', because in many ways its contents provided the first intelligent discussion of money, trade and credit in French writings, a first the merit of which needed to be appreciated, particularly by those who came after the subject had been greatly improved by writers of the calibre of Montesquieu, Cantillon, Hume, Quesnay and Gournay.[30] If the supposition expounded here about Melon's general influence on Hume's economic writings is correct, then Hume may likewise have appreciated Melon's merit, which made his general system a perfect butt for the criticism of economic policy Hume produced in his *Essays*.

In that sense, Hume's *Essays* demonstrate the wider influence of French economic writings from the 1730s and 1740s by providing so much of the inspiration for the work on the subject they contained.

Steuart, Adam Smith and French economics

During the decades when Steuart and Smith wrote their respective treatises, French economics gained theoretical dominance. Both works by these Scottish political economists bear the mark of this temporary French hegemony; interestingly, Steuart's to a lesser extent than Smith's. This can be elucidated simply by the fact that the French authorities cited by Steuart tended to be pre-physiocratic, while Smith had the full benefit of physiocratic theoretical advances at the start of the decade during which he wrote his *Wealth of Nations*. The treatment of these two authors as a third case study is therefore fully justified insofar as only one of them marks the tremendous importance of physiocracy for the development of political economy in the period after 1770.

The French authorities cited by Steuart in his *Principles of Political Oeconomy* can be easily abstracted from the lists of authorities he cited prepared by Steuart's editor and by other leading commentators.[31] It is useful to classify these authorities into several categories. In the first instance, Steuart made use of standard French references on trade and other subjects such as Ricard's *Traité Générale du Commerce*, first published in 1686, Savary's *Dictionnaire Universel du Commerce*, first published in 1723, the legendary Memoirs of the Duc de Sully, and Du Hamel's *Eléments d'Agriculture*, first published in 1753. Second, Steuart drew extensively on the major authorities on the French financial system of the early eighteenth century. Apart from the books by Melon, Du Tot and Paris du Verney which were also referred to by Hume, Steuart cited Desmaret's *Mémoires sur l'Administration des Finances* published in 1716. Third, Steuart on several occasions made reference to Vauban's *Dîme Royale*, drew heavily on Montesquieu's famous work, and utilised the important historical contributions of Goguet. Most importantly for the present purpose, Steuart also drew on a number of French works first published in the 1750s. These included the work ostensibly written by Nickolls, *Remarques sur les Avantages et Desavantages de la France et de la Grande Bretagne* (1754), Ange de Goudar, *Les Intérêts de la France Mal Entendus* (1756), the anonymous *Le Reformateur* (1756), Mirabeau's *l'Ami des Hommes* (1756) and, perhaps most interesting of these authorities, Quesnay's article 'Grains', which was published in the *Encyclopédie* in 1757. It should be stressed that Steuart used the pre-physiocratic edition of *l'Ami des Hommes*, while there is no evidence that Steuart had read the anonymous but theoretically very crucial contribution on 'Farmers' by Quesnay published in the *Encyclopédie* in 1756. In short, Steuart only benefited from some of the contributions whose publication Gournay had organised, and which thereby prepared for the dominance of French economics during the 1750s and 1760s.[32] His knowledge of its physiocratic fruits appears to have been confined to Quesnay's position on the grain trade as presented in the *Encyclopédie*.

Before discussing these 1750s references and their potential impact on Steuart's work more fully, some observations are necessary on the use Steuart appears to have made of the work of the French financial writers. Although they provided much of the factual detail for his extensive discussion of Law's system and hence more generally on his views of banking, credit and monetary circulation,[33] Melon's book seems to have been more widely useful to Steuart, hence supporting the remarks on its importance for the development of eighteenth-century economics made in the previous section. Such a judgement is facilitated by Skinner's useful editorial notes, which suggest the variety of Melon's possible impact on Steuart's economics. Examples include Steuart's discussion of the meaning of 'system', population, luxury, the balance of employment doctrine as a guide to trade policy, and the role of the statesman, on the last of which Melon is extensively quoted. More interestingly, Steuart singles out for special notice Melon's errors on banking and his failure to grasp its principles, confirming thereby the value of Melon's work in stimulating criticism, hence assisting the production of better explanations for such phenomena. This characteristic of Melon likewise illustrates the ease, as Steuart put it, by which 'common sense may become nonsense … a thing by no means peculiar to France, but quite peculiar to *man*'.[34]

Steuart's direct use of the French sources from the 1750s seems relatively minimal. Goudar is quoted as a modern writer opposed to 'bringing mechanism to perfection';[35] Nickolls (that is, Plumart de Dangeul) is quoted on the temporal effect of a plentiful harvest on national food reserves, an observation which Quesnay reproduced from the same source in his article 'Grains';[36] *Le Reformateur* is cited on land tax reform in France, as is Vauban's *Dîme Royale*, the last being also noticed on problems associated with beggars and the need for an accurate population census by occupational groups.[37] This leaves Mirabeau's *l'Ami des Hommes*. The one direct reference Steuart made to this work is on population in relation to luxury and, more specifically, 'prodigal uses' of land, a reference in fact critical of Mirabeau's position on this point.[38] Skinner's editorial notes provide guidance on other potential uses Steuart may have made of Mirabeau's work. Not surprisingly, given the subject matter of Mirabeau's book, these concentrate on population. In addition, they deal with the notion of pyramidal class structure, stages of economic growth, and the need to avoid discussion of theological issues on the legality of interest in an economic treatise.[39] It can therefore not be said that French economics profoundly influenced the structure of Steuart's work.

Steuart's relationship with physiocracy needs some further discussion. It is here difficult not to agree with Sen's conclusion that Steuart owed little to physiocracy. This is evident from the fact that he seems to have taken his notion of agricultural surplus and its importance from Petty's account or, possibly, from that of Cantillon.[40] Careful study of 'Grains', of which Steuart's work in actual fact presents no traces, could have acquainted him with the physiocratic conception of product net, and aspects of their complex price theory in relation to production and accumulation, the two contributions of that article subsequently singled out by Du Pont de Nemours.[41] It could also have alerted Steuart to Quesnay's work on agricultural production in the article 'Farmers', and to the distinction drawn between 'la grande et la petite culture', during which Quesnay's observations on the productivity of capital in agriculture are so strikingly put forward. However, from the contents of the *Principles*, this likewise seems not to have been the case, perhaps because by the time 'Grains' came into Steuart's hands, he had virtually completed the initial draft of the first two books of his treatise, the preparation of which, given the nature of their contents, would have benefited most from a prior acquaintance with physiocratic economics.[42]

This picture of physiocratic influence alters considerably when the final case study for this chapter is introduced: Adam Smith's *Wealth of Nations*. There is no doubt that Smith took full advantage of the extensive developments in French economics which took place during the 1750s and 1760s when writing his famous treatise. This is demonstrable not only from the very representative collection of French work on economics in his library, but in the long list of sources Smith explicitly acknowledged in writing his book. The negative impacts on his economics from his acquaintance with physiocracy he explicitly highlighted in the chapter devoted to their work; its more positive manifestations, although accurately delineated by Cannan many years ago, require more careful elaboration.[43]

The extent of Smith's acquaintance with French sources is revealed from the contents of his library. Its catalogue shows:

> Smith owned Condillac's *Le Commerce et le gouvernement*, Dutot's *Réflexions politiques sur les finances et le commerce*, four works by Forbonnais including the *Elémens du commerce*, Le Trosne's *Recueil de plusieurs morceaux économiques*. Melon's *Essai politique sur le commerce*, Mercier de la Rivière's *L'ordre naturel et essentiel des sociétés*politiques, three works by Mirabeau the elder, namely *L'Ami des hommes, Théorie de l'impôt and Philosophie Rurale*, Montesquieu's Works, three works by Morellet, Necker's *Législation et commerce des grains*, Quesnay's *Physiocratie* (edited by Du Pont de Nemours), as well as ten volumes of the *Journal de l'agriculture, du commerce, et des finances* for 1765 to 1767 and the complete run of the Ephémérides from 1766 and 1769 inclusive which includes the major part of Turgot's *Réflexions* as well as many other writings by the leading Physiocrats.[44]

The index of authorities appended to the Glasgow bicentenary edition of *Wealth of Nations* indicates that Smith used most of these sources, albeit in varying degrees, when writing his treatise, including the many physiocratic works present in his library.[45]

The effects of that use on the contents of the *Wealth of Nations* was effectively summarised by Cannan, more on the basis of intuition than careful textual analysis. Roughly comparing the contents of Smith's final treatise with his earlier *Lectures*, and this comparison continues to hold when extended to cover the early draft of the *Wealth of Nations* subsequently discovered by Scott, the additions to the contents of the *Wealth of Nations* attributable to contact with the physiocrats were said to include

> the introduction of the theory of stock of capital and unproductive labour in Book II, the slipping of a theory of distribution into the theory of prices towards the end of Book I, Chapter vi, and the emphasising of the conception of annual produce. These changes do not make so much real difference to Smith's own work as might be supposed. ... But to subsequent economics they were of fundamental importance. They settled the form of economic treatises for a century at least.[46]

Cannan's last sentence suggests the more permanent influence French economics as developed by the physiocrats exerted on the future evolution of economic thought. However, it cannot really be said, as Cannan also attempted to argue, that the elimination of Book II, or at least its three chapters 1, 3 and 5 inspired by physiocratic influence, would not be missed from his analytical framework. As Hicks has pointed out,[47] the core of the *Wealth of Nations* is contained in its Book II, chapter 3. Smith himself in the introduction to his work implied the contents of this chapter explained the second cause of the *Wealth of Nations* he identified, that is, second after the primary importance of the impact of the division of labour on labour productivity, which for him was the crucial factor in securing substantial economic growth. That second cause was the production of the national labour force employed in useful or productive labour.[48]

Smith's chapter on productive and unproductive labour also illustrates a striking similarity between his economics and Quesnay's analysis of economic growth in the *Tableau Economique*. Eltis[49] has clearly demonstrated that the propensity to consume commodities produced in the productive sector was a key factor for Quesnay in explaining economic growth. This follows from the fact that when the demand for such products is translated into additional production, it also generates (additional) surplus product, something the productive sector (by definition) is only capable of doing. Increased surplus combined with buoyant demand for productive sector output allows a growth process to become cumulative for all sectors of the economy. Although Smith extended the definition of the productive sector to include manufacturing, he maintained Quesnay's principle of its distinguishing feature, that is, ability to generate a surplus. Hence Smith strongly associated higher proportions of the labour force used for productive purposes with greater surplus and greater rates of economic growth. In its essentials, Smith's explanation of the second cause of the *Wealth of Nations* strongly resembles the type of growth analysis offered by Quesnay's zig-zag version of the *Tableau Economique*, the implications of which Smith appears to have clearly grasped.

Likewise, Smith drew a number of important features of his capital analysis from suggestions offered by Quesnay's economics. An important illustration is the distinction between fixed and circulating capital, which resembles, but is not identical with, Quesnay's division of capital into annual and original advances.[50] More interestingly, the peculiar Smithian analysis of employments of capital, with its important implications for the natural progress of opulence model Smith developed in Book III, derived from French contributions, more specifically Turgot's work. However, its comparative estimates of profitability between sectors derive largely from a more general physiocratic perspective.[51] Other factors of similarity may be noted in the context of the theory of rent, where both Smith and Quesnay assign to rent a positive influence on price determination, instead of simply seeing it as a price-determined surplus. These are further hallmarks of Smith's physiocratic stance on some issues. That Smith borrowed the French word 'distribution' from Quesnay (or Turgot) to describe his own theory of pricing productive services, seems still the most plausible explanation for the entry of that meaning for the word into English usage, while Smith's conception of annual produce and its division into gross and net portions, discussed by him in the context of capital theory, seem likewise physiocratically inspired.[52] No wonder that Smith at one stage intended to dedicate his *Wealth of Nations* to Quesnay, whose work he clearly recognised and acknowledged as an important inspiration of parts of his own system. Smith's major criticisms of the agricultural system did not stand in the way of his adaptation of some of its key features for his own economic analysis.[53]

The extensive holdings of French economics in Smith's library indicate he was aware of more than just physiocratic work. It has often been shown that the influence of Montesquieu on Smith's work was extensive, particularly with respect to the scope of his research programme. In addition, the extent of Turgot's influence on the *Wealth of Nations*, long a matter of debate, has now been satisfactorily resolved.[54] However, for reasons that should by now be rather obvious, it is more interesting to make some remarks on the use Smith made of Melon's work. Melon is only indirectly referred to in the *Wealth of Nations*; all three identified occasions contained in Smith's chapter on the public debt. There he is referred to as the author who emphasised benefits from a substantial supply of public debt to economic activity, and the person who identified internal debt as an unimportant transfer payment owed by the right hand to the left, a remark to which Hume had earlier drawn attention. Finally, Melon's *Essai* may well have been used as a source of fact for remarks Smith made on debasement of the coinage in France, as a strategy for debt redemption policy Smith himself frowned upon.[55] However, Smith's fairly detailed account of Law's system in his *Lectures* does not seem to have used Melon's account to any extent; its factual basis tended to rely on accounts by Du Verney and Du Tot, the last despite Hume's warning that its factual accuracy needed to be treated with suspicion.[56]

After Smith, French influence on British economics during what remained of the eighteenth century, was partly indirectly diffused through Smith's work itself. However, physiocratic impact continued to be felt in more direct ways, as did the influence of other notable French economic writers, including Turgot.

The impact of French thought on Malthus and on English under-consumptionists at the turn of the century is a case in point.[57] Pursuing these matters takes this chapter well beyond its self-imposed scope based on the four specific case studies just presented. Their significance can now be assessed to bring the paper to its conclusion.

Conclusions

The four case studies examined show a gradual increase of French influence on British economics, rising to a crescendo in the case of Smith. This is not surprising. The authors in question all wrote at discrete time intervals, over which the importance of French economics in the literature gradually rose to that peak in the 1750s and 1760s largely represented by the work of the physiocrats. Their critical analytical impact on Smith's work preserved that influence to a significant degree, since much of it was transmitted by Smith, albeit in a qualified form, to future generations. To a lesser extent, the same type of diffusion process of specific French influence can be seen in Cantillon's work, in the sense that it acted as a vehicle for spreading some of Boisguilbert's notions to later generations, to the degree to which Cantillon had himself absorbed them.

The case studies of Steuart, and especially Hume, show the importance of another type of influence. This is the influence exerted by novel but erroneous ideas as a stimulus to criticism and new explanation. Melon's well known and well read *Essai* was identified as the key example of this type of influence. Steuart implied that its wrong ideas on banking and credit stimulated his own search for better explanations of the mysteries and consequences of financial systems. In the context of Hume's economic essays, it was suggested that Melon may have been the irritant who, by becoming the general target for Hume's criticism, generated the broad range of issues of economic policy whose form and scope determined the contents of Hume's essays. Nearly half a century after its first appearance, Turgot had recognised in Melon's work its potential for such catalytic influence. Melon's *Essai* also signified the growing impact and authority of French economics during the 1730s and 1740s, preparing the way for the peak performance of the 1750s and 1760s.

Quesnay's influence on Smith demonstrates the analytical importance of French eighteenth-century influence on the future development of the subject. Cannan's classification of the physiocratic contribution to the *Wealth of Nations* enables identification of its crucial components, the importance and nature of which is, however, more clearly grasped from more recent work. The accumulation of capital as a separate requisite of production and growth is a prime example of the importance of Quesnay's legacy for economics, particularly when combined with its division into fixed and circulating capital, where the basis for that division is the extent to which the capital is consumed during the (for Quesnay annual) production process. The notion of gross and net revenue, especially as the focus for analysing the annual reproduction of wealth, is another major part of Quesnay's legacy. The same can be said for his use of the word 'distribution' to define the dispersal of annual product among classes, the disposal of which in turn generated the means and opportunities for its annual reproduction. Finally, Quesnay's division of the economy into productive and unproductive sectors, and the implications of this he drew for the growth process, remains one of his lasting contributions, exerted largely through the manner in which it was developed by Smith. Taken together, these four major influences on Smith make Quesnay undoubtedly the major innovatory force in French eighteenth-century economics, as Smith himself clearly recognised.

The discussion of the previous section also reveals that Quesnay was not the only French influence of note. From the start of the century, impact was exerted by Boisguilbert and Vauban especially, although the first to a surprisingly hidden degree. Towards the end of the first half of the century, French influence was exerted on British economics from the remarkable group of financial economists France produced, and more fundamentally from the work of the great Montesquieu, whose role in the development of political economy within a new secular social science was so extensive. Finally, even during the period of the 'golden age' of French economics in the 1750s and 1760s, when the physiocrats and other French writers dominated the field, to the benefit of English and other national schools of economics, Quesnay shared his dominance with other important writers, of whom Turgot was undoubtedly the most important.[58] The four case studies here presented help therefore to capture both the changing pace, and the nature of, the substantial and varying influences French economics exerted on British political economists during the eighteenth century, the one century for part of which it can be said that French economics dominated the subject.

Appendix

Table 6.1 The contents of Melon's *Essai Politique sur le Commerce* and the titles of Hume's economic essays[a]

Chapters	*Melon's* Essai	*Hume's essays*
I	Foundations	Of commerce
II	Of corn	Of refinements in the arts
II	Of the increase in population	
IV	Of colonies	Of money
V	Of slavery	Of interest
VI	Of exclusive companies	Of the balance of trade
VII	Of martial government	
VIII	Of industry	Of the jealousy of trade[b]
IX	Of luxury	
X	Of exporting and importing	Of taxes
XI	Of the freedom of trade	Of pubic credit
XII	Of specie as money	Of the populousness
XIII	Of the ratio of coin to specie	Of ancient nations
XIV	Of the rebellion against Philip the Fair	
XV	Of the coinage during the reigns of Saint Louis and Charles VII	
XVI	Of debasement of the coinage	
XVII	Of the dearness of commodities	
XVIII	Replies to some objections	
XIX	Various observations on the coinage	
XX	Of the exchanges	
XXI	Of the rate of interest	
XXII	Of the balance of trade	
XXIII	Of public credit	
XXIV	Of political arithmetic	
XXV	Of systems	
XXVI	Conclusions	

Notes:
[a]As given in the editions by Daire and by Rotwein used in this chapter.
[b]Added to the economic essays in 1758.

Notes

1 Terence Hutchison, *Before Adam Smith* (Oxford, 1988) for example, p. 12.
2 Peter Groenewegen, 'Pietro Verri's mature political economy of the Meditazioni: a case study in the highly developed international transmission mechanism of ideas in pre-revolutionary Europe', paper presented at a Conference on 'Political Economy and National Identity', Luigi Einaudi Foundation, Turin, September 1992, Tables 1 and 2.
3 Antoin Murphy, *Richard Cantillon: Entrepreneur and Economist* (Oxford, 1986) esp. pp. 246–51.
4 David Hume, 'My own life', in *The History of England* (London, 1802) vol. 1, esp. pp. vi–vii, ix, xii–xiii.
5 See for example Terence Hutchison, *Before Adam Smith*, pp. 164–5; Murphy, *Richard Cantillon*, ch. 13; Anthony Brewer, *Richard Cantillon, Pioneer of Economic Theory* (London, 1992), esp. ch. 9 which fails to explore French predecessors and potential influences.
6 A. Aspromourgos, *Studies in the Formation of Classical Economics* (London: Routledge, 1996) esp. chs 5 and 7.
7 Murphy, *Richard Cantillon*, esp. pp. 248–50, 274–9.
8 Richard Cantillon, *Essai sur la nature du commerce en général*, ed. Henry Higgs (London, 1959) pp. 105, 159, 187 for references to Boizard, Vauban and *Etat de la France* respectively.
9 Jacqueline Hecht, 'Bibliographie commentée', in *Pierre de Boisguilbert* (Paris, 1966) vol. 1, p. 520; and see in the same volume, J. J. Spengler, 'Les théories économique de Boisguilbert', p. 3; Higgs' attribution of the *Etat* to Boulainvilliers is made in the index to his edition of Cantillon's *Essai*, p. 393. Inspection of Boulainvillier's *Etat* (London, 1727–8) vol. I, esp. p. 55, indicates that Cantillon's specific remarks on the decline of the Mantes wine industry cannot easily be attributed to this source.
10 Evidence for the presence of these propositions in Boisguilbert's work is conveniently provided in Jacques Nagels, *Reproduction du Capital selon Karl Marx: Boisguillebert, Quesnay, Leontiev* (Brussels, 1970) pp. 26–51; Gilbert Faccarello, *Aux origines de l'économie politique liberale: Pierre de Boisguilbert* (Paris, 1986); *Boisguilbert parmi nous*, ed. Jacqueline Hecht (Paris, 1989).
11 Anthony Brewer, *Richard Cantillon*, ch. 9, esp. pp. 124–5.
12 Peter Groenewegen, 'Marx's conception of classical political economy: an evaluation', *Political Economy: Studies in the Surplus Approach* (3) 1987, pp. 19–35.
13 An examination of the Kress Catalogue for these decades reveals the following characteristics. Although English-language literature, not surprisingly, predominates in its holdings, much of it is peripheral and as compared with French economic literature for these decades introduces few new important authors. Examples of exceptions are Jacob Vanderlint, *Money Answers All Things* (1734); George Berkeley, *The Querist* (1735); Sir Mathew Decker, *Essay on the Decline of the Foreign Trade* (1744); and Josiah Tucker's *Brief Essay on the Advantages and Disadvantages of Great Britain and France with Respect to Trade* (1749). These are slight relative to the work by Melon, Du Tot and Montesquieu published in France, thereby showing that by this time French economics was at worst on a par with English writing on the subject, heralding the dominance it gained for some time during the 1750s and 1760s.
14 Hume, *Writings of Economics*, ed. Eugene Rotwein (London, 1955) p. 6 n1; Jean François Melon, *Essai politique sur le commerce*, in *Economistes financiers du 18e siècle*, ed. E. Daire (Paris, 1843) p. 800.
15 Hume, *Writings on Economics*, p. 39, n1.
16 Melon, *Essai politique*, pp. 763, 796–7.
17 Hume, *Writings on Economics*, pp. 92–3, note.
18 Melon, *Essai politique*, pp. 802–3, 805–7.

19 Hume, *Writings on Economics*, pp. 95–6, editorial note and cf. editor's introduction, p. lxxxv.
20 Melon, *Essai politique*, p. 802.
21 A comparison of the table of contents of Melon's *Essai* and the titles of Hume's essays is an easy manner of testing this hypothesis, as shown in the appendix to this chapter, above, p. 139.
22 Hume, *Writings on Economics*, pp. 92–3; Du Tot, *Réflexions politiques*, in *Economistes financiers du 18e siècle*, pp. 972–3.
23 Hume, *Writings on Economics*, p. 39n; Du Tot, *Réflexions politiques*, pp. 972–3.
24 Hume, *Writings on Economics*, p. 39 and note; Du Tot, *Réflexions politiques*, esp. pp. 941, 965, provides only loose support for this quotation from Hume. However, Du Tot in analysing the consequences of increased monetary circulation on prices suggests that logically three possibilities are open, proportional price adjustment and prices in greater or lesser proportion relative to the increased quantity of money. Time lags play a factor in this argument, as does Du Tot's realisation that price levels are influenced by real as well as by monetary factors (Du Tot, *Réflexions politiques*, pp. 972–3).
25 J. M. Keynes, *General Theory of Employment, Interest and Money* (London, 1936) p. 343 n3. It should be noted that Keynes says nothing in this context about the possibility of French influence on Hume on this subject.
26 It also neglects any further reference to Paris du Verney, who is mentioned together with Melon and Du Tot as a French author unaware of the beneficial consequences of a gradual increase in money; as unlikely in his case as in the case of the other two. I have discussed the importance of Montesquieu to the development of economics in the second half of the eighteenth century elsewhere. See my 'Turgot, Beccaria and Smith', in *Italian Economics Past and Present*, eds Peter Groenewegen and Joseph Halevi (Sydney, 1983) esp. pp. 48–50 (above, pp. 3, 33–5).
27 Du Bos, *Les intérêts d l'Angelterre mal entendus dans la guerre présente* (Amsterdam, 1704) pp. 44–6, esp. p. 46; Hume, *Writings on Economics*, pp. 65–6 and note. Du Bos' pamphlet is ostensibly a translation from an English pamphlet attributed in the preface to J. Child, an implausible attribution since Child had died in 1699. It is exceedingly well informed on the British literature, citing among others Sir William Petty, Sir William Temple and Sir Charles Davenant.
28 Vauban, *Dîme royale*, 1707, pp. 26–27; as in the case of Du Tot noted above, the citation is not exact (see note 24 above).
29 Hume, *Writing on Economics*, pp. 83–9, esp. pp. 86–8, and Turgot to Hume, 7 September 1766, Hume to Turgot, late September 1766 and Turgot to Hume, 25 March 1767, in *ibid.*, esp. pp. 211–13. The final editions of Hume's essays which he revised himself were published in 1768, 1770 and 1777. Hume's attack on the proposition that all taxes fall on the landlord was in the first instance directed at Locke, who had presented this position in his *Considerations* of 1691.
30 Turgot to Caillard, January 1771, in *Oeuvres de Turgot et documents le concernant*, ed. G. Schelle (Paris, 1913–23) III, pp. 499–500.
31 That is, A. S. Skinner (ed.) Sir James Steuart, *An Inquiry into the Principles of Political Oeconomy* (Edinburgh, 1966) Appendix C, pp. 739–40; S. R. Sen, *The Economics of Sir James Steuart* (London, 1957), Appendix C, p. 198, and earlier, E. A. J. Johnson, *Predecessors of Adam Smith* (New York, 1960) pp. 409–10.
32 For an evaluation of the Gournay contribution to the diffusion and encouragement of French economic thinking in the mid-1750s, see Antoin Murphy, *Richard Cantillon*, pp. 307–11.
33 That is, Steuart, *Principles*, Book IV, Part II, chs XXIV–XXXV, which occupy a good fifty pages of the second volume in the original edition. This discussion had essentially a critical purpose in stimulating Steuart to develop his own, superior doctrine on banking and credit. For all too rare evaluations of Steuart's theory, see A. R. Sen,

The Economics of Sir James Steuart, esp. pp. 96–100; Douglas Vickers, *Studies in the Theory of Money 1690–1776* (London, 1960) ch. 12, esp. pp. 261–70; and Roy Green, *Classical Theories of Money, Output and Inflation* (London, 1992) esp. pp. 116–19.

34 Steuart, *Principles of Political Oeconomy* (Skinner edition) pp. 8n, 537n, on 'systems', 30n and 43n on population, 136n on luxury, 291n on the balance of employment, 325n on statesman, pp. 539, 548–9 on issues in banking, including the passage quoted in the text.

35 Steuart, *Principles*, p. 121 and note.

36 *Ibid.*, p. 111 and note; Quesnay, 'Grains', in *François Quesnay et la physiocratie* (Paris, 1958) pp. 493–4; and for the attribution of 'Nickolls' ' work to Plumart de Dangeul, p. 471 n9.

37 Steuart, *Principles*, pp. 727–8, 78–9; Vauban's procedures for constructing such a census are criticised by Steuart relative to the more modern and useful practises in this regard adopted by Prussian states.

38 Steuart, *Principles*, pp. 135–6.

39 *Ibid.*, pp. 30n, 31n, 37n, 110n on population; 77n on pyramidal class structure; 181n on stages of growth; and 447n theology and interest.

40 A. R. Sen, *The Economics of Sir James Steuart*, pp. 45–6; Skinner, introduction to Steuart, *Principles*, pp. lxv, lxix, lxx and pp. 677–8n, the last of which comment on similarities between some views on taxation of Quesnay and Steuart. On the possibility that Steuart may not have seen Cantillon's *Essai*, see *ibid.*, p. 30n but for a contrary opinion, see E. A. J. Johnson, *Predecessors of Adam Smith* (New York, 1960) p. 409, where specific references to Cantillon are indicated in material on the Bank of Amsterdam omitted from the Skinner edition (however, Skinner, 564 n2, implies that these references could equally well have come from Melon's *Essai*). (And see below, Chapter 9.)

41 Quesnay, 'Grains', p. 459 n1, where Du Pont's remarks are cited. In comments on a draft of this paper, Tony Aspromourgos has noted that Steuart used the term 'fundamental price', a concept he possibly derived from physiocracy.

42 A. R. Sen, *The Economics of Sir James Steuart*, p. 46. The absence of any detailed analysis of capital in Steuart's work, or of the interdependence of circulation, exchange and distribution in a circular flow analysis, supports this contention.

43 That is, Adam Smith, *Wealth of Nations*, Book IV ch. ix, in which the physiocratic system is both criticised and praised. Cannan's basically correct identification of the major analytical contributions for which the physiocrats were responsible is in the introduction to his edition of the *Wealth of Nations* (New York, 1937) pp. xxxviii–xli. There is an enormous literature on this subject, to which reference is made in what follows.

44 Peter Groenewegen, 'A New Catalogue of Adam Smith's Library', *Economic Record* (44) 1968, p. 503 (below, Chapter 21, p. 383).

45 Adam Smith, *An Inquiry into the Nature and Causes of the Wealth of Nations*, eds R. H. Campbell and A. S. Skinner (Oxford, 1976) pp. 1009–18.

46 Cannan, introduction to the *Wealth of Nations*, p. xxxix.

47 John Hicks, *Capital and Growth* (Oxford, 1965) pp. 36–40.

48 Adam Smith, *Wealth of Nations*, p. 10; Peter Groenewegen, 'Adam Smith and the Division of Labour: a Bicentenary Estimate', *Australian Economic Papers* (16) 1977, pp. 162–5 (below, Chapter 22).

49 Walter Eltis, *Classical Theories of Economic Growth* (London, 1984) pp. 15–21, 75–7 and esp. pp. 315–20; and his 'The Contrasting Theories of Industrialisation of François Quesnay and Adam Smith', *Oxford Economic Papers*, 40, 1988, esp. pp. 275–81; cf. Peter Groenewegen, 'Rehabilitating the Classical Notions of Productive and Unproductive Labour with Special Reference to Their Relevance to Taxation', in *Taxation and Fiscal Federalism. Essays in Honour of Russell Mathews*, eds Geoffrey

Brennan, Bhajan Grewal and Peter Groenewegen (Canberra, 1988) ch. 6, esp. pp. 85–7.

50 Smith, *Wealth of Nations*, Book II, ch. I, cf. Marx, *Theories of Surplus Value* (Moscow, 1963) Part I, pp. 44.

51 Smith, *Wealth of Nations*, Book II, ch. V, Book II, ch. IV, pp. 356–9, Book III ch. I, pp. 377–80; Peter Groenewegen, 'Turgot and Adam Smith', *Scottish Journal of Political Economy* (16) 1969, pp. 279–81 (below, Chapter 20).

52 See Cannan, *Theories of Production and Distribution* (London, 1953) esp. pp. 144–9, esp. 145; Peter Groenewegen, 'Pseudo-distribution', in *The New Palgrave Dictionary of Economics*, eds John Eatwell, Murray Milgate and Peter Newman (London, 1987) vol. 3, p. 1037.

53 Dugald Stewart, 'Account of the Life and Writings of Adam Smith', in Adam Smith, *Essays on Philosophical Subjects* (Oxford, 1980) p. 304.

54 I have done this in my 'Turgot and Adam Smith', pp. 171–87, and 'Turgot, Beccaria and Smith', pp. 31–78, and see the references there cited on Turgot and on Montesquieu's impact on Smith (above, Chapter 1; below, Chapter 20).

55 Adam Smith, *Wealth of Nations*, pp. 924 and n50, 926 and n52, 932 and note. Hume's use of Melon's perceptions of domestic debt as a transfer payment was mentioned in the previous section.

56 *Ibid.*, pp. 515–9; and see note 24 above for Hume's warning about the accuracy of Du Tot's factual observations.

57 See for example R. L. Meek, 'Physiocracy and the early Theories of Under-consumption', 'Physiocracy and Classicism in Britain', in *The Economics of Physiocracy* (London, 1962) pp. 313–63; Samuel Hollander, 'On Malthus' Physiocratic References', *History of Political Economy* (24) 1992, pp. 369–80.

58 In his comments on a draft of this paper, Tony Aspromourgos indicated that Turgot was undoubtedly the more intrinsically advanced theorist as compared with Quesnay, if only because of his generalisation of the importance of capital to all spheres of production, and his associated analysis of equalisation of rates of return of capital used in its various employments. His model of development likewise departed from Quesnay's agricultural 'kingdom' by moving on to the fourth, commercial stage of development. However, Quesnay's innovations made these advances possible, as Turgot himself indirectly admitted in his remarks on Melon cited previously.

7 Employment and machinery

Two classical debates on the effects of automation

The introduction of labour-saving devices, especially on a massive scale, in an important productive sector, has generally produced a dilemma for the policy-maker. On the one hand, there are the important benefits in the form of reduced costs and prices, and, for a trading nation, the not unimportant consideration of increasing the competitiveness of exports. On the other hand, there is the social cost of structural unemployment, which becomes of even greater importance when the society is already operating at a less than full employment level. Furthermore, structural unemployment, due to lack of labour mobility in the full sense of the word, has always been painful to the workers involved and has generally led to considerable labour unrest.[1] It is therefore not surprising that this question was discussed at length by some of the best economists of the eighteenth and nineteenth centuries.

The purpose of this paper is to investigate two of these debates on the machinery question in order to study the solutions offered to this problem by the classics. Since the problem of 'automation' is still present today, probably on an even larger scale than was experienced in the previous two centuries, a study of these solutions is of considerable interest in that the analysis of two intellectual controversies of the past may still yield some practical results.

The first of these debates, conducted in the second half of the eighteenth century, arose from an adverse comment on the social consequences of machinery in the influential book, *l'Esprit des Lois*, by the distinguished French lawyer and sociologist, Montesquieu. His view was attacked by various economists on both sides of the Channel who argued that the benefits of labour-saving inventions outweighed their costs.[2] This last proposition entered English classical economics through Adam Smith's *Wealth of Nations*, where it was clearly stated that the introduction of machinery was always useful.[3] As a result of Smith's undoubted authority, this proposition gained general acceptance during the next fifty years, despite the fact that part of this period saw large structural unemployment in England.[4]

Smith's opinion on the machinery question was not seriously challenged until the publication in 1817 of John Barton's *Condition of the Labouring Classes of Society*. This pamphlet demonstrated that the introduction of machinery could lead to large-scale unemployment, consequently a fall in wages, and that for these reasons the opposition of workers to labour-saving devices was far from irrational.[5] Barton's unorthodox views gained authority when David Ricardo, the leading economist of the period, publicly changed his mind on the issue by inserting a chapter devoted to the subject in the third and final edition of his *Principles*.[6] Other leading economists of the early nineteenth century, notably Malthus and MacCulloch, entered the debate on the effects of machinery.[7]

This chapter will be divided into three parts. The first will deal with the eighteenth-century debate on Montesquieu's views; the second with the controversy arising from the Barton-Ricardo position; while the third will discuss the relevance of these debates to the twentieth-century problem of automation.

I

Opinion in the first half of the eighteenth century was on the whole favourably disposed to the introduction of machinery, since it reduced the labour costs of manufactured commodities and, in the case of exports, made them more competitive abroad. The fact that structural unemployment could also occur from such a policy was on the whole ignored by the advocates of the benefits of machines.[8] This view was critically examined by Montesquieu who, in an argument relating to population and 'the arts', expressed the following general conclusion which threw doubt on the universal acceptability of labour-saving devices:

> The machines designed to abridge labour are not always useful. If a piece of workmanship is of moderate price, such as is equally agreeable to the maker and the buyer, those machines which would render the manufacture more simple, or, in other words, diminish the number of workmen, would be pernicious. And if water-mills were not everywhere established, I should not have believed them so useful as is pretended, because they have deprived an infinite multitude of their employment, a vast number of persons of the use of water, and a great part of the land of its fertility.[9]

Machines, Montesquieu clearly argued, if applied to certain manufactures, would lead to bad results even if they lowered costs and prices. Of these bad results, the worst, in his opinion, was the loss of employment opportunities to the workmen. The advantages of machinery were therefore offset by important social costs, which would have to be eliminated before a technical improvement could become acceptable to society.

Montesquieu's argument was taken up by Postlethwayt,[10] who discussed the advantages and disadvantages of machinery in his *Universal Dictionary*. Machines, by 'keeping the price of labour low', would give the nation that introduced them

> the best chance to gain the trade of foreign markets; for besides that machines generally do the work truer and better than by hand, the labour

> saved by them is so very great, that, if the materials are equally plentiful, they who use the machine, must undersell the other in a vast proportion.[11]

A trading nation could therefore ill afford not to use machinery. 'A people without commerce', on the other hand, 'may safely refuse to admit stocking-looms, sawing mills, throwing engines, weaving and spinning engines', since these would add unnecessarily to the number of 'unemployed poor'.[12] For this case, Postlethwayt suggested the following criteria to judge whether the machine should be used:

> 1. When they do such business as cannot be performed by hand at all. Of this kind are pumps, fire-engines, water engines, looms, wine and oil presses, hand-mills for grain, and perhaps horse-mills. 2. Where the commodities wrought by them are such as would not be used at all, except they were done by the machine, either being not cheap enough, or not good enough for consumption, when prepared by hand. Under this head are the mills for making paper, those for forging, drawing, slitting, iron, copper, fulling of cloth and leather, and making gun powder.[13]

For a non-trading nation Postlethwayt conceded qualified acceptance of the use of machinery since the unemployment effect could outweigh other benefits, unless the machine did work which either could not be done manually or which human labour could only do uneconomically or inefficiently. Unfortunately, he did not give examples of machines which would have offended these criteria, so that it is difficult to see where he would have drawn the line. For a nation which depended on exports, the matter was clear: machines were always advantageous.

Six years later, Josiah Tucker discussed the unemployment effects of machinery in considerable detail. He argued that machinery was always worthwhile, despite popular prejudices against it. For example, he attributed the lack of innovation in the woollen industry, and its consequent deterioration, to

> the mistaken Notions of the infatuated Populace, who, not being able to see farther than the first link in the chain, consider all Inventions, as taking the Bread out of their Mouths; and therefore never fail to break out in Riots, and Insurrections, whenever such things are proposed.[14]

Tucker put forward that those who claimed that machinery created unemployment only looked at the primary effect. The secondary employment effects of machinery, which arose partly from the increased demand for the commodity produced by the machine as a result of the fall in its price and partly from the indirect effects of increased production, would outweigh the primary unemployment effect. In considering these indirect consequences, he argued:

> the first Step is, that Cheapness, *caeteris paribus*, is an Inducement to buy – and that many Buyers cause a great Demand – and that a great Demand

> brings on a great Consumption; – which great Consumption must necessarily imploy a vast variety of Hands, whether the original Material is considered, or the Number and Repair of Machines, or the Material out of which these Machines are made, or the Person necessarily imployed in tending upon and conducting them: Not to mention those Branches of the Manufacture, Package, Porterage, Stationary and Book-keeping, &c. &c. which must inevitably be performed by Human Labour.[15]

The major part of Tucker's argument depends on the elasticity of demand of the affected commodity and on the precise nature of the labour-saving effect of the new techniques. If the demand was highly elastic, and if the machine was not too labour-saving, the increased production could re-employ the originally displaced workers. If these conditions were not met, and if the supplementary employment effects were small, machines could create unemployment. Tucker appears to have assumed a very elastic demand, as is clear from his critique of Montesquieu's contention on the effects of machinery.[16]

Francois Quesnay, in a paper written in 1758, also considered the issues involved in the unemployment effects of machinery. Since machines were generally beneficial in other respects, he suggested three policies which could overcome the unemployment problem. First, alternative employment could be found for the displaced workers in a similar industry.[17] Second, the innovation could be introduced gradually, thereby discouraging new entrants into the affected occupation so that the number of labourers threatened with redundancy 'would diminish little by little until they had died out'.[18] Finally, in cases where these policies would not work, due to specific labour immobility or to the impossibility of gradually changing technique, he suggested a compensation principle in the following manner:

> At Lyons, they have forbidden the introduction of a machine for the manufacture of taffeta, which would have saved the labour of a great number of men employed and reduced the price of the commodity. People were worried about what would happen to the men employed in this work who had no other trade to earn their living by. But they would have done better to support these workers for the rest of their lives than to suppress the machine and keep them on. It would have cost them less to support the men when they were doing nothing, and to allow them to die out, than to exert themselves to give permanent employment to them in such expensive work.[19]

Steuart also supported the introduction of machinery, and failed to see why 'the great Montesquieu finds fault with water-mills' but had no 'objection against the use of the plough'.[20] Machines, despite the fact that they could cause unemployment, were of 'the greatest utility to man' and should therefore be used. 'Peace', he argued by analogy, also caused unemployment, 'yet nobody, I believe, will allege that, in order to give bread to soldiers, sutlers, and undertakers, the war should be continued'.[21]

The statesman, however, has to see that a remedy is found for the unfavourable consequences of machinery, and in this connection Steuart recommended policies similar to the first two proposed by Quesnay: that is, the gradual introduction of the innovation, and the provision of alternative employment. On the whole, he argued that the application of machinery is beneficial to society, as he summed up neatly in his concluding remarks on the subject:

> Upon the whole, daily experience shows the advantage and improvement acquired by the introduction of machines. Let the inconveniences complained of be ever so sensibly felt, let the statesman be ever so careless in relieving those who are forced to be idle, all these inconveniences are only temporary; the advantage is permanent, and the necessity of introducing every abridgement of labour and expence, in order to supply the wants of luxurious mankind, is absolutely indispensible, according to modern policy, according to experience, according to reason.[22]

The above sentiments admirably express the feeling of the next fifty years on this question.

II

By the beginning of the second decade of the nineteenth century the machinery question appeared to be settled on the lines suggested by the economists whose views were discussed above. By the end of that decade, however, the question was completely reopened: by Barton's argument that machinery could lead to considerable unemployment since it displaced labour; and by Malthus, who claimed that its introduction would lead to overproduction and a consequent glut on the market due to deficient demand. Barton's argument was supported by Ricardo, and that of Malthus by the socialist economist, Sismondi.[23] The defence of machinery, especially against the attacks of Malthus, was undertaken by MacCulloch and J. B. Say, who both denied that machinery could lead to long-term unemployment and overproduction.

Barton's argument was relatively simple. In his *Wealth of Nations*, Smith had argued that the demand for labour, and hence the real wages and living standards of the workers, depended on the accumulation of capital.[24] According to Barton this proposition was wrong. In the first place, the rate of capital accumulation had to be compared with the rate of population increase before conclusions could be drawn about the progress of wages. Second, 'it does not seem that every accession of capital necessarily sets in motion an additional quantity of labour'.[25] The investment of new capital into machinery did not necessarily lead to an increased demand for labour, as Barton illustrated with a simple example.

Assume a manufacturer with a capital of £1,000 which he uses to employ twenty weavers at an annual wage rate of £50. Further assume an increase of his capital to £2,000, and that he invests £1,500 of this new capital by means of the purchase of a new machine which can do the work of twenty weavers with the aid of five labourers. 'Are there not then fifteen men discharged in consequence of the manufacturer having increased his capital?'[26] This is an example of an increase in the supply of capital which leads to a decrease in the demand for labour, and consequently to a fall in wages and the living standards of the workers.

The immediate unemployment effect of the investment in machinery is, however, ameliorated in the longer run. In the first place, the machine needs maintenance and renewal, which will annually employ three additional labourers on Barton's calculations. Second, with the increase in capital, and the same rate of profit of 10 per cent, the manufacturer's next revenue has doubled, thereby allowing him to employ two additional men at £50 each as domestic servants. This means employment for a further five men, so that it can be concluded that prior to the employment of the machine, 'with half the capital, and half the revenue, just double the number of hands were set in motion'.[27] The introduction of machinery, which entails the creation of fixed capital, diminishes the demand for labour. The demand for labour can only be increased by an accumulation of circulating capital, so that the interest of the labouring classes is threatened by too great a proportion of fixed capital investment in total capital accumulation.

Barton's argument is open to a serious objection: he fails to allow for the fall in value product which is required to maintain the average rate of profit. To maintain the average rate of profit of 10 per cent, the machine would have to produce annually £200 for profit, as well as £250+£100+£50=£400, being the wages of the five men attending the machine, the depreciation of the machine (which is assumed to last for fifteen years), plus the annual wages for the labour of repair. This gives a total value product of £600. The machine is, however, assumed to produce 'the same quantity of work' as twenty weavers did without it, which in value terms would equal £1,100, being £1,000 in wages and £100 in profits on capital. This discrepancy between the products implies a drop in value of the final product after the machine has been introduced of approximately 45 per cent, since the two techniques produce the same quantity of physical product. With such a steep fall in value or price, and with a relatively elastic demand, the demand for physical output could easily double, and, on Barton's own assumptions, this doubling of output under the new technique would re-employ the displaced workers.[28]

On the appearance of Barton's pamphlet, Ricardo still held orthodox views on the machinery question. In his early writings he had argued that machinery, through the fall in price in which its introduction resulted, benefited all classes of society by raising their real incomes. The unemployment effect, in his view, would be shortlived. As he wrote to MacCulloch in 1820, 'the employment of machinery. ... never diminishes the demand for labour'.[29] His 'Notes on Malthus', written in the same year, showed a slight alteration in this opinion, and, as Sraffa has reported, the first real indication of his change of mind is in a letter of Malthus to Sismondi (12 March 1821) 'which mentioned that Ricardo had altered his views on machinery'.[30] The conversion was made public by the addition of chapter 31 to the third edition of his *Principles* which appeared during May 1821.

In the new chapter, 'On machinery', Ricardo clearly stated the basic conclusion 'that the substitution of machinery for human labour, is often very injurious to the interests of the class of labourers'. This new and more correct view on the machinery question came from the proposition that an increased net income did not always mean an increase in gross income.[31] Like Barton, he illustrated his argument with an arithmetical example.

Assume a society with a total capital of £20,000 which is divided into £7,000 of fixed and £13,000 of circulating capital. The rate of profit is 10 per cent so that total profit, and net revenue, is £2,000. Since the circulating capital is completely paid out in wages, gross revenue for the year equals £15,000, depreciation of the fixed capital being ignored.[32] Further assume that, in the following year, the society decides to increase its stock of fixed capital by devoting half of its capital to the production of a machine, the remainder being devoted as usual to consumption goods production. Gross and net revenue would remain at £15,000 and £2,000 respectively, but at the end of the year the society would have £14,500 in fixed capital but only £5,500 in the form of circulating capital for the payment of wages in the following year. At the end of the third year, net income would remain unchanged at £2,000, but the wages fund having declined to £5,500, gross revenue would decline to £7,500. At this point the arithmetical example stops.[33]

All that Ricardo wished to demonstrate with this example was that:

> the discovery and use of machinery may be attended with a diminution of gross produce; and whenever this is the case, it will be injurious to the labouring class, as some of their number will be thrown out of employment, and population will become redundant, compared with the funds which are to employ it.[34]

Ricardo's example raises several questions in the minds of the reader. First of all, since the rate of profit is assumed to be unchanged, it is difficult to see what incentive the capitalists have to employ the machine, unless they derive satisfaction from obtaining an increased relative share of the gross produce. Second, the example conveniently stops at the end of the third year without taking into account the increased output which would result from the employment of the machine. If the production of consumption goods substantially increased, the wages fund would increase, and unemployment would be greatly reduced in the subsequent year. Finally, since a new technique generally tends to raise the rate of profit, thereby causing a relative fall in wages, the demand for labour may increase, as Wicksell pointed out.[35] None of these possibilities was explored by Ricardo, despite the fact that they could have invalidated the strength of his conclusion.

A few comments must also be made on Malthus' less sophisticated attacks on machinery. In one of the later editions of the *Essay on Population*, he had argued that machinery and the resultant manufacturing system were harmful to the labourers 'with respect to health, and the fluctuations in wages'.[36] His more important attack occurred in the *Principles of Political Economy*, published in 1820. In chapter VII, section 5, he argued that full use could not be made of machinery without the extension of the market, and since this would not always occur, machinery could lead to harmful effects, including unemployment.[37] Malthus' argument hinged on the assumption of a closed economy, where the mechanised industries produced for the domestic economy only. In this case, he argued,

> is it in any degree probable that the mass of vacant capitals [as a result of the change in technique], could be advantageously employed, or that the mass of labourers thrown out of work could find the means of commanding an adequate share of the national produce?[38]

Malthus' views on the machinery question were critically examined by MacCulloch in a article in the *Edinburgh Review*.[39] In this article, MacCulloch argued that 'want of a ready market' could cause 'the distresses of the manufacturers and agriculturalists of this country', but that machinery could not be blamed, because the fall in price following its introduction allowed a more competitive export industry, and thereby extended the market. As he put it:

> If, not withstanding all the contrivances of our Arkwrights and our Watts, to save labour and expense in the production of commodities, we are still in danger of being undersold by foreigners, it is certain that, without these contrivances, we would not have been able to withstand their competition for a single twelve-month. ... It is not to the general introduction of machinery, but to the factitious and exclusive commercial system that we have adopted and to the oppressiveness of taxation, that all our distresses are to be ascribed.[40]

Given free trade, together with a reduction in taxation, the unemployment ascribed by Malthus to machinery and deficient demand would quickly disappear.

MacCulloch contended that even in a closed economy the argument that machinery caused unemployment was invalid. In the first place, the lower price caused by the improved production methods would raise the demand for the product and re-employ a large part of the displaced workers. Second, where the demand for the commodity produced by machinery was already fully satisfied, the displaced labour and capital could move to other industries where an improvement had not occurred.[41] A general glut in the market, such as Malthus envisaged, was of course impossible for a staunch adherent of the 'law of markets' like MacCulloch.[42] J. B. Say, the French economist, fully supported him on this issue.[43]

It is therefore understandable that MacCulloch was thunderstruck by Ricardo's change of heart. In a letter written to Ricardo after receiving a copy of the third edition of the latter's *Principles*, MacCulloch wrote that he was amazed to find that Ricardo had joined his former adversaries Malthus and Sismondi on the machinery question.[44] In the letter, MacCulloch clearly indicated the weak spots in Ricardo's arguments: the failure to explain the motive for the adoption of the new technique, the exclusion of the effect of the increased productivity of the new method on the demand for labour, and the omission of any reference to the durability of the machine.[45] He concluded by stating: 'If your reasoning and that of Mr. Malthus be well founded, the laws against the Luddites are a disgrace to the Statute Book'.[46]

In his reply to MacCulloch, Ricardo failed to answer these arguments convincingly,[47] and it is presumably for this reason that MacCulloch for once did not adopt a Ricardian standpoint on this question. In his own *Principles of Political Economy*, published in 1825, he concluded that although Ricardo's example in the machinery chapter was logically possible, 'it may, nevertheless, be safely affirmed, that it has never hitherto actually occurred, and that it is extremely unlikely it ever will'.[48]

With these exchanges, the second classical debate on the machinery question concluded. Most of Ricardo's most ardent expositors, such as De Quincey and the two Mills,[49] failed to come to grips with the issue by attempting to solve the problem more satisfactorily. Half a century later, the problem was considered once more by the neo-classics who re-emphasised the benefits of machinery, and who treated its unemployment effects as a special problem in political economy.[50]

III

The conclusions derivable from the two debates on machinery are not only of historical interest but also of some practical importance to the twentieth-century problem of automation. The debates clearly showed that automation entailed costs as well as benefits, and that, while the private problem of whether to adopt a new technique was easily solved by the individual capitalist, the social problem arising through the unemployment effect required careful study and possibly government intervention. It can be fairly stated that all the participants in the debates recognised the substantial benefits from labour-saving devices in the form of lower-priced commodities and increased competitiveness of exports. Similarly, there would be general agreement today on the benefits of automation.

It was the social cost of machinery, namely the possibility of unemployment, which caused the argument. Here there were three divergent views. First of all, there was the opinion that the adoption of new techniques was not always in the interest of the labourers, and that therefore some inventions should not be used. This was the view adopted by Montesquieu, Barton, Malthus and Sismondi, and by Ricardo in the *Principles*. Second, it was held – by Tucker,

MacCulloch and J. B. Say – that although machinery could lead to unemployment, this would be the short-run effect only. Indirect employment effects would re-employ all the displaced workers. Third, there was the view – of Postlethwayt, Steuart and especially Quesnay – that the unemployment effect could be overcome by policy measures implemented at the introduction of the new technique. Each of these views may be briefly examined.

The first view, that machinery should not always be used, is a short-sighted policy and can be rejected. As was shown earlier, Montesquieu had not argued the case for this proposition at all; Malthus' and Sismondi's arguments rested on a fear of overproduction, not entirely relevant to the problem at hand,[51] and, as MacCulloch had shown, part of its validity depended on unrealistic assumptions. Finally, the conclusion of Barton and Ricardo failed to be convincing because of the highly restrictive assumptions in their arithmetical examples. For these reasons, it can be argued that there was no adequate case against the adoption of machinery.

The second view, which claimed that the unemployment effects would be short-run only, must also be dismissed since it too rests on not altogether satisfactory assumptions. For this proposition to hold, the elasticity of demand for the commodity produced by the new method would have to be greater, the more labour-saving the new technique. Furthermore, the indirect employment effects in associated trades, mentioned by Tucker, would not always be realised. Even if the validity of these assumptions was greater at the time of their writing, it is very doubtful if the unemployment effects of twentieth-century automation would cure themselves in this fashion.

Finally, there was the view that the benefits of machinery always outweighed the costs, since there were policies which could solve the unemployment problem. First, and where possible, the new technique should be gradually introduced, thereby making sudden adjustments, so painful to the labourer, unnecessary. Second, there was the possibility of transferring the displaced labour to other occupations, a policy which could require state aid in retraining and resettlement schemes to give labour the requisite mobility. Third, there was Quesnay's compensation principle for those cases where neither of the other two policies applied. If the new technique was sufficiently productive, the redundant workers could be compensated for their loss of employment from the increased output resulting from the change in production methods. These policies are still applicable today, and could solve some of the problems arising from automation.

One aspect of the machinery question has so far not yet been discussed. This is the real benefit which may flow from labour-saving devices: i.e. the rise in living standards in the form of increased real incomes. This promise, embodied in the machine age and a vision also applicable to the age of automation, was recognised by MacCulloch, who eloquently described it in his defence of machinery:

> If the labourer's command over the necessaries and comforts of life were suddenly raised to ten times its present amount, (and this would really be

> the effect of the improvement in question), the consumption as well as the savings of the labourer would doubtless be very greatly increased; but it is not at all likely that he would continue to exert his full power. In such a state of society we should no longer hear of workmen being engaged 12 or 14 hours a day in hard labour, or of children being immured from their tenderest years in cotton mills. The labourer would then be able, without endangering his means of subsistence, to devote a greater portion of his time to amusement, and to the cultivation of this mind.[52]

This picture of plenty rather than of distress as a result of new techniques and machines forms a good conclusion to the subject-matter of this chapter.

Notes

1 See, for example, Paul Mantoux, *The Industrial Revolution in the Eighteenth Century*, London, 1961, pp. 226, 264, 401–6, 444; A. E. Bland, P. A. Brown and R. H. Tawney, *English Economic History*, London, 1914, pp. 321, 442, 544; E. F. Heckscher, *Mercantilism*, 2nd edn, London, 1955, I, pp. 264f, II, pp. 126–9; and cf. T. S. Ashton, *The Industrial Revolution*, London, 1960, pp. 154–5.

2 See Montesquieu, *l'Esprit des Lois*, in *Oeuvres de Montesquieu*, Paris, 1964, p. 690; Postlethwayt, *Universal Dictionary of Trade and Commerce*, London, 1751, articles 'Labour' and 'Machine'; Josiah Tucker, *Instructions for Travelers*, London, 1757, pp. 20–2; Quesnay, 'Hommes', in *Francois Quesnay et la Physiocratie*, Paris, 1958, II, pp. 562–3 and n12; James Steuart, *Principles of Political Economy*, London, 1767, Book I, ch. XIX.

3 Adam Smith, *An Inquiry into the Nature and Causes of the Wealth of Nations*, Modern Library edition, New York, 1937, pp. 271–2. Smith virtually ignored the issue of structural unemployment in connection with machinery.

4 See for example Arthur Young, *Political Essays concerning the Present State of the British Empire*, London, 1772, pp. 215–19; Sir Frederic Morton Eden, *The State of the Poor*, London, 1797, I, pp. 441ff; Lauderdale, *An Inquiry into the Nature and Origin of Public Wealth*, Edinburgh, 1819, pp. 157–64, J. B. Say, *A Treatise on Political Economy*, New York, 1964, Book I, ch. VII. Malthus was against machinery on the grounds that it caused the social and moral degradation of labour in the factory system, and industrial depressions through deficient demand. See *Essay on the Principle of Population*, Everyman edition, London, 1960, II, pp. 130–1; *Principles of Political Economy*, London, 1820, pp. 185, 401–13. For evidence as to labour unrest during the period see C. R. Fay, *Life and Labour in the Nineteenth Century*, Cambridge, 1920, pp. 23–4; G. D. H. Cole and Raymond Postgate, *The Common People*, London, 1938, pp. 175, 180–2, 206–9, 234, and the reference to Mantoux in note 1 above.

5 John Barton, *Condition of the Labouring Classes of Society*, Hollander reprint, Baltimore, 1934, esp. pp. 16–17.

6 See David Ricardo, 'Principles of Political Economy and Taxation', in *Works*, Scraffa edition, Cambridge, 1953, I, ch. XXXI, esp. p. 386; and 'Notes on Malthus', in *ibid.*, II, esp. notes 149, 153 and 235.

7 See James Mill, 'Elements of Political Economy', in *Selected Economic Writings*, edited by Donald Winch, Edinburgh, 1966, p. 230; cf. Ricardo to Mill, 18/12/1821, in *Works*, *op. cit.*, IX, p. 127; J. R. MacCulloch, 'Machinery and Accumulation', *Edinburgh Review*, March, 1821, pp. 108–23, and his *Principles of Political Economy*, London, 1870, Part II, section IV; and the correspondence between MacCulloch and Ricardo in *Works*, *op. cit.*, VIII, letters 417–18, 421–2, 424, 428–9, 431, 433–4.

8 See, for example, 'Considerations on the East-India Trade', in J. R. MacCulloch (ed.) *Early English Tracts on Commerce*, Cambridge, 1954, pp. 580–90; Daniel Defoe, *Giving Alms No Charity*, London, 1704, pp. 18–19.
9 Montesquieu, *l'Esprit des Lois*, in *Oeuvres de Montesquieu*, Paris, 1964, p. 690.
10 Postlethwayt, *Universal Dictionary of Trade and Commerce*, London, 1751, II, p. 121.
11 *Ibid.*, pp. 4–5.
12 *Ibid.*, p. 5.
13 *Ibid.*, p. 121.
14 Josiah Tucker, *Instructions for Travelers*, London, 1757, p. 21.
15 *Ibid.*, pp. 21–2.
16 *Ibid.*, p. 22. Cf. J. R. MacCulloch, 'Machinery and Accumulation', *Edinburgh Review*, March, 1821, p. 114, where he explicitly assumes an elasticity of demand greater than one in this connection.
17 Quesnay, 'Hommes', in *François Quesnay et la Physiocratie*, Paris, 1958, II, p. 563, n12.
18 *Ibid.*
19 *Ibid.*
20 Steuart, *Principles of Political Economy*, London, 1767, I, p. 119.
21 *Ibid.*, I, pp. 120–2.
22 *Ibid.*, I, pp. 123–4.
23 Sismondi, *Nouveaux Principes d'Economie politique*, Geneva, 1819, II, pp. 324–6.
24 Adam Smith, *An Inquiry into the Nature and Causes of the Wealth of Nations*, Modern Library edition, New York, 1937, pp. 68–74; cf. James Mill, 'Elements of Political Economy', in *Selected Economic Writings*, edited by Donald Winch, Edinburgh, 1966, p. 230, where he made the same point as Smith for which he was criticised by Ricardo.
25 John Barton, *Condition of the Labouring Classes of Society*, Hollander reprint, Baltimore, 1934, p. 16.
26 *Ibid.*, p. 16.
27 *Ibid.*, p. 17.
28 This appears to have been Ricardo's view as late as 1820, though not his reasoning. See Ricardo to MacCulloch in Ricardo, *Works*, Sraffa edition, Cambridge, 1953, VIII p. 171.
29 Ricardo, *Ibid.*, VIII, p. 171. This paragraph has drawn heavily on Sraffa's excellent introduction to Ricardo's 'Principles', in *ibid.*, I, pp. lvii–lviii.
30 Sraffa, introduction to Ricardo's 'Principles', *op. cit.*, p. lx; cf. Hollander's introduction to the reprint of Barton's *Condition of the Labouring Classes of Society*, Hollander reprint, Baltimore, 1934, pp. 4–5, which includes the details of Mallet's claim to the responsibility for Ricardo's change of mind.
31 Ricardo, 'Principles', in *Works*, Sraffa edition, Cambridge, 1953, p. 388. By gross income Ricardo meant the sum of wages, profits and rent; in net income he included profits and rent only.
32 *Ibid.*, pp. 388–9. Ricardo assumes an individual capitalist but implies that his argument applies to a society as a whole.
33 *Ibid.*, pp. 389–90.
34 *Ibid.*, p. 390.
35 Cf. Wicksell, *Lectures on Political Economy*, London, 1951, pp. 134–41; and Blaug, *Economic Theory in Retrospect*, London, 1964, pp. 124–5.
36 Malthus, *Essay on the Principle of Population*, Everyman edition, London, 1960, II, p. 131.
37 Malthus, *Principles of Political Economy*, London, 1820, pp. 401–4.
38 *Ibid.*, p. 404. Ricardo criticised this part of Malthus' work in his 'Notes on Malthus', *op. cit.*, notes 236–44.

39 MacCulloch, 'The Opinion of Messrs. Say, Sismondi, and Malthus, on the Effects of Machinery and Accumulation, Stated and Examined', *Edinburgh Review*, XXV, March, 1821, pp. 108–23.
40 *Ibid.*, pp. 107–8.
41 *Ibid.*, p. 112.
42 *Ibid.*, pp. 106–7.
43 J. B. Say, A *Treatise on Political Economy*, New York, 1964, pp. 86–8.
44 MacCulloch to Ricardo, 5/6/1821, in Ricardo, *Works*, Sraffa edition, Cambridge, 1953, VIII, pp. 381–2.
45 *Ibid.*, pp. 383–4.
46 *Ibid.*, p. 385.
47 Ricardo to MacCulloch, 18/6/1821, in *ibid.*, VIII, pp. 386–90.
48 MacCulloch, *Principles of Political Economy*, London, 1870, p. 103.
49 See De Quincey, 'Logic of Political Economy', in *De Quincey's Collected Writings*, Masson edition, London, 1897; James Mill, 'Elements of Political Economy', in *Selected Economic Writings*, edited by Donald Winch, Edinburgh, 1966; J. S. Mill, *Principles of Political Economy*, London, 1902, Book I, ch. VI, pp. 58–63. J. S. Mill's position is a qualified defence of machinery which does not attempt a solution of the difficulties in Ricardo's chapter XXXI.
50 Wicksell, *Lectures on Political Economy*, London, 1951, pp. 133–44; A. C. Pigou, *Unemployment*, London, 1913, esp. ch. II.
51 The broader truths in this contention fall outside the scope of this chapter, since they are concerned with general, rather than with structural, unemployment.
52 MacCulloch, 'The Opinion of Messrs. Say, Sismondi, and Malthus, on the Effects of Machinery and Accumulation, Stated and Examined', *Edinburgh Review*, XXV, March, 1821, p. 105.

8 The notion of the subsistence wage in pre-Smithian classical political economy

Some reflections inspired by the surplus approach

(with Tony Aspromourgos)

Introduction

Garegnani (1983; 1984; 1987; 1989) has done much to demonstrate the importance of the classical approach to wage theory, as a feature distinguishing it from marginalist economics in its analysis of the problem of value and distribution. Their approach to wage theory, in many respects relying on an exogenously determined wage, nevertheless constitutes part of the core of the basic 'surplus approach' to economic analysis.[1] Given net social product, aggregate wages for the classical economists are taken to be sufficient to determine the surplus product of the economy in the form of shares other than wages, that is, profit, interest and rent. In addition, the classical approach to wages leaves room for the possibility of unemployment in the analysis, even when the natural wage rate rules in their system. Such an approach to wages, Garegnani (1989: 118) emphatically points out, stands in strong contrast to subsequent wage theories based, as they generally tend to be, on a form of supply and demand analysis. The classical view amounts to an entirely different relationship between income distribution and relative prices – an element of *independence* of distribution from relative prices ('value through exogenous distribution' – Bharadwaj 1963); and, at the same time, an essential interdependence between wages as a distributional variable and commodity prices. These distinctive features of classical wage theory emphasise the relevance of the first part of our title, *pre-Smithian* classical political economy, since they occurred in preliminary form well before 1776.

Before the relevance of that emphasis can be demonstrated, the notion of classical political economy needs some comment. For many historians of economics, and for those familiar with the run-of-the-mill histories of economics, classical economics is seen as a largely British phenomenon, the dominant form of economics for the first half of the nineteenth century. Classical economics is seen to start with the path-breaking work of Adam Smith, and to conclude with the system of political economy developed by John Stuart Mill in his *Principles of Political Economy* (1848 in the first edition, 1871 for the seventh and last) or, in some cases, with the final defence of the Millian system by J. E. Cairnes during the late 1870s. This conveniently enables Smith's predecessors to be labelled as non-classical, as mere precursors or pre-Adamites, a type of classification which enables a particular slant to be placed on the interpretation of Smith, and to ignore the many important non-British contributions which Smith, a cosmopolitan and citizen of the world, gratefully absorbed into his system. This view, moreover, glosses over the other meanings which have been ascribed to classical political economy: that of Marx, that of Keynes, and, in the wake of Sraffa (1960), that which bases itself on the surplus approach as the central framework of classical doctrine with respect to distribution (cf. Pivetti 1987: esp. 872). Of these, Marx's approach in particular, and to a lesser extent, the surplus approach to classical political economy, have the quality of embracing the tradition in economic literature prior to Adam Smith, more specifically in the case of Marx, commencing the period of classical political economy with Sir William Petty in England and Boisguilbert in France at the end of the seventeenth century. This gives classical political economy a virtual century of history before one of its great peaks, Adam Smith's *Wealth of Nations* (see Marx 1859: 56; and, for a detailed discussion, Groenewegen 1987). For the purposes of this paper, the Marxian perspective on the history of classical political economy is particularly pertinent since it allows a discussion of both the British and the French economic literature on the subject of wage theory before Adam Smith's treatise was published in 1776.

Some further remark needs to be made by way of introduction. Much of the focus in this discussion of pre-Smithian classical wage theory is on the conceptualisation, and application, of the subsistence wage in that literature in both France and England. The first section of the paper looks at the idea of the subsistence wage in the general literature of economics in the century from 1650 and at the limited use which was made of it in these writings. This sets the stage for a more detailed examination in the second section of a number of selected authors (Petty, Cantillon, Steuart) who can be said to have developed the notion of a subsistence wage in the context of an economic system based in essence on the surplus approach. A third section looks at three French post-1650 contributions to the concept of a subsistence wage. A fourth and final section offers some conclusions. The chapter's thrust falls within Garegnani's research questions (see Garegnani 1989: 118) which stressed the need for more detailed examination of the more formative stage in the classical theories of wages before Adam Smith.

It may likewise be useful to identify the various stages in which a relationship between subsistence and surplus can be examined. A good starting point is to separate the notion of subsistence from wages. The surplus can then be identified without any reference to wages by the simple subtraction from the product of the necessary consumption (subsistence) of the workers who are required in the production of that product. The analysis is then firmly placed within the sphere of production. An additional step then becomes possible, establishing the proposition that the wages of labour tend to equality with the value of subsistence. This enables emergence of the classical connection between production and distribution, and allocation of the surplus becomes synonymous with the distribution of non-wage income (interest, profits, rent, and in some cases, entrepreneurial income). Principles additional to the identification (or determination) of wages with (by) subsistence are required to explain the distribution of the surplus between profits, entrepreneurial income, interest, rent and taxes. This conceptual framework of the relationship between subsistence and surplus allows a different explanation of content ordering. Section 2 looks at aspects of the second stage; identification of wages with subsistence, in arguments which are generally independent of the first stage. Sections 3 and 4 discuss authors who had tended to cover the first two stages of the argument in varying degrees, and some of whom, towards the end of the period, had begun to tackle the third stage. Of the latter, Turgot is the leading example.

Primitive views on subsistence and wages

The notion of an association between the labourer's wage and cost of living came easily in societies with a long tradition of wage setting in accordance with movements in the price of provisions. In medieval, Tudor and early Stuart England, 'wage fixing had to be carried out in a manner closely resembling the modern calculations of a rise in the cost of living, by referring to "the prices of all kinds of victuals, full rayment and apparel, both linnen and woollen and also of house rent"' (Heckscher 1955: 229; cf. Furniss 1920: 43–4, 164–73; Lipson 1956: III, 271–7; and the statutes reprinted in Bland *et al.* 1914: 329, 342). France had a similar tradition of wage setting in terms of food prices, and of supplementary, regional controls over the price of bread, which lasted longer than their British counterpart.

The simple subsistence theory of wages rested on the proposition that there existed a straightforward direct relationship between the rate of wages and the prices of provisions. If money wages were high, it was only a result of the high prices workmen paid for the necessities needed for their living; and if these prices fell, then wages would fall as a necessary consequence. Anything that caused the price of provisions to change, whether from tax rises, restraints on trade or natural causes such a harvest failure, subsequently induced a change in wages.

That this simple relationship existed in the period as an explanation of the causes of high or low wages can be seen from the following quotations:

> the hire of Labourers and Servants carrieth with it a resultance of the prices of all things necessary for a man's life.
>
> (Rice Vaughan 1675: 108, cf. 105)

> As the food and rayment of the poor is made dear by Excise, so doth the price of their labour rise in proportion.
>
> (Mun 1664: 102)

If malt, coals, leather, and other things bear a great price, the wages of servants, workmen, and artificers, will consequently rise.

(Davenant 1696: II, 199)

We must consider that Wages must bear a rate in all Nations according to the Price of Provisions, when Wheat is sold for one Shilling *per* Bushel, and all things suitably, a labouring Man may work for three Pence *per diem*, as well as can for twelve Pence, when it is sold for four shillings ... you cannot fall Wages, unless you fall Products.

(Cary 1695: 144–5)

the different Cheapness or Dearness of Provisions in several Countries, must be allowed to make amends for different Wages.

(Fleetwood 1707: 165)

Where Provisions are dear, Work and Wages will rise in Proportion and ... should a *Fishery* make Provisions in *England* but one tenth part cheaper, Wages would fall in proportion.

(Puckle 1707: 40, 42, cf. 44)

Rates of Labour are always settled and constituted of the Price of Victuals and Drink.

(Vanderlint 1734: 6)

all Wages must be proportioned to the Price of the Necessaries of Life.

(Lindsay 1733: 36)

For the *Incomes* of such Families are the *Measure* of their *expenses*; and they cannot *eat*, *drink*, or *wear* more in a Year, than they earn in that Time, so that if the intended *Tax* should be laid, and their *Wages* are to continue at the *same Rates* as heretofore, nothing can be plainer, or more certain than that all Money which such a *Tax* would cause to be taken more than usual out of their *Incomes, must be PINCHED* from the *BELLIES* and *BACKS* of the *Labouring Families*, whose wages, as Matters now stand, do but barely provide them with *Necessary* Meat, *Drink*, *Cloathing*, *Firing*, *etc*.

(Massie 1760: 10)

Flesh-meat was tolerably cheap, before bread became dear, but now both stand at a pretty high rate, and of consequence must proportionably raise the price of labour.

(Anonymous 1758: 23)

Several quotations from the opinions just cited mention the frequent outcries against the dearness of provisions in times of harvest failure, such as those which occurred in 1757–9 and 1766–8. Others referred to the impact on wage rates of an excise on the necessities consumed by the poor. This concern was sometimes on humanitarian grounds, but more generally was inspired by a desire to safeguard the export trade from the uncompetitiveness of high wages.

Real analytical depth embodied in this causal relationship between provision prices and wages was generally missing. There was little awareness of the forces which determined the prices of provision apart from the immediate causes such as tax increases, harvest failure and import prohibitions which induced the complaints. Nor was the relationship analytically used to heighten understanding of the economic system. An exception is Child (1690), who built in a migratory population mechanism to explain wage levels, as well as a link between population, employment opportunities and wage levels. 'For much want of People would procure greater Wages; and greater Wages if our Laws have encouragement, would procure us a supply of People without the charge of breeding them' (Child 1690: 175); or, alternatively:

> Such as our employment is for People, so many will our People be; and if we should imagine we have in England employment but for one hundred People, and have born and bred amongst us one hundred and fifty people, I say, the fifty must away from here, or starved, or be hanged to prevent it, whether we had any foreign Plantations or not.
>
> (Child 1690: 174)

However, these remarks were not integrated into a consistent theory of wage determination in terms of subsistence. Another exception can be found in the work of Locke, who used the assumption of a subsistence wage in his argument designed to demonstrate that the ultimate incidence of all taxes was on the landlord who paid it from rent:

> The Poor Labourer and handicraftsman cannot [bear this increase in taxes]; for he just lives from hand to mouth already, and all his Food, Clothing, and Utensils, costing a quarter more than they did before, either his Wages must rise with the Price of things, to make him live, or else, not being able to maintain himself and his Family by his labour, he comes to the Parish and then the Land bears the burden in a heavier way.
>
> (Locke 1696: 92)

If the wages of labour were regulated by the need for subsistence, a tax could not effectively be placed on labourers. They would pass it on; either through wage increases, or else through demands for poor relief, whose burden via the poor rates would fall on landlords. The direct, or indirect, effects of the tax-induced wage increases would likewise impact on landlords' incomes, either through the rise in prices following on a rise in wages for the commodities landlords consumed, or through a rising wage bill for the domestic servants and retainers they hired. The analytical importance of the subsistence wage assumption for this tax incidence result perceived by Locke at the end of the seventeenth century, was grasped equally by the physiocrats in their analysis of the efficiency of a single, direct tax on net product, and by their contemporary Steuart. Its analytical importance was also implied in the work of Petty and, more strongly, Cantillon. This is discussed in the subsequent sections.

Tax incidence analysis, implicitly in the case of Locke, and more explicitly in that of some subsequent writers, raises the issue of surplus in relation to the subsistence wage. A number of British authors of the seventeenth and eighteenth centuries grasped, in varying degrees, the analytical importance of a given subsistence wage for the determination, allocation and distribution of the economic surplus. Their contributions, qualitatively distinctly superior to the simple views looked at in this section, can now be considered.

Petty, Cantillon and Steuart

The central conceptual significance of subsistence in early and mature classical economics is that it provides a fundamental link between production on the one hand, and functional income distribution on the other. Subsistence is identified with the necessary consumption of labour employed in production – this consumption per worker per given time period is the means of reproducing the workforce through time. In this sense, the notion of subsistence itself signifies a kind of production process for labour. The economic system's gross outputs net of direct commodity inputs defines 'net product' as commonly understood; net product net of total labour subsistence defines the social surplus. Hence with regard to production, the notion of subsistence is essential to conceptualising the surplus. Then, if a critical supposition can be added – that the purchasing power of the wages of labour is equatable with subsistence – a direct and clear-cut connection between the social surplus and income distribution can be drawn. Assuming that competition of some kind ensures a uniformity of prices and wages of homogeneous commodities and labour through time – and that production costs are at least covered by prices – then the surplus is realised as non-wage income. That is to say, if the production system produces a surplus, and wages are restricted to subsistence, then prices must allow non-wage income – which is just the point Sraffa (1960: 3–10) makes concerning the transition from pricing in a subsistence system, to pricing with production of a surplus. The question of the allocation of the surplus then become synonymous with the question of the distribution of non-wage income.

It seems evident enough that William Petty's seminal articulation of a notion of economic surplus is closely connected with a selfconscious methodological stance – derived primarily from Hobbes – which is guided by objectivism, economism and a thoroughgoing commitment to mathematics as the model for rational inquiry (See Aspromourgos 1996: ch. 4). Indeed, the very notion of a set of physical quantities of commodities (subsistence) which may be treated as given, for the purposes of an economic inquiry, is an expression of an objectivist stance – pointing as it does towards a social characterisation of consumption, *contra* the particular methodological individualism of post-classical marginalism, which treats consumption as individually idiosyncratic, save for its logical structure. More particularly, in this the earliest account of surplus with analytical significance, subsistence is conceived as a *social* datum not a physiological one: 'sugar, tobacco and pepper, which custom hath now made necessary to all sorts of people'; 'climate disposes men to a necessity of spending more or less'; subsistence understood as 'the easiest-gotten food of the respective countries of the world' – oatmeal (Ireland), rice (India), and so on (Hull 1899: 90, 181, 275).[2] Not invisible, and *impossible to observe*, 'preferences', but observable social behaviour, is the point of departure for analysis. In its most abstract form this approach enabled Petty to define the social surplus by deducting from gross product a single physical magnitude. This he could do by assuming (in an engagingly quaint and selfconscious way) that necessary labour consumption is constituted by a single commodity, homogeneous with the output of a particular sector or activity:

> I premise these suppositions: First ... suppose there be in a territory a thousand people. Let these people be supposed sufficient to till this whole territory as to the husbandry of corn, which we will suppose to contain all necessaries for life, as in the Lord's Prayer we suppose the word 'bread' doth. ... Suppose ... that a tenth part of this land, and tenth of the people, *viz*, an hundred of them, can produce corn enough for the whole.
>
> (Hull 1899: 89, also 30–1, 42–4, 50–1)

This novel construction was noticed by the young Sraffa (1925: 324n, also 279), who noted also that it had caught the attention of Alfred Marshall. It amounts to a production system which employs just one basic commodity.

In Petty, the notion of surplus is deployed for both explanatory and normative purposes. The world Petty's theory and doctrine inhabit is entirely precapitalist. His primitive treatment of the relation between surplus and incomes has ground rents and tax revenues as the income forms in which surplus is realised. Profits on capital advanced are nowhere to be found. The major purpose to which the surplus theory is devoted is analysis of labour allocation in society and extensive proposals for economic reform (i.e. proposals to *re*allocate social labour). In one such discussion Petty notes that the burden of the church on the social product could be substantially reduced by restoring celibacy to the English clergy; making the observation that

> forasmuch as there be more males than females in England ... it were good for the ministers to return to their celibacy. ... And then our unmarried parson might live as well with half, as now with the whole, of his benefice.
>
> (Hull 1899: 25, also 73, 79–80)

Any doubt that this is intended facetiously is dispelled by a knowledge of Petty's temperament (see Aspromourgos 1996: ch. 2). Furthermore, in the context of his famous (or infamous) political arithmetic, Petty actually makes some attempts to empirically measure surplus product, surplus labour and surplus land:

> The moderate labour of 12 million, not over … 12 hours per diem upon necessary business, will so cultivate 72 million of acres as to be sufficient maintenance for 19 millions of people … 3 acres, 2 thirds [of land] well cultivated, will maintain … at a medium of man, woman and children.[3]

> 18,000,000 of acres, 3,500,000 boves, 1,000,000 of sheep and 300,000 people may feed 1,200,000,000 [in Ireland]; and consequently … there being 1,200,000,000 in all … 900,000 are spare hands and may be employed to luxury, ornament, war sciences, superstitions [i.e. religion] etc.
>
> (Matsukawa 1977: 45–7)[4]

With regard to wages and subsistence in particular, the precapitalist character of Petty's thought is manifest in his comments on regulation of wages:

> if it were proclaimed that labourers' wages … should not rise at all upon … [a doubling of money prices] then would this Act be as only a tax upon the said labourers, as forcing them to lose half their wages; which would not be only unjust but impossible, unless they could live with the said half (which is not to be supposed). For then the law that appoints such wages were ill made, which should allow the labourer but just wherewithall to live. For if you allow double then he works but half so much as he could have done and otherwise would;[5] which is a loss to the Public of the fruit of so much labour.
>
> (Hull 1899: 87)

> It is observed by clothiers and others who employ great numbers of poor people, that when corn is extremely plentiful, that the labour of the poor is proportionally dear and scarce to be had at all (so licentious are they who labour only to eat, or rather to drink).[6] Wherefore, when so many acres sown with corn, as do usually produce a sufficient store for the nation, shall produce perhaps double to what is expected or necessary, it seems not unreasonable that this common blessing of God should be applied to the common good of all people, represented by their sovereign; much rather than the same should be abused by the vile and brutish part of mankind.
>
> (Hull 1899: 274–5)

> Now the price of labour must be certain (as we see it made by the Statutes which limit the day-wages of several workmen); the non-observance of which laws, and the not adapting them to the change of times, is by the way very dangerous, and confusive to all endeavours of bettering the trade of the nation.
>
> (Hull 1899: 52; also 30–1, 118–19, 220 with 299)

Petty's regulatory views amount to keeping the hourly or daily real wage at a rate which stabilises labour supply at desirable levels – either by targeting the corn price or adjusting the money wage.

Where Petty's corpus of published writings consists of a collection of tracts – albeit with a considerable underlying unity of doctrine and purpose – Cantillon's extant contribution to economics consists of a single work, which is a genuine treatise. Here the treatment of wages and subsistence leaves absolutely no doubt concerning the social and conventional character of necessary labour consumption. For now customary consumption is not only historically and geographically determined, but also *class* determined. That is to say, there are *multiple* customary subsistences at any particular time and place, with a different consumption for different categories of labour. In a striking illustration of this in relation to consumption and human reproduction, Cantillon observes:

> most men desire nothing better than to marry if they are set in a position to keep their Families in the same style as they are content to live themselves. That is, if a Man is satisfied with the produce of an Acre and a half of Land he will marry if he is sure of having enough to keep his Family in the same way. But if he is only satisfied with the produce of 5 to 10 Acres he will be in no hurry to marry unless he thinks he can bring up his Family in the same manner …
>
> [with regard to the nobility,] as the largest share of the Property is usually given to the Eldest sons, the younger Sons are in no hurry to marry …
>
> …In the lower classes … most … would consider themselves to do an injustice to their Children if they brought them up to fall into a lower class than themselves. … All the lower orders wish to live and bring up Children who can live like themselves.
>
> (Cantillon 1755: 77–9)

This notion of multiple subsistence and 'class reproduction' (so to speak) raises the question of *who* is necessary for production in Cantillon's scheme of thinking; that is to say, what categories of labour (and hence also their customary subsistence) constitute necessary input to the production system, and what labour or activities (and hence also their consumption, subsistence or otherwise) are surplus. The issue is complicated by the fact that, unlike in Petty, in Cantillon profits begin to enter the economic picture in a systematic manner. But these profits are not the profits of capital advanced; rather, they are profits of entrepreneurship, and in particular, of risk-bearing. Entrepreneurship for Cantillon is linked with non-wage income other than rents, interest receipts and taxes. The profits of entrepreneurship are linked with self-employment:

> Undertakers[7] of all kinds adjust themselves to risks … [and] live at uncertainty; except the Prince and the proprietors of Land, all the Inhabitants of a State … can be divided into two classes, Undertakers and Hired people

> … all the Undertakers are as it were on unfixed wages and the others on wages fixed so long as they receive them.
>
> (Cantillon 1755: 53–5)

Hence farmers are entrepreneurs, as – for example – are chimney-sweeps and water carriers; whereas generals and courtiers are hired labourers (Cantillon 1755: 43–55). The precise domain of the surplus and its correspondence with income distribution thereby become somewhat unclear. Are entrepreneurial incomes – in particular, farmers' incomes – to be associated with the social surplus or not? The best judgement one can form on the basis of Cantillon's text is that they are now, with the surplus accruing exclusively as rents, taxes and interest payments (see Aspromourgos 1996: section 7.3).

The conception of subsistence wages as the means of reproduction of a (heterogeneous) labour force is brought into sharp focus in Cantillon's conception of a parity of value between land input and labour input in production. In essence, this equation involves Cantillon determining the quantities of land required to reproduce each category of labour, in the sense of the quantities of land required to produce their customary (subsistence) consumption (see Cantillon 1755: 31–43; Aspromourgos 1996: ch. 6, esp. section 6.2). In other words, it is a reduction of labour (as a reproducible input) to a quantity of land – in Cantillon's system, implicitly the only primary input. This is evident in Cantillon's conception of value as being determined by direct and indirect land input:

> the intrinsic value of any thing may be measured by the quantity of Land used in its production and the quantity of labour which enters into it, in other words by the quantity of Land of which the produce is allotted to those who have worked upon it.
>
> (Cantillon 1755: 41)

The land value of labour – that is, the land input directly and indirectly required to produce customary labour subsistence – is a measure of the real cost of labour reproduction, with the price of labour (the money wage) equal to cost of production (the money price of customary subsistence) (Cantillon 1755: 19–21, 123–5, 177). Cantillon makes this notion of cost-of-labour-reproduction most explicit with respect to slaves, by comparing them to cattle; analytically, the value of non-slave labour is formulated in exactly the same way as for slave labour.[8] As to the *content* of subsistence, Cantillon generally seems to identify it with the product of a vertically integrated rural sector which includes production of its own manufactured inputs to agricultural output (Aspromourgos 1996: 80).

Steuart is a figure contemporaneous with Adam Smith, though the development of Steuart's theory of distribution and value is more really contemporaneous with Quesnay. Here, there is what appears to be a departure from the doctrine of subsistence wages; but whether this marks an *advance* upon the achievements of Petty and Cantillon is another matter. The *Inquiry into the*

Principles of Political Oeconomy (1767) is often ambivalent and somewhat obscure on the issue of the relation between wages and subsistence (see Aspromourgos 1996: ch. 8). Certainly Steuart articulates a clear conception of subsistence (with agriculture the primary element), and its social or conventional character. This he does by drawing a distinction between 'physical-necessary' and 'political-necessary'. The former is defined as 'ample subsistence where no degree of superfluity is implied'. On the other hand, political-necessary, which varies according to social rank, is conventional:

> The nature of man furnishes him with some desires relative to his wants, which do not proceed from his annual oeconomy, but which are entirely similar to them in their effects. These proceed from the affections of his mind, are formed by habit and eduction, and when once *regularly established*, create another kind of necessary.
>
> (Steuart 1767: 269–70; cf. 155)

As in Cantillon, there are multiple customary subsistences. Steuart seems to expect the wages of the majority of labourers to be governed by physical subsistence, though by no means all, where physical subsistence is itself divided into three classes:

> it is requisite that the individual of the most puny constitution for labour and industry, and of the most slender genius for works of ingenuity … should be able … to gain the *lowest* degree of the physical-necessary; for in this case, by far the greatest part of the industrious will be found in the second [middle] class, and the strong and healthy all in the first [highest]. The difference between the highest class and the lowest, I do not apprehend to be very great …
>
> What we mean by the *first class* of the physical-necessary, is … [what] a strong healthy person should be able to gain by the exercise of the lowest denominations of industrious labour, and without a possibility of being deprived of it, by the competition of others of the same profession.
>
> Farther … this *physical-necessary* ought to be the highest degree of ease, which any one should be able to acquire with labour and industry, where no peculiar ingenuity is required. … The *physical-necessary*, therefore, ought to be the reward of *labour* and *industry*; whatever any workman gains above this standard, ought to be in consequence of his superior *ingenuity*.
>
> (Steuart 1767: 272–4; cf. 114–16, 269–76, 297, 302, 377–8, 400–1, 681)

It would be possible, in one sense, to perceive this ambivalence concerning that confluence of subsistence and wages as analytical progress: to the extent that wages are being uncoupled, to some extent, from subsistence, labourers are no longer merely being theorised like cattle (or houses – Steuart 1767: 401). But what seems more significant concerning the relation between wages and subsistence in Steuart is that the ambivalence is an expression of a deep problem which renders his *magnum opus* qualitatively and decisively inferior to that of Adam Smith in this regard. Steuart draws no clear functional distinction between labour and capital, and hence, not between wages and profits. Indeed, he really has no theory of capital at all. The 'profits' which appear in the *Principles* are really the profits of artisans, craftsmen, merchants and traders; and so are largely the profits of species *of labour*: 'the price of a manufacture is to be known by the expense of living of the workman, the sum it costs him to bring his work to perfection, and his reasonable profit' (Steuart 1767: 340). In this sense, (surplus) wages and profits become interchangeable terms (for example, Steuart 1767: 161, 288, 684, 695).

This failure analytically to distinguish wages and profits in an adequate manner manifests itself also in another, and quite striking, line of argument which Steuart pursues concerning distribution and subsistence, and which is worth noting here. Steuart raises the possibility that customary subsistence might itself become a function of above-normal wages (or 'profits' as quasi-wages):

> if the scale of demand … keeps profits high … not only the immediate seller of the goods, but also every one who has contributed to the manufacture, will insist upon sharing these new profits … and by such profits subsisting for a long time, they insensibly become *consolidated* … into the intrinsic value[9] of the goods. … [T]hese profits become, by long habit, virtually *consolidated* with the real value[10] of the merchandize.
>
> So soon as … profits become *consolidated* with the intrinsic value, they … cease to have the advantage of profits, and, becoming in a manner necessary to the existence of the goods, will cease to be considered as advantageous.
>
> [One cause of high price is] consolidation of high profits with … real value … This cause operates in countries where luxury has gained ground, and where domestic competition has called off too many of the hands.
>
> (Steuart 1767: 192–3, 194, 246; cf. 204, 240, 248–52, 259, 684, 695)

Profits are metamorphosed, so to speak, into customary necessary consumption and hence production costs of commodities. Garegnani (1984: 320 n49) raises a similar issue, concerning the possible dependence of subsistence upon market wages – though in his case it is deployed as an implied critique of classical closure (the notion of a 'natural' real wage with respect to which market wages are regulated). In Steuart's case, 'consolidation' leads to no alternative closure – in fact, he is left with a system of value and distribution with no closure or determinacy at all. Marx's (1967: III, 783–4) comment is accurate enough, and applies as well to Steuart: 'Petty, Cantillon, and in general those writers who are closer to feudal times, assume ground-rent to be the normal form of surplus-value in general, whereas profit to them is still amorphously combined with wages'.

Boisguilbert, Quesnay and Turgot

In the French writings of the period, the views of Boisguilbert, Quesnay and

Turgot deserve particular attention. This is not because there were no other writers who drew relationships between wages and subsistence. An examination of Boisguilbert is interesting because of the particular emphasis he gave to workers' subsistence in the context of profits of agriculture and employment opportunities (cf. Bharadwaj 1987: 544). Quesnay developed arguments on the subsistence wage in connection with taxation and the distribution of the total product into net product and necessary expenses; a position which Turgot elaborated on and built into formal propositions about the competitive necessity for a subsistence wage.

In Boisguilbert's economic system, subsistence was associated with the livelihood of the workers, defined as those with nothing to sell but their 'arms' or bodily strength (Boisguilbert 1704: 834). Analytically, they are linked via the price of grain and opportunities for employment. A low grain price is condemned by Boisguilbert, even though at first sight it seems an advantageous situation for the poor. Boisguilbert's reasoning in support of a more appropriate, higher grain price is based on two factors: it enables a higher level of agricultural activity from the higher incomes it gives to landlords and farmers which, in addition, raises economic activity levels cumulatively and generally. It thereby provides greater opportunities for work, and work combined with higher grain prices provides better conditions for poor labourers than unemployment combined with low grain prices and relatively cheap bread (Boisguilbert 1704: esp. 828–9, 843–4).

Contrary to the claim of Van Dyke Roberts (1935: 289–90), Boisguilbert does not really posit an explicit subsistence wage theory. However, he clearly suggests the necessity of the provision of subsistence for workers before profits can be paid or extracted, using the analogy of a coach horse which must be adequately fed before profits can be drawn from its services. This analogy likewise suggests the fact that subsistence has to be advanced to the workers (human or animal) before the produced output is sold. The necessity of subsistence for Boisguilbert arises not only from physical requirements, but from what he calls the 'obligations of religion, humanity, justice and politics'. These also make it mandatory that the labourer and his family get their subsistence, together with the opportunity to earn it from their daily labour (Boisguilbert 1707: 1003; cf. Van Dyke Roberts 1935: 289). Boisguilbert's comments clearly illustrate the validity of Garegnani's remark that classical economists associated the notion of a subsistence wage with social custom and convention as well as recognition of the possibility of unemployment.

What constitutes customary subsistence in Boisguilbert's writings is something needing further discussion. The starting point is the important role of corn in the food requirements of the ordinary people:

> No one contests that in France corn alone constitutes the food of the ordinary people [*menu peuple*] without any assistance of beverages or vegetables as everywhere else, and even less of meat and fish; by contrast in England, it is bread which holds the least place in the customary daily food of the

> people. Meat and fish are there quite plentiful and consequently lowly priced, thereby relieving corn of three quarters, and often even all of the functions which it has in France of almost feeding the people by itself.
>
> (Boisguilbert 1704: 868)

Earlier, Boisguilbert (1704: 864) had discussed the 'necessities for workers' in terms of the abundance of the harvest, and talked of their 'customary subsistence' ('la subsistence ordinaire') in connection with the need for grain exports to revive and stimulate agriculture. Not surprisingly, therefore, there is a link between wages and corn prices; a high corn price 'justifies raising the price of workers' (Boisguilbert 1704: 875).

There are qualifications to the emphasis on the almost exclusive importance of corn in the French labourer's diet. Some workers are able to supplement their corn diet with 'salted meat and a broth made of boiled meat'. During periods of prosperity associated with high corn prices, high employment and high incomes, workers' consumption of meat can be as much as tripled in Boisguilbert's view, hence well above subsistence in leaner times. High surplus is therefore linked with high real wages via the demand for labour it generates (Boisguilbert 1704: 868–9). In the context of a discussion of military supplies, including timber frames for fortifications and metallic products for armaments, Boisguilbert (1707: 1002) mentioned 'bread, wine, meat and clothing' as essential supplies for the soldiers. Boisguilbert's customary subsistence standards therefore admit of considerable flexibility, not only on the basis of international comparisons with England and Holland, a flexibility many of the classical economists admitted, but in terms of the relative degree of prosperity which existed in a particular region or country at a particular time.

Much of the content of Boisguilbert's subsistence wage views can be found in Quesnay's work. His earlier economic writings simply linked wages to the price of subsistence, especially to that of corn, as the commodity which featured most prominently in workers' budgets. A rise in the price of corn could therefore entail a rise in wages:

> A man consumes three setiers of corn (per annum); if because of the proper price ['bon prix'] of corn he pays four livres more for each setier, this price increases his expenditure by a sou per day, and his wages will rise in this proportion.
>
> (Quesnay 1757: 509)

Like Boisguilbert, Quesnay did not advocate low wages, since this was incompatible with his views on the appropriate price of corn. High corn prices were required to stimulate agricultural production, the size of the net product and hence induce economic prosperity. Moreover, low corn prices tended to make workers 'less industrious, lazy and presumptuous so that farmers, as employers of labour, were better off when bread and corn were dear for this reason as well (Quesnay 1757: 509).

In later work, Quesnay introduced some additional factors into his discussion of wages. These related to migratory shifts of labour when 'corn is too low and earnings are in proportion' – a situation he, also like Boisguilbert, linked to diminished employment opportunities for labour (Quesnay 1758: 635). A competitive labour market was implied which linked the level of prices relative to costs of consumption with the state of employment and the supply of available workers via migratory population changes. If the balance between prices and wages was disturbed, that between prices and costs would also be altered, changing both the employment situation (an increased margin over cost raising, and a reduced one, lowering employment opportunities) and the incentives of workers to immigrate or emigrate according to the attractiveness of the circumstances. High prices and commensurate wages provide incentives to hire labour and induce an influx of workers to meet that demand from neighbouring regions with less favourable conditions. As Bharadwaj put it (1987: 544), this constituted a marriage between the ideas of Boisguilbert and Child on the subject.

In one of his last economic papers, Quesnay showed that this mechanism would ultimately lower wages to some minimum:

> The level of wages, and consequently the enjoyments which the wage-earners can obtain for themselves, are fixed and reduced to a minimum by the extreme competition which exists between them. If a nation seeks through a tax to force these wage-earners doubly to restrict their enjoyments, they will migrate in order to settle in other nations where their subsistence is more assured and their industry more protected. Then the small number of them who remain in the country, being less constrained by competition, will lay down the law to the first distributors of the expenditure, and force them to pay the normal wages, plus the tax and the costs of the land into the bargain. The result is that these first proprietors of renascent products bound to the land through their possessions, will necessarily bear the whole burden of this destructive tax. If the wage-earners, whose enjoyments it is sought to restrict by means of the tax, are unable to emigrate in order to get back to their former level, they will become beggars or thieves, a kind of arbitrary and walking tax, which is very burdensome to the first distributors of the expenditure.
>
> (Quesnay 1767: 984–5)

Whether there is an implication in this argument that Quesnay saw this subsistence level as a physical minimum is doubtful. His reference to workers' enjoyments as part of that subsistence suggests customary levels and standards, or a normal consumption pattern above the physically necessary which varied slowly over time. At the same time, the tax incidence theory, as in the case of Locke, required the notion of a given subsistence wage in order to reach the desired result that landlords pay all taxes directly and indirectly. A given subsistence wage seems also to be assumed for the intricate analyses of accumulation, input/output relations and the necessary distribution of output which were part and parcel of his *Tableau Economique*.

Turgot, the last of the major French economists before Adam Smith, produced the most theoretically satisfying subsistence wage theory. His most famous work, the 'Reflections' (Turgot 1766: 45–6) enunciated this by the statement that competition limits the wages of workers to subsistence. A letter to Hume written not long thereafter clarified the matter further. Although wages were competitively determined by supply and demand, labour like all commodities also had a 'fundamental value' which, 'for the wages of the artisan … is the cost of his subsistence'. As in the general theory of value, market prices under competitive conditions in the long run adjust to the fundamental value, even when subsistence, the basis for the fundamental price of the worker, contained an element of 'superfluity, which if need be, can be reduced' (Turgot 1767a: 211–12).

Turgot (1767b: 126–7) explained this more fully by examining the interrelationship between the price of agricultural products, profits, the level of wages and the size of the population. High wages increase the cost of production as part of these costs and lower profits. 'Is there any type of work in which profits are not diminished by the dearness of labour?' Furthermore, higher wages increase population, either by immigration, a fairly rapid effect, or by encouraging marriage and births: 'the increase in people in turn lowers wages through competition'. A similar argument, but in more detail, was presented three years later in Turgot's letters on the grain trade to l'Abbé Terray (Turgot 1770: 174–6, 177 and cf. 170). In this argument, the profits of the farmers are directly linked to the demand of labour. In addition, the passage explains the meaning Turgot gave to subsistence in more detail:

> It is certain that competition, by causing wages to be at a lower level, reduce those of the simple unskilled workers to what is necessary to their subsistence. It should not be thought, however, that this necessary is thus reduced to the essentials for avoiding starvation to such an extent, that nothing remains outside it, which these men may have at their command either to obtain some little luxuries, or, if they are thrifty, to create a little movable fund which becomes their resort in unforeseen causes of sickness, or times of high prices, or unemployment. When the objects of their expenditure increase in price, they first begin to cut down on this little superfluity and the enjoyments it can procure for them. But it is of this type of *luxury* especially, that it can be said that it is *a most necessary thing*, it is essential that there is a little of it, just as it is necessary that there is *some play* in every machine. A watch of which all the wheels would work into each other with mathematical precision and without the smallest gap, would soon cease to go. If by an unexpected decrease in wages or increase in expenses, the worker can put up with being reduced to strict essentials, the same causes which had forced wages to rise a little above the necessary of yesterday, continue to operate and cause them to rise once more until they

> attain a higher level, in the same proportion with the necessary of today. If an absence of the ability to pay stands in the way of this return to the natural proportion, if the decrease of the revenue of the proprietors persuaded them to resist this increase in wages, the worker would go elsewhere to look for the competency without which he cannot exist; population would diminish up to the point where the decrease in the number of workers, by curtailing their competition, enables them to lay down the law and to force the proprietors to raise wages.
>
> (Turgot 1770: 168)

Once again, the import of the remark is that the notion of subsistence is a flexible one; it allows for the requirements of the workers and their dependents in a progressive manner, that is, relative to the changes in these requirements over time, and enabling variation with the circumstances. The last can be documented from a remark on the high wages paid in Holland. These 'exceed the needs of those who earn them', partly because the advantageous location of Holland favours high labour productivity. This enables saving by workers, an opportunity not available in some of the views on subsistence which have been quoted (for example, that of Massie 1760) as well as the taxation of wages or wage goods (the notorious Dutch excise) to defray public expenditure (Turgot 1767b: 131).

Concluding comments

From the modern standpoint, looking at the classical treatment of wages in relation to subsistence in retrospect, we may raise a number of questions, premised upon an observation: it seems obvious that in modern capitalist economies real wages are in general normally above subsistence. (1) What does this 'uncoupling' of wages from subsistence mean for the plausibility of the classical approach to economics today? (2) Does the notion of subsistence labour consumption itself even retain any meaning in the modern context? And if it does not, how can the surplus approach retain any plausibility since, as indicated above, the social surplus cannot be defined in the absence of a concept of necessary labour consumption?

1

The classical surplus approach to distribution and value in particular, proceeded in two steps. First there is the conception of production as a 'circular' system which generates a surplus over and above replacement of used up means of production, including necessary labour consumption – a *re*production system, so to speak. Such systems may be growing through time, depending upon the uses to which the surplus is put, which may itself be connected with income distribution. Second, in a framework of generalised capitalist competition wherein wages, prices, profits and other returns are arbitraged, some principles for determining the distribution of the surplus must be deployed. In the classical framework, the subsistence theory of wages was one such principle (the principle of differential rents was another). Now Sraffa (1960) has rigorously shown that in a classical framework along these lines, given the real wage and output levels, the technique of production in use will determine relative prices simultaneously with the remaining distributive variables; so that the distribution of the surplus, in terms of 'functional' income distribution, is fully determined. None of these results hinges essentially upon the real wage being equal to necessary labour consumption (and certainly does not hinge upon the real wage being constant). All that is required is that the real wage be determined independently of prices and other distributive variables (see Aspromourgos 1996: section 10.3). The only resulting difference is that wages will share in the social surplus, rather than it resolving exclusively into non-wage income shares – and some alternative principle for determining real wages must be posited. If the wage rate is to be maintained as a variable independent of relative prices and other distributive variables, then the most obvious such alternative principle in the modern era is money-wage indexation; but the failure of modern wage indexation systems to endure is noteworthy. In fact, the *lack* of dependence of the surplus approach upon a subsistence wage assumption is evident from the very beginning – in one of Petty's surplus models, in which consumption is allowed to vary above subsistence (Hull 1899: I, 89–90).

It is possible to take a *further* step away from classicism: to propose not only that real wages share in the social surplus, but also that real wages cease to be the independent distributive variable, to be replaced by the general rate of profit on capital (it is evident that the latter step presupposes the former). This is overwhelmingly what those who have followed Sraffa's lead in the rehabilitation and reconstruction of the classical surplus approach have suggested – and Sraffa himself. But there has been a division of opinion as to what principles are to be looked to for determining the rate of profit: the rate of accumulation, in the manner of the Cambridge Growth Equation (e.g. Pasinetti 1977: ch. VII, esp. 217–18); or a rate of interests determined by monetary forces, together with money-wage bargaining (e.g. Pivetti 1991). Garegnani (1984: 320–1) would appear to favour the latter (also Sraffa 1960: 33), the position with which the present authors agree. Certainly the latter approach is more consistent with the projection of a 'Sraffa-Keynes synthesis'. The point to emphasise here is that even this two-step departure from classicism retains the surplus approach: all that has altered is the character of the principles deployed for determining the distribution of the surplus.

2

What of the notion of subsistence itself? It has been seen in the above examination of notions of subsistence in pre-Smithian classical economics that subsistence was always conceived as a conventional or socio-historical phenomenon, from the very beginning of the tradition. The possibility that necessary consumption so understood might itself be a function of *above*-subsistence wages – as Steuart recognised, without grasping its full significance – might well do fatal damage to the classical *theory of wages*, insofar as it deprives the 'natural' wage of independence from the market wage (Garegnani 1984: 320 n49). But it does not seem to do any such damage to the notion of subsistence conventionally conceived itself; and so, neither to the concept of social surplus. This kind of 'hysteresis of subsistence' merely exposes more clearly the fact that subsistence and surplus *really are social phenomena*, not 'natural' phenomena. (It was one of Marx's fundamental criticisms of the classical school, that it mistook historically specific categories for natural phenomena.) In the developed world, access to electricity is a necessity not a luxury, and the telephone is not far off this status as well.[11] It would not seem a wild claim to suppose that at some time in the future, access to computer technologies will acquire similar status as a virtual necessity in large parts of the world. (Of course, there remains a *geographical* element to the notion of subsistence as well: that which is a necessity in one place might simultaneously be a luxury in another – or even quite useless.) If a *tangible* expression of subsistence is to be sought for in the developed world, then it is likely to be found in the character and content of the various social security and related income support systems in the developed economies. These systems, in a very real sense, constitute the various social conceptions of the minimum acceptable standard of life in modern economies. That these systems have themselves evolved as functions of technical progress, labour productivity and real wages, as well as other social forces, in no way vitiates the distinction between necessity and luxury.[12]

This line of argument also points to why the labour movement in particular, and wage earners in general, have a quite direct material interest in the provision of social security and income support, *even if they individually never have recourse to those systems*: if real wages in the modern world are endogenously determined, ultimately by reference to an exogenous profitability of capital, this mechanism would still be constrained by a lower bound for real wages, determined by reference to subsistence. If this socially determined subsistence is constituted by social security, then the preservation and enhancement of such systems is synonymous with the preservation and enhancement of the lower bound of the spectrum of possible distributive outcomes, within which central bank determination of interest, interacting with money-wage bargaining, will determine the actual distributive outcome.

Notes

1 Garegnani defined this specifically in terms of the relation between distribution of the surplus and relative prices.
2 In all quotations from Petty, spelling and punctuation have been modernised.
3 This is from the unpublished *Petty Papers*, vol. I, item 22, p. 4 – as catalogued by Slatter (1980). The *Papers* are now held by the British Library.
4 Other illustrations of this empirical conceptualisation are provided in Aspromourgos (1996: ch. 3; esp. section 3.5).

5 This phenomenon, which was not only observed by Petty, is sometimes described as a 'backward bending' labour supply curve. It might better be described as a 'rectangular hyperbola' supply curve: the worker seeks to adjust labour time worked as the real wage (time-) rate varies with the price of 'provisions' or 'corn', in order to maintain a desired or normal consumption level. If Sh is supply of labour hours per week, wh is the hourly time-rate of money wages, pc is the money price of corn, and c is normal labour consumption per week; then:

$$S_h \cdot w_h = p_c \cdot c$$

$$Sh\ (w_h/p_c) = c$$

The relation between hours supplied per week and the hourly real wage is a rectangular hyperbola.

6 The notion of 'corn' as a generic for subsistence is generally interpreted in terms of 'bread' as a staple – much like rice in much of Asia. Smith (1976: 175–6) makes this point, suggesting the possibility of potatoes replacing corn in parts of Europe. (If classical economics, and capitalism, had originated in the latter part of the world, we would no doubt speak now of a 'rice model', rather than a 'corn model'.) It is therefore worth noting that corn was the basis for distilling alcohol as well as baking bread. Petty makes this explicit in one characterisation of surplus:

> If we know how many people there are and the facilities of each, we can tell how much corn will make them bread *and beer*; how much wool and skins, clothes; what cattle will afford them flesh, butter and cheese; how many men's labour in nets and boats will find them fish and fowl. By all which, and by knowing how much of all these the intrinsic virtue of the country will produce, and with what labour, we know as followeth, viz:
>
> Whether we can live.
>
> What we can spare and export.
>
> How many of our whole number need actually to labour.
>
> (Lansdowne 1927: I, 89–90; emphasis added)

7 This is Higgs' translation of the word *Entrepreneurs*.

8 In initially assuming subsistence labour consumption, Sraffa (1960: 9) also likens wages to 'feed for ... cattle'. Cantillon's notion of labour being 'worth' its cost of production or consumption appears to have heightened Rousseau's indignation against modernity – and he also explicitly refers to men being evaluated like herds of cattle (see Aspromourgos 1996: 200 n16, with 101). See also Steuart (1767: 401).

9 This is an expression for cost of production.

10 This is a synonym for intrinsic value, at least in this context.

11 During the 1990s in Australia there has been some controversy surrounding provision of telephones to the poor – telephones which can take incoming calls, but cannot make outgoing calls. It is interesting to note that the controversy has not really been over whether the poor should have such access – only over whether they should be required to pay an installation fee. This implies that at least being able to receive phone calls is coming to be regarded as a 'necessity'.

12 The very proposition that wages are above subsistence is premised upon the concept of subsistence *retaining* meaning. In fact, the notion of subsistence has been engaged in modern marginalists (neo-Walrasian) economics as well – though in a rather more

physiological than conventional sense – because of the so-called 'survival problem'. That is to say, the problem that at an equilibrium vector of prices, with the endowment of the economy arbitrarily distributed among agents, there is no guarantee that all agents will be able to subsist – unless it is *assumed* that each agent's endowment already contains the subsistence bundle of commodities.

References

Anonymous (1758) *The Cries of the Public*, London.

Aspromourgos, T. (1996) *On the Origins of Classical Economics: Distribution and Value from William Petty to Adam Smith*, London: Routledge.

Baradwaj, K. (1963) 'Value through Exogenous Distribution', repr. in G. C. Harcourt and N. F. Laing (eds) (1971) *Capital and Growth*, Harmondsworth: Penguin Books, 183–95.

——(1987) 'Subsistence', J. Eatwell, M. Milgate and P. Newman (eds) *The New Palgrave. A Dictionary of Economics*, vol. 4, London: Macmillan, 543–5.

Bland, A. E., Brown, P. A. and Tawney, R. H. (eds) (1914) *English Economic History. Select Documents*, London: G. Bell and Sons.

Boisguilbert, P. (1704) 'Traité de la Nature, Culture, Commerce et Intérêts des Grains', in *Pierre de Boisguilbert ou la Naissance de l'Economie Politique*, Paris: Institut National d'Etudes Démographiques, 827–78 (1966).

——(1707) 'Dissertation de la Nature des Richesses, de l'Argent et des Tributs', in *Pierre de Boisguilbert ou la Naissance de l'Economie Politique*, Paris: Institut National d'Etudes Démographiques, 973–1012 (1966).

Cantillon, R. (1755) *Essai sur la Nature du Commerce en Général*, trans. and repr. by H. Higgs, London: Macmillan, for the Royal Economic Society (1931).

Cary, J. (1695) *An Essay on the State of England in Relation to Trade*, Bristol.

Child, J. (1690) *Discourse about Trade*, London.

Davenant, C. (1771) 'An Essay on the Probable Method of Making the People the Gainers of the Balance of Trade', repr. in W. Whitworth (ed.) (1969) *Political and Commercial Works of Charles Davenant*, London.

Fleetwood, W. (1707) *Chronicon Preciosum, or an Account of English Money, the Price of Corn and other Commodities for the last Six Hundred Years*, London.

Furniss, E. S. (1920) *The Position of the Labourer in a System of Nationalism*, New York: Houghton Mifflin.

Garegnani, P. (1983) 'The Classical Theory of Wages and the Role of Demand Schedules in the Determination of Relative Prices', *American Economic Review*, 73(2) May, 309–13.

——(1984) 'Value and Distribution in the Classical Economists and Marx', *Oxford Economic Papers*, 36(2) May, 291–325.

——(1987) 'Surplus Approach to Value and Distribution', in J. Eatwell, M. Millgate and P. Newman (eds) *The New Palgrave. A Dictionary of Economics*, vol. 4, London: Macmillan, 560–7.

——(1989) 'Sraffa: Classical versus Marginalist Analysis', in K. Bharadwaj and Bertram Shefold (eds) *Essays on Piero Sraffa. Critical Perspectives on the Revival of Classical Theory*, London: Routledge, 112–41, 148–58.

Groenewegen, P. D. (1987) 'Marx's Conception of Classical Political Economy: An Evaluation', *Political Economy: Studies in the Surplus Approach*, 3(1) 19–35.

Heckscher, E. F. (1955) *Mercantilism*, revised edn by E. F. Söderlund, London: Allen & Unwin.

Hull, C. H. (ed.) (1899) *The Economic Writings of Sir William Petty*, 2 vols, Cambridge: Cambridge University Press.

Lansdowne, H. (ed.) (1927) *The Petty Papers*, London: Constable.

Lindsay, P. (1733) *The Interests of Scotland Considered*, Edinburgh.

Lipson, E. (1956) *Economic History of England*, London: A&C Black.

Locke, J. (1696) *Some Considerations on the Consequences of the Lowering of the Interest and Raising the Value of Money*, London.

Marx, K. H. (1859) *A Contribution to the Critique of Political Economy*, trans. N.I. Stone, Chicago: Charles H. Kerr and Company (1913).

——(1967) *Capital: A Critique of Political Economy*, 3 vols, ed. F. Engels, New York: International Publishers.

Massie, J. (1760) *Reasons Humbly Offered Against the Laying any Further Tax Upon Malt and Beer*, London.

Matsukawa, S. (ed.) (1977) 'Sir William Petty: an Unpublished Manuscript', *Hitotsubashi Journal of Economics*, 17, 33–50.

Mun, T. (1664) *England's Treasure by Forraign Trade*, repr. in J. R. McCulloch (ed.) (1952) *Early English Tracts on Commerce*, London: Cambridge University Press.

Pasinetti, L. L. (1977) *Lectures on the Theory of Production*, New York: Columbia University Press.

Pivetti, M. (1987) 'Distribution Theories Classical', in J. Eatwell, M. Milgate and P. Newman (eds) *The New Palgrave. A Dictionary of Economics*, vol. 1, London: Macmillan, 872–6.

——(1991) *An Essay on Money and Distribution*, New York: St Martin's Press.

Puckle, J. (1707) *England's Path to Wealth and Honour*, London.

Quesnay, F. (1757) 'Grains', in *François Quesnay et la Physiocratie*, Paris: Institut National d'Etudes Démographiques, 459–510 (1958).

——(1758) 'Interesting Questions on Population in Agriculture and Trade', in *François Quesnay et la Physiocratie*, Paris: Institut National d'Etudes Démographiques, 619–66 (1958).

——(1767) 'The Second Economic Problem', in *François Quesnay et la Physiocratie*, Paris: Institut National d'Etudes Démographiques, 977–92 (1958).

Slatter, M. D. (1980) *Calender of Literary and Personal Papers of Sir William Petty (1623–87) at Bowood House, Calne, Wiltshire*, reproduced London: Royal Commission on Historical Manuscripts.

Smith, Adam (1976) *An Inquiry into the Nature and Causes of the Wealth of Nations*, eds R. H. Campbell and A. S. Skinner, Oxford: Clarendon Press.

Sraffa, P. (1925) 'Sulle Relazioni fra Costo e Quantità Prodotta', *Annali di Economia*, 2, 277–328.

——(1960) *Production of Commodities by Means of Commodities: Prelude to a Critique of Economic Theory*, Cambridge: Cambridge University Press.

Steuart, J. (1767) *An Inquiry into the Principles of Political Economy*, edited with an introduction by A. S. Skinner, 2 vols, Edinburgh and London: Oliver and Boyd, for the Scottish Economic Society (1966).

Turgot, A. R. J. (1766) 'Reflections on the Production and Distribution of Wealth', in P. D. Groenewegen (ed.) (1977) *The Economics of A. R. J. Turgot*, The Hague: Martinus Nijhoff, 43–95.

——(1767a) Letter to Hume, 25 March 1767, in Eugene Rotwein (ed.) (1955) *Economic Writings of David Hume*, London: Nelson 210–13.

——(1767b) 'Observations on a Paper by Graslin', in P. D. Groenewegen (ed.) (1977) *The Economics of A. R. J. Turgot*, The Hague: Martinus Nijhoff, 123–32.

——(1770) 'Extracts from "Letters on the Grain Trade"', in P.D. Groenewegen (ed.) (1977) *The Economics of A. R. J. Turgot*, The Hague: Martinus Nijhoff, 164–81.

Vanderlint, J. (1734) *Money Answers All Things*, London.

Van Dyke Roberts, H. (1935) *Boisguilbert. Economist of the Reign of Louis XIV*, New York: Columbia University Press.

Vaughan, R. (1675) *A Discourse of Coin and Coinage*, London.

9 Sir James Steuart and Richard Cantillon

Introduction

There has been a strong presumption in the literature that Sir James Steuart was familiar with the work of Richard Cantillon. In his English/French edition of the *Essai sur la Nature du Commerce en Général* of 1931, Henry Higgs, by then the leading authority on Cantillon, claimed that Sir James Steuart cited Cantillon's *Essai* in his *Works* (Higgs 1931: 392). Higgs was followed in this surmise, but not in his reference,[1] by Johnson (1937: 337); by Sen (1957: 198), who cites the same reference as Johnson; by Groenewegen (1983: 51–3; 1994: 28) and by Hutchison (1988: 337). Vickers (1960: 244, 253) is more cautious: he refers comparatively to Cantillon's work in his chapter on Steuart but draws no inferences about indebtedness. Brewer (1992: esp. 175–6) is likewise cautious:

> there is no evidence that Steuart knew Cantillon's work (though he did refer to Philip Cantillon, whose book, *The Analysis of Trade*, was based on Richard Cantillon's *Essai*) but sections of the *Inquiry* read very much as if they were based on Cantillon.[2]

A more recent book on Steuart (Yang 1994) makes no comment on whether Steuart had read Richard Cantillon's *Essai* or not, but compares Cantillon's work with that of Steuart on several occasions, sometimes in considerable detail (Yang 1994: 22, 50 n43, 111 n34, 112, 282 n16, chs 2 and 3, app.: 20–3, 68–77). This suggests an implicit assumption on Yang's part that Steuart had read Richard Cantillon's *Essai*.[3] Most of the relatively few commentators on Steuart have tended to assume that Steuart either had, or must have, read the *Essai*.

There seem to be only a few dissenters from this general claim. In his 1931 essay on Cantillon, Hayek (1991: 242) states, 'James Steuart cites Cantillon with reference to Philip Cantillon's garbled English *Analysis of Trade*', hence by implication denying that Steuart had read Cantillon's *Essai*. Hayek based the argument on Legrand (1900: 9) who had reached this conclusion without presenting evidence. More pointedly, Andrew Skinner in his introduction to the reprint of an abridged version of Steuart's *Inquiry* indicates that

> while he [i.e. Steuart] cites Philip Cantillon's *Analysis of Trade*, it is not entirely certain that he read the *Essai sur la nature du commerce en général* (1755). The work usually cited as the *Essai* by Steuart is Melon's.
>
> (Skinner 1966: 30 n2)

This careful statement raises doubts about Steuart having read Richard Cantillon without ruling out the possibility, while at the same time pointing implicitly to earlier wrong references to Steuart's alleged citations of Richard Cantillon which confused his work with that of his cousin Philip, or its abbreviated title with that of Melon.

This chapter examines the evidence on whether Steuart had read Richard Cantillon's *Essai* to decide whether there is any real, positive case for saying that he did so. The next section looks at the internal evidence obtainable from the text of Steuart's *Inquiry*. The section following suggests that if Richard Cantillon's *Essai* was not read by Steuart, the many similarities between the two works can nevertheless be explained by his access to Philip Cantillon's *Analysis*, which incorporated substantial slabs, but by no means all, of Richard Cantillon's earlier *Essai*. A final section presents conclusions on the implications of this discussion.

Did Steuart read Richard Cantillon?

The internal evidence from Steuart's *Principles* determining whether he read or did not read Richard Cantillon's *Essai* is both direct and indirect. On direct evidence, it can be noted immediately that there are no actual citations from Richard Cantillon's *Essai* anywhere in the *Principles of Political Oeconomy*. There are references to Philip Cantillon's *Analysis of Trade* (Steuart 1767: 2, 17, 18, 48), one of which apparently induced Henry Higgs to make the claim about a Richard Cantillon citation in Steuart's book. These Philip Cantillon citations were mentioned in the commentary literature by Legrand (1900: 9); Hayek (1991: 252); Johnson (1937: 409) and so on. Legrand correctly emphasised its significance with respect to Steuart's knowledge of Richard Cantillon: 'James Stuart qui le [i.e. Richard Cantillon] cite d'après l'ouvrage de Philippe Cantillon'. Hayek seems to have followed Legrand in this sentiment. This aspect is pursued more fully in the next section.

Other commentators (especially Johnson 1937: 409; Sen 1957: 198) have claimed to find a reference to Richard Cantillon in Steuart's *Inquiry* from his references to the 'author of the Essay on Commerce' (Steuart 1767: 2 241, 304). The second of these is quite explicit on details of the text consulted, enabling a clear demonstration that Steuart is talking here about Melon's *Essai Politique sur le Commerce* and not about Richard Cantillon's *Essai*:

> The author of the *Essay on Commerce*, reckons it [that is, the treasure of the Bank of Amsterdam] at four hundred million of guilders, and the

> Amsterdam edition carries in the margin a correction, which gives to understood, that it amounts to between eight and nine hundred millions.
> (Steuart 1767: 2 304)

Not only the Amsterdam edition to which Steuart explicitly referred, but all editions[4] of Melon's *Essai Politique sur le Commerce* with reference to the Bank of Amsterdam, in fact argued: 'Celle [that is, the Bank] d'Amsterdam est la plus grande & la plus fameuse; on la [that is, 'les fonds' or the capital] croit de trois ou quatre cens millions de florins', which a note in the bottom 'margin' corrects to 'huit à neuf cens millions (Melon, 1734: 255n*; 1735: 241fn†; 1761: 304).

Richard Cantillon's *Essai* provides no similar information in his brief discussion of the Bank of Amsterdam (Cantillon [1755] 1931: 505–7). As Skinner indicated in his edition of the *Inquiry* (Skinner 1966: 30 n2) and Cabrillo (1988: 175–7) argues at some length, the author of the *Essay on Commerce* mentioned by Steuart refers to Melon and not to Richard Cantillon.

Although Steuart's *Inquiry* contains many sections and arguments which are reminiscent of Richard Cantillon's work, there are no real reasons to presume that such similarities have to be explained by the fact that Steuart had studied Richard Cantillon's *Essai* itself. As Legrand (1900: 9) first suggested, Steuart cited Richard Cantillon indirectly 'after', that is, *from* the version contained in Philip Cantillon's *Analysis of Trade*. Much of Philip Cantillon's text is not 'garbled', as Hayek, following Jevons, wrongly suggested; often it repeats Richard Cantillon's text word for word. On other occasions it alters the argument to make the text more contemporary, that is to fit the circumstances of the late 1750s rather than the late 1720s of Richard Cantillon's text. Other sources for Richard Cantillon's economic ideas were available to Steuart. Brewer (1992: 175–6) indicates (without developing the matter in any detail) that in addition to Philip Cantillon's *Analysis*, Steuart may have derived some knowledge of Richard Cantillon's ideas from Mirabeau's *l'Ami des Hommes*, which had used Richard Cantillon's manuscript extensively, particularly in connection with the subject of population.[5] Moreover, Steuart knew Joseph Harris (Steuart 1767: 2 99), and presumably his *Essay Upon Money and Coins* (Harris 1757), the first part of which likewise embodied many of Richard Cantillon's views, particularly on value, though Steuart most likely knew them indirectly via Postlethwayt's *Dictionary* (Higgs 1931: 386). Whether Steuart had access to Malachy Postlethwayt's publications, especially his *Universal Dictionary of Trade and Commerce*, is not clear. However, if he did, here is yet another way by which Steuart could have gained access to important selections of Richard Cantillon's text without the need to have looked at the original source.[6]

In short, similarities between Steuart's and Cantillon's texts, of the type noted in considerable detail by various commentators (for example, Skinner 1966; Brewer 1992; Yang 1994; Aspromourgos 1996) cannot constitute proof that Steuart had read Cantillon's *Essai* unless it can be shown that the similarity in question has no real counterpart in the texts of Philip Cantillon, Mirabeau,

Harris or, in case Steuart had used his works, Malachy Postlethwayt. None of these commentators appear to have carried out such textual analysis.

However, there is some negative evidence that Steuart had probably not read Richard Cantillon's *Essai*. In his discussion of the determination of the par in foreign exchange rates, Steuart (1767: Book III, part II, ch. II) claims that in such determination due allowance has to be made for seigniorage, or the cost of minting bullion into coin levied by the Crown. This, Steuart argued, was particularly important in the context of estimating the par in foreign exchange between the coin of a nation like Britain, which did not levy a seigniorage on the coinage, and one like France, which did (Steuart 1767: 2 18–19). Steuart (1767: 2 23) in fact claimed originality on this point, which, he stated, had not been made in any of the literature on the foreign exchanges with which he was familiar. This specifically includes Philip Cantillon's *Analysis of Trade*, which is cited in the general treatment of foreign exchange (Steuart 1767: 2 17, 18) and, more specifically, on the particular issue of the French-British exchanges (Philip Cantillon 1759: 99–100). It is therefore interesting to note that Richard Cantillon (1755; 1931: 261–3) was quite aware of the fact that seigniorage affects the par of the foreign exchanges and that Britain, not levying seigniorage for coining bullion at the mint, is disadvantaged in this respect in comparison with countries such as France, which charged seigniorage. Given Steuart's limited inclination to claim originality on any point, together with his relative generosity in acknowledging the work of others, this episode seems to suggest that he had not read Richard Cantillon's work. After all, Richard Cantillon had made the connection between seigniorage and calculating the par in his *Essai*, the absence of which connection, according to Steuart, made all methods of estimating the actual par on foreign exchange incorrect (Steuart 1767: 2 19).

Given that Steuart nowhere explicitly cited Richard Cantillon's work, it is likely that Cantillon's *Essai* never crossed his path. This probability is heightened by the fact that on one matter in relation to which Steuart claimed no one writing on the subject had made the point before him – that is, in connection with the importance of including seigniorage costs when estimating the real par on foreign exchange between two countries – Richard Cantillon's account of the matter does mention the omission which Steuart had identified. This makes it virtually certain that Steuart had not read Richard Cantillon's *Essai sur la Nature du Commerce en Général* when writing his *Inquiry*.

Steuart and Philip Cantillon's *Analysis*

It seems surprising in this context that the similarities between Philip Cantillon's work and that of Richard Cantillon have never been systematically explored. Jevons most misleadingly referred to Philip Cantillon's *Analysis* as 'the garbled translation of 1759' (Jevons [1881] 1931: 338–9) and wrongly suggested (333–4) that the two works had been confused by McCulloch (1845: 52).[7] Higgs (1931: 376–8) provides a more careful picture of the *Analysis of Trade*, including the suggestion that Philip Cantillon used the French published version of Richard Cantillon's *Essai* rather than the original French manuscript. Nevertheless, his treatment strongly implies that Philip Cantillon's work should be treated as if it was designed to replicate fully Richard Cantillon's material. To this account, Higgs adds rather mysteriously that '[c]ollation of the *Analysis* with the *Essai* has proven unfruitful', without indicating the nature of the results obtained, or expected, from this activity.[8] Legrand (1900) also does not attempt a detailed comparison between the texts. However, the issue raised in his paper makes such a comparison imperative, and its details are included in Tables 9.1 and 9.2.

Table 9.1 References to Richard Cantillon's *Essai* [1755] (1931) in Skinner (1966), and their counterpart in Philip Cantillon's *Analysis* (1759)

Skinner (1966)	*Richard Cantillon [1755] (1931)*	*Philip Cantillon (1759)*
p. 32 n5	p. 83	pp. 122–3
p. 53 n7	Pt II ch. 3	p. 115
p. 56 n1	Pt I chs 3–6	pp. 6–14
p. 88 n3	pp. 71, 83	pp. 120–2
p. 119 n5	p. 83	pp. 122–3
pp. 160–1 n2 Pt I ch. 10	pp. 21–2	
p. 173 n2	Pt II ch. 2	pp. 28–9
p. 196 n3	Pt II ch. 8	pp. 47–9, 186–93
p. 205 n1	pp. 195, 235[a]	
p. 291 n1	Pt III ch. 1[b]	
p. 312 n1	p. 97	pp. 34, 86[c]
p. 324 n2	p. 131	p. 44[d]
p. 341 n12	pp. 161, 163	pp. 52–5
p. 349 n17	p. 179	pp. 28–9,[e] 52
p. 450 n2	Pt. II ch. 9	[f]

Notes:

[a] I found it difficult to see the resemblance between the argument on these pages and Steuart's text indicated.

[b] Also resembles Mirabeau, *l'Ami des Hommes* Part III, ch. 2.

[c] 'Intrinsic worth', the phrase used by Steuart, is used by Philip, but not by Richard, Cantillon.

[d] The gaming example used by Steuart is also used by Philip, but not by Richard, Cantillon.

[e] The wheat example used by Steuart is likewise used as an illustration by Philip, but not by Richard, Cantillon.

[f] This argument is not in Philip Cantillon, but it resembles passages in Hume.

Table 9.2 Concordance of Richard Cantillon's *Essai sur la Nature du Commerce en Général* [1755] (1931) and Philip Cantillon (1759)

Richard Cantillon [1755] (1931)		*Philip Cantillon (1759)*	*Further observations*
Part I	'Of Wealth'		
Chapter I	paras 1–3	pp. 1–2	
Chapter II	'Of Human Societies'		
	paras 3–5	pp. 6–8	
Chapter III	'Of Villages'		
	para 1	pp. 8–9	
Chapter IV	'Of Market Towns'		rough paraphrase only
	para 1	pp. 9–10	
Chapter V	'Of Cities'		
	paras 1–3	pp. 13–14	
Chapter VI	'Of Capital cities'		paraphrase in part
	paras 1–2	pp. 14–15	
Chapter VII	'The Labour of the Husbandman is of less value than that of the Handcrafts-man'		
	paras 1–3	pp. 15–16	
Chapter VIII	'Some handicraftsmen earn more, others less, according to the different cases and circumstances'		
	paras 1–2	pp. 16–17	
	para 4	pp. 19–20	
Chapter IX	'The Number of Labourers... is naturally proportioned to the demand for them'		
	paras 1–2	p. 20	
	para 5	pp. 20–1	
	para 7	p. 21	
Chapter X	'The Price and Intrinsic Value of a Thing. . .'		
	paras 1–2	pp. 21–2	
Chapter XI	'Of the Par or the Relation between Land and Labour'		frequently paraphrase of argument
	paras 1–5	pp. 22–5	
	para 7	pp. 24–5	
	para 17	p.25	

Table 9.2 Continued

Richard Cantillon [1755] (1931)		*Philip Cantillon (1759)*	*Further observations*
Chapter XII	'All Classes and Individuals. . . subsist or are enriched at the Expense of Proprietors of Land'		frequently paraphrase of argument
	paras 1–6	pp. 114–16	
	paras 8–10	pp. 117–18	
Chapter XIII	'The Circulation and Exchange of Goods. . . are carried on in Europe by undertakers, and at risk'		paraphrase of argument
	paras 1,3,5,6	pp. 126–7	
	para 11	p. 127	
Chapter XIV	'The Fancies. . . of the Prince. . . determine the use to which Land is put in a State'		
Chapter XV	'The Increase and Decrease of the Numbers of People. . . depend on the Taste, the Fashions and Modes of Living of the Proprietors of Land'		
	paras 1–3	pp. 119–21	
	para 5	p. 121	
	para 7	p. 122	
	para 19	p. 122	
Chapter XVI	'The more Labour there is in a State, the more rich it is esteemed'		paraphrase only
	para 11	pp. 127–8	
Chapter XVII	'Of Metals and Money, especially Gold and Silver'		in part only approximately and with alterations
	paras 1–3	pp. 86–7	
	para 4	p. 26	
	paras 12–13	pp. 97–9	
Part II Chapter I	'Of Barter'		argument replicated
	para 3	pp. 28–30	
Chapter II	'Of Market Prices'		
Chapter III	'Of the Circulation of Money'		similar in analysis of problem only
	paras 13–14	pp. 43–4	

Table 9.2 Continued

Richard Cantillon [1755] (1931)		*Philip Cantillon (1759)*	*Further observations*
Chapter IV	'Further Reflections on Circulation'		
Chapter V	'Of the Inequality of the Circulation. . .'		
Chapter VI	'Of the Increase and Decrease in the Quantity of Hard Money in a State'	pp. 52–3	only reflects some of this content
Chapter VII	'Continuation of the same subject'		
Chapter VIII	'Further Reflections on the same subject' para 5	 p. 126	with respect to bullion as sign of comparative wealth
Chapter IX	'Of the Interest of Money, and its Causes'		some arguments replicated
Chapter X	'Of the Causes of the Increase and Decrease of the Interest of Money in a State para 5	 pp. 66–7	profits, interest and risk
Part III Chapter II	'Of the Exchanges and their Nature' paras 2–7 paras 11–12 para 13	 pp. 74–8 pp. 79–80 p. 82	similar in content
Chapter III	'Further explanations of the Nature of the Exchanges' para 6 para 8 para 10	 pp. 78–9 p. 83 pp. 83–4	rough paraphrase only
Chapter IV	'Of the Variations. . . of Values. . . [of] Metals which serve as Money' paras 1–6 para 7 [for two sentences] para 11 para 15 paras 16–20	 pp. 87–91 p. 91 pp. 91–2 p. 95 pp. 93–7	some with variations not exactly paraphrase rough summary
Chapter V	'Of the Augmentation and Diminution of Coin in Denomination'	pp. 102–4	only rough approximation

Table 9.2 Continued

Richard Cantillon [1755] (1931)		*Philip Cantillon (1759)*	*Further observations*
Chapter VI	'Of Banks and their Credit'		
	paras 1–4	pp. 169–72	
	paras 6–11	pp. 173–6	
Chapter VII	'Further Explanations and Enquiries as to the utility of a National Bank'		rough, similarity on Bank of Venice
	para 1	p. 185	rough paraphrase
	paras 6–7	pp. 185–6	
	para 10	p. 182	
	paras 15–18	pp. 183–4	
	para 20	pp. 180–2, 184	
	para 24	pp. 184–5	
Chapter VIII	'Of the Refinement of Credit of General Banks'		

Table 9.2 shows the extent to which the contents of Philip Cantillon's *Analysis* (summarised by way of a table of contents in the Appendix to this chapter) replicates those of Richard Cantillon's *Essai*. Most of the topics raised by Richard Cantillon are discussed by Philip Cantillon nearly thirty years later, although, and this is important, the amount of detail which the latter included on many of these topics was greatly reduced. Only seven of Richard Cantillon's thirty-five chapters find no counterpart whatsoever in Philip Cantillon's *Analysis*. However, many of Richard Cantillon's more lengthy chapters among the other twenty-eight are only very partially summarised by Philip Cantillon or are only selectively quoted. In some cases, only such brief summaries are presented; in others, Richard Cantillon's argument is expanded by summaries or quotations from Hume's essays, from Locke's works or, much less frequently, from authorities such as Davenant and the author of *The Universal Merchant*. Hume's influence is particularly apparent in the preface (which has no counterpart in Richard Cantillon's *Essai*), in chapters XIII–XVIII dealing with money, its circulation, its effects on prices and on interest, and in the chapter on foreign trade. In short, textual comparison of the two works indicates that Philip Cantillon presented what his title promised to do: to analyse trade, commerce, coin, bullion, banks and the foreign exchanges on the basis of the work of Richard Cantillon, the 'late London merchant now deceased', suitably adapted to present conditions and circumstances.

Even though Philip Cantillon's *Analysis* therefore does not attempt to reproduce all of Richard Cantillon's *Essai*, it is not unfair to say that Philip Cantillon's book does contain nearly all of the major concepts and basic analyses which Richard Cantillon provides. (However, he invariably failed to include the detail, the rich illustrations, and many of the other finer points so abundantly contained in the earlier work.) There are some major exceptions to this broad generalisation. There is no match in Philip Cantillon's *Analysis* for Richard Cantillon's discussion of agricultural surplus and the social division of labour presented in Part I, chapter XVI (Richard Cantillon [1755] 1931: 87–93), probably on the basis of Petty's similar discussion in *A Treatise of Taxes and Contributions*. Second, Philip Cantillon leaves out much of the material on 'undertakers' ('entrepreneurs'), not only from the chapters on the rate of interest (*ibid.*: 199–211) but from the preliminary discussion in Part I, chapter XIII. However, as implied in Table 9.2, the notion of undertakers is briefly explained by Philip Cantillon, not only on the basis of Richard Cantillon's argument in the early, definitional chapter but also in the context of the discussion of the rate of interest. Hence, irrespective of its deficiency in analytical detail, Philip Cantillon's *Analysis* was a very useful source from which to draw the conceptual advances provided by Richard Cantillon's *Essai*, though nearly always without the rich illustrations and analytical background in which they were situated within the *Essai*.

The significance of this comparison for the subject matter of this chapter is that for virtually every topic on which Steuart's arguments have been said to resemble Richard Cantillon's work there is a corresponding similarity with Philip Cantillon's work. To test this hypothesis, a number of examples can be taken from Skinner's many footnote references to Richard Cantillon's *Essai* in his edition of the text of Steuart's *Inquiry* (Skinner 1966). These are shown in Table 9.1, together with the pages of Philip Cantillon's work where similar arguments to those made by Richard Cantillon are to be found. As the notes to Table 9.1 indicate, Skinner provides no passages from Cantillon's *Essai* in this context, of which the substance cannot be found in either Philip Cantillon's *Analysis*, or in sources such as Mirabeau's *l'Ami des Hommes* and Hume's *Essays*, with which Steuart was acquainted. More interestingly, on a number of occasions, as indicated in notes c, d and e, the passages in Steuart resemble more closely the argument as presented by Philip Cantillon than as presented in Richard Cantillon's *Essai*. Given the fact that there are no passages indicated in Skinner (1966) where Richard Cantillon's *Essai* can be unambiguously identified as the only possible source, this exercise suggests that Philip Cantillon could have been appropriately substituted for Richard Cantillon in these comparative references.

Repeating the exercise with a number of other commentators who have compared Richard Cantillon's *Essai* with Steuart's *Inquiry* yields very similar results. Brewer's (1992: 175–83) discussion of Steuart and Cantillon turns more on differences between the two than on similarities. Where Brewer identifies similarities, these can all be explained by alternative sources or, by way of Table 9.2, by the contents of Philip Cantillon's *Analysis of Trade*. The same conclusion obtains when the exercise is applied to Yang (1994) and to Aspromourgos (1996). In short, it seems difficult, if not impossible to build up a case for Steuart's direct indebtedness to Richard Cantillon's *Essai* by pointing to issues or passages which can only have their foundation in that particular source.

Legrand's supposition that Richard Cantillon enters Steuart's system via Philip Cantillon's *Analysis* appears to have been correct.

Conclusions

What other conclusions can be derived from this study of Steuart and Richard Cantillon? Perhaps the most interesting is the corollary it suggests to the frequently made statement that Richard Cantillon was the economists' economist during the second half of the eighteenth century, by indicating that the transmission of his views could occasionally be indirect. This seems to have been the case with Steuart. However, on the available evidence, it was not the case for many of the other great economists of the period. Quesnay, Turgot, Beccaria, Verri and Adam Smith all drew directly on Richard Cantillon's *Essai*, which they specifically cited and more than likely had studied *in toto*. The case of Steuart and Richard Cantillon provides therefore an interesting variant to the transmission during this part of the history of economics: indirect transmission of ideas by means of the incorporation of essential features of an economist's argument in the work of others. For Richard Cantillon's work, the scope of this indirect transmission has been inadequately appreciated with respect to Philip Cantillon's *Analysis of Trade*. This last remark also suggests the conclusion that accepting propositions from authorities without adequate proof can sometimes be a dangerous procedure in the history of economic thought.

Appendix

Table of contents: Philip Cantillon (1759)

Introduction
Chapter

I	Riches
II	How states may be formed
III	How villages may be settled
IV	How market towns may be established
V	How cities may be established
VI	How capital cities may be established
VII	The labour of the plowman is of less value than that of the handicraftsman, and the reasons why this is so
VIII	Some handicraftsmen in certain trades, earn more than others, according to the circumstances of the time
IX	The number of labourers and handicraftsmen is proportioned to the demand for them
X	The price of anything, in general, is estimated by the value of the land which produces it, and the labour and time taken in forming it into use
XI	Of the par and equality between land and labour
XII	Of mines and barter

XIII	Of money and its value
XIV	Of circulation of money
XV	Of the ways and means by which real species increase and decrease in a kingdom
XVI	Of the consequential effect, which the increase and decrease of the current coin of a country, has on the community
XVII	Of the interest of money
XVIII	Of inland and foreign exchange
XIX	Of trade and money, particularly gold, silver and copper, their proportional value and variations with respect to the use made of them
XX	Of the increase and decrease of coin in denomination
XXI	All orders of men in a community, or state, subsist and are enriched at the expense of the proprietors of land
XXII	The increase and decrease of the number of people in a state or kingdom, principally depend on the manner of living of the age, the taste and luxury of the great proprietors of land
XXIII	Of the inland and foreign trade
XXIV	Of bankers and banks
XXV	The subject of the exchanges continued

Notes

1 Higgs mentions Steuart's *Works* (3: 22) as the place of citation; Johnson (1937: 409) indicates correctly that this was a reference to Philip Cantillon's *Analysis of Trade*. Johnson argues that the citation to Richard Cantillon's *Essai* occurs in Steuart's *Works* (3: 391, 408).
2 Brewer suggests that these similarities are partly explicable by Steuart's access to Mirabeau's *l'Ami des Hommes*, which had plagiarised Richard Cantillon's *Essai* on important points.
3 Aspromourgos (1996: ch. 9) makes similar claims.
4 I am indebted to Arnold Heertje, who allowed me to pursue the matter in his splendid library which contains many editions of Melon, including no less than three Amsterdam editions and two distinct variants of the 'first edition'.
5 On Cantillon and Mirabeau, see esp. Hayek (1991: 273–8).
6 On Cantillon and Postlethwayt, see Higgs (1931: 383–6, app. A); on Postlethwayt more generally see Johnson (1937: 185–208, app. B).
7 Since McCulloch does not appear to have known of the existence of Richard Cantillon's *Essai* while he described the contents of Philip Cantillon's *Analysis* quite accurately, it is Jevons who confused the issue of the relationship between the two works.
8 An exception is Higgs (1931: 5n*), where a variant of the texts is indicated, a variant incidentally replicated in the version of the argument presented by Postlethwayt, as Higgs also indicates.

References

Aspromourgos, Tony (1996) *On the Origins of Classical Economics: Distribution and Value from William Petty to Adam Smith*, London: Routledge.

Brewer, Antony (1992) *Richard Cantillon: Pioneer of Economic Theory*, London: Routledge.

Cabrillo, Francisco (1988) 'Who was the author of the Essay on Commerce? A note on Sir James Steuart's doctrinal sources', *History of Economics Society Bulletin*, 10 (2) 185–7.

Cantillon, Philip (1759) *The Analysis of Trade*, London: for the author.

Cantillon, Richard (1755, 1931) *Essai sur la Nature de Commerce en Général*, edited with an English translation and additional material by Henry Higgs, London: Macmillan for the Royal Economic Society.

Groenewegen, P. D. (1983) 'Turgot, Beccaria and Smith', in P. D. Groenewegen and J. Halevi (eds) *Italian Economics Past and Present*, Sydney: Frederick May Foundation, 31–78 (above, Chapter 1).

——(1994) 'La "French Connection": influences Françaises sur l'économie politique Britannique', *Dix-Huitième Siècle*, 26, 15–36 (above, Chapter 6).

Harris, Joseph (1757) *An Essay Upon Money and Coins*, London: G. Hawkins.

Hayek, F. A. (1991) 'Richard Cantillon (c. 1680–1734)', in F. A. Hayek, *Collected Works*, vol. III, *The Trend of Economic Thinking*, London: Routledge, ch. 13.

Higgs, Henry (ed.) (1931) *Essay on the Nature of Commerce in General*, London: Macmillan for Royal Economic Society.

Hutchison, T. W. (1988) *Before Adam Smith*, Oxford: Blackwell.

Jevons, W. S. (1931) [1881] 'The nationality of political economy', in Higgs, Henry (ed.) *Essay on the Nature of Commerce in General*, London: Macmillan for Royal Economic Society, 333–60.

Johnson, E. A. J. (1937) *Predecessors of Adam Smith*, Homewood: Prentice Hall.

Legrand, Robert (1900) *Richard Cantillon –un Mercantiliste Précurseur des Physiocrates*, Paris: V. Giard and E. Brière.

McCulloch, J. R. (1845) *The Literature of Political Economy. A Classified Catalogue*, London: Longman, Brown, Green and Longmans.

Melon, Jean François (1734) *Essai Politique sur le Commerce*, 1st edn, n.p.

——(1735) *Essai Politique sur le Commerce*, Amsterdam: François Chauguion.

——(1761) *Essai Politique sur le Commerce*, new edn, n.p.

Sen, S. R. (1957) *The Economics of Sir James Steuart*, London: G. Bell and Sons for the London School of Economics.

Skinner, A. S. (ed.) (1966) *Sir James Steuart, An Inquiry into the Principles of Political Economy*, Scottish Economic Classics, Edinburgh: Oliver and Boyd.

Steuart, Sir James (1767) *An Inquiry into the Principles of Political Economy*, London: A. Miller and T. Cadell.

Vickers, Douglas (1960) *Studies in the Theory of Money 1690–1776*, London: Peter Owen.

Yang, Hong-Seok (1994) *The Political Economy of Trade and Growth. An Analytical Interpretation of Sir James Steuart's 'Inquiry'*, Aldershot: Edward Elgar.

10 Editing the classics in the Antipodes

With special reference to the problem of identifying anonymous authors

Editing economic texts has a variety of purposes as well as problems. Before focusing on some of the specific problems of editing economic texts in more remote areas of the globe like Australia, and the even more specific editorial problem posed by anonymous texts, it is useful to focus briefly on the range of aims and objectives the editor may have to keep in mind. The editing talent gathered at this conference provides an indication of this variety. It includes the objectives of the editing of collected writings, which may be open-ended or restricted; the editing of a new edition of a major reference work; editing correspondence; editing specific volumes within a wider collected works; editing diaries and editing specific single items, large or small. Translation may, as in my own case, sometimes be a part of the editorial task, as is the transcription (quite difficult in some cases) of unpublished manuscript material.

The purposes of these various editorial roles are not always easy to identify. Some are overt, others more hidden or disguised. Thus the aims of the collected Ricardo have been said to have been appropriate only to the Moscow State Publishing House (Hutchison, 1952, p. 421) since no other clear rationale to the reviewer in question appeared persuasive enough to justify this gigantic editorial task. Others have seen the editing of Ricardo as an opportunity for enhancing the understanding and interpretation of the work of one of the major, if not the major, economist of the nineteenth century. The second manner of justifying Ricardo's collected works points to the major objective of the editorial task: presenting the work of an individual author in such a way as to facilitate its comprehension and interpretation. This objective of the editor can be described in another way. The editorial task is designed to make the text in question more accessible to its potential readers. The notion of enhancing accessibility for the reader has, of course, various dimensions. These need to be elucidated to provide the necessary background for the types of editorial problem to be discussed in this chapter.

Enhanced accessibility for readers is achieved in several ways. Most obviously this is done by collecting the various works of a particular author in a single set of volumes where the degree of accessibility produced is closely associated with the degree of comprehensiveness of the collection aimed at. Posthumous publication of previously unpublished material in the form of manuscripts, letters and diaries can significantly enhance that comprehensiveness, and thereby the understanding of an author's ideas and hence its interpretation. Where degree of comprehensiveness in the collection of works is constrained by economic factors of cost and time, accessibility is invariably reduced, particularly with respect to future readers. This arises from the fact that selection criteria which seem reasonable at the time they are made, because they reflect known current and past interests, may become unsatisfactory for future readers when new interests and questions replace the old. A selection procedure which is too restrictive can therefore produce a false economy, since a large-scale collected works incomplete through omissions, perhaps dictated by costs, may flaw that collection for ever as a collected works (cf. Patinkin, 1975, esp. pp. 250–3). Accessibility is also enhanced through translation, as demonstrated by the importance attached to this objective by initial publications of the International Economic Association. Accessibility is likewise enhanced through the textual notes and introduction an editor provides, in order to facilitate the reader's comprehension of the text by supplying the essential background to its construction and content. Accessibility to a text can, of course, also be improved by the device of the variorum edition, where the reader benefits from seeing the changes introduced in successive editions and thereby becomes privy to the vagaries in the development of its author's thoughts.

Enhanced accessibility from introduction and textual notes is a feature of the editorial task which bears further exploration. This task crystallises many of the problems faced by the editor on the periphery of the 'economic world', including the anonymous author problem which forms the specific focus of this chapter. In addition, interpreting the function of the introduction and the textural notes to be provided imposes important responsibilities on the editor. Certain types of information provided by such editorial vehicles can reduce accessibility of the text to future readers by steering them into predetermined interpretative directions. The appropriate content of the editorial introduction and textual notes as an aspect of editorial responsibility, which, it may be added, have a particular bearing on the subject matter of this chapter, need also to be more fully explored. This is all the more necessary because of the potentially controversial issues they raise.

Enough has been said to indicate the line of argument to be presented in this chapter. In its next section, it addresses the desirable role for an editor's introduction and editorial notes. The subsequent section looks at the problems specifically faced by the Antipodean editor of economic texts. The penultimate section examines problems invoked by the anonymity of the author of the edited text. This section also enables some comment on the role of biography in enhancing understanding of the text to be edited and its significance. A final section presents some brief conclusions.

I

No edited text is without an introduction, and virtually all edited texts provide editorial notes to the text. In addition, translated texts invariably provide notes on the translation, particularly that of specific terms and concepts to assist the reader in interpreting the translated text. Are there rules as to the type of material that should go into these introductions, and on the nature of the textual notes designed to assist the reader in mastering the text? General practice suggests certain implicit conventions as to the acceptable content of such editorial intrusions which seem to be followed by most editors of economic texts, while there likewise appears to be an implicit tradition as to what ought not to be included in such material designed to assist the readers of the edited text.

Take introductions first. Most editorial introductions provide a perspective on both the text and its author, linking the two by elaborating on the circumstances under which the text was produced. The first segment of an introduction generally concentrates on the significance of the text edited, features of its contents and, if appropriate, the various editions and versions in which it has been published, often restricted to those which appeared during the author's lifetime or immediately thereafter. Emphasis on significance of the text is frequently designed to justify the editing task itself, though with the work of more famous authors this tends to be understated and often is taken as self-evident. However, where publication involves previously unpublished material from an established author with a secure reputation, the significance of the new material is often defended in terms of the advantages of the new edition for interpreting and understanding that author's previous, and known, work. Emphasis in the introduction on the various versions of the text in question is essential, to indicate to readers the version of the text actually edited and the manner by which the editor has drawn attention to variations in other editions. Although often expounded at vastly differing lengths, this type of subject matter forms a standard part of editors' introductions.

To what extent features of the publication's contents should be discussed in the introduction is a more delicate matter of judgement. Reflection on my own practice, guided by that of others, especially that of Sraffa's Ricardo – have suggested a number of rules as appropriate. First, a general rule of parsimony seems applicable in elaborating contents of the text to be edited in its editorial introduction. This parsimony is essential to preserve for the readers themselves the task of discovery of that content and not to impose on them the editor's perceptions and preconceptions. Parsimony in this matter does not, however, mean silence. Features of content need to be almost invariably introduced in addressing the question of the significance of the text to be edited. Here the rule of parsimony indicates that this be done as briefly and objectively as possible, by pointing to the subject matter itself rather than to its interpretation.[1] Second, features of content have often to be introduced to discuss the circumstances in which a text is written, and, in the context of texts with more than one edition, to explain how variations in texts arose. As shown subsequently, in the case of anonymous authors, features of their text's contents need often be highlighted as clues to the discovery of author identity. Beyond this, the editor's role becomes gradually transformed into that of interpreter, with consequences not only inimical to the reader for reasons already advanced, but also from making the editor's text more liable to obsolescence. Explanatory comment on the text tends to have a longer life if this rule is followed. References to interpretative sources rapidly date the publication to the fashions and perspectives of the time they are made, a feature particularly relevant to economics, where fads and fashions too often obtrude in the subject matter.

How much should be said about the nature of the edition and that of the author in question? If a new collected works includes extensive biographical material in one of its volumes (for example, as, in volume X of Sraffa's Ricardo, and as originally intended for the Bicentenary Collected Works of Adam Smith), only that biographical detail which illuminates the specific text under consideration needs to be provided by way of introduction, generally to highlight and supplement the manner in which that text came to be written. Where this is not the case, or where biographical material on the author is rather scarce, the biographical content of the introduction can be considerably expanded. Biography, as elaborated more fully below, provides context to the text which assists the reader in its interpretation and comprehension. Generally speaking, however, such biographical detail ought to be confined in the editorial introduction to what is considered essential for understanding the text in question.

Editors in my view have also a responsibility in discussing the circumstances in which the text they are editing was written. Many economic texts can frequently be attributed to specific events, whether in the economic situation of a particular country or in the context of specific intellectual debate and argument. Presenting this background enhances accessibility to the readers, who may neither have sufficient knowledge nor the opportunity to provide such information for themselves. The extent to which this is done is once again a matter for editorial judgement. Elaboration of this consideration may be helpful. The law of parsimony provides guidance on this matter as well. Relative availability of the information necessary for the reader should dictate the amount of detail required in the introduction. Where little comprehensive information exists, the editor should explain the material and intellectual context of the writing in some depth, as part of the editorial responsibility for facilitating readers' access to the text. Where the text in question constitutes a specific departure for its author in terms of subject matter, the responsibility of the editor in illuminating this shift becomes all the greater. Such explanation and information draws attention to potential limitations of such an early text, and assists in situating its contents within the author's subsequent work.

One final matter can be mentioned here, though it fits in just as well with the consideration of textual notes. To this editor, following here precedents established by Jacob Hollander's Johns Hopkins reprints of economic classics, preserving the original pagination of the edited texts seems essential, only obviated when the text in question is reproduced facsimile. This enables doubled access to the text with respect to commentary literature past and future. Where differences with earlier editions are more complex, a concordance becomes essential (as usefully included, for example, in Sraffa's Ricardo, Skinner's Steuart, the bicentenary edition of the *Wealth of Nations* and my own edition of

Turgot's *Réflections*). When texts have been translated, such page references to the source of the translation facilitate checking of the translation's accuracy by those with an inclination to do so. To me this seems a procedure superior, because potentially more comprehensive, to the device of providing a glossary with the introduction to indicate translation practice with respect to specific words and phrases.

The second aspect of the editorial task involves notes to the text. Here practice needs to be circumscribed and guided by Jacob Viner's dictum that 'footnotes are not free goods'. More is intended by this than the need to save printing costs. Sraffa confined editor's footnotes to 'attempts to indicate Ricardo's sources in particular passages and to complete his references to authorities' (Scraffa, 1951–73, I, p. lxii). In addition, he used them to indicate variations in text between editions, to complete or correct quotations where warranted, and to provide cross-references to other parts of the text. With particular reference to his editing of Ricardo's correspondence, his editorial notes provide information on persons, events and writings referred to by the correspondents in their letters, in order to assist the reader's grasp of their contents. Last but not least, in the editing of older texts, it may be helpful to contemporary and future readers to explain classical allusions, and to translate quotations in the original language where this is not done by the author in question (for the growing necessity of this, see Malthus, 1989a, p. xv).

Two general rules can be identified from this practice. First, notes are designed to give factual information and not to intrude interpretative material. Second, with few exceptions, the information provided should relate to aspects contemporary to the author in question, and avoid more recent comment, particularly if of an interpretative nature. Apart from preserving the readers' freedom to make up their own minds in interpreting the text, and only assisting them by elaborating the context of the work where necessary, this device delays dating of the editorial work. References to contemporary interpretation of an author's text rapidly become obsolete when new interpretations come to hand, a danger particularly great in a subject like economics for reasons already mentioned. Factual information of the type indicated, on the other hand, only becomes dated when new evidence comes to light, a matter over which the editor can exercise considerable control by the thoroughness with which the editorial task is undertaken. In this matter also, editorial restraint has considerable advantages.

II

The requirements of the editorial task as identified in the previous section enable specific comments on the problems faced by the editor in the Antipodes who edits classical economic texts, written by authors in other countries and under circumstances geographically and temporally quite different from those of the editor. As is so often the case, technological advance has altered the nature of many of these problems, and the disadvantages of the Antipodean editor of economic texts have been greatly reduced as a consequence. The spatial difficulties I faced in my editorial work on Turgot, to take a specific example, were far greater than those faced a decade later in the editing of my series of economic classics. Most of these problems relate to access to relevant information, and either impose greater research costs or curtail the effective search opportunities such as those involved in the identification of an anonymous author.

Take first the problems encountered from restricted access to necessary sources. As an editor residing in Sydney, I have within easy reach a substantial array of library resources; those at my own university, at the State Library of New South Wales and, via inter-library loans, those of many other Australian collections. Most economic texts are accessible in this way. In addition, the microfiche of the Kress Collection at Harvard and the collection of the Goldsmiths' Library at the University of London give direct access to two major collections of scarce economic literature. Unavailability of the second at the time I was working on Turgot makes for one significant difference between editorial resources at my disposal then and now. However, even for the Turgot much of the material required was obtainable from other libraries on microfilm or other means of reproduction. Increased caution by the custodians in libraries of scarce material over making photographic reproductions of that material may make this avenue less certain for the Australian, as well as for other researchers.

The manner of gaining access to research material mentioned in the preceding paragraph suffers from a major inherent problem which is not faced by those who have direct access to the major library collections. Seeking resources from other libraries requires specific knowledge about the items wanted and almost by definition precludes the search for material through browsing along library shelves or other forms of personal inspection of material related to the subject at hand. Such casual methods can often yield important benefits, when clues are sought for identifying anonymous authors or other forms of background information where the precise nature of the information sought is not clearly defined or specified. Where the relevant material is unpublished, there are even greater problems with the data. Particularly if the manuscript sources in question are large, not adequately catalogued or even classified, physical searches through it are indispensable. Costs are thereby invariably raised for the editor, both in time and money, and quantitatively at least, geographical location makes these greater for the Antipodean scholar. Fortunately, such problems are not insurmountable. John Pullen's magnificent variorum edition of Malthus' *Principles* (Malthus 1989b) shows such projects can be completed in Australia, if the requisite research time and research funds are made available. Hence location as such imposes no absolute bar to major editorial projects.

Just as in the case of collected editions of the writings of an author, comprehensiveness can be constrained by economic cost factors, with a detrimental effect on the quality of the final outcome, so the tyranny of distance for the Antipodean editor can impose costs in the form of reduced quality of edited output. Inability to check a potential source whose value is uncertain, because of geographical barriers which can only be overcome at very substantial costs, requires the judgement whether the game is worth the candle, that is, whether the source can be safely ignored. In editing *Some Thoughts on the Interest of Money in General* (Groenewegen, 1982) a number of such decisions had to be made, as mentioned in the subsequent section.

One final problem for the Australian editor of economics texts can be mentioned. A look at the volumes, for example, of the works of Cesare Beccaria published for Mediobanca (Beccaria, 1984) shows how ready Italian banks appear to be to sponsor substantial, and handsome, editions of Italian economic writers, not to mention other contributions from this source to publications in the history of economics. This finds few imitators in Australian financial circles. Likewise professional societies, of which the Royal Economic Society and the Scottish Economic Society are prime examples, have shown themselves willing to gamble on the venture of sponsoring collected or selected works of major economists, of which the Malthus' variora are the most recent example, and the Marshall correspondence John Whitaker is editing, the most glittering prospect. Australia provides only one example of this type of activity. This is the facsimile of the complete *Australian Economist*, the journal of the Australian Economic Association, which flourished for some years after 1888 to survive until 1898. Its publication was financed by the Economic Society of Australia (and the Economic History Society) with assistance from several financial institutions, an exercise in cooperation which owes much to the coincident bicentenary of white settlement in Australia (see N. G. Butlin *et al.*, 1988; and, for an evaluation of its contents, Groenewegen and McFarlane, 1990, ch. 4). However, the splendid edition by G. L. S. Tucker (1976) of William Huskisson's *Essays on Political Economy* of 1830 could not find a sponsor who was willing to finance a more elegant form of publication than that which the Economic History Department of the Australian National University eventually supplied.

These are the major problems faced by the Australian editor of economic texts when the emphasis is on Australian; problems attributable to both the tyranny of distance and to the cultural backwardness of its entrepreneurial elite in business. Other problems are those faced by all editors, irrespective of location, on which this paper has so far only focused with respect to content selection for introduction and editorial notes to the text. A further general problem facing the editors of anonymous texts can now be addressed: that of identifying the author of the text to be edited.

III

Anonymous tracts, books and articles feature frequently in the early (pre-1850) economic literature, and many battles have subsequently been fought over the attribution of authorship in some of the more famous anonymous contributions. Examples from the nineteenth century include the authorship of the review of Samuel Bailey's *Critical Dissertation on the Nature, Measure and Causes of Value* in the *Westminster Review* in 1826, and the well known review article on 'Mr. Owen's Plan for National Distress' in the *Edinburgh Review* for 1819. Cases from the pre-nineteenth-century literature concern the authorship of the *Natural and Political Observations … upon the Bills of Mortality*, the 1701 *Considerations on the East India Trade*, and, an example with which I am particularly familiar from my own editorial practice, the 1738 pamphlet *Some Thoughts on the Interest of Money in General*. Anonymity is of course not the preserve of English economic literature. The degree to which the practice flourished in other parts of Europe, especially France, is demonstrated by the availability of important reference works on the subject, of which A. A. Barbier, *Dictionaire des Ouvrages Anonymes* and J. M. Quérard, *Les Supercheries Littéraires Devoilées*, are early examples.

When an editor wishes to reissue such tracts or articles,[2] either as part of a collected works or as an individual item, the authorship question is invariably raised. For example, when McCulloch, to pay tribute to an early British editor of scarce economic literature, reprinted the text of *Considerations on the East India Trade* in his *Early English Tracts on Commerce*, he was 'half inclined to suppose that it might have proceeded from the pen of Mr. Henry Martin, who contributed some papers to the *Spectator*' (McCulloch, 1856, p. xv). However, some negative circumstantial evidence on this subject provided in his earlier *Literature of Political Economy* (McCulloch, 1845, p. 102) deterred him from doing so. Although McCulloch's introduction to this text is minimal relative to the editorial responsibilities an earlier section of this paper imposed (his knowledgeable readership drawn from the Political Economy Club is a likely justification), the desire in an editor to name a potential author for an anonymous tract is seen from this example as invariably strong.

Authorship puzzles in economics do not, of course, intrigue only editors, but have cast a spell over all 'who enjoy a good mystery … and provide the raw material for many good who-wrote-it's' (Stigler, 1983, p. 547). Historians of economics have shared this fascination with other literary historians. For an editor, on the grounds advanced in an earlier section of this paper, searching for the authorship of an anonymous text they are editing is of such importance as to make it almost obligatory. Identification of a plausible author greatly assists in providing that context to the work designed for making it more accessible to its readers, a context of which the biographical details of the author are invariably an important part. Hence the skills of literary and historical detection become part of the editor's toolbox. The literature of political economy contains remarkable examples of such detection skills. Some of these can be found in the magnificent editorial work in Sraffa's Ricardo,[3] others include the attribution of the 1830 *Essays on Political Economy* to William Huskisson (Tucker, 1976) and of the anonymous editor of the posthumous second edition of Malthus' *Principles* to Cazenove (Pullen, 1978). Statistical analysis often brought to bear on this problem (the most recent example in economics being that of O'Brien and Darnell, 1982)[4] has been found wanting (Stigler, 1983). Careful collection of the circumstantial evidence remains the best that is on offer in determining authorship questions, with the result that these can only be conclusively settled on the basis of incontrovertible documentary evidence linking author and publisher.[5]

Although there have been many spectacular identifications[6] of authorship in the literature of economics, some of which have already been referred to, the example I wish to take relates to that of the authorship of *Some Thoughts on the Interest of Money in General*. I attributed its authorship to William Pulteney (1684–1764) on the basis of strong circumstantial evidence derived through literary and historical detection. The internal and external sources which induced this attribution provide a case study of this particular aspect of the editorial role. This may be of use to other editors who may at some stage be faced with the anonymity problem.[7]

Examining internal sources provided by the text of the anonymous work under consideration for clues as to possible authorship is the obvious initial stage of literary detection. The subject matter of *Some Thoughts on the Interest of Money in General* provided two general clues which proved of great value. The first was the author's detailed discussion of the events in Parliament relating to proposals for reducing public debt interest to 3 per cent per annum, a proposal which is the main theme in the pamphlet. The proposal itself, made by Sir John Barnard in the House of Commons in March 1737, allowed checking of the accuracy of this detailed discussion by reference to the parliamentary debates as given in *Cobbett's Parliamentary History* (see Groenewegen, 1982, pp. viii–ix). The degree of accuracy of the discussion in the pamphlet, including the technical taxation issues involved, suggested the 'author was highly familiar with the parliamentary debates on the subject which took place in 1737, indicating the strong possibility that he was in fact a Member of Parliament' (p. ix). On the strength of this supposition, the participants in these House of Commons debates immediately became strong candidates for authorship of the pamphlet.

The second initial internal clue was the scholarly nature of the writing, combined with its author's substantial knowledge of the economic literature then available for those writings on the rate of interest. This was evident from the sources cited. These included Locke's *Some Considerations of the Consequences of the Lowering of Interest and Raising the Value of Money*, Bishop Fleetwood's *Chronicon Preciosum*, two works by Charles Davenant, in the citation of which the author realised the importance of Gregory King's work reproduced therein, Petty's *Political Arithmetick*, Pufendorff's *Of the Law of Nature and Nations*, and a specialist work by Weyman Lee on *Leases and Annuities*. In addition, there is evidence to suggest the author was familiar with more contemporary economic writings, such as Gee's *Trade and Navigation of Great Britain Consider'd* and Jacob Vanderlint's *Money Answers All Things*. The skilful use of the statistical material evident in the work, together with the accuracy of the quotations, provided the basis for a second assumption about the author: the person was likely to have been highly educated and, given the high price of books and the virtual absence of public library facilities, wealthy. The general quality of the argument, relative to that in much of the contemporary literature, reinforced the presumption of a highly educated author (*ibid.*, p. xi).

External sources come into play at this stage of the literary detection. The list of possible authors from the members of the House of Commons who took part in the debates on the 1737 Barnard proposal for lowering the interest of money, is a use of such external sources which has already been mentioned. Given the additional qualifications of education and wealth as necessary attributes of the author, a check of this list with the type of information available in the *Dictionary of National Biography* and the Catalogue of the British Library left only one feasible contender, Sir William Pulteney, subsequently Earl of Bath. Pulteney was a longstanding Member of Parliament; a matriculant to Christ Church, Oxford and graduate of that University, who continued his education by the customary continental tour. He was also a man of considerable wealth in his own right, enhanced by his marriage to a wealthy woman. More importantly, he was a person to whom a significant number of economical tracts had already been attributed. These included a 1727 pamphlet on the *State of the National Debt*, which McCulloch considered of sufficient merit to reprint it for the members of the Political Economy Club (*ibid.*, pp. x–xii).

Unfortunately no full-scale biography of Pulteney is available. However, he was sufficiently famous, if not notorious, to feature in many contemporary accounts, biographical studies of his famous contemporaries and friends (who, among others, included Bolingbroke and Dean Swift), correspondence, and the usual English periodical sources of the eighteenth century such as the *Monthly Review* and the *Gentleman's Magazine*. This provided much helpful circumstantial evidence relating to his strong political opposition to Walpole, particularly on fiscal matters; his skilful use of the pen therein; his election to the Royal Society in 1744; his personal opportunity and interest to write the pamphlet in the period when it can be supposed to have been written, including a recognised pecuniary interest in the outcome of the policy debated; while even formal previous association with the publisher/bookseller of the 1738 pamphlet could be established with a high degree of certainty (*ibid.*, pp. xii–xv). Of necessity, all this evidence remains circumstantial, and direct proof of authorship seems now to be impossible, given the fact that Pulteney's private papers were said to have been burned shortly after his death in 1764 by his heir and brother, General Henry Pulteney.[8]

With the availability of Pulteney's other economic writings, internal evidence came once more into play in comparing the text of *Some Thoughts on the Interest of Money in General* with the economic writings firmly attributed to Pulteney. Internal evidence from shared authorities in these writings, with special reference to Locke's *Some Considerations on the Consequences of the Lowering of Interest and Raising the Value of Money*, was found to be very useful in this. Locke's tax incidence argument that all taxes ultimately fall on the land was approvingly taken up in *Some Thoughts on the Interest of Money in General*, as well as in Pulteney's other work, the *Case for the Revival of Salt Duty* and his *Review of the Excise Scheme* (both pamphlets directed against Walpole's fiscal policies). It is also used in Pulteney's better known *The State of the National Debt*. Another common authority shared by Pulteney and the author of *Some Thoughts on the Interest of Money in General* is Davenant's *Essay Upon Ways and Means*, which is accurately quoted in Pulteney's *The Budget Open'd* and in the anonymous work in question.

Shared use of Davenant's work, including his political arithmetic, is in fact a more general feature of Pulteney's known economic writings and *Some Thoughts on the Interest of Money in General*. Not only is the great concern with statistical material and calculation of these writings of interest in this context, the accuracy and skill with which the data is handled and the similarity of the problems solved heighten the relevance of this comparison for attributing authorship to Pulteney. A 'knack for figures' was an acknowledged attribute of Sir William Pulteney, strikingly demonstrated in his *State of the National Debt* and replicated to an extraordinary degree in the calculation of the effect of an interest rate reduction in the pages of *Some Thoughts on the Interest of Money in General*. Although it is possible to ascribe such similarities to mere coincidence, or to some familiarity of the author of the 1738 piece with Pulteney's writings, neither explanation seems plausible. The probability of coincidence is low when it is acknowledged that statistical accuracy was rare in the eighteenth-century literature. Moreover, the 1738 pamphlet was noteworthy as already indicated, for its, by eighteenth-century standards, fairly explicit acknowledgment of authorities and accuracy of quotations, so that the question arises of why Pulteney's work was not acknowledged if it had been found useful by its author, unless of course that author was Pulteney himself. Use of Locke's incidence analysis in eighteenth-century literature prior to the work of the physiocrats was sufficiently rare to raise further the improbability of a coincidence explanation. Other similarities between the use of Pulteney's work and the author of the 1738 pamphlet can be noted, some of them dealing with concepts and language likewise sufficiently uncommon to prevent explanation by way of coincidence.[9] Until evidence to the contrary is produced, I see no reason to abandon my attribution of William Pulteney as the author of *Some Thoughts on the Interest of Money in General*, as made on the basis of this strong internal and external circumstantial evidence.

Moreover, I think this attribution enriched the content of my editorial introduction and proved the usefulness of good editorial notes on the principles elucidated in the first section of this chapter. It thereby also brings further support to the potential contribution of biographical data to understanding economic argument and the interpretation of earlier economic work. In the context of Pulteney's connection with the 1738 publication of *Some Thoughts on the Interest of Money in General*, two avenues for further research and historical interpretation were opened up. First of all, attribution of this pamphlet to Pulteney together with that of the authorship of *The State of the National Debt* and a number of minor fiscal writings already firmly assigned to his pen, makes him a far more formidable figure in early eighteenth-century economic writing. He is of a stature comparable to, say, the figures of Child and Barbon in the literature of the seventeenth century, but he is, of course, rarely acknowledged as such. His identification as author therefore focuses on the importance of his omission from general accounts of the history of classical economic thought, a blemish of some importance in the accuracy of that historical record. Second, ascribing the pamphlet to Pulteney opens intriguing possibilities of linking this work to the author of the *Wealth of Nations* via Adam Smith's friendship with William Johnstone (Pulteney). Smith's friend may well have inherited his more famous namesake's library via his wife, Frances, including therein the pamphlet in question, thereby providing greater justification for Marx's casual description of the author of that pamphlet as 'the anonymous predecessor of Adam Smith', and a clearer explanation for the sources of aspects of Smith's theory of value hitherto more difficult to explain. The last speculation at this stage lacks any solid foundations, and in any case takes the discussion well beyond the purposes of this chapter. However, it does reinforce the potential of literary detection for suggesting new problems, and the interest if not importance of biography, and the search for biography, in editorial work.

IV

This paper has ranged widely and discursively over the tasks of editing economists and of the economist editor. This discussion had both a general aspect and a more narrow focus on the specific problems experienced by the Antipodean editor of economic classics, and by those involved in identifying anonymous authors as part of their editorial role.

Despite the various objectives of individual editorial ventures, so widely represented at this conference, initial general discussion in the opening section was able to conclude with some specific rules. A law of parsimony needs to be applied by the editor in writing introductions and in providing textual notes. Beyond the worth of a general maxim of economy in these matters by not providing more than is strictly necessary for the purpose at hand, this law of parsimony seeks to protect readers of the text from unwarranted editorial intrusions into interpretation instead of sticking to the provision of factual background to the text and its author. To use the phrase frequently employed in that section: the name of the game is increasing accessibility to the text for the reader. An editor's interpretative material can reduce such accessibility and, in addition, is liable to more rapid obsolescence.

The Antipodean editor faces all of these problems together with two specific ones. More limited access to necessary sources, particularly if these are manuscript or highly specialised, is a problem imposed by the tyranny of distance and in principle capable of solution through financial assistance and technical innovations. Such technical progress in photographic reproduction and electronic searches has reduced the problem of distance but not eliminated it. The cultural backwardness of Australian institutions in the private sector, visible in their lack of financial support, creates a further problem for Australian editors as compared to their European (especially Italian) counterparts, but this matter is also surmountable. Government research assistance is increasingly available for this purpose, and it is hoped that Australian private enterprise will improve its record in this regard.

The final section discussed the problem of anonymous authors of texts to be edited. It gave some examples of the long-standing interest of economists' editors and economists as editors in identifying anonymous authors, before proceeding to illustrate the use of both internal and external evidence to a specific case of anonymous author identification. This concerned the circumstantial evidence in favour of attributing authorship of *Some Thoughts on the Interest of Money in General* to the minor economic writer and politician Sir William Pulteney. Apart from highlighting aspects of the methodology in such searches, together with the difficulties involved, including the special problems which can be experienced in this task by those not near the scene of the action, this case study demonstrated the enhancement of editorial information by solving such anonymity problems. It also indicated that in this case there were some interesting spin-offs for the doctrinal historian awaiting further exploration. However, irrespective of the value of this case study as an example, there are no foolproof ways of discovering the identify of anonymous authors. The task is arduous, time-consuming and expensive, and eventual success frequently involves considerable luck in research.

The last point applies equally to the editorial task, particularly in the Antipodes. However, the task of editor has its own rewards, not only in terms of final product and the feeling that through such efforts the work of some deserving economist has been made more accessible to future readers, but also in the opportunities it gives for exchanges such as this. To compensate for this pleasure, I hope that this idiosyncratic account of the experiences of one economists' editor and editing economist has been of value to others of this important species.

Notes

1 Whether Sraffa's famous interpretation of the Ricardo corn economy (Sraffa, 1951–73, I, pp. xxxi–xxxii) transgresses this rule is presumably debated by Professor Porta in his paper 'Sraffa: Master of Economists' Editors', also presented at this conference.

2 I have also edited 'Mr. Owen's Plan for National Distress' as part of Robert Torrens, *The Economists Refuted (1808) and other Early Economic Writings* (Groenewegen, 1984), in which the introduction comments on Torren's claim to authorship as against those made for McCulloch (see Groenewegen, 1984, pp. vii, n4, n6, xix–xx).

3 See Sraffa (1951–73) III, pp. 427–34 and IV, pp. 99, 279, 415–16, for two well known examples of Sraffa's undoubted literary detection skills – the 'ingenious calculator' of Ricardo's *Economical and Secure Currency and Plan for a National Bank* and the 'Mr. – of the Bullion Report'. At least one of these, however, remains 'tantalisingly inconclusive' (see O'Brien and Darnell, 1982, pp. 3–4, 209 n9).

4 There is a strong tradition of involvement by economists and economic statisticians in such literary detection ventures. Examples include Edgeworth's work on the meter of Virgil's verses (mentioned by Stigler, 1983, p. 550) and Yule's statistical investigation of Graunt as author of the *Natural and Political Observations ... upon the Bills of Mortality* (see O'Brien and Darnell, 1982, pp. 5–6).

5 A good example of such a direct link is Henry Brougham's list of contributors to the *Edinburgh Review* preserved at University College, London (see Groenewegen, 1988, p. 435 n6, which also acknowledges my indebtedness to John Pullen for this information).

6 The most spectacular wrong identification of 'authorship', in this case involving translation, is that of Adam Smith as the unknown translator of the 1793 English version of Turgot's *Réflexions* in Lundberg (1964).

7 Lest it be thought that my talents at identification verge on the infallible, let me indicate two failures in the context of my recent excurses into nineteenth-century Australian economics. There I failed to penetrate the pseudonym of 'Cinderella', the author of the 1890 *Manual of Political Economy for Free Men* and anything more than the name of J. E. Goodwin, the named author of the 1878 *Scientific Legislation or the Theory of Calculated Labour Equivalent* (see Groenewegen and McFarlane, 1990, pp. 18–19, 21).

8 I may note that in the context of the previous section it was here that distance became important to my editorial work. Had I lived in England, two issues could have been more systematically pursued. One relates to seeking further information on J. Roberts as publisher of Pulteney, sources for which were largely inaccessible in Sydney. The other relates to checking the destiny of Pulteney's estate, including the degree of accuracy to be attached to the statement in the *Dictionary of National Biography* that his private papers were destroyed. Independent confirmation of this statement would have been useful, while in addition and for reasons explained in the final paragraph of this section, the details of the inheritance by William Johnstone (Pulteney), the friend of Adam Smith, would have been useful. This inheritance came through his wife, Frances Pulteney, cousin and heir of General Henry Pulteney who inherited the property of his more famous brother, William (see Groenewegen, 1982, p. xi n26 and p. xv and n36).

9 Both Pulteney and the author of the 1738 pamphlet had a shrewd appreciation of the details of Locke's monetary theory. This includes shared emphasis on the 'slowness and quickness of circulation', a concept often accredited to Cantillon, while the nature of money supply is widely interpreted by both, another unusual feature in the literature of the time. Last but not least, both Pulteney and the anonymous author suggest that Locke did not oppose legal regulation of interest rates if such regulation *followed* the movement of the natural rate (for details, see Groenewegen, 1982, p. xviii and n40–1).

References

Beccaria, Cesare (1984) *Opere*, Milan: Mediobanca.

Butlin, N. G., Fitzgerald, V. W. and Scott, R. H. (eds) (1988) *The Australian Economist 1888–1898* Canberra: Pergamon Press.

Groenewegen, P. D. (ed.) (1982) *Some Thoughts on the Interest of Money in General* (1738) attributed to Sir William Pulteney, Sydney: Economics Department, University of Sydney, Reprints of Economic Classics series 2, no. 1.

——(1984) *Robert Torrens, The Economists Refuted (1808) and Other Early Economic Writings*, Sydney: Economics Department, University of Sydney, Reprints of Economic Classics series 2, no. 3.

——(1988) 'Pickering's Collected Malthus', *Journal of Political Economy*, 96(2) April, 429–46.

Groenewegen, P. D. and McFarlane, B. (1990) *A History of Australian Economic Thought*, London: Routledge.

Hutchison, T. W. (1952) 'Some Questions about Ricardo', *Economica*, n.s., 19(3) November, 415–32.

Malthus, T. R. (1989a) *An Essay on the Principle of Population*, ed. Patricia James, variorum edition, Cambridge: Cambridge University Press, for the Royal Economic Society.

——(1989b) *Principles of Political Economy*, ed. John Pullen, variorum edition, Cambridge: Cambridge University Press, for the Royal Economic Society,

Lundberg, I. C. (1964) *Turgot's Unknown Translator*, The Hague: Martinus Nijhoff.

McCulloch, J. R. (1854) *The Literature of Political Economy: A Classical Catalogue*, London: Longman, Brown, Green and Longmans.

McCulloch, J. R. (ed.) (1856) *Early English Tracts on Commerce*, London: printed for the Political Economy Club.

O'Brien, D. P. and Darnell, A. C. (1982) *Authorship Puzzles in the History of Economics*, London: Macmillan.

Patinkin, Don (1975) 'J. M. Keynes: From the *Tract* to the *General Theory*', *Economic Journal*, 85(338) June, 249–71.

Pullen, John (1978) 'The Editor of the Second Edition of T. R. Malthus' *Principles of Political Economy*', *History of Political Economy*, 10(2) summer, 286–97.

Sraffa, P. (ed.) (1951–1973) *The Works and Correspondence of David Ricardo*, edited with collaboration of M. H. Dobb, Cambridge: Cambridge University Press for the Royal Economic Society.

Stigler, S.N. (1983) 'Economic Thought and Doctrine: Review of O'Brien and Darnell (1982)', *Journal of Economic History*, 43(2) June, 547–50.

Tucker, G. L. S. (ed.) (1976) *William Huskisson, Essays on Political Economy 1830*, Canberra: Australian National University, Department of Economic History.

Part III

11 Laissez-faire

Reflections on the French foundations

The foundations of laissez-faire in French thought in the sense of origins are well understood. Mill's classic article on 'The Economists' for the *Encyclopaedia Britannica*' was already able to refer to this issue (Mill, 1824, pp. 708–9). First use of the phrase 'laissez-faire' has been attributed to the merchant, Le Gendre, who is alleged to have said to Colbert in response to his question what the government could do for trade: 'laissez-nous faire'. This account originated with Turgot's well known *Eloge de Gournay*, which in the passage where this attribution is made, treats Le Gendre's phrase and the word 'freedom' virtually as synonyms (Turgot, 1759, p. 40, n29). This essential characteristic of the phrase had also been put forward by D'Argenson, in his posthumously published journal and memoirs, and in an essay to which he gave the title. 'Pour gouverner mieux, il faudrait gouverner moins'. In his memoirs, he emphatically declared that 'Laissez-faire, telle devrait être la devise de toute poussance publique'. Earlier, and contemporaneously with the merchant, Le Gendre, the magistrate-political economist-historian, Boisguilbert, combined the phrase, 'laissez-faire' with both 'freedom' and the 'natural order', (see Boisguilbert, 1707, pp. 891–2, 897–8),[1] arguing that freedom was the agent of nature in these matters. If foundations are held to be identical with the 'trivial' question of origins (cf. Gide and Rist, 1949, p. 30, n5), then this catalogue of early usage exhausts knowledge on the subject: the phrase which can be said to have ruled political economy in its practical applications for well over a century was a policy recommendation casually produced by a French merchant *circa* 1680. During the subsequent half-century it was treated as an axiom of good government by both a magistrate, and a son of the Keeper of the Seals under the Regency. It was codified by Turgot in his *Eulogy of Gournay*, and interpreted in considerable detail by his contemporaries, the physiocrats, in their discussion of the natural order required for the good government of society. Two of these aspects constitute the point of departure for these reflections on the French foundations of laissez-faire. The first of these reflections examines the use which the physiocrats made of the phrase in their general writing; the second links Boisguillebert's use of it with some theological developments associated with Jansenism and the conception of order inherent in the doctrine of this religious sect – incidentally, the French sect closest to the Anglo-Saxon phenomenon of puritanism. The second of these should particularly be seen as emphasising the need for further work rather than presenting firm conclusions.

It can be noted at the outset that the physiocrats in their writings of the 1750s, 1760s and even 1770s, only infrequently used the phrase 'laissez-faire'.[2] What the physiocrats, however, did in their writings, and in this context Mercier de la Rivière's treatise (1767) stands out, was to systematically develop the political, social, legal and economic implications of a social order in which liberty was present. In other words, they explained the meaning to be ascribed to good government which refrains from governing too much. In practice, these duties of government appear to be very similar to those assigned to the sovereign by Adam Smith (1776, Book V, ch. 1), but their development by the physiocrats is within the context of the distinction between rights and obligations on which their view of natural order rests.

Irrespective of whether government authority was despotic, monarchic, aristocratic or democratic (cf. Quesnay, 1765, p. 52), its authority entailed obligations as well as rights in the same way as all other sections of society, its social classes, enjoyed rights and owed responsibilities. Du Pont (1772, p. 378) summarised the responsibilities of the governing authority in terms of three major functions: 'the protection of every type of property', supervision over the implementation of the 'laws of natural order', and 'upkeep and improvement of the public patrimony', consisting of 'highways, roads, temples, harbours, bridges, water ways'. Elsewhere, these responsibilities of the state were more succinctly summarised by Du Pont (1772, p. 377) as 'public education, defence, and upkeep and improvement of the public's fundamental capital ["avances foncières"]'. These social responsibilities of the state implied a charge against the surplus product created by society to be acquired through taxation; in short, the state's right to a share of the national wealth was concomitant to the state's public responsibilities. It is not difficult to see the resemblance between this summary of public responsibilities and the functions of defence, justice and public works including education which Adam Smith declared to be the duties of the sovereign (Smith, 1776, Book V, ch. 1).

In the work cited, Du Pont had only outlined these duties of government for the instructions of the Margrave of Baden; they were elaborated in considerable detail in the treatises on physiocracy of Mercier de la Rivière (1767) and Baudeau (1771). In what follows the discussion is largely based on Baudeau's more systematic account of the matter.

Public education was regarded as an essential state activity by the physiocrats for several reasons. In the first place, it contributed generally to the formation of mind and character as well as imparting skills and the habit of industry in the people. Second, the physiocrats stressed the social role of education by instilling the proper morality into the people, including full appreciation of both their rights and obligations under the natural order of society. Hence public education can be described equally as being part of the upkeep and improvement of the national heritage through skill formation; and being a tool in ensuring the successful implementation of the natural order (Baudeau, 1771, pp. 670–3; cf. Mercier de la Rivière, 1767, pp. 91–2; and Adam Smith, 1776, pp. 784–6, 788).

Baudeau indicated that protection was the second duty of the sovereign power, second, because if public education had been properly established, the state's role in protecting property would be considerably reduced. This followed from the fact that such education prevents many of those encroachments on property for the prevention of which the state's protective role was originally required. In Baudeau's exposition of the state's duty of protection, the first two of Smith's duties are included. Protection is concerned with what he called civil or legal protection, and political or military protection. Both types of protection were intimately connected with guaranteeing security of ownership for property-owners, an essential condition of liberty in the manner in which that notion was developed by the physiocrats (Baudeau, 1771, pp. 673–8, esp. 673).

Baudeau conceived his duty of public administration to encompass the third of the responsibilities Du Pont had assigned to the governing authority, that is, the maintenance and improvement of the 'public patrimony'. Baudeau in fact described this responsibility as the most constructive and expensive duty of the sovereign.[3] In addition, public administration is concerned with the appropriate funding of these responsibilities through the administration of taxation, a responsibility which has to be conducted in such a way that the basic liberties guaranteed by the natural order of society are not destroyed. It is well known that the last objective was ensured in physiocratic political economy when the state directly partakes of the nation's surplus product by means of a single direct tax proportional to that product. This single tax on national disposable wealth is the *quid pro quo*, the right of the state, arising from the duties which the natural order of society has imposed on it (Baudeau, 1771, p. 678–88).

Enumerating the duties of the sovereign in this matter, also calls for a comment on the relationship between those duties and the right to make laws. For the physiocrats, governing authorities in general had no need to make laws, a proposition inherent in their perspective on a well regulated state. For such a state, laws derive immediately from the social law emanating from the rights and obligations of the people which counterbalanced those of its governing authority. These social laws are uniquely concerned with the 'preservation of the rights of property' and 'liberty'. These are interdependent because there can be no property without liberty, and there can be no real liberty without the security provided by the protective agencies of the state (Du Pont, 1768, pp. 346–7).

A summary list of the social laws and institutions founded on the natural order can be quoted extensively from the same article by Du Pont (1768, pp. 362–4). Such extensive quotation is essential because this list of social laws and institutions strikingly indicates the inter-dependence between physiocratic economic propositions and the political and social framework required for their successful implementation.

> Here then is the abstract of every social institution founded on the natural order, on the natural constitution which restricts men and all other beings.

Personal property established by nature, by the physical necessity for each individual to dispose of all resources in his person to obtain things proper to satisfying his needs on pain of sufferance or death.

Freedom to work, inseparable from personal property, of which it is a constitutive part.

Moveable property, which is only personal property, considered in its practice, its aim, in its essential extension as things acquired by the labour of his person.

Freedom of exchange, of commerce, of the use of their wealth, inseparable [qualities] of personal and moveable property.

Husbandry, which is an employment of personal and moveable property and of the liberty which is inseparable from property; gainful, necessary, indispensable employment, in order that population can increase in consequence of the multiplication of essential produce for the subsistence of men.

Landed property, essential attendant of husbandry and the only preservation of personal and moveable property used for work and essential preliminary expenses to put the soil into a state fit for cultivation.

Freedom of employment of his land, of every type of his husbandry, of every contract related to its exploitation, to the grant, retrocession, exchange, sale of his land, inseparable to landed property.

Natural division of crops into *returns of the farmers* or wealth whose use must indispensably exist for perpetuating husbandry, under pain of diminishing both crops and population; and *net product* or disposable wealth whose size determines the prosperity of society, whose use is left to the whims and interests of the landed proprietors and which for them constitutes the natural and legitimate reward for the expenses which they have made and the labours to which they have devoted themselves in getting the soil to a state fit for cultivation.

Security without which property and freedom would only be a right and not a fact, without which the *net product* would soon be destroyed, without which husbandry could not exist.

Protecting sovereign authority to procure that essential security necessary to property and freedom, and which discharges this important service in promulgating, in causing implementation of the laws of natural order by which property and liberty are established.

Magistrates, to decide in individual cases, what must be the application of the laws of natural order transformed into positive laws by sovereign authority and who have the overriding power of comparing the ordinances of kings with the laws of justice itself, before beginning to accept these positive ordinances for guiding their verdicts.

Public and favoured instructions in order that citizens, authority and magistrates can never lose sight of the invariable laws of natural order or allow themselves to stray by the influence of opinion into the temptation of individual exclusive interest which, as soon as they are exclusive, are always misunderstood.

Public revenue to provide strength and power necessary for sovereign authority to meet the expenses of its protective service, the important functions of the magistrates and the essential public instruction into the laws of natural order.

Direct taxation, or distribution of the territorial net product between landed proprietors and sovereign authority to constitute public revenue in a manner which restrains neither property nor liberty and which consequently is not destructive.

Essential and necessary proportion of direct taxation with the net product so that it gives society the greatest possible public revenue and consequently the greatest possible degree of security without which the situation of the landed proprietors is not the best situation which can be enjoyed in society.

Hereditary monarchy in order that all the present and future interests of those entrusted with sovereign authority are essentially tied to those of society by the proportional distribution of the *net product*.

(Du Pont, 1768, pp. 362–4)

In Du Pont's own words, these social laws and institutions follow naturally from human nature and are the 'essential laws of a government made for mankind' (Du Pont, 1768, p. 364). Included in this legal and social framework are some specific segments associated with 'economic freedoms' underpinned by the motto, 'laissez-faire', or, rather, synonymous with it. These are 'liberté de travail', 'liberté de l'emploi de sa terre' and 'liberté d'échange, de commerce, d'emploi de ses richesses'. For the physiocrats, the doctrine of laissez-faire was therefore a simple deduction from the necessary conditions of that natural society they wished to establish. Many of their political and economic perspectives hinged on the rights of property and other aspects of personal liberty on which that social order was constructed, and which they saw as in the interest of all members of society irrespective of class, because the economic consequences of this natural order enhanced everyone's potential for enjoyment with minimum effort.

Du Pont's list of institutional pre-requisites describes the conditions, for example, which Quesnay summarised in his assumption of 'good cultivation in an agricultural kingdom', the assumption on which he constructed the original analysis of his *Tableau Economique*. Departures from this social framework based on the natural order induced the detrimental consequences for production and living standards, which Quesnay was able to demonstrate by means of this analytical apparatus. In this manner, laissez-faire in its concrete manifestation of specific economic freedoms, was an essential feature of physiocratic economic analysis.

However, it should also be noted that the practical application of these economic freedoms was qualified in the work of the leading physiocrats.

Unrestrained freedom in both trade and the disposal of property was demonstrably destructive for the prosperity of an agricultural kingdom on the terms of their own analysis. Although in Du Pont's summary which was quoted in full, 'liberté d'échange, liberté de commerce' appears completely unqualified, in practice, this freedom tended to be confined to free domestic trade (Baudeau, 1771, pp. 728–32; Mercier de la Rivière, 1767, ch. 37, which emphasise the usefulness of foreign trade as a device to raise the market for agricultural produce; cf. Gide and Rist, 1949, pp. 46–7; Vaggi, 1987, pp. 109–14). Second, the personal use of, and right to dispose of, wealth was constrained in at least two fundamental ways. The first of these was to avoid 'luxe de décoration' in such disposal, since that direction of demand towards the unproductive manufacturing or trade sector was destructive over the longer term to economic growth, as the *Tableau Economique* was designed to demonstrate. Disposal of wealth should be directed at 'luxe de subsistence' or luxury spending which raised the demand for agricultural production, and which, from its generation of surplus product, was necessarily conducive of economic growth. The physiocratic position on the economically sound disposal of wealth was particularly argued by Baudeau (1767; and see 1771, pp. 734–7). Second, disposal of property by way of lending was constrained by the maximum rate of interest which could be charged if interest was to be charged at all. For Quesnay (1776, pp. 763–8) interest derived from net product of land, and the maximum interest rate which the state should enable lenders to charge was determined naturally by the rate of return to land.[4] In short, physiocratic analysis of economic growth through the development of agricultural production only required free international trade if the market for agricultural produce was to be expanded while freedom of disposal of wealth was likewise constrained by the need to maintain a domestic market for agricultural produce and to restrain farmers' costs by keeping interest rates low.

These restrictions on the application of economic liberty (or laissez-faire) enable also a comment on the distinctive treatment of laissez-faire by the school of Gournay and more specifically, Turgot. The latter, it is well known, fully supported the freedom of lending at interest without legal constraint (Turgot, 1776; 1770, e.g. pp. 7–82, 153–63). The former, credited with the phrase 'laissez faire, laissez passer' by Du Pont (1808, I, p. 258) in fact may have been more favourable to the 'laissez faire' part of the motto only, that is, the freedom to manufacture without restrictions, rather than the freedom to trade enshrined in 'laissez passer' (see Tsuda, 1983, pp. 446–8). The French foundations of the second half of the nineteenth century therefore at best only crudely approximate the interpretation they were given in the middle of the nineteenth century.

II

The second part of these reflections on the French foundations of laissez-faire concerns Boisguilbert who, as already mentioned, likewise used this phrase in his later economic work. Boisguilbert has always been somewhat of an enigma in the history of economic thought. Praised as the French founder of classical political economy by Marx (1859), his work is nevertheless rarely discussed in texts on the history of economic thought, although its general importance has been recognised in several specialist studies. Boisguilbert has also long been recognised as an anticipator of the physiocrats, and was indeed seen by them as an important precursor of their views. Cantillon was acquainted with his work and quoted it in his *Essai*, as was Davenant, who drew on it in 1698 according to Hecht (1966, p. 160).

Of particular relevance in the context of this paper, a recent study of Boisguilbert (Faccarello, 1986) has interpreted his economic work as an important aspect in explaining the origins of a liberal political economy. Contrary to earlier commentators (in particular Hecht, 1966, pp. 160–1), who have tended to ascribe the foundations of Boisguilbert's economic work to English sources, either directly, or indirectly, via the writings of Dubos (1703), Faccarello ascribes the construction of Boisguilbert's work entirely to French sources. These French sources can be subdivided into three distinct groups. The first of these are political writings, of which the work by Bodin is undoubtedly the more important. The second are more generally scientific writings, particularly those devoted to mechanics, more especially the Cartesian perspectives on the subject. Third, and most interesting for the purpose at hand, are writings in the Jansenist theological tradition, in particular those by Domat and Nicole, which emphasised the role of enlightened self-interest in the securing of economic and civil order. Viner (1978, pp. 130–50) had commented on these authors, linking this aspect of Jansenist thought with the work of Mandeville and Adam Smith, which it resembled and foreshadowed.[5]

Viner did not discuss the potential impact of Jansenist thought in this respect on French economic thinking. This is strikingly done by Faccarello (1986, chs 3, 4) in the case of Boisguilbert. Both textual evidence and external evidence are used to demonstrate the likely impact of these aspects of Jansenist thought on Boisguilbert's conception of economic freedoms. Given the comparative evidence presented in Faccerello and the fact that Boisguilbert commenced his education in the Jansenist school of Port Royal (see Hecht, 1966, 132–3), the likelihood of the influence of this Jansenist thought is strong and his argument convincing. What are the implications of this for a discussion of the French foundations of laissez-faire?

Hutchison's interpretation of Faccarello's work leaves no room for doubt. From the Jansenist premises abundantly available in the work of Domat and Nicole, that enlightened self-interest and the lust for gain secures the reciprocal utility of an exchange and mutual want satisfaction on which both the harmony of the world and the maintenance of the state relies, it was an easy step for Boisguilbert to link the achievement of this result to a situation of unrestrained competition. If nature is left alone and not interfered with, the harmonious reconciliations of self-interest with the good of society is naturally assured. In general, the role of government is confined to the preservation of justice and peace; in the particular case of the grain trade, the government has to ensure the subsistence of the people by positive intervention (Hutchison, 1988, pp. 111–14).

If this position is correct, and I personally have reservations about whether Hutchison's summary does justice to both the spirit of Boisguilbert's work and that of the Jansenists, the French foundations for laissez-faire as a rule for the guidance of government in economic affairs have to be sought in French theology as interpreted by a French tax reformer. Given the fact that the Jansenists were the group of French religious thinkers closest to the views of English puritans, there may here be another possibility of linking aspects of 'Protestant' thought and an essential feature of '(the spirit of) capitalism'. Irrespective of the merits of such a hypothesis, there remain many questions about the seventeenth-century foundations of laissez-faire in France. The nature and implications of Boisguilbert's perception of leaving nature alone need more clarification, something which involves closer study of Boisguilbert's perception of the role of the state than has been given in the literature. Furthermore, what, if any, is the connection between Jansenist theology and the (possibly apocryphal) remarks attributed to Legendre on the subject? Did these have similar philosophical foundations, or were they the simple reaction of a practical businessman operating in a highly regulated market when asked by the chief regulator what was the best way to let his business (and that of the nation) thrive?

The brevity of this second reflection reveals the amount of work to be done on some of its basic aspects: the content of the Jansenist literature and the precise context in which it was produced; combined with an absence of systematic study of Boisguilbert's considerable writings from the perspective of his views on the functions of the state. As a necessary precondition for the latter, considerable knowledge is required of the economic history background of sixteenth and seventeenth-century Europe, to which he made many allusions and gave many illustrations during the diagnosis he presented of what was wrong with the French economy of his day.

III

Only a few specific conclusions can be derived from these reflections on the French foundations of laissez-faire, apart from the general observations that nineteenth-century interpretation has been misleading in reading into laissez-faire positions of the physiocrats the perspectives of liberalism current in their own century. This type of critique is now a commonplace in contemporary historical examination of the phenomenon.

More precisely, let me draw attention to some more specific tasks for future research which these reflections suggest.

1 *Boisguilbert's economics*: Despite Faccarello's interesting work on its association with Jansenist thought and French contemporary political and

scientific thought, Boisguilbert's role in the birth of modern economics needs more work, as does indeed the comprehensive understanding of his substantial economic writings. More directly in the context of this workshop, the meaning he gave to 'laissez faire' and the implications he derived therefrom need more work than they have received so far, and many take us far beyond Hutchison's facile picture of Boisguilbert as a liberal forerunner.

2 *Gournay's perspectives on laissez-faire*, including Tsuda's insightful distinction between 'laissez faire passer' and 'laissez faire' in this context, also needs further study because of the potential light it can shed on French economic policy thinking of the eighteenth century. Antoin Murphy's important work on Gournay as organiser of translations in his study of Cantillon has bearing on this, as has closer study of Turgot's policy implementation both as intendant and finance minister.

3 The physiocrats' implied notion of laissez-faire as liberty in the economic sphere in the context of their characterisation of an essential natural and social order also needs more work than it has received. Issues involved are their qualifications of this freedom, and their conclusion implicit in the support they gave to enlightened legal despotism 'that there is no *necessary* link between economic and political liberalism' as historically contemplated. (Bronowsky and Mazlish, 1963, p. 384, n1). Further investigation of the interrelationship between the political, the social and the economic in the complex physiocratic system, may therefore even pay dividends in contemporary discussion of these interconnections, highlighted in at least some interpretations of events in Eastern Europe and the Soviet Union.

In short, these brief (and all too casual) reflections on the French foundations of laissez-faire suggest that revision of some well worn preconceptions on the subject may be quite in order.

Notes

1 In the context of the second of these reflections on the French foundations of laissez-faire, these isolated remarks by Boisguilbert are worth quoting.

> Ce n'est qu'à la pointe de l'epée que la justice se maintient dans ces recontres; c'est néanmoins de quoi la nature et la Providence se sont chargées. Et comme elles ont établi des retraites et des moyens aux animaux faibles pour ne devenir pas tours la proie de ceux qui, étant forts, et naissant en quelque manière armés, vivent de carnage, ainsi, dans le commerce de la vie, elle [i.e. la nature] a mis un tel ordre que, pourvu qu'on la laisse faire, il n'est point au pourvoir du plus puissant, en achetant la denrée d'un misérable, d'empêcher que cette vente ne lui procure sa subsistance; ce qui maintient également l'opulence, à laquelle l'un et l'auitre sont redevables de leur subsistance proportionée à leur état.
>
> On a dit, *que pourvu qu'on laisse faire la nature*, c'est-à-dire qu'on lui donne sa liberté, et que qui que ce soit ne s'en méle que pour y procurer de la protection et empêcher la violence.
>
> (Boisguilbert, 1707, pp. 891–2)

> Ainsi ces deux articles du désordre des tailles et des blés coûtent la moitié des quinze cents millions de perte arrivés au royaume depuit 1660, d'autant plus aisés à rétablir que ce n'a été l'effet, d'aucun intérét particulier, mais seulement manqué d'attention dans l'un, et de trop d'attention dans l'autre, savoir, les grains, Il n'y avait qu'à laisser faire le nature, comme partout ailleurs, et la liberté, qui est la commissionaire de cette même nature, n'aurait pas manqué de faire une compensation avantageuse, qui aurait formé un très grand bien de deux très grandes misères.
>
> (Boisguilbert, 1707, pp. 897–8)

2 See Baudeau (1771, p. 723), who stated:

> *Laisse les faire*, comme disdait un célèbre intendant du commerce [i.e. Gournay] ... Qu'on les *laisse faire*, c'est la vrai legistation, c'est-à-dire le fonction de l'autorité garantissante. Elle *doit* assurer à toute homme quelconque cette portion précieuse de sa liberté personelle, d'employer son intelligence, son temps, ses forces, ses moyens ou ces avances à donner aux productions de la nature, dont il sera le légitime acquéreur, le forme qu'il jugera convenable, soit pour ses propres jouissances, soit pour celles d'une autre homme avec lequelle il espérera faire quelque échange agréable à l'une et à l'autre.

3 The reason for this is that Baudeau, like subsequent nineteenth-century liberals, had high hopes for the consequences for peace from a free international trade. See, for example, 1771, pp. 808–18.

4 As Böhm-Bawerk (1890, pp. 63–9) argued, a circular procedure since the rate of return to land implied by a specific net (surplus) product can only be calculated if the price of land is known, the last being nothing but the net product capitalised by the current rate of interest.

5 See Groenewegen (1989, pp. 137–40; above, pp. 78–80) which comment on this from a different perspective.

References

Baudeau, L'Abbé Nicolas (1767, 1913) *Principles de la science morale et politique sur le luxe et les loix sumptuaires*, ed. A. Dubois, Paris: Marcel Rivière.

——(1771, 1846) *Première introduction à la philosophie economique ou analise des états policés*, in E. Daire (ed.) *Physiocrates*, first part, Paris: Guillaumin, 657–821.

Böhm-Bawerk, E. von (1890, 1957) *Capital and Interest*, trans. William Smart, reprinted New York: August M. Kelley.

Boisguilbert, Pierre (1707, 1966) *Factum de la France*, in *Pierre de Boisguilbert ou la naissance de l'économie politique*, Paris: INED, 879–956.

Bronowski, J. and Mazlish, B. (1963) *The Western Intellectual Tradition*, Harmondsworth: Penguin.

Dubos, J. B. (1703) *Les intérèts de l'Angleterre mal-entendus dans la guerre présente*, Amsterdam [i.e. Paris].

Du Pont de Nemours, Pierre Samuel (1768, 1846) *De L'origine et des progrès d'une science nouvelle*, in E. Daire (ed.) *Physiocrates*, first part, Paris: Guillaumin, 335–68.

——(1722, 1846) *Abrégé des principes de l'économie politique*, in E. Daire (ed.) *Physiocrates*, first part, Paris: Guillaumin, 367–85.

Faccarello, Gilbert (1986) *Aux origines de l'économie politique libérale: Pierre de Boisguilbert*, Paris: Editions Anthropos.

Gide, Charles and Rist, Charles (1949) *A History of Economic Doctrines*, 2nd English edn, London: Harper.

Groenewegen, P. D. (1989) 'New Light on the Origins of Modern Economics', *Economic Record*, 65(189) June, 136–79 (above, Chapter 3).

Hecht, Jacqueline (1966) 'La vie de Pierre le Pesant, Seigneur de Boisguilbert', in *Pierre de Boisguilbert ou la naissance de l'économie politique*, Paris: INED, 121–244.

Hutchison, T. W. (1988) *Before Adam Smith: The Emergence of Political Economy 1662–1776*, Oxford: Blackwell.

Mercier de la Rivère, Pierre-Paul (1767) *L'ordre naturel et essentiel des sociétés politiques*, 2 vols, London and Paris.

Mill, James (1824) 'Economists', *Supplement to the Fourth, Fifth and Sixth Edition of the Encyclopaedia Britannica*, vol. 3, Edinburgh: Constable, 708–24.

Quesnay, François, (1765, 1961) 'Natural Right', trans. in R. L. Meek, *The Economics of Physiocracy*, London: Allen & Unwin, 43–56.

——(1766, 1958) 'Observations sur l'intérét d'argent', in *François Quesnay et la physiocratie*, Paris: INED, 763–68.

Smith, Adam (1776, 1976) *An Inquiry into the Nature and Causes of the Wealth of Nations*, eds R. Campbell, A. S. Skinner and W. B. Todd, Oxford: Clarendon Press.

Tsuda, Tarumi (ed.) (1983) *Traités sur le commerce de Josiah Child et remarques inédites de Vincent de Cournay*, Tokyo: Kinokuniya.

Turgot, A. R. J. (1759, 1977) 'In Praise of Gournay', in P. D. Groenewegen, *The Economics of A. R. J. Turgot*, The Hague: Martinus Nijhoff, 20–42.

——(1766, 1977) 'Reflections on the Production and Distribution of Wealth', in P. D. Groenewegen, *The Economics of A. R. J. Turgot*, The Hague: Martinus Nijhoff, 43–95.

——(1770, 1977) Paper on Lending at Interest, extracts translated in P. D. Groenewegen, *The Economics of A. R. J. Turgot*, The Hague: Martinus Nijhoff, 149–63.

Vaggi, Gianni (1987) *The Economics of François Quesnay*, Durham NC: Duke University Press.

Viner, Jacob (1978) 'Religious Thought and Economic Society', four chapters of an unfinished work, eds Jacques Melitz and Donald Winch, *History of Political Economy*, 10(1) spring, 1–192.

12 The physiocrats

The origins of scientific political economy and the single tax

In Book II, chapter IV of his *The Science of Political Economy*, Henry George (1898, p. 148) argued that the physiocrats were 'the first developers in modern times of something like a true science of political economy'. George's claim did not arise from a profound study of either the history of economic thought or of physiocratic writings. There is abundant evidence that his knowledge of the history of economics was rather slender, and on his own confession he had himself never read any of the works of Quesnay or his followers. For him, they were 'fellow travellers' and anticipators of his own ideas, and their importance arose from the fact that in the previous century they had arrived at proposals very similar to this own.

George's account of how he first gained knowledge of the doctrines of the physiocrats (George, 1898, pp. 163–4) is revealing because it explains the subjective basis for his admiration of their work.

> In what is most important, I have come closer to the views of Quesnay and his followers than did Adam Smith, who knew the men personally. But in any case there was certainly no derivation from them. I well recall the day when, checking my horse on a rise that overlooks San Francisco Bay, the commonplace reply of a passing teamster to a commonplace question, crystallized, as by lightning-flash, my brooding thoughts into coherency, and I there and then recognized the natural order – one of those experiences that make those who have had them feel thereafter that they can vaguely appreciate what mystics and poets have called the 'ecstatic vision'. Yet at that time I had never heard of the physiocrats, or even read a line of Adam Smith.
>
> Afterwards, with the great idea of the natural order in my head, I printed a little book 'Our Land and Land Policy', in which I urged that all taxes should be laid on the value of land, irrespective of improvements. Casually meeting on a San Francisco street a scholarly lawyer, A.B. Douthitt, we stopped to chat, and he told me that what I had in my little book proposed was what the French 'Economists' a hundred years before had proposed.

> I forget many things, but the place where I heard this, and the tones and attitudes of the man who told me of it, are photographed on my memory. For, when you have seen a truth that those around you do not see, it is one of the deepest of pleasures to hear of others who have seen it. This is true even though these others were dead years before you were born. For the stars that we of to-day see when we look were here to be seen hundreds and thousands of years ago. They shine on. Men come and go, in their generations, like the generations of the ants.

More elaborate reasons for George's admiration for the physiocrats are found in the earlier and more influential writings, *Progress and Poverty* and *Protection or Free Trade*. In the first, the physiocrats are praised because they advocated the single tax on land values. George's presentation of 'Indorsements and Obligations' (Book VIII, ch. 4) to his fundamental proposal of the single tax mentions support for the measure from Ricardo, McCulloch, John Stuart Mill and Millicent Fawcett, but the physiocrats are singled out for particular praise.

> There has been a school of economists who plainly perceived ... that the revenues of land, ought to be appropriated to the common service. The French economists of the last [i.e. eighteenth] century, headed by Quesnay and Turgot, proposed just what I have proposed, that all taxation should be abolished save a tax upon the value of land.
>
> (George, 1879, pp. 423–4)

Praise for the physiocratic contribution is continued in the opening paragraph of the next book, which asserts that 'the elder Mirabeau ... ranked the proposition of Quesnay, to substitute one single tax on rent (the *impôt unique*) for all other taxes, as a discovery equal in utility to the invention of writing or the substitution of the use of money for barter. (George, 1879, p. 433)[1]

George's subsequent 'Protection of Free Trade' was dedicated 'to the memory of those illustrious Frenchmen of a century ago, Quesnay, Turgot, Mirabeau, Condorcet, Du Pont, and their fellows, who in the night of despotism, foresaw the glories of the coming day' (George 1886, frontispiece). Less poetically, he explained in the preface (*ibid*., p. iv) that his praise arose from the fact that those illustrious Frenchmen 'organised the motto *Laissez faire* and. ... grasped a central truth which free traders since their time have ignored'. The superiority of the physiocratic free trade position is further explained as follows:

> These French economists were what neither Smith nor any subsequent British economist or statesman has been – true free traders. They wished to sweep away not merely protective duties, but all taxes, direct and indirect, save a single tax upon land values. This logical conclusion of free trade principles the so-called British free traders have shirked, and it meets today as bitter opposition from the Cobden Club as from American protectionists.
>
> (George, 1886, p. 15)[2]

These remarks are reiterated in the concluding chapters, where Henry George explained them on the ground that the physiocrats envisaged their fiscal reforms and free trade policies not as isolated deductions from their political economy, but as a manifesto for 'the complete reconstruction of society [by] the restoration to all men of their natural and equal rights to the use of the earth' (George 1886, p. 310). As noted briefly by Gide and Rist (1949, p. 62, n3) this tribute and inference that 'they were his masters … loses its point somewhat when we remember that he admitted that he had never read them' (for George's admission of this, see 1879, p. 424; 1898, pp. 154–6).

The greater part of this lecture is devoted to establishing the proposition that although Henry George was quite correct in drawing the attention of economists to the important services rendered by the physiocrats to the development of a science of political economy, he did so for quite the wrong reasons. It can be added that in many respects he was not alone in this. As indicated by my title, two major sections of the lecture concentrate on this issue. One of these critically examines a number of other prominent views which have associated the physiocrats with the foundation of scientific political economy. It thereby provides reasons why this school of eighteenth-century French economists is so important in the history of economic thought, which are often superior to those advanced by George. The other major part of the lecture demonstrates that the physiocrats were not the first to argue in favour of the single direct tax on land. It does so by presenting a brief history of the single tax followed by a discussion of some associated matters. A final section presents some broad conclusions from this discussion.

By way of prologue, something must be said about physiocracy itself, since, particularly in the early nineteenth century, comments on its doctrines were frequently marked by ignorance of its texts (a fault already noted in Henry George). This has led some more recent commentators into wrongly attributing *physiocratic* influence on early British thought. In this context it can also be noted that until recently there were still commentaries which regard the analytical masterpiece of physiocracy – the *Tableau économique* of Quesnay – as 'an embarrassed footnote' and 'a vast mystification … treated gingerly by commentators rendered uneasy by the feeling that they do not quite understand what they are talking about' (Gray, 1931 – but still in print in 1984 – p. 106).[3]

I

Who, then, were the physiocrats, or the Economists, to use the name by which they were long known in economic circles, or the French philosopher-followers of Quesnay, as Smith preferred to call them? It is easiest to define them by listing the members of the school. Apart from their self-acknowledged leader and master, François Quesnay, in order of importance the school included Victor Riquetti, Marquis de Mirabeau, Pierre-Paul le Mercier de la Rivière, Pierre Samuel Du Pont de Nemours, Abbé Nicolas Baudeau and Guillaume le Trosne. The writings of the last five consist largely of explanations, elaborations, systematisations and popularisations of Quesnay's doctrines,[4] hence the use of the word 'school' is most appropriate. This was important, because Quesnay's economic and philosophical writings were published as articles rather than a treatise. Although these formed a coherent system of thought, succinctly summarised by Quesnay in the various editions of the *Tableau économique*, they were nevertheless sufficiently fragmented to need the type of systematisation which was provided in the more important writings of his five leading followers.[5]

Although up to the mid-nineteenth century (cf. Sargant, 1867, p. 14 and 14n), the school was generally known by the title 'The Economists',[6] both the term 'physiocrats' – derived from the title Du Pont gave to his edition of Quesnay's collected works (1767) – and Smith's description of them as 'French philosophers' (1776, p. 644) are more appropriate.[7] The new science that they were very conscious of creating (Du Pont, 1768) was intended as a science of society, providing a blue print for an ideal social order based on the laws of nature of which the laws of political economy were an important but not predominant part. This is clearly indicated by the titles of some of the major works in which the physiocrats popularised the ideas of Quesnay. For example, the title of Mercier de la Rivière's book is *L'ordre naturel et essentiel des sociétés politiques* (1767),[8] Baudeau produced a *Première introduction à la philosophie économique ou analyse des états policés* (1771); Le Trosne's major work is called *De l'ordre social* (1777) and Mirabeau's major elaborative work on which the 'master' had himself collaborated, is entitled *Philosophie rurale* (1763).[9]

The nature of physiocracy, as it was understood by the physiocrats themselves, can be conveniently summarised from the resumé given by Du Pont (1768, pp. 362–4) of the 'social institutions founded on the law of nature' which provided the essential foundation for all political and social laws. The first and most important of these institutions was the right of private property, established by nature and sanctioning all persons to use their resources in any manner they chose to obtain objects suitable for the satisfaction of their wants. This starting point implied more specific rights which featured strongly in the physiocratic catalogue of essential freedoms. Among these Du Pont included complete freedom in the use of labour ('liberté du travail') and personal property in the form of capital, the right to free trade ('liberté d'échange'), and the right to use landed property for whatever purpose desired combined with the need and duty to share the produce with the farmers according to the necessary costs of production. To enable full exercise of the right of personal property, it was essential for the state to provide for its security, ensuring this by registration of land titles, by administration of law and by public instruction, a role best exercised by the state through a hereditary monarchy. To enable the state to enforce the law, public revenue had to be raised through the appropriation of the state's rightful share of the net product of land by the single tax (*l'impôt unique*). The demonstration that such a social and economic order produced the best possible results for society was developed in the economic argument for which the physiocrats are now largely remembered. The analysis of the ideal would then also be used to devise policies to improve the far-from-ideal existing French situation.[10]

The active life of the school was relatively short.[11] Quesnay's first economic contribution had appeared in 1756, his last economic article was published in 1768 (Quesnay, 1958, pp. 307, 313). The school itself was formally founded in 1757 through a meeting between Quesnay and Mirabeau (Meek, 1962, pp. 15–18) but as Weulersse (1910, I, p. vi) pointed out, by 1770 it was no longer possible to speak of a physiocratic movement. There was, however, a temporary revival of physiocracy in 1774–6 when Turgot was Finance Minister. The last major physiocratic work (Le Trosne, 1777) appeared a year after Turgot's dismissal. Physiocratic ideas were influential in the early years of the French revolution, partly through the initiatives of Du Pont and Condorcet. However, by the early nineteenth century, there were few who appear to have been familiar with their doctrines at first hand, even though Du Pont, the last survivor of the original physiocrats, was still defending their doctrines against J. B. Say as late as the second decade of the nineteenth century (McLain, 1977, ch. 7).

Some more recent commentators (Meek, 1951a; 1951b; Semmel, 1964–5) have alleged that physiocracy was of considerable importance in Britain in the early nineteenth century, particularly in the context of underconsumption theories associated with Spence (1808), Malthus (1820) and others. However, it is easy to exaggerate this, because close examination of the evidence reveals that the physiocratic content of these British followers of the 'French Economists' was at best rather slight. It can be argued, in fact, that with the exception of a few Scottish economists, most of these English 'physiocrats' had not studied the works of their French counterparts in any detail and had derived knowledge about their doctrine from Adam Smith's summary and critique thereof in the *Wealth of Nations* (1776, Book IV, ch. 9). Apart from setting the historical record straight, this digression on physiocracy in Britain in the early nineteenth century is useful for putting the discussion of the following two sections into proper perspective.

There is ample evidence (see Groenewegen, 1983a; this volume, Chapter 1) that Smith had been a close and careful student of the doctrine of the physiocrats, and that he had a keen appreciation of the tremendous value of the analytical apparatus contained in their work. This is clear from aspects of his theory of accumulation and growth (1776, Book II, ch. 3), taxation (cf. Horner, 1803) and the concise summary he gave of their doctrines in the chapter (Book IV, ch. 9) set aside for that purpose. Dugald Stewart's (1794) remark that Smith would have dedicated his *Wealth of Nations* to Quesnay had he not died prior to its publication is further evidence of his admiration for this 'speculative physician'. However, Smith's misleading suggestion with which he commenced this discussion that, unlike the mercantile system, physiocracy had experienced no practical application (1776, p. 663), combined with its relative brevity and critical tone, indicate that he did not wish to emphasise their importance unduly.

This attitude may have been inspired by motives similar to those that had led him to ignore Sir James Steuart's *Principles* completely.[12]

Dugald Stewart, Professor of Moral Philosophy at Edinburgh, is presumably the reason why the works of the physiocrats continued to be studied in Scotland. In any case it can be noted that in the early nineteenth century, accurate knowledge about the physiocrats backed with citation from their work, was largely a Scottish monopoly confined to Stewart's students and other members of his circle, especially the early economic contributors to the *Edinburgh Review*. These included Lauderdale, Francis Horner, Henry Brougham, James Mill and later John McCulloch. Thomas Chalmers, the under-consumptionist, may also have imbibed his physiocracy from this source.[13] However, English writers who discussed the works of the 'French Economists' at this time do not appear to have been serious students of their work. The case of three leading examples from this group of English economists – Torrens, Malthus and Spence – is briefly investigated to emphasise the real decline of physiocracy in England by the early nineteenth century.

It is not difficult to show that Malthus, Torrens and Spence display little detailed knowledge of physiocratic writings. In the case of the last two, they may have been as innocent of having studied such writings as Henry George confessed himself to be. Although in his *The Economists Refuted* (1808, p. 4) Torrens made a reference to the opinions of 'M. Quesnoi' (*sic.*), he actually only examined the anti-commerce views of Spence and Cobbett. In later work Torrens (1821, p. 110) referred to 'the error involved in the agricultural theory of the French economists' as having 'its origin in their indulging in arbitrary abstractions', but this assertion is not supported by evidence in the form of textual quotation. This supports the view that Torrens never examined any of their writings.

Despite the fact that Spence has been widely regarded as the archetypal English physiocrat (Mill, 1824, p. 324; Meek, 1951a, pp. 358–9; 1951b, pp. 322–4; Semmel, 1964–5, p. 523), he, likewise, seems to have been unfamiliar with their doctrines at first hand. His general introductory summary of Quesnay's views (Spence, 1808, pp. 12–15) contains nothing which cannot be found in Smith's discussion of the subject in the *Wealth of Nations* and includes no reference to any of their works. No citations to physiocratic literature can be found in the rest of the book despite Spence's rather unusual habit for the time of providing fairly specific references to the sources he cited.[14] His under-consumptionist views, attributed by Meek (1951b, p. 324) to a clear understanding of the pattern of production and demand in Quesnay's *Tableau économique* (an assertion for which Meek provided no evidence) appear more likely to have been derived from Spence's reading of Berkeley's *The Querist* (1735), which he cited twice (1808, pp. 59, 69).[15] In connection with the title of this chapter, it may also be noted that Spence (1808, pp. 41–2) opposed the physiocratic doctrine of the single tax.

Malthus' case is perhaps the most intriguing. Both Meek (1951a; 1951b) and Semmel (1964–5) have discussed the considerable physiocratic influence they claim to see in his work from the publication of the first edition of the *Essay on Population* (1798) to the posthumous second edition of the *Principles of Political Economy* (1836). However, Malthus' first economic work (1798, pp. 114–16), although for example, it expressed his preference for the Economists' definition of wealth, provides no evidence that at that stage he had studied any of their works. Subsequent editions of the *Essay on Population* provide two specific citations of physiocratic work.[16] Likewise, his 1814 and 1815 pamphlets on rent provide no evidence to suggest that Malthus had ever scrutinised physiocratic writings very closely,[17] even though Ricardo (1815, p. 37) thought that some of Malthus' opinions in these pamphlets appeared 'to be more consistent with the doctrine of the Economists, than with those which he has maintained'. Finally, Malthus' *Principles* (1820) contain a number of references to the Economists on wealth, productive and unproductive labour, trade and so on, but none of these are backed up by specific references to their texts. It may also be noted that Malthus, like Spence, did not approve of the physiocratic doctrine of the single tax.[18] The case of Malthus is a clear warning that references to the Economists in English works supporting the landed interest cannot be taken for evidence that the author in question had studied, let alone understood, physiocracy.

What then, are the 'findings' of this prologue? Briefly, they are as follows. After enjoying considerable and mixed success in their native France for (at best) two decades (from 1757 to 1777), the work of the physiocrats was used, criticised and to some extent ridiculed by Smith in his *Wealth of Nations* (1776). Their works were then largely ignored or forgotten, except for a small circle of Scottish political economists who studied their writings at first hand, but whose names have not become *very* prominent in the history of political economy. A group of more prominent English economists, of whom Malthus and Torrens are leading examples, either supported or criticised some of their views; in their case without serious study of their work. By the 1820s they had degenerated into figures of fun because of their exaggerated views on agriculture, manufactures and commerce, even though it was recognised that they had rendered a valuable service in the eighteenth century, by supporting general free trade and defence of private property as key features of economic development. This hardly seems the stuff of which developers of a true science of political economy are made.

II

By the 1890s, however, this is exactly what the physiocrats had become. In his *Principles of Economics* (1890, Book I, ch. IV; 1920, app. B, pp. 756–7) Marshall suggested,

> The first systematic attempt to form an economic science on a broad basis was made in France about the middle of the eighteenth century by a group of statesmen and philosophers under the leadership of Quesnay. The corner stone of their policy was obedience to Nature. They were the first to

> proclaim the doctrine of free trade as a broad principle of action ... the chief motive of their study was ... to diminish the suffering and degradation which was caused by extreme poverty. They thus gave to economics its modern aim of seeking after such knowledge as may help to raise the quality of human life.

Some features of this strong praise for the contribution of the physiocrats may be usefully highlighted.

Manuscript notes on the physiocrats in the Marshall Library suggests that Marshall developed these views in the *Principles* on the basis of a careful study of both the writings of the physiocrats (in Daire, 1846), and secondary source material.[19] Further, the material quoted shows that his reasons for praising the physiocrats were not unrelated to his own work: he himself was an ardent believer in free trade and associated economic freedoms, while in addition he had himself depicted remedies for poverty as a major reason for scientific interest in economic questions (Marshall, 1920, pp. 3–5). Finally, the praise of the physiocrats, generous though it appears to be, is rather backhanded. First, he attributed little 'direct value' to their work, though its 'indirect influence' is judged to have been great. Second, and more important, the subsequent section on Adam Smith suggests that 'the greatest step that economics has ever taken' occurred with the publication of the *Wealth of Nations* (Marshall, 1920, pp. 656–7). Like Henry George, it may be said that Marshall praised the physiocrats for rather personal reasons.[20]

Much of the tone of Marshall's praise of the physiocrats, though not all of its emphasis, may have come from his study of the writings of McCulloch on the history of economic thought. These had regularly appeared in more or less the same form over three decades after their first presentation in 1824 in the *Discourse on the Rise, Progress, Peculiar Objects and Importance of Political Eocnomy*.[21] In one of these versions, McCulloch (1825, pp. 30–5) ascribed to 'the celebrated M. Quesnay' the unquestionable merit 'of having first attempted to investigate and analyse the sources of wealth, *with the intention of ascertaining the fundamental principles of Political Economy*, and who thus gave it a systematic form, and raised it to the rank of a science'. In his discussion of this proposition with which his treatment of the physiocrats commences, he clearly reveals that he had read some of their writings (particularly Du Pont, 1767; 1768). However, although he mentions 'the *Economical Table*' as a formula intended to demonstrate 'the production of wealth with its distribution', the *Tableau* is not further discussed, presumably because its systematic treatment was beyond McCulloch's rather limited analytical powers. The discussion therefore switches to recognition of the physiocratic contribution as a 'liberal system of commercial intercourse' and to their defects in ascribing exclusive productivity to agriculture. Despite the shortcomings he concluded that their 'labours ... contributed to accelerate the progress of economical science'.[22]

McCulloch's discussion of the physiocrats and their importance, although in itself rather feeble, did fulfil the useful function of keeping the memory of their work alive in England.[23] Hence some discussion of their views became almost obligatory in the early versions of the history of economics by Travers Twiss (1847), Richard Jones (1847) and J. K. Ingram (1888), McCulloch's successor as contributor of the article on Political Economy to the *Encyclopaedia Britannica* (9th edn, 1888). None of these accounts added to a real understanding of physiocratic work, because they continued to depict this exclusively in terms of advocating free trade, laissez-faire, natural law and wrong-headed views on 'exclusive productiveness of agriculture' (Ingram, 1888, pp. 60–70).

Real appreciation of the analytical contributions of the physiocrats in the nineteenth century came with Karl Marx. It seems likely that Marx first came across their writings in the period 1862–3 and that he had solved the major aspects of the analysis of the *Tableau économique* by the beginning of July 1863. It was then that he wrote the sections of *Theories of Surplus Value* (Marx, 1862, pp. 44–67, 299–334) which revealed the first clear understanding of the work of the physiocrats since Smith had adapted their doctrines to his purposes in the *Wealth of Nations*. Marx's reading of their work allowed praising them in very specific terms at the start of his general treatment of their doctrines:

> The analysis of *capital*, within the bourgeois horizon, is essentially the work of the physiocrats. It is this service that makes them the true fathers of modern political economy. … In addition to the analysis of the material elements in which capital consists … the Physiocrats established the forms which capital assumes in circulation (fixed capital, circulating capital, even though as yet they give them other names), and in general the connection between the process of circulation and the reproduction process of capital. … The minimum of wages … correctly forms the pivotal point of Physiocratic theory. … [They] transferred the inquiry into the origin of surplus-value into the sphere of direct production. … Quite correctly they lay down the fundamental principle that only that labour is *productive* which creates a *surplus-value*.
>
> (Marx, 1862, pp. 44–5)

Unlike McCulloch, therefore, Marx is quite specific about which analytical contributions to the theory of production and distribution constitute the basis for his claim that they were the founders of the modern science of political economy.

Marx did not praise the physiocrats only for this impressive list of contributions. His major reason for admiring their work in economics was Quesnay's analysis of reproduction in the *Tableau économique* and its auxiliary explanations by other physiocrats such as Baudeau (1776). Marx saw the 'five lines which link together six points of departure or return' in Quesnay (1766) as

> an attempt to portray the whole production process of capital as a *process of reproduction*, with circulation merely as the form of this reproductive

> process ... this was an extremely brilliant conception, incontestibly the most brilliant for which political economy had up to then been responsible.
> (Marx, 1862, p. 334)

Marx correctly perceived that Adam Smith had taken over this 'inheritance of the Physiocrats and classified and specified more precisely the separate items in the inventory', particularly in his analysis of accumulation (Smith, 1776, Book II, ch. 3). In addition he indicated in a letter to Engels (1863) how his own analysis of circulation and reproduction had developed from Quesnay's conception, as can be seen more fully in the analysis of simple and expanded reproduction in the final parts of Volume I (Marx, 1867) and in Part III of Volume II of *Capital* (Marx, 1885). Quesnay is explicitly credited with having analysed the conditions under which such simple reproduction can take place, the role of which in the development of Marx's theory of economic growth is now widely recognised.[24]

For the purpose of this chapter, some further comments have to be made on Marx's discussion of the physiocrats. In the first place, his recognition of their importance – again like George and Marshall – was partly inspired by the fact that he saw them as anticipators of his own ideas. However, he was able to transcend this type of praise by showing how the physiocratic tools of analysis could be used to solve important problems in a different historical context from the one in which they had lived. In this way, he was one of the very few economists of the nineteenth century who realised what Smith had realised: that underneath their assumptions about the nature of agriculture there was an analytical system worth investigating, adapting and hence using to explain the dynamics of the capitalist economy.[25] Second, the limited access to the works of the physiocrats enjoyed by Marx should also be appreciated. The edition used by him, Daire (1846), though it reproduced some of the major physiocratic works, omitted a number of important texts, particularly interpretative material on the *Tableau*. At least two consequences flow from Marx's limited access to physiocracy. First, it made it more difficult for him to appreciate some of the disequilibrium features of the *Tableau* which had largely been analysed in works not included by Daire. Second, and perhaps more important, the omissions from Daire (1846) included Quesnay's analysis of value and national income-accounting from the essays 'Hommes' and 'Impôt', which had been lost and were in fact not rediscovered until more than two decades after Marx's death. This meant that Marx's analysis of the *Tableau* and of physiocratic economics stressed the physical aspects of the analysis and not its fairly sophisticated value forms.[26]

The value and limitations of Marx's analysis and praise of physiocratic economics have been increasingly recognised in subsequent work, published largely after the second world war. However, an earlier economist who appreciated these insights was Schumpeter (1912). He fully endorsed Marx's views that the physiocrats were the founders of modern economic analysis because of 'their discovery and intellectual formulation of the circular flow in economic life' (Schumpeter, 1912, p. 43).[27] In addition, Schumpeter's account very perceptively recognises the enormous impact which the physiocrats had exercised on the work of Smith and Marx (*ibid.*, p. 46). Finally, he emphasised the physiocratic contribution to the vision of conceiving economic society in terms of a general equilibrium of mutual dependence between production, exchange and distribution, which was demonstrating its usefulness not only in the work of Marshall, but especially in that of Walras (*ibid.*, p. 53).

Emphasis on growth, economic development, economic planning, input-output analysis and econometrics after the Second World War provided a particularly propitious climate for a general rehabilitation of Quesnay's thought, which at last ensured physiocracy its rightful and very important place in the history of economics. This position is strikingly put by Meek in the opening paragraph of the introduction to his translations of Quesnay's major works:

> The French Physiocrats are at once the most exciting and the most contemporary group of economists in the whole history of economic thought. The most exciting, because the birth of Physiocracy was in fact the birth of the science of economics in the broad general form in which it has come down to us today. The most contemporary, because the Physiocrats' major preoccupations, in both the theoretical and the practical fields, were strikingly similar to those of present-day economists.
>
> (Meek, 1962, p. 9)

Meek's view can be fully substantiated from the important interpretations of Quesnay's work which have appeared from the early 1950s onwards. Apart from his own work (included in Meek, 1962) reference should be made to Schumpeter (1954, pp. 223–43); Phillips (1955), Eagley (1969) and Eltis (1984). In addition, Sraffa (1960) has opened up a further avenue for assessing their importance as founders of classical political economy by noting the enormous contributions they made via the 'surplus approach' (cf. Pasinetti, 1977). In short, and to conclude this section of the paper: Henry George was quite correct to describe the physiocrats as the developers of a true science of political economy, but the reasons advanced for this proposition by current economic research would be as mysterious to him as to a McCulloch, a Marshall or a Gray.

III

In his *Progress and Poverty* (1879, p. 423–4), Henry George seems to credit the physiocrats with being the first to propose that taxation ought to be solely placed on land values because the common expenses of the public services needed to be provided from the revenue of the land. Although it is undoubtedly true that the physiocrats did support the superiority of the single direct tax on land on efficiency grounds and also appeared to have accepted an equity case for this proposal (e.g. Quesnay, 1958, pp. 959–60; Du Pont, 1768; Mirabeau, 1760, esp. ch. VII; Turgot, 1763, esp. pp. 102–8), it has to be pointed out that they were by no means the first to make this discovery. They also displayed little unity on the precise form the single tax was to take and on its implementation.

Showing that the physiocrats were not the first to suggest the policy of the single tax is quite easy. This proposition was established by Stewart (1794, pp. 340, 343) as early as the 1790s, though textual evidence from the earlier work by Locke and Vanderlint revealed similar views. Locke (1691, pp. 256–61) had advanced the argument that all taxes 'in a country, where their great fund is in land, for the most part terminate upon land … those taxes which seem least to affect land, will most surely of all other fall the rent', a view he supported by a careful analysis of tax shifting. This, incidentally, makes Locke's work a pioneering effort in tax incidence analysis.[28] Likewise, Vanderlint (1734, pp. 108–9, 160) had argued that all taxes fall on the land and that if only they were placed there in the first instance, the 'nett Rent left out of their [Landlord's] Estates' would be greater 'than they have now the Taxes are almost wholly levied on Goods'. He did not support these propositions with a detailed incidence analysis of the type offered by Locke, but such an analysis was clearly at the back of his mind. As Coxe (1798, I, p. 376) has argued, the great Walpole excise debate of 1733–4 during which Vanderlint's pamphlet was published, brought out a considerable number of references to Locke's land tax incidence analysis. Vanderlint's lack of detailed discussion of this point may therefore be explained as a reasonable presumption on his part of familiarity with Locke's analysis on the part of his readers.

Vanderlint was therefore not the only economic writer in the first half of the eighteenth century to use Locke's land tax incidence analysis. Locke's views were approvingly cited by William Pulteney on at least three separate occasions (1727, pp. 168–9; 1733, pp. 21–3; 1738, pp. 40–3). It was also used by Weyman Lee (1737, p. 109) and briefly referred to by Mathew Dekker (1744, p. 22 but cf. pp. 4–5), the last proposing a single tax on housing (a more substantial tax base than landed estates) as a solution to contemporary British fiscal problems.

At the start of the second half of the century, the idea of the single tax was authoritatively attacked by Hume (1752, p. 359). In this criticism he portrayed the opinion that 'all taxes fall on the land at last' as a device to encourage the preservation of trade and industry by abolishing taxes on consumption essential in a legislature composed largely of the landed interest. The fact that this doctrine had first been presented by a 'celebrated writer' (that is, Locke), was the reason Hume gave for its wide acceptance (*ibid.* p. 359 n1). From the 1760s, and following Hume's quarrel with Turgot on the subject, the later editions of his essay 'Of Taxes' criticised the notion of the single tax on land as follows: 'It is an opinion, zealously promoted by some political writers [i.e. the physiocrats] that since all taxes, as they pretend, fall ultimately on land, it were better to lay them originally there, and abolish every duty upon consumptions' (*ibid.*). In correspondence with Turgot (1955, pp. 206–13) Hume denied this proposition on the ground that taxes on consumption need not be passed on by the labourers but can be absorbed by them either through a reduction in expenses or by an increase in their labour. Hume also suggested the profits of capital to be as fit an object of taxation as the rent of land. Physiocratic incidence analysis was also not accepted by Sir James Steuart (1767, esp. II, p. 494), who noted that it was as 'absurd to say ... that all taxes fall ultimately upon land ... [as it is to] pretend that they fall upon trade.' The notion of a single tax on land therefore enjoyed considerable vogue in England during the first half of the eighteenth century,[29] but not thereafter.

The doctrine of the single tax was also advanced in France at the turn of the seventeenth and eighteenth centuries as a method of drastically reforming the tax system, particularly the *taille*. Most prominent was Marshall Vauban, a military engineer who in his *Dîme royale* (1707) proposed to eliminate all existing forms of taxation in order to replace them with a single tax levying one-tenth of the gross product of the land.[30] Boisguilbert,[31] Vauban's contemporary and generally regarded as an anticipator of many physiocratic economic ideas, saw Vauban's proposal as simplistic and not at all an appropriate reform of French taxation. He instead proposed the abolition of tax-farming and administrative improvements to the assessment and collection of the *taille* to ensure that all paid their share.

It is therefore not difficult to demonstrate that the idea of a single tax on land values, either in the guise of an incidence analysis suggesting all taxes fall on rent or in the form of a specific tax reform proposal, was around well before the writings of the physiocrats.[32] Henry George is therefore misleading in associating the development of this proposal exclusively with them, as he is indeed with the details of the proposals for the single tax on which there was considerable debate among the physiocrats themselves.

The second aspect of the single tax question, where George's praise of the physiocrats seems to have been exaggerated because of his lack of familiarity with their work, arises from aspects of its implementation. As a starting point, it is useful to quote the concise statement on the issue by the leader of the physiocrats, Quesnay, in maxim V of his 'General Maxims for the Economic Government of an Agricultural Kingdom':

> That taxes should not be destructive or disproportionate to the mass of the nation's revenue; that their increase should follow the increase of the revenue; and that they should be laid directly on the net product of landed property, and not on men's wages, or on produce, where they would increase the costs of collection, operate to the detriment of trade, and destroy every year a portion of the nation's wealth. That they should also not be taken from the wealth of the farmers of landed property: for THE ADVANCES OF KINGDOM'S AGRICULTURE OUGHT TO BE REGARDED AS IF THEY WERE FIXED PROPERTY REQUIRING TO BE PRESERVED WITH GREAT CARE IN ORDER TO ENSURE THE PRODUCTION OF TAXES, REVENUE, AND SUBSISTENCE FOR

> ALL CLASSES OF CITIZENS. Otherwise taxation degenerates into spoliation, and brings about a state of decline which very soon ruins the state.
>
> (Meek, 1962, p. 232)[33]

Apart from the analytical reason for the single tax based on its perceived fiscal incidence on the net product of land, the physiocratic case for the single tax rested largely on the efficiency losses associated with the existing forms of French taxation. As in current tax analysis, such efficiency losses were evaluated in terms of resource allocation effects of particular taxes and administrative inefficiencies. In the context of the latter, some physiocrats presented estimates suggesting that the net yield to the state was about one third of what was actually taken from the taxpayers, a system of tax assessment and collection clearly not in tune with what Smith was to call the maxim of 'economy'. However, the economic efficiency argument, largely in terms of the disincentives to capital intensive farming from existing taxes, raised issues on the precise implementation of the single direct tax, on which there was considerable controversy among the physiocrats.[34]

The issue of implementing the land tax was systematically discussed by Turgot (1763, pp. 102–8) in an unfortunately unfinished memorandum addressed to the Contrôleur-Général. After a critical discussion of other taxes, Turgot raised a number of difficulties in connection with the introduction of the *impôt unique* in which he showed himself highly familiar with the contemporary literature on the subject (see 1763, pp. 104, n12, 106 n13, 107 n14). First, though to some extent left implicit, are the difficulties Turgot saw in defining the tax base, a matter of importance since if taxation fell on the income of the farmer or on the gross product, many of the economic advantages of the single tax would be lost.[35] Second, existing privileges of the nobility and the church provide an impediment to the introduction of the tax (1763, p. 104). However, Turgot appears to suggest that these difficulties may be overcome by direct assessment methods, of which two are possible in principle. The first is to demand a fixed and constant proportion of their net revenue from each landlord (as proposed by Mirabeau [1760; 1763] as well as in the existing English land tax). The second method adapted from the existing system of the *taille* provided an annual distribution of the national tax burden among provinces and municipalities, which would then in turn assess individual landlords according to their respective prosperity. In the absence of detailed land value records, Turgot condemned both methods of self-assessment as incentives to fraud and dishonesty. In addition, he suspected the second direct assessment method of infringing equity principles, since small landholders would be overburdened because of the political power wielded by large ones.[36]

Turgot's pessimism about the feasibility of rapid fiscal reform through the introduction of the *impôt unique* undoubtedly arose from his practical experience as an administrator whose duties included annual advice to the central government on the assessment of his province. Another former administrator, Le Mercier de la Rivière[37] (1767, chs 1–5), in a far longer treatment of the subject, was more optimistic about the matter. For example, although he discussed the possibility of fraud more fully, he rejected it as a practical possibility (1767, pp. 461–2) reflecting a rather naive faith in human nature to which some present day tax discussion of the advantages of the personal income tax is not immune.[38] The greater part of his discourse of public finance with which his book starts is devoted to justifying the measure of the single tax by stressing its advantages, and not in attempting the very difficult but practical problems with its implementation (1767, pp. 477–92).

What can be concluded from this part of the argument? It has already been stated that Locke and some other English economists were the first to espouse the virtues of the single tax. However, it can be said George shared their naivety (excepting here Turgot) about the implementation of this panacea. Furthermore, although Quesnay had proposed the remedy of the single tax as a solution to the enormous fiscal problems of a highly corrupt and inefficient revenue system, where even its imperfect administration would have been an enormous improvement, George proposed it a century later when much of the worst features of eighteenth-century tax administration had already disappeared.[39] In addition, Quesnay, specifically assumed that the single tax was a policy suitable for the needs of an *agricultural kingdom*, a condition likewise no longer matched by the economic realities of the United States in the 1880s and 1890s.

IV

What other conclusions can be derived from this discussion? In order not to make an already long chapter any longer, the following broad conclusions can summarise the essentials of the argument. First, it is abundantly clear that the physiocrats played an enormous part in the origin of scientific political economy, through the adaptation of their analysis of reproduction first by Smith and later by Marx. This made them the first real theorists of the process of expanded reproduction which stressed the interdependence between production, circulation and distribution in a surplus-producing economy. The full significance of this contribution is still being assessed, but I suggest that evaluations of their importance going back to Marx if not to Smith will long outlive the reasonings of McCulloch, Marshall and Henry George. Second, some specific conclusions of value to historians of economics can be offered. The second part of the lecture suggests a strong temptation for economic theorists to identify founders of their science by searching for early anticipators of the specific features of their own doctrine, a fault which this chapter has associated with George, Marshall, and, with some qualifications, also with Marx. In addition, the first section demonstrated the dangers of equating expressions of approval for doctrines of the Economists with actual knowledge of their writings, a problem associated with the interpretations of Meek and Semmel, but also of George. Finally, the chapter has provided a contribution to the history of the single tax, a history far more complicated and different from that which

Henry George assumed when he praised the physiocrats in that context. On this score, there is some justification for this long historical excursus on the physiocrats, the emergence of economics as a science and the single tax.

Notes

1 No reference for this startling and false claim is given, but it undoubtedly derives from George's misreading of Adam Smith (1776, p. 679) where Smith quotes the following from Mirabeau's *Philosophie rurale* (1763):

> There have been, since the world began, three great inventions which have principally given stability to political societies, independent of many other inventions which have enriched and adorned them. The first, is the invention of writing, which alone gives human nature the power of transmitting, without alternations, its laws, its contracts, its annals, and its discoveries. The second is the invention of money, which binds together all the relations between civilised societies, the third, is the Oeconomical Table, the result of the other two, which completes them both by perfecting their object; the great discovery of the age, but of which our posterity will reap the benefit.

It seems that apart from not knowing their doctrines at first hand, George was not able to distinguish Quesnay's taxation proposals from his *Tableau économique*. George repeated this erroneous claim in *Protection or Free Trade* (1866, p. 310).

2 For Australian readers it is interesting to note in this context that through Henry George (who visited Australia in March 1890) sections of the then embryonic Labor Party supported free trade because it implied direct taxation, particularly that of land values. Initially, Labor opposition to indirect taxation therefore implies opposition to protection. This was reversed with the deals done in the name of 'new' protection, in which Labor was assured of a share in the benefits, in return for support in the federal parliament for the Deakin-led government party.

3 Similar profundities from Dühring (1871) were brilliantly exposed by Marx's critique of his 'critical history' (Marx, 1878).

4 Turgot, although he held views similar to them on a variety of topics, including the principle of a single tax on land values, was not a member of the school. This is made clear not only in his own writings, but also in his extensive correspondence with Du Pont de Nemours. See, for example, Turgot to Du Pont, 8 November 1767, in which during comments on Du Pont's introduction to his edition of Quesnay's writings under the title *Physiocratie, ou constitution naturelle du gouvernement le plus avantageaux au genre humain*, he argued:

> Your analysis of Quesnay's ideas appears to me to be neither complete nor very exact. Their systematic development is too systematic, too compressed, too much shortened by essential omissions; it borders on servitude to the ideas of the master; however, respectable that may be, no exception can be made to the rule which says that there is no need for this in matters of science.
>
> (Schelle, 1913–23, II, p. 677, my translation)

5 Quesnay's works themselves were collected on several occasions, starting with Du Pont (1767) mentioned in the previous note. The best edition is Quesnay (1958), from which Meek (1962) prepared his translation. Quesnay's first paper is now available in English translation in Groenewegen (1983b).

6 The Supplements of the fourth, fifth and sixth editions of the *Encyclopaedia Britannica* which remained current till the middle of the century contained an article

by Mill (1824) on 'The Economists', which analysed their work as a contribution to the 'science of politics' and an article by McCulloch on political economy reproduced in expanded form as a 'sketch on the rise and progress of the science' in his *Principles* (1825).

7 The use of the name 'physiocrats' to describe the school must have been considerably enhanced from the fact that their major works (but not those by Mirabeau) were collected together under the title *Physiocrates*, in volumes V and VI of the Guillaumin *Collection des principaux économistes* (Daire, 1846).

8 Smith (1776, p. 679) called this 'the most distinct and best connected work of this doctrine', a view endorsed by Mill (1824) which greatly draws on this work. It became the butt for Voltaire's malicious wit in his famous satire of physiocracy, *l'Homme aux quarantes écus* (Voltaire, 1768).

9 See Meek (1973, pp. 103–13) and Quesnay (1958, pp. 687–728).

10 The best secondary source discussion of these social and political foundations of physiocracy remains Gide and Rist (1949, ch. 1). Good analyses of the policy implications are provided by Meek (1962) and Eltis (1984), but as shown later, Marx and Smith were the first to fully appreciate the analytical significance of their argument. Both adapted physiocratic analysis to suit their own explanations of the operation of an economy. To a very large extent, the same can be said for Turgot, and to a lesser extent, the Italian economist Beccaria. See Groenewegen (1983a) (Chapter 1 above).

11 The history of the physiocratic movement in France has been exhaustively analysed by Weulersse (1910) which remains the standard work on the history of the school in France. See also his posthumous volumes covering the post-1770 period (Weulersse, 1950; 1959). The success of physiocracy abroad has not yet been given serious study, but they were in vogue at various times in Poland, Russia, Tuscany, Austria-Hungary and above all the Principality of Baden, whose ruler as a convert conducted physiocratic experiments in his domain under the distant but watchful eyes of his two correspondents, Mirabeau and Du Pont (Knies, 1892).

12 Smith was rather inaccurate in this diagnosis because aspects of the physiocratic policy package had been implemented in the 1760s and 1770s by their sympathisers. Examples include Bertin's 1763 Edict restoring the domestic free trade in corn (abolished in 1770 by Terray and reintroduced by Turgot in 1774) and Turgot's reform of the corvée in Limoges. Just before the publication of the first edition of the *Wealth of Nations* (March 1776), Turgot's attempts (February 1776) to implement a physiocratic policy package in his famous six Edicts ended in failure (May 1776) and in his dismissal from the finance ministry not long thereafter (see Faure, 1961). As Smith recalled almost ten years afterwards in a letter to le Duc de la Rochefoucauld (1 November 1785), he had been sent many of the relevant documents by Turgot himself and had fully appreciated the significance for France of these reform measures (see Mossner and Ross, 1977, p. 386). On Smith's attitude to Steuart's work, see his letter to William Pulteney, 3 September 1772 (in *ibid*., pp. 163–4).

13 Stewart (1794) demonstrates a solid general knowledge of the physiocrats and economic thought. Lauderdale (1804) frequently cited from both Du Pont (1767) and Mirabeau (1763); Horner (1803) and Brougham (1804) likewise cite Du Pont (1767); Mill (1824) shows considerable familiarity with both Du Pont (1767) and Mercier de la Rivière (1767). McCulloch's knowledge of physiocracy is mentioned in the next section, but it may be noted here that it was more 'historical' than 'analytical' in contrast to the knowledge of physiocracy of Horner or Lauderdale. Du Pont (1767) was, of course, his edition of Quesnay's economic writings.

14 Apart from Smith (1776, Book IV, ch. 9), Spence gathered information about the work of the physiocrats from the pages of the *Edinburgh Review*, in particular Horner (1803) and Brougham (1804).

15 As Hutchison (1953, pp. 61–3) has shown, Berkeley's *Querist* contains underconsumptionist argument similar to those of Spence, a matter also acknowledged by Meek (1951b, p. 318 n3).

16 Malthus (1803, p. 48 and note b) cited Du Pont's *Physiocratie*, volume II on the importance of a high price of corn for agriculture, without apparently realising that this work was a collection of Quesnay's writings with an introduction by Du Pont. The sixth edition of the *Essay on Population* (Malthus, 1826, II, p. 144, n3) cites Mirabeau's *l'Ami des hommes* from a 1762 edition of Mirabeau's *Works* in nine volumes. It can also be noted that the admittedly very incomplete catalogue of Malthus' books at Jesus College, Cambridge (Gray *et al.*, 1983) includes no physiocratic works whatsoever, though it does include the Du Pont edition of Turgot's *Works* which Malthus cited in the *Principles* (Gray *et al.*, 1983, p. 175, which notes that Malthus cited Turgot in the *Essay on Population*; Malthus 1820, pp. 54–5).

17 Semmel (1964–5) strongly argues that these pamphlets were heavily influenced by the physiocrats, but as far as I can see they contain only general remarks on the doctrines of the Economists. However, a letter to Horner (dated 14 March 1815), in which Malthus critically comments on Ricardo (1815), stated *inter alia* that 'the Economists assume that one third of the raw produce obtained by the farmer is advanced to the sterile (*sic*¡) classes'. This statement may have been inspired by one of Mirabeau's versions of the *Tableau* or by Quesnay's *Analyse* of 1766. These suggest a ratio of 2:1 between the annual advances of farmers and the 'sterile' class, which may justify Malthus' attribution of the assumption to them that one third of the raw produce (produced by the farmers) is advanced to the 'sterile' class. See Malthus to Horner (1815, p. 187) and cf. Meek (1962, pp. 147, 158) for two examples of this relationship between annual advances of the productive and 'sterile' class assumed by the physiocrats. The second reference, to Meek's translation of Quesnay's *Analyse* (1766), was to a work apparently accessible to Malthus since it was included in the first volume of Du Pont (1767), while Mirabeau's works in the 1762 edition referred to appears also to have been accessible to him (see note 16 above).

18 Malthus (1803, pp. 440–1 fn) described the single tax doctrine as a principal error of the physiocrats; in Malthus (1815, p. 61) he denied 'that all taxes fall on the neat produce of the landlords' while the later editions of the *Essay on Population* described the single tax doctrine as '*the* principal error of the Economists' (my italics). Cf. Semmel (1964–5, p. 531 n5). The first edition of the *Principles* (Malthus, 1820) contains no specific references to physiocratic work, nor does the second (Malthus, 1836). It may also be noted that the Inverarity Manuscript (Pullen, 1981) has a long set of questions on the physiocrats prepared by Malthus for his students (*circa* 1828–30) at Haileybury, one of which cites Mirabeau on wealth, possibly from the 1762 edition he used for the sixth edition of the *Essay on Population* (see above, note 16).

19 Marshall Library, Marshall Papers: Box 5 Item 6: History of Economic Theory I, contains a detailed set of notes on the physiocrats. These draw on Lavergne, De Tocqueville, McCulloch, and most importantly on Daire. On his notes on the *Tableau économique*, is scrawled 'not important' in Marshall's handwriting but from a later period. Possible reasons for this comment are raised in note 20.

20 In a letter to Price, 19 August 1892, perhaps commenting on an article Price (1893) was writing for the *Economic Journal*, Marshall wrote

> in the early seventies, when I was in my full fresh enthusiasm for the historical study of economics, I set myself to trace the genesis of Adam Smith's doctrines … I found so much in the Physiocrats which I had thought to belong to Adam Smith, that at first I got quite set against him. But afterwards I thought that many of these things were in substance older even than the Physiocrats; and

> that it was the form of his thought rather than the substance that he owed to them.
>
> (in Pigou, 1925, pp. 378–9)

This letter seems to date the notes previously mentioned to the early 1870s, a dating consistent with the handwriting. The remark, 'not important', on notes dealing with the *Tableau* appears to be in Marshall's writing of the late 1890s or early twentieth century, reflecting his subsequent dissatisfaction with at least one aspect of physiocracy.

21 As indicated in note 6 above, this lecture was transformed into the article 'Political Economy' for the supplement to the *Encyclopaedia Britannica*; was then reprinted in McCulloch, 1825 (his *Principles*, which went through several editions), formed the foundation for the notes on various writers in the *Literature on Political Economy* (1845) and for the introductory discourse to his edition of Smith's *Wealth of Nations*, the edition used by Marshall. As suggested in note 13 above, Stewart (1794) which McCulloch cites in this context (McCulloch, 1825, p. 33 note*) is the probable source of these views.

22 McCulloch, by realising the significance of the *Tableau* for the physiocrats but not understanding its purpose, joins a distinguished line of commentators including Gray (1931) and Marshall (1890). McCulloch's reason for selecting the physiocrats as founders of the science is like that of George and Marshall, influenced to a considerable extent by his definition of the science in terms of the production and distribution of wealth.

23 As noted earlier, their works were rescued from oblivion by Daire (1846), and in the 1850s were translated into Italian under the direction of Ferrara. A study of their work, therefore continued, and some examination of their system was presented in early European histories of economics such as that of Blanqui (1838) and the Germans Kautz (1860) and Dühring (1871). Like McCulloch's efforts, these discussions were rarely analytical, and invariably failed to come to grips with the content of Quesnay's *Tableau* (cf. above, p. 224 and n3).

24 Marx (1885, p. 359); Marx's important contributions to the theory of economic growth are discussed for example, in Robinson (1952).

25 Another economist who used Quesnay's *Tableau* analytically was De Lissa (1896), an economist working in Australia. See Goodwin (1962) and Groenewegen (1968) for a discussion of the use made by this economist of Quesnay's *Tableau*.

26 This has been analysed in detail by Vaggi (1982; 1983). The articles 'Impôt' and 'Hommes', rediscovered in 1902 and 1908 respectively, and the early editions of the *Tableau* were the more important omissions from Quesnay's works in Daire (1846). A more complete edition of Quesnay's works was published by Oncken (1888), but what appears now as the definitive edition was not available till Quesnay (1958) was published.

27 Schumpeter's major praise for the physiocrats as the analysists of the 'circular flow' in a form emphasising its general equilibrium connotations, is clearly associated with the emphasis on circular flow and general equilibrium as the foundation for the analysis of economic growth and development. See Schumpeter (1911, ch. 1).

28 It is not clear to me why Locke's argument appeared in a 1691 pamphlet largely devoted to questions about the inadvisability of legally reducing interest rates and currency debasement associated with the recoinage controversy of the 1690s (cf. the remarks of Hume, 1752, p. 359, cited in the subsequent paragraph). It may also be noted that land tax in its modern form has been introduced by 1 William and Mary (1688) but substantial alterations were introduced by legislation (4 William and Mary c. 1) in 1692, the date for this reason frequently selected to mark the start of the modern British land tax. It may be that Locke, as a staunch adherent of the Whigs, inserted this argument on tax policy to win over part of the landed interest

in Parliament to support his views on the recoinage question. Davenant (1771, I, pp. 77, 269) also accepted this notion, arguing in his *Essay on Ways and Means* that

> All taxes whatsoever, are in their last resort a charge upon land; and though excises will affect land to no degree like taxes that charge it directly, yet excises will always lie so heavily upon the landed man, as to make them concerned in parliament, to continue such duties no longer than the necessity of the war continues.
>
> (1771, I, p. 77, and cf. p. 269)

It may also be noted that Locke's contemporary Sir William Petty (1662, ch. 4) in his discussion of land taxes suggested a more complex incidence analysis, in which it is concluded that 'a Land-taxe resolves into an irregular Excize upon consumptions', although initially, before renegotiation of leases is possible, landlords may bear it. (Petty, 1662, pp. 39–40). Petty suggested as well that a twenty-fifth part of the national income ('the proceed of all their Lands and Labours') was probably sufficient to meet the public charges (*ibid.*, p. 38). Part of this discussion may have been prompted by Hobbes (1651, ch. 24) in which Hobbes discussed the power of the sovereign over land and his right to levy tax on it, of which Hobbes appears to disapprove (*ibid.*, pp. 131–2).

29 As Horner (1803, pp. 70–2, 73–4) noted,

> we are rather inclined to believe, that the same train of reasoning, which thus [by incidence analysis] proves that all taxes on land are paid by the proprietor alone, requires very little extension, in order to lead us to a more general conclusion, that all taxes whatever ultimately fall on the neat surplus of the annual reproduction.

He added, that if Smith's conclusions that no taxes could fall on wages or profits was taken seriously, then taxes levied on consumption 'are all ultimately paid from rent'. Henry George does not appear to have grasped this feature of Smith's analysis of taxation.

30 The relevance of Vauban's proposal to this discussion may be denied, since he did not propose the single tax on net product but on gross product. Though this is true, it also appears that there was some confusion on this issue in the work of some of the physiocrats.

31 Boisguilbert to Chamillart, 13 June 1700, see Roberts (1935, pp. 34–6) and Boisguilbert (1966, pp. 663–740).

32 Spence (1808, p. 41 n*) indicated that Gibbon had suggested that the notion of the single tax was first developed by Ataxerxes. This probably derived from Gibbon's remark in chapter VIII attributing Atexerxes with the view that 'all taxes must fall at last upon agriculture' (Gibbon, 1887, I, p. 346).

33 Quesnay appended a long note to this maxim, which explained in detail the argument for justifying the single tax on net product. This included the view that a single tax is no real charge on anyone in the long run because of its capitalisation in the price of land. This neglected the burden imposed on landlords by the initial impact of the measure, which perhaps was one of the reasons why this part of the physiocratic policy was so strenuously opposed by the aristocracy. Because it implied abolition of the very profitable investment opportunity in tax farming (for a discussion see Matthews, 1958; Hincker, 1971) there was vigorous and organised opposition from these influential financiers. It may also be noted here that the one work by a physiocrat completely devoted to the single tax question (Mirabeau, 1760) secured its author a short period in gaol followed by exile (see Fling, 1908, pp. 117–20). Mirabeau's punishment succeeded in silencing the physiocrats from 1760

to early 1763, when they were able to resume publication, perhaps partly because of the more sympathetic influence of Bertin, then Contrôleur-Général, who in 1763 had restored domestic free trade in grain.

34 See, for example, Quesnay, note on maxim V, where taxes assessed are estimated at three times taxes received (Meek, 1962, p. 239). Quesnay had discussed this issue as early as 1756 in his first contribution to the *Encyclopédie*, the article 'Farmers' (in Groenewegen, 1983b, pp. 24–5). Mirabeau (1760, pp. 99–124) used similar estimates to criticise the general tax farm (see note 33 above).

35 Following Quesnay, Turgot argued that the tax base (net product) depended on physical gross product, prices and the expenses of production. To arrive at net product, the value of the gross product should be reduced by

> firstly, all the expenses or annual advances; secondly, the interest on the original advances; thirdly, their maintenance and replacement of their inevitable decay; fourthly, the subsistence and reasonable profit of the entrepreneur farmer and his agents, the wages of their labour and industry.
>
> (1763, p. 103)

None of these calculations were easy, but the need to make them correctly was essential if the efficiency advantages of the single tax were not to be lost.

36 Turgot, 1763, pp. 107–8. The argument of the unfinished paper stops at this point.

37 Le Mercier de la Rivière was a lawyer by training, an occupation he initially followed as Councillor of the Parlement de Paris from 1747 to 1759. He was governor of the island of Martinique from 1759 to 1764, when he was dismissed because he had compromised himself by violating the colonial trade restrictions imposed. Martinique was probably not the practical administrative training ground for problems of French taxation, which Turgot experienced as Intendant of Limoges from 1761 to 1774.

38 An Australian audience need hardly be reminded of the naivety with which some defend the equity of the personal income tax with steep progressive rates, ignoring the incentives to fraud and dishonesty which are now a major feature of its implementation, and which thereby destroy the very equity qualities for which it is praised.

39 It may be noted here that Turgot (1777) had prepared a paper for Benjamin Franklin in which he extolled the virtues of land taxation for the new republic as against the British system of consumption taxation and revenue customs duties. In 1895 extracts from Turgot's writings on taxation were submitted by the United States in the Supreme Court of the United States in nos. 893 and 894 (Library of Congress Catalogue, item HJ 4654. 1895. P. 33).

References

Baudeau, Nicolas (1771, 1846) *Première introduction à la philosophie économique ou analyse des états policés*, in E. Daire (ed.) *Physiocrates*, vol. 2, Paris: Guillaumin, 657–821.

——(1776) *Explication du*Tableau économique *à Madame de …*, Paris: Delalain.

Berkeley, George (1735) *The Querist*, in J. Johnston (ed.) *Bishop Berkeley's Querist in Historical Perspective*, Dundalk: Dundalcan Press, 1970.

Blanqui, J. A. (1838, 1880) *History of Political Economy in Europe*, trans. E. J. Leonard, New York: Putnam.

Boisguilbert, Pierre (1966) *Pierre de Boisguillebert ou la naissance de l'économie politique*, Paris: INED.

Brougham, H. (1804) 'An Inquiry into the Nature and Origin of Public Wealth', *Edinburgh Review*, no. 8, July, 343–77.

Coxe, William (1798) *Memoirs of the Life and Administration of Sir Robert Walpole*, London: Cadell and Davies.

Daire, E. (ed.) (1846, 1971) *Physiocrates: Quesnay, Du Pont De Nemours, Mercier de la Rivière, L'Abbé Baudeau, Le Trosne*, Paris: Guillaumin, reprinted in one volume, Geneva: Slatkine Reprints.

Davenant, Charles (1771) *The Political and Commercial Works*, ed. Charles Whitworth, London: Horsfield, Becket Cadell and Evans.

Dekker, Mathew (1774) *An Essay on the Causes of the Decline of the Foreign Trade*, London: John Brotherton.

De Lissa, Robert (1896) *Production, Distribution and Quesnay's 'Tableau Economique'*, Sydney: McCarron, Stewart.

Dühring, Eugen (1871, n.d.) *Kritische Geschichte der Nationalokonomie und des Socialismus*, 4th edn, revised and enlarged, Leipzig: Verlag von Theo Thomas.

Du Pont de Nemours, Pierre Samuel (1767) *Physiocratie, ou constitution naturelle du government le plus avantageaux au genre humain*, Ypres [i.e. Paris]: 1767.

——(1768, 1846) *De L'origine et des Progrès d'une science nouvelle*, in E. Daire (ed.) *Physiocrates*, vol. 1, Paris: Guillaumin, 335–66.

Eagley, R. V. (1969) 'A Physiocratic Model of Dynamic Equilibrium', *Journal of Political Economy*, 77(1) Jan-Feb, 66–83.

Eltis, Walter (1984) *The Classical Theory of Economic Growth*, London: Macmillan.

Faure, Edgar (1961) *La disgrâce de Turgot*, Paris: Gallimard.

Fling, F. M. (1908) *Mirabeau and the French Revolution*, New York: G. P. Putnam's Sons.

George, Henry (1879, 1971) *Progress and Poverty*, New York: Robert Schalkenbach Foundation.

——(1886) *Protection or Free Trade*, London: Kegan Paul, Trench.

——(1898) *The Science of Political Economy*, London: Kegan Paul, Trench, Trubner.

Gibbon, Edward (1887) *The History of the Decline and Fall of the Roman Empire*, ed. William Smith, London: Murray.

Gide, Charles and Rist, Charles (1949) *A History of Economic Doctrines*, 2nd English edn, London: George Harrap.

Goodwin, C. D. W. (1962) 'Alfred de Lissa and the Birth of the Multiplier', *Economic Record*, vol. 68, March, 74–93.

Gray, Alexander (1931) *The Development of Economic Doctrine*, London: Longmans, Green and Company.

Gray, Edward *et al.*, (1893) *The Malthus Library Catalogue*, New York: Pergamon Press.

Groenewegen, P. D. (1968) 'Some Comments on De Lissa's Multiplier', Economic Society of Australia and New Zealand, Economic Monograph no. 295, June.

——(1983a) 'Turgot, Beccaria and Smith', in P. D. Groenewegen and Joseph Halevi (eds) *Italian Economics Past and Present*, Sydney: Frederick May Foundation of Italian Studies (above, Chapter 1).

Groenewegen, P. D. (ed.) (1983b) *Quesnay, 'Fermiers' (1756) and Turgot (1767) 'Sur la grande et la petite culture'*, Sydney: Department of Economics, University, Reprints of Economic Classics, series 2, no. 2.

Hincker, François (1971) *Les Français devant, l'impôt sous l'ancien régime*, Paris: Flammarion.

Hobbes, Thomas (1651, 1927) *Leviathan*, Everyman edition, London: J. M. Dent.

Horner, Francis (1803, 1957) 'Canard's *Principes d'économie politique*', in *The Economic Writings of Francis Horner in the Edinburgh Review*, ed. F. W. Fetter, London: LSE Reprint.
Hume, David (1752, 1875) 'Of Taxes', in *Essays Moral, Political and Literary*, eds T. H. Green and T. H. Grose, London: Longmans, Green and Co.
——(1955) *Economic Writings*, ed. E. Rotwein, London: Nelson.
Hutchison, T. W. (1953) 'Berkeley's Querist and its Place in the Economic Thought of the Eighteenth Century', *British Journal for the Philosophy of Science*, IV(13) 52–77.
Ingram, J. K. (1888) *History of Political Economy*, Edinburgh: A&C Black.
Jones, Richard (1847) 'Primitive Political Economy', *Edinburgh Review*, no. 172, April, 426–52.
Kautz, Julius (1860) *Die Geschichtliche Entwickelung der National-Oekonomik and Ihrer Literatur*, Vienna: Verlag Carl Gerald's Sohn.
Knies, Karl (1892) *Carl Friedrich von Baden's Brieflicher verkehr mit Mirabeau und Du Pont*, Heidelberg: Carl Winter.
Lauderdale, James M. (1804) *An Inquiry into the Nature and Origin of Public Wealth*, London: Longman and Rees.
Lee, Weyman (1737) *An Essay to Ascertain the Value of Leases and Annuities*, London: S. Bert.
Le Trosne, G. (1777, 1980) *De l'ordre social*, Paris: Debure; facsimile reprint, Munich: Kraus.
Locke, John (1691, 1870) *Some Considerations on the Consequences of Lowering Interest and Raising the Value of Money*, reprinted with J. R. McCulloch, *Principles of Political Economy*, London: Murray.
McCulloch, J. R. (1825, 1870) *Principles of Political Economy*, reprinted London: Murray.
McLain, J. J. (1977) *The Economic Writings of Du Pont de Nemours*, Newark DE: University of Delaware Press.
Malthus, T. R. (1798) *Essay on the Principle of Population*, 1st edn reprint, New York: Ann Arbor, 1959.
——(1803) *An Essay on the Principle of Population*, 2nd edn, London: J. Johnson.
——(1815, 1934) *An Inquiry into the Nature and Progress of Rent*, London: John Murray; Jacob Hollander Reprint, Baltimore: Johns Hopkins Press.
——(1815, 1952) Letter to Horner, 14 March, in P. Sraffa (ed.) *Works and Correspondence of David Ricardo*, vol. VI, Cambridge: Cambridge University Press, 186–8.
——(1820) *Principles of Political Economy*, London: Murray.
——(1826, 1958) *Essay on the Principle of Population*, Everyman edition, London: J. M. Dent.
——(1836) *Principles of Political Economy*, 2nd edn, London: William Pickering.
Marshall, Alfred (1890) *Principles of Economics*, 1st edn, London: Macmillan.
——(1920) *Principles of Economics*, 8th edn, London: Macmillan.
Marx, K. H. (1862, n.d.) *Theories of Surplus Value: Part I*, Moscow: Foreign Languages Publishing House.
——(1863, n.d.) letter to Engels, 6 July, in *Marx-Engels Selected Correspondence*, Moscow: Foreign Languages Publishing House.
——(1867, 1959) *Capital*, vol. 1, Moscow: Foreign Languages Publishing House.
——(1878, 1954) 'From the Critical History', in F. Engels, *Anti-Dühring*, 3rd edn, Moscow: Foreign Languages Publishing House.
——(1885, 1957) *Capital*, vol. 2, Moscow: Foreign Languages Publishing House.

Matthews, G. T. (1958) *The Royal General Farms in Eighteenth Century France*, New York: Columbia University Press.

Meek, R. L. (1951a, 1962) 'Physiocracy and Classicism in Britain', *Economic Journal*, March; in R. L. Meek, *The Economics of Physiocracy*, London: Allen & Unwin.

——(1951b, 1962) 'Physiocracy and the Early Theories of Under-consumption', *Economica*, August; in R. L. Meek, *The Economics of Physiocracy*, London: Allen & Unwin.

——(1962) *The Economics of Physiocracy*, London: Allen & Unwin.

——(1973) *Precursors of Adam Smith*, Everyman edition, London: J. M. Dent.

Mercier de la Rivière, Pierre-Paul (1767, 1846) *L'Ordre naturel et essentiel des sociétés politiques*, in E. Daire (ed.) *Physiocrates*, vol. 2, Paris: Guillaumin, 445–638.

Mill, James (1824) 'Economists', *Supplement to the Fourth, Fifth and Sixth Edition of the Encyclopaedia Britannica*, vol. 3, Edinburgh: Constable, 708–24.

Mirabeau, Victor R. Marquis de (1760) *Théorie de l'impôt*, n.p., n.pl.

——(1763, 1972) *Philosophie Rurale*, 1st edn, Amsterdam, 1764 [i.e. 1763]; reprint Aalen: Scientia Verlag.

Mossner, E. L. and Ross, I. S. (eds) (1977) *The Correspondence of Adam Smith*, Oxford: Clarendon Press.

Oncken, A. (ed.) (1888, n.d.) *Oeuvres économiques et philosophiques de F. Quesnay*, reprinted New York: Burt Franklin.

Pasinetti, L. L. (1977) *Lectures on the Theory of Production*, London: Macmillan.

Petty, Sir William (1662, 1965) 'A Treatise of Taxes and Contributions', in C. H. Hull (ed.) *Economic Writings of Sir William Petty*, New York: Kelley Reprint.

Phillips, A. (1955) 'The "Tableau Economique" as a Simple Leontief Model', *Quarterley Journal of Economics*, vol. 69, February, 137–44.

Pigou, A. C. (ed.) (1925) *Memorials of Alfred Marshall*, London: Macmillan.

Price, L. L. (1893) 'Adam Smith and his Relation to Recent Economics', *Economic Journal*, vol. 3, June, 239–54.

Pullen, John (1981) 'Malthus: The Inverarity Manuscript', *History of Political Economy*, 13(4) winter, 794–811.

Pulteney, William (1727, 1966) 'A State of the National Debt as it Stood at December 24th, 1716', in J. R. McCulloch (ed.) *A Select Collection of Tracts on the National Debt and the Sinking Fund*, New York: Kelley Reprint.

——(1733) *A Review of the Excise Scheme*, London: H. Haines.

——(1738) *Some Thoughts of the Interest of Money in General*, London: J. Roberts.

Quesnay, François (1766, 1958) 'Analyse de la formule arithmétique du Tableau Economique', in *Quesnay et la Physiocratie*, ed. L. Salleron, Paris: INED, 793–812.

——(1766, 1958) *Quesnay et la Physiocratie*, ed. L. Salleron, Paris: INED.

Ricardo, David (1815, 1951) 'An Essay on the Influence of a Low Price of Corn on the Profits of Stock', in P. Sraffa (ed.) *Works and Correspondence of David Ricardo*, vol. IV, Cambridge: Cambridge University Press.

Roberts, Hazel van Dyke (1935) *Boisguilbert, Economist of the Reign of Louis XIV*, New York: Columbia University Press.

Robinson, Joan (1952, 1964) 'The Model of an Expanding Economy', in Joan Robinson, *Collected Economic Papers*, vol. 2, Oxford: Blackwell, 74–87.

Sargant, Willliam Lucas (1867) *Recent Political Economy*, London: Williams and Norgate.

Schelle, G. (ed.) (1913–23) *Oeuvres de Turgot et documents le concernant*, Paris: Félix Arcan.

Schumpeter, J. A. (1911, 1961) *The Theory of Economic Development*, trans. R. Opie, Oxford: Oxford University Press.

——(1912, 1954) *Economic Doctrine and Method*, trans. R. Aris, London: Allen & Unwin.

Semmel, B. (1964–5) 'Malthus: "Physiocracy" and the Commercial System', *Economic History Review*, vol. 17, 522–35.

Smith, Adam (1776, 1976) *An Inquiry into the Nature and Causes of the Wealth of Nations*, eds R. H. Campbell, A. S. Skinner and W. B. Todd, Oxford: Clarendon Press.

Spence, William (1808) *Britain Independent of Commerce*, London: T. Cadell and W. Davies.

Sraffa, P. (1960) *Production of Commodities by Means of Commodities*, Cambridge: Cambridge University Press.

Steuart, Sir James (1767) *Principles of Political Oeconomy*, London: T. Cadell.

Stewart, Dugald (1794, 1980) 'Account of the Life and Writing of Adam Smith LL D.', in W. P. D. Wightman, J. C. Bryce and I. S. Ross (eds) *Adam Smith: Essays on Philosophical Subjects*, Oxford: Clarendon Press.

Torrens, Robert (1808) *The Economists Refuted*, London: S. A. & H. Oddy, C. la Grange.

——(1821, 1965) *An Essay on the Production of Wealth*, London: Longman, Hurst, Rees, Orme and Brown; reprinted New York: Augustus M. Kelley.

Turgot, A. R. J. (1763, 1977) 'Plan for a Paper on Taxation in General', in P. D. Groenewegen (ed.) *The Economics of A. R. J. Turgot*, The Hague: Martinus Nijhoff.

——(1777, 1844) 'Comparison of the Tax on the Revenue of the Proprietor with the Tax on Consumption', in E. Daire (ed.) *Oeuvres de Turgot*, vol. I, Paris: Guillaumin, 409–15.

Twiss, Travers (1847) *View of the Progress of Political Economy in Europe since the Sixteenth Century*, London: Longman, Brown, Green and Longmans.

Vaggi, G. (1982) 'Surplus and Effective Demand in Physiocracy', *Studi Economici*, no. 18, 55–90.

——(1983) 'The Physiocratic Theory of Prices', *Contributions to Political Economy*, vol. 2, 1–22.

Vanderlint, Jacob (1734) *Money Answers All Things*, London: T. Cox.

Vauban, Sebastian Le Prestre de (1887) *Dîme royale*, ed. G. Michel, Paris: Guillaumin.

Voltaire, François Marie Arouet (1768, 1927) *L'Homme aux quarante écus*, English translation in *The Works of Voltaire: Romances and Philosophy*, New York: Walter J. Black.

Weulersse, Georges (1910) *Le mouvement physiocratique en France de 1756 à 1770*, Paris: Félix Arcan.

——(1950) *Les Physiocrates sous les ministères de Turgot et de Necker*, Paris: Presses Universitaires de France.

——(1959) *La physiocratie à la fin du règne de Louis XV*, Paris: Presses Universitaires de France.

13 Quesnay's first publication in economics

The article 'Fermiers' for the *Encyclopédie* – an introduction

The two essays now reproduced for the first time in English translation are both important pioneering contributions to the theory of capital applied to agricultural economics and, especially in the case of the second, practical taxation policy as well. This by itself warrants their reprinting. In addition, the first of them, the 1756 *Encyclopédie* article 'Fermiers', is the first piece on economics by François Quesnay, the founder of physiocracy. Its importance is therefore enhanced by the fact that it presents in rudimentary form the arguments in support of some of the more basic assumptions lying at the foundation of Quesnay's more celebrated analysis of the circular flow in an agricultural kingdom through his *Tableau économique* of two years later. Ten years after the publication of 'Fermiers', Turgot wrote a short defence and cogent elucidation of one of Quesnay's major contributions from his 1756 article – the controversial distinction between *la grande et la petite culture*. This common subject matter justifies reprinting these contributions to agricultural economics from two eminent economists of the eighteenth century between two covers.

Although the greater part of the economic work of Quesnay and Turgot no longer needs an introduction for the English reader,[1] this is unfortunately not the case with the two contributions here reprinted in translation. It is true that there are some specialist studies as well as more general commentaries on *la grande et la petite culture*,[2] but few of these are recent and with some notable exceptions, few are available in English.[3] In addition, some aspects of the contents of these pieces deserve more attention. These include the interesting illustration of the *classical* view of choice of technique embodied particularly in Quesnay's careful study of the two 'modes of production' analysed in his paper, and the value-theoretic points made by him which have been neglected if not suppressed by most commentators on physiocracy.[4]

This introduction highlights some of the more novel aspects which make 'Fermiers' an important contribution in its own right, while in addition it attempts to provide more background to the writing of this article than has hitherto been done.[5] One aspect of this is to provide a more satisfactory explanation for Quesnay's interest in economics than has so far been provided. In addition, it provides some evaluation of the sources of Quesnay's data and their accuracy, in the light of contemporary controversy involving such notable contemporaries as Forbonnais and Voltaire,[6] as well as other background required for a clear understanding of Quesnay's argument.

Background to the publication of 'Fermiers'

The article 'Fermiers' was published under the signature of 'M. Quesnay le fils' in volume 6 of the *Encyclopédie*. This volume also included another of Quesnay's articles, 'Evidence', though this was published anonymously.[7] It can be said that these articles constitute a significant point of departure for Quesnay. In the first place, they were his first published work for nearly three years; his previous publication being the two-volume *Traité des fièvres*, published in Paris in February 1753. Second, they were the first essays published by Quesnay not dealing with medical matters, the subject on which he had built his substantial reputation and from which he earned his living. Third, they were publications in the *Encyclopédie*, a work constantly under threat from the censor and already prohibited on a number of occasions, and hardly the type of publication to which a personal employee of the royal household should contribute. Finally, and most importantly, 'Fermiers' turned out to be the first of a series of economic essays which Quesnay was to publish over the next decade and on which his current place in the history of ideas is based.[8]

The origins and development of Quesnay's interest in economics is a matter which requires some explanation. Unfortunately little information of a satisfactory nature appears to be available on this subject. Oncken[9] argues that Quesnay's move to economic studies took place during the years 1753–6, but no real evidence for this is presented apart from the fact that economic speculation according to him was *à la mode* in France at that time, particularly as a result of the translation efforts by the school of Gournay. The selection of 1753 as the starting year for Quesnay's economic studies is undoubtedly inspired by the fact that Quesnay's last major medical work, as indicated in the previous paragraph, appeared in February of that year. Hecht,[10] in her discussion of Quesnay's relationship with the *Encyopédistes* suggests that Quesnay turned to studies outside medicine – starting with philosophy and only later turning to economics when he first moved into the Entresol at Versailles on becoming physician to Madame de Pompadour. This hypothesis dates it around the spring of 1749, and is plausible because this move would have provided financial security and leisure to allow such wider interests, while at the same time, the intellectual interests of Madame de Pompadour herself would have encouraged such activities.[11]

Hecht also reports that only two slight pieces of evidence remain about Quesnay's debut in other studies. The first is a letter to l'Abbé le Blanc, a protégé of Madame de Pompadour and the translator of Hume's political discourses, which can only be very roughly dated at 1754 or 1755 and which apparently contains some notes which Quesnay's reading of Hume are said to have inspired. The second, precisely dated at 16 January 1756, is a letter to a Professor of Botany, François Bossier Sauvages de la Croix, in which Quesnay provided criticisms of the latter's theory of the relationship between the soul and bodily movement.[12]

Little is also known about Quesnay's life at the Entresol at Versailles during this period which relates to his economics, and which, more importantly for the present purpose, can be precisely dated. For example, the more relevant anecdotes from the memoirs of Madame du Hausset, lady's maid to Madame de Pompadour – such as the story about *prelinpinpin* (or the necessity of money) and the discussions of farming in Normandy and Poitou she had with him and which he encouraged – are impossible to date since these memoirs do not appear to have been printed in chronological order.[13] Similarly, the *Mémoires de Marmontel* which provide a picture of Quesnay at the Entresol busy from morning till night with calculations and system-building about rural political economy cannot be easily dated. Although one passage from these *Mémoires* refers to 1757, it cannot be concluded therefrom that the earlier references to Quesnay deal with a period prior to that year.[14]

It should further be noted that there was complete silence on the topic of what inspired Quesnay in the mid-1750s to turn his talents to economics among his close physiocratic collaborators, both during his lifetime and after his death in 1774. For example, the *Eloge funèbre de M. François Quesnay*[15] by Mirabeau does not dwell on this subject at all. Du Pont de Nemours in his *Origine et progrès d'une science nouvelle* only refers to the fact that Quesnay gave the articles 'Fermiers' and 'Grains' to the *Encyclopédie* as the first exposition of the new science which Quesnay, according to Du Pont, had developed from his observations of and speculations on nature.[16] A year later[17] he discussed Quesnay's early contributions to economics in some detail, including therein the article 'Fermiers', but once again no real explanations are offered on the origins of Quesnay's interest in economics. The importance of 'Fermiers' to the beginnings of physiocracy is reaffirmed in Du Pont's much later autobiographical sketch.[18]

The other eulogies, however, link Quesnay's interest in political economy to the second edition of this book *Essay physique sur l'économie animale*, which had appeared in 1747 with much new material, some of which loosely related to psychology and the social sciences.[19] The *Eloge historique de M. Quesnay* by the Comte d'Albon is most explicit on this. 'Après avoir terminé son travail sur *l'Economie animale*, Quesnay se trouva naturellement conduit à s'occuper de *l'économie politique*'.[20] D'Albon based this hypothesis on the view that there is a natural progression from reflections on the influence of ailments of the soul on the body to the beneficial influence of good government (or that detrimental of bad government) on the happiness of the people. In his brief exposition of this argument d'Albon suggests that Quesnay was naturally led to an examination of the sources of human happiness and sorrow, that he easily related these to the essential enjoyments of mankind, and that these were just as easily associated by him with his youthful experience of rural life. Hence his awakened interests in human happiness and good government led him to investigate the political economy of agriculture, which provides the essentials of human existence and enjoyment.[21] In another eulogy anonymously published in London in 1775, the attributed author – Marquis de Mesmon – suggests a similar explanation for Quesnay's move from medicine for the human body to preventitive medicine and cures for the ills of the body politic. Quesnay discovered the latter in political and economic speculation on agricultural acitivity.[22] This material therefore elaborates on the observed proclivities of medical men of the seventeenth- and early eighteenth century to study political economy, which has already been noted.[23]

Quesnay's interest in agriculture may also have been influenced by the fact that he became a substantial landowner in 1755, after his elevation to the nobility by the king in October 1752 which entitled him to purchase a 'noble' landed estate. The estate purchased was situated in the parish of Saint-Germain-en-Viry, about twenty-four kilometres from Nivers, and included a castle, stables, woods for the chase fish ponds and an ornamental garden with fountains, and lakes. It was given to and farmed by his son, Blaise-Guillaume, who turned out to be a successful farmer. Although the soil was not of high quality, good yields were nevertheless obtained from it, as was reported by Quesnay's friend and disciple Pattullo. The royal gift of a title in 1752 and the consequent possibility of becoming a real landowner by having the right to purchase a noble estate may also have influenced and inspired Quesnay's detailed interest in practical agricultural economics of the type he produced in the article 'Fermiers'.[24]

The place of publication of Quesnay's early economic writings can be easily explained by his personal acquaintance with both editors of the *Encyclopédie*. Quesnay's election to the Académie des Sciences on 11 August 1751 for his services to medicine probably gained him the acquaintance of d'Alembert, who by then had been a member for about a decade. D'Alembert's later personal friendship with Quesnay is attested to by the fact that he published an *éloge* of Quesnay in the *Mercure de France* for 15 November 1778, supplementing the official eulogy of Quesnay produced for the Academy.[25] Diderot's knowledge of Quesnay as a surgeon can be dated back at least to the end of 1748, while Quesnay appears to have been contemplated by Diderot as a possible contributor to the *Encyclopédie* as early as January 1753. Diderot noted at that time in a letter that Quesnay was 'the physician, friend and confidant' of Madame de Pompadour, which suggests that his invitation to write for the *Encyclopédie* may have been partly at least a diplomatic gesture to secure the patronage and protection of the *Encyclopédie* from the royal mistress, via her physician. By February 1753, Diderot refers to Quesnay as a go-between in his discussions with Madame de Pompadour, while her assistance in protecting the early volumes of the *Encyclopédie* from the censor can be easily documented. The censorship problems experienced in 1754 and 1755 may well have made Quesnay an even more useful ally for Diderot, and may indirectly have led to the publication of Quesnay's work on subjects on which he was not an acknowledged expert, in order to secure his assistance in obtaining the royal favour required for publication. It may even be suggested that had it not been for such assistance, Quesnay's initial views on economics may not have seen the light of day. This aspect of Quesnay's life needs considerably more investigation.[26]

The economic content of 'Fermiers'

In light of the many critics of Quesnay's first article on economics, including contemporaries and later commentators, some observations on the more important features of its contents must be made.[27] As indicated at the start of this introduction, these relate to the classical view of choice of technique embodied in the paper, on the capital-theoretic implications of the analysis, and on the consequences of this for Quesnay's later value and distribution theory. These aspects of the foundations of Quesnay's economic system are clearly of great importance in the history of economic thought.

The greater part of Quesnay's article is devoted to a detailed comparison of two agricultural techniques which are characterised in the third paragraph of the article (p. 1) as farmers ploughing with horses and sharecroppers or *métayers* ploughing with oxen. As Turgot had to point out a decade later against Quesnay's critics, this manner of defining the two methods is a shorthand for examining two quite distinct methods of production then being utilised in French agriculture.[28] The first is a fairly primitive – it is tempting to use the word feudal – and in any case largely pre-capitalistic method of cultivation, that of sharecropping or *métayage* carried out by poor cultivators or peasants on a relatively small scale. The second method, which Quesnay purposefully dignifies with the name of 'farming', is a more capital-intensive form of cultivation, implying long leases on more extensive ground and considerable wealth on the part of the entrepreneur-farmers. This position cannot only be easily demonstrated from Quesnay's essay on the subject, it is clearly the inference which Turgot drew from it in a more concise and clear manner.

The feature of this juxtapositioning of agricultural techniques which requires more attention than it has been given is its emphasis on discontinuous choice of technique and the relatively fixed proportion of factor inputs embodied in them. This feature, which can be regarded as an essential characteristic of classical political economy, can be illustrated from quite a large number of Quesnay's remarks on the basis of the distinction. These can be summarised as follows:

(a) quite distinct capital requirements of the two techniques (p. 11);
(b) the different soil terrain suitable for ox-ploughing as against horse-ploughing cultivation (pp. 2–3);
(c) different by-products (dung and butchers' meat) from the two techniques (pp. 3–5);
(d) different crop rotation possibilities under the two techniques which substantially influence yields (p. 6); and

(e) different land-subdivision and enclosure requirements under the two techniques (p. 8).

As Eltis to some extent indicated in his analysis of Quesnay's work, these matters constitute not only economic differences between the two techniques but also institutional ones, a point which Turgot, who was much more sociologically and historically inclined than Quesnay, fully grasped when in his 'Reflections' he described these two techniques as chronologically the last two methods in the historical succession of methods by which landlords extracted the surplus produce from the land.[29]

The essential point arising from Quesnay's comparison of these two techniques, as he made abundantly clear in his famous interview with Mirabeau in July 1757, was to demonstrate the need for more capital using farming techniques, and hence to show that capital accumulation rather than population growth is the way to wealth, prosperity and a strong nation.[30] In 'Fermiers', Quesnay explicitly argued the fallacy of the proposition that labour shortages are the cause of agricultural distress (pp. 22–5) and pointed instead to what he considered to be the real causes of the poor performance of French agriculture. Nearly all the policies to improve agriculture he was to elaborate in his later work are mentioned in this first paper, at least in outline. These include wrong grain trade policy, faulty encouragement of manufacturing and trade in luxuries, wrong taxation policy and insufficient government appreciation of the benefits and importance of agriculture. Quesnay's arguments in this essay (e.g. p. 21) also point to the interdependencies between the various sectors of industry and the need to use agriculture as the engine of economic growth.

It is this emphasis on the role of capital in production which of course was one of Quesnay's major contributions to economics, as was first realised by Marx.[31] Although this paper does not explicitly introduce the concept of *avances primitives* and *avances annuelles*, the costing exercises which Quesnay constructs for the purpose of comparing the two techniques in terms of investment outlay required (pp. 4–5) and their yields, indicate that the basis for this distinction was already firmly implanted in his mind (pp. 14–15). The first explicitly embodied in the calculation the interest cost of capital calculated in terms of its length of life, as well as depreciation and scrap value. In the later yield estimates he shows himself fully conversant with the distinction between annual operational costs and longer-term capital costs. It seems clear that Quesnay's position on capital theory was nearly completely formulated by the time he wrote 'Fermiers' for the *Encyclopédie*.

Two further important aspects of Quesnay's first economic paper should be noted. The first relates to the careful definition of cost of production implied in the table on yield (pp. 14–15), which includes operational expenses such as various wage costs, harvest and threshing costs, incidental expenses, capital costs, including what could be regarded as the minimum supply price of capital,[32] as well as costs such as taxation and rent which must be met by the individual farmer. From these the unit costs of wheat can be calculated at 14 livres per *setier*, a cost which is more or less covered when the price of quality wheat is 16 livres the *setier* which averages out at 14 livres per *setier* for the crop as a whole. This shows the importance of the notion of *bon prix* for Quesnay's agricultural policy, since only a good price for wheat (that is, well above unit cost of production) will provide the substantial returns to the farmer required for the financing of improvements in productive methods. Quesnay's cost calculations also show that for him the net product of agriculture was a value rather than a physical concept.[33]

The other interesting feature of this essay is the frequent use which Quesnay makes of the word 'profit', both as noun and verb. In this paper, in contrast with some of his later work, profits are recognised as an essential stimulus and prerequisite for the investment of capital in agriculture (e.g. pp. 17–19). In the light of Meek's analysis[34] of profits in physiocracy, this paper is instructive since it suggests, as Vaggi[35] has noted, that profits play an important role in the physiocratic model and that the exemption of profits from taxation is an essential part of their growth policy emphasising capital accumulation.[36] This, together with the previous considerations, demonstrate that 'Fermiers' is an important paper for understanding the economics of physiocracy and not a minor and preliminary contribution devoted largely to technical issues of agricultural economics only.

Before concluding this section on the economic content of 'Fermiers', some comments should be made on the sources used by Quesnay in his early writings on economics. These undoubtedly were few. Apart from the cross-reference to the preceding article by M. le Roy (p. 10 n3), the only references in the text are the citation of population data from Dupré de Saint-Maur's *Essai sur les monnoies*, which may have been derived via Herbert's *Essai sur la police des grains* (p. 11 n4, 5), the map ascribed to M. de Cassini on the area of France (p. 11 n6) as well as the citation of Locke's alleged comparison between trade and gambling (p. 24 and n11). When Quesnay's other three early economic essays are examined these sources are not greatly increased. In the article 'Grains' there are references to Plumart de Dangeul, *Avantages et désavantages de la France et de l'Angleterre*[37]; *to* Le financier citoyen *by De Naveau;*[38] an agricultural treatise on *Prairies artificielles* by La Salle de l'Etang[39] and a reference to Cantillon's *Essai sur la nature du commerce en général.*[40] In 'Hommes', there is an interesting reference to an article in the *Journal économique* (June/July 1757) which included translated extracts from Petty's *Political Arithmetick* as well as a reference to an agricultural work by François de Vivens. This article once again makes reference to population estimates by Dupré de Saint-Maur.[41] The final early article, 'Impôts', adds a reference to the *Testament politique du Cardinal de Richelieu* as well as one to Mirabeau's *Mémoire sur les éstats provinciaux.*[42]

The small number of directly acknowledged sources must be supplemented by a number of other works which Quesnay appears to have studied. Hecht, without stating her authority, lists Vauban, Boisguilbert, Melon, Eon de Beaumont and O'Heguerty, in addition to those listed in the previous paragraph. To these names those of Hume and Montesquieu must be added. This list can undoubtedly be further expanded.[43] Nevertheless, it can be concluded that Quesnay's original ideas were largely derived *de novo* and were not inspired to any marked extent by the work of others.[44]

The reception of 'Fermiers': critics and admirers in France and abroad

Quesnay's article 'Fermiers' attracted little attention on publication in 1756, and received in fact little discussion in France until after the work of the physiocrats had become more famous in the mid-1760s. As Hecht put it, only Henry Pattullo, the physiocrat's first foreign disciple, praised the essay and publicised it in his short *Essai sur l'amélioration des terres* published in 1758.[45] During the 1760s the importance of the contents of these early essays was mentioned on a number of occasions by Du Pont de Nemours, as has already been noted.[46]

Quesnay's *Encyclopédie* articles, including 'Fermiers', fared better in Italy, where they were studied and approvingly quoted by at least one prominent Italian economist of the second half of the eighteenth century. This was Beccaria, who in his *Elementi di economia pubblica* (in the second part devoted to agriculture) included a chapter on 'Della piccola e grande coltura delle terre', in which the article 'Fermiers' was approvingly cited and some of Quesnay's calculations were reproduced verbatim.[47] Beccaria's plan for agricultural improvement follows physiocratic lines developed by Quesnay in the article 'Grains' as does his division of society into classes.[48] Beccaria's physiocratic views on agriculture, but not those on the grain trade, were criticised by his friend Pietro Verri, who also criticised the physiocratic theory of taxation.[49]

In England, comment on Quesnay's article 'Fermiers' appears to have been largely confined to some critical remarks by Arthur Young on the attacks made on the use of oxen in husbandry by French agricultural writers, among whom Quesnay is explicitly listed. Young can only attribute this criticism to what appears to him as the poor feeding practices with respect to oxen in France by 'turning them into the commons for their food'. From this he concluded that 'if this is the case, no wonder that ox culture is so unprofitable'.[50]

French reactions to physiocracy in the second half of the 1760s became more and more hostile, and in some cases this hostility included critical remarks on Quesnay's early article, 'Fermiers'. This is partly illustrated by Voltaire's sarcastic critique of physiocracy, first published in 1768, in which, in a dialogue with a geometer, some of Quesnay's exercises in political arithmetic appear to be ridiculed.[51] Two years later in the *Questions sur l'Encyclopédie* commenced in 1770, Voltaire critically discussed Quesnay's articles on the subject of agriculture with special reference to *la grande et la petite culture*. Although the article 'Fermiers' (wrongly entitled 'Ferme' by Voltaire) is regarded as one of the better contributions to this massive reference work, the validity of the distinction between these two methods of cultivation is questioned, partly on historical grounds, and ploughing with oxen is regarded as advantageous as that with horses.[52]

A seemingly sympathetic but nonetheless hostile reaction can also be found in two of Diderot's agricultural articles written for the *Encyclopédie*. In the first of these, 'Agriculture', reference is made to the distinction between ploughing with oxen and horses. Little is made of this by Diderot apart from noting some of the special features associated with ox-ploughing husbandry and mentioning that although those two forms of cultivation are practised in France they are far from general: buffaloes are said to be used for ploughing in Italy and donkeys in Sicily. After a detailed chronological discussion of agricultural tasks, the article concludes with an examination of the views on the subject of Jethro Tull and Duhamel du Monceau, two noted authorities. The last few pages provide some calculations of the cost of ploughing drawn from Tull's figures rather than those provided by Quesnay.[53] In the article 'Laboureur', Diderot strongly argues the importance of advances of capital for good cultivation and indicates the necessity of wealthy husbandmen for profitable cultivation but there are no references made in this context to Quesnay's earlier propositions on the same subject.[54] In both pieces, Quesnay's work is studiously ignored.

Undoubtedly the most virulent analytical critic of Quesnay's articles in the *Encyclopédie*, and in fact of physiocracy in general, was François Véron de Forbonnais, who devoted his *Principles et observations économiques* almost entirely to this task.[55] Part III of this lengthy work is virtually exclusively devoted to the articles 'Grains' and 'Fermiers', including therein much factual criticism as well as methodological criticisms of the specific assumptions on which so many of Quesnay's calculations depend.

Forbonnais' first criticism of Quesnay is devoted to a brief comparison made by him on the price of grain during the reign of Charles IX and that of Louis XIV (see p. 13 for the relevant paragraph). This is described as an ahistorical comparison because it ignores the many traumatic events which occurred in between these periods. These are listed as civil wars, famines, troop movements, foreign wars, commercial difficulties and a half-hearted *police des grains*. All these events would have caused far wider fluctuations in grain prices than suggested by Quesnay's analysis. This point is supplemented by citations about price movements designed to show that actual grain prices moved well outside the range of prices which Quesnay mentioned in the paragraph cited.[56]

More important for the purpose of this introduction is Forbonnais' criticism of some of the factual assumptions which provide the basis for Quesnay's comparison between ox and horse cultivation. For example, he argues that oxen are, generally speaking, preferred for work on small properties, that pastures in those districts are not only used for plough oxen but also for reeding cows which produce meat and milk, that dung produced on these pastures need not necessarily be lost but can be recovered for farming, and that the ratios of horses for oxen presented by Quesnay are rather far-fetched. He also suggests that if in Quesnay's calculation the price of horses and oxen is lowered to 250 and 150 livres respectively, the profit estimated by Quesnay on the use of horses is turned into a loss.[57] Similar comments are made on the harvest yield assumptions in Quesnay's articles, which are called 'metaphysical', and this introduces

Forbonnais' second methodological criticism. Quesnay's calculations are exercises in political arithmetic, which is a conjectural science analogous to medicine.[58]

Although Forbonnais also provided criticism of other aspects of Quesnay's analysis in 'Fermiers' – for example, his attack on the proposition that *petite culture* is of necessity inferior cultivation, his criticism of Quesnay's excessive concentration on wheat cultivation in his examples, and his ignoring of luxury demand in the case of silk production, the main charges levied against Quesnay are the ahistorical nature of the analysis and the calculations based on conjecture rather than facts.[59]

It must of course be agreed that much of Quesnay's calculations have the major characteristic of political arithmetic, that is, they are deduced 'facts' from assumed 'facts'. It is also true, however, that he utilised much fact gathered by others, notably those by Dupré de Saint-Maur and Herbert, and that, generally speaking, he used these accurately. He also encouraged the search for facts. In view of the enormous regional differences in France in the eighteenth century, generalisations made from such particular observations invariably constituted dangerous practice, and one possibly carried too far in Quesnay's work. However, even if his data was not, and probably could not have been, completely correct, his calculations and numerical relationships provided a logical foundation for his coherent theoretical system.[60]

Notes

1 The more important of Quesnay's economic works, particularly those connected with the *Tableau*, have been translated by Ronald L. Meek, *The Economics of Physiocracy* (London: George Allen & Unwin, 1962); a comprehensive set of translations of Turgot's major economic work is included in my *The Economics of A. R. J. Turgot* (The Hague: Martinus Nijhoff, 1977). The standard editions of the works of these economists are *François Quesnay et la physiocratie* (Paris: Institut National d'Etudes Démographiques, 1958) and G. Schelle (ed.) *Oeuvres de Turgot et documents le concernant* (Paris: Felix Alcan, 1913–23), five volumes. All references to Quesnay's and Turgot's works will be to these editions, with the exception of 'Fermiers'.

2 The most important of these is Charles Rebeyrol, *De la grande et de la petite culture chez les physiocrates*, Paris: Jouve & Cie, 1912); and see also O. Thiele, 'François Quesnay und die Agrarkrisis im Ancien Regime. Dargestellt auf Grund zweier Briefe', *Vierteljahresschrift fur Sozial und der Wirtschaftgeschichte*, vol. IV, 1906, pp. 515–62, 633–52; Karl Knies (ed.) *Carl Friedrichs von Baden brieflicher Verkehr mit Mirabeau und Du Pont* (Heidelberg: Carol Winter's Universitatsbuchhandlung, 1892), introduction, pp. CXXX–CXXXII, CXLIII–CXLIV; and the work of A. Oncken, *Geschichte der National-Okonomie. Die Zeit vor Adam Smith* (Leipzig: C. L. Hirschfeld, 1902) pp. 361–3, 373–4; and *Oeuvres économiques et philosophiques de François Quesnay* (Frankfurt am Main: Joseph Baer, Paris: Jules Peelman, 1888) pp. 159–92). Early English commentary on the subject matter of 'Fermiers' is provided by Henry Higgs, *The Physiocrats* (London: Macmillan, 1897), pp. 26–29. The matter of *la grande and la petite culture* is most exhaustively treated in Georges Weulersse, *Le mouvement physiocratique en France de 1756 à 1770* (Paris: Felix Alcan, 1910) vol. I, pp. 333–6, vol. II, pp. 297–322.

3 A recent English appreciation of the importance of the contents of 'Fermiers' is Walter Eltis, 'François Quesnay: A Reinterpretation', *Oxford Economic Papers*, vol.

27, no. 2, July 1975, esp. pp. 169–74. On the other hand, Meek played down the importance of the article 'Fermiers', because it 'contains very little than can properly be called an anticipation of basic Physiocratic theory' (Meek, *op. cit.*, p. 267, but cf. pp. 346–7 where he argued that 'even in the earlier works … the emphasis on the importance of capital is quite unmistakable'). Meek's playing down of 'Fermiers' may have been partly inspired by the derogatory comments by Louis Salleron in the INED edition of Quesnay's works (see esp. p. 427 n1 and p. 459 n1) but possibly owes more to the fact that it caused difficulties for Meek's interpretation of the physiocratic theory of value and profit. See Meek, *op. cit.*, pp. 301–3. See also note 4 below, and the references there cited for the importance of the article in the context of value theory and its relationship with physiocratic economic policy.

4 See G. Vaggi, 'Prices, Markets and Reproduction: A Study of the Role of a Theory of Value in Physiocracy', Ph.D. thesis, University of Cambridge, September 1980. Part of the argument is presented by Vaggi in his 'The Physiocratic Theory of Prices', *Contributions to Political Economy*, no. 2, 1983. (The thesis has now been published as G. Vaggi *The Economics of François Quesnay* [Durham NC: Duke University Press, 1987].)

5 This subject is raised by Jacqueline Hecht, 'La Vie de François Quesnay', in INED edition of Quesnay's works, esp. pp. 253–4. The only reasons she gives are the propensity of medical men to engage in the 'social medicine designed to heal the body politick' as had earlier been done, for example, by Petty, Barbon, Mandeville and Locke, and the fact that things agricultural, with which Quesnay had been familiar from his youth, had become highly fashionable from the beginning of the 1750s onwards. (This issue is treated at length in Peter Groenewegen [ed.] *Physicians and Political Economy* [London: Routledge, 2001] chs 2–6.)

6 That is, François Véron de Forbonnais, *Principles et observations économiques* (Amsterdam: M. M. Rey, 1767) and Voltaire *Questions sur l'Encyclopédie* (1770) in *Oeuvres complètes de Voltaire*, 2nd edn, Paris: Baudovin, 1825) vol. 51, pp. 143–59, esp. pp. 149–51. For a general discussion of the critics of physiocracy, see Henry Higgs, *The Physiocrats* (London: Macmillan, 1897) lecture V, pp. 102–22.

7 *Encyclopédie ou Dictionnaire raisonné des sciences, des arts et des métiers, par une société de gens de letters* (Paris: Briasson) vol. 6 (published January 1756) pp. 146–57 ('Evidence'); 528–40 ('Fermiers'). Jacqueline Hecht, from whose bibliography following her biography of Quesnay (*op. cit.*, p. 307) these particulars are drawn, gives January as the date of publication. Due to censorship problems this volume may not have appeared till later, perhaps not till April 1756. See Georges Roth (ed.) *Denis Diderot. Correspondence 1713–1757* (Paris: Editions de Minuit, 1955) vol. I, p. 208.

8 These biographical details are drawn from Hecht, *op. cit.*, pp. 306, 252–5.

9 A. Oncken, *Geschichte der National-Okonomie. Die Zeit vor Adam Smith* (Leipzig: C. L. Hirschfeld, 1902) pp. 316–317.

10 Hecht, *op. cit.*, pp. 252–3, 239.

11 For a discussion of these see Nancy Mitford, *Madame de Pompadour*, (Penguin Books, 1958) esp. chs 11 and 12, the second of which gives details of her considerable library.

12 Hecht, *op. cit.*, pp. 252–3. The latter is important since Quesnay wrote a piece on the function of the soul ('Fonction de l'âme') which he submitted together with 'Evidence' for publication in the *Encyclopédie*. The latter, together with 'Evidence' were listed as anonymous contributions by the same author in the introduction to vol. 6, p. vii, but according to the alphabetical ordering, it should not have appeared till vol. 7. The original version of this piece has been lost, but in 1760 Quesnay published some of its contents in *Aspects de la psychologie*. Matters concerning the soul were also included in Quesnay's *Essai physique sur l'economie animale*, 2nd edn, 1747, which followed material on natural law. See the extracts given in Oncken,

Oeuvres de Quesnay, in A. Oncken, *Geschichte der National-Okonomie. Die Zeit vor Adam Smith* (Leipzig: C. L. Hirschfeld, 1902) pp. 747–63. This work was linked to Quesnay's work on economics by two of his earlier biographers, a matter pursued later in this introduction.

13 See *Secret Memoirs of the Courts of Louis XV and XVI taken from the Memoirs of Madame du Hausset* (London: Grolier Society, n.d.) esp. pp. 23–6, 76; the relevant extracts in French are included in Oncken, *op. cit.*, pp. 117–19, 125. The references to Normandy and Poitou and Quesnay's interest in the farming there (including interest in the wealth of the farmers there) is interesting since these parts of France were identified as provinces of *la grande culture*.

14 Extracts included in Oncken, *op. cit.*, pp. 139–42. In these memoirs, and also in the context of 'calculs d'économie rustique' and 'le produit net', Marmontel mentions 'jolly dinners' at the Entresol with Diderot, D'Alembert, Duclos, Helvetius, Turgot, and Buffon (*ibid.*, p. 141) meetings which would have taken place at quite different time periods, while the earlier extract also refers to Pattullo's *Essai sur l'amélioration des terres*, which was published in 1758 and based on Quesnay's two economic *Encyclopédie* articles. Pattullo's work is looked at a later stage in this introduction and in note 45).

15 This is included in Oncken, *op. cit.*, pp. 3–14.

16 Included in E. Daire (ed.) *Physiocrates* (Paris: Guillaumin, 1846) pp. 335–66, esp. pp. 338–9.

17 Du Pont de Nemours, *Notice abrégé des différents écrits modernes qui ont concouru en France à former la science de l' économie politique*, first published in the *Ephémérides du Citoyen* in 1769, included in Oncken, *op. cit.*, pp. 145–58, and see esp. 148–150.

18 In this later autobiographical sketch, Du Pont argued that on the advice from the Marquis de Mirabeau he had pursued his economic studies by absorbing the articles in the *Encyclopédie* 'into which Monsieur Quesnay had incorporated the first principles of his doctrine'. See Du Pont de Nemours, *L'enfance et la jeunesse de Du Pont de Nemours* (Paris: private edition, 1906) pp. 210–11, cited in J. J. McLain, *The Economic Writings of Du Pont de Nemours* (Newark DE: Delaware University Press, 1977) p. 69, n18. This should be compared with the remarks he made on these articles in his *Notice abregée*: 'Le mot *Fermiers* présentait quelques idées *mères* d'une grande science. Dans le mot *Grains*, on voit cette science formée et prèsque complète' (in Oncken, *op. cit.*, p. 150).

19 See Hecht, *op. cit.*, pp. 237, 305; the first edition of this work had appeared in 1736. Oncken, *op. cit.*, pp. 747–63 reprints extracts from the third volume of this work as well as a 1748 critical essay of the book from a German scientific periodical (*ibid.*, pp. 739–47).

20 In Oncken, *ibid.*, p. 53. The *Eloge* was first published in the *Nouvelles Ephémérides*, no. 5, 1775, of which d'Albon was one of the editors (see *ibid.*, p. 39, n1).

21 This is a paraphrase of d'Albon's argument in the *Eloge*, *ibid.*, p. 53. Cf. also Oncken, *op. cit.*, p.340.

22 Included in Oncken, *op. cit.*, p. 85, esp. and see *ibid.*, p. 72, n1 on the bibliographical details of this *Eloge*.

23 See note 5 above. See also Schumpeter, *Economic Doctrine and Method* (London: Allen & Unwin, 1954, first published in German in 1912) p. 55 but cf. his *History of Economic Analysis* (London: Allen & Unwin, 1959) pp. 223–43, esp. pp. 239–42.

24 See Hecht, *op. cit.*, pp. 243–7 for details for these matters from which this paragraph has been largely drawn. Pattullo's comment in his *Essai sur l'amélioration des terres* (Paris: Durand, 1758, pp. 77–78) on Quesnay's estate is cited on p. 246 as is the amount of annual revenue drawn from meadows, woods, fishing and mills from the estate, which amounted to 4,675 livres. Georges Weulersse, *Le mouvement physiocratique en France de 1756 à 1770* (Paris: Felix Alcan, 1910) vol. I, pp. 43–4 implicitly associates the purchase of the estate with the early material on economics. The title

of this property may have been a noble *francsaleux*. For details on this type of title see Alexis de Tocqueville, *The Old Regime and the French Revolution* (New York: Anchor Doubleday, 1955) p. 299.

25 See Hecht, *op. cit.*, pp. 249, 318. D'Alembert's eulogy of Quesnay is unfortunately not available to me since it is not included in the editions of the works to which I have access. It may also be recalled that Marmontel in his *Mémoires* mentions dinners hosted by Quesnay and attended by Diderot and d'Alembert. See note 14 above.

26 See Diderot to de Morand (16 December 1748) in Georges Roth (ed.) *Denis Diderot. Correspondence 1713–1757* (Paris: Editions de Minuit, 1955) vol. I p. 60; Diderot to Caroillon La Salettte (January 1753) in *ibid.*, p. 149); to the same (17 February 1753) p. 155. For Madame de Pompadour's association with the *Encyclopédistes* see Nancy Mitford, *op. cit.*, pp. 131–134, and Diderot to Madame de Pompadour and her reply (Winter 1753) in Roth, *op. cit.*, vol. I, pp. 159–61; and for the censorship problems experienced in 1754–1755, *ibid.*, pp. 165–171. It should be noted that Hecht, in her otherwise excellent *Vie de Quesnay* does not deal with this subject at any length (see pp. 252–253). However, she appears to suggest that Quesnay's intended contribution 'Fonction de l'âme' was rejected by the editors of the *Encyclopédie* while his published articles, 'Evidence' and 'Fermiers' were much criticised by contemporaries. See Hecht, *ibid.*, p. 253. No reasons for this are given nor are inferences drawn, though the section of Hecht's biography in which this material appears is followed by a brief discussion of Quesnay's religious views. As noted earlier (note 12 above), 'Fonction de l'âme' had been announced in vol. 6 (*op. cit.*, introduction, p. vii) as appearing in that volume and being by the same anonymous author as the article 'Evidence' which did appear. It could not be included there for reasons of space (vol. VII commenced with FOI words) but 'Fonction de l'âme' did not appear in it. As noted below, Quesnay's material on agricultural economics in the *Encyclopédie* was criticised at a later stage by Diderot and Voltaire.

27 See above, notes 3, 4 and 6, where some of these critics are mentioned, and the subsequent section in this introduction where some of these criticisms are reviewed together with views of the admirers of Quesnay's article (pagination in the text is to the reprint translation, i.e. *Quesnay, 'Fermiers' 1756 and Turgot, 'Sur la grande et la petite culture'*, Sydney: Faculty of Economics, Reprint of Economic Classics, series 2, no. 2, 1983).

28 Walter Eltis, 'François Quesnay: A Reinterpretation', *Oxford Economic Papers*, vol. 27, no. 2, July 1975, p. 170, argues that Quesnay distinguished three techniques of production: the cultivation of land with labour alone; cultivations with ox-drawn ploughs, and cultivation with horse-drawn ploughs. Although Quesnay briefly refers to peasants or labourers scratching a living from small plots of land (e.g. pp. 17–18, 22) this is not really envisaged as a separate technique of production, but is seen as a consequence of rural poverty associated with sharecropping. The techniques compared are *la grande* and *la petite culture*, as Quesnay specifically indicated (pp. 21–3). But cf. Forbonnois, *Principes et observations économiques*, vol. 2, pp. 44, 57–61.

29 See Eltis, *op. cit.*, p. 270–1; Turgot, 'Reflections on the Production and Distribution of Wealth', in Groenewegen, *op. cit.*, pp. 50–6, esp. sects 25–6 on pp. 54–5. Turgot wrote the 'Reflections' at about the same time as his piece on *la grande et la petite culture*. Turgot also clearly indicates that these methods of production are distinguished by the fact that in *métayage* the landlord supplies the capital, while in farming the farmer-entrepreneur supplies the means of production. See 'Reflections', *ibid.*, paras 62–4, pp. 71–2. On the significance of this, see my 'Turgot, Beccaria and Smith' (Chapter 1, above).

30 See Meek, *op. cit.*, p. 15–18, esp. 17 which quotes extensively from Mirabeau's own account of this interview in a letter written to Rousseau ten years later.

31 K. Marx, *Theories of Surplus Value* (Moscow: Foreign Languages Publishing House, 1962) part I, p. 44.
32 This interest may also be interpreted as depreciation, as Quesnay did in 1766 in his *Analysis of the Arithmetic formula of the Tableau Economique*, reprinted in translation in Meek, *op. cit.*, p. 154. However Pattullo, *Essai sur l'amélioration des terres* (Paris: Durand, 1758) p. 95, interpreted this as interest on the money advanced in the enterprise.
33 This argument is put strongly by G. Vaggi, 'Prices, Markets and Reproduction: A Study of the Role of a Theory of Value in Physiocracy', Ph.D. thesis, University of Cambridge, September 1980, esp. ch. III.
34 Meek, 'The Physiocratic Concept of Profits', in Meek, *op. cit.*, pp. 297–312.
35 See G. Vaggi, 'Prices, Markets and Reproduction: A Study of the Role of a Theory of Value in Physiocracy', Ph.D. thesis, University of Cambridge, September 1980, Chapter VII.
36 See 'Fermiers', *op. cit.*, p. 19, 24–5.
37 A translation from an English tract allegedly inspired by Gournay. See 'Grains', *op. cit.*, p. 471 notes 9 and 7, 493 n22.
38 *Ibid.*, p. 473 n*, 497 n17; it is also cited in 'Impôts' in *ibid.*, p. 591 n(3).
39 'Grains', *op. cit.*, p. 481.
40 *Ibid.*, p. 482 n17 and see also pp. 483–4 where the editor has noted further similarities between Quesnay's and Cantillon's work.
41 'Hommes', in Quesnay, *op. cit.*, p. 518 n*; for the work by De Vivens see p. 543 n* and for the references to Dupré de Saint-Maur, *ibid.*, p. 514–15. There is also a reference on the first of these pages to Pierre Doisy, entitled *Détail de Royaume de France*, published in 1753.
42 That is (Paul Hay, Marquis de Chastellet) *Testament politique de Cardinal de Richelieu* (1st edn, Paris, 1688) cited in 'Impôts', *op. cit.*, p. 591, n(2), and Mirabeau, *Mémoire concernant l'utilité des etats provinciaux* (Rome: Carabioni, 1750) cited *ibid.*, p. 616, n22.
43 See Hecht, *op. cit.*, p. 254 and cf. Georges Weulersse, *Le mouvement physiocratique en France de 1756 à 1770* (Paris: Felix Alcan, 1910) vol. I, pp. 52–4. On Quesnay's early acquaintance with Hume's writings, see above and n12; Montesquieu's work was explicitly commented on by Quesnay with respect to colonies in an article produced in 1766. See 'Remarques sur l'opinion de l'auteur de *l'Esprit des lois*', *op. cit.*, pp. 781–92.
44 The one exception is Cantillon, whose analysis of circulation in part II, ch. 3 of the *Essai*, must have inspired essential features of Quesnay's *Tableau économique*. For a discussion of this see Meek, *op. cit.*, pp. 266–9.
45 See Hecht, *op. cit.*, pp. 254–5; and cf. 'Questions intéressantes sur la population, l'agriculture et le commerce', prepared by Quesnay and Marivelt as a questionnaire to obtain information on these matters in the provinces and dated 1758. The section on agriculture provides a bibliography on the subject which lists Pattullo's essay immediately after Quesnay's published *Encyclopédie* articles. Pattullo in fact reproduced the greater part of these in his work, see *Essai sur l'amélioration des terres* (Paris: Durand, 1758) esp. part II, pp. 163–284; 'Fermiers', and Quesnay are explicitly referred to in the introduction, p. 9 and on p. 151.

The bibliographies in 'Questions intéressants … ' appear to provide the basis for Hecht's supplementation of Quesnay's sources discussed above. It is also a case of that self-citation of which Forbonnais was to complain. Below and note 58.
46 See above and notes 16–18.
47 Cesare Beccaria, *Elementi di economia pubblica*, written *circa* 1769, in S. Romagnoli (ed.) *Cesare Beccaria: Opere* (Florence: Sansoni, 1958) vol. I pp. 447–52. Quesnay is cited on p. 451, while the cost calculations of investing in oxen and horses (pp. 4–5) are reproduced on pp. 451–2.

48 Beccaria, *op. cit.*, pp. 452–91.

49 Pietro Verri, *Meditazione sulla economia politica*, first published in 1771, in R. de Felice (ed.) *Del Piacere e del dolore ed altri scritti* (Milan: Feltrinelli, 1964) pp. 213–20, 237–42. See also his *Reflessioni sulle leggi nel commercio de'grani* (written in 1769 in *ibid.*, pp. 267–408, esp. pp. 311–20 on French practice and p. 311 n70, which provides a bibliography of the major physiocratic literature on the subject. Schumpeter's reference in *History of Economic Analysis*, *op. cit.*, p. 224, that the leading Italians – Beccaria, Verri and Genovesi – were friendly is even more peculiar, since I can find no trace of such feeling in Genovesi's main work.

50 Arthur Young, *A Six Months' Tour through the North of England* (London, 1770) vol. IV, pp. 295–6. Sir James Steuart may also have been familiar with Quesnay's 'Fermiers', since he cited the article 'Grains' in his *Principles of Political Oeconomy* (London, 1767) vol. I, p. 110. Some of his discussion of agriculture is quite physiocratic in flavour but this may also have been due to his acquaintance with the work of Cantillon and Mirabeau.

51 Voltaire, *l'Homme aux quarante écus*, first published in 1768, reprinted in English translation in *The Works of Voltaire: Romances and Philosophy* (New York: Walter J. Black, 1927) pp. 315–23, esp. pp. 316–17 on the area of arable land in France and the type and value of its product. It should be noted that Quesnay's last works included two treatises on geometry, as is shown in Hecht's bibliography, *op. cit.*, pp. 314–15.

52 Voltaire, *Questions sur l'Encyclopédie*, article 'Agriculture', in *Oeuvres complètes de Voltaire* (2nd edn, Paris: Baudovin, 1825), vol. 51, pp. 143–59, esp. pp. 149–51 which deals specifically with *la grande et la petite culture*. Voltaire's final criticism on the profitability of ox-ploughing husbandry which is based on the meat value of oxen is unfair to Quesnay, since he had made explicit provision for this in his calculations.

53 See *Oeuvres complètes de Diderot*, ed. J. Assézat (Paris: Garnier frères, 1876) vol. 13, p. 251 and pp. 256–65, esp. pp. 262–4, for Tull's calculations. Although the article *Feuille* and other articles from the *Encyclopédie* are referred to, Quesnay's 'Fermiers' is not mentioned, thereby indicating that in 1751 this article had not been contemplated. In this context, cf. the remarks of Diderot's association with Quesnay in note 26 above.

54 *Oeuvres complètes de Diderot*, *op. cit.*, vol. 15, pp. 407–9. This article was not published till 1765.

55 I.e. Forbonnais, *Principes et observations économiques* (Amsterdam: M. M. Rey, 1767) vol. 2, part III entitled 'Observations sur divers points du sistème contenu dans les articles Grains et Fermiers de "Enciclopedie" [*sic*.] dans le prétendu Extrait des Oeconomies roiales et ailleurs'. The critical references to 'Fermiers' are largely on pp. 9–26, 43–84 and 92–112, the other material in part III relates to criticism of 'Grains' and the appended 'Maximes du gouvernment économique'. Forbonnais himself had contributed the article 'Culture des terres (comm. polit)' to the *Encyclopédie* (vol. 4, 1754) pp. 552–66. On p. 566 a cross-reference to 'Grains' is provided but there is no cross reference to 'Fermiers'. This may mean that 'Fermiers' was not planned till after the completion of vol. 4. Cf. notes 26 and 53 above.

56 Forbonnais, *Principes et observations économiques*, *op. cit.*, pp. 9–26. The previous pages were devoted to a critical examination of the ahistorical nature of the eulogy of the reign of Henry IV and of Sully made by the physiocrats and Quesnay in particular.

57 Forbonnais, *ibid.*, pp. 46–51, the criticism of the calculation (p. 51 n1) depends on the assumption made about the price which oxen fetch as butcher's meat at the end of their working life. If this is likewise reduced by 50 livres then the loss remains proportional to the loss estimated, as Quesnay explicitly pointed out (p. 5) in anticipation of such criticism.

58 *Ibid.*, pp. 93–9; this methodological point is made on pp. 96–7. Cf. Voltaire's *l'Homme aux quarante écus*, first published in 1768, reprinted in English translation in *The Works of Voltaire: Romances and Philosophy* (New York: Walter J. Black, 1927), p. 316, where a similar derogatory comment is made. Forbonnais also strongly objected to Quesnay's practice of citing facts from his *Encyclopédie* articles as seemingly independent evidence in his later works. An example is given in note 45 above. For this criticism of self-citation from 'Fermiers' and 'Grains', which is highly justified, see *ibid.*, p. 37.

59 See *ibid.*, pp. 43–4, 57–61, 68–70 and 103–5. It should be noted that Forbonnais also diagnosed a third agricultural technique in Quesnay's work – *la culture à bras* (*ibid.*, pp. 57–61) as was done more recently by Eltis. See above, note 28.

60 One interesting and relevant difference in the 'facts' as observed by Quesnay and Turgot can be noted here. In 'Fermiers' (p. 8) Quesnay accepts an estimate that seven eighths of the kingdom is cultivated by oxen; Turgot in his paper on *la grande* and *la petite culture* (p. 29) states that *la petite culture* occupies at least four sevenths of the kingdom. It may also be noted that this distinction was accepted by at least one French economic historian, H. Sée; see for example his *La France économique et sociale au XVIIIe siècle* (Paris: Armand Colin, 1969) ch. 2.

14 Du Pont de Nemours on the origins and progress of a new science

Du Pont de Nemours' *De l'origine et des progrès d'une science nouvelle*, recently published for the first time in English translation,[1] is an important text of physiocracy, produced, as it were, at its very zenith and not long before its demise in intellectual acceptance induced by the stunning attacks of Voltaire in 1768 and Galiani two years later.[2] Published as a little eighty-four-page book in 1768, its aim was essentially twofold: to explain the history and intellectual development of physiocracy and its association with other thought; and to summarise the more fundamental aspects of physiocratic doctrine as a system of natural and social order essential to the good government of society, in the manner in which it had been codified by Mercier de la Rivière in his monumental *l'Ordre naturel et essential des sociétés politiques*, which had appeared the year before in 1767.

This dual purpose of Du Pont's text gives it the character of an important classic in physiocracy, and justifies making it more readily available to those interested in the development of classical political economy. The first quarter of its contents, as discussed more fully later in this introduction, is an attempt at the history of the new science, thereby constituting an early history of economics itself. More importantly, the fact that it attempted to summarise the most systematic (and most long-winded) exposition of physiocracy, generally also regarded as the most authoritative one,[3] makes it a very useful text for students interested in a more complete picture of physiocracy as a political and economic system. Such a picture is difficult to obtain at present because there is no English translation of the physiocratic work contemporary to Du Pont's book, the treatise by Mercier de la Rivière on which it was based.

The French text itself is not rare. Published in 1768 in Paris, it went through a number of editions over the next few months.[4] An edited version appeared among the collection of the writings of major physiocrats (Quesnay, Du Pont de Nemours, Mercier de la Rivière, Baudeau, Le Trosne) edited by Eugene Daire in his *Physiocrates* for the Guillaumin collection *des économistes*;[5] a reprint was issued in 1909 as number one in a series of reprints of texts by physiocrats and social reformers in eighteenth-century France under the editorship of A. Dubois;[6] while a facsimile reprinted from the 1768 text was published in 1992 by the Cooperativa Universitaria Editrice Catanese di Magistero, with an introduction by Gino Longhitano, as part of a series of French eighteenth-century economic texts which he edits.[7]

The importance of Du Pont's little book can be further illustrated from the following. McCulloch, in his *Literature of Political Economy*[8] used §XXI (pp. 30–4) of Du Pont's text to indicate in summary form 'the various institutions the Economists held to be necessary for the good government of a country'. In their very valuable chapter on physiocracy, Gide and Rist[9] praised Du Pont's piece, and used it extensively in their summary of the essential philosophical, political and institutional content of the physiocratic system. In his study of Du Pont de Nemour's economic writings, McLain calls it 'the clearest explanation of the origins, philosophy, economics and politics of the physiocratic doctrine and the nature of the society envisioned by the physiocrats in terms that were easy to understand'.[10]

Enough has been said to indicate the importance of the text and the value of presenting it in English dress. The remainder of this introduction attempts the following. The next section gives a brief overview of Du Pont de Nemours's life and work as essential background to this important text. A subsequent section discusses the content of the text reprinted in translation, emphasising some highlights, in particular those associated with its picture of the development of the new science.

Pierre Samuel du Pont de Nemours (1739–1817)

Pierre Samuel du Pont was born in Paris on 14 December 1739. His father was a watchmaker, and Du Pont himself was later apprenticed in that craft. His mother before that tried to secure him a good, general education, and at one stage he toyed with the idea of taking up medicine. During his apprenticeship, his horologist master brought him into contact with Diderot, and thereafter study of the art of watchmaking was combined with philosophical reading. In 1763 he published a pamphlet dealing with aspects of taxation, *Réflexions sur l'écrit intitulé: richesses d'état.* This attracted the attention of Mirabeau, who introduced Du Pont to Quesnay. The latter arranged for Du Pont to assist the Intendant of Soissons in undertaking a land survey, a task which occupied him until 1765. It was at this time that he met and befriended Turgot, with whom he corresponded until Turgot's death and whose works he edited in the early nineteenth century.[11] In 1765, Du Pont became the editor of the *Journal d'Agriculture*, which he turned into an organ for physiocratic research. When it subsequently folded in 1766, he continued his agricultural and economic studies until in 1768 he became editor of *Ephémérides du Citoyen* as successor to Baudeau on his conversion to physiocracy. He continued this task until 1772, when government proscription of the *Ephémérides* was a good excuse to terminate publication. During this period he also became involved with the Margrave of Baden as his personal adviser on agricultural matters and even as tutor to his son, a task carried out by regular correspondence. In June 1774 the Polish royal family invited him to become tutor to the royal children as well as an education administrator. However, after the death of Louis XV, the appointment of Turgot as Minister of Finance by his successor Louis XVI brought him back to France to become the assistant to his friend of long-standing in his new office. After Turgot's dismissal in 1776, Du Pont returned for some time to his country estate at Nemours, bought with the money granted him as Turgot's assistant to compensate him for giving up the Polish appointments. Subsequently he was recalled by Necker, who had become Turgot's successor at the finance ministry, to assist him. Du Pont continued with similar tasks under his successor Calonne until 1787. Advancing free trade became an important part of this work. In 1783 he created the free port of Bayonne; in 1786 he helped to liberalise French-American trade and laid the groundwork for the Anglo-French Commercial Treaty signed in that year. During the years of the French Revolution, Du Pont was active as a reforming deputy, first in the Estates-General and later in the National Assembly, where he represented Nemours. Here he contributed to economic debate and reform, but gradually found himself increasingly at odds with the radicalised majority of the Assembly, being particularly vocal in his criticism of the assignats (paper money backed by confiscated land) as a form of financing the government. He at one stage apparently also physically defended the monarchy in the form of the King himself. He was arrested for some time in 1794, and again very briefly in 1797, but unlike Turgot's other close friend Condorcet was not executed during the Terror. After his second arrest he removed himself from domestic politics. In 1800 he moved to America but returned to France in 1802, partly for business reasons but largely because he missed France too much. He returned to America in 1815, where he died in 1817.

Du Pont's gradual conversion to physiocracy from 1763 produced its first visible fruit in 1764 when his *De l'exportation et de l'importation des grains*, a plea for free trade in grain, was published. Thereafter, as editor of the *Journal de l'Agriculture*, he wrote articles and editorial comment, some of them criticised by Turgot in his correspondence with Du Pont.[12] The period between the demise of the *Journal de l'Agriculture* and his start as editor of the *Ephémérides*, a nineteen-month interlude, produced the work here reprinted in translation. It coincided with two other major publishing events in the history of physiocracy: the publication of Mercier de la Rivière's *L'ordre naturel et essentiel des sociétés politiques*, of which Du Pont's 1768 book was a broad summary, and the publication of *Physiocratie, ou constitution naturelle du gouvernement le plus avantageux aux genre humain*, which in two volumes reprinted most of Quesnay's major economic writings, preceded by an introduction and summary by the editor, Du Pont de Nemours.

Turgot described Du Pont's introduction in the following terms not long after he had received a copy of the *Physiocratie*:

> I received the *Physiocratie* before my departure and thank you for it with all my heart. I have read the preliminary discourse en route, interrupting my reading occasionally to put my hands back in my muff.

> I will speak to you with the frankness which you merit. I can only say that I found it very honest, very nobly and very eloquently written. The analysis of the ideas appears to me to be neither complete nor very exact. Their systematic development is too systematic, too compressed, too much shortened by essential omissions; it borders on servitude to the ideas of the master; however respectable that may be, no exception can be made to the rule which says that there is no need for this in matters of science. You are better equipped than any one to proceed by yourself. Besides, what you have written is really what is the best, not altogether for the work, but for the author; for opinions are formed, steps are retraced, what has only been seen imperfectly is seen better the second time, errors are recognised and truth put in their place, but where the soul and talent are lacking this cannot be claimed. On this note I embrace you.[13]

Du Pont's *On the Origins and Progress of a New Science* likewise conforms to this judgement. It is well and clearly written, perhaps a little too systematic, and it slavishly follows the views of the master, Quesnay, and those of the major propagator of the whole physiocratic system, Mercier de la Rivière. However, the coincidence of the last's monumental work on the physiocratic system together with Du Pont's own editing of the major works by Quesnay provided a perfect opportunity to review the doctrine in its entirety, thereby making its summary in *Origins and Progress of a New Science* all the more authoritative when it was written during that same, busy year of 1767.

There is no need to review the subsequent progress of Du Pont's own work during the 1770s in the context of editing the *Ephémérides*; assisting Turgot, as well as the Margrave of Baden; or the work during the 1780s for the Ministry of Finance and the subsequent activities in connection with the French Revolution. Those interested are referred to the substantial literature available on the topic.[14]

On the Origins and Progress of a New Science (1768)

The first seven pages of Du Pont's book discuss the origins and progress of the new science from its inception in the 1750s. The remaining pages look at its principles in outline. Given the opposition to physiocracy already encountered at the time of writing, the opening pages draw attention to the difficulties in getting new ideas accepted in all scientific and philosophical endeavour. Such difficulties are all the greater, Du Pont suggests, in the science dealing with national prosperity and human happiness, the subject matter of the greater part of his book. After acknowledging and praising the work of Montesquieu in the science of government, Du Pont comments that even this giant among thinkers had failed to grasp the real truth about the essential, natural and social order which restricts all human society to following one constitutive and fundamental law in its organisation and government. This was discovered by Quesnay in nature – hence physiocracy, the rule of nature. It was published by him as providing the content of the physical laws of society, in an argument which also detailed their foundations and consequences. The time of publication was also favourable to the dissemination of the newly discovered ideas because similar conclusions had been reached simultaneously but through a different route by Gournay, a merchant and government official. Moreover, after their publication by Quesnay in 1756–8 in his encyclopaedia articles 'Farmers' and 'Corn', and in his *Tableau économique*, the dissemination process was greatly assisted by two others persons of ability, Mirabeau and Mercier de la Rivière. Du Pont briefly discusses Mirabeau's conversion to physiocracy by Quesnay, his recantation by revision of previously published views, before mentioning the two events of 1767 – publication of Mercier de la Rivière's *Ordre naturel et essentiel des sociétés politiques* and his own edition of *Physiocratie* – which emboldened him to present an abstract of this thought in the subsequent pages. No predecessors are acknowledged at this stage; Montesquieu the only, albeit partial, exception. The historical prologue is therefore designed to demonstrate how Du Pont as author of the book arrived at the important and self-evident truths about the natural laws and order for a prosperous agricultural kingdom.

The subsequent twenty-one sections develop these themes. Rights and duties are declared to be permanent and in existence from the dawn of society. The former comprise freedom to provide for subsistence and ownership of property; the later imply respect for the freedom and property of others (§I). Perpetuation of the species requires production, combining labour, capital advances and landed property. The fruits of production are the only incentive to acquire, and to work property (§II). Capital advances are subdivided into landed advances, original advances and annual advances whose nature needs to be explained (§III). Product over and above the annual replacement of the advances is net product, which belongs to the owner of the land. This net product is the source of all human prosperity (§IV). Competition and security of property ensures the continuation of this process in the most effective manner (§V), preconditions which can only be guaranteed through the institutions of society (§VI–VII). Sovereign authority therefore enforces rather than creates the laws which govern society, assisted in this enforcement by a separate magistrature (§VII–XI), public instruction on the natural law (§XII), the costs of which are to be met from taxation (§XIII). Taxation has its own natural order, summarised by the proposition that only the net product can contribute to taxation if the country is not to stagnate, making state and landowner co-proprietors of the national landed wealth and guaranteeing their mutual interest in the natural order. The natural order therefore also defines the nature of the sovereignty of the monarch (§XIV–XIX). A hereditary monarchy, the only natural form of sovereignty, has therefore a self-evident interest in seeing the net product as large as possible, something which can only be secured by obedience to the natural law and submission to the natural order (§XX). The last is summarised in the final section (§XXI, esp. pp. 30–1) and the institutions of natural order there outlined conform to the inalienable and eternal human rights of freedom and property. Such, Du Pont concludes his outline of the new science of physiocracy, are the 'paramount truths' of 'physiocratic government' (p. 33), unassailable because self-evident. This is the ABC of physiocracy, resembling the later ABCs of socialism and communism published in the early twentieth century. It is a powerful performance of simplification and abstraction of the complex notions and theories of Quesnay, as partly enshrined in the work of Mercier de la Rivière.

Notes

1 As number 7 in Reprints of Economic Classics, series 2 (Sydney: Centre for the Study of the History of Economic Thought, 1995). All references in the text are to this version of Du Pont's essay.

2 That is, Voltaire's *Homme aux quarante écus*, published in 1768, which devastatingly criticised the physiocratic notion of the single tax on land rent as a form of unjust taxation; and Galiani, *Dialogues sur le commerce des bléds*, published in 1770 which, in a witty dialogue, cast doubt on the practicality and value of one of the other major physiocratic policies, the free trade in corn as a means to overcome the hardships caused by periodic harvest failures. Although there were other important critics of physiocracy at this time, such as, for example, Mably, it was perhaps the humour of Voltaire and Galiani that effectively destroyed the brief popular and fashionable appeal physiocracy enjoyed in French society (cf. Jacob Viner, *Essays in the Intellectual History of Economics*, ed. D. A. Irwin, Princeton: Princeton University Press, 1989, pp. 33, 34, 229–30, 314).

3 See Adam Smith, *An Inquiry into the Nature and Causes of the Wealth of Nations*, eds R. H. Campbell and A. S. Skinner, Oxford: Clarendon Press, 1976, p. 679; James Mill, 'Economists', *Supplement to the Fourth, Fifth and Sixth editions of the Encyclopaedia Britannica*, Edinburgh: Archibald Constable and Company, 1824, vol. 3, pp. 705–24.

4 Versions were published in other places, ostensibly including Yverdon, Amsterdam as well as Paris, perhaps simultaneously.

5 That is, Eugene Daire, *Physiocrates*, Paris: Guillaumin, 1843, vol. I, pp. 334–6.

6 That is, P. S. Dupont de Nemours, *De l'origine et des progrès d'une science nouvelle*, edited with an introduction by A. Dubois, Paris: Paul Geuthner, 1909.

7 That is, Pierre Samuel de Pont de Nemours, *De l'origine et des progrès d'une science nouvelle*, facsimile reprint, Textes économiques français du XVIIIe siècle, choisis et presentés par Gino Longhitano, Catania: CUECM, 1992.

8 J. R. McCulloch, *The Literature of Political Economy*, London: Longman, Brown, Green and Longmans, 1845, pp. 9–10.

9 Charles Gide and Charles Rist, *A History of Economic Doctrines*, trans. R. Richards, London: Harrap, 1949, ch. 1, pp. 21–68.

10 James J. McLain, *The Economic Writings of Du Pont de Nemours*, Newark DE: University of Delaware Press, 1977, p. 86.

11 Selections from the Turgot-Du Pont de Nemours correspondence are included in Reprint no. 6, *Turgot: Extracts from his Economic Correspondence* ed. P. D. Groenewegen, Sydney: Centre for the Study of History of Economic Thought, 1992.

12 Turgot to Du Pont de Nemours, 20 February 1766, in *Turgot: Extracts from his Economic Correspondence*, *op. cit.*, pp. 3–12.

13 Turgot to Du Pont de Nemours, 18 November 1767, in *Turgot: Extracts from his Economic Correspondence*, *op. cit.*, pp. 22–3.

14 See James J. McLain, *The Economic Writings of Du Pont de Nemours*, Newark DE: University of Delaware Press, 1977; Manuela Albertone, *Fisiocrati, istruzione, cultura*, Turin: Einaudi Foundation, 1979, ch. 5, pp. 95–130; *La pensée économique pendant la revolution française*, eds Gilbert Faccarello and Philippe Steiner, Presses

Universitaires de Grenoble, 1990, esp. the chapters by Bernard Delmas and Thierry Demals (pp. 123–40) and M. Albertone, 'Le crédit public en France et la naissance des assignats', pp. 405–29.

15 Reflections on Pietro Verri's political economy[1]

This paper offers observations on Verri's *Meditazioni sull'economia politica*, derived from my recent experience as its editor and co-translator into English, and that gained as a student of eighteenth-century economic thought in England, France and Italy for over a quarter century. In addition, Verri's *Meditazioni* have much to offer to the student of public finance, my other major research interest, because a substantial part of this work was devoted to that *scienze della finanza* to which Italian economists have so extensively contributed over the centuries (see Buchanan, 1960).

This paper draws largely on the English edition of Verri's *Meditazioni* I helped to prepare[2] and offers brief observations on the following matters. First, Verri's work on economics following his introduction to the subject is briefly examined to illuminate the extent of his preliminary studies. Second, the major sources of Verri's economics are identified and some comment is presented on the similarity between these sources and those available to some of the other major economic thinkers of the late eighteenth century. Third, some theoretical highlights of Verri's mature work are considered before looking by way of conclusion at a number of historical issues in relation to Verri as an important eighteenth-century economist. These address in particular eighteenth-century reactions to Verri's work, posing some problems on which Italian scholars may be able to shed further light; his lack of recognition in the nineteenth century in England, and finally, whether, as some have argued, it is appropriate to describe Verri as the Italian Turgot or Smith.

It may be noted at the outset that I regard Verri's work as a great and very important contribution to the classical political economy tradition, though his *Meditazioni* also exhibit what might be called neo-classical traits, on which I comment only briefly. In any case, his work is clearly one of the many examples in the economic literature which during the quarter century after 1750 marks the emergence of political economy as a separate science.

I

Verri was introduced to the study of economics by the enigmatic General Henry Lloyd, whose career has been examined in detail by Venturi (1979). Lloyd's importance for understanding Verri's later career clearly arises from his interests in mathematical economics which were shared by Verri, his emphasis on the usefulness of general inquiry into the progress and development of civil society, and his strong influence on Verri's decision to make himself a useful member of that society by becoming an enlightened reformer. Verri's early steps in educating himself in the science of civil society were guided by four eighteenth-century intellectual giants of the enlightenment: Montesquieu, Voltaire, Rousseau and Helvétius. In combination, these particularly informed his emerging views on law and civil society, the importance of historical understanding, his utilitarian tendencies and, more specifically, economic issues associated with trade, money, credit and taxation. More specifically with respect to his economic education, Verri by 1760 seems to have closely studied Forbonnais' *Elémens du commerce* together with that author's French editions of King's *The British Merchant* and Uztariz's *Theory and Practice of Commerce*; the accounts of Law's famous system of money and credit by Melon and Du Tot, and perhaps most importantly, Hume's philosophical essay and history of England. All of these sources are reflected in Verri's mature economic work of the *Meditazioni*, particularly the work by Hume. By the end of 1760 Verri had prepared his first economic work, *Degli elementi del commercio*, whose introductory remarks refer to the new science of political economy as a science of wealth and power particularly relevant to the legislator and other servants of the state.

During the 1760s, in many ways his most productive decade as an original economic thinker, Verri greatly developed his economic skills and increased his economic publications. In the first place, he produced a number of works on monetary issues (recently edited with a splendid introduction by Alberto Quadrio Curzio and Roberto Scazzieri, 1986) as well as detailed investigations of the economic and commercial conditions of the Milanese state, most of which were not published till later in his life or posthumously. In 1763, he published anonymously his *Meditazioni sulla felicità*, with its utilitarian overtones undoubtedly inspired by his early study of Helvétius, its comments on the association between wealth creation, incentives and motivations inspired by self-interest and duty, and the historical remarks on the development of civilised society reminiscent of the opening passages of the later *Meditazioni sull'economia politica*. All this shows a breadth of vision on Verri's part far wider than contemporary neo-classical perspectives on such issues. In 1764, there followed an essay on luxury (*Considerazioni sul lusso*) dealing with sumptuary laws, equality and incentives in production, themes which were also dealt with in the *Meditazioni sull'economia politica*, and in the interesting *Memorie storiche sull'economia pubblica nello stato di Milano* written in 1768 but not published till much later. Most importantly from the perspective of this chapter, he published in 1769 what can be described as a veritable dress rehearsal for the *Meditazioni*: *Riflessioni sulla legge vincolante principalmente nel commercio dei grani*, of which the first part enunciated many of the general principles covered in more detail in the later work.

The above-mentioned economic writings were combined with practical reform measures on fiscal issues such as tax farming, tariff reform and trade policy, in which Verri became increasingly involved from the mid-1760s onwards. These produced important studies and memoranda on the need for reform based on general principles and supported by facts and figures, as well as the eventual abolition of tax farming in Milan and major internal and external tariff reforms (for details see Venturi, 1969; 1987). This reformist zeal, and the general principles on which it was based and enunciated in the *Meditazioni* in a systematic manner, form the basis for claims that he can be aptly described as the Italian Turgot or Smith.

II

Verri's *Meditazioni sull'economia politica* contain no references whatsoever to the literature used in its preparation, nor mention by name any of the authorities to whom Verri refers in refuting or supporting their propositions. This contrasts sharply with Verri's practice in his other economic writings on economics, particularly the 1769 *Riflessioni* with its copious references to the literature. This change may be explained by the fact that Verri wrote the *Meditazioni* in less than a month (see Venturi, 1978) and in this respect it therefore more closely resembles Turgot's *Réflexions* (1766) than Smith's carefully prepared *Wealth of Nations*, the writing of which took well over a decade. However, examination of the pre-1770 work of Verri and Verri's extensive correspondence provides detailed evidence of the English, French and Italian economic literature with which he appears to have been acquainted (Groenewegen, 1986, pp. xiii–xxiii).

Verri was first of all acquainted with many of the Italian writings on economics. He cited material by Davanzati, Montanari, Carli, Genovesi, Pagnini, Tavanti and Neri, as well as work by his friend Beccaria. However, and highlighting the dangers of this method in researching influence, there are at least two important omissions from this list. The first and most important is undoubtedly Ferdinando Galiani's *Della Moneta*, which first appeared in 1751, although this absence of citation may be explained by the fact that the work was originally published anonymously and that Galiani had only publicly made his name in economics by 1770 when he published his *Dialogues sur le commerce des blés*.[3]. It seems equally surprising that Verri was unacquainted with Antonio Serra's classic work on money and trade (cf. Quadrio Curzio and Scazzieri, 1986, pp. 31–3).

Verri's acquaintance with French economics was also impressive. His early study of the major work by Montesquieu, Forbonnais, Melon and Du Tot has already been noted. By the end of the 1760s these authors can be supplemented by Savary's *Le négociant français*, Dupré de Saint-Maur on money, Cantillon's *Essai*, Boisguilbert's *Détail de la France*, Vauban's *Dîme royale*, Mirabeau's *Théorie de l'impôt* and a very substantial amount of French writings on the grain trade, including Herbert on the *Police générale des grains*, Du Pont's *De l'exportation et de l'importation des grains* and Baudeau's *Avis au peuple sur son premier besoin*. Impressive and comprehensive though this listing is, it raises at least two puzzles.

As revealed by his citation practices, Verri only showed a very limited knowledge of the major physiocratic literature of the time, particularly the writings of Quesnay, Mercier de la Rivière and Mirabeau's *l'Ami des Hommes* and *Philosophie rurale* with their important analytical contributions by Quesnay. It can be assumed that like Beccaria (see Groenewegen, 1983, pp. 51–2 and n20) Verri knew of Quesnay's *Encyclopédie* articles, while there is evidence in the *Meditazioni* (Groenewegen, 1986, pp. 60 n30, 107 n63) that his acquaintance with Mercier de la Rivière's major work is probably a safe assumption. Verri's apparent lack of detailed knowledge of Mirabeau's major economic work is all the more surprising because Longhi, one of Verri's associates from the *Il Caffè* days (1763–5) had corresponded with Mirabeau (Venturi, 1969, p. 674).

Equally surprising is Verri's lack of knowledge at this or at a later stage of Turgot's work, although the period covered by the citations was of course before Turgot's period of greatest European fame when finance minister from 1774 to 1776. Two matters may be particularly noted here. Verri shared a number of Turgot's more intimate friends, including Morellet, Trudaine and Condorcet, the first of whom sent him his prospectus for an economic dictionary while the third corresponded with Verri on price theory. In addition, Turgot's activities as intendant during the period of harvest failure at the end of the 1760s, ought to have been familiar to Verri from his extensive reading of the French literature of the period. Equally surprising is the fact that Turgot's huge library (see Tsuda, 1974) contains no copies of Verri's work, unlike the library of Adam Smith, which contained the 1772 Livorno edition of the *Meditazioni* (Bonar, 1932, p. 190).

Verri's familiarity with English economic writings came largely through translations, either into Italian (for example, Genovesi's translation of Cary) or more generally into French. Verri's use of Forbonnais' rendition of King's *British Merchant* has been mentioned, as has his solid knowledge of Hume's major writings on history, economics and philosophy. In his early writings, Verri cited Gresham, Locke and Newton on monetary subjects, and in addition made references to the work of Bacon, Culpeper, Child (on the abatement of interest), Davenant, Mandeville, Robert Wallace (on population), Cary, Decker and Nickolls (on trade).

Citations reveal that Verri was well versed in the economic literature of the time and that his knowledge of the subject as indicated by his potential sources was very similar to those used by Turgot, Steuart, Smith and his compatriot and friend, Beccaria (see Groenewegen, 1983, pp. 47–53, Table 1.3 above). This again reinforces the proposition that the advances in the construction of economic treatises from the end of the 1760s were made possible by the available accumulation of knowledge on the subject amassed in three countries over the previous century or so. In particular, this crucial period in the emergence of economics as a separate science owed much to the work of the major contributors whom Turgot had identified in the 1770s as crucial to this process: Montesquieu, Hume, Cantillon, Quesnay and Gournay; the first four of whom were a shared legacy among all the among economic treatise writers from this period (Groenewegen, 1987).

III

In a letter written to Verri (November 1771), Condorcet summarised the thrust of Verri's *Meditazioni* which Verri had sent him, in terms of the two leading principles which Verri had so clearly established in this work. First, Verri clearly identified the interest of the ruler with leaving every freedom consistent with the constitution to his people; second, Verri demonstrated that wise laws and just administration were the best means to increase annual reproduction, and hence the strength and revenue of the state. This identified the core of the new science of political economy, as Verri had first formulated it as early as 1760 in his *Elementi del commercio*, and as he reiterated it in the preface to the sixth Livorno edition of the *Meditazioni* in 1772. Aspects of this general view of political economy can be further elucidated.

Verri defined the objectives of political economy in a variety of ways in the text of the *Meditazioni*. In §V, for example, the operations of political economy are described as actions to promote industriousness within a people thereby increasing population, resources, national strength and reproduction, a set of actions summarised by a general policy prescription to increase the number of sellers relative to that of buyers (pp. 19–20, cf. p. 36).[4] Verri subsequently gives these aims an almost marginalist flavour (reminiscent, for example, of Jevon's *Theory of Political Economy*) when the economic problem is alternatively defined as:

> to increase annual reproduction as much as possible with the least possible labour, or, given the amount of labour, maximum effect in terms of reproduction, or, given the amount of reproduction, obtain it with the minimum of labour.

These operations by which Verri summarised the problem of political economy (p. 66) were turned by Verri's friend Frisi into simple maximisation/minimisation problems subject to solution by the calculus (Theocharis, 1961, p. 33).

The aim of political economy to increase national power, strength and happiness is achievable through increased population, incentives to labour, increased production and an appropriate balance between it and consumption (an alternative way, as shown subsequently, by which Verri described his general policy principle of reducing buyers relative to sellers). Success in achieving this policy objective can be measured by at least three different means in the absence of reliable national output data, as Verri indicates at various points in his treatise. These are the balance of trade, which he regarded as an imperfect measure; the level of the rate of interest, which he saw as a better measure, and population size and characteristics, which he saw as the best measure because it could be most accurately measured.

Verri considers the study of finance to be a part of the science of political economy (§XXIX) even though it is guided by somewhat different principles. This may be illustrated by the fact that direct laws are seen as useless in promoting the aims of political economy, while such laws and regulations are seen as absolutely essential in financial administration. However, the operations of finance, that is, public expenditure and taxation, should interfere as little as possible with the achievement of maximum reproduction, the aim of political economy.

The structure of Verri's Meditazioni

Given these considerations, the structure of the *Meditazioni* can be best indicated by dividing it into its three parts. The first, covering the first five sections, presents the general principles of the science by explaining economic development and growth, circulation, production, exchange, money and prices in general terms. These general principles are supplemented and elucidated in §§XIII, XIV and XVII on money, industry, interest and circulation and §XXI on population. Part II then applies these principles to a number of policy questions in political economy: the distribution of landed property (§VI), guilds and other forms of restrictive practices through privilege (§§VII, X), price controls (§§XII, XV), controls over sales (§§VIII, IX), sumptuary laws (§XI) and some observations associated with population (§§XXII–XXVI) and agriculture (§§XXVII–XXVIII). Part III presents the theory of finance (§§XXIX–XXXVII) while the last three sections act as a sort of summary of the policy implications of the material presented.

Space allows only a discussion of the general principles and theoretical model on which Verri's argument depends. This stresses the interdependence between population, reproduction, consumption, circulation, money and trade and exchange (buyers and sellers) in a model of cumulative causation. Verri's model can be seen as a growth model, with major emphasis on demand factors identified with monetary growth and circulation and little emphasis on the reproductive process itself. The model is unfortunately never completely articulated and it is not easy to interpret formally. Verri generally expresses his argument in terms of two basic ratios or balances, production and consumption, buyers and sellers, which in some situations seem to be taken as equivalents. This can be explained further.

In §III Verri relates the proportion between annual production and consumption to growth and stagnation via the trade balance and the rate of accumulation, since both the tradeable surplus and the volume of savings depend on this relationship. When annual domestic consumption is below annual reproduction, growth occurs from both the stimulus of trade and accumulation; when the two are equal, the economy is stationary; and when over a period of time, consumption exceeds production, the economy stagnates and declines. This notion of a balance between reproduction and consumption was of course not uncommon in late eighteenth-century economic literature, underlying for example, Quesnay's analysis of economic growth. It may be noted, however, that in Verri's *Meditazioni* it is not supplemented by any analysis of capital accumulation which highlights its benefits for output growth and higher productivity.

In addition, Verri makes much use of a ratio of buyers and sellers which acts as a proxy in the determination of various key variables in the system. It is introduced in §IV (Verri, 1771, esp. pp. 15–16) as a simple explanation for price determination and the benefits of competition, when under simplifying conditions the number of buyers are related, if not identified, with the quantity demanded, and the number of sellers with the quantity on offer or available supply. Many sellers, *ceteris paribus* a sign of competition, is associated with the benefit of low price. Second, the ratio is used as a proxy for determining the value of money on quantity theory grounds. The number of buyers is then seen as reflecting aggregate monetary demand (money supply and velocity of circulation), the number of sellers represents the volume of transactions so that buyers/sellers determine the price level and sellers/buyers the value of money. Third, the ratio has implications for the trade balance, since a high domestic seller/buyer ratio indicates a large tradeable surplus, while a high total buyer/seller ratio (where total buyers reflect aggregate domestic and foreign demand and sellers reflect domestic supply) indicates the size of the tradeable surplus in value terms. Finally, if domestic buyers are interpreted as a proxy for annual consumption, while aggregate domestic sellers reflect annual reproduction, the two ratios underlying Verri's analysis become equivalents.

The issue is complicated by the interdependence of buyers and sellers in a dynamic situation, where gradual increases in buyers (aggregate demand, sometimes interpreted in terms of increased money supply, which in turn can reflect increased foreign demand) generates increased incentives for production by increasing both the size of the market and the price. The ratio of buyers to sellers also guides much of the policy discussion, partly because Verri displays a general preference for increasing the number of sellers rather than lowering the number of buyers, as the former is more easily achieved by removing restraints on trade and production. Furthermore, the reduction of buyers would have a depressing effect on economic activity, since Verri stresses the expansionary effects from increased buyers via gradual expansion of the money supply and its effects on activity levels. In assessing the gains from circulation though a steady monetary inflow from trade, the enhanced reproduction is on one occasion linked to technical progress and increased productivity (Verri, 1771, p. 44). The influence of Law, Melon, Du Tot, Cantillon and even Hume is shown in this argument, since Verri does not regard money as a veil but as a positive influence on output and activity levels.

A number of more general problems in this analysis can be highlighted. First, the price analysis based on supply and demand is linked implicitly to an analysis of fundamental price or necessary cost of production on some occasions. However, this classical feature of the price analysis is not very explicitly developed. Second, the lack of emphasis on capital in the theory of production has already been noted, and this is reflected in the emphasis on the importance of population in an almost Cantillon-like manner. However, low interest is associated with increased opportunities to embark on capital-intensive projects such as irrigation projects, canal construction and land improvement (Verri, 1771, pp. 46–7). Verri's *Meditazioni* also contain no theory of distribution, whether conceived as an analysis of wage, profit or rent determination or as an analysis of the shares of output going to classes of society, that is, labourers, capitalists and landlords. In fact, when classes are discussed, in §XXIV, it is in terms of occupational groupings of producers, middle-men, consumers, administrators and so on.

Although aspects of his theory of public finance could also be highlighted, enough has been said to indicate the major theoretical features of Verri's work. Verri's *Meditazioni* contain a systematic presentation of the main features of political economy interpreted as a science of government and legislation, designed to enhance the wealth and strength of the nation through increased reproduction, trade and population. Many of the more specific aspects of these aims still reflect what may be described as mercantilist concerns. However, the policy by which these aims are to be achieved is liberal and free trade oriented, emphasising the importance of reduced regulation and restraints on trade and a positive role for government in setting the scene for faster economic development. This policy perspective places Verri with Smith, Turgot, the physiocrats and other enlightened economists of the period; analytically his framework is less developed, particularly with respect to price, production and distribution theory. However, this shortcoming in the argument may be explicable in terms of the lower stage of economic development in Italy as compared with that reached in France, and more importantly, England.

IV

When it first appeared in 1771, Verri's *Meditazioni* was well received. Much of this initial reaction to the book has been carefully documented by Venturi (1978). This discusses the Italian criticism from Carli, Frisi and Greppi, the reviews of the book which appeared in Italy and France, and the praise combined with tempered criticism in Condorcet's correspondence with Verri. It is difficult to improve on Venturi's fine account of this matter, apart from raising a few queries about aspects of these eighteenth-century reactions, on which, unfortunately, it is impossible at this stage to provide conclusive answers. These queries relate respectively to an Italian, a French and a Scottish reaction.

The first of these queries concerns what seems to me to be the substantial influence Verri must have had on Filangieri's work, the *Science of Legislation* (1780). Say (1880, p. xxxvii) argued for example, that the 'principles Verri laid down are followed by Filangieri, and even received from him a more complete development'. It is well known that Verri greatly praised Filangieri's work on its publication (Filangieri, 1780, p. 166) perhaps because so much of its argument resembled his own views in the *Meditazioni* both with respect to the general objectives of economic legislation and political economy, and, more specifically, in the details of particular policy proposals concerning taxation, public expenditure, the benefits of small-scale land ownership and the advantages of population growth. In addition, Filangieri's (1780, pp. 172–3) views on the natural progress of wealth from agriculture to manufactures to commerce, the associated hierarchy of employments and the limited but important role of government in this process, are reminiscent of Verri's views. Likewise, their emphasis on the limited nature of economic freedom and the positive duties for government this entails by removing excess or redundant regulations and providing essential infrastructure, is too similar to be mere coincidence. It would be interesting to know what supporting evidence there is for such a hypothesis, since Say's views on the matter are suspect for reasons indicated below.

A second puzzle is associated with the conflicting evidence on Voltaire's supposed reaction to Verri's book. De Felice (1964, p. 127) reports Voltaire's description of Verri's *Meditazioni* as 'the truest, wisest and clearest' book he had ever read on the subject of political economy, but no letter from Voltaire to Verri or any other similar reference to Verri's work can be found in the standard collected edition of Voltaire's works. However, Caspari (1980, p. 662) mentions Voltaire's thanks to Verri for sending him a copy of the *Meditazioni*, dating it precisely at 19 March 1772 on the authority of Mauri (1929, p. 240 and note). Given what is known about Verri's wide distribution of his book to friends and acquaintances (Venturi, 1978, p. 532) and what is known of Verri's great admiration for Voltaire (cf. Caspari, 1980, pp. 361, 375–6, 609), it would be interesting to discover whether Verri had in fact sent his *Meditazioni* to Voltaire and what other reactions this produced from the sage of Ferney.

Finally, what were Smith's reactions to Verri's work? It has already been noted that Smith owned a copy of the sixth Livorno edition of the *Meditazioni*, while his reading ability in Italian is well documented. In 1866, the Dutch economist Pierson, in a review of the Custodi edition in the Dutch *Economist*, argued that it would not surprise him if Smith, whose work did not appear till 1776, may have been substantially indebted to Verri's book for the clear insights into the deficiencies of systems of protection which it contained (Pierson, 1866, p. 95). With equal justice, it can be argued that there are strong resemblances between Verri's discussion of the duties of the state (Verri 1771, pp. 76, 83, 107) and those of Smith, just as there are basic similarities between Verri's five principles of taxation (§XXX) and the four, more famous, taxation canons presented by Smith. However, there is one passage in the *Wealth of Nations* (Smith, 1976, pp. 497–8) where the striking resemblance of language may be more than coincidence, and which echoes essentials of Verri's argument on the balance of produce and consumption. Although Smith strongly differentiated the balance of production and consumption from the balance of trade (an implicit but direct criticism of Verri?), its importance for the 'prosperity or decay of every nation' is strikingly acknowledged. Perhaps Verri may therefore be added to the list of authors whose work was used as one of the many sources for the patient inquiry into the nature and causes of the wealth of nations conducted by Smith in the 1760s and 1770s.

Although praised by Say (1880, p. xxxvi) as the author who most closely approached correct laws of production, distribution and consumption before Adam Smith,[5] and by McCulloch as the most eminent of the Italian eighteenth-century economists, by the second half of the nineteenth century Verri was only a name in the English speaking world for those interested in the history of economics. The only exceptions to this in the twentieth century are Monroe (1923) and Schumpeter (1954). The same conclusion applies elsewhere if Italy is excepted. Marx praised some aspects of Verri's thought, but it was only the Dutch economist N. G. Pierson who appreciated the value of Verri's economic works and gave them critical praise (Pierson, 1866, pp. 43–6, 65–67, 75, 92–105). In the second edition of *The Encyclopaedia of Social Sciences*, Verri did not even rate a mention.

Finally, to what extent can Verri be called the Italian Turgot or Adam Smith? If such comparisons are worthwhile at all, it seems more reasonable to describe Verri as the Turgot of the Duchy of Milan than to liken him to the Scottish moral philosopher and economic writer. As already noted, there are resemblances between ideas of Smith and Verri, but parallels in career between Turgot and Verri are much more notable. Both were heavily involved in issues of practical administration after a decade of study during which most of the major new ideas were formulated. Both were greatly interested in tax reform by way of rationalising and simplifying the tax system as it existed in their own countries, on reform of the guilds, sumptuary laws and legal regulation of interest rates. Even the major works they composed, as already noted, resemble each other in the haste in which they were written and the conciseness and elegance in which the thoughts and principles they contained were expressed. As also indicated, there are no reasons to believe that Verri had studied Turgot's *Réflexions*. Though Verri's argument on the effect of a low rate of interest on productive works (Verri 1771, pp. 46–7) is reminiscent of a similar passage in the *Réflexions* (1766, p. 88), this is probably coincidence when it is recalled that had he read Turgot's text, a coherent capital and distribution theory would not have been absent from his work. As Ferrara (1852, pp. XVIII, LXIII) noted, it is Verri's breadth of knowledge, rectitude of mind, untiring industriousness and purity of aims which ranks him with Turgot and other great reforming ministers. It is, furthermore, the 'moderation, order and tidiness of his thoughts, and the clarity in which he expressed them, which assures him, the decided superiority in any comparison with the other Italian economists of his time', thereby ranking him with the best economic writers of the world in that highly productive period at the end of the eighteenth century. Like his illustrious contemporaries, Verri produced in his *Meditazioni* a classic contribution to the new science of political economy.

Notes

1 Paper presented at a seminar at the Università Cattolica del Sacro Cuore in Milan on Tuesday, 17 May 1987. I am indebted to the participants at the seminar for improvements to the observations on Verri contained in the paper. I first studied Verri's economic writings when visiting the Istituto di Storia delle Dottrine Economiche at the Università degli Studi di Firenze in September/October 1976 at the invitation of Piero Barucci.

2 That is, Pietro Verri, *Reflections on Political Economy*, 1771, translated from the Italian by Barbara McGilvray in collaboration with Peter Groenewegen, edited with notes and an introduction by Peter Groenewegen, Reprints of Economic Classics, series 2, no. 4, Department of Economics, University of Sydney, Sydney 1986.

3 It is very likely that Verri was acquainted with this work when he wrote the *Meditazioni* (see Groenewegen, 1986, p. 32 n14, where some evidence is presented for such a proposition).

4 All page references to Verri's *Meditazioni* relate to my edition in English translation. There is a misleading translation of Verri in the opening paragraph of §XI (Verri, 1771, p. 36) which should speak of achieving the *best* possible domestic ratio of buyers to sellers and not the *highest* ratio.

5 In view of my argument that Verri did not have a theory of distribution, this statement by Say seems strange. Pierson (1866, p. 15 n1) cites Gioja's opinion that Say did not really understand Italian, in the context of his own criticism of Say on this point.

References

Bonar, James (1932) A *Catalogue of the Library of Adam Smith*, London: Macmillan.

Buchanan, J. M. (1960, 1983) 'La Scienza della Finanza: The Italian Tradition', in Peter Groenewegen and Joseph Halevi (eds) *Italian Economics Past and Present*, Sydney: Frederick May Foundation of Italian Studies, University of Sydney, 79–115.

Gaspari, Gianmarco (1980) *Viaggio a Parigi e Londra (1766–1767) carteggio di Pietro e Alessandro Verri*, Milan: Adelphi.

De Felice, Renzo (1964) Introduction and notes to Pietro Verri, *Del piacere e del dolore ed altri scritti di filosofia ed economia*, Milan: Feltrinelli.

Ferrara, Francesco (1852) Preface to *Trattati italiani del secolo XVIII, biblioteca dell'economista*, series 1, vol. III, Turin.

Filangieri, Gaetano (1780, 1976) *The Science of Legislation*, extracts reprinted from the English translations of the American Philosophical society, vol. 66, part 6, reprinted in P. L. Porta and A. Pellanda (eds) *Freedom and Community in the Italian Liberal Tradition*, for the Liberty Fund, Verona, May 1987.

Groenewegen, P. D. (1983) 'Turgot, Beccaria and Smith', in Peter Groenewegen and Joseph Halevi (eds) *Italian Economics Past and Present*, Sydney: Frederick May Foundation of Italian Studies, University of Sydney, 31–78 (above, Chapter 1).

——(1986) Introduction and notes to Pietro Verri, *Reflections on Political Economy 1771*, Sydney: University of Sydney, Department of Economics, Reprints of Economic Classics series 2, no. 4.

——(1987) 'The International Foundation of Classical Political Economy in the Eighteenth Century: An Alternative Perspective', in S. Todd Lowry (ed.) *Pre-Classical Economic Thought*, Boston MA: Kluwer, 211–20.

Mauri, A. (1929) *La dottrina economica di Pietro Verri*, Milan.

Monroe, A. E. (1923) *Monetary Theory before Adam Smith*, Boston MA: Harvard University Press.

Pierson, N. G. (1866, 1910) 'Bijdrage tot de geschiedenis der economische studien in Italië gedurende de 17e and 18e eeuw', *De Economist*, 451–558, reprinted in N. G. Pierson, *Verspreide Economische Schriften*, vol. II, ed. C. Verrijn-Stuart, Haarlem, 1–130.

Quadrio Curzio, Alberto and Scazzieri, Roberto (1986) Introduction to *Sul disordine delle monete a Milano nel settecento: Tre saggi di Cesare Beccaria e Pietro Verri*, Milan: Banca del Monte di Milano.

Say, J. B. (1880) *A Treatise of Political Economy, or the Production, Distribution and Consumption of Wealth*, Philadelphia: Claxton, Remsen and Haffelfinger.

Smith, Adam (1776, 1976) *An Inquiry into the Nature and Causes of the Wealth of Nations*, eds R. H. Campbell, A. S. Skinner and W. B. Todd, Oxford: Clarendon Press.

Theocharis, R. D. (1961) *Early Developments in Mathematical Economics*, London: Macmillan.

Tsuda, Takumi (1974) *Catalogue des livres de la bibliothèque de Turgot*, Tokyo: Hitotsubashi Institute of Economics.

Turgot, A. R. J. (1766, 1977) *Réflexions sur la formation et la distribution des richesses*, English translation in P. D. Groenewegen (ed.) *The Economics of A. R. J. Turgot*, The Hague, Martinus Nijhoff, 43–95.

Venturi, Franco (1969) *Settecento riformatore da Muratori a Beccaria*, Turin: Einaudi.

——(1978) 'Le *Meditazioni sull'economia politica* di Pietro Verri', *Rivista Storica Italiana*, 90(3) 530–94.

——(1979) 'Le avventure del Generale Henry Lloyd', *Rivista Storica Italiana*, 91(2–3) 369–433.

——(1987) *Settecento riformatore. L'Italia dei lumi (1764–1790)*, Turin: Einaudi.

Verri, Pietro (1771, 1986) *Reflections on Political Economy*, edited with an introduction by Peter Groenewegen, Sydney: Centre for the Study of the History of Economic Thought, Reprint series no. 4.

16 A re-appraisal of Turgot's theory of value, exchange and price determination

Although so important an authority as J. A. Schumpeter has stated that only the Turgot specialist should look beyond the 'Reflections' for his economic doctrines, those interested in Turgot's contribution to the general theory of value, exchange and price determination would miss a great deal of important material if they took Schumpeter's advice.[1] The 'Reflections' devote relatively little space to the analysis of value as such,[2] and although this contains the analysis of price determination as well as comments on the measure of value and the theory of exchange, it contains by no means the whole of Turgot's 'sophisticated treatment of value'.[3]

For Turgot, the theory of value was not only a matter of theoretical interest; it was also a matter of great practical importance, since its principles, in his opinion, would demonstrate the disadvantages of price regulation as well as the undoubted advantages of free trade. His detailed criticism of the regulation of interest rates and the grain trade, as well as his more general defence of laissez-faire, depended on the careful development of theoretical propositions which were intended to reveal the undesirable consequences of regulated markets and the benefits of free competition.[4] It is therefore not surprising that Turgot devoted a great deal of attention to the subject of value, exchange and price determination.[5]

Apart from the 'Reflections', Turgot presented an essentially subjective theory of value and exchange in his unfinished paper of 1769, 'Valeurs et monnaies';[6] he also dealt with the theory of value and exchange, especially that between present and future goods, in his 'Mémoire sur les prêts d'argent', which was written in the same year.[7] Finally, he presented an equilibrium analysis in the classical manner which connects market price and cost of production: this was put forward in a letter to Hume and in his 'Observations sur le mémoire de M. de Saint-Péravy'.[8] When these pieces on the theory of value are combined, an analysis emerges which can be regarded as a most important contribution on this subject in the eighteenth century.

It is the purpose of this chapter to reappraise Turgot's theory of value, exchange and price determination and to compare his contribution with those of the leading economists of the eighteenth century. The first section below will deal with value concepts as analysed and defined by Turgot, the second will deal with his remarks on the problem of value measurement, the third will deal with his theory of exchange and price determination, while the final section will present some conclusions on the importance of his contribution for the history of economic thought.

Foundations of the theory of value

The foundations for a general theory of value were painstakingly laid by Turgot in his paper 'Valeurs et monnaies'. In this paper, the basic definitions of the value concepts required for a theory of price determination are put forward in terms of subjective phenomena which find their origin in the work of Aristotle, of some of the scholastics, and of the Italians such as Lottini, Davanzati and Galiani.[9] This is illustrated in Turgot's very definition of the word 'value'. This word, he says,

> expresses the suitability relative to our needs by which the gifts and the goods of nature are regarded as fit for our enjoyment and for the satisfaction of our desires. … The adjectives *bad, mediocre, good, excellent* describe the different intensities of this type of *value*. It must be observed, however, that the noun *value* is not nearly as much used in this sense as the verb *to be worth* [*valoir*]. But if it is used, it can only be understood to mean the suitability of an object for our enjoyment. Although this suitability is always relative to ourselves, yet we have in view, when explaining the word *value*, a real quality which is intrinsic to the object and through which it is fit for our use.[10]

The intrinsic quality to which Turgot refers in this quotation is the usefulness (*utilité*) of the object. This quality, which is so essential to the value of an object, is, however, not 'susceptible to measurement' when considered apart from the usefulness of other objects.[11] Only when two objects are compared can this usefulness or intrinsic quality be measured, because then 'a person will be able to prefer one to the other, find an orange more agreeable than chestnuts, a fur better to keep out cold than a cotton garment'.[12] Value in this sense is therefore essentially relative; the value of an object can be discussed only with reference to another object through the expression of preference of one object over another.[13]

Value of this type is given the name 'esteem value' (*valeur estimative*), 'because it is in fact the expression of the degree of esteem which man attaches to the different objects of his desire'.[14]

Turgot argues that esteem value is influenced by three considerations. The first of these is the usefulness of a commodity for the satisfaction of a particular want, because for each type of want there are several commodities which can satisfy it with various degrees of efficiency. The second is the storability of the commodity; a more perishable commodity, even if it has the same efficiency in satisfying a want, is less convenient for the person whose want is to be satisfied.

The third consideration is 'the degree of difficulty which a man meets in procuring the objects of his desires'. This last is also referred to as the relative scarcity of the object.[15]

At this stage of the discussion, Turgot digresses from the main line of his argument in order to return to the question of the measurability of esteem value. This leads him to a variant of what Marshall was to call the real cost theory.[16] This argument is as follows.

To obtain objects for the satisfaction of his wants, man has only his strength and capacity. 'Each particular object of enjoyment costs him cares, fatigue, labour, or, at least, time'. These form, 'as it were, the price of the object'. Nature supplies isolated man with nothing, 'unless he pays for it by his labor, the use of his ability, and his time'.[17] This suggests that the measure of value for an isolated man is that proportion of his resources of labour, abilities and time, which he has to surrender in order to obtain the object which can satisfy his wants. In other words, the value of a commodity is measured by the labour and time given up to obtain it.[18]

So far the concept of value for only an isolated man has been considered. With the introduction of exchange and commerce, esteem value merges with a more general concept which can be regarded as an average of individual esteem values. This concept is variously called 'appreciative value', 'exchange value', 'current price' and 'mean price',[19] terms which Turgot appears to treat as synonyms. It is the equilibrium price resulting from a process of isolated exchange and 'is essentially of the same nature as esteem value'.[20] Elsewhere it is defined as the price 'which is established by the relationship between supply and demand'.[21]

Turgot introduces one other concept into his discussion: 'fundamental value'. This is defined as 'what the thing costs to him who sells it, that is, the raw material costs, the wages of his labour, and the profits of his stock'.[22] Fundamental value has the characteristic of being relatively stable as compared with exchange value, and appears to have the function of minimum supply price or long-run equilibrium price. This is clearly expressed in the following argument:

> The fundamental value is fairly stable and changes less frequently than the exchange value. The latter is ruled by supply and demand; it varies with needs, and often a single event sufficies to produce very considerable and sudden fluctuations. It is not in any essential proportion to the fundamental value, but it has a tendency to approach it continually and can never move far away from it permanently. It is obvious that it cannot remain below it for a long time; for as soon as a commodity can be sold only at a loss, its production is discontinued until the resulting scarcity has again raised it to a price above its fundamental value. The price can similarly not be much above the fundamental value for any length of time, for the high price, implying high profits, would call forth the commodity and generate lively competition among the sellers. Now the natural effect of this competition

would be to lower the price until it again approaches the fundamental value.[23]

Turgot therefore put forward three different concepts of value, which are closely interrelated: esteem value, current price (which he also called appreciative value, exchange value or mean price) and fundamental value. Esteem value is the purely subjective evaluation of a commodity by an individual, and is based on the suitability and efficiency of a commodity in satisfying a particular want, as well as on its relative scarcity. In an exchange, individual esteem values are merged into a uniform current price, which is determined by competition or by supply and demand.[24] The current price, determined in the market, is in turn influenced by the fundamental value, or cost of production, since in a competitive market there can be no long-run divergence of the current price from fundamental value, as was shown in the quotation above. Esteem value determines current price, current price is limited by fundamental value under competitive conditions. As will be shown later, these three concepts occurred in the writings of earlier economists, but nowhere was their interrelationship more clearly illustrated than in Turgot's work.

Problems in value measurement

Apart from playing such an important part in the theory of the determination of relative prices, the concept of value is also important in that it conveys the possibility of value measurement and, therefore, of comparing commodities according to their value. This point is discussed by Turgot in connection with his theory of money,[25] and even though on his own admission[26] this discussion is not sufficiently detailed, it contains the essence of the problem of value measurement.

In his paper, 'Valeurs et monnaies', Turgot starts his discussion by posing the problem of discovering a standard or common term of measurement. This is the basic problem in the measurement of value, just as it is in the measurement of weight, volume, length, etc. 'The common term of all measures of length, area, or volume, is only the actual size, of which the different measures adopted by different people are but arbitrary divisions which can. … be compared and reduced to one another'.[27] Similarly, in value measurement the common term to be discovered is that of value itself.

Unlike measures of length, area and volume, which suggest their own useful common standard, a *useful* common standard for value measurement is more difficult to find. For an isolated man, concerned with valuing a single commodity, value 'is not susceptible to measurement', since it 'is not being compared with other values'.[28] In theory, a measure for valuing a single commodity can be found in terms of the 'time and trouble' required to obtain that commodity, relative to the isolated man's total resources of time and trouble. This is a type of 'real cost' measure, which Turgot explains as follows:

> What is here his measure of value? What is his scale of comparisons? It is obvious that he has no other than his actual resources [of time and trouble]. The total sum of these resources is the only unit of his scale, the only fixed point of departure, and the values which he attributes to each object are the proportional parts of this scale. It follows from this that the *esteem value* of an object, for the man in isolation, is precisely that portion of his total resources which corresponds to the desire he has for that object, or what he is willing to use to satisfy that desire.[29]

This particular solution to the problem is not satisfactory to Turgot. The method of measuring value in terms of 'real costs' is impossible in practice, because the unit of measurement is indefinite, because the measurement of 'time and trouble' hinges on so many questions and imponderables, and because it would involve 'a labyrinth of calculations, of which all the elements are indeterminate'.[30]

Turgot derives the following conclusions from these difficulties: 'It is impossible to express value in terms of itself; and all that human language can express in this regard is that the value of one thing equals the value of another'. The value of a commodity can be expressed only by reference to the value of another commodity.[31]

The problem of value measurement is therefore essentially that of pricing one commodity in terms of another, that is, the problem of exchange value. Once the current price has been established in an exchange, the value of one commodity can be expressed in terms of another. In an exchange of wine for corn, the price of a bushel of corn can be expressed as so many pints of wine, while the price of a pint of wine can be expressed as so many bushels of corn.[32]

In the same way it can be said that every commodity can be used as a measure of value. Any commodity can be valued in terms of wine or corn or sheep or anything else, after the exchange relationships have been determined.[33] Because some commodities – sheep, for example – vary in quality, convenience has designated as basic measures of value commodities which do not vary in quality, even though they do vary in quantity and therefore in value. These commodities are the metals, especially gold and silver, which can be refined to a high degree of purity and which can therefore serve as measures with a standard quality.[34]

This should not be taken to mean that Turgot regarded gold and silver as *perfect* measures of value. They themselves vary in value, both 'as compared with the other articles of Commerce and with one another'. He states this clearly:

> This value is susceptible to change, and in fact does change continually; so that the same quantity of metal which corresponded to a certain quantity of such or such a commodity ceases to correspond to it, and more or less money is needed to represent the same commodity. When more is needed, the commodity is said to be dearer, and when less is needed it is said to be

> cheaper; but one might just as well say that it is the money that is cheaper in the first case and dearer in the second. Not only do silver and gold vary in price as compared with all other commodities: they vary in price among themselves according as they are more or less abundant.[35]

Custom has therefore made money the acceptable measure of value, and convenience has made gold and silver the money of the world. Gold and silver share these properties with all other commodities, and have been selected as money and measures of value only because they are 'more divisible', 'easy to transport', and 'more unalterable' in quality. It is therefore for practical and not theoretical reasons that gold and silver are the measure of value and the units in which prices are expressed.[36]

Money, the practical measure, must therefore not be confused with the real measure of value, which is based on esteem value and on the virtually immeasurable degree or proportion of 'real costs' required.[37] 'Value' itself is the rigorously precise measure of value, which cannot be used for practical purposes; 'price', the monetary expression of exchange value, is the convenient and practical measure of value. This fundamental theoretical distinction between 'value' and 'price' was very clearly stated by Turgot.[38]

Unfortunately, Turgot drew no final conclusions from his discussions on the subject of the measure of value. The 'Reflections' was not the place for such a final conclusion,[39] while 'Valeurs et monnaies' would probably have dealt with the subject at length, had it been completed. I think, however, that it can be safely concluded that Turgot's conclusion in this connection would have been similar to that arrived at by Cantillon on this subject.[40] He would have argued that a perfect measure of value is impossible to find in practice; and that money, though imperfect, is the best practical measure that can be used for this purpose. Both sentiments are clearly expressed in his works. It may also be said that a general acceptance of these propositions would have saved a great deal of controversy on this topic in the following fifty years.[41]

Theory of exchange and price determination

Turgot solved the problem of price determination by means of his theory of exchange. In an exchange, whether isolated or multiple, individual esteem values are transformed into a current price or, as Turgot sometimes called it, an appreciative value, an exchange value, or a mean price. The theory of isolated exchange is discussed with a great deal of elegance in 'Valeurs et monnaies',[42] while the problem of multiple exchange is sketched in the 'Reflections'.[43] In these and in one other of his works Turgot dealt with no fewer than six different exchange situations, which can be listed as follows.

1 Exchange between two individuals of two commodities which have zero esteem value at the margin: the 'valueless surplus' commodities case
2 Isolated exchange proper: two individuals, two commodities

3 Isolated exchange: four individuals and two commodities[44]
4 Multiple exchange: many individuals, two commodities
5 Multiple exchange: many individuals and many commodities[45]
6 Intertemporal exchange: present against future goods[46]

Each of these cases has to be considered in turn.

Isolated exchange: 'valueless surplus' commodity case

Turgot's first case of exchange is based on certain assumptions. Assume two isolated individuals, A and B, who each own a single commodity. A owns more fish than he can use, so that he owns a valueless surplus of fish, since fish cannot be stored for long; B owns a large quantity of hides, more than he needs for shelter and clothing, so that he also owns a valueless surplus. With the possibility of exchange, these respective surpluses obtain value, since B is willing to exchange hides for fish, while A is willing to exchange fish for hides. Since in this case the valueless surpluses are exchanged, 'the discussion on the conditions of exchange will not be very animated; each would let the other take, one all the fish, the other all the hides, which he himself does not need'.[47] From the assumption that 'both are more than abundantly provided with the things they posses', Turgot concluded that only the surpluses will be exchanged and that these surplus quantities will determine the exchange ratio.[48]

This case is an interesting starting point for the analysis, because it is an extreme case of the gains derivable from exchange. Because both A and B are exchanging what are for them useless things (with no esteem value) for useful things (with positive esteem value), their gains must be great. The exchange ratio is of course indeterminate, since, without knowledge of the esteem value schedules of A and B, it cannot be concluded that only the surpluses will be exchanged and that A will stop exchanging fish for hides as soon as his fish have positive esteem value, and that B will stop exchanging hides for fish as soon as his hides have a positive esteem value.[49] Since this case is unrealistic, Turgot varied his assumptions for the second case.

Isolated exchange proper

In his second case, Turgot changed the assumptions by changing the commodities owned by A and B. A now owns the sole supply of corn, B the sole supply of firewood. He also assumed that this supply cannot be increased, so that for both, the whole stock of their respective commodity has positive esteem value. However, A needs firewood, as 'he is in danger of perishing for want of wood', while B requires corn if he is not to starve. Both therefore want some corn and some firewood, and exchange can take place.[50]

The exchange will come about on the basis of the subjective estimation of value which A and B place on their respective commodities. Turgot assumed that initially A values 3 units of corn at 6 units of wood, while B estimates the value of 6 units of wood as 9 units of corn. A overvalues corn, and B wood, and these overvaluations are the limits between which the final exchange ratio must fall:

> With this in mind, each will keep secret the mental comparison which he has made of the two interests, of the two values which he attaches to the commodities for exchange, and he will sound out the owner of the commodity he desires by lower offers and higher demands. Since the other will follow the same procedure, they will discuss the conditions of the exchange, and as they both have a great interest in coming to an agreement, they will finally do so. Slowly each of them will increase his offers and reduce his demands, until they finally agree to give a certain quantity of corn for a certain quantity of wood.[51]

Turgot assumed, as an example, that the final exchange ratio will be 4 units of corn for 5 units of wood. A has lowered his wood price for corn, while B has lowered his corn price for wood. Nevertheless, each will value the total quantity he receives more than the quantity he gives up. This is a necessary and sufficient condition for exchange or, as Turgot put it, 'the sole motive for it'. If people do not profit from an exchange, then the exchange will not take place. So far Turgot has derived two basic conclusions from his analysis: first, both gain from the exchange; second, the actual exchange ratio must lie between the esteem values of the two parties.[52]

At a later stage of the argument, Turgot attempted to provide a more precise solution to the determination of the exchange ratio in an isolated exchange. The exchange value, he argued, 'which is equal for the two objects exchanged, is essentially of the same nature as the *esteem value*. It differs from it only insofar as it is the *average* esteem value'.[53]

Turgot here appears to argue that given the individual esteem values in an isolated exchange, the exchange ratio can be determined by averaging the two esteem values, so that the exchange ratio is precisely midway between the limits based on those esteem values. With the given, original esteem values of A and B in this example, this would yield an exchange ratio of 1 unit of corn for 1 unit of wood.[54] In connection with isolated exchange, Menger has pointed out that this midway price will be established only 'if the two bargainers are otherwise equally situated'.[55] In view of later discussion on the subject of isolated exchange, where the problem was shown to be indeterminate, it is difficult to see what Menger means, especially as he does not explain what he means by the phrase 'otherwise equally situated'.[56] Turgot's midway price therefore cannot be described as a correct solution. Nevertheless, his discussion of the problem is a remarkable performance for an eighteenth-century economist.

Isolated exchange: four individuals and two commodities

The final case of exchange discussed by Turgot in the unfinished 'Valeurs et monnaies' is that of four individuals and two commodities. Besides A and B of the preceding analysis, Turgot assumes two further individuals: C, an additional corn owner, and D, an additional wood owner. A and B are assumed to have already determined an exchange ratio of 4 units of corn for 5 units of wood. What happens with the introduction of C and D?[57]

As an initial step in his solution, Turgot assumes that C and D conclude a separate bargain which yields an exchange ration of 5 units of wood for 2 of corn:

> Let us now bring our four men together, let us allow them to communicate, to learn of the condition offered by each of the owners, either of wood or of corn. It follows that he who would agree to give four bags of corn for five armfuls of wood will no longer be willing to do so when he discovers that one of the owners of wood agrees to give five armfuls of woods for only two bags of corn. But the latter, learning in turn that four bags of corn may be had for the same quantity of wood, will change his mind too, and will no longer content himself with two. ... The conditions of the projected exchange will thus be changed and a new evaluation will take place, a new appreciation of the value of wood and of corn.[58]

The result of this further evaluation of the corn owners and the wood owners will be a new exchange ratio which is equal for all parties. A will try to lower his corn price for wood, while D will try to raise his wood price for corn.[59] The paper unfortunately ends before a full solution for the final exchange ratio is offered. On the principles established previously, Turgot presumably would have argued that the new exchange ratio would be a midway price, based on averaging the esteem values of the four individuals. This would give a final ratio of 5 units of wood for 3 of corn. Again, the economic validity of this solution must be doubted, though Turgot's description of the exchange process is correct.

Multiple exchange: many individuals, two commodities

For Turgot's solution of the multiple-exchange problem for two commodities, his brief analysis in the 'Reflections' must be examined. Here it is the competition among the various sellers of the two commodities which determines the price through a series of offers and counter-offers:

> The value of corn and wine [the two commodities] is no longer debated between two isolated individuals in relation to their relative wants and resources; it is fixed by the balance of the wants and resources of the whole body of Sellers of corn with those of the whole body of Sellers of wine. For he who would willingly give *eight pints* of wine for a *bushel* of corn will only give four when he learns that an owner of corn consents to give *two bushels* of corn for *eight pints*. The price mid-way between the different offers and the different demands will become the current price, whereto all the Buyers and Sellers will conform in their exchanges; and it will be true to say that

> *six pints* of wine are the equivalent of *a bushel* of corn for everyone if that is the *mean* price, until a diminution of the offer on the one side or of the demand on the other causes this valuation to change.[60]

Once more, the basic solution to the problem of price determination is the same. In a two-commodity case, with 'perfect' competition, the exchange ratio (or current price) will be the average of all individual esteem values, that is, a 'mean price'. The reasoning and the conclusion are the same as in the other three cases.[61]

Multiple exchange: many commodities, many individuals

Turgot also presented some conclusions on multiple exchange proper, when many commodities are traded among many individuals. The general solution to this problem is not stated – presumably because such a complex analysis had no place in an elementary pamphlet like the 'Reflections'.[62] All that is available on this topic is the following paragraph:

> Corn is exchanged not only for wine, but for all other articles which the owners of corn may need; for wood, leather, wool, cotton, etc.: it is the same with wine and with every other kind of commodity. If *one bushel* of corn is the equivalent of *six pints* of wine, and *one sheep* is the equivalent of *three bushels* of corn, the same sheep will be the equivalent of *eighteen pints* of wine. He who having corn needs wine can, without inconvenience, exchange his corn for a sheep, in order afterwards to exchange this sheep for the wine he stands in need of.[63]

This is, unfortunately, the only contribution by Turgot on this subject, and presents therefore no solution. The only conclusion which can be derived from the quoted passage is that for general equilibrium in the market, the exchange ratios for pairs of commodities must be compatible.

Intertemporal exchange: present against future goods

The final exchange situation which Turgot analysed is the exchange of present for future goods, which, appropriately, is discussed in the 'Mémoire sur les prêts d'argent'. In this paper, Turgot argued that in ordinary exchange transactions equal values are exchanged for equal values through the establishment of a current price by competition.[64] In intertemporal exchange, especially in that of present money for future money, the issue is more complicated, since although the esteem values of the quantities of money exchanged will still be equal, the actual physical quantities of money metal exchanged will not be equal. This difference in the physical quantities which equalises the esteem values in intertemporal transactions is precisely the rate of interests. As Turgot put it:

> Is not this [physical] difference well known, and is not the trivial proverb, *a bird in the hand is better than two in the bush*, a naïve expression of this well-known fact? Now, if a sum actually owned is worth more, is more useful, is preferable to the assurance of receiving a similar sum in one or several years' time, it is not true that the lender receives as much as he gives when he does not stipulate interest, for he gives the money and only receives an assurance. Now, if he receives less, why is not this difference compensated by the assurance of an increase in the sum, proportional to the delay? This compensation is precisely the rate of interest.[65]

In this short paragraph, Turgot foreshadowed one of Böhm-Bawerk's three grounds for the existence of interest.[66] From the basis underlying exchange transactions – that is, individual esteem values – interest can be simply explained on the ground that the esteem value of a commodity today is generally higher than the esteem value of that commodity in the future. Interest has to be paid in order to equalize the intertemporal esteem value in this type of exchange transaction.[67] The solid foundation of Turgot's exchange theory is illustrated by his application of it to the problem of interest determination.

This completes the discussion of Turgot's theory of exchange. From the concept of esteem value – the basis for a theory of price determination – an analysis is presented for isolated, multiple and intertemporal exchanges. From this analysis Turgot correctly concluded that under competition the current price will be equal for all parties in the exchange. The solution to the problem of price determination presented by him, based on the concept of a midway price obtained by averaging individual esteem values, is of course not correct. Despite this shortcoming, the analysis can still be described as an important contribution to the theory of exchange and price determination.

Concluding remarks

Having outlined Turgot's general theory of value and price, I should like to place it in the context of eighteenth-century economics in order to appreciate the significance of his contribution. This can be done by comparing his value concepts and the analysis based on them with the contributions of some of his contemporaries and predecessors.

As indicated earlier, subjective considerations in the theory of value date back to Aristotle and the schoolmen, whose works Turgot would have been familiar with.[68] In the first half of the eighteenth century, Hutcheson had argued that 'difficulty of acquiring' and 'usefulness' jointly determined the exchange value of commodities, but Turgot may not have known the *System of Moral Philosophy* in which this analysis was contained.[69] Usefulness, in connection with the theory of value, had also been discussed by Galiani, Quesnay and Graslin, authors with whose work Turgot was familiar.[70] In Turgot's analysis, however, the concept is more fully discussed and its inherent difficulties are more fully appreciated.

The analysis of a competitive market also occurred in the seventeenth and eighteenth centuries. Locke and Law, in their then well known works, had discussed the role of demand in the process of price determination, while Cantillon had improved on their work by discussing the actual bargaining process in some detail.[71] Again, these authors were familiar to Turgot.[72]

Finally, the concept of fundamental value or cost of production was often used in value analysis. Cantillon and Harris, for example, discussed an intrinsic value concept based on land and labour costs;[73] Quesnay had defined the fundamental price of commodities as 'determined by the expenses or costs which have to be incurred in their production or preparation', and it is presumably from this source that Turgot obtained the name 'fundamental value'.[74] These three authors had also related market price to cost of production – Harris in almost as precise a manner as Turgot.[75]

In connection with the problem of value measurement, Cantillon's conclusions have already been cited as being comparable to those of Turgot.[76] There was, however, no other economist prior to Turgot who argued that the problem of value measurement was impossible to solve in a precise manner, because value itself was immeasurable. As is shown above, Turgot argued that the value of a commodity could be expressed only in terms of the value of another commodity or in terms of the 'labour and time' needed to acquire it, and neither of these could be accurately measured. Only money, despite its imperfections for this purpose, could serve as a practical measure of value.

Finally, there is the theory of exchange, the major contribution of Turgot on this subject. Here, as Kauder has shown,[77] he has no peer in eighteenth-century economics in the elegance with which the exchange models are developed. They resemble contributions of the neo-classical school much more than those offered by Turgot's contemporaries. The analysis, although wrong in attempting to solve the exchange problem by means of a midway price obtained by averaging esteem values, and clumsy and incomplete through lack of geometrical illustrations, stands as a tribute to Turgot's theoretical powers. Had his major contribution on this subject, 'Valeurs et monnaies', been completed, even greater praise might have been in order.

It can therefore be argued that Turgot's performance in this field deserves a recognition which it has not been accorded by the general commentators.[78] His theory of exchange is a fine analysis of price determination, while in the classical manner Turgot also shows that the competitive price determined in the market is limited to some degree by cost of production. The law of diminishing marginal utility is unfortunately missing, as is the concept of continuous esteem value functions. Despite these shortcomings, Turgot's theory can be safely called a brilliant achievement for an eighteenth-century economist.[79]

Notes

1 See J. A. Schumpeter, *History of Economic Analysis* (London, 1959) p. 248.

2 See A. R. J. Turgot, 'Reflections on the Formation and Distribution of Riches', ed. and trans. William J. Ashley (New York, 1963) paras 31–9.

3 R. L. Meek, *The Economics of Physiocracy* (London, 1962) p. 389, n1.

4 See 'Mémoire sur les prêts d'argent', in *Oeuvres de Turgot*, ed. E. Daire (Paris, 1844) 1:106–52, esp. 124–30; 'Lettres sur la liberté du commerce des grains', *ibid.*, 1:159–256, esp. 193–4; 'Eloge de Gournay', *ibid.*, 1:262–91, esp. 271–2; and, as early as 1754, in his 'Plan d'un ouvrage sur les commerce, la circulation, et l'intérêt d'argent, la richesse des états', in *Oeuvres de Turgot*, ed. G. Schelle (Paris, 1913–23) vol. 1, esp. pp. 382–5.

5 This also explains why Turgot did not analyse price determination under conditions of monopoly.

6 This (cited below as 'Valeurs') was written in 1769 for Morellet's proposed venture of a *Dictionnaire du commerce* of which only the prospectus was published. See E. Kauder, 'Genesis of the Marginal Utility Theory', *Economic Journal*, 63 (1953) p. 645, n3.

7 'Mémoire sur les prêts d'argent', in *Oeuvres de Turgot*, ed. E. Daire (Paris, 1844) esp. pp. 123–30, 141–4.

8 Turgot to Hume, 25 March 1767, reprinted in *Economic Writings of David Hume*, ed. E. Rotwein (London, 1955) pp. 102–13; 'Observations sur le mémoire de M. de Saint-Péravy', in *Oeuvres de Turgot*, ed. E. Daire (Paris, 1844) 1:418–33.

9 See E. Kauder, 'Genesis of the Marginal Utility Theory', *Economic Journal*, 63 (1953) pp. 638–45. Turgot was familiar with the work of Aristotle and with many of the scholastic writings. See 'Mémoire sur les prêts d'argent', in *Oeuvres de Turgot*, ed. E. Daire (Paris, 1844) pp. 122–24; he was also familiar with Galiani's treatise *Della moneta*, which is cited in 'Valeurs et monnaies'. See *Oeuvres de Turgot*, ed. E. Daire (Paris, 1844) 1:83.

10 'Valeurs et monnaies', in *Oeuvres de Turgot*, ed. E. Daire (Paris, 1844) p. 80.

11 *Ibid.*

12 *Ibid.*

13 This argument implies the rejection of the measurability of utility, and could be argued to foreshadow the essence of indifference analysis, which is concerned with the preference relationships between goods. In this sense, Turgot could be called an early 'ordinalist'. The passage also illustrates Turgot's failure to grasp marginalist-utility analysis, since he did not see the significance of the fact that utility is a function of the quantity held.

14 'Valeurs', p. 82. Turgot appears to consider esteem value as a ratio. Thus if a person esteems 3 units of commodity A as equal to 2 units of commodity B, his esteem value of A in terms of B would be 3:2, and of B in terms of A, 2:3. Cf. below, part III, where Turgot's theory of isolated exchange is discussed and where this concept of esteem value as a ratio is more clearly illustrated.

15 'Valeurs et monnaies', in *Oeuvres de Turgot*, ed. E. Daire (Paris, 1844) pp. 81–2.

16 Cf. Marshall, *Principles of Economics*, 8th edn (London, 1938) pp. 347ff; cf. also S. M. McVane, 'Analysis of Cost of Production', *Quarterly Journal of Economics* 1 (1887): 481–7, esp. 483.

17 'Valeurs et monnaies', in *Oeuvres de Turgot*, ed. E. Daire (Paris, 1844) pp. 82–3.

18 *Ibid.*, p. 83.

19 *Ibid.*, pp. 86–9; A. R. J. Turgot, 'Reflections on the Formation and Distribution of Riches', ed. and trans. William J. Ashley (New York, 1963) pp. 30–1.

20 'Valeurs et monnaies', in *Oeuvres de Turgot*, ed. E. Daire (Paris, 1844) p. 87.

21 Turgot to Hume, 25 March 1767, p. 211.

22 'Observations sur le mémoire de M. de Saint-Péravy', in *Oeuvres de Turgot*, ed. E. Daire (Paris, 1844) p. 431n; cf. Turgot to Hume, 25 March 1767, p. 211.

23 *Ibid.*, p. 431n.

24 The transformation of individual esteem values into a current price will be fully discussed in part III of this article, which deals with Turgot's theory of exchange.

25 'Valeurs et monnaies', in *Oeuvres de Turgot*, ed. E. Daire (Paris, 1844) esp. pp. 75–79; and A. R. J. Turgot, 'Reflections on the Formation and Distribution of Riches', ed. and trans. William J. Ashley (New York, 1963) pp. 30–42.

26 See 'Reflections', *op. cit.*, p. 41:

> A thousand different causes concur to fix at each moment of time the value of commodities when compared either with one another or with money, and to cause them to change incessantly. The same causes determine the value of money, and cause it to vary when compared, either with the value of each particular commodity, or with the totality of the other values which are actually in Commerce. It would not be possible to disentangle these different causes and to unfold their effects without going into very extensive and very difficult detail, and I shall abstain from entering upon that discussion.

27 'Valeurs et monnaies', in *Oeuvres de Turgot*, ed. E. Daire (Paris, 1844) p. 75.

28 *Ibid.*, p. 80.

29 *Ibid.*, p. 83.

30 *Ibid.*, p. 89; cf. pp. 90–1.

31 *Ibid.*, and cf. the remarks in notes 13 and 14 above.

32 A. R. J. Turgot, 'Reflections on the Formation and Distribution of Riches', ed. and trans. William J. Ashley (New York, 1963) pp. 29–31.

33 *Ibid.*, p. 31; and cf. 'Valeurs et monnaies', in *Oeuvres de Turgot*, ed. E. Daire (Paris, 1844) pp. 89f.

34 A. R. J. Turgot, 'Reflections on the Formation and Distribution of Riches', ed. and trans. William J. Ashley (New York, 1963) pp. 32–8.

35 *Ibid.*, pp. 40–1.

36 *Ibid.*, pp. 38, 39, 42.

37 'Valeurs et monnaies', in *Oeuvres de Turgot*, ed. E. Daire (Paris, 1844) pp. 88–90.

38 See *ibid.*, esp. p. 90.

39 The 'Reflections' was not intended as a detailed theoretical treatise, but as a handbook to a questionnaire handed by Turgot to two Chinese students in 1766. See Turgot to Du Pont, 9 Dec. 1766, 29 Nov. 1769, in *Oeuvres de Turgot*, ed. G. Schelle (Paris, 1913–23) 2:519, 3:72.

40 See R. Cantillon, *Essay on the Nature of Commerce in General*, ed. H. Higgs (London, 1959) p. 41. Cf. his remarks in ch. 17, part 1, esp. p. 111.

41 See Adam Smith, *An Inquiry into the Nature and Causes of the Wealth of Nations*, Modern Library (New York, 1937) book. 1, ch. 5, esp. pp. 32–7; T. Malthus, *Principles of Political Economy* (London, 1820) ch. 2, esp. §§4–8; D. Ricardo, *Principles of Political Economy and Taxation*, ed. Sraffa (Cambridge, 1953) esp. pp. 43–51. Ricardo arrived at the same conclusions as Turgot and Cantillon: a perfect measure could not be found in practice, and money is the best practical measure available despite its many obvious imperfections. Cf. also Cournot, *The Mathematical Principles of the Theory of Wealth* (Homewood IL, 1963) chs 2, 3, esp. pp. 19–24.

42 'Valeurs et monnaies', in *Oeuvres de Turgot*, ed. E. Daire (Paris, 1844) pp. 84–8, 92–3.

43 A. R. J. Turgot, 'Reflections on the Formation and Distribution of Riches', ed. and trans. William J. Ashley (New York, 1963) pp. 28–31.

44 These three cases are discussed in 'Valeurs et monnaies', in *Oeuvres de Turgot*, ed. E. Daire (Paris, 1844) pp. 84–8, 92–3. Turgot's analysis of isolated exchange proper is similar to that of Menger and Wicksell. See Carl Menger, *Principles of Economics* (Glencoe IL, 1950) pp. 194–7; K. Wicksell, *Lectures on Political Economy* (London, 1951) 1:49–51.

45 Cases 4 and 5 are discussed in A. R. J. Turgot, 'Reflections on the Formation and Distribution of Riches', ed. and trans. William J. Ashley (New York, 1963) pp. 29–31.

46 Case 6 is discussed in 'Mémoire sur les prêts d'argent', in *Oeuvres de Turgot*, ed. E. Daire (Paris, 1844) pp. 124–30.

47 'Valeurs et monnaies', in *Oeuvres de Turgot*, ed. E. Daire (Paris, 1844) p. 84.

48 *Ibid.*

49 Turgot appears to have assumed discontinuous esteem value schedules which show constant positive esteem value for one part of the total quantity owned by A or B, while the remainder is a valueless surplus. He does not seem to have had a concept of gradually diminishing esteem values, presumably because he did not see the problem geometrically. His schedules can be illustrated by a diagram (Figure 16.1). Here OT is the total quantity of fish or hides. OS has positive and constant esteem value; ST, the surplus, has zero esteem value, since S, the saturation point, has been reached. After trade, A gains ST hides, and B gains ST fish, with positive esteem value for them.

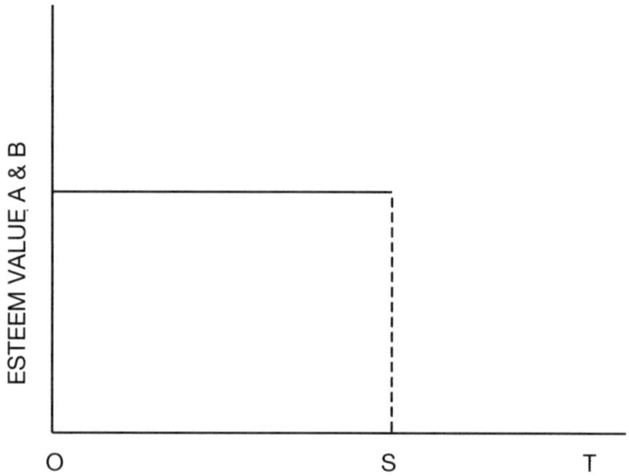

Figure 16.1 Turgot's esteem value schedules

50 'Valeurs et monnaies', in *Oeuvres de Turgot*, ed. E. Daire (Paris, 1844) p. 85.

51 *Ibid.*, p. 86.

52 *Ibid.* As stated in note 14 above, esteem value is a ratio based on the subjective comparison of the quantities of two commodities.

53 *Ibid.*

54 A's corn price for wood is ½, B's corn price for wood is 1½; this gives an exchange ratio of 1:1.

55 See Carl Menger, *Principles of Economics* (Glencoe IL, 1950) p. 196.

56 I.e. by Edgeworth and Wicksell. See F. Y. Edgeworth, *Mathematical Psychics*, LSE Reprint (London, 1932) pp. 43ff; 'The Pure Theory of Monopoly' in *Papers Relating to Political Economy* (New York, n.d.) 1:116–26; K. Wicksell, *Value, Capital and Rent* (London, 1954) pp. 61–70. Cf. Carl Menger, *Principles of Economics* (Glencoe IL, 1950) p. 196.

57 'Valeurs et monnaies', in *Oeuvres de Turgot*, ed. E. Daire (Paris, 1844) p. 92.

58 *Ibid.*, pp. 93–4.

59 *Ibid.*, p. 93.

60 A. R. J. Turgot, 'Reflections on the Formation and Distribution of Riches', ed. and trans. William J. Ashley (New York, 1963) p. 30.

61 In essence the reasoning, but not the conclusion, is similar to that of Walras and Wicksell, while it probably derived from Cantillon. See R. Cantillon, *Essay on the Nature of Commerce in General*, ed. H. Higgs (London, 1959) pp. 117–19; L. Walras, *Elements of Pure Economics*, trans. W. Jaffé (London, 1965) pp. 84–6; K. Wicksell, *Lectures on Political Economy* (London, 1951) 1:53–5.

62 See the remarks in note 39 above.

63 A. R. J. Turgot, 'Reflections on the Formation and Distribution of Riches', ed. and trans. William J. Ashley (New York, 1963) pp. 30–1.

64 'Mémoire sur les prêts d'argent', in *Oeuvres de Turgot*, ed. E. Daire (Paris, 1844) pp. 126–7.

65 *Ibid.*, p. 127; and cf. pp. 129–30. The first reference to time preference that I know of is by F. Galiani, *Della moneta*, 2nd edn (Milan, 1831) 2:186, which anticipated Turgot by nearly two decades. Turgot was familiar with this work, as noted in note 9 above.

66 See E. von Böhm-Bawerk, *Positive Theory of Capital*, trans. Smart (London, 1891) book 5, ch. 1.

67 Turgot explained the divergence of present from future esteem value on three grounds: first, the risks of lending; second, the loss of the use of the commodity lent; third, the profit which could be made from the use of the commodity during the period of the loan. See 'Mémoire sur les prêts d'argent', in *Oeuvres de Turgot*, ed. E. Daire (Paris, 1844) pp. 118–20.

68 See the references in note 9 above.

69 See Frances Hutcheson, *System of Moral Philosophy* (Glasgow, 1755) 2:53–4. Schelle has argued that the physiocrats were influenced by Hutcheson, but gives no evidence. See *Du Pont de Nemours et l'école physiocratique* (Paris, 1888) p. 158. Turgot may have known Hutcheson's work through his acquaintance with Hume and Adam Smith.

70 I.e. F. Galiani, *Della moneta*, 2nd edn (Milan, 1831) esp. pp. 43–70; F. Quesnay, 'Hommes', in *Quesnay et la Physiocratie* (Paris, 1958) 2:526–7; J. J. L. de Graslin, *Essai analytique sur la richesse et sur l'impôt* (London, 1767) part 1, ch. 2, esp. pp. 25–8. It should be noted that both Galiani and Quesnay also had a cost-of-production theory of value. In a recent article, 'The Transition of Turgot's Theory of Value', Yoshio Yamakawa argues that Turgot's subjective theory was an important change from an earlier position, which he describes as a cost approach. This change is attributed to Turgot's acquaintance with Graslin's work in 1767. See *Waseda Economic Papers*, vol. 3 (1959) esp. pp. 31, 47. Since the exchange analysis in the 'Reflections' does not in any way conflict with that of 'Valeurs et monnaies', as I have demonstrated above, I fail to see this 'transition' in Turgot's theory of value, since the 'Reflections' was written before the publication of Graslin's *Essai*.

71 John Locke, *Some Considerations on the Consequences of Lowering Interest and Raising the Value of Money* (London, 1696) pp. 45–6; cf. pp. 59, 61; John Law, *Money and Trade Considered with a Proposal for Supplying the Nation with Money* (Edinburgh, 1705) pp. 4–5; R. Cantillon, *Essay on the Nature of Commerce in General*, ed. H. Higgs (London, 1959) pp. 117–19.

72 Turgot refers to both Locke and Law in his 'Lettre à l'abbé de Cicé sur le papier suppléé à la monnaie', in *Oeuvres de Turgot*, ed. E. Daire (Paris, 1844) 1:97, 99. Cantillon is referred to by Turgot as one of the leading economists of the eighteenth century in a letter to Caillard, 1 January 1771, in *Oeuvres de Turgot*, ed. G. Schelle (Paris, 1913–23) 3:500.

73 R. Cantillon, *Essay on the Nature of Commerce in General*, ed. H. Higgs (London, 1959) pp. 27–9; Joseph Harris, *An Essay upon Money and Coins* (London, 1767) part 1, pp. 5–6. As noted in note 70 above, Galiani also had a cost-of-production theory.

74 F. Quesnay, 'Hommes', in *Quesnay et la Physiocratie* (Paris, 1958) p. 529. Although this paper was not published during Quesnay's lifetime, Turgot would have been familiar with it. See *ibid.*, 2:511, n1, and 579, n1.

75 R. Cantillon, *Essay on the Nature of Commerce in General*, ed. H. Higgs (London, 1959) p. 29; Joseph Harris, *An Essay upon Money and Coins* (London, 1767) p. 9; Quesnay, 'Hommes', *op. cit.*, p. 530. Turgot does not appear to have known Harris' work, which, in any case, was published in the same year as that in which Turgot wrote his 'Observations sur le mémoire de M. de Saint-Péravy'.

76 See note 40 above.

77 E. Kauder, 'Genesis of the Marginal Utility Theory', *Economic Journal*, 63 (1953) pp. 646–7, where it is shown that Turgot was the only eighteenth-century economist with a theory of isolated exchange. Kauder, however, fails to develop the various models which Turgot put forward.

78 See, for example, E. Cannan, *Review of Economic Theory* (London, 1930) p. 163, where Turgot's value theory is called 'disappointing'; cf. E. Roll, *History of Economic Thought* (London, 1956) p. 134; and J. A. Schumpeter, *History of Economic Analysis* (London, 1959) pp. 249, 302, 308. Even Yamakawa (see note 70 above) fails to emphasise the tremendous step forward which makes Turgot's exchange models such important contributions.

79 I am indebted to Mr F. M. Dunn and Professor R. M. Singh, who read this paper in manuscript and provided interesting suggestions and modifications. The errors that remain are, of course, the author's responsibility.

17 A re-interpretation of Turgot's theory of capital and interest[1]

Turgot's theory of capital and interest, although often praised by commentators in the past,[2] still lacks a complete interpretation. This can be explained by the fact that Turgot's analysis of capital and interest, as in the case of so much of his other economics, must be put together from the various papers in which he dealt with the subject. The commentators who have dealt with his theory in some detail[3] have based their opinion on the material contained in the 'Reflections', and have generally neglected his 'Mémoire sur les prêts d'argent' as well as some of his other relevant writings.[4] Their treatment is therefore incomplete, and this alone is reason for a new interpretation of Turgot's theory of capital and interest.

Furthermore, it can be argued that some of his commentators have in fact misinterpreted Turgot's theory. Böhm-Bawerk, for example, who devoted a separate chapter to Turgot's theory of interest in his critical history, was wrong when he described it as a fructification theory on the ground that Turgot had justified and explained interest rates by appealing to the rate of return to land.[5] It can easily be shown that this is a misrepresentation: first of all, in the 'Mémoire sur les prêts d'argent', which dealt exclusively with the topic of justifying interest on loan transactions, Turgot makes no reference at all to a relationship between the rate of interest and the rate of return to land; second, in the 'Reflections', he explicitly argued that the price of land was determined by the current rate of interest.[6]

Cassel's interpretation, although correct, is incomplete because he failed to do full justice to Turgot's treatment of 'the causes which govern the *demand* for capital', despite his contention that what Turgot 'has to say on this subject is. … of the highest value'.[7] Similarly, Schumpeter, although he praised Turgot's contribution as 'by far the greatest performance in the field of interest theory the eighteenth century produced' and as one which 'foreshadowed much of the best thought of the last decades of the nineteenth century', failed to interpret Turgot's theory in the context of the general theory of exchange,[8] which is an important omission. The three leading commentators on Turgot's theory have therefore either misinterpreted or else omitted important features of his analysis of capital and interest.

It is the purpose of this chapter to re-interpret Turgot's theory of capital and interest in order to complete and correct this particular episode in the history of economics. It will facilitate the discussion to divide the chapter into four parts. In the first, there will be an examination of Turgot's analysis of interest determination as part of the general theory of exchange; in the second and third part his discussion of the forces lying behind the demand for and the supply of capital will be considered respectively; while in the final part Turgot's theory will be compared with that of his leading contemporaries who contributed to interest theory, in order to highlight the significance of his contribution on this subject.

I

In his earliest as well as his later writings on the subject, Turgot maintained that the rate of interest was determined in the market through exchange. In his 'Remarques sur les notes qui accompagnent la traduction de Child', written in 1753 or 1754, he argued that interest, or 'the price of money, like that of any other thing, must be settled by the relation between the supply and demand, and not by laws'.[9] Five years later, he wrote that interest should be determined by competition and not by state regulation.[10] The 'Reflections', his most important economic work, written in 1766, offers a similar approach to interest determination, but in contrast to the earlier writings also gives a detailed explanation of the forces lying behind the supply of loanable funds and the demand for them.[11]

The reasons for Turgot's emphasis on a market determination of the rate of interest are not difficult to find. They arose from the restraints imposed on the capital market through the legal regulation of interest rates by the French usury laws which embodied 'the extreme prejudice about usury' inherited from the middle ages and its canon law, which was based on a misunderstanding of 'the meaning of Scripture' and 'natural right'. Although these laws were not generally observed and were often legally evaded, they continued to exist and were 'even still partly observed'. This entailed great disadvantages for commerce, industry and agriculture.[12]

Furthermore, there were leading French economic authorities who supported or condoned this legal regulation of interest rates,[13] thereby offending against Turgot's principles of unrestricted trade. In his writings on the subject, especially the 'Mémoire sur les prêts d'argent', he therefore paid particular attention to the analysis of the market forces determining interest rates in order to show both the futility and the detrimental effects of a policy of legal regulation.[14]

In the 'Mémoire sur les prêts d'argent', which is an explicit attack on the usury laws, Turgot presented his most detailed analysis of the exchange aspects of a theory of interest determination. Money, Turgot argued, should be regarded:

> as a genuine commodity, whose price depends on agreement, and varies, like that of all other commodities, according to the ratio between offer and demand. Interest being the price of loanable funds, it rises when there are more borrowers than lenders; it falls, on the contrary, when there is more

> money offered than is demanded for borrowing. It is in this way that the normal rate of interest is established, but this normal rate is not the only rule which is followed, nor should it be allowed to fix the rate of interest for individual transactions. The risks which the capital may run in the hands of the borrower, the needs of the latter, and the profit which he hopes to draw from the money which he borrows, are the circumstances which, when combined in different ways, and with the normal rate of interest, will often carry the rate to a higher level than it is in the ordinary course of trade.[15]

Loan transactions are therefore very similar to ordinary exchange transactions, except for one important difference. In an ordinary exchange, commodities are immediately exchanged for commodities, including money here in commodities; in a loan transaction, the lender exchanges a sum of money now for a promise to pay a sum of money in the future, just as in a foreign exchange transaction, 'money in one place is given in exchange for the receipt of money in another place'.[16]

It has to be concluded that a sum of money available now, and a promise of that same sum of money in the future, have different values, because 'if it is assumed that a thousand francs and a promise of a thousand francs are exactly of the same value ... why do people borrow?'[17] It is this difference in value between money now and a promise of money in the future which makes it worthwhile for the borrower to pay the interest which compensates the lender for surrendering the use of the principal over the period of the loan. This is clearly expressed by Turgot in the following quotation:

> Is not this difference well known, and is not the commonplace proverb, *a bird in the hand is better than two in the bush*, a simple expression of this notoriety? Now, if a sum currently owned is worth more, is more useful, is preferable to the assurance of receiving a similar sum in one or several years' time, it is not true that the lender receives as much as he gives when he does not stipulate interest, for he gives the money and only receives an assurance. Now, if he receives less, why should this difference not be compensated by the assurance for an increase in the sum proportioned to the delay? This compensation is precisely the rate of interest.[18]

The promise of the payment of interest as well as the repayment of the principal therefore motivates the lender, but why are lenders able to demand interest, that is, why is present money more valuable than future money? Turgot's answer to this question is that money in the present is scarce relative to the demand for it. The theory of interest determination is therefore incomplete until there has been an examination of the factors influencing the supply of loan money and the demand for it.

Before turning to Turgot's discussion of the factors determining the demand for and the supply of loan money, a further point has to be made. Although his analysis of interest considered so far has been dealt with in monetary terms, it should be made clear that it is not a monetary theory of interest. Loan transactions, Turgot argued, are only considered in money terms because individuals regard money as 'equivalent to real objects, and that money in this sense is indispensable to all productive works'.[19] A loan transaction is therefore the transfer of command over real resources or 'moveable wealth' as Turgot called them, and not of money.[20]

II

The demand for loans or the motives for borrowing vary widely from person to person according to Turgot.

> People borrow with every kind of purpose and with every sort of motive. This one borrows to undertake an enterprise which will make his fortune, this other to purchase an estate, another to pay a gaming debt, another to make up for the loss of his revenue of which some accident has deprived him, and another to keep himself alive until he can get something by his labour.[21]

The basic motives for borrowing can, however, be divided into three: borrowing for consumption purposes, borrowing to purchase a landed estate and borrowing for productive purposes, that is, to invest the proceeds of the loan into agricultural, industrial or commercial enterprises.[22] Turgot's examination of these three motives can be looked at in turn.

The first two motives do not need a great deal of explanation. The fact that people borrowed for consumption purposes was considered as self-evident by Turgot, and therefore did not require discussion, even though the motive as such had to be recognised.[23] The motive for borrowing to purchase a landed estate needs a little more discussion, since it would not now be listed separately when the demand for loanable funds was dealt with. For Turgot, however, it was an important individual motive needing separate listing for the following reasons: first of all, the ownership of landed property was socially desirable since it yielded income with a maximum of leisure, a not unimportant consideration for the eighteenth century, when engaging in trade lowered a person's social status; second, it was a relatively safe investment which, when 'leased to an entirely solvent Farmer', yielded a steady return; third, the income from such an investment was fully 'disposable'.[24] It was presumably for these reasons that Turgot listed investment in land as a special motive for borrowing.[25]

The third type of demand for loans, that for investment purposes, is discussed by Turgot in detail. From a study of his 'Reflections' it becomes apparent that he had a very good idea that capital is not only required, but that it is essential to the process of production, especially in a period of technical change. Whereas in the early stages of development, the earth supplied the rudimentary tools with which man could labour, with more advanced methods of production, which are due to the 'separation of professions', or the division of labour,[26] a greater quantity and a more complex form of capital are required. Prior to a thorough division of labour:

> when the same man that cultivated the earth provided by his labour for his other needs, he required no other advances: but when a large part of the Society had only their arms to maintain them, it was necessary that those who thus lived on their wages should begin by having something in advance, either to procure the materials upon which to labour, or to maintain them while waiting for the payment of their wages.[27]

With a more advanced form of division of labour, a greater investment of capital is required in the process of production. The reason for this lies in the technical organisation of more modern industry. The division of labour, as well as producing better and cheaper commodities,[28] also creates a class of wage labourers who do not own any means of production.[29] It also introduces other new problems in the sphere of production. In the solution of these problems lies the need for capital in agriculture, industry and commerce, and hence the motive for borrowing for productive purposes.

In the first place, Turgot argued that in many industries where there is a division of labour the process of production takes a fairly long time, that is, there is a fairly long temporal gap before the raw materials are transformed into final products. This increase in the length of the period of production has some important consequences. It means that the entrepreneur or the producer must have sufficient stocks of raw materials and money for wages on hand, in order to allow the continuation of the production process from raw materials to final consumer goods. He must also provide buildings to house his workers and tools with which they can work. Besides these, there are other commitments such as the training of apprentices and the provision of social overhead capital in the form of roads, canals, market halls, etc.[30] A great deal of capital has to be invested before a productive enterprise can be set up, and before the final product can be sold so that the initial costs can be returned to the entrepreneur.[31]

The technical requirements of production under a division of labour make for an increasing demand on the capital stock of a nation.

> It will be one of the possessors of capitals, or of moveable accumulated values, who will employ them [i.e. the capitals] partly in advances for the construction of the establishment and for the purchase of the materials, partly for the daily wages of the workmen who labour in the preparation of the commodities. It is he who will wait for the sale of the product to return him not only all the advances but a profit as well.[32]

The waiting which becomes essential once more technical production methods are adopted has to be compensated by a profit. The profit motive becomes one of the explanations as to why capital is demanded.[33]

Turgot has so far conducted his argument in terms of technical conditions of production. The purchase of raw materials, the advances of wages for the employees, the erection of buildings, the provision of tools and machinery; all these require capital advances and waiting by the capitalist. Because of this waiting, the capitalists demand a profit from the enterprise. The question is now: how does this return arise and what constitutes this return?

Turgot described this quite clearly. At the end of the period of production, and when the final commodities are sold, the capitalists should earn

> a profit equal to the revenue they could acquire with their capital without labour; the wages and price of their labour, of their risk, and of their industry; and that wherewith to replace annually the wear and tear of the property employed in their undertaking.[34]

The waiting of the capitalist is therefore to be rewarded by a return which can be subdivided into three categories. The first is the depreciation of the capital invested in the enterprise; the second includes the 'wages of superintendence and direction' as well as the risk premium; the third one is the pure return on his capital which he could have earned if he had not employed it in industry.[35]

The act of waiting, which is essential in a modern productive process, must therefore be compensated by a net return to the capitalist, and this net return is at least equal to the current rate of interest on the capital invested in the business. If this net return is not paid by the investment, then the capital will not be put into the enterprise.[36]

The demand for capital is then explained by Turgot as follows.[37] The technical conditions of production under the division of labour require that capital advances are made for the payment of wages, the purchase of raw materials, etc. Owing to the length of time which elapses between the original investment and the sale of the final product, waiting has to be done by the capitalist who supplies the initial resources. This waiting is compensated by the net return which the capitalist hopes to gain from his investment and which should be sufficient to pay the current rate of interest on his advances. Capital is therefore demanded because the entrepreneur can draw a profit from its employment and because waiting is essential to capitalistic production.[38]

III

The supply of capital must also be investigated before a satisfactory theory of interest can be given. The rate of interest, after all, depends on the supply of, as well as on the demand for, loanable funds, and the motives for saving and accumulation must now be discussed. How and why is capital accumulated? What is the effect of the rate of accumulation on the supply of capital and on the rate of interest? These questions are also discussed by Turgot.

In the first place, Turgot correctly argues that what is accumulated by the capitalist is not money, despite the fact that most savings are actually made in money. 'To suppose that saving and hoarding are synonymous, what a confusion of ideas, or rather of language'.[39] Money facilitates the accumulation of capital but the accumulation of money is hoarding, not saving. Only when money savings are translated into commodities essential for production does capital accumulation occur. This is forcefully expressed in the following passage from the 'Reflections':

> We have seen that money plays scarcely any part in the sum total of existing capitals; but it plays a great part in the formation of capitals. In fact, almost all savings are made in nothing but money; it is in money that the revenues come to the proprietors, that the advances and the profits return to undertakers of every kind; it is, therefore, from money that they save, and the annual increase of capitals takes place in money: but none of the undertakers make any other use of it than to convert it *immediately* into the different kinds of effects upon which their undertaking depends; and thus this money returns to circulation, and the greater part of capitals exists only in effects of different kinds, as we have already explained above.[40]

In these observations on Saint-Péravy's *Mémoire sur les effets de l'impôt indirect*, Turgot expanded considerably on his saving-investment analysis and on the role of hoarding.[41] The conclusions he derived from this analysis are worth quoting in full:

> It follows. ... that money which is saved, accumulated, put aside for the formation of capitals, is not lost to the circulation and that the sum of monetary values which are counterbalanced in the transactions of commerce with the other values to settle their price, neither decreases nor increases by it. In a nation where agriculture, industry and commerce flourish, and where the interest of money is low, the stock of capitals is immense, and yet it is well known that the quantity of money placed in hoards is quite negligible; almost all the existing capitals are represented by paper which is equivalent to money because the assets which are responsible for their soundness are equivalent to money. *But there really is no money in the tills other than what is required to meet the daily payments necessary for the flow of trade*. ... I believe to have shown. ... that in fact saving does not really withdraw from circulation the money it puts aside.[42]

Turgot's saving-investment analysis clearly foreshadows the classical analysis on this subject which denied the possibility of leakages from the process of exchange and hence the possibility of a general glut. Money balances are only held for transaction purposes, and hoards for any other purpose, apart from the fact that they are considered to be negligible relative to the total stock of capital, are implicitly regarded as the result of irrational behaviour. As Schumpeter has pointed out, this analysis changed little from the time of Turgot's writing to that of Ricardo and J. S. Mill and perhaps up to that of

Marshall at the end of the nineteenth century.[43] In the process of capital accumulation, Turgot held the view that money was nothing but a veil.

Having dealt with the role of money in the accumulation process, Turgot discussed the question as to how savings originated. 'As soon as men were found whose property in land assured them an annual revenue more than sufficient to satisfy all their wants, there were sure to be found men who, either because they were anxious about the future, or for mere prudence, put in reserve a part of what they gathered each year; either to meet possible chances, or to increase their comforts'.[44]

Savings can therefore be defined as the excess of income after consumption needs have been satisfied. This surplus income is saved because people are anxious about the future or because they wish to be able to meet contingencies, or 'to increase their comforts'. Only if income is more than sufficient to meet the necessary consumption needs can capital be accumulated.

The greater the difference between income and consumption, the greater the amount of savings and the greater the accumulation of capital. If people are thrifty and cut down on their consumption needs, their savings will increase. The same applies to the nation. The greater the national 'spirit of economy', the greater the rate of accumulation.[45]

Having considered the origin of and the motives for saving, Turgot discussed the effect of accumulation on the rate of interest. This effect of accumulation is seen as the cause of a falling rate of interest and rate of profit,[46] and is demonstrated as follows. An increase in the accumulation of capital increases the stock of capital in the community, and *ipso facto*, the amount of capital available for lending. This will cause a fall in the rate of interest, since interest is determined by the supply of and the demand for loanable funds.

When interest falls, borrowers can invest capital resources in enterprises which would not have paid an adequate return before the fall in the rate of interest. This means that industry in general can now work at a lower rate of profit, which spreads throughout the economy as a result of free competition. 'It is the abundance of capitals which animates all undertakings; and the low interest of money is at once the effect and the indication of the abundance of capitals'.[47]

A change in the rate of accumulation, through the effect it has on the rate of interest, changes the allocation of capital resources.

> As soon as the profits resulting from an employment of money, whatever it may be, increase or diminish, capitals turn in that direction and withdraw from other employments; and this necessarily alters in each of these employments of money the relationship between the capital and the annual product.[48]

Furthermore, Turgot's analysis carries the implication that changes in the rate of profit affect the capitalistic nature of production.

> The current rate of interest on money placed on loan can then be regarded as a kind of thermometer of the abundance or scarcity of capital in a nation, and of the extent of the undertakings of every kind on which it may embark.[49]

Since the rate of interest reflects the relative scarcity of capital, it also gives an indication as to how capitalistic enterprises can afford to be.

The supply of capital is affected by the rates of accumulation and saving, which in themselves depend on the difference between income and consumption. If people are thrifty, there will be a high rate of accumulation. This will increase the stock of capital, lower the rate of interest, *ceteris paribus*, and, by diverting capital to less profitable enterprises, lower the rate of profit in turn. Turgot explained the process of accumulation and the fall in the rate of profit simultaneously.[50]

IV

It has been shown that the essence of Turgot's theory is the supply and demand analysis of the determination of the rate of interest. This feature of the analysis was, of course, not new, and it seems undoubtedly correct to say that Turgot derived this basic proposition of his theory from the work of Locke, of Cantillon and of Hume.[51] The same may be said for his stress on real, rather than monetary factors in interest rate determination,[52] while he appears to have owed the distinction between present and future goods in the analysis of time preference to Galiani's *Della Moneta*.[53]

Turgot's analysis of the demand for capital, on the other hand, contains many original features. In the first place, he related motives for borrowing systematically to the various 'employments of capitals', thereby anticipating Smith's later analysis on this point in *Wealth of Nations*.[54] Second, there is his analysis of the role of capital in the productive process, which, according to Schumpeter, 'foreshadowed much of the best thought' on this subject in the 1880s and 1890s.[55] The stress on the time element of production as a consequence of the division of labour, as a cause of the relatively capital-intensive production methods and hence a demand for capital, constitutes an excellent performance in this part of his theory.[56] Finally, his division of the return to the capitalist into pure interest, depreciation, and entrepreneurial remuneration including a risk premium, marked a step forward in the analysis of profit.[57] It is therefore not surprising that both Schumpeter and Cassel praised this part of his work.[58]

In this connection it must not be forgotten that Turgot was acquainted with Quesnay's work on the theory of capital, which contributed substantially to his analysis. It was Quesnay who introduced capital into economic analysis as an important factor of production, while his most important work, the *Tableau économique*, showed that large productions were impossible without large 'original' and 'annual' advances.[59] Quesnay's writings, however, were only concerned with agricultural production, but this shortcoming was repaired by Turgot, who applied the analysis of capital to all productive sectors of the economy. Furthermore, Quesnay's writings contained only an implicit awareness of the time element in production, while in Turgot's writings this aspect was given considerable prominence. Turgot's theory of capital can therefore be described as an important improvement on that of Quesnay.[60]

Turgot's discussion of hoarding, saving and capital accumulation also contains important original contributions. His saving-investment analysis with its discussion of the role of money in capital formation was to change little up to the time of Marshall, and his arguments on the almost immediate transformation of saving into investment was not really successfully challenged till the publication of Keynes' *General Theory*. Turgot was probably the first economist who attempted a rigorous demonstration of the improbability of leakages from the circular flow in the form of hoarding.[61]

Turgot's remarks on the motives for saving, his emphasis on thrift, and his analysis of the effects of capital accumulation on the rate of interest and the rate of profit, although basically not new, also contained some novel features. The broad elements of the theory were present in Cantillon's *Essay* and in Hume's 'Of Interest', but Turgot's discussion of the effect of a change in the rate of interest on the allocation of capital resources is not argued in their work. The relationship between income and saving, which is explicit in Turgot's economic writings, also finds no place in those of Cantillon and Hume.[62]

A good measure of the quality of Turgot's work in this field is to compare his performance with that of Adam Smith. As Schumpeter has pointed out, Smith's analysis of capital, 'though infinitely more prolix, falls far short of Turgot's, despite the similarity of their basic analytical framework'.[63] Like Turgot's, Smith's analysis is one of supply and demand; supply depending on the rate of accumulation,[64] demand on the various employments of capital and uses of borrowed funds.[65] His analysis is also conducted completely in real terms.

At this point the similarity stops and differences start to appear. In the first place, Smith did not integrate his remarks on the time element of production[66] into his analysis of the demand for capital; second, his theory of accumulation and saving-investment lacks the subtle insights displayed by Turgot, that is, the distinction between saving and hoarding, the role of money in the accumulation process, and the individual motives for accumulation; third, Smith displayed no awareness of the role of time preference in the determination of interest rates. Again, to quote Schumpeter, 'A. Smith stereotyped the doctrinal situation. … in doing so he dropped precisely the most promising suggestions proffered by Hume and (if he knew the *Réflexions*) by Turgot'.[67] Since Smith rather than Turgot became the authority for future generations of economists in the early nineteenth century, some of the points made by the latter had to be rediscovered in the years that followed.

For these reasons it is difficult to understand why Turgot's theory of capital and interest has been so studiously ignored by the commentators, with the exception of Böhm-Bawerk, Cassel and Schumpeter. For example, Roll devotes no space in his discussion of Turgot's economics to capital theory; Cannan's chapter in his *Review of Economic Theory* makes no reference to Turgot, while some of the more modern texts on the history of economic thought, like those of Blaug and Rima, follow their predecessors in this regard.[68] It is hoped that this analysis of Turgot's theory of capital and interest has repaired this important omission in the history of economic analysis, by demonstrating that his work on the subject was superior to that of all other economists of the eighteenth century. This can indeed be described as a remarkable performance by Turgot.

Notes

1 I am indebted to Professors R. L. Meek and B. A. Corry, and to Mr J. R. Wilson for helpful comments and suggestions for the improvement of this paper. The errors that remain are of course entirely the responsibility of the author.

2 See, for example, E. von Böhm-Bawerk, *Capital and Interest: A Critical History of Economical Theory* (Smart translation, London, 1890) p. 61; G. Cassel, *The Nature and Necessity of Interest* (London, 1903) p. 22; J. A. Schumpeter, *History of Economic Analysis* (London, 1959) p. 332.

3 See Schumpeter, *op. cit.*, pp. 248–9, 332–3; E. von Böhm-Bawerk, *Capital and Interest: A Critical History of Economical Theory* (Smart translation, London, 1890) pp. 63–4; G. Cassel, *The Nature and Necessity of Interest* (London, 1903) pp. 20–2.

4 I.e. A. R. J. Turgot, 'Mémoire sur les prêts d'argent', in *Oeuvres de Turgot*, ed. G. Schelle (Paris, 1913–23) III, pp. 154–202; 'Remarques sur les notes qui accompagnent la traduction de Child', in *ibid.*, I, pp. 372–6, and also, 'Eloge de Gournay', and 'Observations sur le mémoire de M. de Saint-Péravy'.

5 See E. von Böhm-Bawerk, *Capital and Interest: A Critical History of Economical Theory* (Smart translation, London, 1890) ch. III, entitled 'Turgot's fructification theory'. Fructification theories, although not common, had occurred in the writings of Petty, Hutcheson and Quesnay. See *The Economic Writings of Sir William Petty*, ed. C.H. Hull (Cambridge, 1899) II, pp. 446–8; F. Hutcheson, *A System of Moral Philosophy* (Glasgow, 1755) II, pp. 71–3; and F. Quesnay, 'Observations sur l'intérêt de l'argent', in *François Quesnay et la Physiocratie* (Paris, 1958) II, pp. 763–9. G. Cassel, *The Nature and Necessity of Interest* (London, 1903) p. 22, explicitly rejects Böhm-Bawerk's interpretation, as does Schumpeter (J. A. Schumpeter, *History of Economic Analysis* [London, 1959] p. 332, n5); but cf. K. Wicksell, 'Böhm-Bawerk's Theory of Interest', in *Selected Papers on Economic Theory* (London, 1958) pp. 177–8. W. L. Taylor, *Francis Hutcheson and David Hume as Predecessors of Adam Smith* (Durham NC, 1965) p. 85, also appears to accept Böhm-Bawerk's interpretation of Turgot's theory, and favourably compares Hutcheson's fructification theory with it. See pp. 85–90. Since this paper argues that Böhm-Bawerk's interpretation is wrong, it would appear to the author that such a comparison is highly misleading.

6 See A. R. J. Turgot, 'Mémoire sur les prêts d'argent', in *Oeuvres de Turgot*, ed. G. Schelle (Paris, 1913–23) esp. pp. 167–70, 174–80, 191–2; A. R. J. Turgot, 'Reflections on the Formation and Distribution of Riches' (Ashley translation, New York, 1963) p. 85, where Turgot argued: 'It is evident that the lower the interest of money is, the greater is the value of landed estates'. Cf. also Turgot to Du Pont de Nemours, 10/2/1766, in A. R. J. Turgot, *Oeuvres de Turgot*, ed. G. Schelle (Paris, 1913–23) II, p. 512, where he wrote that he had made some critical notes on Quesnay's 'Observations sur l'intérêt de l'argent', which have unfortunately not been found. These may have included critical comments on Quesnay's fructification theory.

7 See G. Cassel, *The Nature and Necessity of Interest* (London, 1903) pp. 20–2, esp. p. 21.
8 See J. A. Schumpeter, *History of Economic Analysis* (London, 1959) pp. 332–3.
9 In A. R. J. Turgot, *Oeuvres de Turgot*, ed. G. Schelle (Paris, 1913–23) I, p. 375.
10 See 'Eloge de Gournay', written in 1759, in A. R. J. Turgot, *Oeuvres de Turgot* (Daire edition, Paris, 1844) I, p. 277.
11 A. R. J. Turgot, 'Reflections on the Formation and Distribution of Riches' (Ashley translation, New York, 1963) esp. pp. 74–80. Turgot's explanation of these forces lying behind supply and demand will be discussed in the second and third sections of this chapter.
12 See A. R. J. Turgot, 'Mémoire sur les prêts d'argent', in *Oeuvres de Turgot*, ed. G. Schelle (Paris, 1913–23) pp. 163–4.
13 See for example, Montesquieu, *l'Esprit des lois*, in *Oeuvres de Montesquieu* (Paris, 1964) pp. 685–6; and F. Quesnay, 'Observations sur l'intérêt de l'argent', in *François Quesnay et la Physiocratie* (Paris, 1958) pp. 763–8, esp. pp. 765–8.
14 See the quotations in the preceding two paragraphs. This attitude to the legal regulation of interest rates is already apparent in Turgot's first paper on economics, 'Lettre à M. L'Abbé de Cicé sur le papier supplée à la monnaie', in A. R. J. Turgot, *Oeuvres de Turgot* (Daire edition, Paris, 1844) I, p. 95. It probably derived from Locke's devastating critique of the legal regulation of interest rates which is referred to in this letter. See *ibid.*, I, p. 97.
15 A. R. J. Turgot, 'Mémoire sur les prêts d'argent', in *Oeuvres de Turgot*, ed. G. Schelle (Paris, 1913–23) p. 169.
16 *Ibid.*, p. 171.
17 *Ibid.*, pp. 179–80.
18 *Ibid.*, p. 177.
19 *Ibid.*, p. 173.
20

> It is not, therefore, the quantity of silver existing as a metal which causes the interest of money to rise or fall, or which brings into commerce more money ready to be lent; it is simply the sum of capitals to be found in commerce, that is to say, the actual sum of moveable values of every kind, accumulated, saved bit by bit out of the revenues and profits, to be employed to obtain for the possessor new revenues and profits. It is these accumulated savings that are offered to the borrowers, and the more there are of them the lower is the rate of interest, at least if the number of borrowers is not augmented in proportion.
>
> (A. R. J. Turgot, 'Reflections on the Formation and Distribution of Riches' [Ashley translation, New York, 1963] p. 79)

For similar statements, cf. *Ibid.*, pp. 75–9, 85–6, 98–9.
21 *Ibid.*, p. 67.
22 Cf. *Ibid.*, p. 81, where Turgot listed the 'five employments of capital' which are similar to these three basic motives for borrowing.
23 As Hume had pointed out, borrowing for consumption purposes was an important part of the total demand for loans in a society dominated by landlords. See 'Of Interest', in *Economic Writings of David Hume*, edited by E. Rotwein (London, 1955) pp. 49–51.
24 24 See A. R. J. Turgot, 'Reflections on the Formation and Distribution of Riches' (Ashley translation, New York, 1963) esp. p. 82. Turgot was still sufficiently physiocratic in his ideas to stress the special importance of landed property and its net product or revenue. Cf. *ibid.*, pp. 90–8.
25 K. Wicksell, 'Böhm-Bawerk's Theory of Interest', in *Selected Papers on Economic Theory* (London, 1958) pp. 177–8, has argued that Turgot's inclusion of purchasing a

landed estate among the motives for borrowing and the uses of capital is wrong (except for individual motives and uses) because it is not an economic or social use of capital, therefore does not affect the supply of capital and hence the rate of interest. Borrowing for the purpose of buying land can affect the rate of interest only if the real supply of capital is diminished through the dissipation of the purchase price by the seller of the land.

26 A. R. J. Turgot, 'Reflections on the Formation and Distribution of Riches' (Ashley translation, New York, 1963) p. 51.

27 *Ibid.*, pp. 51–2.

28 *Ibid.*, pp. 5–6.

29 *Ibid.*, p. 52.

30 *Ibid.*, p. 53.

31 A. R. J. Turgot, 'Mémoire sur les prêts d'argent', in *Oeuvres de Turgot*, ed. G. Schelle (Paris, 1913–23) pp. 156–7, 168–9; cf. Turgot, 'Reflections on the Formation and Distribution of Riches' (Ashley translation, New York, 1963) paras 59–60, 62, 64, 66–7, 70.

32 *Ibid.*, p. 53.

33 *Ibid.*, p. 71.

34 *Ibid.*, p. 55.

35 It is from this phrase, 'a profit equal to the revenue they could acquire with their capital with labour', that Böhm-Bawerk constructs his fructification theory as an interpretation of Turgot's theory of capital. For him this phrase can only mean that Turgot sees the origin of interest in the rate of return to land. As Cassel has argued, this could imply a type of opportunity cost; the entrepreneur must at least obtain a rate of return equal to the current rate of interest before he will invest his capital in the enterprise. See *ibid.*, pp. 57, 65.

36 *Ibid.*, p. 86.

37 Neglecting the demand for consumption loans and for loans to purchase a landed estate, which are less important than the demand for productive loans.

38 A. R. J. Turgot, 'Reflections on the Formation and Distribution of Riches' (Ashley translation, New York, 1963) pp. 64–5.

39 Turgot to Du Pont de Nemours, 23/3/1770, in A. R. J. Turgot, *Oeuvres de Turgot*, ed. G. Schelle (Paris, 1913–23) III, p. 384. This excerpt from the letter was presumably inspired by an unauthorised change by Du Pont in Turgot's 'Reflections', section 70. In the correct version, the 1788 French edition, the first paragraph of that section clearly differentiates money saving and real investment; the version in the Ashley edition, based on that in the *Ephémérides* and the Schelle text, leaves some material out, and appears to make saving synonymous with hoarding. See *Réflexions sur la formation et la distribution des richesses*, n.p., 1788, p. 87, Ashley edition, p. 64, cf. Turgot, *Oeuvres de Turgot* (Daire edition, Paris, 1844) I, p. 46. Cf. Turgot to Caillard, 16/3/1770, *ibid.*, II, p. 812.

40 A. R. J. Turgot, 'Reflections on the Formation and Distribution of Riches' (Ashley translation, New York, 1963) pp. 98–9.

41 'Observations sur le mémoire de M. de Saint-Péravy', in A. R. J. Turgot, *Oeuvres de Turgot* (Daire edition, Paris, 1844) I, pp. 424–34, esp. pp. 432–4.

42 *Ibid.*, I, pp. 432–3; my italics in the quotation.

43 See J. A. Schumpeter, *History of Economic Analysis* (London, 1959) pp. 324–5 and n2; cf. P. D. Groenewegen, 'Turgot and Adam Smith', *Scottish Journal of Political Economy*, vol. XVI, no. 3, November 1969, pp. 278–9 (below, Chapter 20).

44 A. R. J. Turgot, 'Reflections on the Formation and Distribution of Riches' (Ashley translation, New York, 1963) p. 43.

45 *Ibid.*, p. 44, cf. p. 80.

46 *Ibid.*, p. 86, cf. 'Eloge de Gournay', in A. R. J. Turgot, *Oeuvres de Turgot* (Daire edition, Paris, 1844) I, pp. 276–7; A. R. J. Turgot, 'Mémoire sur les prêts d'argent', in *Oeuvres de Turgot*, ed. G. Schelle (Paris, 1913–23) III, pp. 193–4.
47 A. R. J. Turgot, 'Reflections on the Formation and Distribution of Riches' (Ashley translation, New York, 1963) p. 86.
48 *Ibid.*, p. 84.
49 *Ibid.*, p. 85, cf. p. 80.
50 Cf. G. L. S. Tucker, *Progress and Profits in British Economic Thought, 1650–1850* (Cambridge, 1960) p. 48.
51 See J. Locke, *Some Considerations on the Consequences of the Lowering of Interest and Raising the Value of Money* (London, 1696) pp. 9–11; R. Cantillon, *Essay on the Nature of Commerce in General* (Higgs edition, London, 1959) p. 199; D. Hume, 'Of Interest', in *Economic Writings of David Hume*, edited by E. Rotwein (London, 1955) pp. 48–9. For evidence that Turgot was familiar with Locke's work, see note 14 above; for an indication of Turgot's admiration for the work of Cantillon and Hume, see his letter to Caillard, 1/1/1771, in A. R. J. Turgot, *Oeuvres de Turgot*, ed. G. Schelle (Paris, 1913–23) III, p. 500.
52 See R. Cantillon, *op. cit.*, p. 215; D. Hume, *op. cit.*, pp. 48–9. Other early writers who had real interest theories, such as Barbon, North and Massie, would probably not have been known to Turgot. Quesnay's work, discussed below, also stressed real factors.
53 See Galiani, *Della Moneta* (Milan, 1831) II, p. 186, and A. E. Monroe, *Early Economic Thought* (Cambridge, 1924) p. 302, for an English translation of this passage. Turgot cited this work in his paper, 'Valeurs et monnaies', in *Oeuvres de Turgot* (Daire edition, Paris, 1844) I, p. 83.
54 See P. D. Groenewegen, 'Turgot and Adam Smith', *Scottish Journal of Political Economy*, vol. XVI, no. 3, November 1969, pp. 280–1 (below, Chapter 20).
55 J. A. Schumpeter, *History of Economic Analysis* (London, 1959) pp. 332–3. The 'best thought' on the subject in this context clearly refers to that of Böhm-Bawerk on the theory of capital. This may explain what I consider to be Böhm-Bawerk's misinterpretation of Turgot's theory, since, as Wicksell has shown, Böhm-Bawerk was especially critical of those forerunners who anticipated important parts of his own theory, such as Ricardo, Senior and Jevons. On the other hand, Wicksell's agreement with Böhm-Bawerk's interpretation of Turgot's capital theory can, in my opinion, only be explained by his hostility to Cassel as well as by the fact that he does not appear to have been familiar with Turgot's economic work at first hand. See K. Wicksell, 'Böhm-Bawerk's Theory of Interest', in *Selected Papers on Economic Theory* (London, 1958) pp. 176–80; and cf. his *Lectures on Political Economy* (Robbins edition, London, 1951) I, p. 235 and n2.
56 Smith, in his *Lectures on Police, Justice, Revenue and Arms* (New York, 1964) p. 181, made a similar point. Cf. A. Smith, *An Inquiry into the Nature and Causes of the Wealth of Nations* (Modern Library edition, New York, 1937) p. 259.
57 Cf. E. von Böhm-Bawerk, *Capital and Interest: A Critical History of Economical Theory* (Smart translation, London, 1890) pp. 7–8.
58 G. Cassel, *The Nature and Necessity of Interest* (London, 1903) pp. 20–2, esp. p. 21; J. A. Schumpeter, *History of Economic Analysis* (London, 1959) pp. 332–3. The relevant passages have been quoted in the introduction to this paper.
59 See *François Quesnay et la Physiocratie* (Paris, 1958) II, esp. pp. 444–5, 453–4, 667–8, 793–802. Cf. K. Marx, *Theories of Surplus Value* (Moscow, 1963) Part I, p. 44.
60 Cf. R. L. Meek, 'Adam and Smith and the Classical Concept of Profit', *Scottish Journal of Political Economy*, 1954, vol. I, pp. 150–1.
61 See the references given in note 43 above.

62 For a full discussion of the seventeenth- and eighteenth-century literature on these subjects, see G. L. S. Tucker, *Progress and Profits in British Economic Thought, 1650–1850* (Cambridge, 1960) chs 2–3.

63 J. A. Schumpeter, *History of Economic Analysis* (London, 1959) p. 324.

64 A. Smith, *An Inquiry into the Nature and Causes of the Wealth of Nations* (Modern Library edition, New York, 1937) Book II, ch. III. The rate of accumulation, according to Smith, depends on the proportion of productive and unproductive labour in the economy, and on the parsimony of its inhabitants.

65 *Ibid.*, Book II, ch. V.

66 *Ibid.*, introduction to Book II, pp. 259–60. Apart from the introduction, there is no reference to this elsewhere in Book II.

67 J. A. Schumpeter, *History of Economic Analysis* (London, 1959) p. 333.

68 See E. Roll, *A History of Economic Thought* (London, 1966) pp. 134–7; Edwin Cannan, *Review of Economic Theory* (London, 1934) ch. VI, but cf. p. 254; M. Blaug, *Economic Theory in Retrospect* (London, 1964) ch. 1; and I. H. Rima, *Development of Economic Analysis* (Homewood IL, 1967) esp. ch. 4. These examples can easily be multiplied, but those given should suffice. But cf. W. Fellner, *The Emergence and Content of Modern Economic Analysis* (New York, 1960) p. 46.

18 Turgot

Forerunner of neo-classical economics?

In his many, highly laudatory comments on the economics of Turgot, J. A. Schumpeter (1959) clearly indicated that he regarded Turgot as an economist writing in advance of his time because he anticipated much of what became important in the economic discussion of the period after the 'marginal revolution'. In particular, Turgot is argued to have close affinities with the Austrian variant of this 'new' economics. For example, Turgot's description of the market mechanism is suggested to be 'very similar to that of Böhm-Bawerk' (Schumpeter, 1959, p. 307), his interest and capital theory are argued to have 'clearly foreshadowed much of the best thought in the last decades of the nineteenth century'[1] (*ibid*., p. 332) while last but not least, the use of marginal analysis is attributed to him in the context of his famous statement of the 'law of variable proportions' (*ibid*., pp. 260–1). Finally, at the conclusion of his reader's guide to Turgot's 'Reflections on the Production and Distribution of Wealth', Schumpeter gives what can be regarded as his greatest praise:

> there are practically no definite errors to be found in this first of all the treatises on Value and Distribution that were to become so popular in the later decades of the nineteenth century. It is not too much to say that analytic economics took a century to get where it could have got in twenty years after the publication of Turgot's treatise had its contents been properly understood and absorbed by an alert profession.
>
> (*ibid*. p. 249)

Schumpeter's views on the 'modern' nature of Turgot's economics have been developed by a number of other authors, especially in the context of his theory of value. Kauder (1953) in his analysis of the genesis of the marginal utility theory, argued that Turgot's explanation of isolated exchange 'is almost identical' with that presented over a century later by Menger and by Wicksell but that, as was the case with other writers of the Italo-French school of the eighteenth century, Turgot wrote on the subject of value 'in vain' and his writings were 'soon forgotten' (Kauder, 1953, pp. 646–67, 650). Similarly, Yamakawa (1959) described Turgot's 'attempt to formulate value theory based on the subjective valuation' as 'one of the most significant contributions' he made to the development of economic theory (p. 30). Further appraisals of Turgot's theory of value have drawn similar conclusions.[2]

Although less has been published on Turgot's theory of capital and interest in recent years,[3] its 'modernity' was greatly appreciated at the end of the nineteenth century in the debate about Böhm-Bawerk's interpretation of Turgot's theory which was initiated by Cassel and drew interventions from Wicksell, Marshall and Böhm-Bawerk. The link between Turgot and Böhm-Bawerk on the subject of capital theory, which, as already noted, was emphasised by Schumpeter, can now be demonstrated by reference to Böhm-Bawerk's 'youthful work' of 1876, which according to him (Böhm-Bawerk, 1959, II, p. 439) established the *basic features* of his capital theory but which in itself is essentially a detailed commentary on Turgot's interest theories as developed by him in the second half of the 1760s.[4]

Aspects of Turgot's theory of production have also been interpreted in this 'modern' fashion. Thurlings (1978, pp. 177–9) heads his discussion of Turgot's theory of production with the title 'production functions', and his interpretation of Turgot's statement of the 'law of variable proportions' attributes to Turgot the view that net product (land rent) is *maximised* when the cost of marginal investment equals marginal product (*ibid.*, pp. 185–6).[5] Schumpeter, as was noted, likewise praised this contribution because it actually used 'marginal analysis' and also emphasised that Turgot's formulation of the 'law' was not surpassed until Edgeworth's clear and explicit formulation of the analytical differences between diminishing average and diminishing marginal returns, at the beginning of the twentieth century (Schumpeter, 1959, pp. 260–1; cf. Stigler, 1941, pp. 112–19).

At first sight, there seems therefore to be considerable evidence which supports Schumpeter's arguments about the modern and advanced nature of Turgot's economics, which were cited in the opening paragraphs of this chapter. This interpretation of Turgot as essentially a forerunner of marginalist economics has, however, been challenged by Meek (1973a; 1973b) and by Finzi (1978; 1979). In the context of Turgot's theory of capital, Meek argued that such an interpretation abstracts the theory from its context, a procedure which not only makes comprehension of his analytical system virtually impossible, but also underestimates his achievements as a system builder. In a comment on Turgot's theory of value, Meek implies an inconsistency between such modern interpretations of Turgot's theory and the essentially classical nature of his economic system.

> What is interesting is that Turgot's attempt to incorporate 'scarcity' into 'utility' was in fact made and that a man of his calibre should have believed that a utility-based theory of value was perfectly comparable with a 'paradigm' not essentially dissimilar from Smith's.
>
> (Meek, 1973b, p. 79)

Finzi (1978, pp. xxviii–xxix, liii, lviiin–lix) has criticised the 'neo-classical' interpretations of Turgot's theory of value, while the ahistorical nature of such exercises and their methodological difficulties are analysed in Finzi (1979). Both Meek and Finzi emphasise the classical nature of Turgot's work, together with its relationship to physiocracy.

In view of these different perspectives on Turgot's economics and interpretation, an examination of whether Turgot can be properly regarded as a forerunner or precursor of neo-classical economics may be a useful contribution to a festschrift commemorating the bi-centenary of his death by clarifying a number of points relevant to the understanding of his work. A prerequisite for such an examination is to define the distinguishing characteristics of neo-classical and classical economics, while in this context the notion of precursor may also be investigated more fully. An examination of Turgot's system of economics, with special reference to his theory of value, may then provide an answer to the question posed in the title of this chapter.

I

The 'new economics' of the post-1870s was defined *ex-post* by Robbins (1935, p. 16) as the 'science which studies human behaviour between ends and scarce means which have alternative uses'. The key aspects of this definition are ends, invariably defined in terms of present or future consumption, scarcity reflected in relative prices, and alternative uses which make substitution possibilities a key feature of the process of economic activity. Robbins' definition can be seen as the generalisation of a Robinson Crusoe allocating a given stock of scarce grain among various alternative direct and indirect consumption uses which equate the marginal satisfaction (return) obtained in each use, and thereby maximise aggregate satisfaction. The analysis can be extended by re-defining the means as a given stock of productive resources which can be combined in various ways to produce the desired set of consumption goods, thereby redefining the problem of production as a general problem of resource allocation. The more general, multi-individual version of the theory preserves the maximising individual with a given stock of resources as the focal point of the analysis, but the individual now maximises satisfactions through the exchange of resources with those of others or through production (the transformation of the resources) into the desired set of consumption goods, given the state of technological knowledge.

Efficient resource allocation is achieved in this general system through exchange in competitive markets, so that the key feature of the new economic system are the relative prices which link the given endowments of resources (means) to the consumer tastes (ends) and thereby reflect their relative scarcity. Since consumer preferences are the ultimate yardstick for the ranking of ends, the prices of the productive services (endowment of original resources) are derived and imputed from the prices of the final consumption goods whose production they aid, so that the problem of distribution (reinterpreted as the pricing of productive services) is solved as a corollary of the general determination of prices in a competitive economic system. The theory of production and distribution is therefore subsumed into a general theory of exchange based on the preferences (utility schedules) of consumers.

Although, as is well known, there are considerable variations in the manner in which the new vision of the operation of an economic system was presented during the 1870s, the essentials of that new version are captured in the previous two paragraphs.[6] In the Walrasian general equilibrium version, for example, there was greater emphasis on the efficient operation of competitive product and factor markets which, through the supply and demand determination of equilibrium (market clearing) prices, ensured (or at least, this was what Walras believed) maximum satisfaction for the consumer. In the Austrian variant, provided by Menger, von Wieser and Böhm-Bawerk, the focus is more on unifying the theory of production and distribution into a general theory of exchange with marginal utility as the central principle, but with less emphasis on general solutions to price determination via general equilibrium supply and demand analysis. Jevons, although he explicitly regarded the allocation problem of the maximising individual as the core of economic analysis, did not fully succeed in reducing the problem of distribution to the general pricing problem in the manner of Menger and the Austrians.

This system of thought can be strongly differentiated from the older classical political economy, particularly when defined in the manner of Marx.[7] The major question for the classical political economists was the explanation of economic progress and prosperity, that is, to use the title of Smith's famous treatise, to elucidate the nature and causes of the wealth of nations. The answer to this question was invariably found in the analysis of the surplus product or net product of the society in question, which involved discussion of the origins, definition and the determinants of the size of this surplus as well as of its distribution and disposal. In the shorthand of the definition of classical political economy which Robbins (1935, pp. 64, 67) explicitly sought to replace, it saw as the task of scientific political economy to analyse the production and distribution of *disposable* wealth.[8]

The notion of a *disposable* surplus focuses on a very important characteristic of classical political economy: the representation of the economic process as continuous reproduction (with or without growth) in which part of the reproduced wealth (product or revenue) has to be set aside to ensure the continuation of the economic system. This part is equivalent to the necessary expenses which constitute *non-disposable* wealth, and which cannot be utilised for other purposes without causing the decline of the economy in question. Such a view of the economic system highlights the interrelationship between production, prices and distribution. Both exchange and distribution play a crucial role in ensuring that at the end of the production period (say, a year) the output is distributed in such a way that the required inputs are available to producers in the right proportion to start the production process afresh. To allow reproduction, these exchanges must take place at necessary prices which are necessary in the sense that they at least cover costs so that producers can obtain the required resources for continuing the production process, and in a competitive surplus-producing economy, they must ensure a profit for all producers at a uniform rate. This vision of the production process is in sharp contrast to the neo-classical production function which views production as the transformation of productive services into final consumption goods, and thereby neglects the reproductive features of the system.

Within this schema of reproduction a number of other features of classical political economy stand out. Surplus is created within the sphere of production, it cannot arise in exchange as a general phenomenon, nor can it be satisfactorily explained in terms of restrictions on trade or other monopolistic practices. Its growth is therefore strongly associated with improvements in labour productivity, caused by the division of labour as in Smith, for example, or by the increased application of machines and other aids to labour. Distribution of the surplus is analysed in terms of social classes, which each play *distinctive* roles in the production, distribution and disposal of the social product. Distribution and disposal of the product are seen as key factors in accumulation and growth, and are in turn related to the behavioural characteristics of social classes rather than of individuals.

As already indicated, the role of prices in this analysis also has characteristic features. Classical political economists from Petty onwards strongly distinguished between necessary (or natural, or fundamental) prices, essential to ensure the reproduction of the system, and market prices which reflected the more superficial vagaries of sudden changes in supply (harvest failure) or demand. Costs, in the sense of necessary inputs required for reproduction, were therefore regarded as fundamental in the determination of prices; usefulness and scarcity were not generally seen as determinants of prices, only as necessary attributes (prerequisites) for commodities to become economically relevant.

As in the case of the founders of marginalist (neo-classical) economics, the major features of classical political economy outlined in the previous paragraphs were present in differing degrees in the writings of the period, such differences frequently reflecting the different economic conditions of the society they were discussing. For example, although the dichotomy of market and natural prices is present in the work of Petty, its nature was gradually refined and made more explicit in the succeeding century and a half. On the other hand, in the analysis of social classes, the earlier predominant role of the landlords (Cantillon, the physiocrats) shifted gradually to that of the capitalists (Smith and Ricardo). Although the degree of homogeneity in the views of the classical school should therefore not be exaggerated, there is a greater danger in only stressing differences and peculiar features in the analysis of particular authors, and thereby eliminating the possibility of any general classification in the construction of dividing lines in the development of economics.

The foundation for the distinction between classical political economy and the later marginalist (neo-classical) school presented in this section is the interpretation of the core of the analysis, in what are seen here as two quite distinct schools of thought. This emphasis on the core as the distinguishing feature has a number of implications which should be made explicit. First, if the identification of the particular core in question is successfully challenged or disputed, then the basis for the distinction is destroyed.[9] Second, concentration on the core implies necessarily less attention to the periphery, consequently in the analysis of the views of any particular author, a distinction must be made between major and minor works and between the essential and less essential features of the system constructed by the author in question. Third, and of particular importance in the context of the aims of this chapter, the emphasis on core implies that a precursor of a school of thought must have anticipated the essentials of the analysis and not some of its peripheral features.

Some further comments on the notion of a precursor are in order. This notion is essentially an *ex-post* one, since precursors can only be identified when the systems of thought or ideas which they are said to have anticipated have been themselves discovered and elaborated. This attribute of a precursor frequently encourages the ahistorical search for what are described as 'neglected economists' whose views have something in common with the current school of thought. This is done by selecting and concentrating on those parts of their thought which bear some resemblance to those of the new 'orthodoxy'. Both the 'marginal' and the 'Keynesian revolutions' have inspired such searches for predecessors and precursors, many of which on closer inspection turn out to be misleading, if not exactly wrong, because of their concentration on some superficial similarities which ignore the essentials of the systems of thought which are to be compared. It is argued in this chapter that this has been the case with some of the interpretations of Turgot, and that the continual rewriting of the history of economic thought to which it leads is misleading in many respects, largely by making the interpretation of the author's views dependent on *current* views on the subject.

II

An examination of Turgot's general economic system is made difficult by the fact that, apart from the seemingly hurriedly composed theoretical sketch in the 'Reflections' completed in 1766,[10] no general view of the scope of political economy embodied in a treatise was left by him. However, in the introduction to his 'Eloge de Gournay', written in 1759, there is a short description of the essential qualities which such a science should have if it is approached from the point of view of the philosopher and the statesman.[11] This passage is worth quoting in full, since it has been rarely commented on in works on Turgot.

> Through diligence and alertness he [i.e. Gournay] found time to enrich his mind with a mass of useful knowledge, without yet neglecting that higher literature, but it was, above all, to the science of commerce that he felt himself drawn and to which he directed his mind in all its vigour. To compare the products of nature and those of the arts in man in different climes, to arrive at the value of these different products, or, in other words,

> their relationship with the needs and the wealth of people at home and abroad, the costs of transport which vary according to the nature of the commodities and the diversity of the routes, the many duties to which they are subject, etc., etc.; in short, to comprehend in its full scope, and to follow in its continual upheavals, the condition of natural production, of industry, of population, of wealth, of finance, of the needs and even the vagaries of fashion in all the nations that are united by commerce, in order to theorise profitably on the basis of a thorough study of all these details this is to be concerned with the science of trade, as a merchant and constitutes only a part of the science of commerce. But to discover the causes and effects of that multitude of upheavals in all their diversity, to search out the elemental forces whose action, always in combination with, and sometimes disguised by, local circumstances, directs all the transactions of commerce; to recognise those special and basic laws, founded in Nature itself, by which all the values existent in commerce are balanced against each other and settle at a certain value, just as bodies left to themselves take their place, unaided, according to their specific gravity; to discern those complicated relations which link commerce with all the branches of political economy; to perceive the interdependence of commerce and agriculture, the influence of the one and the other on the wealth, the population, and the strength of states, their intimate connection with the laws and customs, and with all the processes of the government, especially with the distribution of its finances; to weigh the assistance which commerce receives from the Navy and that which it renders to it in return, the changes it produces in the respective interests of States, and the weight it places in the political balance of nations: in fine, to select, from among chance events and principles of administration adopted by the different nations of Europe, the true causes of their progress or of their decline in commerce, this is to approach the subject as a philosopher and a statesman.
>
> (Turgot, 'Eloge de Gournay', in Groenewegen 1977, p. 21)

This passage is instructive since it reveals first of all the breadth of vision which Turgot desired in a science of political economy fit for philosophers and statesmen. It is also interesting because by implication it illustrates some of the imperfections and omissions from his sketch on the production and distribution of wealth. The 'Reflections', albeit briefly, cover the laws of value, the interdependence of commerce and the other branches of political economy (particularly with regard to agriculture, industry, and commerce), its effects on wealth, but it largely ignores its effects on population, the strength of the state, its connection with laws and customs,[12] the distribution and disbursement of state finances, and so on. The 'Reflections' contain brief comments but no systematic discussion of the causes of the progress or decline of commerce. In some instances, such as taxation, interest, value, money, production and reproduction, the contents of the 'Reflections' can be supplemented by those of Turgot's other economic works.[13]

On examining the actual contents of the 'Reflections', it is easily seen that its major thrust is classical in the sense in which that was defined in the previous section. This is already apparent from the opening paragraph, which highlights the importance of economic surplus for general economic progress by demonstrating the severely limited possibilities for such progress inherent in a hypothetical subsistence economy. The implications of the existence of a surplus are then directly and indirectly examined in the remainder of the work, first in the setting of an agricultural society (§§2–28), and then in that of a commercial (capitalist) society (§§29–101). In the first part, surplus is related to exchange, the division of labour and labour productivity (§§2–5); agricultural surplus also creates the first wages fund for the hiring of propertyless wage earners (§§5–6) after the general appropriation of land as private property (§§9–10), although Turgot is careful to point out that there are historical variations in this use of labour in cultivation which allowed landlords to draw the surplus product from their property (§§19–28). The last of these methods, capitalists farming with long-term leases and fixed money rents (§§26–7) introduces capital to the discussion, the implications of which are then analysed in considerable detail. Original accumulation of capital is associated with agricultural surplus, and the necessity of capital in manufacturing, agriculture, and commerce is discussed in detail. The 'Reflections' concludes with a discussion of interest, saving-investment analysis and an analysis of the components of national wealth.[14]

Turgot's distinction in the 'Reflections' between an agricultural society and a capitalist society is shown to have particularly important consequences for the analysis of social classes and the distribution of wealth. The characteristics of agricultural society analysed in the first part of the 'Reflections' demonstrate the validity of the physiocratic class structure of proprietors, who own the land and hence its surplus product; the cultivators, who produce the agricultural surplus; and third, an artisan class maintained from the surplus through exchanging their products for the revenue of the other two classes (§§8, 13, 15). With the explicit introduction of capital as an additional form of surplus income (§29) and after the analysis of capital in agricultural, manufacturing (no longer described as carried out by artisans but by entrepreneurs) and commerce, a further subdivision occurs within the producing classes in agriculture (the productive class) and in the stipendiary class of manufacturers and traders: that of 'the Entrepreneurs or capitalists who make all the advances, and that of the mere wage-earning workman' (§65). The emergence of a new class structure and new income shares is a qualitative change induced by the transformation of society through an accelerated rate of capital accumulation and the associated increased capital intensity of industry.

What was identified as one of the key features of classical political economy – the representation of the economic process as continuous reproduction with or without growth – is also strongly emphasised by Turgot in the 'Reflections'. For example, the description of the need for capital in manufacturing, agricultural and commercial enterprises (§§60, 62, 66, 67) all stress the continuous nature of production, and the requirement that the sale of the product should enable the return of the capital to be used afresh 'for new purchases to furnish and maintain [the] manufactory by this continuing circulation [of products]' (§60). Turgot therefore implicitly recognises that exchanges (sales by the entrepreneur) must take place at prices which allow the continuation of production through the replacement of the capital used up, and that such prices must allow a return on advances sufficient for the capitalist not to withdraw his investment. In this analysis, Turgot also emphasises the interdependence of manufacturing, agriculture and trade in keeping the process going. This is summarised in the following quotation:

> From what has just been said it can be seen that the cultivation of estates, manufacturers of all kinds, and all the branches of trade, depend upon the mass of capitals, or of moveable, accumulated wealth, which, having been first advanced by the Entrepreneurs in each of these different classes of work, must return to them again every year with a steady profit; that is, the capital to be again invested and advanced in the continuation of the same enterprises, and the profits for the more or less comfortable living of the Entrepreneurs. It is this advance and this continual return which constitutes *what ought to be called the circulation of money*; this useful and fruitful circulation, which gives life to all the labour of society, which maintains all the movement and life of the body politic, and which is correctly compared to the circulation of the blood in the animal body. For if, by any disorder whatsoever in the sequence of expenditure of the different classes of society, the Entrepreneurs cease to get back their advances with such profit as they have a right to expect, it is evident that they will be obliged to reduce their enterprises; that the amount of labour, of the consumption of the fruits of the earth, of the production and of the revenue would be equally diminished; that poverty will take the place of wealth, and that the common Workman, ceasing to find employment, will fall into the deepest misery.
>
> ('Reflections', §68)

This summing up of the interdependence of production, circulation and distribution (and its interrelationship with the prosperity of society) as illustrated in the section of the 'Reflections' quoted above, is not an isolated instance in Turgot's writings but a recurring feature of much of his economic work. For example, in 1763, in his 'Plan for a Paper on Taxation in General', Turgot had briefly but clearly indicated the importance of the distinction between gross and net product, the role of the profit motive and the interrelationship between exchange value, net revenue and the process of reproduction. These innovations are correctly attributed to Quesnay (in Groenewegen, 1977, pp. 102–3). A similar set of observations is provided in his commentary on Graslin written in 1767, but which in some ways even further develops the interrelationship between exchange value, reproduction, net product, capital accumulation, social classes and distribution of the product (in Groenewegen, 1977, pp. 123–7). Similar arguments were presented in his fifth letter to l'Abbé Terray on the grain trade, written at the end of 1770. All three versions of the argument referred to in this paragraph were utilised to illustrate the validity of the physiocratic analysis of the incidence of taxation.

It is now time to examine the role of the theory of value and price in Turgot's theory of the interdependent process of production, circulation and distribution, since as has already been indicated, Turgot's views on this subject can only be inferred from the passages already cited. Unfortunately, the material on value in the 'Reflections' is not of much assistance here. This discussion of value is largely confined to the determination of a current value through competition in the market, that is, some brief elucidation of the supply and demand determination of market price (§§31, 32) followed by a lengthy examination of the measure of value and money. Turgot warns the reader at the end of this discussion (§46) that the treatment of the *causes* of value in the 'Reflections' is far from complete. Fortunately, there are both contemporary, and later, discussions of value in Turgot's writings which shed further light on the matter, and which at the same time allow some comments on the consistency of his value theory with his general model of reproduction in a capitalist society, and on the neo-classical features which some commentators have observed in that value theory.

The major additional source for Turgot's theory of value is his unfinished paper, possibly written 1769, entitled 'Value and Money'.[15] This paper contains what has been described as Turgot's subjective theory of value as well as his models of isolated exchange and price determination based on his notions of esteem value and appreciative value derived therefrom. It is undoubtedly true that the tone of this paper is subjective, as is shown by Yamakawa (1959) and by Meek (1973b).[16] It is equally clear that the exchange models contained therein bear resemblance to those of the Austrians, particularly Böhm-Bawerk but also Menger and Wicksell. However, it is not easy to interpret the status of the views on value contained in this essay, because of its clearly unfinished nature, and because of the very specific limitations placed by Turgot on the analysis contained therein.

What are these specific limitations of the analysis in 'Value and Money'? First, this analysis is totally confined to considerations of exchange in the complete absence of any considerations of production. In addition, the analysis appears to be confined to isolated individuals in a *primitive* state of society. For example, the definition and meaning of esteem value is presented for an 'isolated savage' while the examples of isolated exchange are similarly confined to 'savages'. The choice of commodities used as illustrations in the exchange analysis suggests savages in the Americas, representing the standard form of the 'society of hunters'. It can therefore be reasonably inferred that the development of society, and in particular, the development of organised production, modify the causes influencing value, as analysed in 'Value and Money' to a considerable extent. But even if, following the 'Reflections' (§§32, 33) these principles inherent in exchanges and price formation are applicable to more modern forms of society, the analysis remains limited to the determination of market price only.[17]

If it is argued, then, that the analysis of price determination in both the 'Reflections' and 'Value and Money' is confined to market price determination, then Turgot's theory of value can be completed by the distinction between current (market) price and fundamental price which he drew in a letter to Hume (25/3/1767) and in his observations on a paper by Saint-Pérvay, written at about the same time (reprinted in Groenewegen, 1977, p. 120 and note). These comments clearly establish the overall classical nature of Turgot's value theory, by demonstrating his firm adherence to this dichotomy in prices, and all its implications, while they also suggest that market value depends on fundamental value rather than the other way round.[18] Since both these comments are clearly intended to apply to value relations in contemporary society, that is, in a developed commercial society, the status of this distinction appears to me to be more general than the incomplete analysis in 'Value and Money', where the completed text relates to primitive society only. It also fits far better the price analysis implicit in the model of circulation in §68 of the 'Reflections' which has already been quoted.[19]

III

On the interpretation of classical political economy presented here, Turgot's economics is clearly in the classical mould, because the main parts of his economic system are essentially concerned with the conditions for reproduction, the importance of economic surplus for capital accumulation, economic growth and progress, and its effects on the whole of society. If his economic system is compared with the core of the post-1870 neo-classical analysis, little resemblance can be found between them, since the resource allocation problem as such is not considered by Turgot at all.

Even in the examination of some of the details of Turgot's theory, and in particular the features to which Schumpeter drew attention, the resemblance between Turgot's views and that of the post-1870 author is not nearly as close as appears at first sight. In the case of his value theory, the subjective elements which appeared in his paper on 'Value and Money' (Turgot, 1769) were largely designed to illuminate the problem of exchange and market price determination, and do not conflict with the dichotomy between market price and fundamental price to which he adhered. Furthermore, there is no attempt, as in the case of the Austrians, to base the whole of the problem of valuation on utility considerations while the notion of *marginal* utility as sole of determinant of value is conspicuously absent from his analysis. In fact, the notion of marginal utility which allows value measurement of a single commodity in terms of its utility at the margin appears to be implicitly rejected (Turgot, 1769, pp. 137–8). Finally, the models of isolated exchange which most resemble the work of the post-1870 economists, as has been indicated (by Kauder, 1953; Groenewegen, 1970), were in all probability derived by him from scholastic thought and designed to illustrate the similarities and differences between the determination of an exchange ratio in an isolated and primitive exchange and that of a current price in a competitive market in modern society (cf. Thurlings, 1978, p. 12).

Similarly, in the case of capital theory, Turgot's 'modernity' can be exaggerated and its proximity to neo-classical thought over-emphasised.[20] Although Turgot's analysis of interest is essentially market-oriented and determines the rate of interest by supply and demand, the problem of capital itself is closely associated with production and the creation of an economic surplus, with class distribution and economic growth. However, as Meek (1973c, pp. v–vii, xliii–xliv) has pointed out, there is at least one aspect of Turgot's analysis of capital and interest which distinguishes it from that of Adam Smith and that of later classical economists. This is Turgot's explicit equilibrium model of interdependence between the returns on capital in both its active employment in agriculture, manufacturing and commerce, and its passive use in loan contracts at interest and in the purchase of a landed estate (see Turgot, 1766, §§83–90). This feature of his analysis was favourably commented on by both Cassel (1903, pp. 21–2) and Böhm-Bawerk (1959, III, pp. 6–7, 18). Nevertheless, as Meek also indicates (1973c, p. vii) this aspect of Turgot's thought is 'quite comparable with the specification of the particular institutional data and class relationships upon which Smith was concerned to lay emphasis', and does by no means imply that class incomes are solely determined by competition in the market. Although the stress on interdependence and competition in the analysis does suggest some of the qualities associated with Walrasian general equilibrium in Turgot's work, it does not weaken the causal chain which goes from profit (surplus product) to accumulation and investment and then to interest (Turgot, 1766, esp. §§82, 90).

In this context it should also be emphasised that the approach to the theory of distribution which Turgot takes in the 'Reflections' is class-oriented in the sense that the problem is conceived in terms of the division of the total product among the various classes of society and the principles by which this distribution is effected. The division of classes itself depends on the specific role assigned to the various members of society in the production of wealth, that is, whether as propertyless persons they have to earn their living by selling their labour, or whether as owners of property they derive an income without working from either landed property or from capital. The distinct determination of the incomes of these three classes reflects their separation in society, and there is no hint in Turgot's work that this problem is a mere corollary of the determination of prices of final consumption goods, which is one of the hallmarks of neo-classical economics.[21] This important aspect of Turgot's work is therefore also firmly within the classical tradition.

The significance of the 'marginalist' features of Turgot's statement of the 'law of variable proportions' can also be easily exaggerated, as indeed it has been.[22] Although Turgot did distinguish in this discussion between what was to be called the intensive and the extensive margin of cultivation, no inferences of significance for marginalist economics are drawn from this distinction. Furthermore, although his analysis is conducted in terms of increments of product and increments of advances, there is no direct application of the analysis to demonstrate marginalist principles of optimal resource allocation. In fact, Turgot used the analysis for the quite specific purpose of demonstrating the invalidity of the widely used physiocratic assumption that advances yielded gross returns in a fixed proportion, and that therefore the specific effects of the imposition of indirect taxes on agricultural production cannot be determined with any precision (Turgot, 1767a, pp. 111–13).

Generally speaking, therefore, it must be concluded that the resemblance between Turgot's economics and that of post-1870 writers is superficial, and that the similarities which exist should not be taken as a sign that Turgot was in any real sense a precursor of this type of economics. Although in some ways there is no real harm in commenting on, or pointing to, such resemblances, this practice becomes more dangerous if it is used to draw spurious inferences about the development of economic thought. Such ahistorical inferences, for example, appear in the work of Kauder (1953, p. 650), where Turgot and other eighteenth-century economists are argued to have written 'in vain', and where there is talk of 'missed chances' in starting 'correct' value theory earlier than actually occurred. Schumpeter's statements on Turgot imply similar hindsight conclusions of a counter-factual nature.[23]

The major point to which this chapter wishes to draw attention is that Turgot is essentially an economist of the classical school whose work contains all the basic characteristics of that school of thought. He was therefore a man of his own time, a product of the eighteenth century, but one who liked to 'be himself and not somebody else', as he wrote to Du Pont in connection with the latter's 'corrections' of the text of his 'Reflections'.[24] It is therefore not surprising that he attempted to move beyond the accepted view on a number of subjects which he regarded as inadequately explained, while staying within the classical framework of the subject, and all the more the pity that many of these novel approaches to aspects of the subject were not elaborated or completed. These features of his economic thought continue to provide challenges to its interpretation, and if this chapter has corrected some former misinterpretations of that thought it stands as a fitting tribute to the living thought of this great Frenchman, in commemoration of whose bicentenery it was first written.

Notes

1 Half a dozen pages prior to the paragraph from which this quotation has been taken, Schumpeter states that Turgot's theory of capital and interest proved to be 'unbelievably hardy', that it is 'doubtful whether Alfred Marshall had advanced beyond it' and that, although Böhm-Bawerk added a new branch to it, he 'substantially subscribed to Turgot's propositions' (Schumpeter, 1959, p. 325).

2 See, for example, Thurlings (1978), pp. 189–90, and my own re-appraisal of Turgot's value and price theory (Groenewegen, 1970, esp. pp. 189–91, 196) (above, Chapter 16, pp. 288–9, 293). Two errors in that paper have been pointed out to me since it was published. Finzi (1978, pp. lviii–lix) has correctly argued that my interpretation

of Turgot's concept of 'valeur estimative' as a 'purely subjective evaluation of a commodity by an individual' is incorrect since it ignores Turgot's attempts to incorporate scarcity as reflected by labour and other resource costs into utility. Darreau, a Ph.D. student at the University of Limoges, has shown that my criticism of Turgot's solution to the determination of the midway price is wrong, and that Turgot's result of the 'valeur estimative moyenne' is in fact a proper solution to the price determined in an isolated exchange, given his assumptions (undated letter to the author, received in October 1981).

3 See my reinterpretation of Turgot's theory of capital and interest (Groenewegen, 1971, above, Chapter 17) and cf. Meek (1973a, pp. 19–25).

4 I have presented a detailed discussion of this subject in a paper presented to the History of Economic Thought Conference held at Exeter College, Oxford in September 1981, entitled 'Turgot's Place in the History of Economic Thought: A Bicentenary Estimate' (below, Chapter 19).

5 As Thurlings put it, 'Turgot is zich bewust van het feit dat het samentreffen van marginale kosten en marginale opbrengsten het punt oplevert waar de totaliteit van de grondrente haar maximum bereikt' (p. 186). I cannot find any evidence for such a proposition in Turgot, although *with hindsight*, it can be inferred from Turgot's following remark:

> I will mention that it would be mistaken to imagine that the point at which the advances yield the most is the most advantageous one which the cultivator can attain, for, although further increments in advances do not yield as much as the preceding increments, if they yield enough to increase the *net product* of the soil, there is an advantage in making them, and it will still be a good investment.
>
> (Turgot, 'Observations on a Paper by Saint-Péravy', in Groenewegen, 1977, p. 112. I have used the word 'increments' to translate Turgot's 'augmentations'.)

6 Cf. Bharadwaj (1978), pp. 36–7, who lists the salient features of what she calls the new 'supply and demand' theories as the reduction of distribution theory into general price theory, the emphasis on the 'individual' making maximising decisions in response to relative prices, and the shift to exchange and the importance of relative prices as the basic factor in exchange.

7 Marx (1971, p. 52) defines classical political economy as beginning with Petty and Boisguilbert in the second half of the seventeenth century and ending with Ricardo and Sismondi at the 1820s. Conventional definitions of classical political economy see the beginnings in Adam Smith and its conclusion with John Stuart Mill. See O'Brien (1975).

8 Cf. Walsh and Gram (1980, p. 5) who see explanation of the 'production, extraction and accumulation of surplus' as the main theme of classical political economy.

9 For example, the dichotomy between classical and marginalist economics is challenged in a statement such as the following: 'Smith's postulate of the maximising individual in a relatively free market and the successful application of this postulate to a wide variety of specific questions is our basic paradigm' (Gordon, 1965, p. 123). On this basis, a number of authors of whom Hollander (1973, ch. 1; 1979, ch. 9) is the most recent and prominent example, argue that the development of economics since Adam Smith has been a steady refinement of the study of the competitive market as a mechanism which efficiently allocates resources via the signals of relative (market) price changes. Such a view rejects a separate core for classical economics and leaves pre-Smithian authors in some sort of limbo.

10 This neglects the juvenile plan for a work on commerce, circulation, interest and wealth, which he prepared at the age of twenty-five (reprinted in Schelle (1913–23) I, pp. 376–87).

11 The addition of statesman is interesting, since it associates the science of political economy with practical policy in the manner also done by Smith (1976, Book IV, introduction, p. 428).

12 The interconnection of economic activity with customs and laws is traced in Turgot's works on the successive advances of the human mind and in his fragment on universal history. For a discussion, see Meek (1973a, introduction, pp. 27–33; 1976, pp. 68–76).

13 As Turgot himself wrote to Du Pont shortly after he had completed the 'Reflections', many questions had been left out and the only subjects which he explicitly regarded as thoroughly treated were the formation and movement of capitals and the interest of money (Turgot to Du Pont, 9/12/1766, in Schelle, 1913–23, III, p. 519).

14 References to the 'Reflections' in this and the succeeding paragraphs are to my edition and translations (Groenewegen, 1977). Since the section numbering of the various editions of the 'Reflections' differs, this gives only an approximate indication of the references provided in the text for most other editions. A concordance of the major French and English editions is given in Groenewegen (1977, appendix).

15 There is considerable ambiguity about the purpose and time during which this paper was written. For a discussion see Groenewegen (1977, pp. xxv–xxvii) and Meek (1973b, p. 77). The most likely time, however, seems 1769.

16 See also Kauder (1953) and Groenewegen (1970) (above, Chapter 16).

17 Unlike Yamakawa (1959, pp. 30–1, 47) I see no essential difference between the determination of current price (market price) in the 'Reflections' and the elaboration of the argument in 'Value and Money', cf. my (1970, p. 194, n70, Chapter 16 above, p. 297 n70). This destroys, in my opinion, any suggestion that Turgot's thinking on value was substantially transformed between 1766 and 1769. Meek speculates that the paper may have been abandoned because Turgot could not solve the analytical difficulties inherent in his exchange models (Meek, 1973b, p. 79) but he presents no evidence, while I have speculated that Turgot's paper may have in fact been the foundation for Morellet's paper on money, etc., printed in the Prospectus for the Dictionary in 1769. See Groenewegen (1977, pp. xxvi–xxvii and notes 77, 80–6).

18

> But we must distinguish two kinds of price level: the *current price* which is established by the relationship of supply and demand, and the *fundamental price*, which for a piece of merchandise is what the item costs the artisan. ... Now, although the fundamental price is not the immediate basis of the current value, it is nevertheless a minimum beneath which the latter cannot sink. ... You increase the fundamental value: the circumstances which previously fixed the ratio of the current value to this fundamental value must up the current value to the point where the ratio is re-established.
>
> (Turgot to Hume, 25/3/1767, reprinted and translated in Rotwein, 1955, pp. 211–12)

19 Continuous reproduction implies a sale price sufficient to cover all costs including the replacement of capital and the profit necessary to induce the entrepreneur to maintain his investment in the industry, that is, the fundamental value. It is clearly the analytical equivalent of Smith's concept of natural price.

20 This does not eliminate the possibility that Turgot's views on this subject may have influenced the work of the young Böhm-Bawerk, as I have suggested (Groenewegen, 1977, p. xxix, n99; 1981 [below, Chapter 19]).

21 In this context I cannot refrain from commenting on the remark by Schumpeter on the 'Reflections' which I quoted at the end of the first paragraph of this chapter. This comment on the 'first of all the treatises on Value and Distribution' is misleading on

two grounds: first, because it misquotes the title as 'value and distribution' rather than as the correct 'production and distribution of wealth'; second, because it implies a link between value and distribution in the style of 'the later decades of the nineteenth century' which just cannot be found. As indicated in the second section, Turgot explicitly stated that the problem of value was not thoroughly explored in his 'Reflections', so that an emphasis on value in the description of its contents, as Schumpeter gives, is misplaced.

22 Cf. my comments on Thurlings (1978) in this context in note 5 above.

23 Since Turgot's work was readily available in the early part of the nineteenth century and was studied by a significant number of economists, who in general did not appear to see in his writings the foundations for a new theory of value, and so on, it is difficult to speak of 'missed chances'. The merit of such ideas, or rather, the apparent merit, was not recognised until the new theories were fully developed.

24 Turgot to Du Pont, 2/2/1770, in Schelle (1913–23) III, p. 374.

References

Bharadwaj, Krishna (1978) *Classical Political Economy and Rise to Dominance of Supply and Demand Theories*, New Delhi: Orient Longman Limited.

Böhm-Bawerk, E. von (1959) *Capital and Interest*, 3 vols in one, South Holland IL: Libertarian Press.

Cassel, G. (1903) *The Nature and Necessity of Interest*, London: Macmillan.

Finzi, Roberto (1978) Introduction to *Turgot, Le ricchezze, il progresso e la storia universale*, Turin: Piccola Biblioteca Einaudi.

——(1979) 'Turgot fra fisiocrazia e pensiero classico', in *Studi in Onore di Paolo Fortunati*, Bologna: Cooperative Libreria Universitaria Editrice.

Gordon, D. F. (1965) 'The Role of the History of Economic Thought in the Understanding of Modern Economics', *American Economic Review*, 55(2) May, 119–27.

Groenewegen, P. D. (1970) 'A Reappraisal of Turgot's Theory of Value, Exchange and Price Determination', *History of Political Economy*, 2(1) spring, 177–96 (above, Chapter 16).

——(1971) 'A Re-interpretation of Turgot's Theory of Capital and Interest', *Economic Journal*, vol. 81, June, 327–40 (above, Chapter 17).

——(1981) 'Turgot's Place in the History of Economic Thought: A Bi-centenary Estimate', paper presented at the History of Economic Thought Conference, Oxford, September (mimeographed) (below, Chapter 19).

Groenewegen, P. D. (ed.) (1977) *The Economics of* A. *R. J. Turgot*, The Hague: Martinus Nijhoff.

Hollander, Samuel (1973) *The Economics of Adam Smith*, London: Heinemann.

——(1979) *The Economics of David Ricardo*, London: Heinemann.

Kauder, E. (1953) 'Genesis of the Marginal Utility Theory', *Economic Journal*, 63(251) September, 638–50.

Marx, K. H. (1971) *A Contribution to the Critique of Political Economy*, London: Lawrence and Wishart.

Meek, R. L. (1973a) Introduction to *Turgot on Progress, Sociology and Economics*, Cambridge: Cambridge University Press.

——(1973b) *Precursors of Adam Smith: Readings in Economic History and Theory*, Everyman edition, London: J. M. Dent.

——(1973c) Introduction to 2nd edn of *Studies in the Labour Theory of Value*, London: Lawrence and Wishart.

——(1976) *Social Science and the Ignoble Savage*, Cambridge: Cambridge University Press.

O'Brien, D. P. (1975) *The Classical Economists*, Oxford: Clarendon Press.

Robbins, Lionel (1935) *An Essay on the Nature and Significance of Economic Science*, 2nd edn, revised, London: Macmillan.

Rotwein, E. (1955) *The Economic Writings of David Hume*, London: Nelson.

Schelle, G. (1913–23) *Oeuvres de Turgot et Documents le Concernant*, Paris: Felix Arcan.

Schumpeter, J. A. (1959) *History of Economic Analysis*, London: Allen & Unwin.

Smith, Adam (1976) *An Inquiry into the Nature and Causes of the Wealth of Nations*, eds R. Campbell, A. S. Skinner and W. B. Todd, Oxford: Clarendon Press.

Stigler, G. J. (1941) *Production and Distribution Theories: The Formative Period*, New York: Macmillan.

Thurlings, Th. L. M. (1978) *Turgot en zyn Tijdgenoten*, Wageningen: H. Veenman & Zonen NV.

Turgot, A. R. J. (1973–54, 1913–23) 'Plan d'un ouvrage sur le commerce, la circulation et l'intérêt de l'argent, la richesse d'états', in Schelle, G. *Oeuvres de Turgot et documents le concernant*, I, Paris: Felix Arcan, 376–87.

——(1759, 1977) 'Eloge de Gournay', in Groenewegen, P. D. (ed.) *The Economics of A. R. J. Turgot*, The Hague: Martinus Nijhoff, ch. 4.

——(1763, 1977) 'Plan for a Paper on Taxation in General', in Groenewegen, P. D. (ed.) *The Economics of A. R. J. Turgot*, The Hague: Martinus Nijhoff, ch. 6.

——(1766, 1977) 'Reflections on the Production and Distribution of Wealth', in Groenewegen, P. D. (ed.) *The Economics of A. R. J. Turgot*, The Hague: Martinus Nijhoff, ch. 5.

——(1767a, 1977) 'Observations on a Paper by Saint-Péravy', in Groenewegen, P. D. (ed.) *The Economics of A. R. J. Turgot*, The Hague: Martinus Nijhoff, ch. 7.

——(1767b, 1977) 'Observations on a Paper by Graslin', in Groenewegen, P. D. (ed.) *The Economics of A. R. J. Turgot*, The Hague: Martinus Nijhoff, ch. 8.

——(1769, 1977) 'Value and Money', in Groenewegen, P. D. (ed.) *The Economics of A. R. J. Turgot*, The Hague: Martinus Nijhoff, ch. 9.

——(1770, 1977) 'Letters on the Grain Trade', in Groenewegen, P. D. (ed.) *The Economics of A. R. J. Turgot*, The Hague: Martinus Nijhoff, ch. 11.

Walsh, Vivian and Gram, Harvey (1980) *Classical and Neoclassical Theories of General Equilibrium*, New York: Oxford University Press.

Yamakawa, Yoshia (1959) 'The Transition of Turgot's Value Theory', *Waseda Economic Papers*, vol. 3, 30–47.

19 Turgot's place in the history of economic thought

A bicentenary estimate[1]

The bicentenary of Turgot's death, which occurred on 18 March 1781 at his house in Paris on the Rue de Bourbon, provides an opportunity for the assessment of Turgot's place in the history of economics. In such an assessment, two questions ought to be considered in some detail. The first concerns the quality of his contributions to economics, such as the presentation of new techniques of analysis, new concepts, or new propositions. The second question relates to the influence exerted by his work on his contemporaries and successors, either because that work acted as an authority which guided the direction of further investigation, or because it was a source of considerable controversy which stimulated fresh thought and analysis. In particular, if influence on later generations of economists is considered to be large, the author ought to be assured of an important place in the history of economic thought.[2]

Although in this context it is useful to look at the antecedents of the thought of the economist in question, this aspect of the assessment of Turgot need not be conducted here, since it has been done recently.[3] In addition, an assessment of the connection between Turgot and Adam Smith, which would have preoccupied the commemoration of the centenary of Turgot's death in 1881, is now largely redundant,[4] while the catalogue of Turgot's library, edited and published with consummate skill by Professor Tsuda,[5] allows an easy evaluation of the written sources in economics available to Turgot.

Because there are therefore so many recent interpretations of Turgot's economics which place his work in the context of the eighteenth century, this chapter concentrates on the two factors identified by Robbins as relevant to assessing a person's more permanent place in the history of economic thought. In the first section, a quick survey of Turgot's major contributions to economics is presented. The second section presents an evaluation of his influence on nineteenth-century economists, subdivided into three subsections: influence on the British and French political economy school of the early nineteenth century, influence on the mid-nineteenth-century school of French liberalism, and third, influence on some early marginalists who were familiar with his work.[6] A final section presents some brief conclusions.

I

A reading of Turgot's major economic works provides abundant evidence of the variety of his contributions to economic analysis and policy. These contributions not only covered value, production, and distribution theory but also the theory of money and international trade, public policy, and taxation theory, as well as an analysis of economic progress which included consideration on the development of capitalism. All these subjects, with only a few exceptions, were developed by him in memoranda connected with his administrative duties as Intendant of Limoges (1761–74) and Finance Minister (1774–6), and were influenced by his strong belief in the benefits of free trade and unrestrained competition. For this reason they were not integrated by him into a single systematic exposition – apart from the short but highly systematic account of the nature of economic development presented in the 'Reflections' – with the consequence that those who rely on that work alone miss a great deal of importance in the economics of Turgot. An exposition of the model of economic progress from the 'Reflections' is presented first and is then supplemented and qualified by matters raised in his other economic writings.

It is easily shown that 'Reflections' presents a model of the consequences of the transformation of an agricultural society by the introduction of a capitalist mode of production, and it can therefore be largely regarded as a discussion of the third and fourth stages of economic progress, namely agricultural and commercial society. In early writings Turgot had discussed the more traditional model of economic progress – the three-stage theory of hunters, shepherds and farmers.[7] The third or agricultural stage is discussed further in the 'Reflections', where it is shown that after the private appropriation of land, the landlords used various methods of obtaining a surplus from their land which changed over time. From cultivation by slaves and, later, cultivation by serfs as direct methods of obtaining revenue from their property, landlords shifted to more indirect means, of increasing sophistication and efficiency, through tenancy agreements: first vassalage, then sharecropping in the *métayer* system, and finally capitalist farming, which implies the letting of land for a fixed annual money rental. These last two methods were practised in Turgot's own France, and crystallised for him the struggle between the older, feudal mode of agricultural production and the modern capitalistic form in which, for the first time in history, the tenant-farmer provided all the advances of cultivation and transformed himself from a peasant into a capitalist-entrepreneur.[8]

The class structure of the older, agricultural society reflects these differences in the method of production. After the appropriation of land, society is divided into owners of land, who live off the surplus product extracted from their property, and workers, the latter being owners only of their labour power, which is sold to the landlord-farmers and from which sale they obtain their livelihood. With exchange and the division of labour, a third class arises which does not directly obtain its living from agriculture but indirectly through the provision of goods and services to the agricultural sector. This class is the 'stipendiary class', maintained from the agricultural surplus, and the class of proprietors, which appropriates it by virtue of its ownership of the land. The analysis of the first part of the 'Reflections' conforms, therefore, largely to the picture presented by Quesnay's *Tableau économique*, adding little apart from the historical analysis of the different methods of appropriating the surplus from the land.

The second and third part of the 'Reflections' move beyond this picture of agricultural society. Turgot here showed that he clearly 'perceived that feudalism was becoming capitalism, and that economic theory could not, accordingly, confine its attention to the land'.[9] Turgot's awareness of this is shown when in the first section of the second part of the 'Reflections' he indicates that apart from the ownership of land, there is another way of being rich, namely by living off the 'revenue of money' or more precisely, the return on capital.[10] The subsequent analysis of capitalist production involves a digression on the theory of value and money, saving and investment, before proceeding to the analysis of the necessity for advances in production, that is, in manufacturing and commerce as well as in agriculture. This new factor in economic development – the use of capital in production – transforms the class structure of society and the distribution of the product.

The introduction of a capitalistic mode of production subdivides the two working classes of society – the productive and stipendiary class – into two classes. The first comprises the entrepreneurs in manufacturing, commerce and agriculture, who are 'all owners of large capitals, which they invest profitably as advances in setting men at work'. The second is that of labourers who own no property and who 'receive no profit but their wages'.[11] The transformation of feudalism into capitalism creates a new class structure from the old one – the new one consisting of landlords with their income share in the form of landed surplus product or rent; labourers, without property, living on wages; and finally, the new class of entrepreneurs who live off the profits from their invested advances. The change in production implies a change in distribution; these changes also mean that the physiocratic analysis of society has become outmoded.

The essence of this model of economic progress contained important consequences for the development of economic theory. Like Smith, Turgot placed great emphasis on the emergence of capital as a third factor of production and on the new class which owned that factor and derived a new income share – profits – from its use. Turgot's 'Reflections' provided the first economic model which presented this complete picture quite clearly; the method of production defines the class relationship in society and the distribution of the gross product; hence economic analysis has to concern itself with the production and distribution of wealth, which in turn implies elucidation of the theory of value, exchange and money. This framework for organising economic discussion was more clearly defined by J. B. Say in the nineteenth century,[12] together with its implications for production and distribution analysis on a three-factor basis in place of the outdated two-factor model. This contribution is one of Turgot's major achievements.

Turgot's basic model of economic progress is further developed both within the 'Reflections' and in his other economic writings. Two aspects of this economic development have already been investigated in detail,[13] so that little has to be said on the theory of value, exchange, price determination, capital and interest. There is, however, a need for a discussion of Turgot's elaboration of the theory of production and distribution and the policy implications he drew therefrom.

In the theory of distribution, apart from his analysis of the determination of interest, Turgot presented also explanations of the determination of the other two income shares. The theory of rent is confined to a discussion of the physiocratic concept of the net product which Turgot accepted with one qualification: the justification of rent as an income share is for him based on the rights of private property, and is not seen in terms of a reward for investment in the form of improvements to the land which become permanent qualities of the soil.[14] The theory of wages, sketched in the 'Reflections' as a subsistence theory,[15] is more fully developed as an 'iron law' in his comments on Graslin and in his 'Letters on the grain trade'. Population changes, induced by departures of the market rate of wages from the fundamental or subsistence rate, ultimately restore the wage rate to its equilibrium level determined by the customary subsistence of the workers.[16] The theory of distribution is therefore confined to an analysis of the determination of the rate of wages and interest, and acceptance of the physiocratic analysis of net product as a theory of rent.

In the elaboration of his theory of production, Turgot made further important contributions to economic analysis. His enunciation of diminishing returns and of the law of variable proportions, the first in the history of economics, is well known and needs no further discussion.[17] His analysis of the circular flow and of economic growth largely followed that of the physiocrats though, unlike these contemporaries, he saw no difficulties arising from saving in the process of circulation. This aspect – which is in fact Turgot's elaboration of the essentials of Say's law[18] – has already been discussed, as has his analysis of the accumulation of capital.[19]

In addition to the above, Turgot also elaborated the conditions he considered favourable to economic growth. These contributions, made largely in the realm of economic policy, concern his general attitude to government intervention in economic affairs, by taxation and by other restrictions placed on trade and industry. In many of these he went much further than the physiocrats. He can therefore be described as one of the major contributors to the rise of economic liberalism in Europe in the eighteenth century.[20]

Turgot's general arguments for laissez-faire are most clearly stated in his 'In praise of Gournay'. They are applied to particular branches of trade in his 'Letter on the "marque des fers"', dealing with protection proposals for the iron industry. All these considerations are based on the general principle that

> every man knows his own interest better than another to whom it is of no concern. ... [consequently] every man ought to be left at liberty to do what

> he likes. In the case of unrestrained commerce. … [it is virtually impossible] for the individual interest not to concur with the general interest.[21]

This policy by itself will always lead to the greatest wealth and welfare for the community as a whole. The reasons often advanced in justification of state interference, that is, the internal and external security needs of the state and its desire to protect the rights of consumers, are wrong, since these needs are in fact best served by the unrestrained competition secured through free trade.[22]

Turgot's arguments in favour of free trade, because of the stimulus to production this policy would yield, can be best illustrated by his practical application of the principle to the iron industry which existed in his province of Limoges.[23] Proceeding from the premise that there is 'no means of stimulating any trade or industry other than that of giving it the greatest freedom' and of freeing it from the burdens of indirect taxation, Turgot revealed the meaning of this maxim for the industry in question by listing a variety of reasons against protection of industry. In the first place, protection to one branch of trade encourages protection to other branches, which raises the overall cost structure of industry and thereby causes a decrease in welfare for the community as a whole through losses in trade and production. Second, protection invites foreign retaliation, resulting in further losses of production and trade. Third, by protecting the iron industry, there is little consideration for the needs of the consumers of that product, who frequently require the importation of types of iron (English and German) which cannot be produced in France. Protection consequently ruins the industries dependent on imports of foreign iron and steel. Fourth, the interdependence of industrial production, and the importance of iron as a raw material in all branches of production, make it important that this item be produced at the lowest possible cost, which can be ensured only through increased competition caused by free trade. Finally, Turgot presented an argument against protection which comes close to the comparative-advantage case for free trade, and which can be quoted in full:

> To persist in opposing. … [the advantages of free trade] from a narrow-minded political viewpoint which thinks it is possible to grow everything at home, would be to act just like the proprietors of Brie who thought themselves thrifty by drinking bad wine from their own vineyards, which really cost them more in the sacrifice of land suitable for good wheat than they would have paid for the best Burgundy, which they could have bought from the proceeds of their wheat.[24]

Turgot also argued that free trade and the resulting increase in competition provided the most effective protection of the rights of the consumer. Far better than government regulations which prescribed in detail the nature and quality of the articles to be produced, and more effective than the supervision over craftsmanship exercised by the guilds, 'the general freedom of buying and selling [will assure] the consumer of the best merchandise at the lowest price':[25] better, because competition will drive the expensive and fraudulent trader out of business; more efficient, since regulations and restrictions impair progress in industry by discouraging experiment, inventions and new products; cheaper also, because in the absence of regulations the bureaucracy of the inspectorate can be abolished.[26] This protection of the interests of the consumer is especially important in the grain trade. There, free trade will guarantee the largest possible output by enhancing the profitability of agriculture; it will secure the largest supply in times of harvest failure through encouraging the movement of wheat supplies, including imports; while, finally, an increased output will raise the real wage rate and thereby increase the living standards of the majority of consumers.[27] Free trade and competition benefit consumer and producer alike.

Some comments must also be made on Turgot's theory of taxation. Like the physiocrats, he advocated the single, direct tax on land rent as the best possible tax, partly on the score of equity but even more on the score of economic development. Taxation of commodities was not in conformity with his basic laissez-faire position – it constituted a barrier to free trade – though its burden is also shown to fall ultimately on the landlords so that it would be more efficient and economical to tax their income directly.[28] Taxes on wages must also be ultimately passed on to the landlords. The discussion of the taxation of profits reveals his ambivalent attitude to this income share. Profits are excluded by him from the net product, and are therefore non-disposable in the sense that they form part of the necessary costs of reproduction. Profits cannot therefore be taxed, since this will lower the rate of return to investment, cause the withdrawal of capital and a consequent fall in output, which in turn reduces the net product so that the burden is effectively transferred to the landlords. On the whole, Turgot's tax analysis shows the rigour of his theory and the clarity of his thought exceedingly well.[29]

Finally, there are Turgot's contributions to monetary and international trade theory. It can be said that in these areas he contributed relatively little that was new, presumably because of his awareness of and agreement with the contribution on these subjects of Locke, Cantillon and especially Hume. In monetary theory, Turgot dealt adequately with the definitions of money and money of account, as well as with the qualities, functions and value of money. On the latter subject, he showed himself a convinced adherent of the quantity theory of money, and metallist in money and banking policy.[30] In international-trade theory, he followed a strong anti-mercantilist position, was familiar with the theory of the automatic mechanism of international specie distribution, and clearly understood the limitations of the balance-of-trade argument.[31] His general arguments against protection and in favour of free trade have already been discussed.[32]

The above constitute Turgot's major contributions to economic analysis which, taken together, make him one of the leading theoretical economists of the eighteenth century. In addition, some other, more methodological features of his economics may be briefly noted. Turgot, for example, was one of the first – if not the first – economist to draw mechanical analogies in his economic reasoning; his explicit use of a concept of equilibrium is a case in point.[33] His definitional precision as shown in the article 'Value and money', for example,[34] and his habit of always proceeding from 'first principles'[35] in the setting out of an argument, provide further reasons why he may be considered as one of the clearest theoretical writers in economics of the century. It is these features, together with his contributions to analysis, especially in the theory of value and interest, that secured his writings considerable appeal and praise in the century that followed.

II

The impact of Turgot's economics on later generations of economists can now be considered. As indicated in the introduction, he exerted some – though generally speaking only minor – influence on three groups of economists: first, on the British and French school of political economy, including herein Jeremy Bentham, James Mill, David Ricardo, Lauderdale, Malthus, Samuel Bailey and J. B. Say;[36] second, on the mid-nineteenth-century French school of economic liberalism, among whom can be numbered Monjean, Chevalier, Bastiat and Léon Say; and finally, on some members of the early marginalist school, that, on Menger, Böhm-Bawerk and Alfred Marshall.

Before proceeding to a more detailed discussion of the extent of this influence, a comment may be made on the general availability of his works, a matter of some relevance. It can be easily shown that Turgot's major economic work was readily available:[37] his 'Reflections', for example, was reprinted on many occasions in the period up to the end of the nineteenth century, in both French and English, while his works were twice made available during the first half of the nineteenth century in the nine-volume edition edited by Du Pont – the edition owned and read by Ricardo and J. B. Say, for example – and by Daire, the edition used by Marx[38] and the marginalists. Finally, Ferrara included Italian translations of Turgot's economic works in his volume, *Fisiocrati*, in the famous reprint series Bibliotecca dell'Economista.[39] Single works were also frequently reprinted during the nineteenth century in a variety of languages.

The classical school

With some exceptions, Turgot's influence on the classical school was slight. Bentham, for instance, in his economic writings refers to Turgot only in his famous letter to Adam Smith published with his *Defence of usury*, and this was only a second-hand reference derived from a passage in Condorcet's *Vie de M. Turgot*.[40] Bentham's friend James Mill was better acquainted with Turgot's works. Although there are no references to Turgot in his economic writings, he wrote to Ricardo in 1818, 'By the bye, have you ever read Turgot's works? I have been at them lateley. They will interest you highly. Did you ever read his life by Condorcet?'.[41] This shows admiration rather than influence.

With Ricardo, similarly, influence was slight, if not non-existent. In reply to Mill's query, quoted above, he wrote:

> About 3 years ago I was very much pleased by reading Turgot's life and works. He was a reformer – but although the abuses which he wished to remove were most convincingly demonstrated by him to be such, what difficulties had he not to encounter and for how short a time was he entrusted with the power of being useful¡ At least this is the impression which remains with me. He was a very able political economist, considering the prejudices of his time.[42]

Although this recollection of reading Turgot during the time of preparation of the *Principles* may account for the inclusion of Turgot's name among the economists who had improved the science,[43] Ricardo was not sufficiently impressed to quote him frequently in his major work. The only two references to Turgot in the text of the *Principles* are inspired by Say rather than Ricardo's own reading of Turgot's works.[44]

Turgot appears to have had a stronger influence on the work of Lauderdale; in fact, he was probably partially responsible for Lauderdale's *Inquiry into the nature of public wealth*. This can be ascertained from the passages underlined in Lauderdale's own copy of the 1788 edition of the 'Reflections'.[45] These are concerned with the accumulation of capital, with the determination of prices by a supply and demand analysis, with the consequences for investment, profits, and employment of a disturbance in the circular flow,[46] the determination of the rate of interest in the market, the sources of accumulation, and finally, the whole of the last section which presents the classic statement of the saving-investment analysis underlying Say's law.[47]

It can easily be presumed that these passages exerted some influence on Lauderdale, as he had owned and read Turgot's major economic work at least a decade before the publication of his *Inquiry*. This impression is reinforced by the fact that it is precisely in the topics to which these passages refer that similarities are most noticeable between Turgot's work and that of Lauderdale. This is the case in the chapter on value, which is completely supply and demand oriented; in the enumeration of the various uses of capital; and in the lengthy discussion on the process of capital accumulation, where Turgot, as well as Smith, is strongly criticised for what Lauderdale felt to be excessive praise of the benefits of thrift.[48]

Turgot also appears to have exerted some influence on the work of Malthus. Malthus' sympathy and acquaintance with the ideas of physiocracy are well known,[49] so that it is not surprising to find that he had studied Turgot's economic work as well. Yet Turgot is quoted on only a few occasions in Malthus' major economic work, *Principles of political economy*, and then only in connection with one subject, that of value.[50] Apart from the explicit references to Turgot in the text, there are indications of other influences by Turgot on Malthus' theory of value. First of all, Malthus' discussion of the determination of value within a subjective framework by individual 'relative estimation' which in turn depends on the desire to own a thing, and the difficulty of acquiring it, is very reminiscent of Turgot's value analysis in the paper 'Value and money'.[51] Second, Malthus' interesting critique of the 'early and rude state of society' model employed by Smith and Ricardo in their labour theory of value analysis, was possibly also partly inspired by Turgot.[52] Although some influence by Turgot on other subjects is also possible, this would be exceedingly difficult to document.[53]

The final case of possible influence by Turgot on an English economist of the period is that of Samuel Bailey, more specifically, on the theory of value as discussed by Bailey in the first chapter of his *Critical dissertation*.[54] Such influence can be demonstrated only from internal evidence; Bailey did not cite Turgot in his book, but this does not necessarily mean that he was unacquainted with the latter's work. As references are made by him to both Lauderdale and Malthus[55] on the subject of value, it is quite possible that Bailey gained an acquaintance with Turgot's economics through these sources. Furthermore, as already indicated, Turgot's works in the Du Pont edition appear to have been readily available to the major economists of the period, so that Bailey too would have been able to get access to them, while Bailey's familiarity with the French language is evident from the use he made of Say's edition of Storch's *Cours ï économie politique*.[56]

The basic propositions established by Bailey in his critique of orthodox value theory, and on which the whole of this critique depends, can all be clearly found expressed in Turgot's 'Value and money'. First of all, Bailey's opening sentence, 'Value, in its ultimate sense, appears to mean the esteem in which any object is held' is strikingly similar to Turgot's definition of esteem value.[57] Bailey's argument that value can rise only 'when objects are considered together as subjects of preference or exchange' is very similar to Turgot's argument that valuation can occur only when values are compared with other values.[58] The emphasis on the relative nature of value, which is so striking a characteristic of Bailey's work, is also very apparent in Turgot. This is illustrated in the following quotations:

> In the circumstances, that it [value] denotes a relation between two objects, and cannot be predicated of any commodity without an express or implied preference to some other commodity, value bears a resemblance to distance. As we cannot speak of the distance of any object without implying some other object, between which and the former this relation exists, so we cannot speak of the value of a commodity but in reference to another commodity compared with it. A thing cannot be valuable in itself without reference to another thing, any more than a thing can be distinct in itself without reference to another thing.[59]

> The only means of expressing value is then, as we have said, to express that one thing is equal in value to another. ... Value, like size, has not other

> measure than itself, and if values are measured by comparison with other values, as length is measured by comparison with other lengths, then in both means of comparison there is no *fundamental unit* given by nature, there is only an *arbitrary unit* given by convention.[60]

The five points in which Bailey summarised his views on the nature of value can also be found in Turgot's paper,[61] while the specific application of them in Bailey's critical discussion of the use of measures of value by his contemporaries presents conclusions similar to those reached by Turgot in his paper on value and in the 'Reflections'.[62]

Although it is possible that the above considerations are coincidental – a further case of that independent discovery so frequent in economics – this does not seem really plausible. Bailey in his *Critical dissertation*, reveals himself as well read in political economy, and the nature of the references to Turgot in Malthus' *Principles* would more than likely have induced him to study Turgot's works. If this is indeed the case, then it can be stated that Turgot was influential in English economics in the early nineteenth century, not by stimulating the orthodox tradition – with the exception of some indirect influences through Smith – but by inspiring the 'underground' critics of that orthodoxy on the theory of value such as Lauderdale, Malthus and Samuel Bailey.[63] This makes the importance of Turgot's direct influence in English classical economics rather slight, but not insignificant.

The same conclusion does not apply to his influence on the French classical tradition, mainly represented by Say's influential *Treatise of political economy*. Say's acquaintance with Turgot's works as edited by Du Pont is easily proved. They are quoted on many occasions in his *Treatise*;[64] furthermore, he is reputed to have said 'that the publication … of the works of Turgot was the most important service rendered by Du Pont to the science'.[65] In spite of this, it seems certain that Say was a great deal less influenced by Turgot than by Adam Smith. It is Smith who is considered the great authority on the subject; Turgot is occasionally discussed with Smith as concurring with the views of the master.[66]

Nevertheless, it seems to be an established fact that J. B. Say was indebted to Turgot on several important points.[67] First of all, Turgot is said to have influenced the general pattern of Say's *Treatise*; second, considerable influence by Turgot can be seen in Say's treatment of value, while Turgot also had influence on Say's theory of capital and interest; finally, Say seems to have been indebted to Turgot on some questions related to the theory of money. The remaining references to Turgot in the *Treatise* deal with the grain trade,[68] slavery,[69] Turgot's reform of duties on fish in Paris,[70] and Turgot's reform of the corvée.[71]

The influence of Turgot on Say's expository scheme is indicated by Prinsep, Say's English translator. In the preface to this translation, he argued that Say's book

> will be found to contain the best and most methodical view of the general theory of wealth that has yet appeared. In treating his subject, the outline

> of Turgot has been observed and extended, from the production, or formation, and the distribution of wealth, to the survey of ultimate consumption.[72]

This was a division which was largely followed by later textbook writers such as James Mill and J. R. McCulloch.[73] Similarly, Say's treatment of the subject matter within these broad divisions, which was based on a threefold classification of the agents of production, owed probably as much to Turgot as it did to Smith.[74]

In connection with the theory of value, Turgot's influence is also apparent. The stress on usefulness in the first chapter is probably due to Turgot and Condillac,[75] as is the emphasis on supply and demand in the determination of value, though this influence is less noticeable in the fourth edition of the *Treatise*, which rephrased the three chapters on value of the earlier editions and condensed them into two, largely under the influence of Ricardo.[76] One of the passages that disappeared in this revision referred directly to Turgot's definition of exchange value as 'valeur appréciative' or the average of individual esteem values,[77] which reveals both Say's familiarity with and his basic agreement with Turgot's value analysis in the paper 'Value and money'. Furthermore, Say's categorical denial of the possibility of discovering an invariable measure of value, and his comments on the usefulness of money as a measure, would probably have been derived from Turgot's similar opinions.[78] The eighteenth-century French tradition of utility analysis in value theory, and the consequent emphasis on the relative nature of value, were preserved by Say partly through Turgot's influence on his writings, though it was subsequently weakened by Ricardo's criticism.

Turgot is also referred to by Say in connection with monetary theory and the theory of capital and interest. On the subject of money, the indebtedness seems to have been confined to discussion on the suitability of the precious metals to serve as money, on the consequence thereof for their value, and on the limited capacity of money to serve as a measure of value.[79] Turgot also influenced Say on the concept of capital and on the accumulation of capital. Turgot is cited in connection with the proposition that thrift has greatly increased relative to the past, as indicated by the reductions in the rate of interest that have taken place,[80] while the whole treatment of the subject of Book I, chapter 11, of Say's *Treatise* is reminiscent of Turgot's analysis in the 'Reflections'. Hoarding, saving and investment are carefully distinguished; the circulation of capital and the role of money in the savings process and in capital accumulation are carefully described.[81] In the theory of interest, Turgot's influence is also apparent; supply and demand analysis, risk, the need for capital and its various uses, are all discussed in a manner which could easily have been derived from Turgot.[82]

This, then, is by and large Turgot's influence on the classical school. The influence, naturally enough, was greater in France than in England, and it was especially strong in areas where his own analysis was at its most original, namely in the theory of value and in capital theory. Although Turgot's influence was not strong in England, it was not entirely absent, and made its appearance in the important field of value theory.

The French liberal tradition in economics

The mid-nineteenth century in France produced a group of liberal economists who, reacting strongly to the socialist experiments of the revolution of 1848 and their inspiration in the writings of Proudhon and Louis Blanc, proclaimed liberty to be the most important conclusion to be derived from political economy. This group, as Schumpeter has shown,[83] became the dominant group in French economics for a considerable period of time.

> They were anti-*étatistes*, that is to say they indulged in the belief to the effect that the main business of economists is to refute socialist doctrines and to combat the atrocious fallacies implied in all plans of social reform and of state interference of any kind. In particular, they stood staunchly by the drooping flag of unconditional free trade and laissez-faire.[84]

This group included Rossi, Chevalier, Bastiat, Leroy-Beaulieu, Yves Guyot, Léon Say and Monjean, to name only the more important.

To this group of authors, Turgot was a hero and great precursor of their views. Under their auspices, some of Turgot's writings were republished,[85] and many eulogies appeared which praised Turgot for his general free trade approach.[86] Furthermore, his works were summarised and systematised in such a way that they stressed the features in harmony with the views of this school as, for example, in Neymarck's summary of Turgot's necessary preconditions for economic development, which can be quoted in full:

> Le principe de la *propriété*, clef de voûte de la société; *la liberté du travail*, c'est-à-dire le libre exercise du droit qu'a chaque individu d'utiliser les facultés de toute nature, talents, forces, ressources, don't il dispose; … *L'abolition* des monopoles, priviléges, corporations, règlementations, interventions inutiles de l'autorité; La *securité*, véritable capital moral; les avantages de *l'instruction* et les bonnes *habitudes* morales des travailleurs. … Ces vérités, nous les avons vues magistralement exprimées, developpées, dans les écrits de Turgot: elles ont été adoptées après lui par les plus grands maîtres de la science économique: J. B. Say, Ricardo, Rossi, Bastiat, Robert Peel, Cavour, Cobden, Michel Chevalier.[87]

Turgot's economic doctrine foreshadowed the views of this economic school in many other respects. For example, his well argued 'Letters on the grain trade' were organised on the basis of class reactions to the policy of free trade and concluded that there is, in fact, substantial harmony in the interests of the four groups analysed – state, landlords, farmers, and consumers – despite appearances to the contrary. This doctrine of the existence of social harmony under conditions of free trade formed the basis of Bastiat's major economic work. Second, Turgot's first essay in monetary theory, with its strong condemnation of the expropriation resulting from the creation of paper money, foreshadowed the critique by Bastiat and Chevalier of Proudhon's system of banking and credit. Turgot's defence of the rights of consumers, which could be safeguarded only by free and unlimited competition, also formed a major part of the doctrine of the nineteenth-century French school. Turgot's attack on the restrictions and regulations imposed by the guilds on the right to work expressed in his preamble to the edict suppressing them, served as a model for the defence of the freedom to work in the agitation of the French liberal school against trade unions and national workshops in the nineteenth century. Finally, his unreserved and unqualified free trade position received their admiration.

The French nineteenth-century liberal tradition in economics was not strong in economic analysis; nevertheless, even here two areas can be indicated in which some influence by Turgot is discernible. The first of these relates to the theory of value, the second to the theory of interest, subjects to which Turgot had contributed substantially in his economic analysis. This can be illustrated briefly by some comments on the similarity between the theories of value, capital and interest of Bastiat[88] and those of Turgot.

Bastiat's general view of the theory of value, and many of its particulars, are reminiscent of Turgot's theory in the paper 'Value and money'.[89] For instance, Bastiat sees the theory as arising out of exchange and not from the intrinsic qualities of commodities, since only through exchange can value be estimated. He further concludes that '*value* must have reference to the *efforts* which men make in order to obtain the *satisfaction* of their *wants*'. At the same time, value is regarded as strictly relative, since it implies 'competition, appreciation, estimation', the last two terms recalling names given by Turgot to two of his concepts of value.[90] Money is seen as an imperfect measure of value; efforts are immeasurable in practice, as is utility.[91]

In Bastiat's discussion of capital and interest, Turgot's influence can also be seen. The purpose of the essay 'Capital and interest' is the justification of the payment of interest on a loan contract, not (as with Turgot) against the prohibition of interest by the church, but against the views of the socialists on the 'sterility of capital'. As in Turgot, loans are described as a form of exchange in which value exchanged for equal value, interest arising from the fact that 'the value of ten sixpences now' is different from the value of 'a crown a year hence'.[92] From this it follows that 'interest is not injurious to the borrower' provided the contract is free, since the borrower can use the resources borrowed with profit to himself. Interest is also necessary to compensate the lender for parting with command over resources for a period of time and thereby losing the opportunity to profit from their use. Elsewhere it is clearly stated that interest is a price determined by supply and demand. Here again there are striking similarities between Turgot's views as expressed in 1770 in his 'Paper on lending at interest' and Bastiat's justification of interest.[93]

This brief discussion of the connections between Turgot's economics and that of the nineteenth-century French liberal tradition highlights two aspects of Turgot's influence on later generations. In the first place, aspects of his theory of value and interest appear to have been utilised once more, even though in a different context. Second, his uncompromising position of economic liberalism was seized upon and fully exploited by the French school and carried to extremes.[94] This aspect is important, since it probably accounts for the neglect which Turgot's economics suffered in the twentieth century. In the zealous portrayal of Turgot as a nineteenth-century liberal offered by the French, and by some British nineteenth-century historians of economics,[95] many other, more important features of his economic analysis were forgotten, only to be rediscovered and reappraised in the twentieth century.[96]

The marginalist school

In an earlier paper, I have argued that some of Turgot's contributions to economic analysis resemble the work of the marginalist school to a far greater extent than those of his contemporaries and more immediate successors.[97] This is especially the case with his theory of value and exchange, and of capital and interest. It is therefore not surprising to find these aspects of Turgot's work appreciated by some of the leading marginalist economists – including Carl Menger, Eugen von Böhm-Bawerk, and Alfred Marshall – all of whom had studied Turgot's works early in their respective careers. Other founders of this tradition, however, seem to have largely ignored his work.[98]

Carl Menger, the famous founder of the Austrian School, was very familiar with Turgot's works and cited them on no fewer than five occasions in his first and best known work, *Grundsätze der Volkwirtschaftslehre*.[99] Three of these references, not surprisingly, deal with the theory of value, the other two are concerned with monetary theory, the final subject discussed in Menger's book. None of these references can, however, really be described as indicating influences by Turgot on Menger's work. They do reveal that Menger had studied Turgot's work as edited by Daire in considerable detail[100] and presumably at an early stage of his economic career, so that minor influences by Turgot may perhaps be presumed.[101]

Although Menger's familiarity with Turgot's work cannot therefore be said to have inspired his own work, it may have been indirectly responsible for Turgot's influence on Menger's famous student and later colleague, Böhm-Bawerk. Böhm-Bawerk's praise for Turgot's theory of interest and his highly critical evaluation of it as a fructification theory are well known[102] but it is less well known that Turgot is also quite frequently cited in the *Positive theory of capital*[103] and in some of the critical essays which followed the publication of Böhm-Bawerk's two volumes of *Capital and interest*.[104] Finally, it should be mentioned that Böhm-Bawerk's 'youthful work which never achieved publication' and 'which contained the basic features of [his] theory of capital' was largely a commentary on Turgot's interest theory.[105]

For the purpose of this discussion, the mixture of praise and criticism with which Böhm-Bawerk treated Turgot in his writings on interest is highly significant; his categorisation of Turgot's analysis as 'circular reasoning' need not be repeated, though the staunch adherence to the interpretation on which this argument rested, and its reiteration in his later critical history should be noted.[106] Similarly, the identification of Turgot's theory with the 'patriarchal' beginnings of the 'colourless theories' smacks of criticism and condescension.[107]

On other occasions, however, Böhm-Bawerk is not sparing with his praise of Turgot's performance in the field. Turgot's work is described as the first real breakthrough on interest theory since the writings of Salmasius of the seventeenth century,[108] while his justification of lending at interest is called a performance executed 'with a skill which was as remarkable as its results were brilliant'. In this context, Turgot's 'remarkable passages ... emphasising the influence of time on the valuation of goods' are praised, even though 'this pregnant idea' was not fully elaborated by him.[109] Praise of this aspect of Turgot's interest theory was repeated on several occasions in the critical history.[110]

Turgot's concept of capital, although criticised, is also given high praise. In the first place, Turgot's interpretation of capital as accumulated goods is described as the second basic step in the formulation of a correct capital concept, though it is criticised for going too far through its inclusion of dwelling houses and consumption goods among capital goods.[111] Second, and more importantly in the chapter on Rae in the critical history, even more significant praise is bestowed on Turgot's capital concept in this passage: '[Rae's] concept of instruments, the distinguishing characteristic of which is the intention of meeting a future need, seems to me to be most closely akin to the idea of capital as defined by Turgot and Knies'.[112] In view of the many favourable comparisons later made between Rae and Böhm-Bawerk's own theory, this is high praise indeed.[113]

Furthermore, a hitherto unmentioned feature of Turgot's analysis of capital and interest is approvingly referred to in one of Böhm-Bawerk's critical essays.[114] In this work, Böhm-Bawerk recognised the importance of Turgot's argument that a variation in the rate of interest affects the allocation of capital to its various uses, since it reflects changes in the relative scarcity of capital in society. A falling rate of interest – an effect and indication of an increased abundance of capital – allows previously unprofitable employments of capital to be utilised with profit.[115] This point is reiterated by Böhm-Bawerk some dozen pages later in the following manner:

> Under certain circumstances the newly accumulated funds must acquiesce in opportunities that have hitherto been rejected. And this fact, which is familiar to businessmen and economists since the days of Turgot, stands in reciprocal relation to an accompanying decline of the interest rate.[116]

The importance of this relationship in Böhm-Bawerk's own analysis of the rate of interest needs no emphasis, even though its theoretical generality is now seen as invalid.

The significance that can be given to these comments so far as Turgot's influence on Böhm-Bawerk is concerned, must now be assessed. In the first place, it can be noted that two of the features of interest theory for which Turgot was especially praised are, not surprisingly, precisely two which themselves form an important part in Böhm-Bawerk's own theory, though, of course, in a much more elaborate manner. These two points are the difference in value between present and future goods, or more precisely, the fact that the value of present goods is greater than that of goods in the future; and, second, the characteristic given to capital goods of being able to meet a future need. This stress on the time element in the phenomenon of interest is the link that connects Turgot with Böhm-Bawerk's explanation of the origin of interest.

A consideration of Böhm-Bawerk's 'Jugendarbeit' becomes now appropriate. This work, the first on the subject of capital and interest by Böhm-Bawerk and written when he was twenty-five years old, is almost completely devoted to a critical evaluation of Turgot's 'Paper on lending at interest'.[117] The time element which, as has been shown,[118] Turgot stressed so frequently in his analysis of capital and interest, also receives the greatest emphasis in Böhm-Bawerk's first paper.[119] In addition, and not without importance, the treatment of interest as an exchange phenomenon, so characteristic of Turgot's theory, formed also a major point of departure for Böhm-Bawerk's own analysis of interest.[120] Even though this early paper contains considerable criticism of Turgot's work, it at the same time seems to prove that Turgot's analysis of interest exerted considerable influence on the young Böhm-Bawerk, since it was the background against which he formulated the foundations of his own celebrated theory.[121]

Before leaving this discussion of Turgot's possible influence on Böhm-Bawerk, one further comment must be made. In a paragraph dealing with Turgot's theory of value, exchange and price, Schumpeter[122] has argued that Turgot's 'description of the market mechanism is very similar to that of Böhm-Bawerk's analysis of price determination'.[123] It appears to follow Turgot's analysis in the 'Reflections', in that it starts with isolated exchange, then proceeds to an analysis of one-sided competition of buyers and sellers, and concludes with a discussion of general competition in a one-commodity- and then in a multi-commodity case. Some of the details of the bargaining process described in this chapter are also reminiscent of Turgot's analysis. It is, however, unlikely that Turgot was influential in this connection, since the same pattern is followed by Menger as well.[124]

Some brief reference must also be made to Marshall's connection with Turgot's economics. It is easily shown, for example, by referring to the Marshall-Wicksell correspondence,[125] that Marshall thought highly of Turgot's theory of interest and that he was acquainted with Turgot's works in the Daire edition. More interesting, however, is a reference by Marshall to Turgot in an early essay on the theory of value, which was published as part of the 1975 edition of Marshall's early writings on economics.[126] At the opening stages of this paper, Turgot's analysis of isolated exchange is approvingly referred to, and this is followed by a brief critical examination of Turgot's extension of the analysis to a larger market. Of influence there is no question. Turgot's analysis is largely used as an illustration.[127] In the *Principles*, there are only a few references to Turgot: he is mentioned as the first economist to give a clear statement of the law of diminishing returns, he is quoted on the subsistence theory of wages, and, finally, he is cited on the 'iron law' of wages as a long-run phenomenon, and its implications for tax policy as seen by him are referred to by Marshall. He is not even given separate treatment in the historical section of the *Principles* on the growth of economic science.[128]

Nevertheless, it can be said that Marshall was appreciative of at least two of Turgot's contributions to economics: his theory of value and his theory of interest. This is illustrated by the fragment on Turgot reprinted from Marshall's lecture notes of the late 1860s (or early 1870s) included among his early economic writings. His work was also described as a 'monument of genius' in a letter to Wicksell in the context of the Böhm-Bawerk controversy, which can now be examined.[129]

This controversy was started by Cassel, who, after a laudatory but incomplete summary of Turgot's theory of capital in his *Nature and necessity of interest*, severely criticised Böhm-Bawerk's thoughts on the subject.[130] The relevant passage must be quoted in full to explain the vehemence of the replies by Böhm-Bawerk himself and by Wicksell, as well as the involvement of Marshall in the controversy against his wishes. Cassel wrote:

> Of course it was impossible for *Turgot*, in dealing with this side of the problem [i.e. the mutual dependence of the return of the various employments of capital], not to state that capital cannot be used in industry, unless it yields at least the same rent as the capitalist is able to secure for himself by buying land. Out of this a modern Austrian critic, *Böhm-Bawerk*, has constructed what he calls a 'fructification theory of interest' – the theory that the possibility of gaining rent from land is the *cause* of interest – and has thus made it easy for himself to pass over the profound investigation of one of the greatest geniuses who worked in our science in the eighteenth century as hardly more than a simple confusion of thought. It indeed may be doubted whether such criticism is more discreditable to the author himself or to those students who have accepted him as an authority without taking even the simplest precautions to obtain confirmation of his statements.[131]

In view of the last sentence of this paragraph it is not surprising that Cassel's discussion drew bitter responses from both Böhm-Bawerk and Wicksell.

Böhm-Bawerk's criticism of Cassel is contained in a full-length essay in which he devoted considerable attention to the point that 'the abstinence theory and the use theory' were correctly considered by him as 'competitive and exclusive of each other',[132] a point rejected by Cassel, who claimed that these two aspects of interest theory provided the explanation for the supply and demand sides of the problem and could therefore be synthesised into a theory of interest as part of the general theory of market prices.[133] This point is crucial for a defence of Böhm-Bawerk's procedures in interpreting interest theories in his critical history, including those used in his interpretation of Turgot.[134] In connection with the latter, Böhm-Bawerk presented no explicit justification of his fructification theory interpretation, but severely criticised Cassel's praise of Turgot as having fully covered the demand side of the problem and furthermore charged him with misinterpretation of Turgot through wrong translation.[135]

The explicit defence of Böhm-Bawerk's interpretation of Turgot's theory of interest as a fructification theory was undertaken by Wicksell. In an article on Böhm-Bawerk's theory of capital and its critics, Wicksell attacked Cassel strongly on this point. He failed to 'discern the 'depth' which Cassel said he had found in Turgot's 'reflections on interest', and argued that 'it does seem indisputable' that a fructification theory 'was in some vague way the line of thought' Turgot had in mind.[136] In a review of Cassel's *Theory of social economy* seven years later, he returned to the attack by describing Turgot's theory as clearly irrational.[137] Prior to these published attacks on Cassel's views, Wicksell had discussed the matter in detail in correspondence with Marshall, presumably as a consequence of the reference to Marshall inserted by Cassel at this point.[138]

In reply to what must have been a query from Wicksell about this reference – a query not included in the correspondence as reprinted by Gårdlund – Marshall wrote as follows:

> I think it is probable I am in considerable agreement with Prof. Cassel. For a student, who had come to Cambridge with the opinion that the founders of Economics of all nations were inferior in common sense to most children of ten, and very much inferior to his worthy self, gave Prof. Böhm-Bawerk as his authority. I replied, 'I do not think Prof. Böhm-Bawerk has caught their real meaning. I regard personal controversies as a great waste of time; but if you will select any one of these authors as a test case, I will give a lecture on his doctrines of interest'. It happened that several other members of this class were present at the conversation, and the notion was approved and they selected Turgot. I therefore did – what I had not done before – compare Turgot's words with Prof. Böhm-Bawerk's account of them; I made full notes for the lecture. I read out alternatively passages from Turgot and from Böhm-Bawerk's account of Turgot. I then gave Turgot and Prof. Böhm-Bawerk's book to the class and asked them to pass these books from hand to hand, adding 'a fortnight hence I will ask the question in lecture – have I done justice to Prof. Böhm-Bawerk's treatment of Turgot'. The answer was yes. I forget details, but I think I found not only that the opinions which Prof. Böhm-Bawerk had read into some of Turgot's passages, were not really there; but also that in other sections to which discussions on these matters properly belonged, Turgot had expressed categorically the exact opposite of the opinions attributed to him. I have lent the notes of

> this lecture to several persons, and I may have lent them to Prof. Cassel; though I do not recollect whether I did or not. No one who has read the notes has questioned the conclusion to which they point.[139]

In his reply to this letter, Wicksell indicated that after reading 'over and over again the passages in Turgot quoted by Böhm-Bawerk' as well as others which were relevant, he still adhered to Böhm-Bawerk's interpretation for reasons similar to those already discussed.[140] He also asked Marshall to lend him his notes on the subject, which Marshall at first refused.[141] Four months later, however, Marshall changed his mind and wrote: 'I send you my notes *for your own use exclusively*. I have not read them through since I wrote them six years ago'.[142] Wicksell remained unconvinced, and returned the notes with the comment that Marshall appeared to 'overrate the earlier writers on interest, especially Turgot'.[143]

The controversy is interesting for several reasons. In the first place, because it shows that Marshall, at least implicitly, supported a more recent re-interpretation of Turgot's theory of capital and interest,[144] in which Turgot's analysis is presented as a supply and demand analysis with the demand side explained by the use of capital in production. Second, it reveals the peculiar nature of Böhm-Bawerk's methods in his critical history, which depended on a rigid separation of various aspects of the interest problem, and which ignored supply and demand explanations as such when they combined more than one of these aspects together. This, as both Cassel and Marshall felt, biased his critique considerably. A third point, which remains largely unsolved, is the reason why Wicksell maintained strong, qualified support for Böhm-Bawerk's interpretation, in spite of the evidence presented by Marshall. This is partly explained by the fact that he believed Böhm-Bawerk's discussion to be basically correct, as shown in his insistence on criticising Turgot's inclusion of the purchase of land as the first – but not necessarily the primary – form of investment of capital. On the other hand, his general hostility to Cassel, which was largely personal, cannot be excluded as an explanatory factor for the vehemence with which Turgot's theory was attacked. Finally, the importance of Turgot's theory in the history of interest theories is attested to by the fact that it was so frequently referred to in a controversy between adherents of contending theories of interest at the turn of the century, which clearly is an important matter for an assessment of his place in the history of economics.

III

The preceding two sections have answered the questions posed at the beginning of this chapter, and have therefore prepared the way for a final evaluation and assessment of Turgot's place in the history of economics. That this is an important place cannot be doubted: the contributions he made to economic analysis were many and were praised by a significant number of diverse authorities during the two centuries that followed their appearance. His major original work, that on value, capital, and interest, was the most influential part of his economics insofar as the work of later generations of economists goes, though his overall influence was not great, except perhaps in the case of Böhm-Bawerk.

To complete the historical interpretation of Turgot's economics, some further comments are in order. In the first place, it should be emphasised that Turgot devoted relatively little time to systematic economic writing after 1761, so that most of his basic contributions were produced in the little leisure he enjoyed during his hectic administrative career, which finally ended in 1776. In contrast with Adam Smith, who spent more than ten years in writing the *Wealth of nations*, Turgot appears to have completed his *magnum opus* in economics, the 'Reflections', in a few months. Nevertheless, that work has occasionally been favourably compared with Smith's treatise, as for instance in the following quotation from Schumpeter's history:

> The ('Reflections') was evidently written in hot haste and never thoroughly revised. It looked as Marshall's *Principles* would have looked if text, notes and appendices were destroyed and only the marginal summaries – and not all of these – were preserved. In fact, it is not more than a very elaborate analytical table of contents written for a bulky but non-existent treatise. Such as it is, however, Turgot's theoretical skeleton is, even irrespective of priority, distinctly superior to the theoretical skeleton of the 'Wealth of Nations'. In order to arrive at this opinion, it is not necessary to impute to Turgot anything he did not say or to credit him with anything that he may not possibly have seen himself. He actually delivered the goods. In calling his work unfinished or a skeleton, I do not mean to say that there is need for any uncertain conjecture or generosity of interpretation in order to finish it. It presents a complete system of economic theory.[145]

Elsewhere,[146] I have shown that the development of this system was heavily indebted to two major sources: English economics, especially that of Locke, Cantillon and Hume; and French economics, especially that of Montesquieu, Quesnay, and Gournay. His system, however, developed much beyond theirs: in contrast with Cantillon and Hume, he greatly developed production and distribution theory; in contrast with Quesnay, he more clearly saw the coming of capitalism and its implications for economic theory. In addition he advanced economics in many other areas and produced arguments and theories which frequently had to be rediscovered by later generations of economists.

His economic analysis was only partly devoted to theoretical matters; his major purpose in studying economics was practical. Much of the economic material he wrote while Intendant of Limoges and all of what he wrote while Finance Minister was concerned with practical issues and was intended to alleviate the hardship, first of the people of his province, and then of the whole of France. His economics was progressive for the age in which it was written, and it was filled with concern for the problems of his time. The epitaph penned by

Malesherbes in honour of his friend neatly summarises this twofold aspect of Turgot's economic labours, and is a fitting close to this appreciation of his economics:

> Il avait le coeur de l'Hôpital et la tête de Bacon

These laudable characteristics of one of the founders of economic science remain most appropriate for economists facing the problems of the 1980s.

Notes

1 This chapter is based on a paper presented at the History of Economic Thought conference at Exeter College, Oxford, in September 1981. The revision of that paper has benefited from the subsequent discussion of its contents.

2 The criteria are those of Lionel Robbins, 'Schumpeter on the history of economic analysis', in *The evolution of modern economics and other papers* (London, 1970) pp. 64–9, where he defends Marshall's place in the history of economics against the criticism of Schumpeter.

3 See Roberto Finzi, 'Turgot fra Fisiocrazia e pensiero classico', in *Studi in onore di Paolo Fortunati* (Bologna, 1979) pp. 2–31, and his introduction to *Turgot: le ricchezze, il progresso e la storia universale* (Turin, 1978) esp. pp. xxiv–lix; Th. L. M. Thurlings, *Turgot en zijn tijdgenoten* (Wageningen, 1978) esp. ch. 6; and P. D. Groenewegen, 'Turgot, Beccaria and Smith', in P. D. Groenewegen and Joseph Halevi (eds) *Italian economics past and present*, Frederick May Foundation of Italian Studies (Sydney, 1983) (above, Chapter 1).

4 P. D. Groenewegen, 'Turgot and Adam Smith', *Scottish Journal of Political Economy* 16 (Nov. 1969) pp. 271–87 (below, Chapter 20); Dieter Stark, *Die Beziehungen zwischen A. R. J. Turgot und A. Smith* (Basel, 1970).

5 Takumi Tsuda, *Catalogue des livres de la bibliothèque de Turgot*, Institut d'Etudes Economiques, Hitotsubashi University (Tokyo, 1974).

6 The question of what constitutes influence by an economist on later generations of economists was discussed following the presentation of this paper at the Oxford conference, but without any real resolution of the issue. In the second section below, influence of Turgot's economics on later economists is conjectured on the basis of similarity of ideas and from knowledge of their acquaintance or possible acquaintance with Turgot's works. Frequency of citation is used as an index of influence, but not exclusively, as a reading of the documentation of this part of the chapter shows.

7 See R. L. Meek, 'Smith, Turgot, and the "four stages" theory', *History of Political Economy*, 3 (Spring 1971) pp. 9–27. This is further developed in his *Social science and the ignoble savage* (Cambridge, 1976) pp. 68–76.

8 'Reflections', §§19–28, in P. D. Groenewegen, *The economics of A. R. J. Turgot* (The Hague, 1977) pp. 50–6. (All references to Turgot's economic writings will be given to my translation in this work, unless otherwise indicated.) The last two methods of cultivation were also frequently described as 'la petite culture' and 'la grande culture' respectively, following Quesnay's analysis of them in his article 'Fermiers', published in the *Encyclopédie* in 1756. Turgot himself published a more detailed analysis of them in an article 'Des caractères de la grande et de la petite culture', in *Ephémérides du Citoyen*, no. 6 (1767) 77–97. Both are included in translation in P. D. Groenewegen (ed.) *Quesnay: 'Fermiers', and Turgot: 'la grande and la petite culture'*, Reprints of Economic Classics, series 2, no. 2 (Sydney, 1983).

9 Harold Laski, *The rise of European liberalism* (London, 1936) p. 189.

10 'Reflections', §29, p. 56.

11 'Reflections', §§61 and 65, pp. 70–1, 72–3.

12 See the second section of this chapter, below, and cf. E. Cannan, *History of the theories of production and distribution from 1776 to 1848*, 3rd edn (London, 1953) pp. 26–8, esp. p. 28.
13 See my 'A reappraisal of Turgot's theory of value, exchange and price determination', *History of Political Economy* 2 (Spring 1970) pp. 177–96; 'A re-interpretation of Turgot's theory of capital and interest', *Economic Journal*, 81, no. 2 (June 1971) pp. 327–40 (above, Chapters 16 and 17).
14 See 'Reflections', §17, pp. 49–50 and n7; 'Plan for a paper on taxation', *ibid.*, pp. 102–8, esp. 102–3.
15 'Reflections', §6, pp. 45–6.
16 See 'Observations on a paper by Graslin', pp. 126–7; and 'Letters on the grain trade', pp. 175–9, esp. pp. 178–9, where Turgot argues that subsistence need not mean minimum physical subsistence. The theory was described as an 'iron law' of wages by Marshall (*Principles of economics*, 8th edn (London, 1920) pp. 505–6 and n1) and by Wermel, *The evolution of classical wage theory* (New York, 1939) pp. 69–70.
17 See 'Observations on a paper by Saint-Péravy', pp. 111–12; cf. 'Observations on a paper by Graslin', pp. 125–6. Turgot's statement of the law of variable proportions was first emphasised by Cannan in his *History of the theories of production and distribution*; and see also J. A. Schumpeter, *History of economic analysis* (London, 1959) pp. 259–61. All references to Schumpeter's work will be given to this edition unless otherwise indicated.
18 See 'Observations on a paper by Saint-Péravy', pp. 115–18. Turgot had first argued that 'sales and purchases are always equal in the long run' in the context of international trade in a letter to Du Pont de Nemours (20 February 1766) in G. Schelle, *Oeuvres de Turgot* (Paris, 1913–23) 2, pp. 510–11.
19 See my 'A re-interpretation', esp. p. 335, and his 'Observations on a paper by Saint-Péravy', pp. 115–22, in which he criticised Saint-Péravy's fear, shared by the physiocrats, that the money 'set aside to create capitals. ... is not immediately returned to the circulation'.
20 In this connection it is interesting to note that Turgot's works on these subjects were reprinted in the years immediately preceding the French Revolution, as well as during its early stages. See P. D. Groenewegen, *The economics of A. R. J. Turgot*, introduction, p. xxi and n57.
21 See Turgot, 'In praise of Gournay', p. 26.
22 *Ibid.* 25–31. In a sense, Turgot's advocacy of laissez-faire went far beyond that of Adam Smith, who, for example, admitted defence as a good reason for some protection in agriculture and shipping.
23 I.e. Turgot's 'Letter on the "Marque des fers"', pp. 182–8. The quotations in this paragraph have been taken from this paper, the last one on economics written by him as Intendant of Limoges.
24 See 'Letter on the "Marque des fers"', p. 187.
25 See 'In praise of Gournay', pp. 26–7.
26 *Ibid.*, 24–5.
27 See 'Letters on the grain trade', pp. 174–81.
28 See 'Plan for a paper on taxation in general', pp. 100–1, Turgot to Hume, 7 September 1766 and 25 March 1767, in J. Hill Burton (ed.) *Letters of eminent persons addressed to David Hume* (Edinburgh and London, 1849) pp. 147–8, 154–7.
29 See 'Plan for a paper on taxation in general', pp. 96–108, 'Letters on the grain trade', pp. 167–9, and the letters to Hume cited in note 28 above.
30 See Turgot, 'Letter on paper money', pp. 2–8; 'Reflections', pp. 61–4, 81–4; 'Value and money', pp. 134–6.
31 'Observations on a paper by Saint-Péravy', pp. 118–19; see also Turgot to Du Pont, 20 February 1766 in *Oeuvres* (Schelle) 2, pp. 507–12. Physiocratic international trade theory, including Turgot's views on the subject, is admirably discussed by

Bloomfield, 'The foreign trade doctrines of the Physiocratics', *American Economic Review*, 28 (Dec. 1938).

32 See 'Letter on the "Marque des fers"', p. 187, for his argument against protection and trade barriers by way of analogy about the production preferences of the inhabitants of Brie, which has already been quoted. He also wrote vigorously against exclusive colonial trade. See, for example, Turgot to Josiah Tucker, 12 September 1770, in *Oeuvres* (Schelle) 3, pp. 421–3; and his 'Mémoires sur les colonies américaines', *ibid.*, 5, pp. 384–420.

33 The notion of equilibrium is explicitly introduced in the 'Reflections', §88, p. 87; in the 'Letters on the grain trade', p. 176, and his letter to Hume, 25 March 1767, in J. Hill Burton (ed.) *Letters of eminent persons addressed to David Hume* (Edinburgh and London, 1849) p. 156. For a different type of mechanical analogy, see his 'Observations on a paper by Saint-Péravy', p. 112. On the significance of this innovation, see my article 'History and political economy: Smith, Marx and Marshall', *Australian Economic Papers*, 21, 38 (June 1982) pp. 7–8.

34 'Value and money', pp. 136–7.

35 See for example, 'Plan for a paper on taxation in general', p. 96; cf. 'Letters on the grain trade', p. 166. Turgot's method here is of course part of the rationalist tradition of the Enlightenment.

36 Some omissions of Turgot's possible influence on British classical political economy may here be noted. The most important of these is Francis Horner, as was pointed out to me by Donald Winch, who also mentioned the possibility that Turgot may have influenced Dugald Stewart's lectures on political economy given at Edinburgh University around the turn of the century. Horner's journal, which he kept from 1797 to 1803 (that is, between the ages of twenty-one and twenty-five, when he commenced serious study of political economy) shows that he read Turgot's 'Reflections' in August 1798, following this by a careful study of Condorcet's *Life of Turgot* (25 April 1799) and that he was sufficiently impressed by the quality of Turgot's work to project its translation, going as far as to sound out a number of potential collaborators and to investigate with a London publisher the commercial viability of this project. (Apart from the 'Reflections', this translation would have included the letters on the grain trade, the paper on interest and on the 'marque des fers', the *Encyclopédie* articles, two papers on public administration – 'Mines et carrières' and 'Municipalités' – as well as a retranslation of Condorcet's *Life of Turgot* supplemented with notes drawn from Dupuy's *Eloge de Turgot*.) This did not materialise, though it shows that Horner was able to get hold of all of Turgot's economic writings which had been published in the eighteenth century (see below, note 37, on the significance of this). His impressions of Turgot's 'Letters on the grain trade' were recorded on 10 August 1800. See *Memoirs of Francis Horner with selections from his correspondence*, revised edn (Edinburgh, 1849) pp. 44, 49–50, 63, 72. Fetter, in his introduction to *The economic writings of Francis Horner*, LSE Reprint no. 13 (London, 1957) p. 5, briefly refers to this aspect of Horner's economic education.

An intentional omission, at which some conference participants expressed surprise, is J. S. Mill, who greatly admired Turgot as a person. See his *Autobiography*, new edn (London: Longmans, Green and Company, n.d.) p. 65, where Turgot is described as 'one of the wisest and noblest of men'. However, Turgot is only referred to once in the *Principles* and then only in connection with his views on the inefficiency of the *métayer* system cited second-hand from Richard Jones. See *Principles of political economy*, Book II, ch. 8, §3, in *Collected works* (Toronto, 1965) 2, p. 302. My knowledge of Mill's work reveals no discernible influence thereon from Turgot's economic writings.

37 The 'Reflections', for example, was reprinted in 1788 and in English translation in 1793, 1795 and 1801. In addition, his *Mémoire sur le prêt à intérêt et sur le commerce des fers* and his *Lettres sur les grains* were republished in Paris in 1788 for the first time

and probably around the same date for the second time, possibly under the auspices of Condorcet (see note 20 above). Two editions of Turgot's works appeared in the first half of the nineteenth century: *Oeuvres de Turgot, précédees et accompagnées de mémoires et de notes sur sa vie, son administration et ses ouvrages*, ed. Pierre Samuel du Pont de Nemours, 9 vols (Paris, 1808–11); and *Oeuvres de Turgot, nouvelle édition*, eds Eugéne Daire and Hippolyte Dussard, 2 vols (Paris, 1844) as vols 3 and 4 of the Guillaumin Collection des Principaux Economistes. Cf., however, the following complaint of Daniel Wakefield.

> After vainly seeking, both in this country and at Paris for a French copy of the 'Réflexions sur la Formation et la Distribution Richesses de M. Turgot', the author found himself under the necessity of forwarding the manuscripts of the present work to the press while only trusting the fidelity of his quotations, from this celebrated Statesman, to the translation published by Mr. Ridgeway.
>
> (Daniel Wakefield, *An essay upon political economy*, 2nd edn [London, 1804] pp. 113–14)

It should be noted that this complaint was made prior to the publication of the Du Pont edition of Turgot's works. See also Francis Horner to William Erskine (23 January 1800) which comments on the scarcity of Turgot's works, in *Memoirs of Francis Horner with selections from his correspondence*, revised edn (Edinburgh, 1849) pp. 62–3.

In the context of 'the translation published by Mr. Ridgeway', referred to by Wakefield, it was hoped that a clue could be found to the mysterious translator of the 'Reflections', thereby to squash once and for all the story presented by I. C. Lundberg (*Turgot's unknown translator* [The Hague, 1964]) which ascribes this translation to Adam Smith. This hypothesis has been convincingly rejected by Jacob Viner in his introduction to the reprint of John Rae, *Life of Adam Smith* (New York, 1965) pp. 128–38, and in my 'Turgot and Adam Smith', part I, esp. n40 (below, pp. 375–6).

38 Marx, although he used the Daire edition of Turgot's works, appears to have studied the 'Reflections' only. But he thought highly of Turgot's work, especially of his theory of capital and analysis of capitalist relations, which he regarded as a considerable advance over the work of the physiocrats. See *Theories of surplus value* (Moscow, n.d.) part I, pp. 53–9. It is interesting to note that Marx, like Böhm-Bawerk (on which see below) ascribed a fructification theory of interest to Turgot. See *Theories of surplus value*, p. 47, and cf. *Capital*, 3 (Moscow, 1959) p. 608.

39 That is, Francesco Ferrara, Biblioteca dell'Economista, prima serie, vol. 1: *Fisiocrati* (Turin, 1850) which reprints 'In praise of Gournay', 'Reflections', 'Value and money', 'Paper on lending at interest', and 'Observations on a paper by Graslin', in Italian translation from the Daire edition.

40 See W. Stark (ed.) *Jeremy Bentham's economic writing* (London, 1952) 1, pp. 188, 190. In the second edition of *Defence of usury*, Bentham appended the passage in question from Condorcet's *Life of Turgot*. For a further association between Bentham's work on usury and that of Turgot, it should be noted that the two were published together in a French edition published in Paris in 1828 and in a Spanish translation published in the same year.

41 David Ricardo, *Works and correspondence*, ed. Piero Sraffa in collaboration with Maurice Dobb (Cambridge, 1951) 7, p. 365.

42 Ricardo, *Works*, 7, p. 382. Both Condorcet's *Life of Turgot*, and the Du Pont edition of Turgot's *Works* were in the library at Gatcombe Park. See *ibid.*, 10, p. 399.

43 Ricardo, *Works*, 1, p. 5.

44 *ibid.*, 1, pp. 238, 280.

45 Lauderdale's copy is at present in the Goldsmith's Library at the University of London. With it is a letter from Lord Hawkesbury to Lauderdale (24 August 1793) which reads as follows:

> Lord Hawkesbury presents his compliments to Lord Lauderdale and returns him herewith M. Turgot's Tract sur la Formation et la Distribution des Richesses which he has read with the greatest Pleasure ... it contains all that Dr. Adam Smith has written on the Influence of Capital on the Commerce of Nation. But M. Turgot develops his principles, in a more elegant and clear manner by far, than Adam Smith, who appears to have borrowed greatly from him.

The passages underlined by Lauderdale occur on pp. 38, 63, 64, 85, 105–10, 135–6.

46 See 'Reflections', 1788 edn, p. 64; in my edition, §68, pp. 75–6, the passage starting, 'For if, by any disorder whatsoever ... ' to the end of the paragraph.

47 See 'Reflections', §101, p. 95. For further comments on this passage and its importance in the history of economic thought, see my 'Turgot and Adam Smith', pp. 278–9 (below, Chapter 20).

48 See Lauderdale, *An inquiry into the nature and origin of public wealth* (Edinburgh, 1804) ch. 1, esp. pp. 21–2, 159–60, and ch. 4, esp. p. 210. Turgot is cited in the last two references, but he is not specifically referred to in the chapter on value.

49 See B. Semmel, 'Malthus: "Physiocracy" and the classical system', *Economic History Review*, 17 (1964–5) pp. 522–35; R. L. Meek, 'Early theories of under-consumption', and 'Physiocracy and classicism in England', both in his *Economics of physiocracy* (London, 1962). This physiocratic influence is especially noticeable in the first two editions of the *Essay on population*. In conversation and correspondence with the author, Walter Eltis has queried this allegation about Malthus' indebtedness to the physiocrats, on the ground that he is not aware of any direct citation of their work in Malthus' writings. This matter appears to be in need of further investigation.

50 See T. R. Malthus, *Principles of political economy*, 1st edn (London, 1820) pp. 54, 87; 2nd edn (London, 1836) p. 51. The second edition dropped the footnote reference to the 'Reflections', and the second reference. The section numbers of the 'Reflections' cited by Malthus indicate that he used a Du Pont version, most probably the Du Pont edition of Turgot's works.

51 Malthus, *Principles*, 1st edn, p. 53; cf. 'Value and money', pp. 137–9, esp. 139.

52 T. R. Malthus, *Principles*, 1st edn, pp. 87–8. This may have been indebted to Turgot's capital analysis in the 'Reflections'.

53 Such documentation is made very difficult because of the alleged physiocratic influence on Malthus' work. See references in note 49 above.

54 Samuel Bailey, *A critical dissertation on the nature, measures and causes of value* (1825; reprinted London, 1931) ch. 1, entitled 'On the nature of value'.

55 Bailey, pp. 243–5.

56 *Ibid.*, p. 251.

57 Bailey, p. 1; 'Value and Money', p. 139.

58 Bailey, pp. 2–3; Value and money', pp. 137–8.

59 Bailey, p. 5.

60 'Value and money', p. 145.

61 Bailey, pp. 33–4; 'Value and money', pp. 145–7.

62 Bailey, ch. 6, esp. pp. 98–9, and see 'A reappraisal of Turgot's theory of value, exchange, and price determination', part II, esp. pp. 183–4 (above, Chapter 16) and the references to 'Value and money' and the 'Reflections' there given.

63 Rauner, the main commentator on Bailey's theory of value, does not discuss the possibility of Turgot's influence on Bailey. In fact, Turgot is mentioned only once in his work, in a reference concerned with the continental value tradition. See R. M. Rauner, *Samuel Bailey and the classical theory of value* (London, 1961) p. 7.

64 See J. B. Say, A *treatise of political economy*, trans. Prinsep (1821) 1, pp. 127, 284, 316, 357; 2, pp. 352–4, 359. These references are not confined to the 'Reflections'.
65 Cited by J. R. McCulloch, *The literature of political economy* (1845; reprinted London, 1938) p. 359. Say corresponded with Du Pont. See F. Ferrara, 'Preface to the doctrine of the Physiocrats', trans. E. Henderson, *International Economic papers*, no. 8 (London, 1958) pp. 8–9.
66 Cf. Du Pont to J. B. Say, 22 April 1815, in Ferrara, pp. 8–9. An explicit example of Say's preference for Smith is given in the *Treatise*, 1, p. 127.
67 See J. K. Ingram, A *history of political economy* (London, 1915) p. 160, where Du Pont's claim that Say was indebted to Turgot in many ways is accepted. Schumpeter, p. 492, claims that

> Say's work grew from purely French sources. ... It is the Cantillon-Turgot tradition which he carried on, and from which he *could* have developed ... all the main features of his analysis including his systematic schema and his entrepreneur. ... Say's work is the most important link in the chain that leads from Cantillon and Turgot to Walras.

It is interesting to note that a recent work on Say – Evert Schoorl, *Jean-Baptiste Say: hoofdstukken uit zijn leven en economisch denken* (Amsterdam, 1980) – makes no reference to any connection between Turgot's economics and that of Say, despite his citations from Schumpeter in this context.
68 Say *Treatise*, 1, p. 284, where Turgot's proof of the inefficiency of government relative to private speculators in the grain trade is approvingly referred to.
69 Say *Treatise*, 1, p. 316, which quotes the opinions of Turgot, Steuart, and Smith on the relative productivity of slave and free labour.
70 Say *Treatise*, 2, pp. 352–4. This passage was critically commented on by Ricardo and constitutes one of the two references in his *Principles* to Turgot. See Ricardo, *Works*, 1, p. 238.
71 See Say, *Treatise*, 2, p. 359, which gives details of the social benefits to the nations from this tax reform.
72 Say, *Treatise*, pp. vii–ix. Cf. note 12 above.
73 I.e. James Mill, *Elements of political economy* (London, 1821); J. R. McCulloch, *Principles of political economy* (London, 1825). Both introduced slight variations to Say's scheme: Mill included a chapter called 'Interchange' between those on 'Production' and 'Distribution' (chs 1 and 2) and that on 'Consumption' (ch. 4); while McCulloch prefaced his parts on Production, Distribution, and Consumption with a historical view of the rise and progress of economics. James Mill followed his father's classification by making the subject matter of his first three books production, distribution, and exchange.
74 Cf. Schumpeter, p. 492.
75 See J. F. Bell, A *history of economic thought* (New York, 1953) p. 403.
76 See Say, *Treatise*, 2, p. 1, n(b).
77 See 'Value and money', p. 143. This passage was adversely commented on by Ricardo in the first and second editions of his *Principles*. See Ricardo, *Works*, 1, pp. 279–80 n2.
78 Say *Treatise*, 1, p. 398; cf. 'A reappraisal of Turgot's theory of value, exchange and price determination', pp. 184–5, and the references to Turgot's work given there (above, Chapter 16).
79 Say, *Treatise*, 1, pp. 341ff, esp. 357, where Turgot is cited.
80 Say, *Treatise*, 1, p. 127. The reference is to Turgot's 'Reflections', §81 (in the Du Pont edition of the *Works*); in my edition, §82, p. 85.
81 Say, *Treatise*, 1, pp. 111–17, 186; cf. with the outline of Turgot's theory given in my 'reinterpretation', pp. 334–7 (above, Chapter 17).

82 Say, *Treatise*, 2, pp. 129–32, 147–52; cf. B. F. Catherwood, *Basic theories of distribution* (London, 1939) p. 96.

83 Schumpeter, p. 841.

84 *Ibid*. These views are admirably illustrated in Bastiat's *Essays on political economy*, which contained explicit refutations of the views of Louis Blanc, Proudhon, and other socialist writers, and which were published in 1848 and 1849. Bastiat's free-trade position is revealed in his other popular work, *Economic sophisms*, which also stressed the association between socialism and protection.

85 See for example, G. Robineau (ed.) *Turgot, administration et oeuvres économiques* (Paris, 1889) which includes the 'Reflections', the 'Eloge de Gournay' and the preambles to the edicts suppressing the corvée and the guilds.

86 See 'De la liberté en général, de la liberté du travail et des moyens d'assurer le bienêtre matériel et moral des classes laborieuses. Ce mémoire est suivi d'une Eloge de Turgot' (Paris, 1848); H. J. L. Baudrillart, 'Eloge de Turgot', *Revue des Deux Mondes* 5e séries, 15 (15 Sept. 1846) pp. 1019–49; Auguste Bouchot, *Eloge de Turgot* (Paris, 1846); Félix Cadet, *Turgot, 1727–1781* (Paris, 1873); A. Mastier, *Turgot: sa vie et ses doctrines* (Paris 1862); Léon Say, *Turgot* (Paris, 1887); C. J. Tissot, *Turgot; sa vie, son administration et ses ouvrages* (Paris, 1862); and M. Chevalier, 'Turgot et la liberté du travail', *Journal des Economistes*, Feb. 1873.

87 Alfred Neymarck, *Turgot et ses doctrines* (Paris, 1885) 1, pp. 336–7; and cf. Léon Say, *Turgot*, pp. 9–10, where the nineteenth century is described as the true century of Turgot, since it was then that the economic policy he espoused was fully accepted. Perhaps we will see a further revival of this type of Turgot literature in the reaffirmation of a laissez-faire faith by the current crop of deregulators, particularly in the United States.

88 The essence of Bastiat's thought on these subjects is contained in his essay 'Capital and interest', in *Essays on political economy* (London, 1853) and in his *Harmonies of political economy*, translated from the third French edition (Edinburgh, n.d.) esp. chs. 4, 5, 7.

89 Although Turgot is not explicitly cited by Bastiat, it is hard to believe that he was not acquainted with Turgot's work. The Daire edition of Turgot's works is implicitly referred to in the chapter on value (*Harmonies*, p. 141) while in connection with value elsewhere (p. 136) he uses the phrase 'a labyrinth of inextricable difficulties', an expression similar to that used by Turgot in his paper 'Value and money', pp. 145–8.

90 Bastiat, *Harmonies*, p. 134; Turgot, 'Value and money', pp. 137–8.

91 Bastiat, *Harmonies*, ch. 5. All these can be found in Turgot's value analysis as indicated above, cf. 'A reappraisal', pp. 183–4.

92 Bastiat, 'Capital and interest', p. 16; cf. p. 17.

93 *Ibid*., 38–9, and the anecdotes on pp. 19–29. Cf. *Harmonies*, pp. 196–217; and Böhm- Bawerk, *Capital and interest*, vol. 1, book III, ch. 3. See Turgot, 'Paper on lending at interest', pp. 152–4, 155–9.

94 This transportation of Turgot's liberal ideas from the eighteenth century to the nineteenth century without adequate regard for the changed historical circumstances is, of course, improper. For example, his suppression of the guilds on the principle of the right to work was undoubtedly a progressive move in the 1770s; to use these arguments against the establishment of national workshops to create employment in the late 1840s was a perversion of his ideas. After all, he himself had established such institutions during the famine as Intendant of Limoges. See Dakin, *Turgot and the* ancien régime *in France* (London, 1939) pp. 114–17.

95 See the references given in note 86 above, and cf. W. B. Hodgson, *Turgot: his life, time, and opinions* (London, 1870) esp. pp. 60–4; and Robert Morley's famous essay reprinted in *Critical miscellanies* (London, 1877) vol. 2.

96 Much of this rediscovery and reinterpretation has been done by non-French historians. See the references cited in notes 3, 4, 5, 7, and 13 above, while reference

should also be made to R. L. Meek, *Turgot on progress, economics and sociology* (Cambridge, 1973). Nevertheless, apart from Schumpeter's *History of economic analysis*, there are few reasonable discussions of Turgot's economics in the general textbook literature, so that the 'rediscovery' has not yet been completed. Most of the French work on the subject of Turgot's economics appeared after Schelle's tremendous contribution in editing the five volumes of Turgot's works (Paris, 1913–23) and prior to the Second World War. Some exceptions are the essays by Edgar Faure, 'Les bases expérimentales et doctrinaires de la politique économique de Turgot', *Revue Historique de Droit Français* 39 (1961) pp. 254–95; 'Turgot et la doctrine du produit net', *Revue d'Histoire Economique et Sociale* 39, no. 3 (1961) pp. 273–86; and his *Le Disgrâce de Turgot* (Paris, 1961). In addition, there is the final volume of Weulersse's history of physiocracy, *Les Physiocrates sous les ministéres de Turgot et Necker* (Paris 1950) and the introductions to two reprints of selections from Turgot's economic writings – Pierre Vigreux (ed.) *Turgot: textes choisies* (Paris, 1947) and Bernard Cazes (ed.) *Turgot, écrits économiques* (Paris, 1970). Reference should also be made to the proceedings of a seminar, *Turgot, économiste et administrateur*, eds Christian Borde and Jean Morange (Paris, 1983) and to the April 1982 issue of *Keizai Kenkyu* devoted to Turgot, 1781–1981.

97 See my 'A reappraisal', p. 196 (above, Chapter 16) and cf. R. L. Meek, introduction to his translation of 'Value and money', in *Precursors of Adam Smith* (London, 1973) pp. 78–9. Such a portrayal has been criticised by Roberto Finzi, introduction to *Turgot: le ricchezze, il progresso e la storia universale*, pp. li–lix, esp. lviii–lix and n13. My earlier (1970) views on this subject have been altered as a result of reading this penetrating study and after further thought on the matter. The topic is further explored in my 'Turgot: forerunner of neo-classical economics?', *Keizai Kenkyu*, 33, 2 (April 1982) pp. 119–34 (above, Chapter 18). The whole issue of the *Economic Review* published by Hitotsubashi University is devoted to Turgot's economics.

98 For example, Walras referred to Turgot only once in his major work, in the first chapter. See *Elements of pure economics*, ed. Jaffé, p. 51. Jevons, although citing Condorcet's *Vie de M. Turgot* in his bibliography of mathematical writings on economics, appears to have been largely unaware of the importance of Turgot's work. See *Theory of political economy*, 4th edn (London, 1911) pp. 323–4. The preface to the second edition (see *ibid.*, p. xliv) does not include Turgot's name among the French writers to whom Jevons felt some affinity. Turgot is, however, cited in connection with the division of labour in his uncompleted *Principles of economics* (London, 1905) p. 100. Edgeworth and Wicksteed do not refer to Turgot in their major economic work; Wicksell, in his *Lectures*, omits any substantial reference to Turgot, though his controversy with Cassel over Böhm-Bawerk's theory of interest reveals his familiarity with Turgot. This controversy, in which Böhm-Bawerk and Marshall also became involved, is discussed below in this section, thereby providing an opportunity to correct an error in my earlier 'A re-interpretation', p. 337 n7 (above, Chapter 17) and interlinking this material on Turgot's influence on some marginalist economists. Taussig, in his *Wages and capital*, is similarly an exception; he devoted several pages to what he described as Turgot's 'remarkable performance' on capital theory. See *Wages and capital* (reprint, London, 1932) pp. 127–9.

99 Vienna, 1871. In Carl Menger, *Gesammelte Werke* (Tübingen, 1968) vol. 1, 80n, 108n, 173n, 258n, and p. 272. This compares with five references for Ricardo, three for John Stuart Mill, and nine for Adam Smith.

100 Menger cites both 'Value and money' and the 'Reflections' in his *Grundsätze*, while his *Untersuchungen über die Methode der Socialwissenschaften* (Leipzig, 1883) cites Turgot's contribution to the philosophy of history, with the implication that Menger had studied more than just two of Turgot's works. See Menger, *Werke*, 2, p. 128 n44.

101 The theory of isolated exchange is one example which has been noted previously. See 'A reappraisal', p. 189 (above, Chapter 16).
102 Eugen von Böhm-Bawerk, *Capital and interest* (South Holland IL, 1959) vol. 1, book I, ch. 4, which starts with the statement that Turgot provided 'the first attempt at a scientific explanation of ordinary interest' which appreciates the problem completely (p. 39). I have discussed Böhm-Bawerk's general misinterpretation of Turgot's theory in my 'A re-interpretation', pp. 327–8 and n5 (above, Chapter 17).
103 Böhm-Bawerk, *Positive theory of capital*, vol. 2, where Turgot is cited on no fewer than eight occasions.
104 Böhm-Bawerk, *Capital and interest*, vol. 3, where Turgot is cited six times in two of the essays contained in that volume.
105 See *Capital and interest*, 2, p. 439 n2. This unpublished paper, entitled 'Böhm-Bawerk's Jugendarbeit über den Kapitalizins', was drawn to my attention by Klaus Hennings, who also supplied me with a typescript copy of the original. I am indebted to Professor Friedrich von Hayek for permission to quote from this paper, the original manuscript of which was given to him by the author's widow in either 1922 or 1923. It was written by Böhm-Bawerk for presentation at Knies' seminar in Heidelberg in 1876, and is therefore his earliest piece on the subject in existence.
106 See *Capital and interest*, 1, p. 72, where it is mentioned in connection with Canard 1:96, where Lauderdale is cited as having rejected Turgot's fructification theory (see Lauderdale's *Inquiry*, p. 158, 1:336 where Turgot's theory is compared with the similar theory of Henry George; and 1:366 where Turgot's theory is once more described as a fructification theory. This interpretation was already made in his 'Jugendarbeit', which is discussed below.
107 *Capital and interest*, 1, p. 54, and cf. p. 72.
108 *ibid.*, 1, p. 25, and cf. p. 39.
109 *ibid.*, pp. 34, 36.
110 *ibid.*, pp. 225, 357; 2, p. 81. This aspect of Turgot's theory was emphasised in the 'Jugendarbeit'.
111 *Capital and interest*, 2, p. 19. Turgot is here criticised specifically for failing to differentiate between goods for consumption and goods 'designed to yield an income for the owners'. Only the latter could properly be included among capital goods, as Smith pointed out (*ibid.*, 2, pp. 22, 27, 39). The inclusion of dwelling houses and of consumption goods is therefore the main criticism of Turgot's concept (and the concepts of Roscher and Knies, whose definitions are regarded as similar). See *ibid.*, 2, pp. 34–5.
112 *Capital and interest*, 1, pp. 464 n9.
113 See for example, Schumpeter, pp. 468–9.
114 *Capital and interest*, 3, pp. 1–23.
115 *ibid.*, pp. 6–7.
116 *ibid.*, p. 18.
117 See 'Jugendarbeit', p. 5, where Böhm-Bawerk wrote:

> Die Betrachtung dieser weittragenden Kontroverse, und im Anschlusse hieran die Prüfing der Ansichten, welche Turgot in seinem Mémoire sowohl als auch in seinem 'Réflexions sur la formation et la distribution des richesses' über das Wesen und der Urspung des Zinses aufgestellt hat, soll die Aufgabe dieser Blätter sein.

118 See my 'A re-interpretation', esp. pp. 333–4 (above, Chapter 17). This interpretation has been implicitly criticised by R. L. Meek in his *Turgot on progress, economics and sociology*, p. 24 n2.
119 'Jugendarbeit', pp. 14, 15, 40, 45, 53–5, 63.

120 See my 'A re-interpretation', pp. 328–31 (above, Chapter 17).
121 This conclusion is reinforced by the many criticisms from Turgot in Böhm-Bawerk's works on capital and interest, which have been already referred to.
122 Schumpeter, p. 307.
123 Böhm-Bawerk, *Capital and interest*, vol. 2, book III, part B, ch. 2.
124 It is undoubtedly Menger who was influential here, as in so many cases of Böhm-Bawerk's work. The connection between Menger and Turgot on the theory of value has been discussed above.
125 Discussed below in this section.
126 In J. K. Whitaker (ed.) *The early economic writings of Alfred Marshall, 1867–1890* (London, 1975) 1, pp. 119–59.
127 The relevant paragraph is as follows:

> In a simple barter, as in the case of Dr. Livingstone exchanging muskets for ivory with a tribe in Central Africa, the considerations which enter are but few. Dr. Livingstone sooner than not to effect the exchange would give a musket for AB ivory, they sooner than not effect would give AC ivory for a musket. Each side tries to delude the other as to the relative value in use to himself of the two commodities. Finally, they come to terms at the rate AD somewhere between AB and AC:

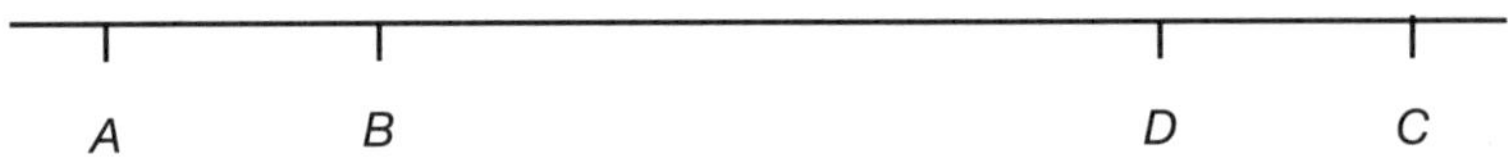

Figure 19.1 Turgot's analysis of isolated exchange

> Turgot (Réflexions sur la formation et la distribution des richesses) commences his account of value by considering a case of this sort, and then says in the case of a large market each side considers the circumstances not only of himself and the man with whom he is bargaining, but all those who are carrying on transactions in these two commodities. But it is not at all easy to do this.
>
> (Marshall, *Early writing*, p. 217)

My attention was first drawn to this paper prior to its publication by Neil de Marchi. Cf. also 'A reappraisal', p. 118 n16.
128 Marshall, *Principles*, pp. 172, 176 n1, 505–6n.
129 Whitaker, *Early economic writings*, 2, pp. 252–3; and see Marshall to Wicksell, 26 August 1904, in T. Gårdlund, *Life of Knut Wicksell* (Stockholm, 1958) p. 342.
130 G. Cassel, *Nature and necessity of interest* (London, 1903) pp. 20–2.
131 *Ibid.*, p. 22. A footnote reference indicates that Cassel was 'indebted to Professor Marshall for some very suggestive remarks on the point' (*ibid.*, p. 22 n2). The students of Böhm-Bawerk referred to in the last sentence of the quotation presumably include Wicksell, against whom Cassel had a bitter animosity which was in fact mutual.
132 Böhm-Bawerk, 'On the historical development of the theory of durable goods within the capitalist theory. Some critical remarks on the interest theories of Cassel and Landry', in Böhm-Bawerk, *Capital and interest*, vol. 3, essay XIII, esp. pp. 196–200.

133 Cassel, *Nature and necessity of interest*, esp. ch. 1, §§6–7; ch. 2, §4. Cassel's analysis and viewpoint was shared in principle by authors such as Carver, Marshall, and Irving Fisher and, at least implicitly, even by Wicksell.

134 Böhm-Bawerk, *Capital and interest*, 3, pp. 199–200. A great deal of the argument in his critical history depends on this rigid classification of use and abstinence theories as separate and exclusive theories of interest, including, as I have argued, his interpretation of Turgot. My re-interpretation follows the supply (abstinence)/demand (use of capital) model which was widely accepted in the late nineteenth and early twentieth century (see the preceding note).

135 Böhm-Bawerk, *Capital and interest*, 3, pp. 197–8, 200, 241 n8. The misinterpretation relates to Cassel's translation of the plural 'valeurs' as used by Turgot in phrases like 'valeurs mobilières, valeurs accumulées', into the singular 'value', which has a quite different connotation. A more suitable translation would be 'values' or 'goods' (i.e. economic goods) though this has no great bearing on the main point at issue between Cassel and Böhm-Bawerk. See also Böhm-Bawerk, *Capital and interest*, 2, p. 401 n7.

136 K. Wicksell, 'Böhm-Bawerk's theory of capital', *Selected papers on economic theory* (London, 1958) pp. 177–8; cf. his 'The new edition of Mengers *Grundsätze*', *ibid.*, p. 196. Wicksell's reasons for his support of Böhm-Bawerk were that the purchase of land, which Turgot lists as the first use of capital, is not an economic use of capital at all; that Turgot did not explicitly state that the demand for capital is not influenced by the purchase of land; and, most importantly, that the rate of return to land is irrelevant to the theory of interest. These points have been discussed already in my 'A re-interpretation', pp. 332 n2, 337 n7 (above, Chapter 17).

137 Wicksell, 'Cassel's system of economics', reprinted in *Lectures on political economy*, 1, p. 235 n2. Wicksell also comments on the fact that Cassel's 'loud praises of Turgot's theory of interest … are now suddenly silenced'. In his *Theory of social economy*, 2nd edn (London, 1932) p. 188, Cassel made only *one brief* reference to Turgot.

138 This correspondence (conducted from July 1904 to January 1905) is reprinted as an appendix to Gårdlund's *Life of Knut Wicksell*, pp. 339–45. For Cassel's reference to Marshall, see above, note 131.

139 Marshall to Wicksell, 26 July 1904, in Gårdlund, pp. 339–40. A letter to Mr Sraffa, when he was Marshall librarian at Cambridge, on the present whereabouts of these notes, elicited the following response: 'the catalogue of the Marshall manuscripts is not very detailed. As far as one can see from the catalogue, the notes on Turgot are not there'. But cf. note 129 above.

140 Wicksell to Marshall, 10 August 1904, *ibid.*, pp. 340–1. These reasons are summarised in note 136 above.

141 *Ibid.*, p. 341, and Marshall to Wicksell, 26 August 1904, where he wrote:

> I fear that if I send you my notes I may be drawn on gradually to waste – from my point of view – much time in arguing a point which has little or no interest to me; and, at the same time to seem to be attacking Prof. Böhm-Bawerk indirectly. If you strongly desire to see my notes, and will promise me that you will not in *any way* bring me into the controversy, I will send them. I have just looked at them again, but without comparing them with the originals; and I have not read Prof. Cassel. But the general effect left on my mind is to confirm my previous opinion that Turgot's doctrine, rightly interpreted, is a monument of genius and falls very little short of the best that is known today about interest.
>
> (*ibid.*, pp. 341–2)

142 Marshall to Wicksell, 19 December 1904, *ibid.*, p. 343. The last sentence of the passage quoted seems to be in contradiction with Marshall's letter of August 26, where he wrote that he had 'just looked at them [i.e. the notes] again', See note 141 above.
143 Wicksell to Marshall, 6 January 1905, *ibid.*, pp. 343–5.
144 That is, my 'A re-interpretation of Turgot's theory of capital and interest' (above, Chapter 17).
145 Schumpeter, p. 248.
146 See my 'Turgot, Beccaria and Smith', esp. §4 (above, Chapter 1). The point is also made in the papers on Turgot published previously in the concluding sections, and is documented as well in the introduction to my *Economics of A. R. J. Turgot*, which, in the discussion of the various pieces of Turgot's economics there translated, also presents the various influences on these works, particularly if supplemented by the editorial notes given throughout the text.

20 Turgot and Adam Smith[1]

> Tout ce qu'il y a de vrai dans ce livre estimable (Richesse des Nations), mais pénible à lire … se trouve dans les *Réflexions* de Turgot … tout ce qu'Adam Smith y a ajouté manque d'exactitude et même de fondement.
>
> (Du Pont de Nemours)

> This essay (Reflections on the Formation and Distribution of Wealth) may be considered as the germ of the treatise on the Wealth of Nations written by the celebrated Smith.
>
> (Condorcet)

The opinions of Du Pont de Nemours and Condorcet quoted above[2] on the possible relationship between Turgot's 'Reflections on the Formation and Distribution of Wealth' and Adam Smith's *An Inquiry into the Nature and Causes of the Wealth of Nations* started what is probably the oldest controversy in the history of economic thought. Time and time again this question has intrigued scholars of various nationalities, and new hypotheses are still being put forward to explain it.[3] This chapter intends to review the controversy, to appraise the evidence, and to give some conclusions on the subject of what has been called the 'Smith-Turgot myth'.[4]

Before proceeding with this inquiry, it is useful to classify the evidence on which the myth has been based. This may be divided into two basic parts. First of all, there is the internal evidence obtained by comparing the text of Turgot's 'Reflections' with that of Smith's *Wealth of Nations*; second, there is the historical evidence which is based on the personal acquaintance of the two authors, the alleged correspondence between them, and the availability of Turgot's economic writing to Adam Smith during the period preceding the publication of the *Wealth of Nations*. The discussion of these two types of evidence will form the basis for what follows in this chapter.

I

The historical evidence can be dealt with relatively briefly, because it has often been discussed in the past.[5] Nevertheless, a summary of this evidence is important since the *origin* of the controversy lay undoubtedly in the fact that the two were personally acquainted when Turgot was writing his 'Reflections'. The basis for the controversy was reinforced by Condorcet's allegation of correspondence between the two and by the availability of Turgot's 'Reflections' to Adam Smith.

The first point to consider is the opportunity of meeting. Adam Smith, on the evidence of both Stewart and Rae, was in Paris from December 1765 to October 1766, a period of about ten months.[6] Turgot, as far as can be surmised from details in his correspondence, was not in Paris for all of this period. He spent the greater part of it in Limoges, as is shown by letters to Du Pont and to Trudaine.[7] On the other hand, he was definitely in Paris from July to September 1766.[8] Smith and Turgot's main opportunity of meeting would therefore have occurred in those three months.

Contemporary references to these personal meetings are, however, few. There are the references to each other in their correspondence with Hume in July–September in connection with Hume's quarrel with Rousseau. These letters provide evidence for two distinct meetings, one of them at the house of Baron d'Holbach.[9] There is also the extract from Morellet's memoirs which refers to several meetings.[10] There seems, therefore, to be direct contemporary evidence for no more than half a dozen meetings.

The biographers of Turgot and Smith have added to these meetings. Dakin[11] mentions a meeting between Smith and Turgot at the Entresol; Rae mentions meetings at the house of Mlle de l'Espinasse and implies that Smith often met Turgot there, 'as indeed he did everywhere he went'.[12] Although there is a strong possibility that these meetings did occur, they must be considered to be pure supposition, as no evidence is offered to substantiate them.

As to the topic of conversation at those meetings, the evidence is even more slender. It is known for certain that they discussed the Hume-Rousseau affair, since they both mention this in their respective letters to Hume.[13] It may be assumed that they discussed economics,[14] but it appears just as likely that they discussed philosophy, history, law, philology and literature.[15] Little more can be said about the Paris meetings unless the diary which Smith is alleged to have kept during his stay in France is discovered.[16]

The second part of the historical evidence concerns the alleged correspondence between Smith and Turgot. This subject was first raised by Condorcet in his *Vie de M. Turgot* without any documentation.[17] Stewart referred to this correspondence but appears to have doubted its existence on the ground that no traces of it have been found.[18] Léon Say, in his biography of Turgot, repeated Condorcet's assertion,[19] while Rae argued that Condorcet's authority for such a correspondence 'cannot altogether be disregarded'.[20]

The story of the correspondence was more or less discredited when Cannan published a letter from Smith in the *Economic Journal*, in which Smith wrote that though he had been acquainted with Turgot, he had never corresponded with him.[21] The relationship between the two economists cannot therefore be explained by correspondence between them, since the evidence seems to point clearly to the fact that no such correspondence ever took place.[22] There was, however, an exchange of books between the two, which is a more relevant factor.[23]

This third type of historical evidence concerns the availability of Turgot's writings to Adam Smith before the publication of the *Wealth of Nations*. The major source for this evidence is contained in the various catalogues of Adam Smith's library,[24] but there is also a great deal of information to be found in the correspondence of both Turgot and Smith from which fairly plausible hypotheses can be constructed. This part of the evidence therefore suffers from the fault of not being fully conclusive, since all the catalogues of Smith's library can be described as incomplete.[25]

This type of evidence was used by Cannan in his rebuttal of Thorold Rogers' opinion on the relationship between 'Reflections' and the *Wealth of Nations*.[26] In the introduction to Smith's *Lectures*, Cannan wrote that Turgot's 'Reflections', 'though written in 1766, was only published six years before the *Wealth of Nations*, and then only in the periodical *Ephémérides du Citoyen*'. Since this was not in the Advocates Library at Edinburgh, nor in Smith's own library as catalogued by Bonar, 'we are not justified in assuming that Adam Smith had so much as seen the work'.[27] As will be shown later, Cannan's opinion on this matter has to be revised in view of the new information now available.

W. R. Scott, in his *Adam Smith as Student and Professor*, also used some of the library data in connection with the alleged relationship between Turgot and Smith.[28] Although he had the use of the greatly enlarged second edition of Bonar's *Catalogue* and a copy of the 1781 manuscript catalogue of Smith's library, he did not use this new material to any extent. He is clearly in error in connection with the volumes of the *Ephémérides*, since he argued that 'Adam Smith had the three years 1767, 1768, 1769 only'.[29] In Yanaihara's reprint of the 1781 catalogue there are, however, four entries for this important French periodical, the three volumes listed by Scott as well as six issues for 1766. These are at present in the Library of New College, Edinburgh.[30] This indicates that Adam Smith's library contained at least two thirds of the 'Reflections' as published in the *Ephémérides*, and that the third part, in the January 1770 issue, was not owned by him in this form.[31]

Although it can therefore be shown that at least part of Turgot's 'Reflections' was in Smith's possession, there have also been attempts to place the 1770 offprint (*tirage à part*) in his hands.[32] H. Higgs, in his review of Cannan's edition of Smith's *Lectures* stated that: 'The late Dr. Hodgson expressed an opinion that Adam Smith was made acquainted with the "Reflections" by Tucker, to whom Turgot sent a copy in 1770; though it does not appear upon which that foundation rested'.[33] Neymarck also seemed to think that it was Tucker who provided Smith with the 'Reflections'.[34]

Lundberg has suggested that Hume may have received a copy, a possible further link to Smith, and that either Du Pont or C. J. Devaines, Turgot's amanuensis, may have sent a copy directly to Adam Smith.[35] Can it be assumed that as Turgot had sent Smith a copy of the *Procès verbal* there is a strong possibility that Smith had been sent a copy of the 1770 *tirage à part*?[36]

This leaves the hypothesis that Smith may have obtained a copy of the 1766 manuscript of Turgot's 'Reflections'. It is possible, as Lundberg assumes, that Smith may have received this personally from Turgot in Paris in 1766.[37] There is, however, no evidence for this, just as there is no evidence that Smith received a copy of the *tirage à part*. On the other hand, it cannot be said that Smith *definitely* did not own a copy of the 'Reflections' in either of these versions, since even the most recently published catalogue of his library is not necessarily complete.[38]

One item which may be called historical evidence need not be discussed here. This is Lundberg's hypothesis that Adam Smith may have been the anonymous translator of the 'Reflections', which was published in 1793.[39] As Viner has pointed out, in a fairly detailed criticism of this book, this thesis cannot be accepted since it does not fit the facts.[40]

This then, is the historical evidence. It can be concluded that there were several meetings between the two economists in Paris in 1766; that, most probably, there was no correspondence between them; and finally, that although there is no proof that Smith owned the whole of the 'Reflections', this possibility cannot be ruled out. In any case, he owned at least two thirds of them. It remains to be seen whether, on internal evidence, there is reason to presume that Smith used some of the arguments from the 'Reflections' in the writing of his *Wealth of Nations*.

II

In the past, the question of internal evidence has been approached in two different ways. On the one hand, there are those writers who have attempted a comparison of Turgot and Smith based on their respective economic systems, methods of analysis and philosophical outlooks;[41] on the other hand, there have been commentators who have tried to settle the issue by detailed textual comparisons from the writings of the two economists.[42] Since both methods lead to interesting results relevant to the controversy, both will be dealt with in this chapter. The second approach of detailed textual comparisons will be discussed immediately below, the first, broader, approach in the section that follows.

As Cannan, Viner and Lundberg have shown,[43] Rogers' textual comparisons are of little importance since they really prove nothing about possible indebtedness. Similarly, Leser's long list of comparative passages[44] and Lundberg's argument about the similarity of certain parts of Turgot's and Smith's economic vocabulary[45] do not yield conclusive results. In my own comparison of the 'Reflections' with the first two books of the *Wealth of Nations*, I have found only five points where similarity may have some significance for the purpose at hand. These points will be discussed in turn.

The first point concerns the definition of 'effectual demanders' which is given some prominence in Smith's analysis of market price and which was not very common in the eighteenth century. Smith's definition not only implies demand for the commodity, but also the means to satisfy that demand. In the 'Reflections', Turgot had written, 'it is always the wants and *the means* of the Consumer that set the price at the sale',[46] but since he wrote to Du Pont de Nemours that 'it is assuredly very obvious that the ability to pay is a strong consideration in demand',[47] a great deal of importance cannot be attached to this similarity.

The second point relates to their treatment of circulating capital. Both Turgot and Smith argued that circulating capital was indispensable to production,[48] and furthermore they stressed its interconnection with the division of labour. In the introduction to Book II of the *Wealth of Nations*, Smith showed that capital accumulation was essential prior to any division of labour in order to bridge the time gap between the production of a commodity and its sale. Turgot also made this point in very similar language.[49] When discussing more advanced and complex forms of division of labour, they both argued that 'this requires a much greater capital than where every man is occasionally employed in every different part of the work'.[50] Although the concept of circulating capital was probably derived by both of them from Quesnay's concept of annual advances,[51] the link between it and the division of labour was new at the time. This may be a point of greater significance, but its importance may easily be overrated.[52]

Third, there is the similarity in their saving-investment analysis, first noted by Schumpeter. His argument may be quoted in full, since it has a direct bearing on the controversy.

> In comparing the *Wealth* and the 'Reflections', some doubt may assail us concerning the value of indication previously mentioned about Smith's independence. For Turgot also says that, at least in the case of entrepreneurs, savings are converted into capital *sur-le-champ* [his italics]. But Smith's 'immediately' certainly is the exact translation of *sur-le-champ*. And this is not unimportant; on the contrary, as will be seen in a moment, it is an essential feature of both theories and indeed their most serious shortcoming. That such a slip should occur independently in two texts is indeed quite possible; but it is not likely.[53]

Since this concept of the immediate transformation of saving into investment became the foundation of classical analysis on this point, Schumpeter's argument is especially significant. However, it may be said that here again the ultimate source was Quesnay, whose *Tableau économique* implicitly contains this idea. On the other hand, I have not come across an *explicit* statement of this argument in the literature prior to Turgot and Adam Smith.[54]

The similarity of their attack on luxury, their praise of thrift, and of their analysis of the effect of saving and accumulation on the rate of interest, which Leser noted, has no real value for settling the controversy, since on these points they were probably both indebted to Hume's essay, 'Of Interest'.[55]

The fourth similarity of interest is their treatment of the determination of the price of land and the profitability of investing capital through the purchase of land. At the end of Book II, chapter IV of the *Wealth of Nations*, dealing with the subject of interest, Smith included a paragraph on the price of land and on two employments of capital not mentioned in the fifth chapter, which is specifically devoted to that subject. This passage may be quoted in full, since it contains arguments which are also put forward by Turgot.

> The ordinary market price of land, it is to be observed, depends every-where upon the ordinary market-rate of interest. The person who has a capital from which he wishes to derive a revenue, without taking the trouble to employ it himself, deliberates whether he should buy land with it, or lend it out at interest. The superior security of land, together with some other advantages which almost every-where attend upon this species of property, will generally dispose him to content himself with a smaller revenue from land, than what he might have by lending out his money at interest.[56]

This paragraph can be compared with the following remarks from the 'Reflections', where Turgot makes the same points in connection with the price of land, and the advantages and disadvantages of the employment of capital in either buying or lending at interest. These passages are as follows:

> It is evident that the lower the interest of money, the greater is the value of landed estates. … The man who invests his money in the purchase of an estate which is leased to an entirely solvent Farmer procures himself a revenue which gives him very little trouble to receive. … There is the additional advantage that land is of all forms of property that whereof the possession is most secured against every kind of accident. He who lends his money on interest has an even more peaceable and free enjoyment of it than the owner of land; but the insolvency of the debtor may cause him to lose his capital. He will not, therefore, content himself with an interest equal to the revenue of the land which he might buy with the same capital.[57]

Both Turgot and Smith stressed the greater security and the lack of trouble involved in investing capital in land as compared to the investment of lending at interest. They also argued that this explained the difference in the rates of return on these two employments of capital.[58]

The significance of this similarity is heightened by the fact that they both placed this discussion in the context of the employments of capital. Smith discussed the other employments of capital immediately after the passage quoted above, while for Turgot investing in land and lending at interest were two of the five employments of capital he analysed. This is shown in the following quotations from their work:

> A capital may be employed in four different ways: either, first, in procuring the rude product annually required for the use and consumption of the society; or, secondly, in manufacturing and preparing that rude produce for immediate use and consumption; or, thirdly, in transporting either the rude or manufactured produce from the places where they abound to those where they are wanted; or, lastly, in dividing particular portions of either into such small parcels as suit the occasional demands of those who want them. In the first way are employed the capitals of all those who undertake the improvement or cultivation of lands, mines, or fisheries; in the second, those of all master manufacturers; in the third, those of all wholesale merchants, and in the fourth, those of retailers.[59]

> I have reckoned five different methods of employing capitals or of profitably investing them. The first is to buy a landed estate … the second is to invest one's money in agricultural undertakings … the third is to invest one's capital in industrial or manufacturing undertakings, the fourth is to invest it in commercial undertakings, and the fifth is to lend it to those who want it, in return for an annual interest.[60]

These passages are not only similar because they use the peculiar and new terminology of 'employments of capital',[61] but also because the classification, which at first sight seems different, is fundamentally the same. The five employments of capital listed by Turgot are easily reconciled with those of Smith. This is the fifth point of similarity which I noted.

It will be remembered that two paragraphs previously – but in another chapter – Smith mentioned two additional employments of capital, buying land and lending at interest, which are the same as Turgot's first and fifth employments. Furthermore, in Turgot's discussion of his fourth employment of capital, that is, 'investing it in commercial undertakings', he clearly distinguished between 'wholesale merchants' and 'retailers' – Smith's third and fourth employments – but grouped them together because they both 'buy to sell again'.[62] This type of argument, as far as I know, was first put forward in the 'Reflections', and it seems difficult to explain this similarity on the grounds of coincidence.

This completes the formal comparison of passages in the two works. Although at least some of the similarities in these passages are difficult to explain away on the ground that they occurred in earlier writers, it cannot be concluded that Smith was greatly indebted to Turgot. It can be concluded that because Smith did own part of the 'Reflections', and possibly the whole of it, it is probable that he used it, like so many of his other sources, in one or two places.[63] One of these places may have been the saving-investment analysis, the other the enumeration of the various employments of capital. There is no real evidence for any other conclusion.

III

In contrast to the textual comparisons approach, which has been dealt with above, there is that of comparing the broad theoretical framework of the two books. In the past, this approach has concerned itself mainly with the laissez-faire aspects of their work, but after the publication of Cannan's edition of Smith's *Lectures*, this aspect was shown to be no longer relevant, because Smith was clearly an independent discoverer of the advantages of economic freedom.[64] With Cannan's edition of the *Wealth of Nations*, the area of similarity where Smith could have been indebted was further narrowed down to the fields of distribution and capital theory only,[65] fields to which Turgot's 'Reflections' devoted a great deal of space.

Since Cannan's work, no more such comparisons have been made. It may therefore be useful as a starting point to compare the broad analytical framework of the two books. For this purpose, the last three books of Smith's treatise may be excluded since their contents have no real counterpart in the 'Reflections'. Table 20.1, based on chapter headings of the *Wealth of Nations* shows that, broadly speaking, the 'Reflections' cover more or less the same ground as the first two books of the *Wealth of Nations*, though there are, it goes without saying, substantial differences in emphasis and treatment of this subject matter.[66]

Table 20.1 Subject matter in the *Wealth of Nations* compared to that in 'Reflections'

Subject	*Relevant chapter in 'Reflections'*[67]	*Relevant paragraph in* Wealth of Nations
Division of labour	Bk I chs 1–3	1–4, 48
Origin and use of money	Bk I ch. 4	30, 41–5, 47, 69
Digression on silver	Bk I ch. 11	46, 78–9
Measure of value	Bk I ch. 5	34–40
Theory of value and price	Bk I chs 6–7	31–3
Theory of wages	Bk I chs 8, 10	6
Theory of profit	Bk I chs 9, 10	60
Theory of rent	Bk I ch. 11	14, 19
The division of stock	Bk II ch. 1	51
Money and stock	Bk II ch. 2	68, 101
Accumulation of capital	Bk II ch. 3	49–50, 53–5, 81–2, 100
Stock and interest	Bk II ch. 4	29, 70–80
Different employments of stock	Bk II ch. 5	51, 59–60, 62, 66–7, 83–90

It is undoubtedly this similarity in contents which struck some of the commentators in the past.[68] However, on closer inspection this similarity can be shown to be not particularly relevant to the subject matter of the controversy. In the first place, as Cannan and W. R. Scott have shown, much of this material was already present in the *Lectures* and in the early draft of the *Wealth of Nations*, and therefore could not have been greatly influenced by Smith's acquaintance with the 'Reflections'.[69] Second, when the ordering of the subject matter of the two works is examined, it can be shown that although the contents are formally duplicated, the line of reasoning which connects the contents is substantially different.[70] This second point should be further examined.

According to its title, Smith's argument in Book I deals with the causes of the improvement in labour productivity and with the theory of distribution, but on inspection of the table of contents it will be found that after the three chapters on the division of labour and labour productivity, and before the four chapters on wages, profits and rent which form the theory of distribution, there are four chapters dealing with money, and with value and price theory.[71]

These chapters of Book I are interrelated by a chain of reasoning which links labour productivity to the division of labour (ch. 1), the division of labour to exchange and the size of the market (chs 2–3), the development of exchange to the origin and the use of money (ch. 4), the theory of money to the concepts of real and nominal price and the problem of the measure of value (ch. 5), the measure of value to the theory of value (ch. 6), the theory of value to the determination of natural and market price (ch. 7), and finally, the three component parts of the natural price, that is, wages, profit, and rent, to the theory of distribution (chs 8–11).

Book II, 'Of the Nature, Accumulation and Employment of Stock', is connected to Book I through the division of labour, since, as Smith argued in the introduction to this book, a division of labour implies a prior accumulation of capital.[72] The three items mentioned in the title of the book form the subject matter for three of its five chapters (that is, chapters 1, 3 and 5) while the other two deal with money and stock, including banking and credit (ch. 2) and the theory of interest (ch. 4).

Turgot's ordering of the subject matter in the 'Reflections' is based on a different principle. The first part of the work as published in the *Ephémérides*[73] deals almost exclusively with production and distribution in an agricultural society. In such a society, there is already a need for the division of labour and exchange (§§1–4) but the non-agricultural occupations are relatively unimportant (§5). Society is therefore divided into proprietors, who own the land, the people concerned in agricultural production who produce the most important part of the society's wealth, and finally, the artisans, who produce commodities required by the first two classes and who receive their subsistence in return (§§7–18). Two types of income share arise in such a society: rent for the landowners, who are the only owners of property (§§19), and wages for those who have no property (§6). In fact, the various modes of agricultural production which have been practised (§§20–8) are all concerned with the extraction of a revenue or rent by the property owners who do not work, from the people with no property who therefore have to earn their living by labour.

In the second part of the 'Reflections', Turgot introduced money (§30), which entails problems of valuation and exchange (§§31–46) but which allows the formation of another form of revenue which can be appropriated without labour. This revenue is the interest of money or the return on capital or moveable wealth (§29). The theory of value and money is followed by a lengthy discussion on the accumulation of capital, the need for capital in all forms of production, and the origin of profit (§§49–55, 59–60, 62–71). Since the two forms of property which allow the receipt of an income without labour have to be distinguished (§§56–8), the division of society into classes put forward in the first part, has to be modified. The group of property owners has to be expanded to include those who own moveable wealth or capital. Society is therefore now divided into the proprietors of real wealth, the landlords who live off the revenue of land; the proprietors of moveable wealth, the capitalists who live off the revenue of capital; and, finally, those who own no property and who therefore have to live on their wages (§§61, 65).

The third part discusses the legitimacy and the determination of interest (§§72–90), the division of wealth into real and personal property, or land and capital (§§91–2), the question whether the revenue of capital is disposable in the same way as the revenue of land (§§93–9), and concludes with some further remarks on the saving-investment process (§§100–1).

From these sketches of the order of contents of the two works, it can be concluded that they differ considerably in emphasis. Turgot highlighted the difference which capital makes to the process of production and distribution by comparing a capitalist society to an agricultural society.[74] Adam Smith, on the other hand, concentrated on the contribution made by the division of labour to the productiveness of labour, the cause of the wealth of nations, and then proceeded to show how the process of valuation distributes this wealth into wages, profit and rent. It is the division of labour rather than capital which receives the emphasis.[75]

On the other hand, there is a broad similarity in the basic conclusions they reached from their respective studies of production and distribution. Although Quesnay had emphasised the role of capital in production of his economic work, he had failed to see its significance for a theory of distribution. Turgot and Smith, on the contrary, clearly recognised that capital implied a transformation in the property relations of society, and that profit or interest, the alternative form of earning property income, had to be added to that of rent, thereby making a threefold division of wealth or income into wages, profit and rent. The recognition of the importance of capital in production *and* distribution theory is another reason why Turgot and Smith were so easily linked.[76]

However, neither the similarity in contents of their respective works, nor their novel conclusion of a threefold distribution schema provides sufficient evidence for such a link in my opinion. It seems to me quite plausible that these may be no more than coincidence,[77] since, after all, there are other instances in the history of economics of simultaneous and independent discovery.

IV

It remains to be seen what final conclusions can be put forward from this survey of the evidence on the Smith-Turgot myth presented here. The historical evidence, it was shown, remains inconclusive except for the fact that it is now known that Smith at least knew part of the 'Reflections' if not the whole of it, so that it can be presumed that he may possibly have used it in writing the *Wealth of Nations*.[78] The internal evidence surveyed in this paper does not lend a great deal of support to this conclusion, since only a few passages can be interpreted as providing further evidence that Smith may have used the 'Reflections'.[79]

On the other hand, there are the broad similarities in contents and basic conclusions of the two works.[80] A comparison of the contents revealed that both authors dealt with broadly similar subjects but that their analytical framework was substantially different. Nevertheless, they both reached a similar conclusion, since they both put forward that as a result of the tremendous importance of capital in the process of production, a point the two probably derived from Quesnay, distribution analysis had to be conducted in terms of three classes and three income shares: capitalists had to be added to landlords and labourers, profit to wages and rent. It is this important, and for the time, novel, conclusion that makes the similarity between their work so striking.[81]

Nevertheless, this similarity disappears when it is more closely examined. There are major differences in emphasis and in the treatment of particular topics, which indicate that Smith was not greatly indebted to the author of the 'Reflections'. Only the idea of including a chapter on the different employments of capital may have been suggested to Smith by Turgot's work, but even here the contents are substantially modified, as is the classification.[82] The question of the broad similarities is therefore not really answered by this type of reasoning.

In order to explain these broad similarities, the simplest answer is probably also the most plausible. They may be partly explained by the common heritage which the two economists shared, especially in the writings of Locke, Cantillon, Hume and Quesnay.[83] Their similar outlook on economic policy, at which they both arrived independently early in their respective careers,[84] explains the similarities that remain. It is not really surprising that people with a similar outlook on economic issues and with common theoretical forefathers would produce books with so many similar ideas.

Notes

1 This paper has benefited greatly from comments by Professor Viner, Professor Meek and Dr Skinner, who read a draft of this paper in manuscript. Many of their

suggestions have been incorporated, but this does not excuse the author for the errors that remain.

2 Du Pont de Nemours, *Eloge de Turgot*, cited by G. Schelle, *Du Pont de Nemours et l'école Physiocratique*, Paris, 1888, p. 159; Condorcet, *Vie de M. Turgot*, cited in *Monthly Review*, XCVII, London, 1795, p. 570.

3 See especially, I. C. Lundberg, *Turgot's Unknown Translator*, The Hague, 1964; and Jacob Viner, introduction to the re-issue of John Rae, *Life of Adam Smith*, New York, 1965, pp. 128–38.

4 By Edwin Cannan. See his introduction to Adam Smith, *Lectures on Police, Justice, Revenue and Arms*, New York, 1964, p. xxiv.

5 See e.g. John Rae, *Life of Adam Smith*, ch. XIV; C. R. Fay, *Adam Smith and the Scotland of his Day*, Cambridge, 1956, ch. 11; J. Viner, introduction to the re-issue of John Rae, *Life of Adam Smith*, New York, 1965, pp. 128–38, and I. C. Lundberg, *Turgot's Unknown Translator*, The Hague, 1964. These four references together present nearly all there is to know on the historical evidence on the 'Smith-Turgot myth'.

6 See Dugald Stewart, *The Works of Adam Smith with an Account of his Life and Writings*, London, 1811, V, pp. 465–6; John Rae, *op. cit.*, pp. 194, 226.

7 See Turgot to Du Pont, 20/2/1766, 9/12/1766, in *Oeuvres de Turgot*, Schelle edition, Paris, 1913–23, II, pp. 504–15, 519; Turgot's letters to Trudaine during February–March 1766 are also dated at Limoges, see *Oeuvres de Turgot*, ed. E. Daire, Paris, 1844, I, pp. 353, 363.

8 See letters 1–3 from Turgot to Hume in J. Hill Burton, *Letters of Eminent Persons Addressed to David Hume*, Edinburgh, 1849, pp. 130–48.

9 Smith to Hume, 6/7/1766, reprinted in John Rae, *Life of Adam Smith*, New York, 1965, p. 208; Turgot to Hume, 27/7/1766, reprinted in Burton, *op. cit.*, esp. pp. 136–7.

10 This passage is as follows: 'M. Turgot, who like me loved things metaphysical, estimated his talents greatly. We saw him several times; he was presented at the house of M. Helvetius; we talked of commercial theory, banking, public credit and several points in the great work he was meditating …' (Morellet, *Mémoires*, I p. 237, cited by C. R. Fay, *Adam Smith and the Scotland of his Day*, Cambridge, 1956, p. 156). From this extract it can be concluded that Turgot met Smith several times in the company of Morellet but not that they necessarily discussed economics together. Cf. Rae. *op. cit.*, p. 201.

11 D. Dakin, *Turgot and the Ancien Régime*, London, 1939, p. 17.

12 John Rae, *Life of Adam Smith*, New York, 1965, pp. 201–3.

13 See the references in note 9 above.

14 Cf. Dugald Stewart, *The Works of Adam Smith with an Account of his Life and Writings*, London, 1811, V, pp. 469–70; John Rae, *Life of Adam Smith*, New York, 1965, pp. 203–4.

15 Both Turgot and Smith had written on these subjects and they therefore shared many more interests than just economics. Cf. S. Feilbogen, *Smith und Turgot*, Vienna, 1892, p. 17.

16 The reference to such a diary is in W. R. Scott, 'Studies relating to Adam Smith during the last fifty years', *Proceedings of the British Academy*, London, 1940, pp. 273–4.

17 Condorcet refers to 'an exchange of letters with M. Smith on issues most important to humanity'. See *Vie de M. Turgot*, in *Oeuvres de Condorcet*, edited by A. Condorcet O'Connor and M. F. Arago, Paris, 1847, V, p. 163.

18 Dugald Stewart, *The Works of Adam Smith with an Account of his Life and Writings*, London, 1811, V, pp. 47, 470.

19 L. Say, *Turgot*, London, 1888, p. 32. Say seems to have had second thoughts since, according to John Rae, *Life of Adam Smith*, New York, 1965, pp. 204–5, he searched the Turgot family archives and found no trace of letters from Smith.
20 John Rae, *Life of Adam Smith*, New York, 1965, pp. 204–5. As evidence he cites Smith to Sir John Sinclair, 24/11/1778, which refers to the fact that Smith had received *Mémoires concernant les impositions* 'by particular favour of M. Turgot'. This letter gives no authority for Rae's assertion that 'an occasional letter ... certainly did pass between them' (*ibid.*)
21 Smith to de la Rochefoucauld, 1/11/1785, *Economic Journal*, VI, 1896, pp. 165–6. The letter also refers to the fact that Turgot had sent Smith a copy of the *Procès verbal* of the *Lit de Justice* in connection with Turgot's six Edicts of 1776.
22 Professor E. C. Mossner, who is at present preparing an edition of the correspondence of Adam Smith, has informed me by letter that no new information on this subject has turned up.
23 I.e. the two books mentioned in notes 20 and 21 above. Both appear in Bonar's *Catalogue of the Library of Adam Smith*, London, 1932.
24 I.e. Bonar, *op. cit.*; Tadao Yanaihara, *Catalogue of Adam Smith's Library in the possession of the University of Tokyo*, Horoshi Mizuta, *Adam Smith's Library*, Cambridge, 1967.
25 Cf. J. Viner, introduction to the re-issue of John Rae, *Life of Adam Smith*, New York, 1965, pp. 127–8.
26 E. Cannan, introduction to Adam Smith, *Lectures on Police, Justice, Revenue and Arms*, New York, 1964, p. xxiii.
27 Cannan, *op. cit.*, p. xxiii.
28 W. R. Scott, *Adam Smith as Student and Professor*, Glasgow, 1937, pp. 125–6.
29 *Ibid.*, p. 125.
30 See Tadao Yanaihara, *Catalogue of Adam Smith's Library in the possession of the University of Tokyo*, p. 98; Horoshi Mizuta, *Adam Smith's Library*, Cambridge, 1967, p. 20.
31 The 'Reflections' appeared in three issues of the *Ephémérides*: those of November and December 1769, and January 1770.
32 Turgot requested 150 of these offprints from Du Pont for distribution to his friends. See Turgot to Du Pont, 23/3/1770, in *Oeuvres de Turgot*, Schelle edition, Paris, 1913–23, III p. 383. Cf. I. C. Lundberg, *Turgot's Unknown Translator*, The Hague, 1964, pp. 20–1.
33 *Economic Journal*, VI, 1896, p. 612.
34 A. Neymarck, *Turgot et ses doctrines*, Paris, 1885, I, p. 229.
35 I. C. Lundberg, *Turgot's Unknown Translator*, The Hague, 1964, pp. 37–8.
36 If Turgot had as high regard for Smith as Morellet maintained, this would seem to be a plausible assumption, especially since Turgot had sent his work to many of his other economist-friends such as Quesnay, Mirabeau, Mercier de la Rivière, Baudeau, Morellet and Tucker. See Turgot to Tucker, 12/9/1770, in *Oeuvres de Turgot*, ed. E. Daire, Paris, 1844, II, p. 801; Turgot to Du Pont, 23/3/1770, in *Oeuvres de Turgot*, Schelle edition, Paris, 1913–23, III, p. 383.
37 I. C. Lundberg, *Turgot's Unknown Translator*, The Hague, 1964, p. 36.
38 Cf. J. Viner, introduction to the re-issue of John Rae, *Life of Adam Smith*, New York, 1965, pp. 127–8, and P. D. Groenewegen, 'A New Catalogue of Adam Smith's Library', *Economic Record*, December 1968, esp. p. 498 n2, and pp. 501, 503 (below, Chapter 21).
39 I.e. I. C. Lundberg, *Turgot's Unknown Translator*, The Hague, 1964.
40 J. Viner, introduction to the re-issue of John Rae, *Life of Adam Smith*, New York, 1965, pp. 128–38. In his comments on this paper, he added the following: 'Incidentally, shortly after the publication of my "Guide" to John Rae, I ran across in my own files ancient notes I had taken on a publication shortly before 1793 by the

same publisher of the same translation in serial form in a periodical. On examining recently the set of this periodical in the Princeton University Library, I find that the translator describes himself – or is described by the publisher – as "A Merchant". So Smith as a translator would have been a deliberate mystificator or liar'.

41 The first approach is put forward in works such as S. Feilbogen, *Smith und Turgot*, Vienna, 1892; E. Cannan, introduction to *Wealth of Nations*, Modern Library edition, New York, 1937; and J. A. Schumpeter, *History of Economic Analysis*, London, 1959, esp. pp. 248–9. Schumpeter, however, also uses the second approach on some occasions.

42 The second approach is contained in E. Leser, *Der Begriff des Reichtoms bei Adam Smith*, Heidelberg, 1874; J. E. Thorold Rogers' edition of the *Wealth of Nations*, Oxford, 1880; I. C. Lundberg, *Turgot's Unknown Translator*, The Hague, 1964; and also by J. A. Schumpeter, *op. cit.*, esp. pp. 323–4.

43 See E. Cannan, introduction to Adam Smith, *Lectures on Police, Justice, Revenue and Arms*, New York, 1964, pp. xxiii–xxiv; J. Viner, introduction to the re-issue of John Rae, *Life of Adam Smith*, New York, 1965, pp. 132–3; Lundberg, *op. cit.*, pp. 58–60. For the passages in question, see Rogers, *op. cit.*, I, pp. 12–14, 24, 31, 58, 71, 151, 280, 290, II, pp. 248, 443, and cf. his statement in the introduction: 'In the first book [of the *Wealth of Nations*], particularly, passages will be found which are almost transcripts from Turgot's divisions and arguments' (*ibid.*, I, p. xxiii).

44 See E. Leser, *Der Begriff des Reichtoms bei Adam Smith*, Heidelberg, 1874, pp. 80–93, where the parallel passages are given in full.

45 See I. C. Lundberg, *Turgot's Unknown Translator*, The Hague, 1964, chs VIII–IX, esp. p. 73. J. Viner, introduction to the re-issue of John Rae, *Life of Adam Smith*, New York, 1965, p. 136 and n37, has severely criticised her contentions and conclusions.

46 Adam Smith, *Wealth of Nations*, ed. E. Cannan, Modern Library edn, New York, 1937, p. 56; Turgot, 'Reflections', in *Oeuvres de Turgot*, Schelle edition, Paris, 1913–23, p. 58. This passage was among those noted by J. E. Thorold Rogers in his edition of the *Wealth of Nations*, Oxford, 1880, I, p. 58.

47 Turgot to Du Pont, 20/2/1770, in Schelle, *op. cit.*, III, p. 378.

48 See Smith, *op. cit.*, p. 267; Turgot, 'Reflections', *op. cit.*, p. 44. This passage was also noted by J. E. T. Rogers in his edition of the *Wealth of Nations*, Oxford, 1880, I, p. 280.

49 Adam Smith, *op. cit.*, p. 259, Turgot, *op. cit.*, pp. 44–5. As Cannan has pointed out, this idea is also expressed in E. Cannan, introduction to Adam Smith, *Lectures on Police, Justice, Revenue and Arms*, New York, 1964, p. 181.

50 Smith, *op. cit.*, p. 326, Turgot, *op. cit.*, pp. 52–3. The quotation in the text is from Smith.

51 See R. L. Meek, *The Economics of Phyiocracy*, London, 1962, pp. 151n, 154–6. Both Turgot and Smith were acquainted with Quesnay's work.

52 Since Smith had made this connection in his *Lectures*, he would not have been indebted to Turgot for it. See note 49 above. Furthermore, Schumpeter has argued in this connection that there is ground for believing that Smith did not use the 'Reflections', since Smith's 'exposition, though infinitely more prolix, falls far short of Turgot's theory of capital' (J. A. Schumpeter, *History of Economic Analysis*, London, 1959, pp. 323–4).

53 *Ibid.*, p. 324 n2. The relevant passages are in Smith, *op. cit.*, p. 321, Turgot, in *Oeuvres de Turgot*, Schelle edition, Paris, 1913–23, p. 98. It is interesting to note that the 1788 edition of the 'Reflections' does not italicise the phrase 'sur-le-champ', while versions edited by Du Pont, do. The Ashley edition, which Schumpeter probably used, also italicises this phrase.

54 See J. A. Schumpeter, *History of Economic Analysis*, London, 1959, pp. 324–5. It is interesting to note that Lauderdale, one of Smith's first critics on this score, under-

lined passages dealing with saving-investment in his copy of Turgot's 'Reflections' (which is at present in the Goldsmith's Library, University of London).

55 On thrift, see Smith, *op. cit.*. p. 321, cf. Turgot, in *Oeuvres de Turgot*, Schelle edition, Paris, 1913–23, p. 80; on interest and saving, see Smith, *op. cit.*, pp. 334–6, Turgot, *op. cit.*, pp. 80, 85–6. E. Leser, *Der Begriff des Reichtoms bei Adam Smith*, Heidelberg, 1874, pp. 85–8, compared some of these passages, but did not comment on their similarity to Hume's analysis.

56 Adam Smith, *op. cit.*, p. 340.

57 Turgot, 'Reflections', in *Oeuvres de Turgot*, Schelle edition, Paris, 1913–23, pp. 82, 85.

58 This explanation of the different rates of return was not new. See e.g. Dudley North, *Discourses upon Trade*, in *Early English Tracts on Commerce*, Cambridge, 1954, p. 518.

59 Adam Smith, *op. cit.*, p. 341. This passage almost immediately follows the passage quoted previously.

60 Turgot, 'Reflections', in *Oeuvres de Turgot*, Schelle edition, Paris, 1913–23, p. 81.

61 Cf. I. C. Lundberg, *Turgot's Unknown Translator*, The Hague, 1964, p. 73.

62 Turgot, 'Reflections', in *Oeuvres de Turgot*, Schelle edition, Paris, 1913–23, p. 61.

63 E. Cannan, introduction to *Wealth of Nations*, Modern Library edition, New York, 1937, p. lv:

> An attentive study of the notes to the present edition will convince the reader that … usually but little, sometimes only a single fact, phrase, or opinion, is taken from each [source], so that few authors are less open than Adam Smith to the reproach of having rifled another man's work. … The *Wealth of Nations* was not written hastily with the impressions of recent reading still vivid on the author's brain. Its composition was spread over at least the twenty-seven years from 1749 to 1776.

With this opinion, I can fully concur. If the above analysis is correct, as I think it is, then Turgot did not inspire Smith to any marked extent and the 'Reflections' becomes just one of the many sources used in the writing of the *Wealth of Nations*.

64 See e.g. W. Hasbach, 'Adam Smith's *Lectures on Justice, Police, Revenue and Arms*', *Political Science Quarterly*, 1897, XII, esp. p. 687; A. Oncken, 'The Consistency of Adam Smith', *Economic Journal*, 1897, VII, pp. 443–50; S. Feilbogen, *Smith und Turgot*, Vienna, 1892, esp. part II, ch. III.

65 E. Cannan, introduction to *Wealth of Nations*, Modern Library edition, New York, 1937, p. xxxix. W. R. Scott disagreed strongly with this particular argument after his discovery of the early draft of the *Wealth of Nations*, from which it is plain, according to him, that Smith had independently arrived at a theory of distribution. See Scott, 'The Manuscript of an Early Draft of the *Wealth of Nations*', *Economic Journal*, 1935, XLV, esp. pp. 433–4; cf. J. M. Keynes, 'Review of *Adam Smith as Student and Professor*', *Economic History*, III (i.e. IV) 1938, pp. 44–5; and for a contrary opinion, R. L. Meek, 'Adam Smith and the Classical Concept of Profit', *Scottish Journal of Political Economy*, 1954, I, pp. 150–1.

66 The need for such a comparison was suggested to me by Dr Skinner. The differences in emphasis on particular subjects are partly revealed by the relative number of paragraphs which Turgot devoted to it, and which vary considerably from topic to topic.

67 The paragraph numbering in this table follows that used by Ashley, which differs from that of the Daire and the 1788 edition. The reader will also observe that some paragraphs have been left out altogether, since they have no parallel in the *Wealth of Nations*: e.g., 7–18 on physiocratic classes, and 20–8 on agricultural modes of production.

68 E.g. Smith, *Wealth of Nations*, ed. J. E. T. Rogers, Oxford, 1880, I, p. xxiii; S. Feilbogen, *Smith und Turgot*, Vienna, 1892, pp. 47–9.

69 See references given in note 65 above. In fact, most of the material in Book I and part of that in Book II, especially the introduction and the lengthy second chapter, can be found in the *Lectures*.

70 This is partly revealed in the table presented above. Smith's ordering of the subject matter is not followed by Turgot, as can be judged from his paragraph numbers.

71 Cf. E. Cannan, *History of the Theories of Production and Distribution from 1776 to 1848*, London 1953, pp. 147–8.

72 Adam Smith, *op. cit.*, pp. 259–61.

73 For the purpose of publication in the *Ephémérides*, Du Pont divided the 'Reflections' into three parts to appear in successive issues. Turgot, as can be seen from his correspondence with Du Pont, seems to have had no objections to the principle on which the material was divided.

74 Turgot, however, did not completely emancipate himself from the economics of an agricultural society. The landlord remains predominant and rent remains the only form of disposable income. See 'Reflections', in *Oeuvres de Turgot*, Schelle edition, Paris, 1913–23, pp. 90–8.

75 In Smith, the role of capital is also highly important since it is the pre-requisite for the division of labour, but it is the latter which ranks first in his treatise.

76 Cf. R. L. Meek, *Economics and Ideology and other Essays*, London, 1967, pp. 30–1.

77 This coincidence may be explained by the fact that the two authors were contemporaries and that they drew on basically the same major sources for their economic education. This second point will be discussed further in the final section.

78 Thereby slightly modifying Cannan's conclusion in the introduction to the *Lectures* (E. Cannan, introduction to Adam Smith, *Lectures on Police, Justice, Revenue and Arms*, New York, 1964, p. xxiii), and to the *Wealth of Nations* (E. Cannan, introduction to *Wealth of Nations*, Modern Library edition, New York, 1937, p. lv).

79 Especially the material on saving-investment analysis and on the various employments of capital, discussed in the second section of this chapter.

80 It does not really need repeating that this comparison only refers to the 'Reflections' and the first two books of the *Wealth of Nations*.

81 On the importance of this modification of the analysis of distribution, see R. L. Meek, 'Adam Smith and the Classical Concept of Profit', *Scottish Journal of Political Economy*, 1954, I.

82 This was discussed in detail in the second section of this chapter.

83 It need hardly be shown that both economists were acquainted with these four predecessors: Smith cited all four in the *Wealth of Nations* and knew their major works; Turgot had a high opinion of the last three (see Turgot to Caillard, 1/1/1771, in *Oeuvres de Turgot*, Schelle edition, Paris, 1913–23, III, p. 500) while he cited Locke in his 'Letter on Paper Money'. See *Oeuvres de Turgot*, ed. E. Daire, Paris, 1844, I, p. 97.

84 Mainly the laissez-faire outlook which is characteristic of both their work. Turgot and Smith arrive at this in the 1750s, long before there was any question of personal meetings, etc.

21 A new catalogue of Adam Smith's library[1]

The history and contents of Adam Smith's library have been of considerable interest to Smithian scholars and historians of economics for a long time. This has, of course, been due to the tremendous importance of the *Wealth of Nations* as a landmark in the history of the science and to the many controversies which have surrounded the supposed origins of Smith's economic ideas.[2] For this reason, the appearance of a new catalogue of the library merits some attention.

The history of the library itself has been well chronicled by Dr James Bonar, the first editor of a catalogue of its contents. On the death of Smith his library passed to his cousin and heir, David Douglas (later Lord Reston), who in turn bequeathed it in equal portions to his two daughters, Mrs Cunningham of Prestonpans and Mrs Bannerman of Edinburgh.

On Mrs Bannerman's death in 1897, the library passed to her son, The Rev. David Douglas Bannerman, who presented part of the collection to New College, Edinburgh, in 1884, adding the remainder in 1894. A large portion of Smith's library is therefore at present housed in the library of a Faculty of Divinity, and has, as yet, not been completely catalogued.[3]

The other portion of the Smith library has a more complicated history. As early as 1862 one of its items was presented by the Rev. W. B. Cunningham, Mrs Cunningham's husband, to the economist J. R. McCulloch. Similar presentations cannot be excluded.[4] On the death of her husband in 1878 Mrs Cunningham sold part of the collection in Edinburgh,[5] while on her death the remainder went to her son, Professor R. O. Cunningham. Part of this remainder went during the lifetime of the latter to the library of Queens College, Belfast; the final part was sold on his death in 1918. In 1920 most of this final part was purchased by Professor I. Nitobe and sent by him to the Imperial University of Tokyo, where it survived both an earthquake and the Second World War.[6]

These leakages from the Cunningham part of the library, as well as the incompleteness of the catalogue of the Bannerman collection, have made the compiling of a catalogue of Smith's library a most difficult task. To this must be added the fact that all the leakages may not have been recorded since there is a great possibility that Adam Smith himself, Lord Reston, the Bannermans and the Cunninghams, made several small and informal presentations like the one to J. R. McCulloch mentioned above.[7] Little else needs to be said on the history of the library at this stage.

The history of the published catalogues of Adam Smith's library is almost as interesting as the history of the library itself. This begins in 1894 when Bonar published the first catalogue, which was immediately praised as an important contribution to the history of economics.[8] The first catalogue possessed so many shortcomings and omissions that its editor prepared a second and much enlarged edition, which was published for the Royal Economic Society in 1932.[9] In 1951 a further catalogue appeared, this time listing the books with Smith's bookplate in the possession of the University of Tokyo, but which also included as an addendum a reproduction of the 1781 catalogue of the library, prepared for Smith himself, and therefore of the greatest importance to Smithian scholars.[10] In the period between the appearance of the second Bonar catalogue and that of the Tokyo catalogue, more than half a dozen notes were published which reported additions to the list compiled by Bonar.[11] Research into the contents of Smith's library is therefore complicated by the lack of adequate information on this subject available in a single source.

Fortunately, the various sources have now been brought together, thanks to Hiroshi Mizuta and once more the Royal Economic Society – through the publication in 1967 of a new catalogue in the form of a supplement to the 1932 catalogue together with a checklist of the whole library. This paper sets out to discuss the contents of the new catalogue, to draw some conclusions relating to the economic contents of the library (insofar as that can now be ascertained), and finally to give some comments on its uses for Smithian studies.

I

The new catalogue is divided into two parts. The first deals with the additions to Bonar's catalogue, while the second provides the checklist to Adam Smith's library as a whole. There is also a useful introduction which gives some interesting additional information.

Part of the information contained in the introduction concerns the places where Smith's books are now to be found. There is, however, no inclusion of changes in location of some of the books, as compared with the location given by Bonar; but on the other hand, Mizuta does list several cases where Bonar's locations are wrong. For example, part of Foxwell's collection of Smith-books is missing, since several of the books marked 'F' by Bonar are neither in the Kress nor the Goldsmiths Library where the major part of the Foxwell collection has ended up. Mizuta gives other examples of books missing from their location as given by Bonar: the presentation copy of *Moral Sentiments* to Bentham is missing from University College, London; the first volume of Rousseau's *Works* is missing from the Kirkaldy Museum; while there are about twenty items which cannot be traced in the New College Library, Edinburgh.[12] It seems a pity that Mizuta did not investigate this sort of thing in more detail, as this could have led to information about leakages other than those chronicled by Bonar.[13]

The supplement adds about 480 titles to Bonar's catalogue, which is an addition of over 40 per cent to Bonar's 1,100 separate books and pamphlets.[14] About 390 of these new additions come from the 1781 manuscript, while the others come from discoveries of Smith's books made in libraries after 1932. Of the additions that were located in libraries or private collections, the majority are in the collections of New College, Edinburgh; the Hutzler collection of Johns Hopkins University, Baltimore; and Queens University, Belfast.[15] Only eighty-two of the new items whose location is known appeared in the 1781 catalogue, so that there are still about 300 items of that document missing.

It is also interesting to note that of the items listed as not being cited in the 1781 catalogue, fifty-six were published before 1781, thereby indicating the possibility that even this manuscript may not be complete.[16] It is a pity, however, that the notes supplied with these additions are not as full as in the case of Bonar's 1932 catalogue.

Among the new additions there are several items of considerable interest to the historian of economic thought. In the first place, there is a copy of Condorcet's *Vie de M. Turgot*, which is at present in the library of Old College, Edinburgh University, being 'part of a donation of books to the Library in 1933, known as the Lady Carlaw Martin Bequest'.[17] Second, it can now definitely be stated that Smith possessed a large run of the physiocratic journal, *Ephémérides du Citoyen*, namely forty-two volumes bound in fifteen, running from 1766 to 1769. These include the first two parts of Turgot's *Réflexions* as edited by Du Pont de Nemours.[18] The third item of interest, also connected with Turgot, is a copy of the 1793 English translation of the *Réflexions*, at present in the Hutzler Collection of Johns Hopkins University, which was first discovered by Jones, commented on by Viner, and has now been properly included in the catalogue of Smith's library.[19]

The other items of interest are more miscellaneous. The first of these are numbers 1–11 of the *East India Examiner*, in the second edition of 1766, which are bound together with the first seven numbers of the *East-India Observer*. These periodicals may have influenced Smith's decided opinions on the East India Company.[20] The second is a copy of the two volumes of Malachy Postlethwayt's *Universal Dictionary of Trade and Commerce* in the third edition of 1766, which is at present in New College, Edinburgh. Smith may have obtained from this source the list of wheat prices printed at the conclusion of his chapter on rent.[21] Third, there is a copy of *Characteristics of the Present Political State of Great Britain*, generally attributed to Robert Wallace, and the first published economic work of that eighteenth-century Scottish population theorist.[22]

Leaving the additions, some criticisms may be mentioned. It is inevitable that errors appear in the compiling of a work like this catalogue, but Mizuta is to be congratulated on having very few of them. One of these errors relates to the entry concerning Morellet's *Réfutation de l'ouvrage qui a pour titre Dialogues sur le commerce des bléds*; this appears in Bonar and should therefore not have appeared in the supplement. Second, it appeared in the 1781 catalogue as reproduced by Yanaihara, a fact which is not reported in the margin.[23] Other examples of items included in the supplement and referred to by Bonar can be cited.[24]

In connection with the entry for *Ephémérides du Citoyen*, the full title given by Mizuta is only applicable for 1767 and following years; in 1765 and 1766 the full title of the journal was *Ephémérides du Citoyen en Chronique de l'Esprit National*.[25]

There are also some annoying printing errors. In the checklist, there is an item entitled *Treatise of affaires maritime*, which could easily be a reference to a French work. In the supplement the entry appears as *A Treatise of Affairs Maritime, & of Commerce*, which clearly makes it an English tract.[26] Fortunately, there are few errors of this type.

On the whole, however, Mizuta's contribution to Smithian studies is a most useful one, although it must be added that it is incomplete without Bonar's much more scholarly 1932 catalogue. It greatly adds to our knowledge of Adam Smith and his work.

II

In connection with these comments on Adam Smith's library, something should also be said about the economic content of that library, a subject on which there is still no authoritative study. This is a pity, since most enquirers into the contents of the library have been historians of economic thought. Some comments on this topic are therefore in order.

A glance through the checklist in Mizuta's catalogue almost immediately reveals the extent of Smith's reading in English, French, and even Italian economics. Most of the leading works of the seventeenth and eighteenth century are represented, though there are also some interesting gaps in his collection. Besides the leading authorities, Smith also possessed many secondary source books on industry, agriculture, commerce and public finance. Out of the 1,600 items in his library, well over 200 are connected with economic science.

Proceeding in alphabetical order through the British authors, Smith possessed copies of the following: Berkeley's *The Querist*, Cantillon's *Essay on the Nature of Commerce in General*, Child's *New Discourse of Trade*, Davenant's *Works*, Fleetwood's *Chronicon Preciosum*, Gee's *Trade and Navigation of Great Britain Considered*, Harris' *Essay Upon Money and Coins*, Horsley's (or Magen's) *Universal Merchant*, Hume's *Essays*, Hutcheson's *Moral Philosophy*, Law's *Money and Trade Considered*, Mun's *Englands Treasure by Forraign Trade*, Postlethwayt's *Universal Dictionary of Trade and Commerce*, Richardson's (or Decker's) *Essay on the Causes of the Decline of Foreign Trade*, Steuart's *Principles of Political Oeconomy*, no less than six of Tucker's economic tracts, Wallace's *Characteristics of the Present Political State of Great Britain*, and six of the early economic works of Arthur Young.

The only really notable omissions from this collection are Petty's economic writings and the monetary essays of John Locke.[27] Another interesting gap in his library is Mandeville's *Fable of the Bees*. There is no record that he ever possessed a copy. This is more than surprising, since it was not a rare work during Smith's lifetime, and because he had criticised it in detail in the *Moral Sentiments*.[28] The omission of Locke's monetary essays and Mandeville's notorious book could indicate the possibility that the 1781 catalogue was not complete.

The leading French economists are nearly as well represented. Smith owned Condillac's *Le Commerce et le gouvernement*, Dutot's *Réflexions politiques sur les finances et le commerce*, four works by Forbonnais including the *Elémens du commerce*, Le Trosne's *Recueil de plusieurs morceaux économiques*, Melon's *Essai politique sur le commerce*, Mercier de la Rivière's *L'ordre naturel et essentiel des sociétés politiques*, three works by Mirabeau the elder, namely *l'Ami des hommes*, *Théorie de l'impôt* and *Philosophie Rurale*, Montesquieu's *Works*, three works by Morellet, Necker's *Législation et commerce des grains*, Quesnay's *Physiocratie* (edited by Du Pont de Nemours), as well as ten volumes of the *Journal de l'Agriculture, du Commerce, et des Finances* for 1765 to 1767, and the complete run of the *Ephémérides* from 1766 to 1769 inclusive which includes the major part of Turgot's *Réflexions* as well as many other writings by the leading physiocrats.

The Italians are represented by Beccaria's *Works* and by Verri's *Meditazione sulla economia politica*, while a Dutch and Spanish economic writer are represented in translation.[29] Smith's library included a large and international collection of books on political economy. When this list is compared with the list of authorities cited in the *Wealth of Nations* which was compiled by Cannan,[30] it is found that most of them were in fact present in Smith's library.

There are some interesting additions to what was previously known about the contents of the library, especially in the French part. It can now be shown that Smith had a much wider acquaintance with French eighteenth-century economics than Cannan, W. R. Scott and Fay indicated in their studies of Adam Smith.[31] W. R. Scott especially tended to minimise the importance of the 1781 catalogue, despite the fact that he was fully aware of its contents when writing his *Adam Smith as Student and Professor* and his last, posthumously published, paper on Adam Smith.[32] It is to be hoped that the new edition of Smith's works to be edited by Andrew Skinner for the University of Glasgow will take account of all this new and important information.[33]

III

The final question that should be discussed is concerned with the use that has been made by scholars of the information contained in the various catalogues of Adam Smith's library. Apart from the aid the 1894 Bonar catalogue must have given to Cannan in his edition of the *Wealth of Nations*, this information has been solely used in the discussion of the Turgot-Smith controversy.[34] Viner, in his excellent introduction to Rae's *Life of Adam Smith*, which has already been referred to, has summarised 'The Use by Scholars of Information concerning the Contents of Smith's Library'.[35] Apart from information contained in Mizuta's new catalogue, his summary is virtually complete. It is to this new information that this section is devoted.

In the first place, Mizuta's supplement gives the answer to the question posed by Viner in connection with Smith's holding of the *Ephémérides*.[36] The forty-two 'tomes' run from 1766 to 1769 inclusive, and not to June 1770 as Viner suggested as a possibility. Smith therefore lacked the third and concluding part of the *Réflexions*.[37]

On the second point, the presence in Smith's library of a copy of the English translation of Turgot's *Réflexions*, Mizuta throws no light. This is an intriguing question in view of Lundberg's hypothesis that Smith himself may have prepared this translation, and therefore deserved some comment by Mizuta. Since this translation was not published till three years after Smith's death, and since this is the only post-1790 volume so far discovered which bears the book-plate, the inclusion of this item in the supplement should have been discussed by Mizuta. Viner's enquiries in connection with this item have not yet been completed, and it is to be hoped that they will be published in the near future.[38]

The final new item of interest is the inclusion of Condorcet's *Vie de M. Turgot* in the supplement, since this work is also connected with the 1793 translation of the *Réflexions* and the Lundberg hypothesis.[39] The 1793 translation, and the 1795 reprint of it, contain on the title page the following quotation from this work of Condorcet: 'This Essay may be considered as the germ of the Treatise on the Wealth of Nations, written by the celebrated Smith'.[40] This statement was evidently considered of so much importance by the translator that it was repeated by him in the *Eulogium*, from which Lundberg concluded: 'the translator, in two deliberate passages on as many pages, was claiming for Adam Smith an indebtedness the eminent Prof. Edwin Cannan would later scout as baseless'.[41] Her further conclusions suggested that only Smith would have known his indebtedness to Turgot, that Smith only could make such a 'public claim', and 'since no other man could venture on virtually an open confession, and no other translator would have a motive for revealing Smith's debt to Turgot, then the translator must have been Adam Smith and no other'.[42]

Although this reasoning is rather forced, one assumption Lundberg had to make in support of her argument can now be verified; Smith did own a copy of Condorcet's *Vie de M. Turgot*, and would therefore have been aware of the statement linking the *Réflexions* with his *Wealth of Nations* to which the anonymous translator gave such prominence.[43] This is all that needs to be said in this connection.[44]

Although the use of the information about Smith's library contained in the various catalogues is therefore small and rather one-sided, this does not mean that this information is unimportant. Mizuta has done historians of economic thought a great service by bringing Bonar's catalogue up to date and by providing a checklist of the whole library. It is now the task of others to use this wealth of information in shedding more light on the works of Adam Smith, and on the origin of his ideas. As Cannan, W. R. Scott, Bonar, Fay, Viner and others have shown, this is a task well worth undertaking.

Notes

1 A review of H. Mizuta, *Adam Smith's Library: A Supplement to Bonar's Catalogue with a Check-list of the Whole Library*, published for the Royal Economic Society (Cambridge University Press, London, 1967) pp. xix + 153. £1 17*s* 6*d*. Throughout these notes, all references to Mizuta are to this work unless otherwise indicated.

2 These controversies dealt with the alleged shift in Smith's philosophical position which occurred between the publication of *Moral Sentiments* and the *Wealth of Nations*, his relationship with physiocratic ideas, and especially with those of Turgot, and his attitude to what were then current topics, such as the role of the East India Company, etc.

3 See the introduction to James Bonar, *A Catalogue of the Library of Adam Smith* (Macmillan, London, 1932) pp. xvi–xvii. I have by me a letter from Mr J. V. Howard, New College librarian, who warns me that 'The New College collection, which appears to comprise about half the total, has never been fully catalogued, and there are, I am sure, omissions and inaccuracies as a result [in Mizuta's catalogue]'.

4 Bonar, *op. cit.*, pp. xvii, 55, 199–200.

5 See *ibid*. p. xvii.

6 *Ibid*. See also introduction, T. Yanaihara, *Catalogue of Adam Smith's Library in the Possession of the University of Tokyo* (New York, 1965).

7 See J. Viner, 'Guide to John Rae's *Life of Adam Smith*', in J. Rae, *Life of Adam Smith* (Kelley, New York, 1965) pp. 126–8, where the possibility of other leakages is discussed.

8 See H. Higgs, *Economic Journal*, vol. IV, December 1894, pp. 705–6; John Rae, *Life of Adam Smith* (Macmillan, London, 1895), p. 327.

9 See James Bonar, *A Catalogue of the Library of Adam Smith* (Macmillan, London, 1932), p. vii.

10 See note 6 above. The 1781 catalogue was found in manuscript among the purchases made in 1920 by Professor Nitobe.

11 See James Bonar, 'Current Topics', *Economic Journal*, vol. XLIV, June 1934, p. 349; Bonar, 'Adam Smith's Library' *Economic Journal*, vol. XLVI, March 1936, pp. 178–83; *The Vanderblue Memorial Collection of Smithiana … in the Kress Library*, Boston MA, 1939; C. Jones, 'Adam Smith's Library: Some Additions', *Economic History*, vol. IV, February 1940, pp. 326–8; MacGarvey, 'Notes on Adam Smith's Library and the Bonar Catalogue 1932', *Economic Journal*, vol. LIX, June 1949, pp. 259–64; Mizuta, 'Adam Smith's Library. Additions and Revisions to Bonar's Catalogue', *Journal of Commerce* (Fukushima University) vol. XXV, 1956, pp. 113–33, 198–231; and Y. Deguchi, 'A Note on the books that belonged to Adam Smith', in *Adam Smith no aji*, Tokyo, 1965, 305–12.

12 Mizuta (1967) *op. cit.*, pp. xii–xiii.

13 See above and the reference in note 7. Mizuta also suggests a leakage from the library when in Lord Reston's possession. See *ibid.*, p. ix.

14 *Ibid.*, p. xi.

15 A quick check revealed the following information about the location of the new items: New College, 97 items; Johns Hopkins, 25; Queens University, 7; Goldsmiths' Library, 9; Tokyo, 15; Old College, 8; Kress, 6; Glasgow University, 8; the remainder are single items in private collections with one exception, that of L. Livingstone, which is now in Glasgow University. See *ibid.*, p. ix.

16 Since many of these books are items from the seventeenth century, they could have been acquired by Smith after 1781. But there are also many pamphlets of the 1750s and 1760s among them, which Smith probably would have acquired when they were published.

17 H. Mizuta, 'Adam Smith's Library. Additions and Revisions to Bonar's Catalogue', *Journal of Commerce* (Fukushima University) vol. XXV, 1956, p.16. This pamphlet

contains the famous statement linking the *Réflexions* with the *Wealth of Nations*. See I. C. Lundberg, *Turgot's Unknown Translator* (Nijhoff, The Hague, 1964, pp. 30–1).

18 They are at present in the library of New College, Edinburgh. See Mizuta (1967) *op. cit*., p. 20, See also J. Viner, 'Guide to John Rae's *Life of Adam Smith*', in J. Rae, *Life of Adam Smith* (Kelley, New York, 1965), pp. 131–2.

19 See C. Jones, 'Adam Smith's Library: Some Additions', *Economic History*, vol. IV, February 1940, p. 327; Viner, *op. cit*., p. 138; Mizuta, *op. cit*., p. 59. The above three links with Turgot will be commented on at a later stage of this paper.

20 Mizuta, *op. cit*., p. 31.

21 *Ibid*., p. 47; cf. Smith, *Wealth of Nations* (Modern Library edition, New York, 1937) pp. 256–8.

22 Mizuta, *ibid*., p. 61.

23 See *ibid*., p. 41, where it is reported as being in Old College, Edinburgh. See also James Bonar, A *Catalogue of the Library of Adam Smith* (Macmillan, London, 1932), p. 120, who reports it as in the possession of Edinburgh University. T. Yanaihara, Introduction, *Catalogue of Adam Smith's Library in the Possession of the University of Tokyo* (New York, 1965) p. 98, reports it as being included in the 1781 catalogue.

24 See Mizuta, *op. cit*., p. 49, item 'Procès-Verbal'; cf. Bonar, *op. cit*., p. 102, who lists it under 'L' as 'Lit de Justice'. Forbes' *Methodical Treatise concerning Bills of Exchange*, which appears in Yanaihara, p. 112, as being in the 1781 catalogue, appears neither in Mizuta nor in Bonar. Morellet's *Examen de la response de* M. *N***, which is listed in the 1781 catalogue (Yanaihara, p. 120) also does not appear in either Mizuta or Bonar.

25 See Mizuta, *op. cit*., p. 20. H. Higgs, *Bibliography of Economics 1750–1775*, gives two entries for *Ephémeridés*. See items 3363 on p. 335, item 3978 on p. 394. The 1781 catalogue gives only the second title.

26 See Mizuta, *op. cit*., pp. 59 and 147. This item could have been: William Horsley, A *Treatise of Maritime Affairs; or a Comparison between the Commerce and Naval Power of England and France* ... See *Kress Library Catalogue through 1776* (Boston MA, 1940), item 4711.

27 Smith did have Petty's *Essay on the Growth of the City of London* and Graunt's (or Petty's?) *Observations on the Bills of Mortality* which were reprinted in A *Collection of the Yearly Bills of Mortality from 1657 to 1758*. See James Bonar, A *Catalogue of the Library of Adam Smith* (Macmillan, London, 1932), p. 120. He also owned Locke's *Two Treatises on Government* (*ibid*., p. 102) and must have been acquainted with Locke's monetary work. See Smith, *Wealth of Nations* (Modern Library Edition, New York, 1937) p. 336.

28 Cf. E. Cannan, introduction to *ibid*., p. li.

29 That is, *De Witt's Political Maxims of the State of Holland*, London, 1743, and Uztariz's *Theory and Practice of Commerce and Maritime Affairs*, which was translated by John Kippax and published in London in 1751.

30 See Smith, *Wealth of Nations* (Modern Library Edition, New York, 1937) pp. 971–6.

31 See E. Cannan (ed.) Smith, *Lectures on Police, Justice, Revenue and Arms* (Kelley and Millman, New York, 1964), pp. xxiii–xxiv; *Wealth of Nations*, *op. cit*., p. xxix; W. R. Scott, 'Adam Smith as Student and Professor', pp. 124–6: *Studies relating to Adam Smith in the Last Fifty Years, Proceedings of British Academy*, London, 1940, pp. 251–3; C. R. Fay, *Adam Smith* (Cambridge University Press, London, 1956) ch. 11.

32 See the references to Scott listed above, and cf. J. Viner, 'Guide to John Rae's *Life of Adam Smith*', in J. Rae, *Life of Adam Smith* (Kelley, New York, 1965) pp. 121–2.

33 To be published in connection with the bicentenary celebrations of the publication of the *Wealth of Nations*.

34 See references in note 32 above, and J. Rae, *Life of Adam Smith* (Kelley, New York, 1965), ch. XIV.

35 J. Viner, 'Guide to John Rae's *Life of Adam Smith*', in J. Rae, *Life of Adam Smith* (Kelley, New York, 1965) pp. 128–32.
36 *Ibid*., pp. 131–2.
37 H. Mizuta, 'Adam Smith's Library. Additions and Revisions to Bonar's Catalogue', *Journal of Commerce* (Fukushima University) vol. XXV, 1956, p. 20. In connection with an enquiry on this matter, Mr J. V. Howard, Librarian of New College, Edinburgh, confirmed that Smith's holding of the *Ephéméridés* includes the first two parts of the *Réflexions*.
38 See J. Viner, 'Guide to John Rae's *Life of Adam Smith*', in J. Rae, *Life of Adam Smith* (Kelley, New York, 1965) pp. 126–7; also Mizuta (1967) *op. cit*., p. 59. The only comment Mizuta gives is as follows: 'Smith's bookplate can only have been attached to this volume after his death in 1790'.
39 See Mizuta, *op. cit*., p. 16; also I. C. Lundberg, *Turgot's Unknown Translator* (Nijhoff, The Hague, 1964) ch. IV.
40 Lundberg, *op. cit*., pp. 30–1.
41 *Ibid*., p. 31.
42 *Ibid*., p. 32.
43 *Ibid*., pp. 30–1.
44 This is not to say that I agree with Lundberg's conclusions. As Viner points out ('Guide to John Rae's *Life of Adam Smith*', in J. Rae, *Life of Adam Smith* [Kelley, New York, 1965], p. 137), the inclusion of this claim by Condorcet may also show that Smith was in no way involved in the translation. After all, the linking of Smith's *Wealth of Nations* to the *Réflexions* would have been a good sales gimmick for the translator, since Smith's treatise was a bestseller and already a well known authority on political economy. In any case, Condorcet's statement drew the attention of the only reviewer of the translator I could find. See *Monthly Review*, London, vol. XCVII, 1795, p. 570.

22 Adam Smith and the division of labour

A bicentenary estimate[1]

The 9th of March 1976 saw the two-hundredth anniversary of the publication of the first edition of Adam Smith's *An Inquiry into the Nature and Causes of the Wealth of Nations* and the development of a new, separate science which is now generally described as economics.[2] That this anniversary needs celebration among economists, who can all be described as the heirs of Adam Smith, does not have to be stressed. Many of these celebrations have been organised across the world,[3] including, on a more limited scale, in Australia. In writing a paper to celebrate this anniversary, an author is faced with a difficult problem of choice. Should he concentrate on a formal analysis of Smith's doctrines, as was so brilliantly done in the 150th anniversary festschrift,[4] or should he analyse the research of Smith scholars in the last fifty years, to use the model adopted by W. R. Scott in 1940?[5] Perhaps a solution to this problem is obtained by combining aspects of these two approaches with that adopted by Professor Recktenwald in a recent paper[6] which emphasises the relevance of the *Wealth of Nations* for 'today and tomorrow'.

Such a combination is perhaps best achieved by concentrating on a particular aspect of Adam Smith's doctrine, by assessing the more recent research of Smith scholars in this area, and by looking at its relevance for today and tomorrow, not only for the historian of economics but also for the economic historian and the economic theorist. What better topic to select for this purpose than the topic particularly close to Smith's heart and which, at the same time, provides the foundation for his model of economic growth? I am referring of course to the division of labour, the starting point of Smith's inquiry into the nature and causes of the wealth of nations, a subject on which a substantial number of papers have been published in the last decade or so,[7] while in addition, Smith's treatment of this subject raises new questions for the economic historian,[8] and for the economic theorist.[9]

This chapter will therefore concentrate on several aspects of the division of labour as the best manner of paying tribute to the sagacity and lasting relevance of the views of the author of the *Wealth of Nations*. The first section of the chapter briefly outlines the importance of the division of labour to the Smithian system; the second looks at the importance of Smith's treatment of the subject in connection with education; the third examines the questions raised by the division of labour for the economic historian of the industrial revolution; while the final part assesses problems associated with the division of labour for the development of current economic theory.[10]

I

The first three chapters of Book I deal with Division of Labour. We are in the oldest part of the building, the part already completed in the Draft. Also, presumably because in his teaching Smith had so often gone over this subject, it is by far the most polished part of the whole. Though, as we know, there is nothing original about it, one feature must be mentioned that has not received the attention it deserves: nobody, either before or after Adam Smith, ever thought of putting such a burden upon division of labour. With Smith it is practically the only factor in economic progress.[11]

There is little need to discuss the contents of these three chapters of the *Wealth of Nations* at length. Smith claims in the opening sentence of the book, that 'The greatest improvement in the productive powers and the greater part of the skill, dexterity and judgement with which it is anywhere directed, or applied, seem to have been the effect of the division of labour.' In the subsequent discussion, he distinguished between the social division of labour or the division of society into occupations and professions, and the division of labour in manufactures or the industrial division of labour. It is the last which gets the greater emphasis – the famous pin example, probably derived from his observations of nail making in Kirkcaldy and his reading of the article 'Epingle', in Volume V of the French *Encyclopédie* – but within this industrial division of labour a further distinction is made on whether 'the great number of workmen' is collected or not collected 'all into the same workhouse'. The pin example most likely would fit the first case, the 'linen and woollen manufactures', referred to subsequently by Smith, the second.[12]

'The great increase in the quantity of work, which, in consequence of the division of labour, the same number of people are capable of performing', is ascribed to three circumstances: increased dexterity, saving of time, and the invention of machines which facilitate labour.[13] Since the division of labour is more easily carried out in manufactures, it is in the manufacturing sector that costs would decline, and it is this sector of the economy, therefore, that is linked with increasing returns.[14] These consequences of the division of labour in turn are responsible for the tremendous rise in living standards experienced by civilised nations in the last hundred years, 'or that universal opulence which extends itself to the lowest ranks of the people'.[15]

Chapters 2 and 3, and the introduction to Book II, discuss both the prerequisites for and the constraints on the division of labour. The division of labour is exclusively ascribed to the human 'propensity to truck and barter, and exchange one thing for another'. Division of labour is therefore only possible in an exchange economy, and hence is limited by the 'the extent of the market'. The greater the market, or the potential demand for final output, the greater the division of labour that can take place. The importance of demand, as well as that of transport and communications, as factors in economic development is clearly illustrated by Smith in these chapters.[16]

A final requirement for the division of labour is given in the introduction to Book II, thereby linking the analysis of capital to that of the division of labour. In the second paragraph of this introduction, Smith demonstrates that a prior accumulation of capital must exist when the division of labour is practised, in order to maintain the labourer, 'and to supply him with the materials and tools of his work till such time' that the production process has been completed and the output has been sold.[17] Later it is argued that the extent of the division of labour is in this way limited by the accumulation of capital and, in addition, that such accumulation encourages further division of labour because the capitalist wants to secure a maximum return for his advances.[18] The division of labour and the accumulation of capital are therefore strongly interrelated.

This summary of Smith's account of the division of labour has done little to illustrate the feature which Schumpeter found so remarkable and to which he drew attention in the quotation at the beginning of this section: the tremendous burden for the whole theory of economic growth which Smith placed on the division of labour. This particular feature of Smith's economics can be demonstrated through the use of the 'growth model' developed from Book II, chapter 3 of *Wealth of Nations* by Sir John Hicks.[19] In this model, the rate of growth of output in the economy is expressed in the following equation:

$$g = k.p/w - 1$$

where g is the rate of growth of output, measured in corn, k is the proportion of productive labour in the total labour supply (the savings ratio),[20] p is the product *per* man year measured in corn (the productivity of labour), and w is the wage rate in terms of corn. This simple relationship provides a useful summary of the essence of Smith's economics.[21]

The rate of growth, the major topic of Smith's treatise as indicated by its title, therefore depends on three variables: the savings ratio, the wage rate and the level of labour productivity. It is clear that a high savings ratio and high productivity imply a high growth rate, while high wages imply a low rate of growth. To appreciate the importance of the division of labour in this system, some comments must be made on Smith's expectations as regards the likely trends in these variables. In so far as k, the savings ratio, was concerned, Smith argued that although accumulation had greatly increased and was still increasing, the 'prodigality of the rich', especially rich landlords, would act as a severe constraint on the size of the savings ratio, so that it was dangerous to place too much emphasis on its increase over time. In connection with wage rates, Smith not only argued that fast growth implied rising wages, but also that this should be the case since development which did not benefit the vast majority of the people was not worth having. In this manner, the effect on growth of the accumulation of capital was counter-balanced by rising wages.

A high growth rate therefore of necessity depended on rapid increases in labour productivity, and such increases, as Smith asserted in the first sentence of his work, depended on the division of labour. The productivity gains from the division of labour in this manner provided the major 'causes of the wealth of nations'. The more important policy conclusions which Smith derived from his critique of contemporary orthodoxy in Book IV to some extent depend on this result. The policy of free trade which Smith there advocated was closely linked with his ideas on the division of labour. If Smith's economic system is interpreted in this manner, it is only logical that the discussion of growth should commence with the division of labour.[22]

II

Smith's discussion of the division of labour was so widely accepted by his economist-successors that it was largely taken for granted and rarely critically discussed. This is illustrated, for example, by the fact that Ricardo in the ten volumes of his works made only four references to the division of labour,[23] none of which advance beyond the treatment of Adam Smith. In the work of Ricardo's leading contemporaries, the treatment of the division of labour, although more extensive, was in the same category.[24]

The one exception to this treatment of the division of labour in subsequent economic writings is associated with those authors who explicitly linked the division of labour with increasing returns. This was done by Nassau Senior,[25] but more strikingly by J. S. Mill, who in his *Principles of Political Economy* devoted a separate chapter to the division of labour which is followed by a discussion of production on a large and on a small scale.[26] Marshall's subsequent treatment of these matters,[27] which brought increasing returns to the forefront of economic discussion in the 1920s and 1930s, also hastened the demise of the division of labour in the economic literature. Increasing returns raised so many difficult problems for marginalist economic theory, that its discussion and that of its progenitor, the division of labour, were largely ignored in the analytical writings that followed.[28]

The above should not be taken to imply that Smith's treatment of the division of labour exerted little influence on the subsequent development of thought. One particular aspect of his discussion of the subject became a matter for considerable controversy in discussions of the social consequences arising from a society in which the division of labour was extensively practised. This controversy relates to Smith's opinion, given in Book V, chapter 1 of the *Wealth of Nations*, that the division of labour also exercised a harmful influence on the 'labouring poor' which required state action in the form of public education.[29]

The harmful influence of the division of labour on the men who were employed in such a system of manufacturing arose from the repetitious nature of the work, and would make them 'as stupid and ignorant as it is possible for a human creature to become'.[30] Similar sentiments were expressed by Adam Ferguson in his *Essay on the History of Civil Society*.[31] These sociological aspects of the division of labour attracted the attention of political and social philosophers at the end of the eighteenth century, particularly in Germany, such as Schiller and Herder. They were particularly concerned to draw out the human consequences of this growing subdivision in the functions of man, and to develop this as a humanistic critique of the new, commercial society. As Schiller put it:

> Eternally tied to a single fragment of the whole, man himself develops into nothing but a fragment. Everlasting in his ear is the monotonous sound of the wheel which he operates. He never develops the harmony of his being, and instead of stamping the imprint of humanity upon nature he becomes no more than the imprint of his occupation and his specialised knowledge.[32]

This reduction in the humanity of man arising from his subdivision in the labour process not only fragmented man himself, as Schiller argued, but also fragmented society. Such a situation, in the view of these philosophers, was in strong contrast to classical Greek society, which formed for them the perfect society, since, being without a massive division of labour, it exhibited the harmony lost in commercial society. This aspect of the social consequences of the division of labour was not fully developed till the work of the mature Hegel and following him, that of Marx.[33]

Like Smith, Schiller saw the solution of this social consequence of economic progress through the division of labour in the extension of education, in particular aesthetic education, which would regenerate not only the human personality but also the cohesion and harmony of society.[34] This idea was taken up by Hegel in his *Philosophy of Right*, in which education is linked with the division of labour in a manner which Marx described as heretical.[35]

Hegel's remarks on the division of labour in this work occupy only a few brief paragraphs which contain all the essential elements of the theory: rising productivity of labour, the interdependence of mankind in the exchange economy and the coordination which this requires, the fact that labour becomes more and more mechanical and therefore less stimulating, 'until finally man is able to step aside and instal machines in his place'.[36]

Education, Hegel argued, has precisely the opposite effect on man:

> The multiplicity of objects and situations which excite interest is the stage on which theoretical education develops. This education consists in possessing not simply a multiplicity of ideas and facts, but also a flexibility and rapidity of mind, ability to pass from one idea to another, to grasp complex and general relations, and so on.[37]

In contrast to the fragmentation of man's personality by his labouring activity conducted under a division of labour, is the 'growth of the universality of thoughts [which] is the absolute value in education'.[38] In this manner education acts as the countervailing force to the harmful social consequences of the division of labour.

It is not the purpose of this section of the chapter to develop the history of ideas on education and division of labour,[39] but rather to raise the question of whether these high expectations of the value of universal education in this connection have in fact been realised, or to put it more strongly, whether they can be realised. At the present time especially, it can be argued that the education process itself has been absorbed into the division of labour, and that man, as a result of his modern, specialised education, has 'become no more than the imprint of his occupation and his specialised knowledge', to quote Schiller's remarks once more. It is this aspect of education and the division of labour, particularly the division of labour in the education of economists, on which I want to make a few comments in this context, though I hasten to add that these comments are not nearly as fully developed as they should be.

It need not be stressed that the division of labour is now practised intensively in the study of economics. It is not only a separate discipline removed from related subjects such as history, sociology and politics; it has also subdivided into branches of learning which are becoming independent specialisations. The broad division of the subject into micro- and macro-economics is one example, the development of a separate labour economics, monetary economics, international economics, public sector economics, development economics and industry economics, indicates a further trend in the process.

As a teacher of the subject it is easy to see the advantages of this phenomenon: everything cannot be taught at once and subdivision as a pedagogic device is useful in the teaching and learning process. At the same time, the explosion in publication and to a lesser extent in knowledge in these areas makes it virtually impossible for the academic to keep abreast with the advances in all these branches of learning. Finally, there are the various occupational pressures which force specific specialisations on particular students.

The disadvantages of this development are less frequently mentioned. For example, the subdivision of the subject in to micro- and macro-economics has had some disastrous consequences, particularly for the study of inflation. Second, the process of specialisation in the study of economics in the universities may lead to the production of graduates who have relatively little or no knowledge of such important aspects as monetary economics, public finance, planning and labour economics, and who can therefore hardly be described as adequately trained economists. Finally, there is the more general problem of the costs involved in the subdivision of economics as a separate subject away from other closely related subjects. During the nineteenth century, and again strongly in the last decade or so, there were and are many people who have lamented the separation of sociology and politics from economics, and the creation of a separate economic history.[40] In the twentieth century there has been as much, if not more emphasis on the fact that the economist's education is not complete without a reasonable degree of knowledge in mathematics and statistics, not to mention econometrics. Others have stressed the importance of legal studies and accounting knowledge for the proper understanding of economic phenomena. Here is another stultifying consequence of the division of labour in economics, with frequently disastrous consequences for the understanding of important economic problems.[41]

Enough has been said on this subject to indicate that education in general is not necessarily the complete answer to the problems raised by a division of labour for society as a whole, since the examples drawn from the education of economists are in principle applicable to virtually every other discipline. Here, therefore, is one question raised by Smith in connection with the division of labour which is one legacy from the *Wealth of Nations* whose value has not been dissipated.

III

The second problem raised by Smith's treatment of the division of labour for contemporary thought is connected with economic history, and in particular with the treatment given to the division of labour in discussions of the causes of the 'Industrial Revolution' in England. Although it is generally agreed that Smith was a shrewd and intelligent observer of economic development in the England and Scotland of his day,[42] and while it has already been demonstrated that Smith regarded the growth of the division of labour as a major factor in this economic development, the division of labour, as far as I have been able to ascertain, receives only scant attention in the economic history discussions of the industrial revolution.[43] It is the contention of this section that Smith himself was partly to blame for this oversight in historical investigation, since his analysis concentrated to some extent on the wrong features of the productivity gains ascribed to the division of labour to the neglect of others.[44]

To simplify this discussion of a complex historical issue, recourse may be had to the, in some ways admirable, *Theory of Economic History* of Sir John Hicks, which includes a general analysis of the industrial revolution.[45] Summarised briefly, Hick's argument is that the industrial revolution is nothing but 'the rise of modern industry' and not the rise of industry as such, which raises the question of the characteristics of *modern* industry. For Hicks, modern industry is characterised by *fixed* capital, while early handicraft and domestic industry is associated with *circulating* capital, capital that is rapidly turned over, and which essentially arose from merchant's capital. For Hicks, the crucial element in the explanation of the industrial revolution is the transformation of circulating into fixed capital or the replacement of handicraft (domestic) industry by factory industry.

This transformation in turn is ascribed to two factors: financial developments in the eighteenth century in England, and science. The first resulted in declining interest rates as capital (loanable funds) became less scarce, while the financial developments were themselves constituted in institutional changes in banking, credit and the capital market which increased the liquidity of investment and thereby made it less risky. Second, there is the factor of science, technological change and innovation, and in particular as Hicks points out (p. 147) the developments of the machine tool industry which allowed construction of machines and which thereby greatly increased the efficiency of mechanisation through greater precision in the tool making process. In this discussion, Sir John Hicks has neglected the role of the division of labour which, I would venture to argue, links his two factors more closely to the historical phenomenon of the Industrial Revolution.[46]

The division of labour, first of all, is strongly linked with this process of the transformation of circulating into fixed capital, a fact appreciated by some eighteenth-century economists but not particularly by Adam Smith.[47] In eighteenth-century England, there were in addition some specific features attached to the role of the division of labour in this transformation process. These arose from the saving in circulating capital which could be achieved by such a re-organisation of production within the one building or factory, because of the particular difficulties associated with domestic industry in this period. To analyse this further requires a brief summary of some of the features of this domestic organisation of industry as practised in the mid-eighteenth century.[48]

Domestic industry in eighteenth-century England was a mode of production in which the workers-craftsmen furnished generally their own tools and equipment, as well as the workshop (generally a part of the home) but in which the materials were supplied by merchants who also disposed of the finished goods. The scanty fixed capital required was therefore supplied by the owner/manufacturer, while the circulating capital in materials, work in progress and finished goods was advanced by the merchant/capitalist. As Ashton points out, 'The larger the time occupied in production, the greater the capital cost' to the merchant, especially to one who was putting out too many domestic workers.[49]

As Ashton also points out, there were many factors at work in eighteenth-century England which made this particular form of the production process lengthy rather than short. 'Many domestic workers were accustomed to give Sunday, Monday, and sometimes Tuesday, to idleness or sport'. Such attitudes to work were possible because the worker himself remained in control of the hours worked, and were encouraged by the low grain prices which characterised the middle of the eighteenth century, and which made vitriolic complaints about the 'idleness of the poor' a common phenomenon in the contemporary economic literature.[50] Such work habits and lack of discipline in the workforce would have greatly lengthened the time period of production and thereby the capital cost.

A further wasteful feature of the domestic system was theft, fraud and embezzlement.

> textile workers mixed butter and grease with the fabric to increase the weight, and nailmakers substituted inferior iron for the rods they had received from the warehouse. Filching of materials was widespread. Acts of Parliament, with increasingly heavy penalties were passed in 1703, 1740, 1749 and 1777, in an attempt to check it, and in the last of these years the

> employers were given the power to enter shops or outhouses for the purpose of search.[51]

Again, it seems an easy conclusion that such practices greatly increased the costs of production of the putting out system.

Finally, Ashton mentions a 'tendency for employers to spread work lightly over a large number of workers, partly to ensure that they would not be short of labour in times of pressure'.[52] When transportation was slow, and above all, expensive, this must have raised the time of production and the costs even further.[53] Is it any wonder, therefore, that this type of manufacturing organisation was spurned by the newly developing industries, because the inefficiency and the costs of the traditional industries were so plain to see to the intelligent observer?

A division of labour which combined these processes under the one roof (a possibility noted and appreciated by Adam Smith)[54] would therefore mean a re-organisation of production, which was particularly productive through the saving of circulating capital obtained by cutting the time period of production, through the elimination of the time and expense of a great deal of transport, by the removal of many opportunities for embezzlement and theft of the materials and finished goods, and, above all, by the supervision and disciplining of a workforce which was characterised by absenteeism, drunkenness and other vices from the point of view of the employer. It is precisely this aspect of the 'productivity' consequences of the division of labour which is absent from Smith's treatment in the *Wealth of Nations*.

Professor Marglin, in his paper, makes this point even more strongly:

> It will be argued ... that the agglomeration of workers into factories was a natural outgrowth of the putting-out system (a result, if you will, of its internal contradictions) whose success had little or nothing to do with the technological superiority of large-scale machinery. The key to the success of the factory, as well as its inspiration, was the substitution of capitalists' for workers' control of the production process; discipline and supervision could and did reduce costs *without* being technically superior.[55]

To prove this point, Marglin brings considerable evidence forward in support of this view from both the contemporary literature and from modern research into English economic history.[56] More relevant for the immediate purposes of this chapter, he also devastatingly criticises the three grounds which Smith had listed[57] in support of his assertion about the high productivity of the division of labour.[58]

The first of these grounds, the saving of time, was indeed important, but not in the sense that Smith meant; enough has been said on this aspect to make further elaboration unnecessary. Smith's second argument about improved dexterity was probably not very important in the areas to which he applied it – unskilled labour quickly gained a high level of proficiency in its simple tasks under a division of labour – the motto, 'practice makes perfect' applies with much greater force to skilled occupations, such as the work of the surgeon, the opera singer, the actor, the musician, the buffoon – all those occupations classified by Smith as unproductive labour. Finally, there is the third ground of a great propensity to invent as a result of the division of labour. Again, in the way Smith presented the matter, the gains from such on-the-job improvements were probably quite small; nevertheless, this particular aspect of the division of labour was important in a sense which was developed further by Marx, possibly from a suggestion in Hegel.[59]

To conclude the argument about the interrelationship between the division of labour and the transformation of circulating into fixed capital, which for Hicks is the essence of the Industrial Revolution, a few final comments may be made. It has been argued that the division of labour, *when carried out in the one building*, saved circulating capital, thereby reducing its relative importance in manufacturing substantially. At the same time fixed capital investment in buildings, and later in machines, substantially increased. This substitution was due not so much to the superiority of the new method of production – the techniques of production remained substantially the same for much of the eighteenth century in those industries where the domestic mode was important – but due to the organisational superiority of the new method. It is these organisational features (which preceded the technical innovations) which are also so frequently neglected in the economic history accounts of the industrial revolution.[60]

The second factor listed by Hicks as important in the rise of modern industry is 'science', or to put it more precisely, technological progress, especially in machine tool development and precision engineering. Here again, there is a close relationship with the division of labour, which Marx analysed in some detail[61] and which he concisely summarised at the end of his chapter on the division of labour:

> One of its [i.e. manufacturing industry under a complex division of labour] most finished creatures, was the workshop for the production of the instruments of labour themselves, including especially the complicated mechanical apparatus then already employed. A machine factory, says Ure, 'displayed the division of labour in manifold gradations – the file, the drill, the lathe, having each its different workman in the order of skill'. This workshop, the product of the division of labour in manufacturing, produced in its turn – machines. It is they that sweep away the handicraftsman's work as the regulating principle of social production.[62]

The argument in this section provides considerable evidence on the importance of the division of labour as a leading explanatory factor of the Industrial Revolution. To a large extent this argument supports and unifies the explanation given by Sir John Hicks, and in this manner transcends it by concentrating on the organisational features of the division of labour and the important consequences that flowed therefrom.[63] Furthermore, this analysis vindicates the intuitive emphasis placed upon the division of labour as a factor in economic development by the author of the *Wealth of Nations*, despite the faults in his analysis which have been noted.

IV

The final task of this paper is to assess the relevance of the division of labour to contemporary economic theory. Earlier,[64] it has been argued that the link between the division of labour and increasing returns in manufacturing industry, which had already been made by Smith, and which was developed in the work of Senior, J. S. Mill and above all Marshall, led to a decline in the treatment accorded to this topic in twentieth-century literature, because increasing returns raised so many difficulties for marginalist economic theory. These difficulties, as is well known, related to implications of increasing returns for competitive theory,[65] and more recently, to the difficulties raised for general equilibrium analysis on the same score.[66]

Little purpose would be served in a general paper such as this, to enumerate the difficulties raised by increasing returns for theories of competitive equilibrium, whether general or partial. Aspects of these difficulties were covered by Marshall's analysis in appendix H of his *Principles*.[67] In addition, increasing returns highlight factors of 'change of another order' which lie, by definition as it were, outside the realm of equilibrium economics.[68]

These factors of change are aspects of economic development associated with increasing returns, that is, with its dynamic and historical connotation, and were emphasised in Allyn Young's very important paper, 'Increasing Returns and Economic Progress', published in 1928. The more important issues raised in this paper were summarised by Young in the following manner:

> the mechanism of increasing returns is not to be discerned adequately by observing the effects of variations in the size of an individual firm of a particular industry, for the progressive division and specialisation of industry is an essential part of the process by which increasing returns are realised. What is required is that industrial operations be seen as an interrelated whole.[69]

The point made here is not a plea for general equilibrium analysis but, as has frequently been pointed out,[70] it is a comment on the relevance of equilibrium economics for understanding the processes of economic progress. As Young succinctly put it elsewhere in his paper, 'change becomes progressive and propagates itself in a cumulative way';[71] something which alters the conditions of industrial activity in one sphere sets up a chain reaction in other, related industries, which in turn affects other industries. Far from the initial change leading to a new, stable equilibrium position, the effect of such changes is to set up a whole series of further departures from equilibrium. In such an analysis, there is no role for the stable equilibrium position of equilibrium economics.

> the securing of increasing returns depends upon the progressive division of labour, and the principal economies of the division of labour, in its modern forms, are the economies which are to be had by using labour in roundabout or indirect ways.[72]

In this way, as Kaldor has argued, the accumulation of capital and consequent capital deepening, 'becomes a by-product rather than a cause of the expansion of production'.[73] This is in fact the picture displayed in the previous analysis of the role of the division of labour in the industrial revolution in England. This interrelationship between capital deepening and the scale of operations also plays down the role of relative factor prices in such a process, as compared with the traditional, Austrian variant of capital theory.[74]

This is not the place to develop these subjects at length, but rather to draw out the basic point of difficulty for equilibrium theory from this process of 'circular and cumulative change'. As Hahn has summarised it, 'at the point, when large historical vision is at issue, equilibrium economics is inadequate to the task'.[75]

These arguments of Kaldor, Hahn, and above all Allyn Young, demonstrate the irrelevance of equilibrium economics to some important economic problems, while they also demonstrate the necessity to give increasing returns far greater prominence in the literature of economics. Without this, a great deal of contemporary economic theory must remain a more or less empty box. It is true that it can be argued with Hicks that such a procedure means the sacrifice of a great deal of elegance in economic analysis and the scrapping of a great many 'economic laws' but surely, in the interest of the economic science whose birth is celebrated in the bicentenary of the *Wealth of Nations*, such sacrifices may in the long run be repaid by the benefits of an increased relevance of the theory and the better understanding of the economic phenomena which are to be studied and explained. To brush increasing returns and the division of labour under the carpet as 'the *usual* assumption of increasing relative marginal costs'[76] may be analytically quite rewarding, but is it good science?

Smith's treatment of the division of labour (which, incidentally, is far more extensive and rewarding than this short chapter can portray) remains therefore as fresh and stimulating in 1976 as it must have appeared in 1776. This is perhaps the greatest tribute that can be paid to an author on the two-hundredth anniversary of the first publication of his *magnum opus*.

Notes

1 Paper presented at a Reserve Bank seminar and as the Smith bicentenary address at a meeting of the Economic Society of Australia and New Zealand (New South Wales Branch). In revising the paper, I am indebted to an anonymous referee of this journal and to Mr F. M. Dunn for valuable comments.

2 For a more detailed discussion of this generalisation, see my 'Thoughts on the Emergence of Economics as a Science', a paper delivered at the Third Conference of Economists, Adelaide (May 1973) (above, Chapter 2).

3 Appropriately, the University of Glasgow, together with the Royal Economic Society and the Scottish Economic Society, have organised the biggest celebration, which took place in April 1976. The History of Economics Society celebrates the event at its annual conference in Chicago this year, the Ninth Conference of Historians of Economics takes place in Glasgow in September, while the Japanese and the Italians also have celebrations.

4 That is, J. M. Clark, J. H. Hollander, G. R. Morrow, M. Palyi and J.Viner, *Adam Smith 1776–1926* (Chicago, 1928).

5 W. R. Scott, 'Studies Relating to Adam Smith during the last Fifty Years', *Proceedings of the British Academy* (London, 1940).

6 Horst Claus Recktenwald, 'Adam Smith Heute und Morgen', *Kyklos*, vol. 28, no. 1, 1975, pp. 5–22.

7 That is, E. G. West, 'Adam Smith's Two Views of the Division of Labour', *Economica*, 31, 1964, pp. 23–32; N. Rosenberg, 'Adam Smith on the Division of Labour: Two Views or One?', *Economica*, 32, 1965, pp. 127–39; R. Hamowy, 'Adam Smith, Adam Ferguson, the Division of Labour', *Economica*, 35, 1968, pp. 249–59; E. G. West, 'The Political Economy of Alienation: Karl Marx and Adam Smith', *Oxford Economic Papers*, 21, 1969, pp. 1–23; R. L. Meek and A. S. Skinner, 'The Development of Adam Smith's Ideas on the Division of Labour', *Economic Journal*, vol. 83, 1973, pp. 1094–1116; V. Foley, 'The Division of Labour in Plato and Smith', *History of Political Economy*, vol. 6, summer 1974, pp. 220–42.

8 See S. A. Marglin, 'What Do Bosses Do?', in *Radical Interpretations of Economic History, Review of Radical Political Economics*, VI, summer 1974, pp. 61–112.

9 See N. Kaldor, 'The Irrelevance of Equilibrium Economics', *Economic Journal*, 82, 1972, pp. 1237–55; N. Kaldor, 'What is Wrong with Economic Theory?', *Quarterly Journal of Economics*, 89, 1975, pp. 347–57.

10 Needless to say, no exhaustive treatment of these topics is offered here. A major intention of this paper is simply to indicate that the division of labour will probably supply sufficient questions to keep researchers going until 2076.

11 J. A. Schumpeter, *History of Economic Analysis* (New York, 1959) pp. 187. Book I is of course Book I of *Wealth of Nations*, while 'the Draft' refers to the early draft (1763) of *Wealth of Nations* published by W. R. Scott, *Adam Smith as Student and Professor* (Glasgow, 1937) pp. 317–60. A full discussion of changes in the treatment of the division of labour in Smith's writings (including the lecture notes taken from his lectures on the subject at Glasgow in the 1760s) is presented by R. L. Meek and A. S. Skinner, 'The Development of Adam Smith's Ideas on the Division of Labour', *Economic Journal*, vol. 83, 1973, pp. 1094–1116.

12 Adam Smith, *An Inquiry into the Nature and Causes of the Wealth of Nations*, edited by E. Cannan (Modern Library edition, New York, 1937) pp. 3–6. All subsequent references will be to this edition. The various types of the division of labour referred to in the text are of considerable importance to the discussion in the third section of this paper.

13 *Ibid.*, pp. 7–10. A more detailed discussion of these three 'circumstances' is given in the third section below, while for the purpose of the fourth section it should be noted that the division of labour was a dynamic concept for Smith, largely used for the analysis of economic growth. In this sense it is quite different from 'increasing returns' as the static concept of modern economic literature.

14 *Ibid.* pp. 6, 242–43. In subsequent pages (pp. 244–45) Smith established the dichotomy so noted in nineteenth-century writings (such as the *Principles* of J. S. Mill and Marshall) of manufacturing industry with increasing returns and agriculture with diminishing returns.

15 *Ibid.*, pp. 11–12.

16 *Ibid*., chs 2 and 3. The theory of development and trade sketched in Book I, chapter 3, and at greater length in Book III, chapters 3 and 4, illustrates Marshall's comment, 'It's all in A. Smith'.

17 *Ibid*., p. 259. A similar passage is contained in Smith's lectures; see E. Cannan (ed.) *Adam Smith's Lectures on Justice, Police, Revenue and Arms* (Oxford, 1896), p. 181.

18 Smith, *Wealth of Nations*, *op. cit*., p. 260.

19 John Hicks, *Capital and Growth* (Oxford, 1965) ch. 4. For the purpose of this analysis, Hicks assumes a simple corn economy. See pp. 36–8.

20 In this simple model of the corn economy, the division of the labour force into productive and unproductive labour is synonymous with the division of output into saving and consumption. The proportion of productive labour in the total labour supply then equals saving as a proportion of output or the savings ratio.

21 It also illustrates a great deal in the development of economics in the next two hundred years, when it is remembered that $p - w/w$ is the rate of profit. When $k = 1$, the simplest assumption of a propensity to save of the capitalists, the equation becomes $g = r$ where r is the rate of profit; this is the foundation of the 'Cambridge theory of profits' developed by Kaldor, Kalecki and Pasinetti. See L. L. Pasinetti, *Growth and Income Distribution* (Cambridge, 1974), esp. pp. 121–2. The crucial difference between Smith and later classical economics (like that of Ricardo) is also illustrated: for Smith, p (labour productivity) rises over time owing to the division of labour; for Ricardo and the classical economists labour productivity falls over time as a result of diminishing returns in agriculture (See below, chapter 23).

22 In light of this interpretation, I find it amazing that S. Hollander, in his recent *The Economics of Adam Smith* (London, 1973) pays so little attention to the division of labour. Chapter 7, on 'Technical Change', devotes less than three pages to the subject, while it does not even have a special reference in the index, being classed instead as 'specialisation'. This arises undoubtedly from the fact that Hollander wants to fit Smith into a neo-classical general equilibrium context, and not into the classical context of accumulation and growth.

23 P. Sraffa (ed.) with the collaboration of M. H. Dobb, *The Works and Correspondence of David Ricardo* (Cambridge, 1951–73) I, pp. 94, 412; II, p. 395; IV, p. 25.

24 See James Mill, *Elements of Political Economy*, in Donald Winch (ed.) *The Selected Economic Writings of James Mill* (London, 1966) pp. 214–16; J. R. McCulloch, *Principles of Political Economy* (Murray reprint, London, 1870) pp. 51–5. In his edition of *Wealth of Nations*, McCulloch provided few additional notes on this subject, thereby indicating that Smith's treatment in this case was still considered the last word on the subject.

25 N. Senior, *An Outline of the Science of Political Economy* (London, 1951) pp. 73–82.

26 J. S. Mill, *Principles of Political Economy*, Book I, chs 8, 9. Mill is critical of some of the advantages of the division of labour as listed by Smith, particularly in section 5 of Book I ch. 8.

27 Marshall, *Principles of Economics*, Book IV, esp. ch. 9. The difficulties raised by increasing returns permeate the treatment of value in Book V, and are raised particularly in appendix H. Edgeworth also linked the two explicitly, in his *Papers Relating to Political Economy* (London, 1925) I, pp. 81–2.

28 Cf. J. R. Hicks, 'Thoughts on the Theory of Capital – The Corfu Conference', *Oxford Economic papers*, vol. 12, no. 2, June 1960, pp. 128–9; F. H. Hahn and R. C. O. Mathews, 'The Theory of Economic Growth: A Survey', in *Surveys of Economic Theory* (London, 1965) vol. II, p. 55. Some of these issues are explored in the fourth section of this chapter.

29 Smith, *Wealth of Nations*, *op. cit*., Book V, chapter 1, article II, 'Of the Expense of the Institutions for the Education of Youth', esp. pp. 734–6.

30 *Ibid.*, p. 734. This view of the division of labour has been described by one commentator as a contradiction to Smith's analysis of the division of labour in Book I. See the papers by E. G. West and N. Rosenberg in *Economica* referred to in note 7 above. To my mind, no such contradiction is apparent from a careful reading of Smith's text: the economic consequences are separated from the social consequences on the ground that the latter require government intervention. They are therefore treated in Book V dealing with public finance.

31 Adam Ferguson, *An Essay on the History of Civil Society* (Edinburgh, 1767) p. 280; see also his *Institutes of Moral Philosophy* (Edinburgh, 1769) pp. 31–2. For a discussion of the interrelationship between the ideas of these two Scottish philosophers on this subject, see the paper by Hamowy cited in note 7 above.

32 Schiller, *Briefe über die Ästhetische Erziehung der Menschen*, in *Werke* (Bonn, 1962) vol. 20, p. 323, cited by R. Plant, *Hegel* (London, 1972) p. 23.

33 The effects of the division of labour on the fragmentation of society are touched upon in the third section of this chapter, since it more properly belongs to the economic history questions raised by this issue. Schiller's views on this subject were re-imported into England by Thomas Carlyle, and others, in the mid-nineteenth century.

34 Schiller, *Briefe über die Ästhetische Erziehung der Menschen*, in *Werke* (Bonn, 1962) vol. 20, p. 326.

35 See K. Marx, *Capital* (Moscow, 1959) I, p. 363 n3.

36 Hegel, *Philosophy of Right*, translated with notes by T. M. Knox (Oxford, 1962) p. 129. To restore cohesion in the exchange economy, Hegel appeals to the state (following Sir James Steuart) rather than to the 'invisible hand' of Adam Smith. His final comment on mechanisation and the division of labour is looked at further in the third section of this chapter.

37 Hegel, *Philosophy of Right*, translated with notes by T. M. Knox (Oxford, 1962) p. 129.

38 *Ibid.*, p. 29.

39 In the first instance, this would require a lengthy analysis of Marx's views on the subject in *Economic and Philosophic Manuscripts* (1844) and in *Capital* (Moscow, 1959) I, ch. 14. Opposing views to this argument were put by editors of Smith's *Wealth of Nations* in the nineteenth century, namely McCulloch and Garnier. See McCulloch's edition of *Wealth of Nations* (Edinburgh, 1850) p. 350 n1. See also E. G. West, 'The Political Economy of Alienation: Karl Marx and Adam Smith', *Oxford Economic Papers*, 21, 1969, pp. 1–23, and the literature there cited, and P. N. V. Tu, 'The Classical Economists and Education', *Kyklos*, vol. 22, 1969, pp. 691–716.

40 For the nineteenth century, two prominent examples are J. K. Ingram and Alfred Marshall; in the twentieth century such views have been expressed in many presidential addresses to economic societies (e.g. those of Phelps Brown and Worswick published in the *Economic Journal*, 1971). Part of this dissatisfaction with the state of economics is reflected in the call for a revival of political economy.

41 The solution to this has been found in interdisciplinary studies, the combinations of subjects offered by faculties, boards of study and schools, but these of course only provide a partial solution.

42 See, for example, S. Hollander, *The Economics of Adam Smith* (London, 1973) and R. Koubner, 'Adam Smith and the Industrial Revolution', *Economic History Review*, vol. X, no. 3, 1959.

43 A check on some standard economic history treatments reveals this lack of concern. This includes early works such as Arnold Toynbee, *Lectures on the Industrial Revolution of the Eighteenth Century in England* and those of William Cunningham, as well as more modern works such as Paul Mantoux, *The Industrial Revolution in the Eighteenth Century* (London, 1961); T. S. Ashton, *An Economic History of England: The Eighteenth Century* (London, 1964) and his *The Industrial Revolution 1760–1830*

(Oxford, 1948); Phillis Deane, *The First Industrial Revolution* (Cambridge, 1967); Charles Wilson, *England's Apprenticeship 1603–1763* (London, 1967); and R. M. Hartwell (ed.) *The Causes of the Industrial Revolution in England* (1967) who, in his 'Essay on Methodology' on the causes of the industrial revolution included in this collection, lists 'more round-about and larger-scale production (e.g. enclosures and factories with greater division of labour)' (p. 58) without developing this to any extent in the subsequent discussion. In his elaboration of technical change, his second cause of the Industrial Revolution (*ibid.*, pp. 68–71) the division of labour is not even mentioned.

44 The inspiration for this section of the paper is derived from S. Marglin's stimulating analysis in S. A. Marglin, 'What Do Bosses Do?', in *Radical Interpretations of Economic History, Review of Radical Political Economics*, VI, summer 1974, pp. 61–112.

45 J. R. Hicks, *A Theory of Economic History* (Oxford, 1969) ch. 9.

46 The only references to the division of labour are in the early sections of the work and are largely related to pre-modern industrial societies. See *ibid.*, esp. pp. 22–3.

47 Adam Smith, in his introduction to Book II of *Wealth of Nations*, largely treats the capital requirements of a division of labour in terms of circulating capital (*op. cit.*, pp. 259–61). Turgot, on the other hand, in the second part of his 'Reflections', linked the division of labour not only to circulating capital but to large-scale fixed capital investment as well. See P. D. Groenewegen, 'A Reinterpretation of Turgot's Theory of Capital and Interest', *Economic Journal*, vol. 81, June 1971, esp. pp. 332–3 (above, Chapter 17).

48 The account of the features of English domestic industry draws heavily on T. S. Ashton's economic work. See especially *The Industrial Revolution 1760–1830* (Oxford, 1948) pp. 49–57.

49 T. S. Ashton, *An Economic History of England. The Eighteenth Century* (London, 1964) pp. 111–112, cf. pp. 100–1.

50 Ashton, *Industrial Revolution*, pp. 51, 54; see also Dorothy Marshall, *The English Poor in the Eighteenth Century* (London, 1926) pp. 32–3; for contemporary accounts see William Temple, *The Case as it stands between the Clothiers, Weavers and other Manufacturers* (London, 1739); *A Vindication of Commerce and the Arts* (London, 1748); J. Cunningham, *Considerations on Taxes as they are supposed to affect the Price of our Labour* (London, 1765). A detailed discussion of this issue is given in E. S. Furniss, *The Position of the Labourer in a System of Nationalism* (New York, 1920).

51 T. S. Ashton, *The Industrial Revolution* (Oxford, 1948) p. 54.

52 *Ibid.*, p. 55.

53 T. S. Ashton, *An Economic History of England. The Eighteenth Century* (London, 1964) p. 102, where he states: 'It is said that in the hosiery trade in the East Midlands as much as two and a half days a week might be taken up in getting orders and materials, returning finished work and collecting wages'.

54 A. Smith, *op. cit.*, p. 4. Cf. the remarks in *ibid.*, p. 260 on the necessity of the capitalist to maximise the return on his advances of circulating capital, which Smith argued elsewhere could be best done by reducing the turnover period of that capital (*ibid.*, pp. 112–14).

55 S. A. Marglin, 'What Do Bosses Do?', in *Radical Interpretations of Economic History, Review of Radical Political Economics*, VI, summer 1974, p. 84.

56 Marglin, *op. cit.*, pp. 81–95, 102.

57 A. Smith, *op. cit.*, p. 7.

58 S. A. Marglin, 'What Do Bosses Do?', in *Radical Interpretations of Economic History, Review of Radical Political Economics*, VI, summer 1974, pp. 64, 66–70.

59 This will be developed later in this part, since Marx's argument was that there was a strong connection between the division of labour and the technological progress in the machine tool industry in the nineteenth century. Hegel's argument (*Philosophy of*

Right, translated with notes by T. M. Knox [Oxford, 1962] p. 129) that as labour becomes more and more mechanical, it is easier to replace such labour by machines, has already been quoted.

60 In his *Economic History of England* (London, 1964) p. 122, Professor Ashton makes the observation that the organisational features of the manufacturing process in the industrial revolution have not received the attention they deserve.

61 Marx, *Capital* (Moscow, 1959) I, pp. 341–2, which gives examples from the tool making industry in Birmingham. See also *ibid.*, pp. 371–86.

62 Marx, *ibid.*, p. 368. The quotation from Ure is from Andrew Ure, *The Philosophy of Manufacturers*, 2nd edn (London, 1835) p. 21.

63 Two of these important consequences are the factory system and the mechanisation of industry; these in turn led to the sharp division of society into a capitalist and a labouring class.

64 See above, the first two paragraphs of the second section of this chapter.

65 See especially P. Sraffa, 'The Laws of Returns under Competitive Conditions', *Economic Journal*, 1926. A good survey of the controversy is in G. L. S. Shackle, *The Years of High Theory* (Cambridge, 1967) ch. 3.

66 See e.g. F. H. Hahn, 'On the Notion of Equilibrium in Economics' (Cambridge, 1973), where he argues:

> The first point to emphasise is that an Arrow-Debreu equilibrium *may* exist when there are increasing returns. Not only is this so when these increasing returns are not internal to the firm, but even if they are, *provided they are not too large*.
>
> (pp. 12–13, my italics)

See also *ibid.*, p. 32.

67 A. Marshall, *Principles of Economics* (London, 1920) appendix H, esp. pp. 805–8.

68 A. Young, 'Increasing Returns and Economic Progress', *Economic Journal*, vol. 38, no. 4, 1928, pp. 528, 533.

69 *Ibid.*, p. 539.

70 N. Kaldor, 'What is Wrong with Economic Theory?', *Quarterly Journal of Economics*, 89, 1975, p. 355; F. H. Hahn, 'The Winter of our Discontent', *Economica*, vol. 40, 1973, p. 327; Joan Robinson, *History versus Equilibrium*, Thames papers in Political Economy, London, 1974.

71 A. Young, 'Increasing Returns and Economic Progress', *Economic Journal*, vol. 38, no. 4, 1928, p. 533.

72 *Ibid.*, p. 539.

73 N. Kaldor, 'What is Wrong with Economic Theory', *Quarterly Journal of Economics*, 89, 1975, p. 355.

74 Cf. *ibid.*, p. 356, and his 'The Irrelevance of Equilibrium Economics', *Economic Journal*, 82, 1972, pp. 1237–55, p. 1242.

75 F. H. Hahn, 'On the Notion of Equilibrium in Economics' (Cambridge, 1973) p. 32.

76 P. A. Samuelson, 'Diagramatic Exposition of a Theory of Public Expenditure', in R. W. Houghton (ed.) *Public Finance*, Penguin Modern Economic Readings, 2nd edn (Harmondsworth, 1973) pp. 191–2 (my italics in the quotation).

23 Productivity of labour, thrift and economic progress

Adam Smith's optimistic view of economic development

It is well known that Adam Smith was a product of the age of enlightenment in the sense that he shared the view of human improvement which was so characteristic of the mid-eighteenth century and its optimistic faith in the potential for the continuous progress of mankind in all its endeavours: social, scientific, political and economic.

This aspect of Smith's vision is already apparent in the four stages theory of human development he espoused. Smith had included such a theory in his lectures on jurisprudence, insofar as can be ascertained from the records of these lectures as he had delivered them in the session of 1762–3 and 1763–4. Especially from the first of these transcripts, or the 'Lothian' manuscript named after its first discoverer (Meek *et al.*, 1978, p. 9), it can be seen that Smith was an important co-discoverer of this view (jointly with Turgot, who had enunciated the theory in France in the early 1750s). The four stages theory argued the materialist position that the mode by which humankind earned its subsistence determined the potential for civilisation such a society could reach, as influenced by the productivity (surplus-creating capacity) of these various modes of production.

As is well known, these four stages of progress were the following: first, that of hunter-gatherers; second, that of the pastoralists; third, that of agriculture; and fourth, and final stage, that of commercial society. Each of these stages, which naturally succeeded each other in the progress of development, can be briefly looked at in turn.

The primitive stage, that of hunter-gatherers or, to use the Rousseauean language in vogue at the time, the state of nature, or that of the ignoble savage (Meek, 1976) In this stage of development, it was difficult to speak of the creation of surplus. Much of the product of the hunt was incapable of prolonged storage. Society was nomadic and property was virtually nonexistent. Exceptions were the implements for the hunt, for the temporary storage of fruits and other gathered products of the soil for clothing and for cover. This stage, in its necessary lifestyle as dictated by the mode of producing its subsistence, was contrary to all trappings of contemporary civilised society.

The hunter-gatherer stage developed naturally into that of the pastoral stage or the age of shepherds Food and clothing could be more effectively supplied if herds were accumulated from some of the animals originally captured in the hunt which were suitable for domestication. These needed to be protected from predators, both in the form of wild beasts and that of humans continuing in the hunter-gatherer stage, so that preservation of property became an important function in this society. Herds were productive of a surplus from natural increase, provided the herd was kept secure and adequately watered and fed. Absence of artificial or cultivated pasture meant the need for constant shifting – hence a continuation of nomadic life – but the fact that this was society with substantial property had novel implications as compared with the previous stage. Inequality in wealth was one such consequence. It entailed social divisions between the rulers and the ruled, employers and the employed. As Smith indicated in Book V of his *Wealth of Nations* (1776, ch. 1), such a pastoral society was also conducive to the martial arts, as evidenced by the history of the Arabs and Tartars. The potential for wealth accumulation in the pastoral stage ensured some of the trappings of civilisation, though these still tended to be rather limited.

Pastoral society naturally developed into agricultural society Nomadic herds were an easy source of animals to be trained for the plough, and cultivation of pasture and other crops (especially grains) provided a more reliable and more permanent source of food for man and beast. Agriculture implied settlement and acquisition of property in land. Much of this landed property initially was acquired in the fertile areas near large rivers, which not only provided access to water for people, the farm animals and the crops, but means of transport and communication, and opportunities for trade in the surplus crops. Ownership in land was a further and more important source of inequality. It created a caste of owners and those without property. The first gained their living from the surplus which agricultural property provided, the rest of society gained it more modestly by labouring in cultivating the fields for the owners of the land. The settled state entailed by agriculture also allowed the building of large and ornate residences for the owners of landed estates and, much more humbly, for the workers. Hence villages gradually developed near the agricultural settlements. The substantial potential for surplus product from a developed agriculture also created a giant fund of subsistence (or wages fund) for those not directly employed on the land such as servants for large landholders, artisans and craftsmen to produce implements for work and for living, as well as luxuries of the rich, and the revenue (through taxation) for government by which it could defray the expenses for the preservation and defence of property against internal and external marauders respectively.

The commercial (and capitalist) stage developed naturally from agricultural society and from the wealth its surplus was capable of producing Such surplus became not only a source of exports to trade for desirable imports from other parts of the world, it became the fund for accumulation *par excellence*, as it constituted the natural wages fund from which wages for hired labour could be paid. Property other than land, that is, in the form of stored commodities and instruments, or what quickly became known as capital, evolved into an additional source of surplus and power. It also created a new class of capitalists and merchants, who employed their capital in manufacturing and trade as well as in the adoption of modern, capital-using, farming techniques. Capital, furthermore, provided opportunities for improving productive processes through an increased reliance on the division of labour, or specialisation. Division of labour could be applied not only to enlarging the structure of the various professions, as it had done for centuries; but also within specific trades and industrial processes. The great productive potential from such subdivision of labour further enhanced the opportunities to accumulate, and growth became a steady cumulative process of increasing wealth. In addition, the wealth created by commercial society and inherent in the nature of its productive activities, brought large towns into existence, and the many additional services and commodities which town and city life initiated and facilitated. Although inequality remained great between the property owning classes (of land and capital) and those who had to rely on them for their employment and subsistence, the growth in productive power (output per head) generated by commercial society held out the prospect for increases in wealth in which all could share, including the humble wage earner. Hence growth in output marched together with rising living standards, even if inequality was not removed.

This was the stage of society which Smith saw developing in Glasgow in the 1750s and early 1760s, buoyant through the steady growth of trade and industry. Not surprising, this is what he also described in some of its essential features, first in his lectures as part of a long process of historical development, and then in his *Wealth of Nations*. The latter version, which provides the mature vision of economic growth and development of the Glasgow philosopher, also provides a lead-in for examining the main features mentioned in the title of this short paper: productivity, thrift and economic progress.

Smith's model of economic growth

In the preface to his *Wealth of Nations*, Smith clearly identified the causes of the wealth of nations, which, after all, constituted the major subject matter of his treatise. The first is the 'skill, dexterity and judgement with which its labour is generally applied, [the second] the proportion between the number of those who are employed in useful labour, and that of those who are not so employed' (1776, p. 10). These causes form the subject matter of the first two books of the *Wealth of Nations*, generally described as the theoretical core of his book. More specifically, Book I deals with the productivity of labour and its major cause, the division of labour, together with its necessary preconditions in the form of sizeable market, the extent and growth of which determines the scope for the division of labour and the potential for its growth. Book II chapter III deals with the accumulation of capital or, to use the alternative title which Smith seems to treat as virtually synonymous, of productive and unproductive labour, in which the use of the former is identified with thrift and the use of the latter signifies prodigality.

Distribution of the product, or of the annual revenue, to use another of Smith's expressions for this important category, is also treated in Book I. It is seen as sufficiently important to form part of the title, 'Of the Causes of the Improvement in the Productive Powers of labour, and of the Order according to which its Produce is naturally distributed among the different Ranks of the People' (1776, p. 13). The logic of the ordering of this subject matter is compelling, as Cannan (1898, p. 146) demonstrated a century ago. Division of labour is discussed first (chapter 1) as the main cause of the productivity of labour (the first aspect of the subject matter listed in the title of Book I). It is limited by the extent of the market (chapter 3), the topic discussed immediately after a thorough examination of the human proclivity to exchange, or mankind's innate propensity to truck and barter (chapter 2). The growth of the market is inexorably linked to the nature and use of money (chapter 4), money is connected with the measure of value and to the distinction between nominal and real prices (chapter 5); measure of value naturally introduces a discussion of the nature of value, that is, natural and market price, and since the former of these regulates the latter, to the component parts of natural price, wages, profit and rent (chapters 6 and 7). The last, following the terminology introduced by the physiocrats, could also be denoted by the theory of distribution, the second aspect of the subject matter specifically mentioned in the title of Book I. Book II, which deals with the nature, accumulation and employment of stock, is linked directly to the division of labour in the introductory remarks to that Book. Once a division of labour has been 'thoroughly introduced', capital needs to have been accumulated beforehand, in order for people, all dependent on each other's activities, to live until they can sell their product to others. Division of labour is generally capital-intensive, hence capital accumulation and division of labour go hand-in-hand. The final three books of the *Wealth of Nations* then look at specific aspects of the theory of growth, to use modern terminology for Smith's subject matter defined as the nature and causes of the wealth of nations. The various paths to economic growth are discussed in Book III; some major policies used to achieve economic growth are then evaluated and found wanting (Book IV); while the more correct role for government in economic growth, and the financing mechanism this entails, conclude the discussion of Smith's treatise (Book V).

The logic of the ordering of Smith's argument is therefore impeccable, given the nature of its content. (It is therefore surprising how frequently it has been misrepresented by various, so-called authorities on Adam Smith, who twist his contents in an order which suits their logic, not that of Smith.) The thrust of Smith's argument has, however, been very neatly captured by some commentators. A good example is Hick's simple exposition of the Smithian growth model. This summarises that model in a simple equation, highlighting the key variables in the theory, as they were identified by Smith himself. This equational summary is so useful for highlighting the major thrust of the paper, that its rationale and derivation should be succinctly explained.

Assume an economy which produces one major commodity, say corn, therefore able to act as the wage good. Let X stand for the corn output of this economy, or for its output as a whole. Last year's corn output can then be written as $Xt-1$. It is available for the employment of this year's labour, so that if w is the wage rate in terms of corn, the labour supply to be employed is $Xt-1/w$. Let p be labour productivity per person year, then this year's output, $Xt = p/w\ Xt-1$. Call the growth rate of the economy,

$$g, \text{ which} = \frac{Xt\text{-}Xt\text{-}1}{Xt\text{-}1}$$

By manipulating this and the previous equation, it is then easy to show that

$$g = \frac{p}{w} - 1$$

However, the analysis has assumed so far that all of this labour is productively employed, an unlikely case in Smith's theory. Assume that only a proportion of the wage fund, k, is devoted to hiring productive labourers (hence $1-k$ of the wage fund is devoted to unproductive labourers, who produce nothing). Next year's output is then smaller, that is $Xt = k.pXt-1/w$, so that

$$g = k.\frac{p}{w}\text{-}1$$

which is the Smithian growth equation according to Hicks (1965, ch. 4).

Although the simplicity of Hick's exposition has sometimes been criticised, this summary of the Smithian growth model can give rise to a number of interesting conclusions. The following can be specifically noted:

(a) For Smith, the growth rate varies directly with the productivity of labour, p, and with the proportion of labour productively employed, k. As shown previously, this is in line with the position he succinctly expressed in the preface to his book. It varies inversely to wages, a matter which needs further explanation. It was indicated previously that Smith was a firm believer in the fact that growth in commercial society would generate rising living standards for all sections of the community, including wage earners. Smith made this abundantly clear in the final paragraph of Book I, chapter I of the *Wealth of Nations*, where 'even the meanest person' is argued to be much better provided for in 'a civilised society' as a result of the division of labour (1776, pp. 23–4).

Identification of these variables in the growth process also enables some comments on Smith's prognostications about the likely prospects for economic growth. There can be no doubt about the fact that Smith had a strong faith in the productivity gains to be made from continuous extensions of the division of labour, as a process which to him seemed to be unlimited. He was far less optimistic, it seems, on the prospects for vast increases in k, the proportion of the labour force productively employed. The growing size of government, as succinctly demonstrated in Book V, chapter I of his work combined with the entrenched prodigality in the lifestyle of the aristocratic land holder, made a more or less constant value of k the best that could be hoped for. Smith's expectation that all would share in the benefits of economic growth in civilised society placed a further constraint on the growth rate through rises in the wage rate, though the extent of these is difficult to fathom. Quality increases are seen as the major benefit from the division of labour for the poor in the concluding segment of Book I, chapter I; rising real wages are strongly argued to be the hallmark of a progressive growing society in Book I, chapter VII. Taken together, these expectations about the three growth variables place an inordinate stress on p, the productivity of labour, if a substantial growth rate is to be achieved. No wonder that Smith gave such an emphasis to the importance of the division of labour in the structure of his argument on economic growth. Furthermore, if free trade extends the market, and an extended market increases the scope for the division of labour, then his vision on growth prospects provides a further strong reason for his advocacy of free trade. The productivity consequences of a vigorously expanding division of labour are the lynchpin of Smith's story of economic growth.

(b) Another aspect of the Smithian growth equation is worthy of comment. The relationship p/w is a clear reflection of the surplus potential of an economy, since the greater output per unit of labour relative to cost per unit of labour, the greater the surplus product. $(p/w)-1$ can be simply rewritten as $(p-w)/w$, which is the rate of profit in a simple system of production which employs no fixed capital (as the case in the simplified Hicks version of the Smith growth model). The proportion of labour productively applied, k, stands for thrift in Smith's analysis of the accumulation of capital (where savings, as Smith argued, were immediately invested). Hence k can be seen as a savings propensity, or s. The equation for Smithian growth can then be rewritten as $g = s.r$, from which the expression known as the Cambridge theory of profits can be simply derived, that is $r = g/s$. This association between the essentials of Smithian growth theory and a proposition of contemporary, post-Keynesian economics, shows the strength of the classical roots of this contemporary development from the economics of Keynes.

(c) A third and final point to be derived from the growth equation leads directly into the topic for the second paper (not reproduced here). During the decades after Smith, economists tended to become more pessimistic about the overall prospects for p, the productivity of labour. This is visible in the growing emphasis on diminishing returns, the introduction of which into classical economics can be largely associated with Malthus' essay on the principle of population. The generation of economists after Smith built diminishing returns firmly into their economic structures. This implied a dramatic shift in their expectations about the value of the variables influential in the growth process. Productivity of labour boosted by the division of labour was heavily reduced in importance – either to an important constancy as diminishing returns in agriculture offset the increasing returns from division of labour in manufacturing or, worse, declining productivity from the overwhelming impact of diminishing returns. Consequently, wages likewise became a constant, stuck over the longer term at customary levels of subsistence. This made thrift or accumulation the major factor in economic growth, and severely limited progress as a continuing prospect for humankind. As a result of these changes, essentially derived from substituting diminishing returns for the benefits in the form of increasing returns from increased division of labour, classical political economy was turned into what was called 'a dismal science' which rejected the optimistic vision of rising living standards through growth and increasing returns bequeathed to them by Adam Smith. This in turn had implications for their vision of the future of society, including the welfare state.

References

Cannan, Edwin (1917) [1898] *A History of the Theories of Production and Distribution in English Political Economy from 1776 to 1848*, 3rd edn, London: Staples Press.

Hicks, J. R. (1965) *Capital and Growth*, Oxford: Clarendon Press.

Meek, R. L. (1976) *Social Science and the Ignoble Savage*, Cambridge: Cambridge University Press.

Meek, R. L., Raphael, D. D. and Stein, P. G. (eds) (1978) *Adam Smith, Lectures on Jurisprudence*, Oxford: Clarendon Press.

Smith, Adam (1976) [1776] *An Inquiry into the Nature and Causes of the Wealth of Nations*, eds R. Campbell, A. S. Skinner and W. B. Todd, Oxford: Clarendon Press.

Index